THE
CHURCHILL
DOCUMENTS

THE CHURCHILL DOCUMENTS

RANDOLPH S. CHURCHILL

VOLUME 4
MINISTER OF THE CROWN
1907–1911

Hillsdale College Press, Hillsdale, Michigan

Hillsdale College Press
33 East College Street
Hillsdale, Michigan 49242
www.hillsdale.edu

Originally published in 1969 by William Heinemann Ltd. in Great Britain and by Houghton Mifflin in the United States.

Printed in the United States of America

Printed and bound by Edwards Brothers, Ann Arbor, Michigan

Cover design by Hesseltine & DeMason, Ann Arbor, Michigan

THE CHURCHILL DOCUMENTS
Volume 4: *Minister of the Crown, 1907–1911*

Library of Congress Control Number: 2007902660

ISBN: 978-0-916308-14-8

First printing 2007

Contents

Note
to the New Edition

Winston Churchill's personal papers are among the most comprehensive ever assembled relating to the life and times of one man. They are so extensive that it was only possible to include in the narrative volumes of his biography a part of the relevant documents.

The Companion Volumes, now titled *The Churchill Documents*, were planned to run parallel with the narrative volumes, and with them to form a whole. When an extract or quotation appears in a narrative volume, the complete document appears in an accompanying volume of *The Churchill Documents*. Where space prevented the inclusion of a contemporary letter in the narrative volume, it is included in the document volume.

Here in these three volumes of *The Churchill Documents*—Volume 3: *Early Years in Politics, 1901–1907*, Volume 4: *Minister of the Crown, 1907–1911*, and Volume 5: *At the Admiralty, 1911–1914*— are set out all the documents relevant to *Winston S. Churchill, Volume II: Young Statesman, 1901–1914*. Mention in these texts of "Main Volume" refers to this second volume of the biography.

The chapter and page numbers for volumes 3, 4 and 5 of *The Churchill Documents* run consecutively through the volumes. The index to all three volumes appears in Volume 5.

10

African Journey

(See Main Volume Chapter 7, pp. 221–238)

═══════════

O N 10 September 1907 WSC left England to attend the French Army manœuvres. He went on from France for a four-month trip through Africa. This was recorded in *My African Journey*, published by Hodder and Stoughton in 1908.

Lady Lytton[1] to WSC

14 September [1907]
Knebworth
(In the train)

Winston mine,

What about a polo pony for the winter? I would like one very much – if you liked the arrangement we made last winter I should be very pleased to look after, keep and ride any of yours you think fit.

I enjoyed Doncaster meeting very much – it was glorious weather – and we had a pleasant party including Goonie who grows ever more beautiful and nice. We talked about you. There were endless cats at the races and a full mustering of the hardy nags – chief among them sly Sarah – whose evil eye shines ever brighter and harder.

I wish you had not left us. If you have not many friends, those you have love you with much strength and loyalty – and I am one of those, perhaps the leader. Don't forget me, and write me just the sort of letter you know I love – and I will answer, and tell you anything good that happens.

Yours
PAMELA

Best luck, and God's – *our* God's – blessing.

[1] Pamela Frances Audrey Lytton (b. 1874), see under Pamela Plowden in Companion Volume I. In 1902 she married Victor, 2nd Earl of Lytton.

Lady Randolph to WSC

EXTRACT

17 September 1907   Lochmore
                                                                Lairg

My dearest Winston,

I wonder how you are getting on with the 'Froggies.' I hope you will find a moment to send me a line. Did F. E. Smith 'wear' as well as you expected? We are still in Scotland as you see. It has been most pleasant here – Shelagh & Bend'or are enjoying life & sport. . . . George has killed as many stags as ever he cd desire. It is very mild up here, but I like the outdoor life, & have taken to fishing which I enjoy. I write all the mornings & have got on with the book. I received the chapters. You were a bit scathing about Chap V but I did not mind as I ought to have told you that V was *quite* in the rough – merely a lot of notes put together which Miss Anning typed in order that you might see them. In any case I shd never have sent the chapter to the *Century* as you saw it. I have added a lot to Chapt 4 & lead up to Ireland. The *Century* have now 4 chapters & I hope they will leave me in peace for a little. We return to SH then 28th. Send me a line there, when you have a moment. I suppose you will stop in Venice on your way south. Your French must be much improved by your intercourse with all those French soldiers – do tell me how you went, & how did the Army impress you compared to the German? In the Memoirs of Mde de Boigne she gives an account of a conversation she had with Napoleon. I have copied it out for you as I know yr keen interest in him. Bless you darling. Thank you so much for looking at my chapters & I forgive you for saying 'Fie!' to your loving

MOTHER

WSC to Lady Lytton

(*Lytton Papers*)

EXTRACT

19 September 1907   Venice

Pamela dear,

Last night I was singing your praises to Sunny and telling him how fond I was of you and what a good & true friend you always were to me – & how you sprang up so unexpectedly yet so certainly to bid me good-bye – & he was agreeing – & now this morning is your letter! Quite true I have vy few friends – but why should I have more? I could make more, but never like those I have; & alas with my busy selfish life – I fear, as it is, I fail too often in the little offices which keep friendship sweet & warm. But you always understand me & pardon, because you know me & care about me; & upon my word you are almost the only person who does – except Jack & my mother – which is different: & Sunny, who is also different again. Well!

Since I left England I have been in incessant movement. The French manœuvres were most interesting & it was a vy pleasant experience to me. . . . The French treated us with almost royal honours and I think even down to the private soldiers they were all genuinely pleased to see us watching their military evolutions.

We were the only foreigners with the army and consequently had all the attention from everybody. I have written a report about it all to Ian Hamilton. Perhaps he will show it to you. But then it is all dull technical stuff – bad for kittens so long accustomed to cream!

Then I motored all down France – from Paris to Fontainebleau, Auxerre, Nevers, Moulins, Vichy, Lyons, Chambery – over the St Bernard 7,000 feet high – down into Italy like Napoleon at Aosta; thence to lovely Baveno where Mr F. E. Smith departs – & then on by Milan & Verona here – where I meet Sunny. We start again tomorrow for Vienna. It will take 3 days; but I so much prefer seeing all the country, & stopping & starting at will – to the methodical discomfort of the railway, that I would rather take a little longer.

Pamela, will you do two things for me? 1st I want several yards of fine, but strong gauze – to make veils like bags even, to hang over my helmet and keep away these detestable poisonous mosquitoes – who tell lies & even truths – & make so much mischief in England, & who in Central Africa bite me to death.

Secondly will you buy me three or four pairs of long, soft, buttonless ladies' gloves (for the same purpose) if you can find any that will be big enough for my masculine paws. Do this for me & give them to Eddie Marsh to bring out – & tell me how much money they cost. Please.

Sunny is vy glad to get me here. All his old friends are in the canals – but he does not dare to go to see any of them except for a minute or two because of gossip. He is all alone: & quite embittered. But he has only to keep his head high & to hold firm for two or three years – for all to come right for him.

Today what a programme for me! First I am going at 10.30 to row about in a gondola with Gladys D. [Deacon, later Duchess of Marlborough] all the morning & then climb the tower of San Giorgio Maggiore. Then lunch with Helen [Vincent]: & afterwards gondola with that other person! Such a dream of fair women. You will think me a pasha. I wish I were. But still believe me it is a greater pleasure to me to write to you – & think of one kind heart that has a responsive palp for me – than to see these strange glittering beings with whom I have little or nothing in common (I shan't tell them this). It is for private circulation only & for the especial delectation of the demure kitten purring & prinking over what I trust will ever be to her the sweet & abundant milk of life.

Always yours
W

Lord Elgin to WSC

25 September 1907   Broomhall

My dear Churchill,

Marsh has been good enough to let me know that he is starting on Saturday to join you and I take the opportunity of sending you a few lines.

I am glad to say that with the exception of our two spoilt children, Newfoundland & Natal, I have not much to say of Office matters.

The first pursues the even tenor of its way: i.e. vehement protest agt anything & everything we attempt. I thought at one moment that there were better symptoms – when Bond actually proposed a *modus* of his own! And I am not clear still that the case is hopeless. There has been no one in the Office who dealt with this matter last year – and the powerful Minutes (& telegrams) have been written by Keith[1]: who with all his ability is not in my judgment a very safe guide. However Hopwood came back yesterday & I think I have managed to keep the door open – if Bond means to be reasonable.

If, as I fear is more probable, he means to follow the same impracticable policy as last year – we must disregard him as we did then. I don't think you need worry about this case: it is full of annoyance – but I do not fear any serious challenge of our policy.

Natal is a much bigger business. Who would have thought that when McCallum in his last letter wrote of Dinizulu[2] being 'flattened out', his

---

[1] Arthur Berriedale Keith (1879–1944), barrister, scholar and civil servant; entered Colonial Office in 1901, taking first place in civil service examination; Secretary to Crown Agents for the Colonies 1903–5; re-appointed to Colonial Office 1905; Clerk to the Imperial Conference 1907; Senior Assistant Secretary to Imperial Conference 1911; Regius Professor of Sanskrit and Comparative Philology, Edinburgh University 1914–44.

[2] Dinizulu, Paramount Chief of the Zulus at the time, was suspected by the Natal authorities of complicity in native rebellions during 1906 and 1907. In November 1907 he was arrested and taken to Pietermaritzburg to stand trial.

successor's first *telegram* would be that an enquiry into that Chief's conduct & his probable deportation was imminent!

Simultaneously came the report of the Commission appointed by the Natal Govt itself which condemns their Native Administration from beginning to end. I have only received to-day – & have not yet read – the comments on this whole subject of the Acting Govr (Beaumont[1]). The point that is before us for immediate decision is whether we shall agree to a movement of Imperial troops to Eshowe to overawe Dinizulu. I had a chance of consulting Haldane when the proposal first came to me and he entirely agreed in my demand for fuller information. It is just a case which during a Session would have come before the Cabinet. As it stands I shall not decide without reference to Haldane & the Prime Minister.

You would be quite entitled on this narrative to remind me of your continued criticism of the methods & policy in Native Affairs of the Natal Gov. You could not have asked [for] a more striking illustration. At the same time, while I admit that the ineptitude has gone further than I imagined, I do not depart from the view that, in the relative positions of white & black, such things must happen. It is a curious coincidence that the question of the treatment of Natives is coming to the front everywhere in Africa. Besides Natal I have before me at this moment despatches from the Transvaal – a letter from Girouard regarding Northern Nigeria – and turning back a little – the Nairobi incident in E. Africa and the question of the Forest concession in W. Africa. On the Transvaal Case which was sent to me to-day I have written a Minute desiring a comprehensive and exhaustive consideration of the whole subject. You will easily believe that this is not likely to be brought to a conclusion before your return, and I commend it to you as a subject well worthy of study on the spot.

I shall look forward with the greatest interest to learning the results of its consideration by so acute an observer as yourself. And I shall not wish in any way to prejudge the question. But I may mention that I have some sympathy with the view, which I believe Selborne to hold, that so long as the Native is excluded from the political rights possessed by the white man, he is better left under a personal rule. There is no doubt some difficulty in combining the 'personal' rule of the Native (which must almost of necessity rest with the Governor) – and the 'self government' accorded to the Colony as a whole, & exercised by the white inhabitants. But I am not satisfied that a compromise is impossible.

Well, I will not weary you with more of these speculations, as yet in an elementary stage, and destined to cover reams of paper. I mention them

[1] William Henry Beaumont (1851–1930), Acting Chief Justice and Administrator Natal 1907; knighted 1910.

because I want to profit by the unique opportunity of your being able to look at them with all your great powers of observation and your knowledge of official information.

Wishing you once more a real good time and success in all your operations.

Yours very sincerely
ELGIN

WSC to Lady Randolph

26 September 1907   Eichhorn

Dearest Mamma,

You must not regard my criticisms as personal. Literary judgements are not worth much – but they are worth nothing unless they are at once impartial & impersonal. I am delighted to hear the political chapter was only in the rough. You have a great chance of making a charming woman's book about the last 30 years, & do I beg you lavish trouble upon it, & banish ruthlessly anything that will hurt other people's feelings. It is well worth while.

I have got the de Boigne memoirs with me – but it was kind of you to send me the passage. Make Mr F. E. Smith come to see you & tell you all about the French Manoeuvres & the journey from Paris to Italy.

Here it is vy pleasant. Sunny, de Forest,[1] H. Farquhar,[2] & me – that's all – but lots of partridges & hares.

I start for Malta on Sunday night from Vienna via Syracuse. It takes 3 days: & I meet the others there late on Wednesday night.

I have had a vy kind letter from the Prime Minister wh I think you will like to see. After reading it you might send it to Cassel or show it to him & say I said he would be interested. Then give it to Miss Anning to file & put away.

I am in hopes that the House will have been let & the Anning in part at least provided for.

With best love, I remain
Your affectionate son
W

---

[1] Maurice de Forest (1879–1968), later Count de Bendern. For an account of his career see Main Volume II, pp. 156–8.

[2] Horace Brand Farquhar (1844–1923), Master of the Household of King Edward VII; Lord Steward 1915–22; MP for Marylebone West 1895–8; PC; baronet 1892; Baron 1898; Viscount 1917; Earl 1922.

Jack Churchill to WSC

EXTRACT

27 September 1907   28 Throgmorton Street

Dear Winston,

I have settled the letting of Bolton Street. Sievier[1] comes in next Monday & stays until the 24th Feb at the rate of £10.10 a week. I tried to get more – but found it dangerous – and so I closed with him for that. Mrs Scrivings is going to stay on. I stipulated that either she or the housemaid should remain to look after things in your interest.

Mrs S consented to remain – although I fear she is very disappointed at not getting a holiday and not being able to go to her children. You must let her have a holiday when you come back, for she has not had one since B. Street started. You might let Scrivings know you appreciate her staying on etc.

Tinto's are a little better. The dividends will be declared in a few days. The pessimists say that it will be 30/–. But Lord R [Rotchschild] tells me he thinks it will be 50/–. If he is right, there should be a good rise. . . .

I am sending this by Eddie – who will give you all the news that there is. It has been very dull here – and I wish I could have come away for a month. But I could not fit it in. Sunny will think it dreadful sacrilege letting the house to Sievier. I have not seen him since Doncaster. Where is FE? There are some of his boxes here, which he never sends for.

Well best of luck to you – you are not much of a correspondent.

Yrs
JACK

I shall pay £110 (half the rent) into your a/c at Cox's tomorrow or Monday.
JSC

Lord Knollys to WSC

28 September 1907   Balmoral

My dear Churchill,

It is very stupid of me, but I cannot remember for *certain* whether or no I answered your last letter (though I believe I did) in which you were good enough to offer to write to the King during your travels, if he would wish you to do so.

I think that under any circumstances it is safer therefore to write now & say that it gives him great pleasure to take advantage of your offer.

[1] Robert Standish Sievier (1860–1939), well-known race-horse owner and trainer; in 1902 his horse Sceptre won four out of the five classic races; see also Main Volume II, p. 237.

I imagine you know that the King is only waiting for General Botha's formal offer of the Diamond to accept it.

You will I am sure have a very interesting & instructive visit to Africa, & I hope everything will go off well.

Pray do not take the trouble to answer this letter.

Yrs sincerely
KNOLLYS

WSC to Jack Churchill

3 October 1907   The Palace
                                                              Malta

My dear Jack,

Well – I accept the *fait accompli* & I quite understand your difficulties; & think it vy kind of you to have taken so much trouble & to have made what is no doubt in itself a thrifty arrangement. At the same time I have strong misgivings about dealing with such a ruffian.

I trust *all* papers & personal effects have been secured.

I have spoken to Scrivings about his wife. I am vy glad she will stay. It is good of her & she must have a holiday at the end of the business.

Jack – what has happened to Cerros? Do please watch this & let me know. A letter will catch me at Port Said.

I am vy sorry you are not with us. Here we are installed in much state in this wonderful old Palace of the Grand Master of the Knights of Malta, & with our *Venus* lying obedient & attentive in the roads. I have spent all day receiving functionaries – the Executive Council – the Archbishop-Bishop & others; & in visiting the batteries & dockyards. It is a wonderful place altogether. But whether worthy to have caused the greatest war in history or not – I cannot tell.

Best love, Yours always
W

WSC to Lord Elgin
(*Elgin Papers*)

4 October 1907   Malta
Private

My dear Lord Elgin,

I am vy much obliged to you for your letter wh Marsh brings me. I must certainly congratulate you on the Newfoundland incident. The course of events seems fully to justify your views & action. Even *The Times* for once is friendly & straightforward, & Bond is clearly coming to be regarded more & more as an impracticable person. I trust his intemperate & undiscriminating advocacy will not be allowed to prejudice the vy strong case wh in my opinion Newfoundland will present to the Hague tribunal, still more to compromise the larger interests of Canada. But it will not be easy to shut him out.

As to Natal – the proposal to deport Dinizulu under cover of a movement of Imperial troops cannot fail to raise Parliamentary issues of importance & much difficulty. At this distance I do not feel inclined to venture an opinion upon the merits of any particular step. But I submit to you this general principle: – that the measure of Imperial assistance must be at least the measure of our right to be consulted effectively upon the native policy. I would not do anything for them without a sufficient return for the benefit of the native as well as for Parliamentary defence. I think you should drive a hard bargain. I was therefore vy glad to read your telegram in reply to Nathan.[1] The question is indeed a delicate puzzle: but I am sure the Natal Government is vy much below the level of its responsibilities to the natives & much too inclined to take everything from us & give nothing in return.

What I saw at the French manoeuvres convinces me that we may safely & properly allow Haldane to put his SA batteries upon a 4 gun basis. The French army already adopt this organisation as their regular war strength; & they do this not on grounds of economy but because they contend that with QF artillery the ammunition supply of a six gun battery can be fired away only too quickly by 4 pieces. If the first artillery nation in the world is prepared to fight European artillery with four-gun batteries, such a system should surely be good enough for our S. African needs which happily exclude the possibility of operations against forces armed with artillery.

I have passed two vy busy but vy interesting & certainly pleasant days in this strange island. General Barron,[2] the Acting Governor, is a vy sensible man, much esteemed by the Maltese whom he treats with great tact & sympathy. He & they are both disappointed the governorship is otherwise bestowed. There is no doubt the Clarkes[3] were far from popular here. They

---

[1] Matthew Nathan (1862–1939), Governor of Natal 1907–9; Governor of Gold Coast 1900–3; of Hong-Kong 1903–7; Under-Secretary to Lord Lieutenant of Ireland 1914–16; Governor of Queensland 1920–26; knighted 1902; PC 1914; Colonel 1914.

[2] Harry Barron (1847–1921), Commanding RA, Malta 1904–8; Governor of Tasmania 1909–13; of Western Australia 1913–17, Major-General Royal Artillery 1904; knighted 1909.

[3] Charles Mansfield Clarke, 3rd baronet (1839–1932), Governor of Malta 1903–7; Quartermaster-General to the Forces 1899–1903; succeeded father 1899.

entertained little, gave themselves tremendous airs, and cut the elected members & all their supporters out of all Government House recognition. Their departure was hailed with general satisfaction.[1]

I called on the Archbishop-Bishop and today he returned my visit. He is a dear old gentleman who is stirred up to write these ugly letters by his Vicar-Apostolic. I made friends with him and we had a frank talk. I told him we had no intention whatever of hurting the feelings of the Maltese Catholics, of restricting their privileges or of allowing irritating demonstrations to be made against them; but that we were bound to secure for Protestants the religious liberty to which they were entitled. And then I told him that his letters had been much misunderstood in England, where people were inclined to think that he wished to deny to others the great liberties his own faith enjoyed at the hands of the British Government – & wh so greatly exceeded any allowed by the Italian Govt to the Pope himself. He was vy meek: & I learn privately that he had a wigging from the Vatican for the letters wh he allowed himself to father.

Then I have visited the elementary schools – wh are really admirable in every respect; & tomorrow I go round the Lyceum & secondary schools, the hospitals, the poor house & the prison. All that I have seen seems vy worthy of the British occupation.

But now of course the *pièce de résistance* has been my meeting with the elected members. On this point I will write to you at greater length than this letter will allow. Their demand for a reconsideration of the Constitutional position was supported by a deputation of the nobility, the Ch of Commerce, & the advocates: & I am bound to say that their complaint – viz that they were never conquered by England, but that now we spend their money without allowing the Maltese any sort of control – is a vy real & to me at least a vy painful one.

I will send you the shorthand report of the interview, & I trust you will approve of the line I took. The Governor & others with whom I consulted fully agreed. My line was that 'the last word had not been spoken,' & that it rested with them by frank cooperation with the Government to establish a case for the reconsideration of the question!

But I think I shall be able to make you some modest proposals which will relieve the local situation without impairing the effective control of all Imperial interests by the Governor. I will draw up a memo on my way from here to Cyprus. I do not like to feel that we are behaving in a highhanded & arbitrary fashion – even with the best intentions; & it is a serious

---

[1] In 1897, when he was Governor of the Madras Presidency, Sir Mansfield Clarke had incurred WSC's wrath by refusing the 4th Hussars polo team leave to take part in the interregimental tournament at Meerut (see Main Volume I, p. 306).

nuisance to have the Maltese giving us a bad name from one end of the Mediterranean to the other.

We sail tomorrow night in the *Venus* for Cyprus, where I shall stay nearly a week. A letter would catch me at Port Said on the 14th I think in case you wish to write to me.

> With good wishes, Believe me, Yours vy sincerely
> WINSTON S. CHURCHILL

Jack Churchill to WSC

EXTRACT

11 October 1907   28 Throgmorton Street

My dear Winston,

I received your letter from Malta – and am very glad you are pacified about Bolton Street.

There are no complaints from Mrs S and I am sure it will be all right. Every paper and every photo has been taken out of the house.

The City is still very bad indeed. The copper market is being jumped about all over the place by these big thieves in New York.

With regard to Cerros I do not think there is anything to be done but to hold on. Wheater has been buying quickly any shares that have been offered for sale – and when everything takes a better turn, he will be in a position to 'make a market' and get the price up. At present it is no use trying to do that. No one will look at anything from Consols to any damned Stinkfontein deep share.

Tinto's have been a great disappointment. They declared a dividend 10/–d increase of that which was expected – and the things go down in sympathy with Americans. Cecil [Grenfell] is for holding on a little longer, but I am afraid we shall have to cut a nasty loss. Old Natty's deal with me the day before you left – has cost him £20,000! This is secret.

Americans are flat again – and no one seems to take an interest in them. Cassel however has begun carefully to buy again. This is also secret – & you must know nothing about it. He has been away and I have not seen him, but evidently he thinks the bottom has been touched. Pray heaven it is, for the depression here gets on one's nerves. . . .

> Yrs
> JACK

WSC to Lord Elgin
(*Elgin Papers*)

TELEGRAM

13 October 1907   Limassol
                                                        Cyprus

Immediate

Confidential

Private. Just leaving Cyprus after five busy days. I am writing to you fully
upon numerous important questions which require attention. Greek unity
demonstration, though aggressive, not hostile to British Government. High
Commissioner for Cyprus very much pleased with general result of visit.
Island has been terribly starved by Treasury and bears deep mark in moral
and material conditions. Propose to call at Berbera after Aden.

WSC to Lady Randolph

19 October 1907   HMS *Venus*
                                                        at sea near Aden

Dearest Mamma,
    You will think me a faithless correspondent, and I confess my short-
comings; but I trust Eddie will have given you some account of our pilgrimage, & in any case there seem to have been pretty full accounts in
the newspapers.
    Of course the Red Sea in October – especially when rough as well as
sultry – is not an ideal condition. But it is nearly over now, and certainly,
apart from nature, nothing could be more comfortable or more ceremonious,
than this method of travel. I have two beautiful cabins to myself – one of
which is quite a large room with a delightful balcony at the end overlooking
the waves. The captain is unceasing in his efforts to promote our comfort, &
all the officers are most civil & attentive. I spend a good deal of every day,
and almost every dawn, on the bridge; & am becoming quite a mariner.
    The Admiralty instructions are to the effect that the Captain is to study
my wishes in respect to visiting any other ports than those originally mentioned; & I have availed myself of this to include Berbera, Somaliland, in
my tour. We shall reach Aden tonight & tomorrow we have to coal there.
During the night of the 20th we shall cross the Gulf & I shall spend I think
two days looking into the affairs of the Somaliland Protectorate – upon
which we spend £76,000 a year with uncommonly little return.

This will delay me three days reaching Mombasa & as I had only allowed 12 days in the EA Protectorates, I propose now to postpone my departure across the Great Lake till a week later than originally intended.

It is vy nice having Gordon [Wilson] with us. He is such a good fellow & such a good tracker. I have worked vy hard at Malta & Cyprus & have had to write several long reports upon things I want to have done. I expect I shall not get much shooting in East Africa. An Under-Secretary is a *rara avis* in these out of the way places & everyone wants to see him. *Now* I send you the CB letter wh I so stupidly forgot to enclose in my last. It is vy warm & friendly. But I do not see much prospect of a change at present. The only thing that might happen would be for me to go into the Cabinet keeping my present office, when Ld Ripon goes. That would suit me vy well. But they are afraid that Elgin's position would become difficult, he being such an unassertive fellow. *Qui vivra!* I must say I did not at all like that rascal Sievier occupying my house. But Jack put his case vy forcibly & well in a letter I had from him at Cyprus & I accept the *fait accompli*. Reading I fear does not make the progress I had hoped. You know what ship life is; & how hard it is to concentrate attention on board.

I hope you admired my aerial summer house at Salisbury H!¹

With best wishes to George, Believe me
Ever your loving son
WINSTON SC

Lady Randolph to WSC

EXTRACT

21 October 1907   The Warren House
                                         Stanmore

Dearest Winston,

I have no idea where this will find you, but I suppose it will reach you in time. I have been following your 'Royal Progress' with the keenest interest. I hear that Sir F. Hopwood has spoken in high praise of your Malta speech – & said it had a very good effect. I have not seen F. E. Smith & therefore have never heard the account of your French manoeuvres – How I envy you your trip! but I could never undertake Uganda on my 10 toes – what will yours & Eddie's be like at the end of your promenade?

... Miss Anning is working for Ld Hugh Cecil.

Your loving
MOTHER

---

¹ WSC had built himself a tree-house in the grounds.

Jack Churchill to WSC

25 October 1907   28 Throgmorton Street

My dear Winston,

It is difficult to find a moment to write to you.

You will have seen from the telegrams that there has been a panic in New York. It has been raging for three days and is not over yet.

Cecil and [I] have decided to hold on to your Unions. They are paid for and need not cause you any concern. This panic has nothing to do with the prosperity of the Railways.

They say that the dividend may be cut down. But I have seen Harriman[1] giving for the call and buying – and while he does that he will not cut the dividend. Cassel has been buying at these panic prices – and so have other big people.

It has been a great crash and has come from over-speculation and from dishonest men being shown up. The immediate cause is interesting. The Railways said they would borrow a lot of money and electrify a great deal of their systems. A great gamble in copper began at once – as of course electrification utilizes copper. Then Roosevelt began and said that the Railways must not borrow anymore. He began the investigation of some of the dishonest Trust people.

Copper slumped – and the Gamblers were ruined. Then the disclosures which came out in Roosevelt's investigations were so startling – that a distrustful feeling began everywhere – which at last culminated in a 'run' on the Knickerbocker Trust. Of course all sorts of small trust companies will follow – and [how] far it will go no one can tell.

If this had happened a year ago there would have been a panic in London. But London people have been very far-seeing. The bankers have taken every precaution. There are no American bills here – and New York has not been able to get any gold from London.

Apart from the losses we have, and they are enormous, I am very glad this has happened. A year ago all the Yankee millionaires were telling us that they were the only people on the earth and that New York was the centre of the financial world. Well most of them are ruined today and money is 100% in New York while it remains 4½% here.

I think the slow and sure system of Threadneedle Street has survived their jeers.

---

[1] Edward Henry Harriman (1848–1909), American railway magnate, owner of Union Pacific Railway; his battle for control of the Northern Pacific Railway led to a famous crisis on Wall Street in 1901. His financial methods were much criticized by President Theodore Roosevelt.

I have no particular news for you. Consuelo has gone to NY and was I see mobbed on her arrival. It was rather soon to go there.

I have sent off by this mail 300 films – which I hope will reach you. If you send home the exposed plates let me know and tell the S. Company to send me some proofs.

I must stop – Mama has written you most of the news. I heave every night until 8 o'clock – watching the crumbling prices. It is not very pleasant. Yes, our finances are not looking their best – I fear we shall have to borrow when you come back.

Best luck
JACK SC

Lady Lytton to WSC
EXTRACT

26 October [1907]   Knebworth

Winston,

You wrote me a very wonderful letter from Venice, and it gave me a lot of pleasure. Here we sit, bodily and mentally shaped by the grey chill of the air, and the damp of the ever-sweating soil, while you I suppose are immensely happy amongst new scenes, strange events; revelling in the freedom of the world under the wide palace of the sun. How I wish Victor and I had come with you, I think you might have managed that, it was awfully stupid of you not to. . . .

Girton Girl is here – and I have been out on her twice and much enjoyed her wild red hot ways, but I am not sure that we shall keep her, because our groom thinks her legs need blistering – we are going to watch her closely.

I care for nothing better just now than learning to ride astride, and I have a very neat suit to do this in – only all my fun has to take place alone, as I have no friends down here, and the house is too small for visitors. Oh! I know so well what I want – and time is going full gallop – and I shall have reached nothing before the end.

To begin with less bills; and more money; fame for Victor; a fatter face; another son; I could write forever on this subject! One has no chance now of selling one's soul for one's heart's desires – but I could almost sell mine to the Devil in return for a strong body, a cold heart and a flashing brain. Could you?

I see Granville Barker's new play, 'Waste' has been censored, and will never appear.[1] I am disappointed.

Antony calls me his dear-hearted Mother, which is rather intoxicating, and he tells me he is *almost* lion-hearted himself already! He is quite divine.

This letter must go. I will write short ones very often, and try to make you feel glad to come home again.

Yours always
P.L.

Licence to shoot Game

2 November 1907   Mombasa

The Rt Honble Winston Churchill & party are granted a complimentary licence to shoot such game as is allowed by the schedules of the game Regulations, during their tour through East Africa.

J. HAYES SADLER
Governor

WSC to Lady Randolph

6 November 1907   Camp Thika
                               (half way between Nairobi – Fort Hall)

Dearest Mamma,

I wish I cld find time to write you full accounts of all this most interesting journey. But my days are occupied literally from sunrise till bed either in shooting & travelling or else in official work wh presses upon me – in state apt for decision – from every side. I must however tell you about the rhinoceros hunt wh was certainly in its way quite as vivid & tingling an experience as any ordinary skirmish with bullets.

We left Mombasa after two days of functions & inspections & speeches, & proceeded up country by the Uganda Railway. Everything moves on the smoothest of wheel for me – a special train with dining & sleeping cars was at my disposal all the way, wherever I wished to stop – it stopped. When it went on, we sat (Gordon & I) on a seat in front of the engine with our rifles & as soon as we saw anything to shoot at – a wave of the hand brought the train to a standstill & sometimes we tried at antelope without even getting down. From the railway one can see literally every animal in the Zoo. Zebras, lions, rhinoceros, antelopes of every kind, ostriches, giraffes all

[1] It was, in fact, licensed in 1936.

– on their day – & often five or six different kinds are in sight at the same moment. At Simba – about 200 miles from the coast we stayed in a siding for two days & made excursions into the country. The first day I killed 1 zebra, 1 wildebeeste, 2 hartebeeste, 1 gazelle, 1 bustard (a giant bird). The third day was the feast of the rhino. We all started at dawn – Gordon, I, the Governor's son & Eddie Marsh, & marched off into the bush. After about two hours walking we saw some ibex – a vy fine kind of antelope with beautiful straight horns. Gordon & I stalked these & I wounded one vy severely. But he made off & we followed him up. Suddenly on turning round the corner of a hill & coming into a great wide plain of dry grass – we saw, almost 500 yards away a rhinoceros quietly grazing. I cannot describe to you the impression produced on the mind by the sight of the grim black silhouette of this mighty beast – a survival of prehistoric times – roaming about the plain as he & his forerunners had done since the dawn of the world. It was like being transported back into the stone age.

After we had united our party we started to sally out against Behemoth & do battle with him: and we started accordingly across this wide plain. We had not gone more than a hundred yards when by the greatest good luck we saw quite close to us under some little trees on our right two more rhinoceros placidly resting from the heat. If we had not noticed them & had gone on & fired at the others, they would have charged up-wind at us and as we should have had one wounded monster on our hands already – it might have been nasty. We changed our plan at once, hurried back to the edge of the plain & sneaked up under the brow of the plateau to within about 150 yards of the two new rhino. Then I fired at the big one with a heavy 450 rifle & hit her plum in the chest. She curved round & came straight for us at that curious brisk trot which is nearly as fast as a horse's gallop, & full of surprising activity. Everybody fired & both the rhino turned off – much to our relief, and then in a few more seconds down came the big one on the ground & the smaller one managed to get away under a heavy fire – this one we followed up & killed later in the day. I must say I found it exciting and also anxious work. The vitality of these brutes is so tremendous that they will come on like some large engine in spite of five or six heavy bullets thumping into them. You cannot resist a feeling that they are invulnerable & will trample you under foot however well you shoot. However all's well that ends well.

I began this letter four days ago at the Thika camp amid beautiful trees & waterfalls on my way to Fort Hall. I have not had *one quarter of an hour* to finish it till now 11th Nov back at Nairobi. All the time I have been moving about so fast, hunting lions, visiting stations, receiving native chiefs & riding through the country, and have been jolly glad to sleep in my clothes at the end of the day. The lion hunting was nervous work – especially beforehand – till one had familiarised oneself with the idea. But of course I had several of the best shots in the country with me: & I don't think there was much danger. I only saw one lion, & he escaped without being shot at. But he was a fine big yellow brute, plunging along through the high grass, & it was vy exciting wading along after him expecting to come upon him at any moment. Gordon however shot one, on the day when I was away at Embo & is delighted. He made a most excellent shot & killed the lion dead, but it leaped back into the reeds & no one could tell how much it was hurt. After waiting an hour & throwing stones, etc to make him move our friends lost patience & vy daringly & vy rashly walked in to the reeds in time to finish him. This is supposed to be the most dangerous thing you can do; & had I been there I would not have allowed it. However after a few yards the royal vermin was discovered lying stiff & cold: & again all's well!

I could only spend the night of the 6th & the morning of the 7th at the Thika camp, as I had to get on to Fort Hall, wh I did by motor-car – about 8 miles an hour over unmetalled roads in the afternoon of the 7th. The 8th, great Durbar of natives: 4000 – with all the chiefs stark naked in all essentials, – and in their full war toggery – men & women all dancing together & chanting in curious rhythms from daybreak on. I was presented by the various chiefs with 108 sheep, 7 Bulls, about £100 worth of ivory, an ostrich egg, many fowls & some vy good leopard skins. All these presents except the skins – wh I have kept – will be sold by Govt & in return presents of slightly greater value will be made to the chiefs. I have told them that each shall have a good bred ram to improve their stock. I also made them a speech wh comforted their anxious hearts.

After the pow-wow I had intended to ride to the Tana rises & then return by motor to Thika where our wild hunting party was assembled – & with that idea all arrangements had been made. But when I reached the banks of the Tana and looked out over the lovely & delicious country that lies beyond stretching gently up by gradual slopes to the mighty snow-clad peak of Mt Kenya – I could not bring myself to turn back. So we chucked lunch, kit and all other petty arrangements to the devil. I took Eddie Marsh, the Provincial Commissioner and a young official named Dundas[1] – who is a vy clever fellow & who amused me a great deal (he says he knows you); & on we went without waiting even for the rest of our train. We rode through all this beautiful country and just got into the little pub at Embo – 26 miles away – before it got dark – having nothing but what we stood up in & only a banana inside us. Embo is a new station opened only last year in a hitherto un-

[1] Kenneth Robert Dundas (1882–1915), Assistant Collector in British East Africa under the Foreign Office 1904–8; District Commissioner 1908; 4th son of 6th Viscount Melville.

penetrated country. The two white officers there were properly astonished as you may imagine to see us swoop down upon them with the night. But they gave us a most excellent dinner & we all slept on floors & chairs & blankets utterly but naturally tired. What a difference to the fag of a London day. My health bounds up with every day I spend in the open air. At dawn we rode back to Fort Hall, where the motor car waited to take me back to Thika. There we hunted lions all yesterday – but without success – only finding great fierce wart-hogs which we killed – galloping one of them down & shooting him with my revolver & so on here (Nairobi) for dinner & delighted Governor who is just made KCMG.

Joyous times – you will say – & indeed it is true. The country across the Tana is much richer than anything I have seen in India or S. Africa. It is no exaggeration to say that in beauty, in verdure, in fertility, in the abundance of running water, in the delicious coolness of the air, in its rich red soil, it will bear a fair comparison with the valley of the Po. I have told the Governor he may now advance further into this country & establish a new station & post at Meru – fifty miles beyond Embo.

This will bring 150,000 more natives under our direct control & add several English counties to our administration area. There will not I think be any bloodshed, as the native chiefs want us to come – & about 100 soldiers will be sufficient. This will operate next month: & we do Secret { not propose to consult the Colonial office till it is an accomplished fact! Thus the Empire grows under Radical Administration!

Well my dear Mamma, goodbye now – I cannot write any more as today I have constant work at papers & with different departments, & also we celebrate the King's birthday with a review & other festivities. Perhaps Sunny would like to see this letter. But do not let any one outside see it.

Your loving son
W

Jack Churchill to WSC

14 November 1907   The Bath Club
34 Dover Street

My dear Winston,

I am writing to tell you that a very wonderful thing has happened. Goonie loves me. I have loved her for a long time – but have always attempted to put thoughts of that kind out of my mind – because I felt that I had nothing to give her – and also chiefly because I never for one moment imagined that she would ever care for me.

About six months ago – I found that she loved me. We had long talks and spoke quite openly to each other. We agreed that it was impossible for us to marry – as there was no money – and I promised always to remain a friend to her. Since you went away until to-night I have not seen her – except on the race-course at Doncaster for a few moments (we were not in the same house). But my love for her was too strong – and at last I wrote and asked her if she would wait for me. She answered that she could not promise to do so. I accepted that. What else could I do? I have nothing in the world to offer her.

But a week afterwards she wrote again and told me her love for me was stronger than anything else. She said that she would sacrifice anything for her love; that her ambition for riches and everything else had all vanished and that she would wait for me until I could come and fetch her. I saw her tonight here in London – and we are agreed that our love is too strong to fight against. I have promised to come for her as soon as I can and we are *secretly* engaged.

This is absolutely secret. Only my Mother and George know about it. Her parents[1] know nothing. Nor must they – until I can come with some proposition.

It is all very wonderful – and one moment I am so happy at having won such love and the next I am driven to despair at the thought of all the difficulties in the way. There is money – there is Religion – there are her parents – who will be very angry.

But if only I can get at some of the former – the rest will count as nothing. I have painted dreadful pictures of what our life may have to be. But she promises that nothing makes any difference to her – and that her love for me is the only thing that counts.

All this has not happened in a hurry. We have both tried to avoid it – but our love has been too strong. I wish you were here to advise and help us. I cannot go on writing all the details of what I hope may happen. The present position is hell. Her family think I am flirting with her – and I may not see her. However it is I suppose a good thing that our love should have to stand a good test before we can marry. But the process is anything but pleasant. I am going to try and arrange for £1000 a year for certain down here. In very bad times I shall have that. In moderate times I ought to get 2 thousand and in good times 3, 4, or even 5 thousand. It is just my luck that this should happen in a year which for financial disasters is a record to any living memory. Also it is my first year as a partner – and therefore I have no reserves to fall back on. I am also rather disturbed to hear that the

---

[1] Montagu Arthur Bertie (1836–1928) succeeded his father as 7th Earl of Abingdon in 1884; married, as his second wife, Gwendeline, daughter of Lieut.-Gen. Hon. Sir James Dormer.

American property and the English 'Will' property are settled on our children and we have only a life interest in these things. The only thing which we absolutely have for our own are the 'settlements' amounting in all to about £13,000.

I cannot think that this is quite right; and I must have a closer look into things.

But you are so far away – that details like this cannot be discussed. I do not know when this will reach you – but it may not be for 6 weeks or more. The main point my dear – is that we both love each other absolutely. It has not been done in a hurry – and every attempt has been made to suggest to each other the impossibility of it all. But it has been of no use – and after 6 months of arguing against it – she has told me – she will only love me – and that she will wait until I can come and fetch her.

For months we have been regarding each other with a kind of mutual distrust. I never dared ask her to wait for me – because I thought she would never be able to be a poor man's wife – and she never thought I would ever ask her, because she thought perhaps my love was not strong enough to face a life of struggle and poverty for her sake.

Do you understand all this? I wish you were here. You were in love really once – and you know what that meant. But you had other things to think of. Your career and your future filled more than half of your life. I love the same way you did – but I have no other thoughts. All dreams of the future – my career and everything else, are wrapped up in one person. Nothing else matters to me in the least. I suppose that sounds very silly – but the only people who think it so are those who have never been able to feel these things themselves.

Well pray God it will work out alright. It seems all very difficult now. But if she means it – and I do not doubt her – as much as I do – then I have no fear. She shall be my wife – and I shall find a way to make her so soon.

I have told her to write and tell you all this – but when our letters will reach you I do not know. If only this beastly city would alter – and the extraordinary position in America become normal – everything would be so much clearer. I have a good position here – but it is just luck that it should be so bad at this time.

Write to Goonie – but I impress on you keep our *secret absolutely*. If her family suspected now – her life at Wytham would be unbearable. I will write to you further developments.

Yrs
JACK SC

Sir Francis Hopwood to WSC

EXTRACT

15 November 1907   Colonial Office

My dear Churchill,

We have followed from the telegrams in the newspapers your progress from place to place with much interest, and I have also had full reports of your speeches both in Malta and Cyprus. They have been read *in extenso* by the Secretary of State.

I am nursing up the Malta Memorandum until your return, as it must be dealt with with considerable circumspection. That relating to Cyprus has been printed and is now under the consideration of Lord Elgin. I have had no word with him upon it at present.

Your promised letter making proposals as to Somaliland, has not yet come to hand. . . . I talked to Lord Elgin on the subject, which was not new to him, for it seems that in former days Somaliland was under the direct jurisdiction of the India Office, and that he, as Governor General of India, was faced with the problem as to how internal order could be maintained in the country merely by retaining coast defences.

Last Saturday, the King's birthday, Solomon and I went to Sandringham to present the Cullinan Diamond. We had received a hint, anonymous it is true, that our train or the carriage in which we were to drive from the station to the house, might be held up and the diamond taken from us! We were accompanied all the way by the two principal members of the detective staff from Scotland Yard, and also by other minor detectives. Fortunately, or unfortunately, nothing happened, and the presentation was duly made in the presence of the King and Queen, the Queen of Spain[1], the Queen of Norway[2] and a large house party, including the Duke of Westminster and Revelstoke. We had an informal luncheon there after the presentation and then returned to town. The King and Queen were very much impressed with the diamond, and arrangements are now being made to have it cut, so that it may be used for the Royal Crown.[3] Needless to say, His Majesty presented Solomon with a KCVO.

We are in the throes of November Cabinets, and the Secretary of State

[1] Victoria Eugénie Julia Ena (b. 1887), daughter of Beatrice, youngest daughter of Queen Victoria, and Prince Henry of Battenberg; niece of King Edward VII; married King Alfonso VIII of Spain in 1906.

[2] Maud Charlotte Mary Victoria (1869–1938), youngest daughter of King Edward VII. Married her first cousin, Prince Christian of Denmark, who in 1905 became King Haakon VII of Norway.

[3] In 1908, the Diamond was sent to Amsterdam and cut into a number of large stones. The largest – a 516½ carat drop-shaped brilliant known as the *Star of Africa No 1* – now forms part of the head of the Royal Sceptre with the Cross. It is slightly less than five times the

has to induce the Cabinet to approve both the Transvaal Chinese Labour Law, and the Transvaal Immigration Law. He has written memoranda for the Cabinet on both these Acts, and I do not assume that there will be any difficulty with regard to either of them.

Smuts has written a very strong Minute against making the administrative changes as to trials of Chinese by Magistrates in compounds in lieu of the use of the ordinary Magisterial Courts etc, and if the Minute is published it would certainly be difficult for us to justify the change in administrative procedure; but in order to make as good a Parliamentary case as we can, I am urging the Chief to keep open the question of making these administrative changes, so that we may be in a position to say that we are pressing for them if we find that the extremists in the House of Commons are disposed to be objectionable. Solomon however tells me he has seen people like Mackarness, Molteno[1] etc, and I have myself seen Seely, and in their present frame of mind there would appear to be little chance of serious opposition. In the meantime the Chinamen are departing month by month, and the market in South African shares is rising week by week. George Farrar[2] has made a speech in which he says that he recognises that the Chinese experiment is dead and gone for ever, and Abe Bailey tells me that they find that they can get on very well without them.

J. B. Robinson has been to see me in really a furious passion, because he did not receive a baronetcy. He says that he spent enormous sums of money, to a great extent at the bidding of the Government, and that he understood from the Prime Minister, and also I gather from you, that it would be alright.

I am taking steps to let the Prime Minister know Robinson's very strong feeling on the subject, because as he is so stoutly backed up by the Transvaal Government, I really think it a pity to give him serious ground for complaint for what is after all a trifling matter.

Wallace,[3] you will be glad to hear, duly appeared in the Honours list. Also Lamb,[4] the member for Rochester, who has been here to see me and express his thanks at the instance of the Whips.

---

weight of the famous Koh-i-noor diamond, also a part of the Crown Jewels. The next largest – a 309$\frac{3}{16}$ carat brilliant known as the *Star of Africa No 2* – is set in the circlet of the Imperial State Crown. Two of the relatively smaller stones were set in the Crown of Queen Mary, George V's consort.

[1] James Tennant Molteno (1865–1936), Member of Cape Parliament 1890–98; Speaker of House of Assembly, Union of South Africa 1910–18; knighted 1911.

[2] George Herbert Farrar (1859–1915), Chairman East Rand Proprietary Mines; knighted 1902; baronet 1911.

[3] William Wallace (1856–1916), Deputy High Commissioner and acting Governor Northern Nigeria 1900–10; KCMG 1907.

[4] Ernest Henry Lamb (1876–1955), Liberal MP for Rochester 1906–10, 1910–18; CMG 1907; knighted 1914; Baron Rochester 1931; Paymaster-General 1931–5.

Talking of the Prime Minister, you will be sorry to hear that he has been very seriously unwell. He has no doubt over-taxed his strength, and in the middle of last Wednesday night was seized·with a more or less dangerous heart attack. I hear good accounts of him privately, but on the other hand the fact that such a thing should have happened must give us cause for anxiety. Should I hear of any unfavourable symptoms, I have it in mind to send you a telegram. He had spoken at the Guildhall last Saturday; was at Windsor on Sunday; spoke again on Monday; was at Windsor for the German Emperor's visit on Monday evening; at a Cabinet meeting on Tuesday morning; made a speech in the City on the same day; went to Windsor again in the evening; received a deputation on Wednesday morning; went to Bristol in the evening to a political demonstration, and was taken ill afterwards. The report to-day is that no further bulletins will be issued.

The Office re-organisation is at last complete,[1] after a good deal of fighting and skirmishing with the Treasury, but your prophecy has come true, and we have got all we asked for. Now we are going to work and by the time you come back I trust we shall be in some semblance of order.

The most important subject we have had before us since the Ministers came back to town is that of the South African garrison. You will recollect that we made an arrangement for the reduction of the number of guns for each battery, and nothing more, but I gather that when the first Autumn Cabinet was held, the Chancellor of the Exchequer and others pressed vigorously for a substantial reduction in the garrison. I telegraphed to Selborne for reasons against it and the Secretary of State, although recognising that as time goes on, it will be impossible to maintain a large garrison in responsible governed colonies, is strenuously opposing any material reduction at the present time. There is, I fancy, considerable difference of opinion in the Cabinet on the subject, and the discussion will be resumed at the next meeting. I have seen Haldane and two or three of them privately and hope that I have at any rate secured a lull until after next September. This will give time for reconsideration.

A Deputation of Swaziland Chiefs arrive tomorrow to pay their respects to the King. They have come principally about the delimitation of their country as between themselves and the old concessionaires, but according to Selborne's advice, they are to receive a flat negative to their petition, so their visit will be really nothing more than ornamental and social. We are making arrangements to give them certain entertainments and some presents.

[1] For details of the reorganization of the Colonial Office see J. A. Cross, *Whitehall and the Commonwealth*, London, 1967.

As far as I can see all goes well. The Education Bill is settled, and the only disturbing political factor at the moment arises from some speech that was made by Lord Tweedmouth, on the subject of Scotch land. He seems to have favoured a handing over to the Scotch County Councils, and this has set our Scotch friends by the ears.

Since writing the above I am led to take a more serious view of the question of reduction of SA Garrison – the Army estimates are going to show a positive increase & this the Cabinet cannot stand. They have a strong memorial from more than 100 of their best supporters against it & in favour of reduction. Great pressure will be put on Ld E to agree to bring away about 2000 men before the end of the present financial year. McKenna & some of them agree that we must keep 10,000 out there but not more.

Yr v sincerely

FRANCIS S. HOPWOOD

WSC to Jack Churchill

17 November 1907   Kisumu
                                                 British East Africa

My dear Jack,

Your letter gives me a most interesting account of the New York crisis, and I am very glad to get it here before I sail. Certainly I do not wish you to sell the Unions; they have been bought and paid for, and I trust are quite a good investment.

The films have arrived safely, only just in time, for we had reached our last roll. I have received a fine offer from the *Strand Magazine* for five articles for £750, which I propose to accept, as it will definitely liquidate all possible expenses in this journey. There will be another £500 in book form.

Here we are at last at the end of the Uganda Railway, on the great Lake, and at one o'clock we start in quite a large, comfortable steamer, for Entebbe and Uganda. Mamma will shew you my letter to her telling her about the rhinoceros, and since then we had a most pleasant day at Lord Delamere's[1] estate, Elmenteita; riding about all over the great plains, swarming with game of every description, some of which we shot, and every now and then large wild pigs with tremendous tusks, whom we rode after and speared, or tried to spear. It generally ended, however, in their having to be finished off with a revolver.

One made a very ugly charge at me, but luckily I plugged him in the neck

---

[1] Hugh Cholmondeley, 3rd Baron Delamere (1870–1931), a pioneer of colonization of British East Africa; succeeded father 1887.

with my spear, so hard that it broke, and the brute escaped with a foot of it sticking in his body.

The Governor came up here with us, and we had a special train, which carried a good many members of the Government, so that in the intervals of these field sports I have transacted a good deal of business of one sort and another; and altogether my tour here has been very profitable and instructive. This is really a wonderful country, and almost every day I have seen landscapes superior to anything which India or South Africa can offer, and some parts really will hold their own with England and Italy. Although we are on the Equator it is quite cool, owing to the great height of all this African plateau. The Railway reaches an altitude of 8,320 feet, and there the climate is just like a cool English May. Here on the Great Lake, 3,700 feet up, we are in July. I am steadily pursuing the road marked out beforehand, and if all goes well I shall be back in England on the 15th January. I wonder if Freddy will be home again, and if so (or, indeed, if not) whether he would let me stay in his house until Sievier clears out of Bolton Street. You might find this out for me, and if nothing can be arranged, engage me some rooms at the Ritz.

Please do make inquiries as to the condition in which Freddy's motor car arrived home. It was all right when it left. I assured him that I took the greatest pains that it should be sent safely back, but Freddy has already left for America, and I do not know who received the car when it arrived. It is always possible that other people use it when it passes out of one's own hands, and then I should get credited with any carelessness which had occurred. Talk to F. E. Smith about this, because I consider he is jointly responsible with me for the safe return of the car, and I have written to him to tell him to find out about it.

I will write to you again from Uganda.

Best love dear old boy, from
Your affectionate brother
WINSTON

General Sir Ian Hamilton to WSC

EXTRACT

18 November 1907

Head Quarters Southern Command
Andover

Dictated

My dear Winston,

Permit me to congratulate you with all my heart on the very able Report you have written concerning the Manoeuvres of the 7th French Army Corps. I have read it with much interest, and after passing it round to the senior Officers in the Command I shall forward it to the War Office, where I hope it may be made some use of and not shoved into a pigeon hole. Indeed, I shall do what lies in me to avert that not unusual termination to many a valuable document by informing Mr Haldane privately of what I am sending in officially to the Director of Operations. . . .

I notice you contrast these life-like French Manoeuvres with the crude absurdities that we saw last year in Silesia. In conversation with one of the German General Staff Officers who were staying with me this autumn for our Manoeuvres, I touched upon the unreal situations that had arisen last year at their Manoeuvres, and he hastened to explain that the new Chief of the General Staff had induced the Kaiser this year to forsake theatrical display for a closer approximation to reality. It will be interesting to see if this will be borne out by the reports of our Officers.

And now, my dear boy, as to yourself. I track your movements by the series of speeches which give the world your line of travel in much the same way as the small pieces of paper left by the school hare show the line of country to the pursuing hounds. All seems well with you, and I do not think you could have chosen a more convenient period to get in touch with the realities of your Dominions.

Lloyd George has had a big success, but he was lucky indeed in having an easy situation to deal with, as neither masters nor men really had any heart for the fight.[1] Otherwise nothing of much interest or greatly affecting the prestige of any politician has occurred. Haldane is going to make a success of his Territorial Army. It is to me a delightful and highly entertaining thought that one of the chief achievements of a Liberal–Radical–Socialistic Government may probably be a fine Military achievement. Unless my instincts deceive me, Haldane's Territorial Army and the South African

---

[1] After negotiations arranged by Lloyd George a threatened railway strike was averted on November 6.

Constitution will stand out in future years as the big things, and the only big things, of the big majority.

Goodbye for the present. Take care of yourself, for your health is precious not only to your friends but to the country.

Yours ever

IAN HAMILTON

Jack Churchill to WSC

21 November 1907   28 Throgmorton Street

My dear Winston,

I wrote to you last week – to explain to you what had happened about myself and Goonie. I hope you received it alright. There is, I am sorry to say, nothing definite to add to my last. I saw Goonie last week in London for the first time since you went away. We have made our promises to each other – and she is ready to wait for me until times are better. She has told her mother – who while disapproving – is sympathetic. Her Father does not yet know – and I am waiting to arrange my financial prospects etc properly before I go to him. I have told Nelke[1] and he is sympathetic. I have asked him to give me a guarantee of £1000 a year. He has not definitely answered yet – but I am sure he will do something for me. I am going to Tring for Sunday – and I shall find out whether Natty will help me – I feel certain he will.

It is all very wonderful & I can hardly realise yet that it is true. I never believed or even hoped that her love for me could be so strong. I told you – I remember one day this summer – that I did not believe she would marry a poor man. But all that was wrong. In spite of my doleful stories of poverty, she says she will wait until I come for her; and that no other man can mean anything to her.

I am so worried about it – and wish I could write and tell you that something was settled. Everything is so *en l'air* and I see so many difficulties in the way. But I believe we shall be able to surmount them.

The financial situation in America is still very critical. But the newspapers will tell you more than I can.

I must send this off as it is to go by messenger, who leaves tonight for Cairo.

Goodbye – send me a line. I am going through a mixture of happiness and fear that is not enviable.

---

[1] Paul Nelke (1860–1925), senior partner of Nelke, Phillips and Company, Stockbrokers, the firm with which Jack Churchill was employed at the time.

Don't tell anyone about Goonie. It would be so tiresome for anyone to know – before things were settled in some form or other.

Yrs

JACK SC

Lady Randolph to WSC

21 November 1907

My darling Winston,

I have not written to you for ages – but I understood from Jack that letters wd only have to wait for you. A 'Confidential pouch' is going to-morrow & probably will reach you sooner than the ordinary post. I was delighted with your one letter – but expected no more. The Press has kept me *au fait* of your movements & speeches – I feel I have so much to say I do not know where to begin. In the first place Jack will have told you *his* news – this will probably surprise you. I sometimes thought you had designs in that quarter – but not serious ones – & Goonie has always cared for Jack. They are both much in love but will have to wait a long time I'm afraid – ways & means are not brilliant – but there is no doubt a couple can do on little, if they have no aspirations to entertain or live in any style. Jack will have written to you his ideas about Nelke etc – therefore I will leave the subject – Goonie is a good girl besides being charming, & she is quite determined to wait for Jack. No one knows a word of it. So do not tell even Marsh. He might write to someone. You will be sorry to hear that we have made up our minds to let SH for a year from January – & take a tiny flat in London. We intend only keeping the Waldens & my maid – George hasn't been able to draw one penny from his business this year – so we have no nest egg to fall back upon. Perhaps things will be better in a year. Anyhow it is the only thing to do. I am making the best of it – for it preys dreadfully on poor George who is getting quite ill over it all. I wonder how CB really is? I hear they won't let him do any work for some time. I fancy there will be a change soon. He will probably go to the H of L's & Sir E. Grey will be Prime Minister & you will be in the Cabinet. Those are *my* views! How I envy you basking in the sun – & how interesting your journey has been.

I hear they say you are much missed here – they want you for speeches! Thank Goodness you are safely away from them! I have been opening an Exhibition of Books today in Bond Street. It has been got up by the *Daily Chronicle*. All the publishers & authors were there – & I made a speech & Mr John Murray proposed a vote of thanks to me. He is very deaf & made a 'fuddly' speech – said 'Mrs Cornwallis – who is an authoress & the mother of an *authoress!*' Shrieks from the Audience – I will send you the report of the proceedings. We are going to stay with George Curzon of K [Kedleston] next week. I will write to you from there & find out his news. The French Press has noticed my first instalment in the *Century* at great length & in most flattering terms. The *Temps* & the *Gaulois* each gave 2 columns! I wish you were here to cast an eye on the new chapters. We talk & think of you so much. Bless you darling – do take care of yourself & give my love to Gordon & Eddie. The latter has not written. The only good thing in our coming to London is that I shall see more of you. I had a letter from Sunny. He is very lonely poor thing. I asked him to come to SH. George & I, & Jack are going to the Ridleys for Xmas. I hear Consuelo is to be there. That does not enthuse me. Now Goodbye & good luck & Many happy returns of the day – altho' it is a bit previous.

Your loving
MOTHER

Mrs Scrivings says all is quite right at No 12. Togo is at SH & has become enormous!

WSC to Lady Randolph

23 November 1907 Jinja
Victoria Nyanza

Dearest Mamma,

Tomorrow we leave steam communications of all kinds and plunge on foot into this tremendous country, to emerge if all's well, at Gondokoro on the 15 December.

Everyone is extremely well & we have all enjoyed ourselves vy much indeed. We are at this moment steaming along in the little steamer *Sir William Mackinnon* from Kampala the Capital of Uganda to Jinja, the point where the Nile plunges out of the great lake & starts on its journey of 3500 miles to the sea. Perfect weather, delicious cool breezes, beautiful scenery, a cheery party – and islands absolutely depopulated by sleeping sickness. A sinister contrast.

You will be glad to hear that I have accepted the offer of the *Strand Magazine* to write them five articles at £150 a piece, or £750 for the series. So that the question of expenses for the expedition is satisfactorily solved. There will also be a book publication, worth perhaps £500 – perhaps more.

We had long interviews with kings, chiefs & missionaries in Kampala & certainly the degree of civilization to wh the natives of Uganda have attained is vy wonderful. More than 200,000 can read & write, & they seem a most peaceful & industrious people.

I am concerned to read of CB's illness. Such attacks however overcome are vy serious at 72. His removal from the scene would lead to many changes; & I should be sorry to lose a good friend who has always shown me kindness. I expect political circles at home will have been busily buzzing. I am vy glad to be out of the way.

With best love, I remain, Your affectionate son
W

PS George ought not to gamble; but I am vy glad he won. The Little King of Uganda[1] is exactly like Consuelo in his expression.

J. A. Spender to WSC

23 November 1907   45 Sloane Street

My dear Churchill,

A Reuter telegram announcing that you have 'not seen a lion' pricks my conscience and reminds me that I promised you a letter which I have never written. I am sorry about the lion, but I hope that you have seen other things which make up for its absence, and have got safely through the fever belt which you told me was to be your portion for a hundred miles or so.

You have missed – in order of demerit – black fogs, the German Emperor, the railway agitation and the triumph of Lloyd George, the baiting of Arthur Balfour at Birmingham, and, I gather, a lively controversy among the most esteemed of your colleagues about next year's estimates. As autumns go it has not been so dull. The Kaiser's visit was really a success and I think will lead to something rather important. Haldane had a great success at Windsor and even the melancholy Metternich[2] was almost cheerful. Some of us newspaper men went to see the potentate, when he came to the Embassy, and he greatly endeared himself to us by his entire lack of discretion and repose. But he was looking ill and much thinner than when one saw him at Potsdam in June.

The Liberal Party? Nothing is changed, but a campaign against the Lords won't run in England on a Scottish Bill. I have been trying to say to some of your colleagues that it will be a great mistake to open the session by reintroducing the Scottish Bills, unless the intention is deliberately to make the Lords question *the* question of next year and to run to a dissolution before many months. My own impression from what I hear is that Arthur Balfour

[1] His Highness Sir Daudi Chwa, Kabaka of Buganda (1896–1939), succeeded his father, King Mwanga of Buganda, 1897; KCMG 1925; KBE 1937.
[2] Count Paul von Wolff-Metternich zur Gracht (1853–1934), German Ambassador in London 1901–12, in Constantinople 1915–17.

doesn't want a dissolution before 1910, but with the Scottish Bills, Education and Licensing for next year, he may be so committed that he must force the pace, especially if Rosebery is driving in the background. The programme for next session ought to have been Licensing, Poor Law Reform and Old Age Pensions, with Education and the Scottish Bills the session after, i.e. if the Government wants to last with credit. What I fear is that the Lords will manage to discredit you next year, and that, in spite of it, you will go on living a filling-up-the-cup existence which means disaster at the next election.

The PM was sharply ill at Bristol – the result of a life disordered by speeches, dinners and Royal junketings, quite unfit for an old gentleman to lead. I am told that the King and the Emperor kept him standing for two hours and a half on end the day before his seizure. Poor old Ripon was so exhausted that he reclined on a table and got Mrs Sydney Buxton[1] to spread her skirts in front of him. The PM, however is not dangerously hurt and his doctors promise him a complete recovery after a month at Biarritz. There was much temporary flutter at the possibility of his withdrawal and I gather that the succession was considered quite secure for Asquith. His only possible rival, Grey, steadily refuses to emerge from the FO, and the Radicals, led by Massingham in the *Nation*, appear to be planning an attack on him and Haldane.

Labour is rather threatening at this moment and the party will have to make up its mind whether it means to do a deal with the Labour men or not. If not, then a Bill for second ballot on Crawshay-Williams's alternative vote becomes imperative and should be introduced next session. At present the policy seems to be to take a high line and do nothing – which is disastrous.

I can imagine how foolish and remote all this will seem to you, if by any chance it reaches you in some wild place under the Equator. I suppose you will annex something on the way – rumour says you will reappear in the Congo, leading the tribes against King Leopold. I am preparing an article 'The real object of Winston Churchill's mission, the truth at last revealed'. In any case do something safe in a reasonably temperate climate, and come back with a whole skin. My wife sends her kindest regards.

Ever yours

J. A. SPENDER

I was going to protest against the late meeting of Parliament, but magnanimously forbore on hearing that you could not be back earlier.

---

[1] Mildred Anne (1866–1955), married Sydney Buxton in 1896 as his second wife; GBE 1919.

Lady Gwendeline Bertie to WSC

EXTRACT

26 November 1907   Coombe Abbey
                                            Coventry

My dear Winston,

Winston *tout court* I call you, in view of my becoming your sister in law in due time. That is what I am going to become to you. Tell me, do you like the prospect? is it agreeable to you? I have fallen in love with Jack, and he with me, and we want to marry each other so much – but we have to wait, as we have no money at present – it will come, the money, some day, & that some day must be soon, and it will be soon – & meanwhile we love each other – Winston – Jack is your brother and you are very devoted to him, and of course you are interested in his welfare. I promise you I will be such a good wife to him, and always his slave. I will make him happy, and I will try my utmost to be worthy of him. Thank you so much for your letter you wrote from the Red Sea. It was so nice of you to write at all, to have remembered that I was existing even! Amongst all the pomp & ceremony of your state progress – I was perfectly delighted when I got that letter, it interested me so much too. You wrote all about the Greek Islands, & Malta, & enclosed a photograph of yourself, surrounded with priests, archbishops in robes. Well since then I have followed you to Aden & Mombassa. The English Press gives the English Public a full account of your doings, & it was this morning in a half penny illustrated that I saw you land at Mombassa, in a big white helmet, & being received by important trading officials dressed in white, the sun blazing, one could feel the heat by looking at the photograph, but you chose to wear a black suit, it made you a conspicuous figure at all events.

The *Punch* has 'Winston day by day' which is always interesting to those who take interest in you; and so on; you are always in the lime light. . . . I will tell you what is very sad, & that is this smash, money smash, American smash – & I cannot tell you how very sorry I am that it has hit George & your mother; & I am as depressed as them, that they have to let Salisbury Hall, it must be so annoying for them; but your Mother is a very wonderful woman & so philosophical – I had lunch with her the other day in London, & in spite of everything, her spirits & her vitality is wonderful. She never gives in – not for a single moment. I expect you know of Pamela more than I do. I have not seen her for ages. She is being gay & admired & looking as radiant as she always does. She has got the dearest little house now in South Audley Street, which makes her very happy, it was her ardent wish to have

it, and bless her, it is fulfilled at last. I wish I could write you a really interesting letter, but I can not, it is a pity.

The suffragettes have been a great trial to the harrassed Ministers. Poor
Herbert Gladstone had to take refuge in flight at Lords a few days ago.
Herbert Gladstone is very stupid, astoundingly stupid, he really is, but he
cannot help it – I am very sorry for him. I have made a new friend in the
person of Mr Alfred Lyttelton. What a charming man, & he is quite conscious
of his charm, but that does not matter – & I will tell you who I think also
very charming, & that is Ld Curzon. He has been at Oxford for a fortnight,
making himself extremely popular in his new office of Chancellor of the
University. But all this is very stupid – what I am telling you – please write
to me again; please find time, & leisure & inclination & the mood to do so!
I wish you all good luck for the rest of your expedition. Forgive the volume
instead of a letter.

Yours sincly
GOONIE

WSC to the King

EXTRACT

In Camp near Mrali
Victoria Nile

27 November 1907

[Copy]

Your Majesty,

I have waited, Sir, until I have been some weeks in Africa before availing
myself of yr permission to write you a letter, in order that I might form some
impressions wh are the fruit not merely of observation but of reflection.

The strongest feeling that I experience is of admiration & wonder at the
beauty & worth of these noble & spacious possessions wh have been so
lately added to YM Dominions. There are large parts of the EA Protectorate wh in fertility, in verdure, in the coolness of the air, in their streams
of running water & their rich red soil, are far superior to anything I have
ever seen in India or SA, & really bear & even challenge comparison with
England & Italy. I allude particularly to the country all round Mt Kenya,
to the Rift Valley, & to the elevated plateau, nearly 9000 ft high, of the
Mau escarpment. Most of all I praise the Kenya district. There never was
a mountain that made so little of its height as Kenya. It rises so gently from
the plain, & by such vy gradual slopes, that one wd never believe that it

was nearly 17000 ft high, but for the beautiful snow peaks at its summit. And it is on these gradual slopes that according to the altitude it is possible to grow every conceivable crop or tree known in the world from the Equator to the Arctic circle.

Here in Uganda we are at a lower level – abt 4000 ft above the sea, & it is of course much hotter than in the Highlands. Yet no one cd call the heat oppressive, or compare it for a moment with the plains of India, & the beauty & intense fertility of the country are inspiring. I cannot doubt that Uganda will be one of the greatest centres of tropical cultivation, & that a steady stream of most valuable & necessary raw materials including esp cotton will flow down the Uganda Ry to supply Br manufacturers.

There is however a reverse to the medal, & it is dark indeed & sinister. The coolness of the air must never lead one to forget that all these lands lie upon the Equator. The direct ray of the sun, & the unusual altitude, seem to produce after a few years evil effects upon the nerves, the memory, & the general health of the European. Like his imported stock, he seems to deteriorate, & if not refreshed by regular periods of residence in temperate climates, it is very doubtful whether he wd live the normal span. In Uganda, many serious diseases – nearly all engendered by insects, exact a heavy & increasing toll of our officers, & the movement & activity wh the colony of the British has produced in the country seems to have stirred slumbering perils. For instance there is the spirillum tick fever wh is our chiefest danger in travelling along these roads & against wh even the best precautions often prove vain. Road after road has become infected, & officer after officer is struck down by these tiny pests with an intermittent fever of the most cruel severity.

But of course, as YM well knows, the worst of all is the sleeping sickness. It is like an-old time wizard's curse. In order that the spell may work, 5 separate conditions must all be present: water, trees, bushes, the tsetse fly & one infected person. Remove any one of these, & the charm is broken. But let them all be conjoined, & the absolute & certain extermination of every human being within the area is only a question of time.

I find that the Govr of Uganda, Mr Hesketh Bell,[1] has dealt with this scourge (by wh at least 200,000 persons have died around the lake shores alone, & by wh whole populous islands have been swept clear) in a vy effective & energetic manner. Wherever it is absolutely necessary to come to the lake – as for instance at places like Entebbe, Kampala Port, Jinja, etc, we have had the trees & bushes all cut away, with the result that the

---

[1] Hesketh Bell (1864–1952), Governor of Uganda 1907–9; Governor and Commander-in-Chief of Northern Nigeria 1909–12; of Leeward Islands 1912–15; of Mauritius 1915–24; KCMG 1908; GCMG 1925.

dreaded tsetse fly quite disappeared, & all danger is at an end so long as one keeps to the clearings. But of course it is not possible to do this except at a few special places, & so from the whole of the lake shore all the population has been withdrawn. Therefore where there are no people there are no tsetses and where there are tsetses there are no infected people to poison them & so spread the disease. Unless a remedy is discovered soon for the sickness, all those infected will die, & there cannot consequently be any hope of greatly reducing the mortality for some years to come. But when this melancholy harvest has been reaped, the field will be clear.

I was sorry to find a good deal of discontent among the white settlers in the EA Protectorate. No doubt the adminsn of the country might be improved in a good many ways, & I have made a long list of suggestions for Ld Elgin as the result of my conversations with the Govr & of my numerous interviews with deputations who came to see me. But making every allowance for many vexations wh the settlers suffer under, I must tell YM that they seem to me to advance vy extravagant pretensions, & do not show themselves sufficiently recognisant of the many benefits & services rendered to them by the officials whose disinterested labours are worthy of the highest praise. There can be no question of our handing over this beautiful Protectorate upon wh we have spent so much, with its 4 or 5 millions of YM native subjects, to the control of the first few thousand white men who happen to arrive in the country. There are of course a gt many vy good people among them, & I was careful not to discourage them in any way by what I had to say; but in the last two or three years there has been an influx of a vy low class of S. African element, & it is to their influence that a great deal of the agitation is due.

I write this letter to YM from a camp about 12 miles W of Mruli. We have come here from Jinja, or Ripon Falls, as it might well be called, by a journey of 3 days march & 3 days in canoes towed by a steam launch across Lake Chioga [Kyoga]. Tomorrow we march on to the Masindi & thence by 3 stages to the Murchison Falls & Lake Albert. This route will enable me to see the two gt waterpower centres wh will one day drive the machinery of vy considerable industries. It also follows the most probable line of the rlway extension from the Victoria & Albert Lakes.

This Sir is perhaps the most attractive work wh shd be taken immediately in hand in this part of the world. Only two short links of rlway are required – one of abt 40 & the other of abt 60 miles length – to unite the two gt Lakes with the navigable reaches of the Nile & with L. Chioga. For 100 miles of rlway construction, wh I am informed by the engineers who have come with me wd cost more than £4000 a mile, an increased radius of steam communication of nearly 300 miles wd be obtained, & it wd be possible to travel from Mombasa to the Albert Lake in less than 90 hours. The effect of this wd be nearly to add a third to the length of the U Rlway at only abt. 1/12 of its cost, & to open into the vy heart of Africa a sure swift road down wh all the trade of the upper waters of the Congo & of this fertile country of Unyoro wd certainly flow. I cannot think of any better method of raising the Uganda Ry to a proper paying commercial position, & of course besides from a military point of view such a line wd place us beyond the reach of rivalry of any kind in Central Africa. I earnestly hope that this enterprise may seem to commend itself to YM, & that in that case I may be able to take part in carrying it through while I have the hon to remain at the CO.

I have been kept so busy with official work & seeing people who desired interviews that I have found but little time for sport. But I was fortunate in shooting a rhinoceros near Simba in EA as well as a good many different kinds of antelope, & Gordon Wilson shot a good lion at the Thika River on the road to Mt Kenya. It is vy pleasant for me to have him with me as a companion, for he is an excellent traveller never out of spirits or tired or bored or vexed whatever may happen. . . .

I hope, Sir, you are enjoying vy good health, and sending my best wishes for a happy Christmas & New Year,

I remain, YM faithful & devoted servant

WINSTON S. CHURCHILL

Sir Francis Hopwood to WSC

EXTRACT

30 November 1907   Colonial Office

My dear Churchill,

Since I wrote to you, there has been a great deal of discussion in the Cabinet on the subject of the South African Garrison.

As far as I can make out that distinguished body was practically unanimous on determining to reduce the garrison to 10,000 men. Lord Elgin pressed strenuously for as much delay as possible, but the emphasis laid by the Chancellor of the Exchequer on the expediency of showing no increase in the coming Army estimates, told very much in the opposite direction. As a result I gather no exposition of policy is to be made, but there is to be a gradual withdrawal of the troops extending over a considerable period of time, until the limit that I indicated has been reached.

Lord Elgin has written a private letter to Selborne in this sense and as the High Commissioner was violently opposed to any further reduction for a period of 5 years, I am wondering what his reply will be.

Since the determination of the Cabinet there has been a disappointing retrocession of unrest in the minds of the Natal Government on the subject of Dinizulu. . . . They feared to move without our help while they thought he was strong, now they ask us for nothing and with evidence of his weakness, propose to break him without our aid. I have told Nathan that he must get in touch with the High Commissioner, because the follies of the Natal Government may at any time fire the train of native unrest which will blaze out in Swaziland and goodness knows where else.

About the Swazis, their deputation is in this country, they have seen Lord Elgin and myself at the Colonial Office and have had an interview with the King. They are paying their own expenses and their personal conduct is anything but above reproach. We are anxious that they should return to South Africa, as soon as possible. They have, however, fallen into the hands of unscrupulous lawyers and although they came over here to urge certain points which they have freely stated and which have been met, they have, on the advice of barristers, now filed a petition, not with the King or with the Secretary of State, but with the Privy Council asking that their independence may be recognised! This method of procedure, quite apart from the demerits of the case, involves the unpleasant possibility of their remaining here for weeks and weeks, and according to the rules of the Privy Council, their petition has to be considered by the King in Council, and nobody knows when that will be.

The Cabinet approved the two Bills for the Transvaal about Indian Emigration and Chinese Labour. In the latter case, I pressed that the request made by the Governor for administrative reform should be kept open, because it appears to me that it would give you something to bargain with, when you have to defend the action of the Government in the House of Commons. On the other hand I have little fear that you will be criticised about the action of the Government by our friends Mackarness and Company. I have seen several of the 'crowd' & they seem content with the visible transportation of Chinamen.

Two of your telegrams to the Office have tried me much too highly, namely, the one about Somaliland and the other the disbandment of the King's African Rifles. I cannot go into the merits and demerits of either of your propositions within the limitations of a letter.

With regard to Somaliland, your propositions promised in your letter of the 22nd of October have not yet come to hand, but the Secretary of State, who had the question before him when he was Governor General of

India, the Foreign Office, I believe the India Office, Cordeaux,[1] Gough[2] and Hannyngton[3] all opposed the proposition to cease the building of forts and the arming of the friendly native tribes, tooth and nail, and without having the details of what you propose and your arguments in support of your proposals before me, it was quite impossible to make headway against such a general and expert opposition. When you return the whole question must be gone into, and among other things we shall have to consider the attitude we have taken up both as regards Italy and Abyssinia.

With regard to the second question, namely the disbandment of the 1st Battalion of the King's African Rifles, I send you a copy of a memorandum which Colonel Gough has written. Lord Elgin is I understand still considering your telegram and as he is away in Scotland I have no opportunity of speaking to him on the subject.

You also sent us a telegram with regard to Chamberlain's land claim, and upon this I have been more fortunate. We have been able to meet your wishes. The same thing applies to the monorail tramway between Kampala and the Lake. The Crown Agents have got an estimate of it – which I have not yet seen – and it shall be cabled to Mombasa.

The Office is very anxious that we should approach the Treasury for a railway from the Congo boundary to the Semike, at a cost of £1,200,000, but I cannot for the life of me imagine that the Chancellor of the Exchequer, in the present state of the money market, will entertain the proposal for a moment.

I had a long conversation with the King a few days ago, and he enquired most kindly after you and said that he followed, in the newspapers, your proceedings with great interest. He also laughed heartily at various whimsical passages which he had read in *Punch* intended to be a travesty on your sporting expeditions. I gave him as far as I could a full sketch of what you had done and what you would do and referred especially to the very interesting speeches you had made both in Malta and Cyprus.

Things here are more or less in a turmoil, as the reorganisation of the Office is just coming into force; – I hope you will find it in full working order.

The Cabinet has separated for the Christmas vacation earlier than usual,

---

[1] Harry Edward Spiller Cordeaux (1870–1943), Commissioner and Commander-in-Chief Somaliland Protectorate 1906–10; Governor of Uganda 1910–11; of St. Helena 1912–20; of Bahamas 1921–6; knighted 1921.

[2] John Edmund Gough (1871–1915), Inspector-General, King's African Rifles, Somaliland; also served in British Central Africa and South Africa; Brigadier General, General Staff, 1913–15; VC 1903; son of General Sir Charles Gough VC (1832–1912).

[3] John Arthur Hannyngton (1868–1918), Colonel serving in East Africa at the time; also served in India, Uganda, and on Western Front.

in consequence of the advice given by the Doctors to the Prime Minister. The unofficial reports about him given by Members of Parliament and such like, are unsatisfactory, but in Ministerial circles I hear nothing which is calculated to cause alarm. He has gone abroad and I hope we shall see him back in the middle of January fit for the session's work.

The Educational and Temperance legislation has I believe been settled, but I hear alarming accounts of the condition of Ireland. Law has gain fallen into disuse and juries are refusing to convict in the clearest cases. I had a long talk with Sir Antony Macdonnell[1] yesterday at the Club, and he is in one of his periodical fits of resignation, he says that the Chief Secretary simply takes the line that as he is not allowed to confer the obligations of self government upon the Irish people he has no responsibility of their proceedings!

Lord St Aldwyn has been with me, his daughter and a Royal lady are going to make a trip, from Khartoum to the Congo and either out at the West of Africa or at Mombasa. You may have met them between Entebbe and Gondokoro.

I hope you are keeping well and Marsh also. We shall welcome you back.

Yours ever
FRANCIS S. HOPWOOD

The Swazis are giving great trouble. They go to see some ladies in Abbey Rd, St John's Wood and have a pretty taste in whisky. This would not so much matter but they have also a passion for law. . . .

We have had a great success with the settlement of the Railway dispute & I am really elated with it. But on top comes Lloyd-George's sad trouble. He has lost his 17 year old daughter after an operation for appendicitis – a clever girl just blossoming into womanhood & simply adored by him, poor fellow.

Private: In case of Macdonnell's resignation, there are 'feelers' for me for Ireland but I hope you will be back to protect me against this unless you think it a matter of duty. HMG have already 'killed me with kindness' & I shrink from any more.

FSH

---

[1] Antony Patrick Macdonnell (1844–1925), Under-Secretary of State for Ireland 1902–8; served previously with Indian Civil Service; knighted 1893; PC 1902; Baron Macdonnell of Swinford 1908.

Sir Ernest Cassel to WSC

30 November 1907   21 Old Broad Street

Dear Sir,

I beg to inform you that I have credited your account £38. 16s. 4., value 29th instant, being six months interest, less tax on $10,000. – Atchison, Topeka & Santa Fe Railway 4% Convertible Bonds which I hold on your account, as per note at foot.

Yours truly

E. CASSEL

6 months' interest $10,000 – @ 4% $200. –

@49 1/32d. per $ =   £40.17. 2

less Income Tax @ 1s/– per £.   2. 0.10

        ───────

        £38.16. 4

        ───────

Lady Randolph to WSC

5 December 1907   Salisbury Hall

My dearest Winston,

I wanted so much to send you a cable for yr birthday on the 30th. But in the first place I did not know where to address it – & in the 2nd – I thought it might be expensive. 'Strange fit of economy' you will say! We spent last week with G. N. Curzon at Hackwood, the place he has taken near Basingstoke a very nice place & charmingly arranged – full of rich colour & comfort. But I thought it pathetic to think of him walking about with silk & velvet patterns under his arms, doing the work Mary C ought to have done. He was not well – & spoke despondently of the future – in fact he thought he had none – as according to him his heart wd get worse & the end was in sight. Poor fellow, I felt very unhappy about him. What a waste of a fine brain & of a loveable nature! We go to Eaton next week – & later to Blagdon then Ridleys for Xmas. I hear Consuelo is to be there. I saw Sunny at Evelyn Ker's[1] wedding – I thought he looked thin & seedy. Jack is going to Blenheim for this Sunday – we have not had an offer for this place yet. We have cut down half the establishment – & have reduced expenditure

---

[1] Lady Evelyn Anne Innes-Ker (1882–1957), youngest daughter of 7th Duke of Roxburghe; WSC's first cousin; married 23 November 1907 Colonel William Fellowes Collins DSO, Scots Greys.

by £1,000 a year. If we let it we intend to go to the Ritz – we find that we shall be able to live there cheaper than in any other decent manner. I see your book is mentioned as coming out in the Strand – I hope you are getting a good price for it?

My 2nd No is out & the papers give columns of quotations; they tell me, it only advertises it. The enclosed may amuse you. Jack's young lady has gone to Holland. There is nothing fresh about the situation which has to be kept dark until he can go to Ld A with your financial plan. I suppose you will be next to 'pop off'; it is always so in a family. I hear Lloyd George was very much cut up about his daughter's death.[1] Poor man. Miss Anning tells me that she has sent you a lot of newspaper cuttings. *Punch* is amusing – I hear Gordon has got a lion. I wonder what you think of the Zulu rising. I suppose 3 or 4,000 natives will be killed – one white man will fall off his horse & so the rising will be quelled. I have been to the dentist today who has hurt me so much that I feel a wreck, & must go to bed. Give my love to Gordon & the Eddie's altho' as he has never written he does not deserve it.

Bless you darling – I shall be very glad to get you back. You seem to have had a right royal tour. I expect to see you looking fit & twice your usual size!

Your loving
MOTHER

Togo is looking beautiful & enormous, Charlin Charlie & Susie Sue are rather jealous but no blood has been drawn as yet!

Sir Francis Hopwood to WSC

13 December 1907   Colonial Office

My dear Churchill,

We are sending you to-day all the telegrams which have passed with reference to the Natal question, and a copy of several Minutes which will give you an insight into our position.

The conduct of the Natal Government has been trying to my nerves and to my temper, but as demobilisation of the troops has now begun I hope we may say that any prospect of bloodshed is at an end. The next thing to do is to secure the fairest possible trial for Dinizulu. Nathan seems alive to the position, and we will keep him up to the point of exercising his influence. I am very much opposed to allowing an indictment for High Treason if we can prevent it, because all sorts of evidence so called, which

---

[1] Lloyd George's eldest daughter, Mair Eilund, died on 30 November 1907 of appendicitis, aged 17. Lloyd George was so upset that he immediately moved house.

is not evidence at all, can I think be let in under that form of indictment; whereas it would be excluded if a strictly criminal charge, such as that of murder was made against the Chief. Anyhow the Natal Government has not yet made up its mind as to what line of action can be taken with the best prospects of obtaining a conviction.

The Transvaal and Orange River Colony Governments have both given notice to retire from the Inter-Colonial Council. What effect this will have upon the railway problem, especially as regards the Orange River, it is difficult to say, but I have discussed matters with Solomon and urged upon him the expediency of some arrangement to take the place of the existing traffic agreement, and he is of the same opinion. You will recollect that the Imperial Government has an interest in this question.

Newfoundland. Bond seems to be making himself offensive to Laurier, and will not render any assistance either to Canada or to us in the preparation of the terms of arbitration. It looks very much as if we shall be driven to settle the matter with Canada without Bond's direct assistance, which will of course cause another grievance with Newfoundland.

There is very little else to tell you. You will get all the current news from the papers we are sending, and we shall telegraph to you in reply to yours of December 10th, any more recent news which may come from South Africa. The accounts of the Prime Minister from Biarritz are satisfactory. I have not heard from him direct, but Vaughan Nash[1] has shown me letters.

I am glad to hear that you are keeping well, and I shall be vastly interested to discuss with you your impressions and adventures.

I am myself over-worked, but hope to get a few days rest at Christmas.

Yours very sincerely
FRANCIS S. HOPWOOD

PS
I take it you will be home before Jan 20th when the next Cabinet will be held. I do not think you should be later than this. There may be changes. Your interests will be looked after as far as can be in your absence but yr presence in town will be desirable.

FJSH

---

[1] Vaughan Nash (1861–1932), Private Secretary to Sir H. Campbell-Bannerman 1905–8; to H. H. Asquith 1908–12; on editorial staff of *Daily Chronicle* 1893–9 and *Daily News* 1901; visited India during famine of 1900 as representative of *Manchester Guardian*; Chairman Development Commission 1912–29; CB 1909; CVO 1911.

Sir Walter Runciman to WSC

13 December 1907   West Denton Hall
                                                   Scotswood-on-Tyne

Secret

My dear Winston,

Your absence from England this Autumn has made a great deal of the
Campaign rather commonplace, but you have missed the Suffragette rows
and that is something to be thankful for. They have devoted their aggressive
attention to the Cabinet ministers – whether for or against them. Even Burns
has not escaped, and Herbert Gladstone, Lulu [Harcourt], Asquith &
McKenna have all been upset at one meeting after another, and although
they made their speeches – in some instances, really excellent speeches,
Asquith's in particular – platform work has been uncomfortable for all of
them. The only men who have done much speaking & have escaped have
been Macnamara[1] and I. Having little or nothing to do at the LGB he has
stumped in 15 or 20 places, and I have been at about a dozen big towns. I
was at Cardiff this week with Ivor Guest and at Liverpool a few days ago,
Glasgow before that, & so on. Everywhere the Tories are making a poor
show, & they have made no progress on their own account, which is not
surprising for they still quarrel over Tariff Reform and cannot combine to
attack us. The Tariff Reformers set out to capture Arthur Balfour, and at the
Annual Meetings of the National Union of Conservative Associations held
at Birmingham in November they set their harmless traps for him. F. E.
Smith & Harry Chaplin compiled a beautiful resolution entirely made up
of snippets of AJB's speeches & the 'Insular Free Trade'. Of course AJB
commended the resolution & congratulated (in a public letter) 'my dear
Harry' on its felicitous phraseology! He has committed himself against Free
Trade, but he evades these simple creatures.

The other Tories have been no good. Lansdowne spoke once or twice
without doing any harm. Walter Long started well, but has succumbed to
Carbuncles. George Wyndham blossomed occasionally after dinner. Austen
pegged away at the old tale, now & again blaming us for the enormous rise
in the wheat prices. And Alfred Lyttelton has once or twice aired his singular
morality.

Our most industrious orator has been Haldane if one may fairly call his
formless & endless speeches oratory. He has been all over England, Scotland

---

[1] Thomas James Macnamara (1861–1931), Parliamentary Secretary to the Local Government Board; Liberal MP North Camberwell 1900–18; Coalition Liberal MP for North West Camberwell 1918–22; National Liberal MP for NW Camberwell 1922–4; Parliamentary and Financial Secretary to the Admiralty 1908–20; Minister of Labour 1920–2; PC 1911.

& Wales, organising County Associations (unsuccessfully for the most part), patting Lord Lieutenants on the back, soothing Welsh Dis-establishers, tickling the ears of philosophers, & occasionally sobering provincial Radicals – everywhere useful, energetic & securing public confidence. He is a great worker.

His Army Estimates for next year gave us a shock, although no one expected much in the way of Economy, alas. But two & a half millions over this year was more than the Cabinet could swallow. Once our economy forces were mobilized he found the resistance was too much for him. McKenna & CB fought him in six Cabinet meetings and at last he realised that either the Army Estimates must go down, or he would. They are to be £500,000 below this year's. Tweedmouth came with his £2,500,000 up, but the Cabinet were convinced that this was unnecessary, & when Charles Beresford joined with Fisher[1] to say in public that our naval strength had never been so supreme, there was no fear of a scare. They are to be well supplied with new vessels, much is to be done on repairs, & Rosyth is to proceed, but this year's figures are to be the limit. That is not yet clinched.

At any rate we are to be well off for Revenue, & Old Age Pensions on a discriminatory basis for a start are to be initiated in the coming session. Economy has saved the situation. The Cabinet Committee on Old Age Pensions is working steadily through its task, & we are proceeding safely along the road.

The Labour men may say the scheme is too small, but I don't believe that they will be able to make much of a row, & however angry they may profess to be in the constituencies I don't believe that they will secure much support. They will be dished. Some of them have been nasty in other people's constituencies. Ramsay MacDonald has been venomous, and tried to outbid Shackleton whose sober sense was an almost intentional contrast.

The only development in their party is the possible adhesion of the entire Miners' group, but there is nothing alarming in that, for the miners will leaven the Labour party, or tone it down. If they go in, Shackleton will become the leader, & Keir Hardie & Ramsay Macdonald will be able to force the pace only as heads of a group within the party. Their strength is that they alone have distinctive ideas.

So long as CB is at work no harm can be done, and how long that will be, who can tell? The poor old man nearly died at Bristol a month ago, and he is now at Biarritz with his doctor, nursing his worn-out heart back to normal work. I should not be surprised to hear at any moment that he has unbuckled his armour, even if he lives. When the first news came of his collapse, all eyes instinctively turned to Asquith. Grey may be a popular figure but

[1] Lord FISHER.

Asquith cannot be passed, and indeed Grey would be a fool to compete with Asquith. No one else is within a decade of them. You should not delay your return, for events may succeed each other rapidly at any moment.

The two dramatic episodes of the Autumn have been: first Lloyd George's intervention in the Railway dispute – a fine piece of negotiation, where geniality, finesse & a certain bold art were the qualities which made his success. The poor fellow's elder daughter died a week ago, & he has been sadly distressed. And the other has been the failure of Birrell in Ireland. Cattle driving has gone completely out of hand. Juries won't convict, Magistrates won't sit. Nationalists won't help him. The country is uncontrolled, & is indeed now quite uncontrollable – by Birrell. He writes me frantic & despairing letters, and to tell the truth he is too much of the tender Christian to carry through the plain task which the Govt must face. His nerve has gone, and his explanation is now simply that 'everybody is behaving as badly & as foolishly as they can'! What do you think of that? I cannot imagine what he anticipated. He said at a meeting yesterday that he is about to introduce an Irish University Bill & if that fails Ireland is to know him no more. Miscarriages are as bad for statesmen as for women.

I wish that you had been here – much happens in a single Autumn, & I would have dearly loved to talk about these disquieting things and all the future possibilities. But I can only say that for my own satisfaction no less than in your own interest, I urge you to waste no time on your homeward journey. May you come back refreshed!

I am ever your friend
WALTER RUNCIMAN

I have been incessantly at the Treasury since the middle of October. It is a hard-worked job. Before that I was at sea, & also for some weeks stalking in the West of Scotland.

Lady Randolph to WSC

EXTRACT

13 December 1907   Ritz Hotel
                                                       London

My darling Winston,

I hope you are well & flourishing. I am here for a night & return to SH with Jack tomorrow. George has been so seedy these last 4 weeks with a cold that the doctors have ordered him off to St Moritz to recruit. Unfortunately owing to the expense I have not been able to go with him – which is depressing for both – as he feels ill & is lonely – & I hate being away from

him as you know. However there it is! I haven't much news to tell you.
I dined with Cassel last night – who asked after you. I hear the German
Emperor who met Leonie at luncheon at Clarence House asked a great
deal after me & said he remembered me in Berlin with R. He also spoke of
you—he seems to have made himself very popular during his stay here.
Punch is very amusing about you this week – as Miss A sends you the cuttings
I will not tell you about it. I saw Consuelo in the distance yesterday looking
very well & quite fat for her. She is going to take the children with her to
Blagdon. Where poor Sunny spends his Xmas I don't know. I'm told that
he is trying to let Blenheim! Might as well let a white elephant! – I am
getting a great deal of notice over the instalments in the *Century*. I hope it
won't spoil the sale of the book. Jack is in one of his reserved moods so I
cannot tell you anything about him or his affairs.

Your loving
MOTHER

WSC to Sir Francis Hopwood

EXTRACT

[Copy] [Undated]

. . . I am examining and will you please consider whether as an expansion
of my Somaliland ideas, it would not be wise to combine the Administration
of that Protectorate with that of Aden. I am sure that a very large economy
in staff would be possible in Somaliland, and so far as Aden is concerned
the advantages of coming under the Colonial Office are indisputable. We
already look after all the other fortresses on the road to India – Malta,
Gibraltar, the Cape, and Aden is only the last link. At present Aden is no
man's child; for the Government of Bombay have many more interesting
outlets for their energy and their cash. No improvement however small can
be made at Aden without reference to

(a) Bombay
(b) Simla
(c) India Office
(d) Foreign Office.

Nothing is ever done in consequence, and there is an air of withered neglect
about the whole place which is melancholy.

But whatever may be thought of this, it is clear that the destinies of Aden
and Somaliland ought not to be separated. Somaliland was occupied almost
entirely in the interests of the fortress of Aden. Aden is the one place where

all the threads of Somaliland tribal politics combine. Close Aden to Somaliland trade and there is not a tribe that cannot be pinched right up to the Abyssinian Border, or in Italian territory. It is their one market, and they can be far better controlled from there than by a cordon at the coast ports in Somaliland. We should therefore confront the India Office with this proposition 'Both or neither'. If they like to have them both as they used to – so much the better for us. But it is wrong to divide the two, and the division produces duplication, confusion and inefficiency.

My plan would be – I think – for this is all in the air – to let the India Office appoint, subject to CO approval, the military governor of Aden, the Hinterland, and the Somaliland Protectorate just as the War Office appoint to Malta and Gibraltar. Under him, resident at Aden, would be the Political Commissioner for the whole area: salary £1000: a humble business-like person concerned with trade and intrigue. Shrink up the Somaliland administration by merging all similar services in the Aden services. Join the armed forces. Interchange the subordinate political officers. Let Aden count on the Somaliland troops if needed for a siege, and re-inforce Somaliland if there is a disturbance. As to finance let us make the existing arrangement the basis. Let both governments pay as at present for their respective children: and when the Administration is finally combined let us either – take a fixed contribution from India – if we manage – or they from us – if they manage or else let us agree to divide future economies pro rata starting from the present basis. Have a talk to Godley about this. I am quite sure it would not be difficult to come to an agreement.

Sir Francis Hopwood to Lord Elgin
(*Elgin Papers*)

EXTRACT

16 December 1907   Colonial Office

. . . 8 long letters from Winston on Saturday! His Somaliland proposals among them. I am having memoranda put into print for your perusal & for registration. . . .

Lady Gwendeline Bertie to WSC

16 December 1907   Wytham Abbey
My dear Winston,
     Letters take a long time to come from the great Lake you know, I have only just got yours written from there, today, it has taken nearly a whole month. It is not astonishing, now that I have looked at a map of the world, which is hanging on the wall in front of me, & why a map of the world is

on the wall is because I am writing from my old classroom at Wytham. You are far away from us all, I had no idea you were so far – it is nice to think that your thoughts are not, and it is nice of you to write to me again. It was only yesterday afternoon that your Mother read out to me bits of your letter to her, while I was driving about with her in the streets of London – & I had not expected to find one for myself waiting for me here – I love surprises, don't you?

Jack & I are so happy; but, Winston, is it not cruel that I am not allowed to see him, & even writing has been forbidden, though I do write all the same! Don't you think that it is positively cruel to impose this on us? You see, this dreadful financial crisis has upset the City & it has upset Jack – & though Mother has been told that we want to marry, Father has not been yet, because nothing definite can be settled about money, and Jack does not know exactly how much he has got & how much he will have & all that, and as my Father is – well, rather difficult to tackle we thought it wd be better to wait & tell him when everything is absolutely straight & square, which it is sure to be very soon – and meanwhile my Mother does not allow me to see him; and we do love to! I know that you love a woman, Winston, very much, and you know what it means – you can imagine what I am going through not been able to be with Jack – I call it positively cruel. Are you still in the Oxfordshire Yeomanry? They are going to camp out in the park here next May I believe, & do their drill in Park Meadow, you know that big flat field about half a mile from here & we must make it a point to be here when they all are under our windows – it will be quite amusing. I landed back in England yesterday from having been on a little tour in Holland, of all places under the sun & of all months of the year to chose to go touring about Holland in! It sounds perfectly insane – but however I thoroughly enjoyed it – it poured with rain, it blew gales, it was pitch dark every day at 3 pm & all the dykes threatened to give way because of the incessant rain, but in spite of all, I enjoyed it, & I enjoyed the pictures; they really are most wonderful, & worth going to see at any distance & under any discomfort. Do you travel in great comfort, or is there a good deal of roughing to do? but I am going back to my Holland. What interested me very much was their ingenious system of dykes and dams & canals and their persistent way of driving the ever encroaching sea off their land, & what's more the way they have driven the sea out of its rightful bed & the way they have planted themselves in it & built large prosperous towns. While in Amsterdam, the German Emperor arrived, & he too seemed to be very interested in dykes, dams & canals for whenever I was 'inspecting' he came too, & what a man with what a brain! his ability & his grasp of every question on every sort of thing, big or little is astounding; & his energy, my dear, he saw more of Amsterdam in 5 hours than any other human being could in two days. I expect you know him though quite well. You will see I suppose a very wonderful system of dams on the Nile. Is it not Sir William Garstin who had to do with the new dam – and you will also see little Sir Eldon Gorst; give him my love, he used to know me as a baby [sketch] when I was this sort of shape & size. Considering all things, I think your Mother is very cheerful & well – of course she is wonderful the way she makes the best of everything & never lets her vitality go down for one minute. Her Reminiscences keep her busy. How interesting they are – & how cruel you are about her little 'potions & histories' – forbidding looking 'no' marked on the margin!!

My dear, I can but write you a most uninteresting & unexciting letter – News, of any description, I have none, not even dull news – I have not seen or heard anything. The Prime Minister is recovering at Biarritz – old Herbert G [Gladstone] came down here the other day, but he was not particularly exciting in general, though very excited about thrashing in prisons, but I do not understand anything about that. As for social 'policies', do not come to me for them, I have never any, though I think it a mistake, I am sure one is more amusing! To think that it will be well into January before you get this, but whenever you get it I am always your affectionate friend.

GOONIE

Cecil Grenfell[1] to WSC

16 December 1907   4 Great Cumberland Place

My dear Winston,

One line to thank you for your letter of November 14th just received. You give me an account of the country and your sport. I shall never forgive you for not taking me with you. Now you want news of this country: I have two homesteads Leicestershire and London – the former is now in a state of siege, on account of burglaries at Brooksby and only on Sunday at Barley Thorpe where our enterprising friends swept away all the Yellow Earl's[2] tokens and presents from the various crowned heads whose friendship he has enjoyed. We all now go to bed with loaded rifles and guns at our side, what use they would be in the dark I am not quite sure, except that they might curtail the deserved pension of some ancient retainer who was trying

---

[1] Cecil Alfred Grenfell (1864–1924), husband of WSC's cousin Lilian Maud, daughter of 8th Duke of Marlborough; Liberal MP for South Cornwall 1910; member of Stock Exchange.

[2] Hugh Cecil Lowther (1857–1944), succeeded his brother as 5th Earl of Lonsdale 1882; notable boxer, yacht-racer and race-horse owner; master in turn of Woodland Pytchley, Blankney, Quorn, and Cottesmore hounds; Lord-Lieutenant of Cumberland 1917–44; GCVO 1925; KG 1928.

to assist at the capture of the elusive enemy. The Leicestershire police have been most active, and regularly issued warnings to all householders after the event. Tell Gordon they entered Brooksby (the burglars) by what used to be my bedroom on the ground floor. London has been steeped in fog – when not foggy it rains which has not helped the financial depression; the clouds do not roll away (I mean the financial ones) as quickly as they might. I fear we have a long period of trade depression before us. The American mess is awful. When you grasp the fact that no Bank is paying in cash, you can realise all – but – can you imagine it and the petty contrivances that rich men with large sums to their credit have to indulge in to get small cash payments made – I could give you numerous instances – but, back to London. Druce case[1] we are bored with – the principal anti-witness being described as the 'champion affidavit maker', he's disappeared. Is Wood guilty of Dimmock's murder? I think No.[2] Politically there is nothing doing, as I wrote to you, CB won't stand much more work. Down with the House of Lords, though right and just, does not raise enthusiasm. Socialism is always attractive but whilst perhaps we are not making much progress the opposition are not gaining, except perhaps as regards Ireland, where, certainly a strong hand is required.

Frank Harris gives me this epitaph, a true one he found in an old English churchyard.

> Under these stones
> Lie the Bones
> Of Abraham Keeling
> And at his feet
> As is most meet
> His wife is kneeling
> Were these alive
> And had some feeling
> She were on her back
> And he was kneeling.

A Merry Xmas to you all and good prosperous 1908.

from
CECIL GRENFELL

[1] The Druce family, financed by a company, were attempting to claim the estates of the Duke of Portland. The grave of T. C. Druce, sometime proprietor of a large furniture business, was opened on December 31 to determine whether it contained the body of the fifth Duke of Portland. It was contended by the Druce family that T. C. Druce and the fifth Duke of Portland were the same person. An examination of the body proved the Druce case groundless and it was dismissed on 6 January 1908.

[2] On December 18, at the Central Criminal Court, Robert Wood was acquitted of the murder of Emily Dimmock. 'The verdict was loudly cheered both inside and outside the court.' *AR 1907.*

Jack Churchill to WSC

19 December 1907   Marlborough Club

My dear Winston,

I was so pleased to receive your nice telegram this morning from the bowels of Africa. Although I have not yet been able to settle anything – things are looking better for me. Nelke has been very affable and has promised to make some new arrangements about me. I am waiting to hear everyday. I am afraid he will jib at giving me £1000 a year.

Phillips[1] has retired at last – and the whole firm is being reorganised. This is lucky for me and means probable promotion. In the meantime Lady Abingdon knows all about the situation – and although I fancy she looks rather askance at me, she is in reality only too willing to do whatever she thinks will make Goonie happy.

We have not told Lord A yet. I am waiting everyday to have a definite settlement with Nelke – and then I shall write to him.

But it is still rather misery – Since I last wrote to you I have only seen Goonie for two minutes at a Railway Station!

Was there ever such a way of making love. She has been at Wytham – and she promised her mother not to see me. So I had to waylay her 'by accident' at the Station one day.

We write pages to each other all day – but I never see her.

However – we love each other very deeply – and these little worries will soon be forgotten.

What fun you must have been having with your rhinos and lions. It must have been most exciting – How I envy you. The city has been frightfully depressing and I have stayed at it all the time. Has Eddy Marsh hit anything or anybody yet with that big revolver? Tell him he is a Pig. He has never written a word either to me or to Mama. She is very cross with him.

I think I shall put out a feeler and see whether Sievier would not be willing to turn out of Bolton Street a little sooner. If that fails how would you like Wimborne House? I am sure they would make you very comfortable there. Failing that, I shall arrange at Ritz. Mama can get some rooms on very good terms I think. Freddy [Guest] is still out West somewhere and there is nothing *monté* in his house.

Send me a cable if you have any views when you receive this.

It is very nice to think of you back again in a get-at-able land. And also somewhat of a relief to find you have come through the sleeping sickness part safely.

---

[1] A partner in the firm of Nelke and Phillips.

Do you mean to dawdle on the way home or do you come back straight?
I think you have been well out of the autumn speech-making. I think politics seem to be a little flat just at the moment.

You will I am afraid have a lot of trouble at Manchester with the women. The Suffragettes have broken up and spoilt a great many meetings. Every Cabinet Minister has had a dose of them – and I think John Burns is the only one who defeated them.

He got hold of his interrupter and roared at her 'When you are married, my dear, you will understand a great deal more than you do at present.' There were roars of applause during which the blushing bitch subsided and was heard no more.

Write to Goonie – and give me a good character. We have loved each other for so long – and I never understood – but thought it was only on my side – and I never dared to think of such things.

I must stop now. I will send you some more from Blenheim next week. I was going with Mama to Rosie R [Ridley] at Blagdon. But Consuelo M was asked then and said she would not meet Mama – I of course at once chucked also. It really is too idiotic.

Yrs
JACK

Sir Francis Hopwood to Lord Elgin
(*Elgin Papers*)

EXTRACT

27 December 1907   Colonial Office

. . . As to Churchill: I destroyed your postscript. I have not circulated his papers but in the case of the Cyprus tribute & I think Somaliland he sent letters or memoranda to the Treasury in the former & Charles Hardinge in the latter case – Dale[1] tells me that he hears that the Ch of Ex & the officials are vastly amused at the Cyprus memo for Churchill has not understood the financial basis of the arrangement & C. Hardinge wrote me a note sometime ago clearly intimating that FO would require a lot of convincing about Somaliland. In fact the stuff Churchill has sent direct has been if anything destructive of his case. There is a good deal to be said for sending the memoranda as from you with a caveat as to your policy because then we shall get a discussion on fair & open lines. The alternative

---

[1] Charles Ernest Dale (1867–1956), Financial Commissioner to Nigeria 1906–1914.

is the usual system of lobbying on C's return. He is most tiresome to deal with & will I fear give trouble – as his Father did – in any position to which he may be called. The restless energy, uncontrollable desire for notoriety & the lack of moral perception make him an anxiety indeed!

Churchill should have reserved his points until he returned home – anybody else would have done so both out of caution or at the dictation of personal convenience – Marsh gives a vivid description of 14 hours work in one day upon these memoranda in the heat & discomfort of the Red Sea.

I am bound to say that in all my relations with him he fully respects your authority & judgement but he can never understand that there is any better way of enforcing an argument than by intrigue & by pugnaciously overstating a case. . . .

Had I followed my own wishes I should not have sent you his letters, which are marked 'private', because I felt that they would not either in style or substance be pleasing to you. But it is always better to have no secrets or reservations. . . .

Jack Churchill to WSC

27 December 1907   Blenheim

My dear Winston,

I have just had a telegram from Mama, about poor Scrivings. What an awful thing. You will never get so faithful a slave again. Mrs S is up in Scotland, but Mama has telegraphed to her and she will come back to-day – when she will be told.

I am writing this in the train, with a very bad 'stylo'. You must therefore excuse the writing – and do not imagine that I have got DT.

Now about your return. Freddy's house is all shut up and he is still in America – so that is no good. I thought of Wimborne House – but that also is shut up and has no servants in it. I spoke to Rosie R [Ridley] and she said she thought that Mat would like to put you up in Carlton House Terrace. But I have not heard anything definite from her. And I am not sure that you would not be more at home, with a couple of rooms at the Ritz. Let me know from Paris – what you would prefer. Sunny wants to meet you in Paris and stay a few days there. But I expect you have been away long enough and will be glad to get back again.

Many of the papers foreshadow changes in the Government. And your appointment has been announced 'on good authority' to every post. I hope there will be a re-shuffle – but still I think it would be a great pity for you to leave the C office. It is very difficult to write here – but I shall only just have time to send this to the C office to have it enclosed tonight with your other letters.

The city is still very bad – and, although the 'panic' is over, confidence is not yet restored and business is at a standstill. You can imagine, with what impatience I wait for things to better themselves.

I sometimes feel very desparing about it all – but still Goonie will wait – and I have no fear about her.

I cannot write anymore, it is too jerky. Let me know what you prefer about rooms etc. I cannot get my mind off poor Scrivings – and I am sure you must feel it very much.

Yrs
Jack SC

WSC to Jack Churchill

28 December [1907]   SS *Ambigol*
Nile

[Copy]

Dictated

My dear Jack,

Scrivings' death was a great shock to me & has cast a gloom over all the memories of this pleasant & even wonderful journey. I hope Mamma either broke it to Mrs S herself, or else entrusted it to you. It is really a terrible thing to think of those poor people struck down by ill tidings on Xmas day. The cause of death was choleraic diarrhoea, & indeed the symptoms so closely resembled Asiatic cholera in its most malignant form, that were it not for the fact that the Soudan is clear of that disease, it wd very likely have been classified as such. We all must have eaten the same dish wh contained the poison – whether it was a tin of ptomaine-poisoned fish, or rotten asparagus, or what, will never be known. The same cause will produce widely different reactions on different constitutions. We were all fit, we had been accustomed to walk 10 or 12 miles a day under the hottest sun & to sweat profusely. Personally I was in much better condition than I had been for a long time. S however sprained his ankle at Fajar, & this kept him in a chair or on his back for nearly 3 weeks, during wh time he was carried by coolies all through Central Africa, & without taking any exercise ate all the abundant food in wh we active ones indulged. The consequence was that his organs were fat & flabby & he was no doubt in a condition to receive bacteriological poison. When he called me at 7 o'clock on the 23rd he seemed all right & I had no idea that he was ill until about 3 o'clock, when just as we were landing at the Palace, Khartoum, Eddie told me he had been vy sick. I thought it was only one of his ordinary bilious attacks, & I consoled him by telling him that we had arrived at last in a really comfortable house, & with first-class doctors he would be all right. He looked vy blue, & his hands a curious leaden colour, wh struck me at the time tho' I did not attach serious importance to it. He walked alone & I had a Dr sent for at once. The Dr did not think anything dangerous was the matter, he only said he had a bad pulse & required careful watching. He was taken at once in a carriage to the Civil Hospital wh is of course at Khartoum equipped with everything. He had 2 English Drs & an English nurse. During the night he was continually sick & had continual attacks of diarrhoea, with a certain amount of cramp & backache. Under these symptoms he seemed to collapse, & twice in the night he vy nearly died. He did not himself think that he was dangerously ill, & he appears during the night to have told an engine-driver, a fellow patient in the hospital, a good deal about himself & his journey with me through Uganda. At about 10 am he collapsed entirely, & died, quite painlessly, without I think being alarmed about himself in any way, & much more suddenly than the Drs expected. It appears from the post mortem that the mitral valve of his heart was incompetent, & it may well be that this gave way at the critical moment, but in any case the form of malignant choleraic diarrhoea from wh he was suffering is nearly always fatal.

We passed a miserable day, & I had him buried in the evening with full military honours as he had been a yeoman. The Dublin Fusiliers sent their band & a company of men, & we all walked in procession to the Cemetery as mourners, while the sun sank over the desert, & the band played that beautiful funeral march you know so well.

Eddie has written at my request an account of this for Mrs Scrivings, & you should read her such parts of this letter as you think fit. Tell her also that I have made arrangements for a monument to be erected over his grave & have written out a long inscription for it. It will be photographed as soon as it is put up, & a copy will be sent home for her to see. You should also tell her not to be worried about her future, as so far as my limited means allow I will endeavour to look after her & her children.

I thought it quite on the cards that some others of us wd be struck down, for we had all eaten from the same dishes; & as you may imagine I passed rather an uncomfortable 48 hours until the danger period was over. It is all the more melancholy that this shd have happened when really all the un-healthy & dangerous part of the journey was over & we had been living for 10 days on a comfortable Nile steamer. But Africa always claims its forfeits!

Please make some arrangements for me on my return. I leave Alexandria on the 9th by the *Heliopolis*, & either meet Sunny at Naples on the 11th or at Marseilles on the 12th, I hope the former. If Sunny comes out to meet me, ask him whether his servant can look after me as well, for I have masses of luggage, & no one. If Sunny cannot come, or perhaps in any case, you might send your servant to meet me at Naples or Marseilles according as I shall telegraph.

On my return I think I shall go to the Ritz Hotel, & please ask Mamma to engage me a bedroom, a bathroom, & a comfortable sitting room, & to make the vy best terms she can with the Manager. She should tell them that if they make me comfortable & do not charge me too much I will in all probability stay a month, but if they overcharge me I will clear out at once & tell everybody what robbers they are.

I will telegraph to you the best address for letters, etc. as time goes on.

We have got a special steamer from the Sirdar, wh is conveying us pleasantly down the Wady Halfa-Assouan reach of the river, & wh stops wherever we want at temples.

[WINSTON S. CHURCHILL]

PS Show this to Mamma with my best love.

Lady Randolph to WSC

EXTRACTS

30 December 1907   Blenheim

My darling Winston,

This may find you at Cairo. Sunny showed me yr wire from Assuan. I received your wire from Khartoum while I was at West Dean where I was spending Xmas. I was greatly shocked at hearing of poor Scrivings' death. He was such a faithful devoted servant & a good fellow. You will miss him terribly. I received yr telegram on the 24th & wired at once to Mrs S that I would go up next day to see her. I was all dressed to go to London Xmas morning and getting no answer from her, I waited. Next day she telegraphed from Scotland where she was with her mother & children. Having prepared her by several telegrams as to Scrivings becoming ill I eventually wrote a long letter enclosing yr telegram. This letter I enclosed to the mother telling her to break the sad news to her daughter & then give her my letter. I am telling you all this in order that you shd know how much trouble I took. I thought as she was with her people it wd be wiser for her to stay with them for a few days with her grief. Poor woman – it is lucky

that she is not dependent on Scrivings for her livelihood. Walden told me he
thought Scrivings wd never return as he used to drink a little & that it wd
be fatal in those hot countries. Walden impressed on him the danger. Poor
man. I have heard of a very good man who might suit you – but we will
discuss this on your return. I suppose you saw the Devonshires at Assouan?
I came here on Sat, Jack being here & George still abroad – F. E. Smith is
here as pleasant as ever. He & Sunny talk of going out to meet you. What a
delightful time you have had & I hope it has set you up in health for a long
time. How I wish you cd have taken George with you. He needs an open air
life. This City grind is very hard for him. I hear old CB is at Biarritz eating
& drinking far too much. I am told that HG will be shunted & that you will
be in the Cabinet. I hope so. We have not as yet let SH & if things get a little
better we may not be obliged to. I see by today's papers that G. Curzon is
going to return to active political life – if you can call the House of Lords
'active'? I am very glad, as it will take him out of himself & his broodings. . . .
I am longing to get you back – but it is cold & grey here. Stay away as long
as you can is my advice.

Yr loving
MOTHER JCW

WSC to Sir Walter Runciman
(*Runciman Papers*)

30 December 1907   Assouan
Private

My dear Walter,

   I am immensely obliged to you for your letter. You have certainly made
good use of the opportunities offered by your position at the Treasury to take
a central view of men and things; and the account you give and one I have
received from Spender really make me feel *au courant* in political affairs.

   I am sorry for Birrell. But it is his own fault. How *could* he ever have introduced that stupid Bill, within three months of becoming Irish Secretary and
before he knew, or anybody would believe he knew, anything about the
subject. That has been our one disaster. But it is a big one; for it leaves us
without an Irish policy, & I fear it has wrecked the brightest hope Ireland
has seen since the Union. It would have been so easy to say 'No bill this year',
and no one could have shaken that position. But instead a vast policy has
been squandered to tide over imaginary Parliamentary emergencies, &
Ireland at the moment is utterly pigged.

   Very few men are able to make more than one really bad mistake. I hope

Birrell will be among the exceptions; but that the next mistake will not entail such far-reaching consequences.

I have thought a good deal about the general situation especially as affected by CB's health. I agree with you that Asquith must be the heir: and I am sure no better workman will have been installed since the days of Sir Robert Peel. As to the work which he will choose – that lies in the mists: but men do come on so much when they are placed on the pinnacle that I should be full of hope.

I do not see how any of these potential revolutions will be likely to affect me, and I have now developed several keen interests in Colonial Office work, to which I propose to devote myself in the coming year. In these our work will fall together. You must help me & I must help you. First about Somaliland. I am more convinced than ever that we are absolutely wasting public money there. I asked Hopwood to give you my memorandum on the subject. If you have not seen it, please ask him for it. I fear great opposition, but I will not myself consent to see forty thousand a year of British money thrown away, because of mere inertia & feebleness: & if you will join in the hunt, I promise you I will ride it to the finish. Besides it is your show.

Then there is the Cyprus tribute which is so vy unjustly & improperly exacted from that wretched island. Have you ever realised that we have actually bled them to the extent of £1,800,000 since the occupation, all clear profit to us, all clear loss to them? Again Hopwood will give you my memorandum.

But more than anything else I want the Victoria and Albert Railway. One hundred miles of line joining the Victoria Lake to Lake Chioga & Lake Chioga to the Albert with Railway ferries on the Lakes, would more than double[1] the radius of the Uganda Railway, at less than 1/10th its original capital charge. I have an elaborate scheme on foot which will enable this railway to be built for about £500,000 (plus ferries) in the course of the next two years. If this be done, and the policy settled soon, I hope to catch the whole Congo trade, including the material for Leopold's railway for the Uganda line; that is to say commercial solvency! I have had long conferences with Wingate, & Gorst and we are absolutely agreed on the policy. There is no question of any clash between British & Soudan interests.

But all this I must explain to you with maps & figures when I come back.

I have had a really wonderful journey and was never in such good health. We were just rejoicing on having escaped all the perils of Central African travel, when my poor servant Scrivings, who you know, was struck down by some deadly form of choleraic diarrhoea and died in a few hours after our arrival at Khartoum. This has been a most keen sorrow to me; for he had

[1] 'Nearly treble' deleted.

looked after me for ten years and I was vy fond of him. His wife – my cook – & four small children were awaiting his return. It is one of the saddest things I have ever known. Africa always claims its forfeits.

Always your friend
WINSTON SC

PS I return the 17th. The NLC [National Liberal Club] have bidden me to a feast on the 18th. Will you dine with me on Monday 20th? I will try to get a few friends together. It must be at Ritz Hotel, as my house is let till February.

WSC

Jack Churchill to WSC

2 January 1908

My dear Winston,

One line, which I hope will reach you somewhere before you get home. I have had many 'confabs' with Nelke. At the New Year, he has given me £500 a year. To-night I told him that that would be of no use to me. He tells me that he will arrange something that will give me in the worst times, £1000 a year. I suggested this £500 a year salary and one % of the profits of the firm, but that the 1% should be guaranteed to me to be worth another £500. This will mean £1000 a year in very bad times – while a good year will mean £2000 or even £3000 and £4000. Many people marry on less. I believe that she will have something given to her. If it is only £200 it is something. Nelke told me to-night that I must not worry; and that if at any time things went wrong, it was to be understood that I could always borrow from the firm.

I am looking forward very much to your return in order to have your advice and your help. Harriman cabled yesterday to Nelke to ask whether it would be possible for 'Churchill' to ask Lord Rothschild to do something for him, as he had been told that I had some influence over R. He added that if I could arrange this, he would give Nelke a good deal of his business in England. I went to New Court and found that R had promised to do the opposite to what Harriman wished. But he now has decided to reconsider his verdict. This has been a feather in my cap – and I have rubbed it in.

Your letters have been very much appreciated, and we are all looking forward to your articles in the *Strand*. Young Wolmer[1] (Selborne's son) who

---

[1] Roundell Cecil Palmer, Viscount Wolmer (b. 1887), eldest son of 2nd Earl of Selborne whom he succeeded in 1942; married Grace, younger daughter of Viscount Ridley in 1910; Conservative MP for Newton 1910–18, Aldershot 1918–40; Parliamentary Secretary to the Board of Trade 1922–4; Assistant Postmaster General 1924; Minister of Economic Warfare 1942–5.

I met at Blenheim told me he went to Mombasa just before your arrival. He said that he found the officials most enthusiastic about you. They said that while they distrusted, in some respects, the present Government, they appreciated you at the Colonial Office. They said that they preferred you even to Mr Chamberlain, because they found you even more sympathetic about 'Empire' than he.

In the meanwhile, things seem to be going pretty badly in the home *ménage*. Poor George, who has little stamina, has knuckled under to the bad times and is in a bad way. I am trying to make him 'buck up' against the bad times – but it is hard work.

Write to Goonie. Poor thing, she is very miserable that we have to wait so long – but at the same time she writes me that she is prepared to wait until I come for her. If six months ago you had told me of this – I should have laughed at you, although I loved her, and told you that perhaps the Conservative papers were right, and that you had a real knowledge of people and things.

I spent a few days last week at Blenheim. F. E. Smith was there and said many nice things about you. He said he was much worried about Manchester. He said he was sure you would soon be in the Cabinet, but that that would necessitate an Election, and that, as he has made himself president of some Lancashire Association about the Education Act, he would find it necessary to have meetings against you at the Election. He said that this worried him greatly. Because he thought that in Politics there was a great difference between arguing against anyone in the H of C and arguing against one at an Election. I told him that he could do as he liked – that you would understand – and that (incidentally) he could do what he liked because it would make no difference to your election!

And now my dear I must 'shut up'. I long for your return, to talk to you about so many things. I cannot get over poor Scrivings. You will never get a man like him again. To be practical, Rosie and Matt will be delighted to give you two rooms on the top floor at Carlton House Terrace. (There is a lift). Cable me what you think of this. You can have my servant if you like him and until you can get another. But if you think 'Ritz' would be more comfortable let me know, and I will arrange that – at the cheapest rate possible.

Good bye.

What a good time you must have had. Yrs
JACK SC

WSC to Lady Randolph

3 January 1908   General's House
                                                 Cairo

Dearest Mamma,

I was surprised not to receive a telegram in answer to my wire about Scrivings' death, & I still hope for a letter from you about his wife.

I was most deeply grieved by this tragic end to our wanderings. It was as unexpected as a lightning flash. The doctors can only say 'choleraic diarrhoea' following the eating or drinking of something causing ptomaine poison. I cannot understand how none of us were stricken too. For Scrivings ate our food always. It was a melancholy & startling event; & to me who have become so dependent upon this poor good man for all the little intimate comforts of my daily life, it has been a most keen & palpable loss. I cannot bear to think of his wife & children looking forward to his return – letters by every post – and then this horrible news to lay them low. It might have happened in England. Anyone who swallowed that fatal mouthful – whatever it was – would almost certainly have perished anywhere. But still – if he had not followed me so faithfully – he might have been spared. Alas, Alas. Few things have grieved me more.

I arrive Marseilles – all being well – on the 12th; I propose to stay two days in Paris with Sunny, coming to London on the 16th. We might try to dine together that night. I shall stay at the Ritz till my house is free. I am quite glad not to reenter it till that unfortunate woman has got over her first grief. I must from ever-straitening resources make some provision for her future.

I thought as I walked after the coffin at Khartoum – I always follow funerals there – how easily it might have been, might then still be, me. Not nearly so much should I have minded, as you would think. I suppose there is some work for me to do. But if I had ended there, Jack could have married without any delay. Poor dear – we must manage to drive that through for him. 'Some gleams of sunshine, mid renewing storms' precious, to be cherished. How happy he must be & how glad he must be & how glad I am he has not married some beastly woman for money. Well well – I wish you had written me a nice letter about it all; but perhaps tomorrow!

I have broken one of my front teeth, shorn off, upon a French plum stone on Lake Chioga. Will you make an appointment for me with Davenport for the morning of the 17th?

                                                 Always your loving son
                                                 W

Lady Randolph to WSC

3 January 1908 The Ladies Automobile Club
Claridge's Hotel

Dearest Winston,

It was stupid of me not to mention in my New Years' telegram that I had received yours from Khartoum. Sir Francis Hopwood wired to me. I have seen Mrs Scrivings. I went to No 12. Poor thing she was very low and sad – but luckily she has a great deal to do. She has had letters from Scrivings a day or two ago – in which he said he did not feel very well and had walked a great deal. Jack has written to you all our news I know. Rosie and Matt offer you for 2 or 3 weeks 2 rooms at the top of their house in C Terrace. As there is a lift I think you should do very well there. Otherwise the Ritz is the best. I can make arrangements for you. George has returned from St Moritz a little better. He will probably have the operation to his nose the end of next week. Poor fellow he never seems to be out of hospital.

Stay away as long as you can. It is icy cold here & rather dreary. I am going to see a play of B. Shaw's tonight *Arms & the Man* & then go to the Guests (A & I) [Alice & Ivor] who are entertaining frozen-out Mothers at supper. Bless you darling.

Yr loving
MOTHER

Sir Francis Hopwood to Lord Elgin
(*Elgin Papers*)

EXTRACT

4 January 1908 The Metropole
Folkestone

... You did not tell me whether I might send the Churchill printed memoranda to Hardinge, Godley, Murray etc, from you. I should like to see them officially before he returns – Churchill's 'man' died somewhere between Entebbe & Khartoum. Winston telegraphed to me to inform his (Winston's) mother so I suppose the man was an old servant probably of Ld Randolph's. ...

Lady Randolph to WSC

7 January 1908   Salisbury Hall

My dearest Winston,

I am writing to send just one line from my bed as I have got a slight chill –
I feel like a boiled gooseberry so do not expect a coherent letter – I wrote
to you before that I had seen Mrs Scrivings. This letter she had written before
I had seen her. She told me she had a great deal to do which is a good thing.
I am looking forward to your return & hope you will let us know the exact
date. Jack will have sent you Sievier's letter to the agent. You will be very
comfortable at Rosie's and it will cost you nothing. George is going to
have his operation to his nose in a few days. I'm afraid it will take a little
longer than he imagines. I had a charming letter from Eddie. I can't write
by this mail but will by next. Bless you darling –

Your loving
MOTHER

Sir Ernest Cassel to WSC

9 January 1908   21 Old Broad Street

My dear Winston,

I have just received your telegram informing me that you will be in Paris
from the 13th to the 15th. If you would like to stay at my apartment 2 Rue
du Cirque will you telegraph to that address to Blanchet stating by what
train and on what day you expect to arrive. I could not manage to be in
Egypt when you were there and I am leaving by the *Heliopolis* from Marseilles on the 18th. I shall leave London on the 16th and it would be too bad
if we missed each other on our respective journeys. Let me know therefore
as early as you can how you propose to travel and we will then see whether
we can arrange to meet by waiting at some place for a later train. I hope
you have thoroughly enjoyed your trip although I am afraid that the loss of
your old servant must have been a severe blow to you. Lady Sarah[1] kept me
well posted about your doings and the papers naturally brought some news
of you.

With every good wish for the new year

Yours always
E C

[1] Sarah Spencer-Churchill (1865–1929), WSC's aunt, daughter of John, 7th Duke of
Marlborough; she married, in 1891, Captain Gordon Chesney Wilson.

A. P. Watt[1] to WSC

9 January 1908   Hastings House
                                Norfolk Street

Private

Dear Mr Churchill,

I am this morning in receipt of your letter from 'on the Nile' and, having had another interview with Mr Greenhough Smith,[2] the editor of *The Strand Magazine*, I am very pleased to be able to tell you that I have succeeded in selling him the two additional articles to which you refer on the same terms as before, viz., £150 a piece. I am writing to Mr Smith this afternoon putting this new arrangement on record and I will advise you immediately I receive his promised letter in confirmation. I have informed Mr Smith that for the £1050 which he has now agreed to pay us, you will give him 35000 words of matter divided into eight articles. Copy of No 1 did not reach us in time to enable Mr Smith to begin the publication of the series in his February number but he tells me that he will be able to begin in his March number and this will mean that the last of the series will be published in the October number of *The Strand Magazine* issued I believe on the first of the month. This will leave you free to publish your book in October, which is of course a very good time.

And now with regard to the book rights, Mr Smith desires me to say that he would be very glad, if, in consideration of their having bought the serial rights you would authorise us to give them the first refusal of the book rights for Messrs Hodder & Stoughton. It appears that the proprietors of *The Strand Magazine* have entered into an agreement with Messrs Hodder & Stoughton under which the former are wherever possible to get for the latter the first refusal of the book rights of any serial story or any serial feature appearing in *The Strand Magazine*. From my own experience, I can assure you that Messrs Hodder & Stoughton are a first class firm and that your book would have full justice done to it if published by them; at the same time, I presume you wish to sell in the very best market and I need scarcely say that I should not advise you to sell your book to any particular firm if I thought I could get you better terms from another.

Looking forward to hearing from you in this matter of the book rights.

                           I am, dear Mr Churchill
                                 Yours sincerely
                                 A. P. WATT

---

[1] Alexander Pollock Watt (1837–1914), founded A. P. Watt and Son, Literary Agents, in 1875.
[2] Herbert Greenhough Smith (d. 1935), journalist; one of founders and editor of *The Strand Magazine* from 1891.

Jack Churchill to WSC

10 January 1908
Warnford Court
Throgmorton Street

My dear,

I am scribbling you a line to catch you at Marseilles. Wire as soon as you can and let us know exactly when you intend arriving.

Mamma has written you details about putting up at Carlton House Terrace. Wire to Rosie and let her know when you arrive.

I have tried to oust Sievier – but he says he regrets he has business in London and must stay on in the house. Will you arrange for me to dine at the Liberal Club on the 18th. You might telegraph to someone about it.

I am sending this to the *Heliopolis* office – and must do so at once.

We are all looking forward very much to your return. But you must wire details about when you mean to arrive. What have you got for a servant?

G was delighted with your letter.

Yrs
JACK SC

Sir Francis Hopwood to WSC

EXTRACT

11 January 1908

My dear Churchill,

I look forward to seeing you again.

Changes are coming & I fear they will in some form or other terminate our association here: still I shall like to see you in the Cabinet.

I want you to give me an evening before Parliament meets for a small dinner at the Reform – not a banquet of Ritzian splendour – altho' by the way I am glad that I can be present on the 20th. . . .

His Lordship is still in Scotland but will be up I take it in about a week.

All accounts *except the most confidential* about CB are good, i.e. Biarritz has braced him up, and he can now go about & enjoy life. Reports on the progress of Haldane's Army scheme are not satisfactory. It is said that the men required cannot be obtained so that if they were the cost of them would seriously run up the Army estimates. Those estimates at first showed an increase but I understand that the Cabinet cut them down until they stand at the same figure as last year. The Navy estimates are 'up'.

The Attorney General is very unwell & his health is giving his people great anxiety.

The Government of NSW with the assent of the Opposition & of the Labour party is petitioning to keep Governor Rawson[1] for another year.

Fortunately the Natal business seems to have blown over – it looked very ugly at one time. . . .

It is beastly cold here, you will feel the change.

Yr v. sincerely
FRANCIS S. HOPWOOD

Lady Randolph to WSC

EXTRACT

12 January 1908   Salisbury Hall

My dearest Winston,

I received your letter of the 3rd from Cairo – last night. I am delighted to think that by now you are so near. First – in regard to my not having wired about poor Scrivings, you will have had my excuse in a former letter – It *was* stupid of me not doing so. And I also explained about Mrs Scrivings. I think you need not dread seeing her. She is very calm and as I said, has so much to do that she has no time to indulge in her grief. Sievier wrote a very civil letter to say that if he had known of your return a little earlier he would have turned out. Since Jack wrote to you I have decided to accept for you the Ridleys' invitation – they themselves are hardly going to be in London at all, as they are going away now for a fortnight & Rosie goes to the West Indies on the 5th of February. Matt will only be up and down when he is not hunting. They give you a large sitting room & a bedroom (lift to take you up) the library & dining room being open downstairs. The house will be practically yours – servants & a cook, & they want you to stay until you get your house. You can lunch and dine at the Ritz. It will save you a lot of money & you will be very comfortable. I do hope you will be pleased with this arrangement. It is very kind of the Ridleys & think how they would be hurt if you did not go. I am lunching with Rosie tomorrow to see your rooms. I am going to Gopsall in the afternoon but shall come up on the 16th to dine with you, & shall stay the night & return to Gopsall next day. I hope you will wire me there should you change the date of your arrival in London. How I wish I could have gone to Paris to meet you! Sunny will be with you. . . . George is better and will have his

---

[1] Harry Holdsworth Rawson (1843–1910), Governor of New South Wales 1902–9; Admiral 1903; knighted 1897.

operation the week after next when I shall come to London. The cold for the moment is intense, 22 degrees of frost. We have been skating at Hatfield where I saw Lord Salisbury & Ld Hugh – the latter very pale after his bad attack of influenza. He asked a great deal after you. I want you to come here next Sunday 19th. We are asking F. E. Smith & I might get Ld Hugh to come over. You have a big dinner the Sat I know. I have heard of various servants for you. One which sounds excellent. Unfortunately the man is married and his wife is a very good cook. But of course you will not part with Mrs Scrivings. I must try again. Thank God you escaped any ill effects of those dangerous dishes. But indeed *le bon Dieu* has work & happiness for you yet. As for Jack he is very happy. Ld Abingdon is very ill at this moment but when he recovers Jack will probably be able to go and make his proposal *en règle*. What a lot we have got to talk about! I shall look forward to your articles which are sure to have a great success. I plod on with the book. It is difficult to find material for all the Chapters. One is full of vulgar twaddle about Sandringham – but I can't help it – on the whole it seems to go down. Bless you my darling boy – I am longing to see you – do telegraph to Gopsall when you make up your mind the actual day & hour you arrive that your 'Mommer' may be there.

Yours lovingly
MOTHER

I wonder if you are at Cassel's or at the Bristol. Will arrange about Davenport.

WSC to Lady Randolph

13 January 1908   Hotel Bristol
Paris

Dearest Mamma,

Very many thanks for all your letters, which relieve my anxiety about that poor woman & the effect upon her of the terrible news I had to ask you to convey. Certainly you did everything possible.

I arrived here this morning after a good & fast voyage in the new *Heliopolis* steamer 12,000 tons, & 20 knots, in wh we were invited to travel as the guests of the company! A desirable economy. I stay here till midday 17th to meet Cassel. I will gladly go to Carlton House Terrace & it is vy kind of Rosie & Matt to put me up. I think I had better arrive at the Ritz in the first instance, so as not to upset them with an unexpected incursion & luggage etc. We can dine quietly lateish on the 17th together. Will you explain? I am writing to them myself too. Masses of letters & papers have met me here: & there is a regular vista of speeches etc before me. There are rumours of changes wh reach me from rather authoritative quarters. But I do not see anything clearly.

How silly of Cornelia to be downhearted about the Government. It never was so strong as at this moment: nor has any Administration ever embarked on its third session under such favourable circumstances & with so much support.

With vy best love, always your affect son
W

I do hope your cold is better. This weather is vy treacherous.

Lord Elgin to WSC

13 January 1908 Broomhall

My dear Churchill,

I want to send one line of greeting to welcome you home – but I am not going to attempt any discussion: the more so as I shall see you so soon.

This Cabinet on Friday has upset my plans – & I think I must if possible get down for the week end again – as Ly E has been unwell & is still in bed.

But I hope I may at any rate have a sight of you. I have been reading the report of your proceedings in E. Africa – but I want to have as much as I can from yourself at first hand. I hope you come back fit and well in spite of all your exertions.

Yours very truly
ELGIN

WSC to Jack Churchill

13 January 1908 Hotel Bristol
Paris

My dear Jack,

All your news about Nelke is excellent. I really do not think you need be anxious about obtaining a speedy conclusion. £1400 a year is quite enough for two sensible people who care about one another. Of course to go the London pace it is a wisp of straw. Besides you have solid & certain expectations upon wh you can in time of need fall back.

Have you told Cassel? If not I think I will – unless you object – when I meet him here on the 17th. His good will must always be a matter of legitimate importance to you: though I expect it is not easy to make him & NR

[Nathaniel Rothschild] run in double harness. I am vy fond of Cassel & know him for a true man & friend. He might be hurt if he were not admitted to your confidence. After all you made your entrée to the City under his auspices.

I will go to Matt's – with pleasure. But on arrival I think to the Ritz. Get me therefore two rooms for the night of the 17th & reserve yourself to dine there.

Yours always
W

PS I have got a sort of servant – an honest rifleman – just time expired – but raw! He will do, till I can look round.

A ticket for the NLC will come to you.

WSC

J. E. B. Seely to WSC

15 January 1908 29 Chester Square

My dear Winston,

Welcome home – You have had a long trek, but we have not forgotten you. I say 'we' because my children have been awaiting your home-coming, so that you might come to Brooke and again delight them with vast engineering works on the sea shore, and wondrous tales either read or invented. As it turns out you have returned too late, and we could not go to Brooke because diphtheria broke out in the household.

You have missed nothing politically – absolutely nothing at all; never was there such a dull autumn so far as speech-making is concerned; things have been moving all the time no doubt, but in what direction nobody seems to know.

I leave here tomorrow for various yeomanry engagements in Hampshire, then to Liverpool for a week with my constituents, so I shall not have a chance to see you till Parliament meets. But it will be good to see you again.

Yours ever
JACK SEELY

Lady Lytton to WSC

EXTRACT

16 January [1908]   Cresta Palace Hotel
                                                     Celerina
                                                     Switzerland

Winston,

This is to welcome you home with all my heart. I wish I was on your doorstep. You have had a splendid time haven't you? What delightful talks I look forward to: Dear, is it true that poor Scrivens [*sic*] is dead? I heard so in a round about way and feel so really sad about him. How he loved you (& no one can do without love) & how incessantly you will miss him. I am sorry for you & I know that you must have been made very unhappy about him.

This is an infernal place – full of death traps & downfalls – quite inhuman – wonderful to see, but hateful to live in. However, Victor is supremely happy, skating about 8 hours a day *magnificently*, & that is why I am here.

I am sure you would fly down the Cresta run if you were with us. This a deadly place & the people fly down on their tummies on iron toboggans, with scarlet faces and terrified eyes looking – to the spectators – as if they were bound for Hell.

The sun is burning hot, but the glare makes one's eyes bleed. Write me a line here please

                                                                    P

Are you *well?* Tell me that.

King of Buganda to WSC

22 January 1908   Mengo
                                                    Uganda

Dear Mr Winston Churchill,

I have sent the pictures which you asked me to send them to you. I have sent two pictures of me; and the other ones are the men which you saw that day when you came to see me. I am quite well, and I hope you are quite well too. Our football are going on very nicely, and the other day the Budu boys came to play football with my boys, and we beat them, but they are learning more. The words on the fortographs mean I am your friend.

I am your friend
DAUDI CHWA

Sir Richard Solomon to J. C. Smuts
(*Smuts Archive*)

30 January 1908 London

EXTRACT

. . . Thanks very much for your telegram yesterday informing me that a settlement on the Asiatic question was in sight. . . . I am sure both Elgin & Churchill will give the T'vaal Government credit for having all throughout acted with the greatest consideration & have never shown any desire to have their pound of flesh. I have written a memorandum for Churchill on Asiatic legislation in the Transvaal since 1885 giving reasons for the necessity for the Immigration Act and the Asiatic Law Amendment Act of 1907. I hope it will be of some use to him should the Government be attacked on this Asiatic question in the Transvaal. . . .

WSC to Lord Elgin
(*Elgin Papers*)

1 February 1908 Colonial Office

My dear Lord Elgin,

I only wanted the Somaliland papers for a moment. I have known for some time that as Governor General you must have been forced to protest against the reckless plunges into the interior which have proved generally injurious to our finances & to our prestige.

It would be a great pleasure to me to talk to you about my various memoranda. I thought you would send for me when you had considered them, and I was reserving myself for that!

Please understand that my letter to Grey – wh he has had printed – was intended by me to be a private & not a state paper. There is nothing in the substance unsuited for circulation, but the style would have been different had I contemplated it appearing in 'cold lead'.

I hope Lady Elgin is better. These week-end journeys in such cold weather must be trying to you.

Yours vy sincerely
WINSTON S. CHURCHILL

Lord Rosebery to WSC

2 February 1908   38 Berkeley Square

My dear Winston,
   I was just about to write to you to propose a walk when I saw you looking
so blossoming at Ritz's. Let us try and take a walk (not Monday or Tuesday).
                                                              Yrs
                                                              AR

WSC to Lord Rosebery
(Rosebery Papers)

3 February 1908

My dear Lord Rosebery,
   Will Wednesday at 9 o'clock suit you?
   I look forward to telling you about Uganda and my projects for pushing
the railway forward to the Albert Lake – which now look quite practicable.
   I wonder whether the enclosed paper on the subject will interest you. It
explains in outline the argument I am building up.
   Also we must talk about things here. It will be a shocking disaster to this
country if through any fault of ours the Tories carry their Tariff. How I
wish you were with us! But any how
                          Believe me always your sincere friend
                                       WINSTON S. CHURCHILL

Sir Richard Solomon to General Louis Botha
(Smuts Archive)

7 February 1908   London

EXTRACT

. . . Last night that great protector of the rights and liberties of the loyalists
in S. Africa, Sir Gilbert Parker . . . moved an amendment to the address on
the question of the retrenched officials of the Transvaal. I posted Churchill
up in all the facts and he told me I had given him a very fine case. He did
not require to use it all as the attack was so miserably weak that it required
only a short speech from Churchill to blow it to atoms. . . .

Sir Francis Hopwood to Lord Elgin
(*Elgin Papers*)

EXTRACT

11 February 1908   Colonial Office

. . . There are a good many Questions about Natal & Churchill has been anxious to send divers telegrams. After a great deal of discussion I fixed on the form enclosed & sent it. I hope you will approve. Churchill liked it so much I am rather alarmed that I may not have detected a latent vice. . . .

WSC to Sir Matthew Nathan
(*Elgin Papers*)

14 February 1908   Colonial Office

TELEGRAM

Private and Personal

Pray send me a full telegraphic report of the situation in Zululand as revealed by your visit and whether there is any reason to think improper methods have been used under martial law to punish natives or obtain evidence.

Lord Elgin to WSC

21 February 1908

My dear Churchill,

I am exceedingly sorry if my Minute on retrenched officials seemed a reflection on you.

I assure you I did not so intend it. I meant to go for Gilbert Parker & Co – who to my mind are not honest in their championship: and for Milner, the extravagance of whose system is more & more apparent.

It might have been better I admit that I had not commented on the word monstrous (I am sure you will agree that I take great care to observe our compact, & to only quarrel out of school, if at all) but my object even there was rather to work up to the other proposition.

My bark has been worse than my bite – for I have communicated with two colleagues to-day regarding one retrenched officer.

So I hope we need not quarrel over this.

Yours ever

E

WSC to Lord Elgin
(Elgin Papers)

22 February 1908   [Colonial Office]

Private

My dear Lord Elgin,
    It would never be possible for me to quarrel with you, because your frank
& invariable kindness always removes at once from my mind any trace of
vexation which may arise from the tiresome course of business.

Yours vy sincerely
WINSTON S. CHURCHILL

WSC to Sir Matthew Nathan

[27 February 1908]   [Colonial Office]
[Copy]

TELEGRAM

Personal & Private

I am anxiously awaiting your reply to S of S telegram of Feb 20th. Meanwhile Parliamentary difficulties are increasing and I only stave off many
awkward questions from day to day. Is it possible that no precise charge
has been formulated against Dinizulu? Whom is he accused of murdering?
Whom has he incited to murder whom? When and how was the incitement
given? In what respects by what specific acts on what days & places is he
charged with high treason? What answer can I give to such questions?

CHURCHILL

Sir Matthew Nathan to WSC

28 February [1908]   [Pietermaritzburg]

TELEGRAM

Strictly private and personal

Please do not press for appt of outside counsel for Dinizulu. Minister will
not agree to it & I do not think it wd be right for me as Supreme Chief to
take action you propose against their advice. They are in a difficult position,
& impolitic to give them grounds for resigning as protest against active imperial interference. If they resigned on such grounds they wd have sympathy

of whole Colony wh at present is as critical of their action as is public at home but with more knowledge of actual state of affairs. Element of ministry most prone to ill considered action in matter of Dinizulu is I believe least popular. The press have all adopted our views of martial law against those of Ministers and have generally expressed satisfaction at quieting influence of my tour and dislike to Mackenzie's[1] operations. I repeat I have no fear but that justice will be done to Dinizulu. He is well looked after by Renaud reputed very capable criminal lawyer and his friends here seem prepared to go to great lengths for his rehabilitation.

NATHAN

WSC to Sir Matthew Nathan

[1 March 1908]   [Colonial Office]
[Copy]

TELEGRAM

Private & Personal

Your telegram of 28th I sympathise sincerely with you in the difficulties and embarrassments with which you are confronted and it would always cause me the greatest regret to add to these in any way. The position is however one of gravity [and] we are bound to press the question of counsel to the end. It would be very hard for me to continue to defend the Natal Government in the House of Commons unless fully satisfied that Dinizulu was not prevented by lack of funds from obtaining the necessary legal assistance which assistance S of S has already explained must include the services of a leader. When it is known that your ministers have refused to become parties in any way to the provision of such assistance, demands with which I entirely sympathise will be made upon HMG to supply the necessary funds. Suppose next week this demand is made and that HMG accede to it will your ministers resign? Observe that the action of HMG will not operate through any direct channel, and we should be in the position of enabling the friends of the accused to sustain the defence and not of sustaining it ourselves. You would not be involved either as Paramount Chief or Governor. Therefore whatever may be the fact the forms of delegated constitutional authority will not have been departed from. If Ministers resign can you form another government? What political strength is there behind your present advisers within and without the Colony? Please let me know your whole mind on these contingencies.

---

[1] Duncan Mackenzie (1859–1932), a Colonel commanding British forces during Natal native rebellion; KCMG 1907; retired as Brigadier-General.

After all that has happened this year and last it is not possible for Imperial Government to rest content with the utter ignominy even of the most friendly & earnest representations upon a point which scarcely any civilised Government would dispute. Do not of course consult ministers or take any executive action however slight except upon instructions from S of S but I rely upon you not to let expense of telegraphing prevent you from giving me a complete & reasoned statement of your view.

CHURCHILL

Rowland Ward Ltd to WSC

4 March 1908   Rowland Ward Limited
                                                    167 Piccadilly

Sir,

In accordance with instructions given on your behalf by Lieutenant Colonel Gordon Wilson, we have in hand the following: —

MODELLED HEADS

1 Rhinoceros,
1 Zebra,
1 Warthog,
1 Wildebeest,
1 Coke's Hartebeest,
1 Grant's Gazelle,
1 Thomson's Gazelle

and the dressing of three Zebra skins, at a total cost of £32. 7. o., (thirty two pounds seven shillings).

We are, Sir, Yours faithfully
per pro ROWLAND WARD LTD

PS We have no instructions to put in hand a Rhinoceros Table. Do you wish us to do so?

We shall be glad to hear.

Rowland Ward Ltd to WSC

25 March 1908   Rowland Ward Limited

Dear Sir,

We have pleasure to inform you that the Wildebeest shot by you, ties with the largest and finest we have yet measured, as will be seen upon reference to Mr Rowland Ward's *Records of Big Game*. The measurement of yours is 29½ inches.

Yours faithfully
ROWLAND WARD LTD

WSC to H. H. Asquith
(*Asquith Papers*)

14 March 1908   Colonial Office

Secret

My dear Asquith,

I was touched by your kindness on Thursday and by your confidence in me. Whatever you decide is best for the Government & in the general interest I will do to the best of my ability. But after our talk I feel I may, indeed I should, put my own view & feelings before you upon the various suggestions on which we dwelt.

I *know* the Colonial office. It is a post of immense, but largely disconnected, detail; & I have special experience of several kinds which helps.

During the last two years practically all the constructive action & all the Parliamentary exposition has been mine. I have many threads in hand and many plans in movement. It would take another at least a year merely to learn the facts: & no one will in this Parliament gain the experience which I have of what you can & can't do in the Colonies & in the House of Commons from the Colonial Office. I venture even to think that I was getting a certain measure of public approval in the Colonies & outside party lines at home. Certainly my return for Manchester would be easier if I remained at the Colonial Office from the support which would be given me by the Cotton trade.

Much of the smooth working of the CO depends upon personal relations. I have been fortunate to establish excellent relations in many quarters, which will not soon be recreated by another. The Government has much to gain from a spirited yet not improvident administration of an Imperial Department. The work is well within the compass of my strength & knowledge; & I should be available for general work in the House, in the country, or upon Cabinet committees whenever wanted.

You also mentioned the Admiralty to me. It is a contingency which I feel a personal difficulty in discussing.[1] The proposition is threefold – Finance, Machinery, & a great Professional service – the last not the least important element. It is of course in its amenities & attractions much the most pleasant

[1] Lord Tweedmouth, the First Lord, was WSC's uncle.

& glittering post in the Ministry. If however I were given my choice between the Admiralty & the Colonial Office, I should feel bound to stand by my own work here upon purely public grounds.

To compare such offices, from the standpoint of personal satisfaction, with the Local Government Board is of course impossible. There is no place in the Government more laborious, more anxious, more thankless, more choked with petty & even squalid detail, more full of hopeless and insoluble difficulties: & I say deliberately that so far as the peace & comfort of my life are concerned, I would rather continue to serve under Lord Elgin at the Colonial Office without a seat in the Cabinet than go there. It is however only on public grounds that I submit the following considerations to you.

I have had very little training in the detail of domestic politics such as would seem necessary at the LGB. I have never piloted a Bill of any importance through Parliament (That kind of work exhausts me). I cannot claim any acquaintance with a proper grounding in the Poor Law or the Law of Rating – two absolutely basic subjects. Five or six first-class questions await immediate attention – Housing, Unemployment, Rating Reform, Electoral Reform, Old Age Pensions administration – I presume, to say nothing of minor measures & exacting day to day administration. On all of these I shall be confronted by hundreds of earnest men who have thought of nothing else all their lives, who know these subjects – as I know military & Colonial things – from experience learned in hard schools, or else men who have served for many years on local bodies.

Dimly across gulfs of ignorance I see the outline of a policy wh I call the Minimum Standard. It is national rather than departmental. I am doubtful of my power to give it concrete expression. If I did, I expect before long I should find myself in collision with some of my best friends – like for instance John Morley, who at the end of a lifetime of study & thought has come to the conclusion that nothing can be done.

Any attempt to grapple with the evils of Unemployment must be concerted between all departments. Youth must be educated, disciplined & trained from 14 to 18. The exploitation of Boy Labour must be absolutely stopped. The Army must be made to afford a life-long career of State Employment to at any rate a large proportion of its soldiers on leaving the colonies. Labour must be de-casualised by a system of Labour Exchanges. The resultant residuum must be curatively treated exactly as if they were hospital patients. The hours of labour must be regulated in various trades subject to seasonal or cyclical fluctuations. Means must be found by which the State can within certain limits and for short periods augment the demand of the ordinary market for unskilled labour so as to counterbalance the oscillations of world-trade. Underneath, though not in substitution for, the immense disjoined fabric of social safeguards & insurances which has grown up by itself in England, there must be spread – at a lower level – a sort of Germanised network of State intervention & regulation.

In all this, as in the Bills I have mentioned, the Local Government Board must inevitably be the fountain. I do not underrate the great honour you have done me in seeming to wish me to encounter such awful labours & responsibilities. I hope your arrangements may permit some other disposition of offices. I am sure you will find people much better qualified than I for service in this arena.

No condition personal to myself shall prevent me from serving you where you wish. It is clear, however, & will not escape your sense of justice, that a department charged with such profound responsibilities ought not – whoever holds it – to be inferior to a Secretaryship-of-State: & you will no doubt consider whether the moment of a change in persons & the accession of a new Government is not the opportunity for such an alteration.

Yours vy sincerely
WINSTON S. CHURCHILL

Lord Esher[1] to Lord Knollys
(*Royal Archives*)
EXTRACT

15 March 1908   Orchard Lee
                                                   Windsor Forest

... I have seen Loulou Harcourt this week, who says that a reconstruction of the Government although not perhaps necessary immediately, must come very soon after Asquith succeeds to the Premiership; because some office must be found for Winston. ...

Mrs H. H. Asquith to WSC

28 March 1908   20 Cavendish Square

Dear Winston,

There are a few moments in life when unwilling decisions seem forced on one. I know them well they make one feel sick & rebellious but I've had luck with mine. I knocked a great love out of my life to make room for a great character & do you suppose we ever regretted it – *never*.[2]

---

[1] Reginald Baliol Brett, 2nd Viscount Esher (1852–1930), permanent member of the Committee of Imperial Defence 1905–18; Liberal MP 1880–5; succeeded father 1899; knighted 1902; PC 1922.

[2] Probably a reference to Peter Flower, brother of Lord Battersea. For a different version of the end of this affair see Margot Asquith, *Autobiography*, i 222–64.

I was *very* touched by yr loyalty & sweetness when you said you wd give of yr best – I know you will & I believe it will be through you if we win in 2 or 3 years the Gen Election. Its being *in* the Cabinet that matters. H & the others need you badly – you must between you make a proper possible measure or programme not overloading the ship now but combining the *same* front of iron courage & concentrating on the same big points. I only write this to cheer you up. CB was so touching when he thanked Henry; he said he was the finest colleague he cd ever have had & that his work had been magnificent. H will tell you the rest tonight if you dine at Alice's. Dull as it sounds no nation can be great that is not sound at core. This soundness largely depends on you & Henry. All Joe's power started from municipal training – he wanted power far more than pomp – Curzon wrecks himself by confusing the 2. Power first & after that you can do what you like. To be loved & backed by the British people added to what you are already, very well known all over the world & much loved personally by the Cabinet. Let us say for short the P Minister wd be my ambition.

ever yr affectionate
MARGOT

General Louis Botha to WSC

3 April 1908 Prime Minister's Office
Pretoria

Dear Mr Churchill,
   With reference to the possible withdrawal of the Troops from the Transvaal, I should like to tell you that I am very anxious for the Troops to remain here. As far as my information goes, there were in the Transvaal on 1st March, 1907, about 8000 Officers and men and on the 1st March this year there were about 7000. If it could possibly be managed my colleagues and I are very desirous that they should not be withdrawn from this Colony.
   As you are aware we have been doing our utmost to obtain unification in South Africa and as soon as that hope will be realized we can begin with the establishment of a strong defence force. The older population of the Transvaal is now beginning to understand the Military better and many petitions have been sent to the Government praying us to assist them in their endeavours to retain the Troops in the Transvaal. Personally I deem it very desirable that they should remain here, not because I foresee any difficulties but you remember the old saying that in order to preserve the peace it is best to be always ready for emergencies.
   I am glad to be able to tell you that matters are going fairly well with us

here and that they are not in that miserable state that Sir Gilbert Parker and Mr Lyttelton would make you believe.

The Anti-Chinese policy has been an unqualified success and I can very well understand why the Conservatives are continually referring to that subject. The Chinese Labour Policy has been an absolute failure in South Africa, and naturally the Conservatives feel sore about it. We are repatriating the Chinese regularly every month without having experienced any shortage of native labour as yet and as far as we can see we will have a sufficient number of Native Labourers to replace every Chinaman who must still go by two Natives. The Natives under Responsible Government are much more satisfied than before and have confidence in the Government, and as far as I can see there is no reason why the Mining Industries should not expand considerably without any shortage of Native Labour being felt.

I am also grateful to say that the relations between Dutch and English are rapidly becoming better.

There has been a considerable agitation here for protection against the other Colonies, but this also is gradually diminishing and I hope will soon give place to a higher and better ideal. One thing I very sincerely hope and that is that the British Government will never think of withdrawing the Government of Zululand from Natal. I think this would be a most deplorable step and I foresee that the other Colonies would sympathise with Natal in the matter.

I believe that Merriman[1] will be bringing up the matter of the Martial Law Proclamation at the forthcoming Conference and I think that what may happen there will be a serious warning to Natal whose action in a certain measure was indefensible – but every Government makes a mistake sometimes, and I think you might safely leave this matter to be dealt with by the South African Colonies.

We were sincerely sorry to hear of the serious illness of Sir H. Campbell-Bannerman and I hope that he will recover soon and live to see the fruit of the good work which he has done for South Africa. We hope while he is still in Office he may see the unification of British South Africa realised.

Your journey in East Africa must have been most interesting and I hope that your next trip will be to our parts, where you can be sure of a good reception, as we appreciate what you are continually doing for us.

With kind regards, believe me, Yours sincerely

LOUIS BOTHA

[1] John Xavier Merriman (1841–1926), Prime Minister and Treasurer of Cape Colony 1908–10; Member of Union House of Assembly 1910–24; PC 1909.

*　　*　　*　　*　　*

WSC to Arthur Wilson Fox[1]

4 January 1908   General's House
                                                             Cairo
Dictated
[Copy]

My dear Wilson Fox,

Would you very kindly examine, illuminate, & fortify the following:—

The main need of the English working classes is Security. In Germany, where the industrial system was developed under State control with all the advantages of previous British experience, uniform & symmetrical arrangements exist for insurance of workmen against accidents & sickness, for provision for old age, and through Labour bureaux etc for employment. No such State organisation exists in England. Its place is supplied by an immense amount of voluntary private machinery in the shape of friendly & benefit societies, trade unions & the like. Comparing the two systems in their practical working, it may be said that what the English system loses in uniformity it gains in flexibility, in spontaneity, and possibly even in economy. But in one respect the German system has an enormous advantage. It catches everybody. The meshes of our safety net are only adapted to subscribers, & all those who are not found on any of those innumerable lists go smashing down on the pavement. It is this very class, the residue, the rearguard, call it what you will, for whom no provision exists in our English machinery, who have neither the character nor the resources to make provision for themselves, who require the aid of the state.

No one would propose to substitute the German for the English system. Such a change is beyond the wit of man to execute. But if we were able to underpin the whole existing social security apparatus with a foundation of comparatively low-grade state safeguards, we should in the result obtain something that would combine the greatest merits both of the English & the German systems.

I should very much like to have your views & information on this. I am to speak at Birmingham on the 23rd, & these ideas of minimum standards of life & wages, of security against going to the Devil through accident, sickness, or weakness of character, & of competition upwards but not downwards, will be my general theme.

                                                Yours sincerely
                                                WINSTON S. CHURCHILL
RSVP to CO

---

[1] Arthur Wilson Fox (1861–1909), Comptroller-General of the Commercial, Labour and Statistical Department of the Board of Trade 1906–9.

WSC to [?]

28 January 1908   Colonial Office
[Copy]

Dear Sir,

I am much obliged to you for your letter, and indeed I am always glad when my constituents take the trouble to write to me.

I agree with you that the debate on the Address is often too long; at the same time it would be a great mistake to think that the House of Commons was intended simply to be a machine for passing bills. If that were the only end in view, it would be perfectly easy to invent an Assembly which would pass all the bills which would occur to the wit of man in a moderate session. What the effect of these bills would be afterwards, what measure of acceptance they would receive from the public are other questions.

Parliament is not a mere legislative machine, but the principal forum where all great matters should be debated; and simply to make it a Committee for disposing of estimates and legislative details would be, in a very short time, to deprive it of its claim upon public respect. The opportunities during the Session for general discussions are few and far between, and I am inclined to think that more latitude ought to be allowed to the House in that respect. Indeed I remember the great injury to public interests which was caused by the refusal of Mr Balfour to afford any opportunities during the close of the Session of 1903 for the discussion of the fiscal policy of Mr Chamberlain which was the most vital factor in the whole political session.

No such opportunity occurred until the debate on the Address in 1904, and had the rule which you suggest been then in force, I really cannot see that there would have been any occasion when the great question would have been thrashed out at all except on private members' nights. In these circumstances, I feel that it is easy to take a too capacious view of Parliamentary proceedings even when they lead to no actual financial or legislative result. The members come back to the House after a long recess, and I think it quite right that whatever great matters have been in dispute in the Autumn should be capable of being debated, and the Government forced to defend themselves for the whole range of their policy.

Yours faithfully
[WINSTON S. CHURCHILL]

WSC to Thomas Horsfall[1]

13 February 1908   Colonial Office

[Copy]

Dear Mr Horsfall,

Many thanks for sending me your papers on town planning. I will read them with the interest which I always derive from your disquisitions on social subjects.

I should like to know more about the proposal to have skilled professional mayors on the German plan instead of our present happy-go-lucky amateur system.

How could you interweave the German plan with the habits of our life in England so as to cause the least possible alteration in the appearance and form of things, the least possible break with the past, and the minimum of disappointment to individuals who may have nourished hopes of civic honour?

What is to happen to a burgomaster appointed, let us say, for seven or eight years, no longer in my opinion under any circumstances, who in his third or fourth year gives general dissatisfaction? Has the town got to stand him until his full term is up? What disciplinary machinery is there for removing such a person even before their new term of office will occur?

What effective method of control have they got over the whole policy of the system? How far can they act in opposition to the will of their council? What proportion do you think right between paid and unpaid members? How much real power have the elected unpaid members against their paid colleagues and the professional mayor?

What do you think is the best system to apply to Manchester as a concrete instance?

Another point occurs to my mind. Would it be a good thing to try to form the municipal and local civil service in the country into one large body of similar character, though necessarily of a somewhat lower standard, to the existing civil service of the crown?

Would it not enhance the dignity and efficiency of surveyors, electricians, boro' architects, poor law officers, sanitary inspectors, and all the body of minor officials indispensable to modern local government, if they found themselves all members of one great organization animated by a high spirit of corporate honour?

Would not the institution of such a service as this have the effect of affording more skilled advice to town councillors and provincial mayors

---

[1] Thomas Coglan Horsfall (1841–1932), writer on art, education and social reform; a founder of the Horsfall Art Museum, Manchester.

who under the present system come into office, in the same way that ministers of the Crown who are new to the work of their new departments are aided by the great body of civil servants?

On any of those points I should be delighted to have your opinion, for I believe the times are now coming when active and increasing social construction and reconstruction will be the order of the day.

[WINSTON S. CHURCHILL]

WSC to Herbert Gladstone

(*Herbert Gladstone Papers*)

24 February 1908

Dear Gladstone,

I send you a file of correspondence which has been sent to me on the working of the Aliens Act.

You will see that the Jewish Board of Deputies were contemplating a Memorial to the Prime Minister on the points which are set out herein. I am afraid his present illness will make it impossible for him to consider these matters at the present time, but I should be glad to know from you what view the Home Office take of these proposals.

Upon the occasion of the Deputation on Naturalisation which was introduced by me to the Prime Minister on March 14th last year, the Prime Minister and the Chancellor of the Exchequer were both understood to have expressed themselves favourable to a reduction of the naturalisation fee to a figure closely corresponding to the actual cost to the State of the process; and this position was accepted gratefully by the Deputation and by the leaders of the Jewish community generally. I understand that the Home Office consider that the figure of £3 would cover the regular expenditure in this connection, but that a question has been raised as to whether the lowering of the naturalisation fee in England will not affect the general question of naturalisation throughout the Empire, which formed the subject of discussion at the Colonial Conference, and is likely in the future to engage the attention of a subsidiary Conference; and that this doubt is an obstacle to action being taken in accordance with the promises which have been made.

There is no possibility of any reduction such as is contemplated clashing with the larger subject of naturalisation throughout the Empire. The question of an uniform fee for the Empire has not been hitherto raised either in the report of the Inter-departmental Committee of 24th July 1901, Command paper 723, or at the Colonial Conference, but even if there were any question of a uniform fee, a reduction in the British naturalisation fee would only be a step towards such uniformity. From the appended table for fees charged in the different self-governing Colonies, it will be seen that no fee is over £1, and that the British fee for naturalisation is at present more than five times higher than any other fee in the British Empire.

Fee for obtaining letters of Naturalisation

Revised Statutes 1906 cap 77	Canada	25 cents
Cll of 1903	Australia	No fee
	New Zealand	No fee for Europeans
Law 2, 1883	Cape of Good Hope	2s 6d
Law 18, 1905	Natal	£1
Ordinance 46, 1902	Transvaal	£1
Ordinance 1, 1903	Orange River Colony	£1
Cap 145	Newfoundland	$2.50

Yours sincerely

WINSTON S CHURCHILL

11

Cabinet and Marriage

(See Main Volume Chapter 8)

ON 6 April 1908 Sir Henry Campbell-Bannerman resigned through ill-health and Mr Asquith was summoned by the King to Biarritz to be asked whether he would form a Government. He accepted and was appointed Prime Minister on April 8. Sir Henry died on April 22.

The law at this time made it necessary for new Ministers to stand again for election in their constituencies. On being appointed President of the Board of Trade, WSC fought and lost a by-election in North West Manchester before being returned for Dundee.

WSC to John Redmond[1]

7 April 1908   Colonial Office

[Copy]

Private

Dear Mr Redmond,

I am vy much obliged to you for yr letter & I fully appreciate the friendly spirit in wh it is written.

Yr countrymen will make a mistake if they fail to support me now. Their alternative is to vote for an ultra-Unionist who has spent some part of the autumn in denouncing the Govt for not applying the Crimes Act to Ireland, & who hopes to secure the Protestant vote by denouncing the University Bill.

My vote for yr resolution will undoubtedly expose me to considerable

---
[1] John REDMOND.

attack, as it will rightly be interpreted as being another step forward on my part towards a full recognition of Irish claim to self-Govt. I shall not however regret it, whatever be the treatment to wh I may be subjected: & yr friends may rest assured that any action they may take – however injurious & as I think miscalculated – will not prevent me from doing my best as opportunity may offer to serve the interests & sustain the hopes of Irishmen, & from promoting that effective recognition of their national claims to the management of purely Irish affairs wh I believe to be right in itself, & entirely compatible with the interests of the British people.

Believe me that the courtesy & consideration of yr letter will always be a pleasant recollection to

Yrs vy truly
WSC

H. H. Asquith to WSC

8 April 1908   Hotel du Palais
                                              Biarritz

Secret

My dear Winston,

With the King's approval, I have the great pleasure of offering you the post of President of the Board of Trade in the new administration.

It is my intention to seek the consent of Parliament to placing the office on the same level, as regards salary & status, while retaining its present title, with the Secretaryships of State. But I am afraid that the change cannot come into effect during the current year.

I shall hail with much gratification your accession to the Cabinet, both on public & on personal grounds.

I return to England tomorrow.

Yours always
H. H. ASQUITH

WSC to H. H. Asquith
(Asquith Papers)

10 April 1908   12 Bolton Street

Secret

My dear Asquith,

I accept the offer of the Presidency of the Board of Trade with which you have honoured me.

I shall exert myself to the utmost on behalf of your Administration. It gives me great pleasure to serve you. I am vy sensible of the kindness of your letter. When can I see you for *a few minutes?* There are two or three matters of urgency connected with the Manchester election on which I need your advice. I could come round at 7.45 if that were convenient.

Yours always most sincerely
WINSTON S CHURCHILL

John Morley to WSC

8 April 1908   Flowermead
                                                                               Wimbledon Park

My dear Winston,

I have read the enclosed[1] with lively interest, you may be sure: first, because I am full of concern and solicitude as to your career: second, because I'm fascinated at every turn and shake of the Irish Kaleidoscope, and always shall be. I don't see what better reply you could make – unless you were in the mood to play Don Quixote. We'll talk about it.

The B of T will bring you into responsible contact with some of the greatest of imperial questions. But for you, at this stage of your life, the department is not all; it matters less than the acquisition and accumulation of influence, authority and power in the Cabinet. That's what you have to build upon the platform & the public you have secured.

Nobody wishes you well more heartily than

Your friend
JOHN MORLEY

WSC to Sir Edward Donner[2]

8 April 1908   Colonial Office

[Copy]

Dear Sir Edward Donner,

If we may judge from newspaper report, and I certainly know nothing to enable me to contradict it – there is likely to be a bye-election in NW M/c next week. On that assumption the writ would be moved in the House of Commons on Tuesday and I should arrive in Manchester either on Tuesday

---

[1] WSC's letter to John Redmond quoted on page 764.
[2] Edward Donner (1840–1934), Governor of the Victoria University of Manchester; baronet 1907.

evening or Wednesday morning. It would give me very great satisfaction if I could feel that you could do me the service of presiding over the work of my election Committee. As you know, at the last election I was supported by Sir J. Southern[1] and his illness will make it impossible for him to take any part in this contest. There is no one who could exert a more useful influence upon our workers than yourself and I earnestly hope that you will find it possible to give me your assistance in a contest which would be (should it occur) of peculiar importance to the Liberal Party and to His Majesty's Government.

[WINSTON S. CHURCHILL]

Sir Edward Donner to WSC

9 April 1908　　　　　　　　　　　　　　　　　　　　Oak Mount
　　　　　　　　　　　　　　　　　　　　　　　　　　Manchester

Dear Mr Churchill,
　It will be a pleasure to me to render any assistance that I can whenever the contest may come.

Yrs very truly
EDWARD DONNER

WSC to Edward Tootal Broadhurst[2]

8 April 1908

[Copy]

Private and personal

My dear Mr Tootal Broadhurst,
　It is very likely that a writ for an election in NW M/c will be moved for on Tuesday next. If so, I shall come forward as the Liberal and Free Trade candidate; and I shall be opposed by a gentleman who is pledged to support the fiscal resolution carried by Mr Chaplin at Birmingham last year. In these circumstances I hope I may count on your support. None could be more valuable or personally more agreeable to me.
　There are of course other issues besides Free Trade, but is there any half so important to Lancashire? The defection of the commercial division of life

[1] James Wilson Southern (1840–1909), Manchester industrialist; knighted 1907.
[2] Edward Tootal Broadhurst (1858–1922), Manchester businessman; baronet 1918.

upon this notable occasion would be a cruel blow to a cause for which you have already sacrificed so much. Yet there are several elements less favourable to my candidature than at the General Election. The Irish voters would be rather estranged by the accession to the leadership of the Liberal party of a minister who they know has no intention of introducing a Home Rule Bill until the country has been specifically consulted on that issue. Their support may easily be given to the Protectionist candidate. I have always regarded the Central Division of Manchester as the citadel of Free Trade, and if it were lost, I believe the harm resulting would be greater even than the advantage of capturing it at the last election.

Your views on social questions leave me no doubt of the sympathy which you feel for the Temperance aspect of the Licensing Bill. With regard to the finance of that measure it is possible – nay it is certain – that some substantial modifications will be made in its passage through both Houses of Parliament; and although I am not prepared at present to accept the actuarial statements which have been produced by the trade as correct, I agree that the time limit should be such as to enable a prudent trader or investor to make provision against the resumption by the State of the monopoly value which has unwisely been surrendered.

I feel I have some claim upon the Free Trade League. It was at their invitation that I came forward three years ago to undertake so desperate – as it then seemed – a contest.

I am not conscious of anything which should justify the withdrawal from me of the support which you and your friends then gave me: and I ask for it again in order that I may continue to defend our Free Trade system – perhaps from a position particularly associated with that duty.

Yours sincerely

WSC

WSC to T. W. Killick

8 April 1908   Colonial Office

[Copy]

Private

My dear Mr Killick,

In the event of a bye-election occurring in M/c next week as a consequence of Cabinet re-arrangement, I trust I can count upon the energetic and wholehearted support of the Free Trade League. Mr Joynson-Hicks has been forced by the Conservative Central Office to adopt Mr Balfour's fiscal policy in its entirety. That policy is, as you know, embodied in the fiscal resolution moved by Mr Chaplin at the Birmingham Conference this year, and is of course a complete and comprehensive Protectionist policy embracing not merely a retaliatory provision against foreign countries but the preferential taxation of bread and meat. It was to counter such a policy as this that I came forward three years ago as Liberal and Free Trade candidate for NW M/c. The invitation which I received on that occasion did not only emanate from the Liberal party in the Division, it was accompanied by a formal invitation from the Free Trade League whose candidate in a very direct sense I was and for whose objects I have not ceased to exert myself. Since the General Election the issue so far from becoming obscured or remote has been made actually more acute. Mr Joynson-Hicks, who on the last occasion presented himself as a mild retaliationist opposed to food taxes and unconnected with any scheme for a general tariff, has now adopted – or been compelled to adopt – what in common parlance is described as the 'platform of the whole hogger'. I remain of the same opinion as when I last appealed for the support of M/c, that is to say that I do not approve of taxation for any purpose other than for revenue. I feel therefore that I have a right by the constitution of the Free Trade League and by my personal association with it to call for its most strenuous exertions during a contest which – if it occurs – will be fraught with the deepest significance to the Free Trade cause.

I do not like to put you to the trouble of coming up to London, but if your arrangements should make that convenient it would give me the greatest pleasure to see you here at the Colonial Office any day this week and almost at any time.

[WINSTON S. CHURCHILL]

T. W. Killick to WSC

9 April 1908   Devonshire Lodge
                                                           Buxton

Private

My dear Churchill,

I am fully in accord with all you write, and have been working hard and continuously to keep the Free Trade League up to the mark.

Liberal and Labour votes are all safe for Free Trade. The problem is to poll the Unionist Free Traders. A few weeks ago it looked as if we should lose most of these in North West Manchester. A suggestion was even made that the League should stand neutral if Mr Joynson-Hicks gave a *partial* Free

Trade pledge. This danger has been averted. The Free Trade Unionists may be led but it would be fatal to attempt to drive them. They realize the vital importance to Free Trade of winning at the coming bye-election. Many of them are trying all ways and means to get as much of their strength polled as possible. Two large and successful Free Trade Hall meetings have been held, and a lot of literature circulated.

I would come up to London to see you if I thought it would be of any use, but I don't think it would; and it would not be advisable for me to be away from Manchester.

Yours very truly

T. W. KILLICK

Sir Alexander Fuller-Acland-Hood to Lord Stanley
(Derby Papers)

[9 April 1908]   St Audries
                                                             Bridgwater

Confidential

My dear Eddy,

I quite understand the difficulties in NW Manchester, and the great importance of getting rid of Winston.

I think however that victory would be too dearly bought, even if it *were* bought, at the price of the compromise you suggest. To put it shortly, we are to accept a temporary alliance with a man (solely for the purpose of turning out Winston) who is openly prepared at the General Election to oppose the Chief Constitution Policy of the Party.

Our Candidate is to bind himself *not* to support the Leader of the Party if that policy is advocated by him in the present Parliament.

I think the result of such a compromise would be disastrous for many reasons.

(1) Of all bye-elections[1] this will be far the most important and all eyes will be on it, every paper will report on it.

(2) The suggested attitude of our Candidate would make all Tariff Reformers luke-warm, if not hostile.

(3) An astute electioneer like Winston would make enormous capital out of it.

(4) A distinct wobble of this kind would have a most deplorable effect in

---

[1] Between January and September 1908, seven Liberal seats were lost to Conservatives in by-elections: Mid-Devon, South Hereford, Peckham, Manchester NW, Pudsey, Haggerston, and Newcastle.

Lancashire when we have been working for months past, and with success, to bring the Party into line.

(5) The effect on other bye-elections, and in certain seats now held by our wobblers, would be bad.

(6) I could not get any speakers from the House of Commons to go and support the Candidate.

(7) How could my Chief send a letter of recommendation to a Candidate who openly avows that he cannot support him in the House of Commons on the Fiscal Question during this Parliament? I need hardly say I am sure Chamberlain would not do it.

Let us have a stand-up fight and do the best we can. Whatever happens, as long as we seem on a straight issue we shall put some heart into our people in Lancashire. I am sorry I cannot visit you Saturday, but I am down here for business and meetings.

William Joynson-Hicks to WSC

10 April 1908   Holmbury
                                                        Dorking

Private

Dear Churchill,

I gather that we are to have another fight & at a most awkward time.

I write to enquire whether you would care for a truce over Easter say from midnight on Thursday to midday on Monday both of us to clear out of Manchester & do no meeting or canvassing.

If you agree I will.

Perhaps you could drop me a line to the Queen's, Manchester.

Yours very truly
W. JOYNSON-HICKS

*   *   *   *   *

Mrs H. H. Asquith to WSC

[10 April 1908]   20 Cavendish Square

Private

Dearest Winston,

I'm told Lloyd George dines with you tonight. I *wish* you wd speak to him & tell him quite plainly that the staff of *Daily Chronicle* have given him away to 3 independent people (better praps keep McKenna's name out) Mr Nash & Runciman. Quite simply told them both that Lloyd George had given them the list. The *only* man the King resented at all (dont say this to a living soul not even to Henry please) was Lloyd George wh seemed so odd! Ld Knollys knows it was LG who split & he says the King will be furious. Lloyd George's best chance if he *is* a good fellow, wh I take yr word for, is *not* to lie about it when H speaks heavily to him but to give up his whole Press Campaign; he will be done as a dog if he goes on. I think *you* might ease him & the Cabinet if you do this courageously. The Editor as well as others told Nash. Do yr d—dest. I've just driven H from the station & he said to me 'he hoped to God Winston would give it him'. He is perfectly furious.

Yrs
MARGOT

Burn this

WSC to H. H. Asquith

(*Asquith Papers*)

10 April 1908   12 Bolton Street
Midnight

Secret

My dear Asquith,
    I broached the matter to Lloyd George. He denies it utterly. I told him that you had said that you learned that several colleagues thought he was responsible; but that you had of course no knowledge yourself. He intends to speak to you to-morrow on the subject, & I have told him he can quote me as having put him the question. It will be a good opportunity for a talk.
    I hope you will let me know if it turned out that you want to replace Kearley at the Board of Trade. I have preserved the silence of an oyster upon minor appointments.

Yours ever
W

D. Lloyd George to H. H. Asquith
(Asquith Papers)
EXTRACT

11 April 1908   5 Cheyne Place
                                                   Chelsea

. . . Winston told me last night that some of my colleagues had rushed to you immediately on your arrival with the amiable suggestion that I had been responsible for the publication of the Chronicle list. I need hardly tell you that I feel very hurt at the accusation & I think I ought to know who it is amongst my colleagues who deems me capable of what is not merely a gross indiscretion but a downright and discreditable breach of trust. . . .

Lord Tweedmouth to H. H. Asquith
(Asquith Papers)
EXTRACT

11 April 1908   HMS *Enchantress*
                                              Portsmouth

. . . I ought to have resigned when the cabinet again and again cut down my estimates. . . . You don't trust me. Why not give me a watch-dog, say Runciman or Winston with a seat in the Cabinet. . . . Forgive me if I am seeming to go beyond my proper rights.[1] . . .

Sir Alexander Fuller-Acland-Hood to Lord Stanley
(Derby Papers)
EXTRACT

12 April 1908   St Audries
                                               Bridgwater

I am glad you agree with me about NW Manchester.

I have never heard a word about Haddock[2] resigning in order to put you in.[3] He spoke to me a fortnight ago about not standing again, and I told him

---

[1] When Mr Asquith announced the members of his new Administration on April 10, Lord Tweedmouth was appointed Lord President of the Council and was replaced at the Admiralty by Mr Reginald McKenna. Lord Tweedmouth resigned because of ill-health in September.

[2] George Bahr Haddock (1863–1930), Unionist MP for North Lonsdale, Lancashire 1906–18.

[3] Stanley's search for a seat ended when his father died in June.

that I thought at his age it would be very foolish to give up Parliament. But your name was never mentioned.

On general grounds I am against vacating seats just now, and for this reason I held up Wimbledon and Hastings as long as I could. In the first place we have quite as much as we could arrange in attacking Radical seats which fall vacant. I have a first class Election Staff, but they are being *very* hard worked.

In the second place a reverse just now when everything is going in our favour would be a disaster.

Haddock's majority was only 179 and if there were a three-cornered fight the seat would be in great danger.

As regards the assurances you ask –

(1) Certainly whenever you stand I will give you the full support of the Central Office.

(2) As I have said above I am not anxious to open Haddock's seat.

(3) Austen Chamberlain is abroad so I cannot get anything from him till we meet again, but I am sure he will agree with me in saying that 'absolute allegiance to Arthur Balfour, coupled with a promise made without any reservation whatsoever to support him is quite sufficient to satisfy the party requirements' – to quote your own words.

I agree with you that it is not a Liberal Unionist seat and that they have no right to interfere.

I am very sorry you should have had all this trouble. . . .

Lord Curzon to WSC

13 April 1908   Hackwood

My dear Winston,

Bravo! at 33 a great record. *Sic itur ad astra.*[1]

No reply.

Yours ever
CURZON

[1] Virgil, *The Aeneid*, ix. 641: So shalt thou scale the stars.

William Joynson-Hicks to WSC

14 April 1908   The Queen's Hotel
                                                Manchester

Private

Dear Churchill,

I'm awfully sick but my people have fixed meetings for me on Saturday (largely because you had done) and they decline to permit the truce.

Of course I shall do nothing on Good Friday or Sunday but do not ask you to agree to the same line.

Again I can only add my sorrows.

Remember me to the Guests.

Yours very truly
W. JOYNSON-HICKS

W. Joynson-Hicks to the Parliamentary Electors of the
North-West Division of Manchester

13 April 1908   Chasefield
                                                Bowdon

Gentlemen,

It is part of the constitution of our Country that when any member of Parliament takes office under the Crown he vacates his seat and must submit himself for re-election.

Mr Winston Churchill has just been appointed to the office of President of the Board of Trade, and, in consequence has necessarily to seek re-election at your hands, and I have been compelled to consider the grave responsibility which would be placed upon myself if I refused the very strongly worded request, which has been presented to me by my friends in Manchester, that I should contest the seat.

I much regret the necessity for doing this, and under other circumstances I might have declined the invitation, but this is the first occasion which South-East Lancashire has had of expressing its opinion upon this Government who in the space of two short years have alienated our Colonies, thrown away the fruits of the Transvaal War, weakened our Navy, attempted to gerrymander our Constitution, increased our Taxation, flouted our religious convictions, let loose chaos and bloodshed in Ireland, and are now setting out to attack every trade and institution who are not prepared to obey the rattle of the Radical drum.

Beyond this I desire especially, that, in this Election, you should speak with no uncertain voice upon two subjects – the Education Policy and the Licensing Policy of the Liberal Government, in both of which they are supported by Mr Churchill. The Education Policy, while doing nothing to improve but much to hinder the cause of Education, has violated the consciences of Churchmen, Roman Catholics, and Jews, and many devout Nonconformists to an extent without parallel in the history of our Country.

Lancashire has been moved in a way in which politics rarely touch the feelings of our people, and were we to allow this opportunity of striking a blow at the Government and their Education proposals to pass by, the Cabinet would naturally and rightly say:—

'Lancashire, which is the heart of the Voluntary School position, dares not take up the gauntlet which Mr Churchill has thrown down, and all their denunciations of our Education Policy may be disregarded.'

Upon the pretext of remedying a grievance under which in some country districts our Nonconformist friends have suffered, and which I would gladly see alleviated, they propose to throw a tenfold grievance upon the shoulders of the supporters of all Voluntary Schools; every clause of their Bill breathing enmity against the Church of England, veiled hostility against the Church of Rome, and a spirit of similar unfairness to the Jewish community.

I had the honour during the autumn of 1906 of taking an active part in the campaign against the Bill of that year and I rejoice, as all honest men must, that the House of Lords came to the rescue of the people of this Country by delivering them from the tyranny of a Radical majority, got together on every pretext under the sun except only that of dealing honestly and fairly with the property and rights of others.

On the rejection of this, their chief measure, by the House of Lords, instead of appealing to the people as a strong Government would have done, the Radical Government, knowing in their hearts that they could not count upon a victory in a fair fight on this question, have taken refuge in threats against the House of Lords and have introduced an even worse Education Bill in the present session.

Not content with introducing the principle of appropriating the property of others, without payment, in their Education Bill, they have embodied it as the cardinal and essential feature of their Licensing Bill which (and I speak as a temperance reformer and a total abstainer) will do nothing for the cause of temperance but strike a determined blow at the rights of property.

This Bill in particular embodies in a naked form pure Socialism, and as such must, I hope, receive the detestation of all who cherish the fundamental doctrines of right and wrong.

In order to get legislation of this character through Parliament the House of Lords must either be muzzled or destroyed, and consequently the Government embarked upon their ill-fated agitation against that House, Mr Churchill himself, in a recent Bye-Election, declaring to the Electors that 'If they rejected the Liberal Candidate at this Election they would be sending a message to the unconstitutional power in the State, the House of Lords, to disregard the votes of Liberals, of Radicals, of Labour men, and of Socialists, in the House of Commons.' (*Times*, March 18th, 1908.)

The answer on that occasion was a decisive victory for the Unionist Candidate, and I appeal confidently to the business community of North-West Manchester to declare for the maintenance of the House of Lords as a protection against predatory and Socialistic Legislation, and to return me as their representative to the House of Commons with a distinct mandate from this great City to oppose measures of this character produced or threatened by the Radical Government.

To one other subject only do I think it right to refer, namely, that of Tariff Reform.

My views on this subject are these:—

I am in favour of a revision of our fiscal policy on the conservative lines laid down by Mr Balfour in his speech at Birmingham in November last.

At a future general election, if I am again your candidate, I shall advocate at greater length this policy, and elaborate it in detail, but in a contest of this peculiar character, the question which each elector must answer for himself is this:—

'Have you, or have you not, confidence in the legislative policy of the present Government?'

My political life has been lived in your midst for the past ten years, and if you elect me to represent you in Parliament it will be my earnest endeavour to merit your confidence by devotion to the interests of the city and of the great industries upon which your prosperity depends.

I have the honour to be

Your faithful servant

WILLIAM JOYNSON-HICKS

H. G. Wells to an elector in NW Manchester

OPEN LETTER

[? 13 April 1908]

My dear Sir,

You are at present considering how you may best vote at this imminent election in your constituency. I take it that, in common with the great mass of active-minded people in this country you have been deeply moved and interested by the Socialist movement, which has been urged upon your attention by every sort of speaker from dukes to dustmen and also by Mr J. St Loe Strachey in a series of letters in the *Spectator* of exceptional distinction. You may not have been made a Socialist, but you will have come to realize how much is just in the Socialist case, how much is fine and possible in its proposals. You desire the development of a constructive State which shall exist *for* all men and be served by all men, the establishment of a wider security and comfort and of a definite minimum of welfare below which no one shall be allowed to fall. You wish to see men living less and less for the mean end of private gain and the accumulation of wealth and more and more for the noble purposes of public service and honour. It is quite possible that, misled by the wide application of the Socialist name, you may think that these ends will be best forwarded by voting for the professedly Socialist candidate, Mr Irving.[1] I want very earnestly to point out to you that this is not so. I want to point out to you that Mr Irving is not a representative Socialist candidate; he has little or no prospect of return, and the diversion of your vote, which would I assume go otherwise to Mr Winston Churchill, will simply favour the return of an exceptionally undesirable person, Mr Joynson-Hicks.

You may think that in spite of that it may be well to vote for Mr Irving, simply because he calls himself a Socialist, for the sake of the demonstration in favour of constructive ideals. That would be all very well if Mr Irving was indeed a good representative of Modern Socialism. Were he a properly accredited candidate, chosen beforehand from out of the constituency and supported by the centre organization of the Independent Labour Party and the Labour vote I should have nothing to say against him. But he is not that. *The Labour Leader*, the official organ of the Independent Labour Party in Great Britain, in its issue of April 17th very distinctly says he is not. The local Socialist organizations did not invite or desire his candidature. He has, I regret to say, decided to come in from outside as a delegate of the so-called Social Democratic Party. Mr Irving has done sturdy work for Socialism in the past, but at this election he is representative not of Socialism as a whole and of the great organizing projects it has developed in the last quarter century, but of that extreme, old-fashioned and implacable type of Socialist theory, limited, doctrinaire and cantankerous, which has done so much to retard the development of a sound and statesmanlike propaganda in Great Britain. Not everyone who calls himself a Socialist is necessarily a representative of our movement; and it is becoming more and more desirable

[1] Dan Irving (1854–1924), secretary and agent to Socialist Party; Socialist MP for Burnley 1918–24.

to distinguish clearly between the two wings of Socialism, or to put it more justly between the main body of British Socialism and the Social Democratic wing, between that broadly constructive and essentially *British* Socialism on the one hand, of which the Independent Labour Party is at present the political expression, standing today for all that is noblest and most hopeful in the awakening consciousness of our democracy, and on the other the extreme and relatively small left wing, harsh, impracticable, insubordinate, a mere disloyal minority, altogether alien to that compromising yet persistently creative disposition, that practicality and clarity and sanity which are the peculiar political virtues both of the British people and of that real and vital Socialist movement which more and more embodies its ideals.

For nothing is more remarkable than the political sanity of the main Socialist movement at the present time, its general and increasing enfranchisement from narrow and intolerant attitudes. We realize fully that the organized State of the future must be made out of such elements of order and progress as exist today. We aim at no sudden revolution, no dramatic replacement of class by class. We work steadily to increase the proportion of labour representation in Parliament and diminish the power of narrow, anti-social and demoralizing propertied interests, but we recognize and welcome the cooperation of all men of good intent. The political system of tomorrow must develop, we are fully persuaded, out of the traditions of the governing class of today. And though Mr Churchill is not a Socialist, though he stands as a member of a party that is strongly tainted by the memories of Victorian Individualism, though he refuses the letter of our teaching, we recognize in his active and still rapidly developing and broadening mind, in his fair and statesmanlike utterances and in particular in his recent assertion of the need of a national minimum, a spirit entirely in accordance with the spirit of our movement and one with which it is both our duty and intention to go just as far as we can.

A man because he is a believer in the vitalizing influence of Modern Socialism is not necessarily bound to vote for a candidate because he labels himself Socialist. Indeed by doing so he may be inflicting a real injury at this moment upon Socialist development. But every voter with any breadth of outlook in NW Manchester, whether he be a Socialist or not, is bound to do his utmost to secure the rejection of Mr Joynson-Hicks. I have no hesitation in saying that Mr Joynson-Hicks represents absolutely the worst element in British political life at the present time, that he stands for debased politics, for the Americanization, in the worst sense, of our public life. He is far more of the type of a party unit in the House of Representatives than an English member of Parliament. He is an entirely undistinguished man and involved, I notice, in all those ridiculous reversals of opinion and self-contradictions natural to a man of his personal indeterminateness. In contrast with Mr Churchill's brilliant career and vivid personality he is an obscure and ineffectual nobody. I know nothing and want to know nothing about his social standing or his private quality, and I do not suppose I should ever have heard of his name before this time, if it were not that I keep myself informed by means of press cuttings of the progress of Socialist discussion. But among the multitude of speakers who were busy last year in bespattering the great constructive proposals of Modern Socialism with insult and misrepresentation his name was conspicuous through his witless use of the clipped and forged quotations which formed the ammunition of the great Anti-Socialist campaign and through his vile abuse of Socialist leaders. For example he called Mr Keir Hardie a 'leprous traitor'. He was industrious with the foolish lie that Socialism is Atheism. He declared, knowing it as he must have done to be childlishly untrue, that 'the very essence of Socialism was that all the Ten Commandments should be swept away'. He invented wonderful unknown Socialist books which he would not 'dare read in an audience of English men and English women.' Nothing indeed seemed too foul or too foolish for Mr Joynson-Hicks to spout at as great and honourable a popular movement as England has ever seen.

I think it is most necessary that NW Manchester should not forget Mr Joynson-Hicks' methods of controversy at the present juncture. This question of fair and decent public discussion is one of supreme importance, far more important than any other single issue before you, land, liquor, Tariff or what not. If we English are to lose our habit of freely and generously expressing and criticising ideas, if one party or movement is to set out to blacken and vilify another public movement, if senseless misstatements of an adversary's opinions are to replace their honest discussion, if such constituencies as yours are to endorse such methods and send the user to Parliament, then it seems to me our national outlook is a gloomy one.

I think this question of elementary decency in public discussion transcends any party lines. Whatever side we back, the fight must be a fair one. I would be the first to admit as a reasonable Socialist that there is a strong case to be made and powerful arguments to be advanced against Socialism. They do not convince me but I acknowledge their validity. I can understand and respect the attitude of such an antagonist as Mr Mallock[1] for example. But this Anti-Socialist propaganda of which Mr Joynson-Hicks is a typical representative has not made out a case. It had failed quite amazingly to

[1] William Hurrell Mallock (1849–1923), author, who declared in *Who's Who* that his 'main object in his political and economic writings has been to expose the fallacies of Radicalism and Socialism'; best known as author of *The New Republic* (1877), a satire on English society and ideas.

make out a case. It is scarcely too much to say it has not attempted to make out a case. Throughout it has treated the ordinary voter as a fool who must be humbugged, and not a man who must be reasoned with. It has been from first to last a campaign of lies and controversial tricks and base imputations, an outrage upon and an insult to the intelligence of our common people and to the splendid constructive dreams they are developing. It has been a campaign to drag in scandal and personalities and in every way to embitter and degrade political life, to foul the names of antagonists, and exacerbate class feeling. The question every Conservative gentleman, every Unionist, every constructive-minded Tariff-Reformer in NW Manchester has to ask himself in the next three days is whether this sort of thing is to be the New Politics. Are men who cannot be trusted to make a quotation to be presently trusted to draft a tariff? And if the new age of politics is not to sink below the old, if the typically English traditions of national compromise, of fairness, moderation and mutual honourableness, of patient collective development in which every class participates, are to be maintained, then I do not see how they or anyone can support Mr Joynson-Hicks. And the effective way not to support Mr Joynson-Hicks on this present occasion is to vote for Mr Winston Churchill.

Vy Sincerely Yrs
H. G. WELLS

WSC to Miss Clementine Hozier
(CSC Papers)

16 April 1908   12 Bolton Street

I am back here for a night and a day in order to 'kiss hands' on appointment, & I seize this fleeting hour of leisure to write & tell you how much I liked our long talk on Sunday [at Lady Randolph's house, Salisbury Hall] and what a comfort & pleasure it was to me to meet a girl with so much intellectual quality & such strong reserves of noble sentiment. I hope we shall meet again and come to know each other better and like each other more: and I see no reason why this should not be so. Time passes quickly and the six weeks you are to be abroad will soon be over. Write therefore and tell me what your plans are, how your days are occupied, & above all when you are coming home. Meanwhile I will let you know from time to time how I am getting on here in the storm; and we may lay the foundations of a frank & clear-eyed friendship which I certainly should value and cherish with many serious feelings of respect.

So far the Manchester contest has been quite Napoleonic in its openings & development. The three days I have been in the city have produced a most happy change in the spirits of my friends, & not less satisfactory adjustments of the various political forces. Jews, Irish, Unionist Free Traders – the three doubtful elements – wh were all alleged to be estranged, have come or are coming back into line, & I have little fear of their not voting solidly for me on Friday.

The Socialist candidate [Dan Irving] is not making much progress as he is deserted by the Labour party. He will however deprive me of a good many votes, and this is the most disquieting feature in a situation otherwise good and rapidly improving.

Even with the risk that a contrary result may be proclaimed before this letter overtakes you, I must say I feel confident of a substantial success. Lady Dorothy [Howard][1] arrived of her own accord – alone & independent. I teased her by refusing to give a decided answer about women's votes, & she left at once for the North in a most obstinate temper. However on reading my answers given in public, back she came and is fighting away like Diana for the Greeks – a vy remarkable young lady in every respect. But my eye what a tyrant! Mind of marble – calm, unerring, precise, ruthless in its logic, devoid of flexibility – a thing to admire, but not to bruise yourself against. Yet – a dear!

I never put too much trust in formulas & classifications. The human mind & still more human speech are vy inadequate to do justice to the infinite variety & complexity of phenomena. Women so rarely realise this. When they begin to think they are so frightfully cock-sure. Now nature never deals in black or white. It is always some shade of grey. She never draws a line without smudging it. And there must be a certain element of give & play even about the most profound & assured convictions. But perhaps you will say this is only the sophistry of a political opportunist. Will you? Well I shall not mind, so that you say it in a nice letter to

Yours vy sincerely

WINSTON S. CHURCHILL

[1] Dorothy Georgiana Howard (b. 1881), 3rd daughter of the 9th Earl of Carlisle; married 14 October 1913, Francis Robert, 6th Baron Henley.

Walter Long to Lord Robert Cecil
(*Cecil of Chelwood Papers*)

EXTRACT

17 April 1908　　　　　　　　　　　　　　　Culworth House
　　　　　　　　　　　　　　　　　　　　　　Banbury

... But to my mind a much graver issue has arisen in Manchester when it is announced that the Free Trade Unionists are working for and supporting Churchill. If this be true & if their action has the approval of yourself & your colleagues then I frankly own I do not see how we can *possibly* continue to act together. Nobody can pretend that Free Trade is now in danger, while WS represents a policy to which we as a Party are bitterly opposed & if Unionists help to put him into Parliament & so give the Gov the most valuable assistance possible & proportionately injure us & our course & if their action is approved by other Free Trade Unionists I am sure the great mass of our Party will never forgive them & for my part I do not hesitate to say that a split becomes inevitable! ...

Lord Robert Cecil to Walter Long
(*Cecil of Chelwood Papers*)

EXTRACT

18 April 1908　　　　　　　　　　　　　　　Gale
　　　　　　　　　　　　　　　　　　　　　　Uckfield

[Copy]

... Personally I could not vote for Winston. Indeed if I had a vote I should probably give it for Hicks though on personal grounds I should dislike doing so. ...

The by-election at North-West Manchester took place on 24 April. The results were as follows:

W. Joynson-Hicks (Conservative)	5417
WSC (Liberal)	4988
D. Irving (Socialist)	276

Lord Loreburn to WSC

25 April 1908   Kingsdown

Dover

My dear Churchill,

I am very grieved over Manchester. I will only say that I would far rather lose as you have lost than win as many win. And you are right that we must all fight on. I have no doubt we shall win in the long run. Nothing can prevent that & you have the youth and the vigour to see the fight right through and to inspire others to victory. Don't answer this.

With hearty sympathy

Vy sincerely yours

LOREBURN

George Cornwallis-West to WSC

25 April 1908   Salisbury Hall

My dear Winston,

There are many points in politics upon which we differ, but this does not prevent my being exceedingly sorry you did not get in on Friday, & I write to tell you so. After all it may be a blessing in disguise. NW Manchester was always a Tory seat. If you had been unseated at the next General election, it might not have been so easy to obtain a safe seat; whereas now there can be no difficulty in finding one which should be a permanency for you. Jack tells me, in confidence of course, that there is a chance of your going to Northampton. I much doubt if such a course would be a wise one.

At the present moment, no doubt the Liberal party can more or less dictate to the Labour Party. The positions may be reversed, or at any rate modified shortly; in which case a Liberal member for Northampton might find himself called upon to swallow more than he could digest.

Doubtless you know better than I do, that this city is, & always has been, a hot-bed of socialism. I do hope that wherever you go, that you will consider your health. Don't overdo it. Au revoir & good luck old man: & that you may get a safe & permanent seat without a contest is the wish of

Yours ever

GEORGE C.W.

Joseph Dulberg to WSC

25 April 1908   260 Oxford Road
                                                     Manchester

Dear Mr Churchill,

I am sorry I had not a chance of seeing you all day yesterday – as I was busy looking after the voters – and also of saying a few encouraging words of farewell to you before your departure.

Do not be disheartened and take care of your health, which is now one of the assets of the nation. Other great and illustrious men have had their moments of defeat and misfortune, but your hours of triumph, like theirs, will surely come again and again.

It is more for the sake of Manchester that I regret yesterday's disaster and we shall have to work hard, very hard, if we are to regain the seat for Liberalism.

To me personally, like to very many others, the parting from you as our member seems almost like a bereavement and I cannot realise it. But I have the satisfaction that I have done my best for your success and that as far as the Jewish electors are concerned, you were not disappointed. Had the other sections of the electorate equally rallied round you, you would have won by a large majority. We reckon to have polled on our side 95% of the Jewish voters.

If at any future time I can again be of the slighest service to you, I shall only be very happy to do it. You have only to say the word.

Meanwhile I remain with the best wishes for your future career which I have no doubt will be a brilliant one.

                                                     Yours very sincerely
                                                     J. DULBERG

A. O. Williams[1] to WSC

26 April 1908   Castell Deudraeth
                                                     N. Wales   ⸝

Dear Churchill,

Would it help you to have this seat of mine, if it can be arranged for me to vacate it for you? I have called a meeting of my executive for Tuesday to ask them if they are willing. I have every reason to think they will be. Of course it would only be for this Parliament, the Merioneth Lib Assn being

[1] Arthur Osmond Williams (1849–1927), Radical MP for Merionethshire 1900–10; baronet 1909.

free to choose its own candidate at the General Election. A letter by return will find me here.

Yours very truly

A. OSMOND WILLIAMS

I do not think there is a chance of your being opposed.

Frank Harris to WSC

26 April 1908   *Vanity Fair*
                                                          33 Strand

My dear Winston Churchill,

I did not congratulate you on your entrance into the Cabinet, because I thought the Cabinet ought to be congratulated; but now I cannot help writing to express sympathy with you over that wretched set-back in Manchester: the voice of the people is always the voice of the devil and has nothing to do with the voice of God. If the masses are saved it will be in spite of themselves, as one saves pigs from cutting their throats in a seaway for higher reasons than the pig dreams of.

I have finished the book which I spoke to you about. I think you will consider it first-rate: it is a little like an electric eel that gives you a shock wherever you touch it, the best thing I have done yet, by far.[1]

When am I to see you? When will you lunch with me? I want an hour of vivifying talk.

Your chance has come, and I know you will use it greatly: Lloyd George is a bad man to follow and beat; but if anyone can do it, you can. 'It is up to you,' as the Americans say, and I am one of those, gradually growing more numerous, who believe that you will make good.

By the bye, I would have sent you the motor-car to Manchester; but to tell you the truth, a damned creditor got hold of it, and I have only just been able to get it out of his clutches. Hurroo!

Yours ever

FRANK HARRIS

WSC to Miss Clementine Hozier
(*CSC Papers*)

27 April [1908]   Taplow

I was under the dull clouds of reaction on Saturday after all the effort & excitement of that tiresome election, and my pen did not run smoothly or

[1] Probably *The Bomb*, a novel, published by John Long, 1908.

easily. This morning however I am again buoyant, and refreshed by a quiet & cheery Sunday here, I set myself to write you a few lines.

It was a real pleasure to me to get your letter & telegram. I am glad to think you watched the battle from afar with eyes sympathetic to my fortunes. It was a vy hard contest & but for those sulky Irish Catholics changing sides at the last moment under priestly pressure, the result would have been different. Now I have to begin all over again – probably another long & exhausting election. Is it not provoking!

The Liberal party is I must say a good party to fight with. Such loyalty & kindness in misfortune I never saw. I might have won them a great victory from the way they treat me. Eight or nine safe seats have been placed at my disposal already. From my own point of view indeed the election may well prove a blessing in disguise. It is an awful hindrance to anyone in my position to be always forced to fight for his life & always having to make his opinions on national politics conform to local exigencies. If I had won Manchester now, I should probably have lost it at the general election. Losing it now I shall I hope get a seat wh will make me secure for many years. Still I don't pretend not to be vexed. Defeat however consoled, explained or discounted is odious. Such howls of triumph from the Tory Press; such grief of my poor friends & helpers; such injury to many important affairs. There is only one salve – everything in human power was done.

We are having hateful weather here – blizzards, frost, raw wind – perfectly vile to everyone: to no one more than to a candidate who has to gad about from morn till night, in & out of hot meetings, speaking in the open air. How I wish I could get away to Florence & the sun. But here I am bound upon the wheel of things.

Lady Dorothy fought like Joan of Arc before Orleans. The dirtiest slum, the roughest crowd, the ugliest street corner. She is a wonderful woman – tireless, fearless, convinced, inflexible – yet preserving all her womanliness.

How I should have liked you to have been there. You would have enjoyed it I think. We had a jolly party and it was a whirling week. Life for all its incompleteness is rather fun sometimes.

Write to me again – I am a solitary creature in the midst of crowds. Be kind to me.

Yours vy sincerely
W

WSC to Sir Edward Donner

29 April 1908   [Board of Trade]

[Copy]

My dear Sir Edward Donner,

I must ask you to convey my sincere thanks to all of those who worked with you to secure the success of the Liberal and Free Trade cause at the late election in North-West Manchester. The energy and public spirit which they displayed in that hard conflict are beyond all aspersion; and their efforts were supported by a thoroughly efficient organisation. An even more powerful concentration of forces and interests has prevailed; and certainly I am not going to underrate the evil consequences of the result. But there is in the heart of every political reverse the dynamic impulse of a future triumph. You must turn the emotions of defeat to the process of recovery, so that the very hour of disaster may become the seed-time of victory.

And in my opinion the figures of the poll ought to carry the highest encouragement to all Free Traders who are in earnest. It is quite clear that the political levels and balance in North-West Manchester have been permanently altered during the last four years. Here in a constituency which since its creation has been regarded as the Blue Ribbon of Lancashire Toryism, at a moment of peculiar national and still more local difficulty, the utmost exertions of the most powerful vested interests in the country have only succeeded in securing an anti-Free Trade majority of 153 upon a poll of unexampled size. And even this exiguous majority was only achieved through the sudden and organised transference of between four and five hundred Catholic votes always hitherto an integral part of the Liberal strength in Manchester to the Protectionist side upon grounds quite unconnected with the main issues.

Now by the general election several important adverse factors may have been removed. The insignificant support secured by the Socialist candidate after so much trouble makes it at least doubtful whether that curious diversion will be repeated. The Licensing Bill will I trust have taken its place upon the statute book and the Liquor Trade may not be in a position to exercise the undue political power which they at present possess. The Catholic voters now estranged will, there is reason to hope, have been conciliated and their apprehensions allayed by some fair and practical concordat in Educational matters. Lastly at the General Election the issue will be sharply defined; and a vote for a Protectionist candidate will not only be a moral injury to the cause of Free Trade in the abstract, but a direct mandate for the immediate erection of a discriminatory Tariff upon a vast number of commodities.

See now what a noble opportunity rises above the horizon. There is no reason in my opinion why with a suitable candidate the seat should not be recovered in such a manner and at such a time as will more than repair the misfortune that has occurred. In such a work I shall be ready to aid in any way in my power: and although my Parliamentary connection with the division has now terminated I shall consider myself under special obligations to help so far as my strength permits to defend Free Trade in the great City to whose prosperity and fame Free Trade is vital.

Yours very sincerely
[Winston S. Churchill]

WSC to Lady Randolph

[?29 April 1908]   Board of Trade

Dearest Mamma,

On the strong advice of the Chief Whips in Scotland and England and with the recommendation of the PM I have accepted the invitation of Dundee.

They all seem to think it is a certainty – and even though a 3 cornered fight will end in a majority of 3,000. It is a life seat and cheap and easy beyond all experience.

Yours ever
W

*   *   *   *   *

H. P. Wood to WSC

4 May 1908

Dear Sir,

Whilst travelling 2 or 3 days ago a conversation was commenced between 5 or 6 gentlemen concerning your fight & unfortunate defeat in North West Manchester. One reason, which was brought forward by one of the gentlemen, whom I should conclude was a Conservative, was an incident which took place whilst you were, I think, a war correspondent in South Africa. It was stated by him that the party (of whom you were a member) who were imprisoned after being captured by the Boers, gave their word of honour not to attempt to escape & that by your subsequent escape your word of honour was broken & the prisoners whom you left behind were severely dealt with because of your escape. I believe he almost went as far as to say that he knew a person who was imprisoned at the same time.

A denial of such an outrageous assertion hardly seems necessary. But I should like very much to be able to inform them that their statements were totally incorrect. I should be delighted to receive a letter from you denying the statements made.

Trusting that your fight in Dundee will prove a great victory for Free Trade & for Progress.

With best wishes for your success.

Yours faithfully
H. PERCY WOOD

PS I said I intended writing you & that I would tell them your reply.
Note by WSC at top: – Ansd absolutely untrue u'taking action for libel agst MC [*Manchester Courier*]

E. Crosfield Pearson to Captain F. Guest

5 May 1908
March, Clayton & Pearson,
Solicitors
Manchester

Dear Captain Guest,

As Mr Churchill will doubtless like to know what is taking place in connection with the Libel Action against the *Manchester Courier*, I write a line to report.

In accordance with the rules of the Court, a Summons for Directions, as to the procedure to be adopted, came before the district Registrar yesterday. He directed that pleadings (a Statement of Claim and Defence) should be delivered in the ordinary way. No order has yet been made as to the mode of trial or place of trial. With regard to the mode of trial – either party has the right to demand a jury. I think in the end that the advisers both of the plaintiff and defendant would prefer a jury. It is however, worth the consideration of Mr F. E. Smith and Mr Churchill whether we should try and persuade the defendants' Solicitors to dispense with a jury and have the Action tried before a Judge alone. The dangers of a jury are, that without knowing it, we might get some strong political opponents, who would doubtless minimise the meaning and effect of the Libel as much as possible.

On the other hand, the Judges who will try actions in Manchester at the Summer Assizes will be Mr Justice Pickford[1] and probably Mr Justice Coleridge,[2] who would, I think, both be good men.

With regard to the place of trial – I think it best to leave this over to see what sort of defence the *Courier* raises. If by any chance they allege that the words complained of were true it might suit our purpose to press for the trial to take place in London, as I gathered from Mr Churchill that he could find a large number of witnesses in London at the present moment who would speak as to the exact facts of his escape. If, on the other hand, the *Courier* do not plead the truth of the words complained of, I think it will be well to keep the trial in Manchester, so as to save the possibility of the case coming before a political partisan such as Mr Justice Grantham.[3]

You may be interested to hear that the Solicitor for the *Courier* seemed surprised that the Action was proceeding and explained that he thought that the issue of the Writ was merely an election dodge. I quickly disabused his mind of this theory, and told him that Mr Churchill regarded the libel as a very serious one.

Perhaps at the proper time you will bring this matter before Mr Churchill. Hoping you are all keeping well in spite of the double strain.

I am, Yours faithfully
E. CROSFIELD PEARSON

Lord Northcliffe to WSC

11 May 1908   22 St James's Place

My dear Churchill,

I was amazed to hear from Mrs Garvin when in Spain that she had heard from her husband that you considered our criticisms a personal matter.

There was a well understood agreement between us that we should use our stage thunder in the furtherance of our mutual interests. You have criticised me very hotly in and out of Parliament and I have never felt the

---

[1] William Pickford (1848–1923), Judge of the High Court of Justice 1907–17; Recorder of Oldham 1901–04; Recorder of Liverpool 1904–07; Lord Justice of Appeal 1914–18; Member of Dardanelles Commission and its Chairman 1917; knighted 1907; Baron Sterndale 1918.

[2] Bernard John Seymour Coleridge, 2nd Baron Coleridge (1851–1927), Judge of the High Court of Justice 1907–23; Commissioner of Assize, Midland Circuit, 1907–8; Liberal MP, Sheffield (Attercliffe) 1885–94; succeeded father 1894.

[3] William Grantham (1835–1911), Judge of the High Court of Justice 1886; Conservative MP for East Surrey 1874–85; Croydon 1885–6; knighted 1886.

least bitterness about it, as you must have seen by our recent meeting at Lord Lansdowne's.

As we have got to live together more or less in public life & in more ways than you know, for, I hope, a great many years I propose that we take a walk in St James' Park some morning this week and thrash this matter out.

Yours sincerely
NORTHCLIFFE

WSC to Lord Northcliffe

14 May 1908   Board of Trade

[Copy]

My dear Northcliffe,

I fully accept yr assurance that you were not inspired by any feelings of personal resentment to me, & that you are in no sense responsible for the libellous statements in the *M/c Courier*. I never thought you were. I will give the most careful instructions that my counsel in any proceedings wh may arise shall not involve you & shall be strictly confined to the *M/c Courier*, & that if yr name shd be mentioned through circs beyond my control a frank disclaimer shall be made on my part, so that it may be known that we are friends & that I make no complaint whatever against you.

I think it wd be an advantage if you had a talk on the whole subject with F. E. Smith who besides being my counsel is one of my closest personal friends. I am only concerned to vindicate myself effectually from a serious charge, & I am sure that you wd not wish me to take any course wh wd afterward expose me to reproach.

I had a visit last night from Mr Nicol Dunn[1] of wh he will perhaps give you an account.

I am vy glad we have again seen something of each other and hope our personal relations will be all the better for the misunderstanding wh you have so completely removed from my mind.

Yrs v s
WSC

---

[1] James Nicol Dunn (1856–1919), editor of *Manchester Courier* 1905–10, *Morning Post* 1897–1905, *Johannesburg Star* 1911–14.

J. Nicol Dunn to WSC

23 June 1908　　　　　　　　　　　　　　*The Manchester Courier*

Dear Mr Churchill,

I enclose a copy of today's *Courier* containing the apology of which you were good enough to approve and in doing so I thank you for all your generosity in the matter. The list of charities has only reached me today, but it will be given in tomorrow's paper. I am, dear Mr Churchill,

Yours faithfully
J. NICOL DUNN

*　　*　　*　　*　　*

Lord Curzon to WSC

6 May 1908　　　　　　　　　　　　　　Hackwood

My dear Winston,

I sympathise with you heartily in having to face this double ordeal. However that is neither here nor there.

This is merely to suggest to you how pleasant for me and others it would be if you were able to look in here at any time between June 6 and 15 when friends will foregather here. Golf and trout fishing will be going on: and some talk ought to supervene.

Choose your own time.

Yours sincerely
CURZON

Lord Knollys to WSC

7 May 1908　　　　　　　　　　　　　　Buckingham Palace

My dear Churchill,

The King desires me to thank you for your letter & for informing him that the 'Strike' in the shipbuilding trade has come to an end through the mediation of the Board of Trade.

He is sincerely glad to hear that an arrangement has been arrived at & he congratulates you on the termination of the 'Strike'.

He much hopes that you will be able to persuade the men to agree to some permanent machinery of conciliation, as he has long felt that this would be the most likely arrangement to prevent 'Strikes', or at all events that it would be the most practical way of preventing their lasting any time.

Yrs sincerely
KNOLLYS

I would have written to you yesterday, but I had to be the whole afternoon at the Exhibition.[1]

The results of the Dundee by-election, held on 9 May, were as follows:

WSC (Liberal)	7079
Sir G. W. Baxter (Unionist)	4370
G. H. Stuart (Labour)	4014
E. Scrymgeour (Prohibitionist)	655

*   *   *   *   *   *

WSC to Lord Crewe
(*Crewe Papers*)

[?13 May 1908]   Board of Trade

Dear Lord Crewe,

The Prime Minister asked me this morning at the Cabinet to take part in the Debate this evening, & it had been arranged that I was to wind up, following Alfred Lyttelton in a short speech.

I now receive a message through Colonel Seely's private secretary to the effect that you particularly desire that I should not do so. Believe me I have not the slightest desire to interfere in the affairs of your department, except in so far as Cabinet policy is concerned. I am therefore communicating with the Prime Minister on the point.

It is a pity your strong opinion was not made known earlier to me as I have been put to a good deal of extra work in consequence of the request wh was made to me.

Yours vy truly
WINSTON S CHURCHILL

---

[1] The Franco-British Exhibition at Shepherd's Bush which was opened by the Prince and Princess of Wales on 14 May.

Lord Crewe to WSC

13 May 1908   Colonial Office

My dear Winston,

I am sorry that any confusion should have arisen over the debate in your House this evening, but I am not to blame. Seely had told me that there would only be time for one speech from our Front Bench, and I therefore concluded that he would speak late in the debate, (a very delicate one, as you know) and I carefully agreed with him the line which he should take. An hour ago I hear for the first time that you tell Seely that you propose to wind up the debate, with no intimation that the Prime Minister had expressed any opinion on the subject. I have not the faintest idea what your views are, or what you would have said, but I should have been bound by them without any previous consultation with you. No department can be conducted on such lines, and certainly none ever will by me.

I asked Seely to point this out to the Prime Minister, in case he should be willing to adhere to the arrangement first proposed. I am exceedingly sorry if you have been put to any needless trouble & we should have mentioned the matter at the Cabinet; but I had imagined that the course of the debate was plain sailing.

Yours sincerely
CREWE

You can of course show this letter to the Prime Minister.

WSC to Lord Crewe
(*Crewe Papers*)

13 May 1908
9.30

Private

Dear Lord Crewe,

I should have thought that if your department were in discussion in the House of Commons, you would have been glad if your colleagues came to its assistance: & that you would sufficiently have trusted me not to commit you beyond the obvious limits of Cabinet policy.

I spent my afternoon, after the Prime Minister's request, in inventing arguments to show that nothing definite could be said upon the future of the SA Protectorates or upon the form & scope of South African Federation.

I cannot now tell what the course of the debate will be. But the Prime

Minister has asked me to watch its progress on behalf of the Government, & if necessary wind it up. It seems to me that the conduct of H of Commons business must rest with the Leader of the House. I shall listen vy carefully to what Seely says, so as to do the best I can to represent your exact views & to do full justice to them.

But in regard to the conduct of this debate, I must clearly discharge the duty wh the Prime Minister has impressed upon me. Perhaps the necessity will not arise!

Yours vy truly

WINSTON S. CHURCHILL

Lord Crewe to WSC

13 May 1908   Crewe House

My dear Winston,

Thanks for your note just received (10 pm). I am really sorry to have moved in the matter, but it seemed to me I had no choice, though it is odious to argue such a point with a colleague, a thing which has never happened to me before. Of course the Prime Minister's judgment is supreme on the conduct of business; but this fact does not relieve any of us from recognizing the fact that all debates are carried on either under instructions from the Cabinet, or from the department concerned. This matter had not been before the Cabinet, so in my opinion you should have communicated with Seely or myself so soon as it was arranged between you and the Prime Minister that you should speak.

If I might suggest a parallel case, I suppose that I have a more intimate knowledge of the Education question than either Runciman or Tweedmouth, but if some resolution on the subject were moved in the Lords, it would not occur to me, though I have had charge of this department since the last Govt was formed, to speak without ascertaining Runciman's views, if the Cabinet had come to no decision. But leaving me out of the question, if you put yourself in Seely's place, I can't help thinking that you would have resented such an arrangement, when you filled the same office.

You must excuse this tedious statement, which needs no reply.

Yours sincerely

CREWE

Lord Elgin to Lord Crewe
(*Elgin Papers*)

EXTRACT[1]

[?] May 1908   [Dunphail, Murrayshire]

Draft

... When I accepted Churchill as my Under Secy I knew I had no easy task. I resolved to give him access to all business – but to keep control[2] (& my temper). I think I may say I succeeded.[3] Certainly we have had no quarrel during the 2½ years, on the contrary he has again and again thanked me for what he had learned and for our pleasant personal relations. I have taken a keen interest in his ability and in many ways attractive personality. But all the same I know that it has affected my position *outside* the *Office* – and the strain has often been severe. On 'questions' alone hours have been spent – (Hopwood who has of late relieved me of much of this work could if he chose tell you many tales). I admit that most of this is personal and perhaps ancient history and I should not have mentioned it had it not been for the Tour of last autumn. That originally was intended to be a purely sporting and private expedition – & I really don't know how it drifted into so essentially an official progress: but if you consult more serious documents than the *Strand Magazine* you will find the character it assumed. And therefore it has left behind it matters with which you will have to deal, for the course is strewn with memoranda – Malta, Cyprus, Somaliland, East Africa, the Nile &c. I do not discuss any of them. I believe most of them hopelessly to be unpracticable at least as they stand. ...

*   *   *   *   *

[1] Lord Elgin was so deeply hurt at being excluded from Mr Asquith's administration that he withdrew from political life and confined himself to his estate, Broomhall, where he remained until his death in 1917. Some months after leaving London his Colonial Office papers, which had been packed in several large tin boxes, were sent by rail to him. Lord Elgin however never again looked at them. At first he was even loth to discuss with his successor, Lord Crewe, the colleagues and officials with whom he had worked for more than two years, and the business in hand when his tenure of office came to an abrupt end. However after Lord Crewe had written a placatory letter to him, Lord Elgin sent a lengthy reply, from which this extract has been taken.

[2] 'of the business' was inserted and then deleted at this point.

[3] The phrase 'but the strain has been severe' originally concluded this sentence.

WSC to Miss Clementine Hozier
(*CSC Papers*)

7 August 1908   Nuneham Park[1]
Oxford

This is only to be a line to tell you how much I am looking forward to seeing you on Monday. But I have a change of plan to propose wh I hope you will like. Let us all go to Blenheim for Monday & Tuesday & then go on, on Wednesday to Salisbury Hall. Sunny wants us all to come & my mother will look after you – & so will I. I want so much to show you that beautiful place & in its gardens we shall find lots of places to talk in, & lots of things to talk about. My mother will have already wired you & Sunny will do so to-morrow. There will be no one else there except perhaps F. E. Smith and his wife.

Jack has been married to-day – *civilly*. The service is tomorrow at Oxford: but we all swooped down in motor-cars upon the little town of Abingdon and did the deed before the Registrar – for all the world as if it was an elopement – with irate parents panting on the path. Afterwards we were shown over the Town Hall & its relics & treasures – quite considerable for so small a place – & then back go bride & bridegroom *to their respective homes* until tomorrow. Both were 'entirely composed' & the business was despatched with a celerity & ease that was almost appalling.

I was delighted to get your telegram this morning & to find that you had not forgotten me. The fire was great fun & we all enjoyed it thoroughly.[2] It is a pity such jolly entertainments are so costly. Alas for the archives. They roared to glory in about ten minutes. The pictures were of small value, & many, with all the tapestries & about $\frac{1}{2}$ the good furniture were saved. I must tell you all about it when we meet. My eyes smart still & writing is tiring.

It is a vy strange thing to be locked in deadly grapple with that cruel element. I had no conception – except from reading – of the power & majesty of a great conflagration. Whole rooms sprang into flame as by enchantment. Chairs & tables burnt up like matches. Floors collapsed & ceilings crashed down. The roof descended in a molten shower. Every window spouted fire, & from the centre of the house a volcano roared skyward in a whirlwind of sparks. The Guests have no responsibility: & the

---

[1] The home of Lord Harcourt.

[2] On August 6, WSC had been staying with his cousin Captain Freddie Guest at a house he had rented at Burley-on-the-Hill, Rutland. The house was destroyed by fire. WSC, clad in pyjamas, an overcoat and a fireman's helmet, directed the firemen in putting it out. He also helped salvage the pictures and the wine cellar.

Finches are I hear well-insured. It is only the archives that must be mourned inconsolably. Poor Eddie Marsh lost everything (including many of my papers) through not packing up when I told him to. I saved all my things by making Reynolds throw them out of the window. It was vy lucky that the fire was discovered before we had *all* gone to sleep – or more life might have been lost – than one canary bird; & even as it was there were moments of danger for some.

Your telegram to my mother has just arrived.

It is my fault that the plan was changed. I thought it would be so nice to go to Blenheim, & I proposed it myself to Sunny. If you have a serious reason for not wishing to go there, I will telegraph to him in the morning & try to stop arrangements; but I fear he will already have asked F. E. Smith & his wife to balance *us*.

I do hope that your reluctance is only due to not quite understanding the change & fancying there was to be a great function or to very naturally requiring some more formal invitation, & not to any dislike of Sunny or harsh unfavourable judgment wh you have been led – perhaps on imperfect information – to form of him. He is my greatest friend, & it would grieve me vy much – if that were so. But I am sure it is not. Write & tell me all about it & about your days at Cowes; & what you have been thinking of; & whether you would have thought of me at all – if the newspapers had not jogged your memory! You know the answer that I want to this.

Always yours
W

WSC to Miss Clementine Hozier
(*CSC Papers*)

8 August [1908]   Nuneham

My dear,

I have just come back from throwing an old slipper into Jack's departing motor car. It was a vy pretty wedding. No swarms of London fly-catchers. No one came who did not really care, & the only spectators were tenants & country-folk. Only children for bridesmaids & Yeomanry with crossed swords for pomp. The bride looked lovely & her father & mother were sad indeed to lose her. But the triumphant Jack bore her off amid showers of rice & pursuing cheers – let us pray – to happiness & honour all her life.

I was vy glad to get your telegram this morning that you will come to

Blenheim on Monday. There will be no one at all except my mother & the Smiths & Mr Clark,[1] my secretary at the Board of Trade, & the Duke and his little son – just blossomed, or rather pruned into Eton jackets. You need have had no apprehensions, for I am as wise as an owl when I try, & never take steps of which I am not sure.

Here at Nuneham we have the *debris* of the wedding party & also of Burley-on-the-Hill. The Harcourts are most kind & hospitable and are entertaining all sorts of aunts, cousins & nieces collected for the event. Among the former – Leonie – who brings me news from Cowes – of a young lady who made a great impression at a dance four nights ago on all beholders. I wonder who it could have been!

We have also cosmopolitan Free Traders to the number of fifty from the Congress which I opened last Tuesday, who are now disporting themselves on the lawn, but who leave happily before dark.

I shall go over to Blenheim quite early on Monday, & mind you come by the first possible train. It is quite an easy journey from Southampton to Oxford *via* Didcot. I will meet you at Oxford in a motor-car if you will telegraph to me *here* what time you arrive.

You have not distinguished yourself very much as a correspondent; for no line of your handwriting has as yet glinted from among my letter-bag. But I suppose you were waiting for me & – I was hampered & hindered by cruel catastrophe. Alack!

Sunny made a charming speech after the breakfast & showed all his courtly address to the greatest advantage. I hope you will like my friend, & fascinate him with those strange mysterious eyes of yours, whose secret I have been trying so hard to learn. His life has been grievously mutilated, & there are many to blame him – not altogether without cause. But any clever woman whom he loved could have acquired a supreme influence over his nature & he would have been as happy as he now is sad.

He is quite different from me, understanding women thoroughly, getting into touch with them at once, & absolutely dependent upon feminine influence of some kind for the peace & harmony of his soul. Whereas I am stupid & clumsy in that relation, and naturally quite self-reliant & self-contained. Yet by such different paths we both arrive at loneliness.

I think you will be amused at Blenheim. It has many glories in the fullness of summer. Pools of water, gardens of roses, a noble lake shrouded by giant trees; tapestries, pictures & monuments within. And on Wednesday we will motor on to Salisbury Hall to humbler if homelier surroundings. For the

---

[1] William Henry Clark (1876–1952), Private Secretary to President of Board of Trade 1905–08; to Chancellor of Exchequer 1908-10; Indian Civil Service 1910–17; UK High Commissioner in Canada 1928–34; in South Africa 1934–9; KCSI 1915; KCMG 1930.

rest I will do what I can to divert the hours, when better company fails. Till Monday then & may the Fates play fair.

Yours always
W

WSC to Miss Clementine Hozier
(CSC Papers)

[12 August 1908]   Blenheim

My dearest,
    How are you?
    I send you my best love to salute you: & I am getting up at once in order if you like to walk to the rose garden after breakfast & pick a bunch before you start. You will have to leave here about 10.30 & I will come with you to Oxford.
    Shall I not give you a letter for your Mother?

Always
W

WSC to Lady Blanche Hozier[1]
(CSC Papers)

12 August 1908   Blenheim

My dear Lady Blanche Hozier,
    Clementine will be my ambassador to you today. I have asked her to marry me & we both ask you to give your consent & your blessing.
    You have known my family so many years that there is no need to say vy much in this letter. I am not rich nor powerfully established, but your daughter loves me & with that love I feel strong enough to assume this great & sacred responsibility; & I think I can make her happy & give her a station & career worthy of her beauty & her virtues.
    Marlborough is vy much in hopes that you will be able to come down here today & he is telegraphing to you this morning. That would indeed be vy charming & I am sure Clementine will persuade you.

With sincere affection, Yours ever
WINSTON S. CHURCHILL

[1] This letter was never delivered. Churchill decided to accompany Miss Hozier to see Lady Blanche in London.

WSC to Lady Lytton
(*Lytton Papers*)

12 August 1908   12 Bolton Street

Pamela,

I am going to marry Clementine & I say to you as you said to me when you married Victor – you must always be our best friend.

Ever yours
W

WSC to Jack Churchill

[? 12 August 1908]   12 Bolton Street

Jack (& Goonie),

It is done & done forever.

I am to marry Clementine almost at once.

I hope we shall be happy like you are, and always all four of us bound together by the most perfect faith & comradeship.

Yours ever
W

WSC to Miss Clementine Hozier
(*CSC Papers*)

[? 13 August 1908]   Blenheim Palace

My dearest,

I hope you have slept like a stone. I did not get to bed till 1 o'clock; for Sunny kept me long in discussion about his affairs wh go less prosperously than ours. But from 1 onwards I slept the sleep of the just, & this morning am fresh & fit. Tell me how you feel & whether you mean to get up for breakfast. The purpose of this letter is also to send you heaps of love and four kisses xxxx

from your always devoted
WINSTON

Lady Blanche Hozier to Wilfrid Scawen Blunt
(*Blunt Diaries*)

EXTRACT

14 August 1908   Blenheim

. . . yesterday, he came to London to ask my consent, and we all three came on here. Winston and I spoke of you and of your great friendship with his father. He is so like Lord Randolph, he has some of his faults, and all his qualities. He is gentle and tender, and affectionate to those he loves, much hated by those who have not come under his personal charm. . . .

WSC to Miss Clementine Hozier

[14 August 1908]   12 Bolton Street

My dearest & most truly beloved –

I send you the King's telegram wh I have *dutifully* answered. There are no words to convey to you the feelings of love & joy by wh my being is possessed. May God who has given to me so much more than I ever knew how to ask keep you safe & sound.

Your loving
WINSTON

King Edward VII to WSC
(*CSC Papers*)

TELEGRAM

14 August 1908   Marienbad

Many thanks for announcement to me your engagement to Miss Hozier & I offer you my best wishes for your happiness.

EDWARD R

Lady Sarah Wilson to WSC

17 August 1908   Marienbad

My dear Winston,

I wired you my congratulations but must add a few more by letter & also to express the wish that I shall soon make Miss Hozier's acquaintance & that we shall be the best of friends. I dined with the 'Duke of Lancaster'[1] on Saturday evening & he at once drew me aside to shew me your two telegrams & his reply to your first one. It was a good idea of yours to reply so promptly to

[1] Edward VII sometimes used to travel under this name.

his congratulations. He was most friendly. I am off Wednesday on my return to England. I feel tons better for being in the wonderful air. Any time you are run down, you should try it.

> With best love & good wishes, Yrs affectly
> SARAH J. WILSON

Muriel Wilson to WSC

15 August 1908   Tranby

My dear Winston,

It was too nice of you to wire & I was most touched & I can't tell you [how] genuinely pleased I am at your happiness – I hope you are absolutely supremely contented – for you deserve everything of the nicest description – I watched you with Clemmie this year & wondered so much if you liked her. She is so extraordinarily beautiful I did not think you could help falling in love with her. I don't know her *very* well – but like her so much & I only hope she realises *how* lucky she is! I really mean this Winston dear – because I want you to be *so* happy & I want everything to go well with you always. I am awfully glad you are going to be married as I know how lonely you are at times & what a help a wife will be to you & I do think Clemmie *is* lucky!! Will you give her my love & tell her how much I congratulate her – & as to you I wish you every luck & happiness from all my heart. I hope I shan't lose a friend? If I thought this, I should be unhappy – but I feel we shall always like each other & remain real true friends – anyhow I shall always count you as such. Bless you dear Winston & I can't tell you how really delighted I was to get your wire.

> Yours affectionately
> MURIEL

Lord Lytton to WSC

15 August 1908   In the train going to
                                                                     Norway

Dear Winston,

A thousand congratulations. I am immensely pleased at your great news and heartily wish you every happiness. Pamela tells me that you are going to have a very short engagement so I suppose you will be already married when I return. I am sorry that I shall not see you to tell you in person how earnestly I hope that the step which you are now taking may be the beginning of many years of delightful companionship and mutual help and sympathy. I can wish you nothing better than to find in marriage all the happiness which it has brought to me.

Only don't let it diminish our friendship which I value greatly.

Ever most affectly yours
LYTTON

Lord Northcliffe to WSC

15 August 1908   Beaulieu Abbey
                                                                      Hants

My dear Churchill,

Lady Northcliffe & I want to be among the hundreds who are writing today to congratulate you on the abandonment of bachelorhood announced today.

You kept your secret well or my young men were not in their usual anticipatory vein, which must be inquired into on my return to town.

Seriously, I hope that Miss Hozier will speedily induce you to relax & rest sometimes, so that you may give yourself the chance to attain that much wished for you by friend & foe alike.

V. sincerely yours
NORTHCLIFFE

No reply please

Lord Curzon to WSC
(*CSC Papers*)

TELEGRAM

15 August 1908   Basingstoke

Am delighted to hear good news and having spent afternoon in futile attempt to decide which is more to be congratulated you or young lady have decided to give it up.

CURZON

Lord Rosebery to WSC

15 August 1908   Hotel du Parc
                                                  et Majestic Palace
                                                  Vichy

My dear Winston,

I have just seen the news of your engagement, and send you at once my heartiest good wishes. I have seen and admired your bride, and honestly believe that you have the fairest prospects of happiness. I am sure too that such a marriage will be an incalculable solace and assistance in your public career, so brilliant and successful and affluent of future distinction.

Marriage is by far the most critical event in life; so much so, that I seldom attend the ceremony, for it fills me with awe rather than joy. But just as an ill-mated marriage is hell, so a fortunate one is the Kingdom of Heaven on earth.

Yours
AR

WSC to Lord Rosebery
(Rosebery Papers)

17 August 1908   Board of Trade

My dear Rosebery,

I am touched by the kindness of your letter, I hope you got my telegram soon after you had written it.

This is a wonderful event in my life & one wh I had never been able to fashion in my mind. It alters the whole poise & balance of one's life & conceptions. I never thought *this* sun would shine for me.

I deeply respond to your good wishes with feelings of loyal friendship to my father's friend & mine.

Yours ever
WINSTON S. CHURCHILL

Lord Curzon to WSC

17 August 1908   Hackwood

My dear Winston,

I was greatly flattered by your sending me the good tidings.

You were quite right in thinking as you did that by no one would the news of your happiness be received with greater delight than myself.

Marriage in private life is capable of being the greatest of all human joys, in public life the most supreme of encouragements and consolations.

May you find it both and may you never know what it is to suffer.

If it is a pleasure to your friends to see you march from strength to strength it will be all the more so when that progress is shared by one so qualified both to adorn and to crown it.

Yours ever
CURZON

Blanche, Countess of Airlie[1] to Lady Randolph

17 August 1908   Airlie Castle

Dear Mrs West,

I must send you my Warmest Congratulations on the engagement of your son to my dearest Grandchild Clementine Hozier, and at the same time I thank you for your loving welcome to her. I hope she will be all you can desire as a wife for your son & I admire her so much & love her so well, that I have no fear that she will not fulfill yr wishes.

Blanche is an old friend of yours. So Clementine will not be quite among strangers.

Pray give my Warm Congratulations to your Son & believe me

Yrs affectionately
BLANCHE AIRLIE

Duchess of Marlborough to WSC

Monday [?18 August 1908]

My dear Winston,

Many thanks for your very nice letter. I am delighted to hear you are so happy and it is a joy to me to think of you so. Please tell me whether you want furniture or silver as I want to give you something that will be useful to you so would like to know. If you are taking a new house perhaps you would prefer furniture. If so tell me what kind.

Yours aff
CONSUELO

[1] Henrietta Blanche, Countess of Airlie (d. 1921), CSC's grandmother; 2nd daughter of 2nd Baron Stanley of Alderley; married 1851 David Graham Drummond Ogilvy, 7th Earl of Airlie.

Lord Hugh Cecil to WSC

18 August 1908   21 Lewes Crescent
                      Brighton

My dear Winston,
 I meant to write before to say how glad I am you are going to be married. It will be excellent for you mentally morally & politically. A bachelor is regarded as morally unprincipled.
 When is it to be? I want to be there if I can. And have you any views as to presents?

                    Yrs ever
                  HUGH CECIL
I am here till Sat: Who is to be best man?

Lord Hugh Cecil to WSC

20 August 1908   Brighton

My dear Winston,
 I shall be charmed to be best man – tho' until just before the day absence & incompetence will make me inefficient I fear.
 You can have two or three or even four clergy to do the ceremony. Are you going to be married by banns or licence? Unless you contemplate a special licence you ought to take steps soon. I fancy the Brd: of Trade will make you a resident in St Margaret's parish. But if not you shd take a room in the West Palace Hotel. After a fortnight's residence (I think) you can apply for an ordinary licence. A special licence costs a lot of money (£30?), so you had better go for an ordinary one or for banns.
 What about music & hymns? Also seating arrangements etc: these things are properly for me to attend to subject to your directions but I am away. Probably you will be wise to go & see Henson[1] (or the curate in charge) & do whatever he tells you.

                    Yrs ever
                  HUGH CECIL

[1] Herbert Hensley Henson (1863–1947), Rector of St Margaret's Westminster and Canon of Westminster 1900–12; Dean of Durham 1912–18; Bishop of Hereford 1918–20; Bishop of Durham 1920–39; Canon of Westminster Abbey 1940–1.

Duke of Marlborough to WSC

18 August 1908   Blenheim

Private

My dear Winston,

Your letter has given me much pleasure and a great deal of satisfaction. It is indeed a joy to feel that you are so happy, and that you realise that in ensuring the content of another being, lies in no small degree the solace and also the enjoyment of life. I earnestly hope that your life and Clementine's may be unclouded, and that the only source of contention between you during the years in front, may be which of you two loves each other the better. You are rich in many things, in friends, in health, ability, and true worth is to be found not in the quantity of one's possessions, but in the capacity for the limitation of one's own personal requirements. She herself Clementine is surrounded by those who admire her, and enriched by those who love her – and whom she loves – : and in addition possesses all those graceful and affectionate qualities of the heart which form the basis of the essential characteristics of a life's companion. You will find that during your engagement that Love is forgetful of Time. I sincerely hope, indeed believe, that Time will not be forgetful of your Love, and that it will remain with you both until that day when by the inexorable laws of the flesh you are to be parted, yet again nevertheless to be united in that world beyond of which all of us know so little and some of us hope so much. I have made arrangements that this house will be at your disposal from the date of your wedding until you wish to journey elsewhere, and I am very glad that you both feel disposed to come here.

I will willingly undertake the task of Trustee since you would like me to act in that capacity. I fear alas! that I shall be unable to be present at your wedding. I have had a long and trying year; I have had to kick curs that would snarl, and stamp on my heel vipers that would bite. The task has left me weary and anxious for repose and solitude. I go to Doncaster for a few days, not that I like racing but my presence there annoys HM, and I also mingle with some of my old friends of bygone years. After that week I am going abroad at once for a month or six weeks. I regard all marriages as solemn events, and in the case of a dear friend and relation the occasion is a trying one. I hope you will allow me to spare myself the mingled pleasure – and pain – of such a ceremony. For their meaning conveys everything or nothing. If the former then it is soul racking, if the latter then it produces only nausea. Forgive me therefore if my decision on this point is final and believe me that my thoughts will be with you, though I myself shall be absent.

The suggestion which you make in the latter part of your letter to me will not be realised; the difficulties are insuperable, the obstacles unsurmountable. The stink of sulphur was in my nostrils for hours after my visit to London!

Let me know sometime your plans for the immediate future and I will make it my business to see you. In the meanwhile fare you well and may every blessing and happiness be your companion.

Your affectionate
SUNNY

Mrs G. K. Wilson[1] *to WSC*

19 August 1908   Little Tranby
                                                            Beverley

My dear Winston,

For the sake of old days, coupled with memories of a charming speech you made one night at supper when *my* engagement was announced (now, alas! over 13 years ago) I *must* bother you with this letter (which please do not trouble to answer) to congratulate you 1000 times and wish you every possible happiness in the world – I think Miss Hozier is very lucky, and am sure that anyone as beautiful and clever as she is will be an endless joy to spend the rest of one's life with.

Once more, endless good wishes . . . and endless happiness.

Yours very sincerely
MOLLY K. WILSON

WSC to Lord Salisbury
(*Hatfield Papers*)

19 August 1908   Board of Trade

My dear Lord Salisbury,

Thank you for your kind letter. This auspicious event in a remote manner connects me with your family: & the union between Churchills & Cecils which was unsuccessfully attempted in two generations in the political sphere, may perhaps now be more prosperously approached from the private side.

Yours vy sincly
WINSTON S. CHURCHILL

---

[1] Adela Mary Wilson (1875–1946), formerly Molly Hacket, married, in 1895, Muriel Wilson's brother.

Lady Airlie to WSC

20 August 1908 Airlie Castle

Dear Mr Churchill,

I thank you for yr very kind letter & wish you & Clementine great happiness in your married life.

Your mother has welcomed her so heartily, this will add to her happiness and she will learn much from her.

I hope to see you here when you come to Dundee. You will find our people full of admiration for you, most of them agree with your speeches & the rest admire your genius – they all love Clementine and are as you know a critical race. So their good opinion is worth something.

I myself trust her to you with confidence. A good son is a good husband.

I am most truly yours
BLANCHE AIRLIE

Edgar Lafone¹ to WSC

20 August 1908 Chief Constable's Office
Maidstone

My dear Winston,

Now that the first torrent of good wishes is perhaps subsiding I want to add my drop to it.

I am so very glad – I never thought you would take the plunge and it is one that does help a man so much. Well done! I wish you all that is best. I remember at Bangalore you asked me to help you write the love scene in your novel as you had no experience! It's alright on the day isn't it?

Pamela was down here last night and told us how happy you are and filled us with the hope of meeting your lady soon.

May you be very happy always, Yours ever
EDGAR M. LAFONE

¹ Edgar Mortimore Lafone (1867–1938), a fellow officer of WSC's in 4th Hussars; married Beryl Plowden, a sister of Lady Lytton; chief constable of the Metropolitan Police 1910–26.

Mrs Waldorf Astor[1] to WSC

Loch Luichart
Rosshire

My dear Mr Churchill,

I am so glad you are marrying and I feel you will be v. happy.

You are both fortunate, especially you as she's v. lovely – and especially her as you are v. domestic and ripe for a nice settled home.

I shall have to send my present later – if you will marry in such a hurry.

V. sincerely yours
NANCY ASTOR

Waldorf adds his good wishes to mine tho' I can't see I've put mine to paper but my heart is full of them.

Lord Morley[2] to WSC

20 August 1908   Skibo Castle
Sutherland

My dear Winston,

I congratulate you with all my heart, and nobody wishes you well with more warmth and sincerity than do I. Pray, be sure of that. I trust that your new alliance will bring you all sorts of new strength, and smoothe the path of high and arduous ascent that is yours. Marriage makes all the difference you may be certain.

Well, I think much of you, with all affectionate consideration, and many confident expectations from your abundant gifts. I beg to make the acquaintance of the young lady; and to assure her that I hope to find myself the friend of both of you, as I am at this moment very warmly yours.

JOHN MORLEY

D. Lloyd George to WSC

23 August 1908   Hotel Esplanade
Hamburg

My dear Churchill,

Once more my heartiest congratulations. Your luck has followed you into the most important transaction of your life.

[1] Nancy Witcher Langhorne [1879–1964], married, first, Robert Gould Shaw, whom she divorced in 1903; second, in 1906, Waldorf Astor, son of 1st Viscount Astor. She was Conservative MP for the Sutton Division of Plymouth 1919–45, and the first woman to take her seat in the House of Commons. CH 1937. As Viscountess Astor, after 1919, a leading hostess at Cliveden, the Astor's Buckinghamshire house.

[2] He had been created Viscount Morley of Blackburn on 12 April.

Are you likely to be in town next week? I arrive Wednesday afternoon and could see you anywhere from Wednesday at 3 p.m. up to Friday morning at 1 p.m. I have so much to talk to you about. Your Swansea speech was tiptop and pleased the Germans immensely.[1]

Ever sincerely
D. Lloyd George

Joseph Chamberlain to WSC

24 August 1908   Highbury

Dictated and Private

My dear Winston,

In my enforced retirement I have heard of your engagement and I most sincerely congratulate you. I should like to be represented by some trifle in your new home and therefore have told Lambert to send you a couple of coasters of George IV's time which I hope you will duly receive and accept as a mark of good will and friendship.

With all cordial wishes for your continued success and happiness,

I remain, Yours very truly
J. Chamberlain

Henry Labouchere to WSC

28 August [1908]   Hotel Schweizerhof
Lucerne

Dear Churchill,

For two days have I wandered into the shops here and flattened my nose against their front windows to find a little present to send to you with my congratulations on your marriage. You have had a narrow escape of William Tell or a bear, a coral adornment for your person, and a clock. At last I found a card case in which it seems to me more easy to put a card in than to get it out which I am sending by parcel post, but which I am assured by the

---

[1] Speaking at Swansea on August 17 Churchill condemned those who regarded the German navy as a menace to Britain. 'There is no feeling of ill-will towards Germany. I say we honour that strong, patient, industrious German people.'

vendor is absolutely necessary to complete the belongings of any self-respecting gentleman, who can manage to live without a William Tell or a bear, and has already a watch. I don't know your address, so I sent it to the Board of Trade, as this letter. I used to know your departed prospective father-in-law, and Lady Blanche very well, & I have a vague recollection of your bride when she was a few years old, but 'from information that I have received' I hear that she is very pretty and very charming. So I wish you and her everything that people wish on such occasions. You and Lloyd George seem to me the only members of the Cabinet that are not afflicted by the armament craze. If these panic mongers had their way, we should in the end all find ourselves in Noah's Ark, heavily armoured, & with huge guns warranted to sink everything within ten miles. One would suppose that an invasion is the simplest of operations to hear them talk. Directly we have all built Dreadnoughts, some Power will build a bigger ship, when we shall have to start afresh the game of beggar my neighbour. A sane country provides against reasonably probable dangers & not against theoretical possibilities. This was always the reply of Sir Robert Peel to the 'Imperialists' of his day.

Yours truly
H. LABOUCHERE

Dr J. E. C. Welldon to WSC

28 August 1908   The Deanery
                                                    Manchester

My dear Winston,
    It was only last night that I got back from Newfoundland & taking up a newspaper this morning I see a reference to your approaching marriage.
    Forgive me if I seem to be late in offering you my most hearty congratulations. I have been spending the last three weeks out of the reach of English news. But I do not think you need me to assure you how strong an interest I feel in an event so full of promise for your happiness in life as your marriage. For ever since your Father asked me to take you into my house at Harrow I have watched your life, both private & public, not of course with unchanging agreement but with that ever closer sympathy which is born of the faith that a man will every year prove better & nobler than he was before. Now you will pass on to the loving care of one who will have a higher title to feel for you than I, yet the relation of a master for his pupils never really dies, & my regard for you has been specially deep & warm; so that every success which may assail you in the coming years will bring pleasure to me, even as

the prospect of your marriage touches my heart with hope & joy. You will let me send you a little present this week as a sign of my good wishes. Perhaps at such a time as this I may be permitted to call myself

Your affectionate friend

J. E. C. WELLDON

WSC to Nathan Laski
(Laski Papers)

29 August 1908   Board of Trade

My dear Laski,

It is vy kind of you indeed to wish to send me a token of your friendship on this great occasion in my life. I will accept the carpet with pleasure, and I am sure it will be most useful as well as beautiful in my home.

Yours vy sincerely

WSC

WSC to Lord Rosebery
(Rosebery Papers)

4 September 1908   Board of Trade

My dear Lord Rosebery,

I have to thank you most sincerely for the beautiful token you have sent me of your friendship, & for the good will which accompanies it.

You know that I shall value it because it comes from you & reminds me of your affection for my father, & your unvarying kindness to me.

Yours always

WINSTON SC

Dr J. E. C. Welldon to WSC

4 September 1908   The Deanery
                                                          Manchester

My dear Winston,

I will not fail you on the 12th. It will be a pleasure to me always to reflect that I was permitted to say a few words at your wedding. They will not take more than five minutes – perhaps not so much.

Believe me, With every good wish, Ever yours

J. E. C. WELLDON

Lord Hugh Cecil to WSC

5 September 1908   Kinloch
                                                   Sutherland

My dear Winston,

I ought to have written before now. But frailty thy name is Linky.

As to the service it is for you & your bride to settle – subject to Welldon. The marriage rite itself is performed by the parties – the congregation are only witnesses. Even the clergyman only judicially pronounces the marriage to be made – it is the parties who by their formal & public declaration of consent actually marry one another. Plainly it is for you & the clergyman to arrange the service. He is the proper ecclesiastical authority under the Bishop & I shall not dispute his decisions but submit *ex animo!!!*

No doubt you will Bowdlerise – wh I disapprove of – for I think there should be a little plain speaking publicly on these topics & it is less offensive in the ordered words of a service than in the spontaneous ones of a sermon.

I earnestly hope you will be both good & happy married; but remember that Xtian marriage is for Xtians & cannot be counted on to succeed save for those who are Xtians. And the marriage vow must be kept altogether – you cannot merely abstain from adultery & leave loving cherishing etc etc to go by the board.

                                                   Yrs ever affly
                                                   HUGH CECIL

WSC to R. B. Haldane
(*Haldane Papers*)

7 September 1908   Board of Trade

My dear Haldane,

I am touched by the kindness wh has prompted you to send me such a beautiful & valuable present for my wedding. I remember the long succession of encouragements and friendly services which you have accorded me during my political life. I look forward to years of fruitful & effective cooperation & comradeship in office & opposition. I am confident that our friendship will never be even ruffled by the incidental divergencies of honest opinion inseparable from the perplexities of politics & affairs.

I thank you most sincerely for this token of your good-will, & believe me I reciprocate in the strongest degree the feelings wh inspired your gift & wh will double its value in my eyes.

                                                   Yours always
                                                   WINSTON S. CHURCHILL

Ian Malcolm to WSC

8 September 1908   Knapton Hall
                                                          North Walsham

My dear Winston,
    I hope you have by this time received and will accept from Jeanne
and me a pair of old wine stands for the decoration of your new dinner
table, and in kindly remembrance of old friends who wish you exceedingly
well.
    I am so glad to see that Hugh is to be your Best Man; I feel a sort of
foster father to the arrangement from having first introduced you to one
another.

Ever Yours
IAN MALCOLM

Earl of Dundonald to WSC

8 September 1908   34 Portman Square

Dear Churchill,
    You are marrying the daughter of an old friend of mine and a late officer
of my old regiment. I wish you happiness with all my heart.
    Life is too short for soreness, though I prefer to think of you as you were in
South Africa than later when with Mr Lloyd George you attacked me for
my action against corruption which in its gross and Canadian sense is little
known in England, happily.
    Mainly owing to this attack my career as a soldier has been ruined and my
life's work thrown away.
    You did not realise all this. I felt it *from you* as I had been always a staunch
friend to you when it was a question of your getting a commission in the
SALH [South African Light Horse] it was I who went to Buller, not
everyone wished you to have it and again I did my best for you to get
reward for your gallant ride – it is all past now.

Yours sincerely
DUNDONALD

Sir Edward Grey to WSC

8 September 1908   Fallodon
                                                         Northumberland

Dear Churchill,

I am sorry I can't be back in London this week as I should have been delighted to dine on Friday.

I am having some Marlborough Literature bound for you to wit Coxe's Memoirs, Marlborough's Letters and Despatches and Wolseley's Life of the Great Man. As Literature I fear it is not up to the high standard of the library in Bolton Street, but you certainly ought to have the chief works on Marlborough in that library.

I am afraid the binding will not be done in time for the 12th, but you will hardly want such solid fare on a honeymoon and the books will I hope be ready when you return.

I should have come up for the wedding, but the ceremony itself has such associations for me that I attend it now no more. But I shall think of you on the day none the less earnestly with wishes for your prosperity and success and happiness.

Yours sincerely
EDWARD GREY

H. H. Asquith to WSC

10 September 1908   Slains Castle
                                                        Aberdeenshire

My dear Winston,

I am sincerely sorry not to be able to be present at the ceremony on Saturday. The 12th happens to be my birthday, which I always keep with my family.

But nowhere will warmer wishes or higher hopes be felt for you & your bride than in this house.

My colleagues & myself are hoping that you will accept a tribute of our collective regard.[1] Owing to the absence of almost all of them from London, we have been obliged to ask you to excuse us for delaying the actual presentation until we meet in October.

Yours always
H. H. ASQUITH

---

[1] His colleagues in the Government gave the couple a splendid scallop-edged silver tray with all their autographs engraved on the back. Asquith himself gave a 10-volume edition of the collected works of Jane Austen.

Lieut-Colonel Sir Robert Hermon-Hodge to WSC

10 September 1908   21 Auckland Road
                                                     Doncaster

My dear Churchill,
    I am sending you tomorrow a silver salver precisely the same as Jack's
from the officers of the Q.O.O.H. with the warmest good wishes for your
happiness. Please allow me this opportunity of telling you how much I
appreciate your work in the Regiment and the way in which you stick to it
in spite of the important claims upon your time.
    Do not trouble to answer this.
                                        Believe me, Yours sincerely
                                            ROBERT HODGE
                                             (Col QOOH)

WSC to Lady Randolph

13 September 1908   Blenheim

Dearest Mamma,
    Everything is vy comfortable & satisfactory in every way down here, &
Clemmie vy happy & beautiful. The weather a little austere with gleams of
sunshine; we shall long for warm Italian suns. There was no need for any
anxiety. She tells me she is writing you a letter. Best of love my dearest
Mamma. You were a great comfort & support to me at a critical period in
my emotional development. We have never been so near together so often
in a short time. God bless you.
    What a relief to have got that ceremony over! & so happily.
                                                    Your loving son
                                                          W
PS I open this letter again to tell you that George [Cornwallis-West] said
he could wish me no better wife or happier days than he had found in you.
                                                          W

WSC to Lady Randolph

20 September 1908   [Venice]

Dearest Mamma,
    I send you another packet of letters, wh pray distribute. I am now quite
determined not to sell Bolton Street without a premium. It is absolutely

necessary to the furnishing of another house. Do try & find a rich bachelor. That is the line.

We have been happy here & Clemmie is vy well. She has written to you of our doings so I will not repeat the tale. We have only loitered & loved – a good & serious occupation for which the histories furnish respectable precedents. With all my affection.

Your loving son
W

Sir John Willoughby[1] to WSC

1 November 1908   2 Down Street

My dear Winston,

I want to give you a little wedding present and it has occurred to me that 5 shares in the South African Option Syndicate would perhaps be more useful than a teapot or butter dishes! The shares today are £7 and with luck may go to anything up to £100. If you will let me know if you would like them I will transfer them to you at once if not please tell me what else you would prefer.

Yours ever
JOHN WILLOUGHBY

[1] John Christopher Willoughby (1859–1918), accompanied Dr Jameson on his raid into the Transvaal 1896; served South Africa 1899–1900; besieged at Ladysmith; in charge of transport at relief of Mafeking; served First World War; succeeded father as 5th Baronet 1866.

12

The Board of Trade

(See Main Volume Chapter 9)

Sidney Webb[1] to WSC

13 May 1908   Board of Trade
Private

Dear Mr Churchill

I send you *in confidence* the scheme of Poor Law Reform that I am advocating on the P.L. Commission – & I think it may be useful to you considering the old age Pension Scheme.

It occurs to me th you might like, either now or when you are more disengaged, to look through the evidence of the Poor Law Commission with regard to Unemployment? Yes, I now send you, in confidence, all the evidence taken before us, which bears on the question.

Warmest congratulations on your great electoral exploits.

Sincly
SIDNEY WEBB

WSC to Lord Crewe
(Crewe Papers)

30 May 1908   Board of Trade
Private

My dear Crewe,

I should'be vy much obliged to you if you would put Marsh – my private Secretary – down on your list for a CMG. He has ten years standing in the

---

[1] Sidney James Webb (1859–1947), socialist, historian and statesman; a founder of the Fabian Society 1884; served on Royal Commission on Trade Union Law 1903–6; on the Coal Industry 1910; on Railways 1917–18; Professor of Public Administration, London School of Economics 1912–27; Labour MP for Seaham 1922–9; President of Board of Trade 1924; Secretary of State for Dominion Affairs 1929–30; for Colonies 1929–31; Baron Passfield 1929; OM 1924; author of many books including *History of Trade Unionism* 1894, *Industrial Democracy* 1897, *Socialism in England* 1890. Married to Beatrice Webb.

CO; was Chamberlain's private Secretary for a long time; & came with me through Uganda where he did extremely well & acquired invaluable experience. I understand this was practically settled when the Cabinet changes took place, & I hope you will feel yourself able to view it with a favourable eye.

Yours sincerely

WINSTON S. CHURCHILL

WSC to the Master of Elibank

11 June 1908   Board of Trade

Copy

My dear Murray,

A difficulty has arisen about Marsh. When I went to the Colonial Office two and a half years ago, he was already a senior, and consequently according to office practice, ineligible for private secretary's work. It was arranged however that he should come to me without the additional allowance of a private secretary, and that this £150 be paid to the Junior whoever he was who was detailed to do Marsh's ordinary departmental work. In this way, the £150 allowance was made available for a junior whose smaller salary such allowances are intended to augment. The transaction was made effective by the following method. Marsh continued to draw the £150 as my private secretary and he gave up from his regular salary as a senior clerk in the Colonial Office an equivalent sum which was transferred to the junior acting for him. Years passed and we come to the Board of Trade. Marsh comes with me. The new Under Secretary of State for the Colonies becomes entitled to the £150 allowance for the private secretary allocated to that office and he makes his own arrangements, employing this time a junior who directly benefits by the allowance. Marsh is transferred to the Board of Trade, and in place of being private secretary to an Under Secretary of State, he becomes secretary to a departmental chief. I fully understood from Sir Francis Hopwood that this arrangement – which is very necessary for my convenience – could be made, and that Marsh would continue to draw his regular salary as senior clerk of so many years standing at the Colonial Office. To this he is clearly entitled as a covenanted civil servant.

He would of course receive no allowance as a private secretary from the Colonial Office, such sum being available for my successor; but I should propose to make him some allowance out of the £400 with which the President of the Board of Trade is provided for these purposes, and in this way his transference from the position of private secretary to an Under

Secretary of State to that of private secretary to a Departmental chief would carry with it an improvement in his pay. This again is perfectly regular, as the private secretaries of cabinet ministers are often senior clerks, & their allowances are additional to their salaries. But now I find that it is proposed to take away from him not only the £150 a year which he would be paid as private secretary at the Colonial Office (which is very proper) but also to take the second £150 from his own pay which he had contributed towards the pay of the junior who had taken his place. This is so manifestly unfair and absurd that I am sure it only needs to be brought to your notice to be put right. Marsh has now done the work of a private secretary for two and a half years without receiving the slightest increase in his ordinary emoluments, and I am sure you will agree with me that it will only be proper in coming here that his services in a more important capacity, should be marked by an improvement in his circumstances. I had therefore arranged to divide equally between my two private secretaries the £400 assigned to the President of the Board of Trade, so that both these officers will be serving on exactly equal terms. But if the proposed deductions were insisted upon, this arrangement would become quite impossible. Let me further remind you that in coming here from the Colonial Office, I have given up the extra private secretary whom the Treasury were good enough to allow me and for whom an extra £150 was provided as a special case to meet the unusual pressure of work which prevailed at the Colonial Office when we first assumed office.

I hope I may hear from you soon that this matter which has caused me a great deal of concern has been satisfactorily arranged.

Believe me, Yours vy sincerely
WINSTON S. CHURCHILL

WSC to Lord Hugh Cecil
(Quickswood Papers)

27 June 1908　　　　　　　　　　　　　　　12 Bolton Street

My dear Linky,

I am vy sorry you cannot & will not dine.

I do not think that any vacancy will occur in the immediate future in the quarter you mention. My information is that the Birthday List will create no seats. But you know how utterly in the dark the underlings of Governments are.

Yours ever
W

WSC to Lord Morley

2 July 1908　　　　　　　　　　　　　　　　　　　Board of Trade

Copy

Private

My dear Lord Morley,

I am very sorry to find that my explanations to you yesterday in Cabinet were after all not conclusive; and still more that you appear to have doubts about my discretion in respect to public documents. The difference wh I fear exists between us in opinion upon the scale of British armaments ought surely not to lead to personal want of confidence. And I should fail in a friendship wh I have greatly valued and wh I earnestly desire to preserve if I did not let you know my feelings.

The Prime Minister has given me permission to read the evidence upon wh the report of your sub-committee was based together with some earlier documents before the sub-committee at that time. It is obvious that no intelligent opinion can be formed of the Report – circulated to the Cabinet Committee on Estimates at *your* suggestion if I mistake not – without reference to these papers. But I do not intend to read them unless you feel able to tell me that you wish me to do so.

Yours v sincerely
WSC

Lord Morley to WSC

2 July 1908　　　　　　　　　　　　　　　　　　　India Office

My dear Winston,

I am petrified! Who has told you that I 'doubted your discretion about public documents'? *Never:* no *never* have I used language of that kind or anything like it.

Nor have I ever demurred to your going into the evidence of the NW Frontier committee. What I have said is wholly founded on the danger to the good working of the CID; if every member of the Cabinet is to have permission for a *roving* exploration of the secrets of the CID the only result would be that the WO, the Admiralty, and the IO, would keep secrets to themselves, and the CID would find itself hamstrung. I think the PM (who is the master of the CID) should make his authorisations rather specific, limited and defined; but I told him today that I for one did not in the least object to your rummaging out evidence taken before my sub-committee. I understood that you sought more than this. Apparently I was wrong.

Let me just add this. We had many sittings of the Sub C. We came to conclusions. They were submitted (not so mightily long ago) to the whole CID, including CB and Asquith, and by them approved. This does not prove that the conclusions were not moonshine. They may have been, but don't be angry with poor me for shedding tears, hot tears, over the discovery that I am convicted of having wasted so many of my dwindling days. As for 'personal confidence', pray don't talk of that!! It will be a very black day for me that interrupts the affectionate feelings entertained for you by

J. MORLEY

Let us have a talk before Thursday?

WSC to H. Llewellyn Smith[1]

8 July 1908   Board of Trade
Secret
Copy

Mr Llewellyn Smith,

Mr Shackleton tells me that the Trade Unions think the time has come for another International Labour Congress (the last was held, I believe, 16 years ago).

It has been suggested to Mr Roosevelt that the US should propose one, & there is much probability that he will issue invitations next year unless some other Power does so sooner.

Labour in this country would warmly welcome any initiative taken in this direction by HMG & there would be much prestige to be gained by the Board of Trade if the Congress took place here.

The case against is that probably many awkward questions would be raised, such as child & woman labour – reforms would be proposed, for which strong cases could be made out & which would no doubt be beneficial – but which it might be difficult & uselessly dangerous for the Govt to adopt in view of the powerful interests affected.

I would like to have your views on the question raised in this Minute as soon as possible, as the proposal if adopted shd be discussed at the Trades Union Congress in September, the agenda for which have to be settled before the end of this month.

WSC

---

[1] Hubert Llewellyn Smith (1864–1945), Permanent Secretary to Board of Trade 1907–19. General Secretary, Ministry of Munitions 1915; CB 1903; KCB 1908; GCB 1919.

WSC to Herbert Gladstone
(*Herbert Gladstone Papers*)

8 July 1908   Board of Trade

My dear Gladstone,

Shackleton told me some little time ago that the Trade Unions think the time has come for another International Labour Congress, & I have also heard that it has been suggested to Mr Roosevelt that he should propose such a Congress next year, & that there is much probability of the United States Government issuing invitations unless some other Power should forestall them.

I have been considering whether it might not be worth our while to endeavour to arrange for a Congress of the kind in London next year. Undoubtedly labour in this country would warmly welcome any initiative taken by the Government in this direction. On the other hand, some embarrassment would certainly arise, if a Labour Congress were being held, or were about to be held, in this country, & the Government were at the same time bringing in Bills on the subjects which were being discussed, or were about to be discussed, by the Congress. We cannot afford to neglect this consideration as the reform of the Poor Law, questions connected with unemployment &c, have to be dealt with during the next two years, & it would unquestionably be inconvenient to have a new Labour programme thrust upon us by the Congress at a time when it would be difficult to carry it through. And after ourselves summoning the Congress, it might involve some loss of prestige if we were unable to give effect to, at any rate, some of the more important resolutions passed by the delegates.

I should much like to know what you think about this. Perhaps a convenient *via media* would be to get the labour leaders here to promote a Congress in London, which the Government could bless without having been responsible for calling it together or for framing its Agenda.

Upon the whole my mind is adverse to Shackleton's proposal.

Yours vy sincerely
WINSTON S. CHURCHILL

Herbert Gladstone to WSC

9 July 1908   House of Commons

My dear Churchill,

The idea is a good one, & with careful organization the Congress might produce good fruit. If held it would be necessary of course to settle its composition and agenda in advance by negotiation more or less in private. I have had some talk with Shackleton & have asked him to let me have privately a sketch of his views. I don't think there need be much danger from a development of a new labour programme. Subjects for discussion would be those which show international variation of treatment by law or administration which is prejudicial to industrial development. I mean Factory & Mines Inspections, limitations of hours, employment of women after childbirth and such like functions. It is of great importance to stimulate industrial movements in other countries especially the backward ones. I will speak to you about it – but I do think it is well worth an effort.

Yours always

H. J. GLADSTONE

WSC to Herbert Gladstone
(*Herbert Gladstone Papers*)

13 July 1908   Board of Trade

My dear Gladstone,

Many thanks for your letter of the 9th about the suggested Labour Congress. I am telling Shackleton that I find you regard the idea with a good deal of favour, & that as Labour legislation is so much more intimately connected with your department than with mine I think he had better communicate mainly with you; while I shall be glad to co-operate in any way I can. I said that you would probably write or speak to him about it.

Yours very sincerely

WINSTON S. CHURCHILL

Memorandum by WSC[1]

Confidential

[July 1908]   [Board of Trade]

A 'Labour Exchange' may be defined as an office for registering on the one hand the needs of employers for workpeople, and on the other hand the needs of workpeople for employers. Properly organised, it should serve

---

[1] This document is based upon a memorandum on Labour Exchanges prepared for WSC by William Beveridge.

two distinct though connected purposes: – (1) the closer adjustment of the demand for, and the supply of, labour by the concentration of the labour market for any given area at a single known centre; and (2) the supply of immediate information as to the state of the labour market and as to industrial conditions generally.

(1) The demand for labour is constantly undergoing both permanent and temporary changes. The former arise from the decay of established industries, their transference from one place to another, or changes in the methods and machinery employed, or from the rise of new industries calling for fresh supplies of labour, or for labour of a new character.

The temporary changes arise from the fluctuations of trade, both general and local. Experience shows that quite apart from the seasonal or cyclical depressions which affect individual industries or all industries simultaneously, there are constantly independent and opposite fluctuations in the work of different employers or different trades; and that scarcity of labour in one district may be coincident with a surplus of similar labour in other districts.

This clearly involves economic waste, some of which, it is suggested, might be saved by increasing the mobility of labour. Another and worse form of waste is represented by the casual occupations in which each employer, to meet sudden fluctuations of demand, has a reserve of men constantly waiting or calling at his gates. These separate reserves are never all employed at the same time; that is to say, taken altogether they make up a chronic over-supply of men in regard to the occupation as a whole. This overstocking of occupations is largely a consequence of the attraction of casual jobs. Its counterpart is the under-employment and chronic distress of the men in reserve. The more irregular and uncertain the demands of employers and the more casual their methods of engagement the stronger is the tendency to overstocking. Consequently, in certain occupations where this system exists, notably those connected with building and with the docks, and many others, which require chiefly unskilled or low-skilled labour, the normal condition of many of the workpeople is under-employment, that is to say, a state of affairs in which men have sufficient chance of work to prevent them effectively seeking work elsewhere, but not sufficient to provide a reasonable subsistence.

The principal object of a well-equipped system of Labour Exchanges would be to remedy these evils by organising the demand for, and the supply of, labour of all kinds (skilled and unskilled, permanent and temporary), and to decasualise labour as much as possible by dovetailing the casual work of the different employers in each area, so that the same man, though constantly passing from one employer to another, should yet be able to obtain a reasonable continuity of work in a group of similar firms where he cannot find regular employment under one employer alone. The rapid transference of the superfluous labour of a district to another district possessed of an inadequate supply, would also be an object, though one which presents special difficulties of its own.

Whilst a system of Labour Exchanges might, if successful, afford a most important advantage by promoting the decasualisation of labour, it is impossible to omit from consideration the fact that any such action will probably entail the more or less complete unemployment of a not inconsiderable number of workmen who at present obtain a precarious and very inadequate livelihood by getting, say, two or three days work a week. The treatment of the problem thus presented is one which will probably be dealt with by the Poor Law Commission in its forthcoming report. In any case, however, this important question is a separate matter, which cannot usefully be treated in this Memorandum. It appears, however, proper to allude to it in order to show that it has not escaped attention.

(2) A system of Labour Exchanges would automatically register the beginning, depth and ending of trade depressions; it would show the need or the absence of need at any given time for emergency measures or relief; and furnish much valuable information at present only inadequately obtained as to the conditions of the labour market, especially amongst those trades which are either entirely unorganised or only partially and loosely organised.

The United Kingdom now stands almost alone among important European countries in its lack of any organised system of public Labour Exchanges. In the Report upon 'Agencies and Methods of dealing with the Unemployed in Foreign Countries,' issued by the Board of Trade in 1904, attention is drawn to the very considerable extension of labour registries in the preceding few years in Germany, Austria, Switzerland, France, and Belgium. The most conspicuous case is that of Germany, where, since the depression of 1893–4, public Labour Exchanges have been set up in nearly every important town, and have developed rapidly until with a few exceptions there is now a public Labour Exchange in every municipality of over 50,000 inhabitants, and many smaller ones. These institutions are of two main types: (a) purely municipal, and (b) maintained by voluntary associations with varying degrees of municipal recognition and support; the general tendency is towards complete municipalisation. In most cases the Exchanges receive some measure of support from the State Government, and lately the Imperial Government has made an annual grant to the General Federation of German Labour Exchanges in order to promote closer co-operation.

It is submitted that an effort to develop a system of Labour Exchanges

C II—PT. II—F

in this county is desirable, and that any such attempt should be based on three main principles:—

1. Whilst it will probably be found impracticable to attempt to call a complete system into being at once, the ultimate objective should be a national system covering the whole country.

2. The Labour Exchanges must be treated as machinery for the organisation of the demand for supply of labour, especially that which is now casual; and not for relief.

3. Labour Exchanges must be regarded as industrial even more than municipal, *i.e.*, as part of the economic organisation of the nation, rather than as a piece of the machinery of local government. They may succeed without municipal support; they cannot succeed without the co-operation of employers and employed, and of employers and employed in association.

The first principle makes it necessary that Labour Exchanges should at least be vigorously started and directed by central government, whose task it should be to co-ordinate their working and to provide a central 'clearing house' of exact and detailed information as to the labour market. The second and third principles point to the Board of Trade as the Government Department to whose existing functions the new work is most closely related, as it is already an industrial intelligence office, receiving continuously and systematically a large amount of information from trade and labour correspondents, officials of employers and workmen's organisations, and others as to local and trade conditions, while it possesses a staff of experienced investigators of its own. As recourse to the proposed Labour Exchange must be purely voluntary, it is obvious that their success would largely depend upon the extent to which employers and workmen can be induced to avail themselves of them.

This same consideration points to the desirability of the establishment of the exchanges by the local authorities or, at least, with their co-operation, in order to secure local interest and support. Perhaps the actual administrative committees should be mixed bodies representing the municipalities and the principal organisations of employers and employed. On the other hand, it is evident that mere central supervision alone (without some inducement to local activity) would be insufficient, and that it would be most desirable for the central government to make substantial grants-in-aid to such Exchanges as reach, in the judgment of the supervising authority, an adequate standard of efficiency.

It would be the task of the Board of Trade, as already indicated, to co-ordinate the work of the Exchanges, to provide a central office through which the various Exchanges may readily and usefully communicate with each other, and to deal rapidly with the statistical information received from them.

It is not possible at this stage to lay down precise plans of organisation, or to determine the extent to which the machinery can or should be set up at once. There are many difficult points, both of policy and administrative detail, which will require very careful and detailed consideration, such as (a) the relations between the proposed Labour Exchanges and the trade union organisations; (b) the position of the Exchanges in regard to non-unionist workmen, and to strikes; (c) the relations of the institutions set up under the proposed scheme to the existing Exchanges created under the Labour Bureaux Act and the Unemployed Workmen Act; and (d) finance.

But should the policy suggested in the present Memorandum be approved, it would be the duty of the Department to make such investigation as may be desirable in order to determine the best lines of organisation and the manner in which a beginning may be made with the most promise of success.

WSC

Sidney Webb to WSC

16 July 1908   The Hermitage
                                                    Luton Hoo

Dear Mr Churchill,

I have practically nothing to criticise in the Memorandum on Labour Exchanges. It seems to me, not only correct, but also a quite admirable statement.

All I can do is to note a few trifling points which might, as it seems to me, be made slightly more accurate in expression.

Page 4. line 6. The parenthesis seems hastily expressed. The Board of Trade returns as to unemployed in Trade Unions are not an accurate sample of *Trade Unions* (being too much drawn from the engineering & shipbuilding trades); nor can they be said to be drawn *from every variety of trades.* The parenthesis might run '(for the most skilled trades often show five or even ten per cent of their members unemployed)'.

There might be added the further argument:

'Moreover, if by an organised system of Labour Exchanges there were increased opportunities of "Dovetailing" employment in one occupation with employment in another every kind of training would become more useful as helping the labourer to pick up the new skill required in the new occupation opened up to him.'

Page 4. par 2. They will show also the *localities* of depressions.

Page 5. line 5. '*Apposite.*'

„   5   par 2. '*sea*sonal' not sessional (?)

„   7   It is an important drawback to local (municipal) Exchanges that, more often than not, the municipal area is not coextensive with the industrial centre – either because the latter has overflowed, e.g. London into West Ham & then into East Ham; into Chiswick & Ealing; really also, into Reading, & Luton & Erith & Croydon. Or because two nuclei have joined, e.g. Manchester & Salford &c, Liverpool, Bootle, Birkenhead &c, Leeds, Bradford &c. In fact the West Riding is nearly all one continuous commercial unit!

Page 8. Is not the precedent of the Mercantile Marine offices exactly apposite? These 110 Labor Exchanges dealing with one great industry are already in existence; & on the estimates.

What is their cost per seaman engaged?

Page 8–9. I think the Central Unemployed Body's Exchanges are on altogether too mean & petty a scale. I do not think the Govt could run the London Exchanges under £1000 a year each. And there would soon have to be more of them (or more accommodation) if any large proportion of the London labor contracts came to be dealt with.

Page 11. No doubt £50,000 would easily suffice *for the first year.*

I do not think I can add any other suggestion—except that (in the present state of feeling!) it might be well from the outset to make it clear that *women* were to be equally provided for. Query, whether any indication should be given as what classes were to be catered for?

There are existing Registry Offices for (i) domestic servants, (ii) scholastic appointments, which might obstruct if about to be competed with. There are also smaller agencies of the kind for hotel servants & waiters, I think. On the whole, the field is pretty clear, & I think there need be *no* limits.

Yours vy truly

SIDNEY WEBB

Arthur Wilson Fox to WSC

17 July 1908   Board of Trade

My dear President,

I am so much obliged to you for your most kind letter of yesterday; and all the more do I appreciate it being aware of the great pressure under which you work.

There is nothing much wrong with me, and I am at the Office again today.

I was chiefly knocked up yesterday, because, for some reason, I had two nights with but little sleep.

It is not at all necessary for me to act on your very kind suggestion and take a month off. If I really felt that it was better to do so I would, because I do not believe in people being at work in a condition when they cannot turn out their best.

But pray do not think that any work which you have initiated, had anything to do with my being a little 'off colour'. This is not the case. I really like work, and most especially constructive work, and I am much looking forward to a very interesting and enjoyable time under your administration of the Office.

I trust that you will always bear this in mind – that, quite apart from any duty I owe to the Department, I am ready & willing at all times and seasons to do anything or go anywhere for you. You cannot ask for too much, and I say this with much sincerity.

Yours very truly
ARTHUR WILSON FOX

Marie Corelli to WSC

27 July 1908   Mason Croft
                                              Stratford-on-Avon

Private

Dear Mr Winston Churchill,

I hope in your busy life you still have some slight memory of me? I read what you said in Hyde Park on Saturday – and I thought you might perhaps be interested to know that my new book which is now advertised – 'Holy Orders' – deals with the Drink subject in a way which I hope may strengthen *all* hands who are fighting for the sobriety of the nation. At any rate that is its intention and object. I take up the troubles of the drunks in *small rural villages all over England,* and as you know I have a very large 'following'. I am not without hope that I *may* be of use in the cause. At any rate, please regard me as a humble worker on your side! I may add that I am *not* a Suffragette!!

Sincerely yours
MARIE CORELLI

Memorandum by WSC

8 August 1908   Board of Trade

I circulate[1] to my colleagues the accompanying Memorandum, which has been prepared in the Board of Trade, upon the state of employment and trade during the first six months of the year, in order to call their timely attention to the conditions which may be apprehended in the autumn and winter.

The amount of unemployment is disquieting for the season of the year. It arises, no doubt, in part from the disputes in the shipbuilding and engineering trades, which have thrown out of work many besides those directly concerned, and have caused a widespread dislocation of the normal course of those industries. But the decline of 16½ millions in our exports of manufactured articles, coupled with other indications, tends to show that these disputes are only a minor and secondary cause; and, taking the figures of unemployment in conjunction with the shrinkage in wages and the comparatively high level of food prices, it is evident that a period of unusual severity for the working-classes has begun, and that conditions may become more stringent in the course of the winter.

On the other hand, it should be remembered that any comparison with last year relates to a very high standard of prosperity which we could scarcely hope to maintain; and some sinister consolation may perhaps be derived from the third part of the Memorandum, which shows that our prospects are certainly no worse than those of France, Germany, and the United States.

WSC

Sir H. Llewellyn Smith to WSC

11 August 1908   Oakfield Lodge
                                                                    Ashtead

My dear President,

I hope you are none the worse after your adventure as fireman.[2] I am here (going up occasionally to the Board of Trade) working a reasonable amount of time daily at such problems as Bankruptcy amendment, casual labour, and sweated trades. The last named question will give some trouble next year after the report of the Select Committee on Home-Workers.

The question will arise: if there is to be legislation on what lines should it

[1] Memorandum on the state of Employment and Trade during the first six months of 1908. Circulated 17 August, 1908.
[2] See p. 798.

proceed, and should it be in charge of the Home Office or Board of Trade? The latter question will be partly determined by the answer to the former.

But a preliminary question is whether the Government mean to do anything, or to leave the initiation of legislation to the private members. In any case it is well to study the problem & its various (attempted) solutions, & this I am doing. By the way Labour Exchanges as a remedy for unemployed do not seem simpler the more they are considered in detail. On the contrary the problem bristles with all kinds of difficulties.

I see the Port of London Bill has been put down for Oct 12th. Is this seriously intended? I hope so.

I shall be available up to Aug 28th, & then shall be away for some weeks I hope.

I am enclosing a private letter from Sir Adam Block[1] (President of the Ottoman Debt) parts of which may interest you. In view of what is going on in Turkey we must be very much on the alert to protect & advance British interests, as what is taking place is bound to affect the relative influence of different Powers, and may lead to quite unexpected results – I am thinking especially of Commerce, Import duties, Railways, Harbours &c.

I am, Yours sincerely
H. Llewellyn Smith

W. P. Byles to WSC

Dictated

18 August [1908]   8 Chalcot Gardens

My dear Churchill,

I am lying limp & helpless on a sickbed: the fever is gone, but gnomes, political shadows & fears crowd my brain as bees haunt a hive.

Yesterday your Cardiff speech came down on them like a shaft of pure, crystal water from the fountain of Hope. To-day the gnomes have crept away & there have come instead fays & fairies, pleasant fancies & radiant hopes. Shall I not thank you for your Ariel work?

The two subjects nearest to me are international amity & Irish reconciliation: & a Statesman has at last arisen – young, valiant, amply equipped – who sees things & does them, & who shall accomplish both these dreams. And in this faith I doze again!

[1] Adam Samuel James Block (1856–1941), President of British Chamber of Commerce, Constantinople 1907–18, CMG 1895; KCMG 1907.

But I took up my pen (or rather my wife's) to say that I am extremely glad you are going to be married. My congratulations to you, &, not less, to Miss Hozier. I paid homage this morning to her presentment in the MG [*Manchester Guardian*]

With me marriage was the wisest step I ever took in a long life. That it may be the same with you is the sincere wish of

Your faithful friend
W. P. BYLES

WSC to Edward Marsh
(*Longleat Papers*)

20 August 1908   Board of Trade

My dear Eddie,

Few people have been so lucky as me to find in the dull and grimy recesses of the Colonial Office a friend who I shall cherish and hold to all my life.

Yours always
W

Sir Charles Hardinge to the King
(*Royal Archives*)

EXTRACT

24 August 1908   Kimbolton

. . . As Mr Lloyd George appeared to be devoting more of his time to matters affecting the Foreign Office than to the study of the working of old age pensions in Germany, Sir E. Grey sent him a telegram to say that the question of Naval armaments was not to be discussed by him during his stay in Berlin nor any other subject of that kind. Sir E. Grey has also pointed out to Winston Churchill the fallacy of some of the statements made by him in his speech of the other day, and the undesirability of his embarking on questions of Foreign Policy in his political speeches in the constituencies. . . .

Memorandum by WSC

1 September 1908   [Board of Trade]

The President of the Board of Trade is causing the following memorandum to be communicated to Chambers of Commerce and Employers' and Workmen's Associations.

Memorandum

1. Under the Conciliation Act of 1896 the Board of Trade has power to appoint a Conciliator in trade disputes and an Arbitrator at the request of both parties. These slender means of intervention have been employed in cases where opportunity has offered, and the work of the Department in this sphere has considerably increased of recent years. In 1905 the Board of Trade intervened in 14 disputes and settled them all: in 1906 they intervened in 20 cases and settled 16: in 1907 they intervened in 39 cases and settled 32: while during the first eight months of the present year no fewer than 47 cases of intervention have occurred, of which 35 have been already settled, while some of the remainder are still being dealt with.

2. It is not proposed to curtail or replace any of the existing functions or practices under the Conciliation Act, nor in any respect to depart from its voluntary and permissive character. The good offices of the Department will still be available to all in industrial circles for the settlement of disputes whenever opportunity offers; single Arbitrators and Conciliators will still be appointed whenever desired; special interventions will still be undertaken in special cases, and no element of compulsion will enter into any of these proceedings. But the time has now arrived when the scale of these operations deserves, and indeed requires, the creation of some more formal and permanent machinery; and, with a view to consolidating, expanding, and popularising the working of the Conciliation Act, I propose to set up a Standing Court of Arbitration.

3. The Court, which will sit wherever required, will be composed of three (or five) members, according to the wishes of the parties, with fees and expenses to members of the Court, and to the Chairmen during sittings. The Court will be nominated by the Board of Trade from three panels. The first panel – of Chairmen – will comprise persons of eminence and impartiality. The second will be formed of persons who, while preserving an impartial mind in regard to the particular dispute, are nevertheless drawn from the 'employer class'. The third panel will be formed of persons similarly drawn from the class of workmen and Trade Unionists. It is hoped that this composition will remove from the Court the reproach which workmen have sometimes brought against individual Conciliators and Arbitrators, that, however fair they mean to be, they do not intimately understand the position of the manual labourer. It is believed that by the appointment of two arbitrators selected from the employers' panel and two from the workmen's panel in difficult cases, thus constituting a Court of five instead of three persons, the decisions of the Court would be rendered more authoritative, especially to the workmen, who, according to the information of the Board of Trade, are more ready to submit to the judgment of two of their

representatives than of one. As the *personnel* of the Court would be constantly varied, there would be no danger of the Court itself becoming unpopular with either class in consequence of any particular decision; there would be no difficulty in choosing members quite unconnected with the case in dispute, and no inconvenient labour would be imposed upon anyone who consented to serve on the panels. Lastly, in order that the peculiar conditions of any trade may be fully explained to the Court, technical assessors may be appointed by the Board of Trade at the request of the Court or of the parties to assist in the deliberations, but without any right to vote.

4. The state of public opinion upon the general question of Arbitration in Trade Disputes may be very conveniently tested by such a voluntary arrangement. Careful inquiry through various channels open to the Board of Trade justifies the expectation that the plan would not be unwelcome in industrial circles. The Court will only be called into being if, and in proportion as, it is actually wanted. No fresh legislation is necessary.

5. Steps will now be taken to form the respective panels.[1]

WSC

A. P. Watt to WSC

8 September 1908   Hastings House

Dear Mr Churchill,

As the result of another interview which I have just had with Mr Greenhough Smith, he authorises me to say that, provided he receives from you or us the 'copy' of your last article not later than the 24th of this month, he will then be able to publish it in the November number of *The Strand Magazine* – actually issued on or about the 1st of November – and if he is able to do this he is willing that Messrs Hodder & Stoughton shall publish the last and the other articles which have appeared in *The Strand Magazine* in book form on the 6th of November. I gather from your letter of yesterday's date that there will be no difficulty about your delivering the 'copy' of the last article before the date mentioned by Mr Smith viz., the 24th of this month.

After seeing Mr Smith I called again upon Messrs Hodder & Stoughton and, as a result of my conversation with them, I am glad to be able to tell

---

[1] Improved machinery of conciliation came into operation in the autumn of 1908. In the following twelve months, courts were set up to settle disputes in the boot and shoe, coal-mining, iron and copper industries. In 1912 a permanent Industrial Council was set up under the chairmanship of Sir George Askwith, which 'died for lack of work' (see E. Phelps Brown, *The Growth of British Industrial Relations*, p. 341).

you that, provided you can let them have the 10,000 words of new matter in time, they are quite willing to waive the clause in the agreement between you and them which provides for publication some time between the 15th and 31st of October, and to publish the book instead on the 6th of November. Under the circumstances they have agreed to withdraw their request that in consideration of the publication of the book being postponed you should supply them with some additional matter over and above the articles which have appeared, and will appear, in *The Strand*, and the 10,000 words of new matter already provided for.

Please let me know if possible by return how soon you expect to be able to let me have the 10,000 words of new matter above mentioned. In the meantime, I understand that, with a view to saving as much time as possible, Mr Hodder Williams will at once put into type all the matter which has appeared in *The Strand*, and if you could let him or us have *some* of the illustrations he would like to be going on with the making of the blocks.

Trusting that all will now go smoothly,

I am, dear Mr Churchill, yours sincerely

A. P. WATT

WSC to A. P. Watt

8 September 1908

[Copy]

Dear Mr Watt,

This is a very satisfactory result. Messrs Hodder & Stoughton should let me have all the *Strand* articles up to date in slip proof as soon as possible; and should also say how many illustrations they contemplate, whether any lithographed photos and what maps they have in mind. I really think it would be better if one of their principals came and talked over with me the general style and presentation of the book, but that is for them to decide. I will undertake to let them have the whole of the copy by the end of the first week in October if that is early enough, but at the worst by the end of September. The greater part of the proofs can be in their hands long before that date corrected, and I shall send them all the illustrations I propose to use before I leave England on the 16th. You may inform Mr Greenhough Smith that he shall have the copy of the last *Strand* article by that date at latest. The photographs shall be sent him on Tuesday next.

Yours &c

WINSTON S. CHURCHILL

WSC to Lord Crewe
(*Crewe Papers*)

19 September 1908   Board of Trade
Private

My dear Crewe,

I have received a vy charming present from you & your wife on my marriage with Clementine which I value vy much & for wh I thank you most heartily. It is vy kind of you to send me a token of your good will & friendship.

Some time ago you suggested that we might pay you a visit at Crewe; & you know how anxious I am to have an opportunity of pouring out my soul to you on Uganda extension, on Cyprus tribute, on Malta Constitution & on Somaliland. My views may not command your agreement. But they were honestly & laboriously formed & I should greatly like to put them before you. I am sure I could tell you in two or three hours what it cost me months of work to acquire.

And the Uganda extension is vy dear to my heart – & the biggest constructive enterprise in any Crown Colony now on the board.

Well how would Sunday 11th Octr do? We are going to Dundee for speeches on the 9th & would travel south on the 10th to arrive Crewe DV in time for dinner. On the Monday I must go to London for a show I have to attend to: & Clementine has promised to go to the Stanleys (of Alderley) till the Tuesday when, alas, I address the United Kingdom Alliance in the FT Hall. Do let me know if this plan pleases you,

& believe me Yours vy sincerely
WINSTON S. CHURCHILL

WSC to Edgar Harper[1]

10 October 1908   Board of Trade
[Copy]

Confidential

Dear Harper,

Will you tell me how you meet this argument: – All taxation falls upon persons, not upon property. The burden of the taxation is measured by the amount of sacrifice involved to any individual. The source of wealth is irrelevant, since wealth-producing properties are freely and frequently interchanged. There is no reason why a thousand a year from mining

---

[1] Edgar Harper (1860–1934), statistical officer to LCC 1900–11; Chief Valuer, Inland Revenue 1911–25; knighted 1920.

royalties should be taxed more heavily than a thousand a year from Consols, except in so far as it can be shown that the property thus specially taxed is specially benefited by the consequent expenditure. The latter is the case in regard to land value, which would be only required to contribute proportionately to the process of their own enrichment. It would therefore appear that the special taxation of fixed charges like ground rents or mining royalties was invidious.

I should be very much obliged if you would think this over in your mind and let me have what you think is the answer, if answer there be. It seems to me to cut very deep.

> Yours very truly
> WINSTON S. CHURCHILL

Herbert Samuel to WSC

10 October 1908   Bedford Hotel
   Brighton

Private

My dear Churchill,

I have been following the question of Unemployment very closely during the last ten years. Your speech of last night is the first made by any leader which has seemed to me on the right lines.[1] To recognise – first, that it is an essential duty of the State to deal with this evil; secondly, that it is a permanent evil, though sometimes of greater and sometimes of less intensity, and must be dealt with not by machinery improvised for the occasion when the need is specially weak, but by a standing organization; thirdly, that, in addition to whatever localities may do, useful works should be organized on a national scale, set into full operation in times of bad trade and reduced to a minimum in times of good trade; fourthly, that a root of the evil is the wrong proportions of unskilled and skilled labour in our society caused mainly by the greater use of machinery for navvy's work, and to be cured mainly by technical combination schools.

To recognize this is, I am sure, the first step to the solution of the problem. I don't think I have ever before troubled any one with a letter about a speech he had delivered, but I must write to thank you for this.

Don't trouble to reply.

> Yours sincerely
> HERBERT SAMUEL

PS My best thanks for what you wrote to me the other day about my work this year.

[1] WSC had spoken on unemployment at Dundee, see Main Volume, pp. 302–4. His speech is reprinted in full in *Liberalism and the Social Problem*.

Cabinet Minute by WSC

10 October 1908　　　　　　　　　　　　　　　　　Board of Trade

This report[1] on the state of employment in the United Kingdom, though not yet complete, presents information relating to a matter of such public importance that I think it proper to communicate it to my colleagues for their consideration now.

In August I circulated to my colleagues the Report of the Board of Trade for the first six months of the year, as the state of industry and employment appeared to require timely consideration. Since then, I have had further special inquiries made throughout the country through various channels open to me. The results of the inquiries are not yet complete; but they already show that the apprehensions which I expressed in my covering note upon the previous report have been fully sustained and even surpassed by the event. There can be no doubt that we have already entered upon a period of exceptional distress and industrial dislocation; and these conditions may be sensibly aggravated as the winter advances.

So far as trade prospects are concerned, however, while it would be premature to expect a trade revival, there are some indications that the present depression will be less severe in duration than in degree.

WSC

C.W. Macara[2] to WSC

27 October 1908　　　　　　　　　　　　　　　　33 York Street
　　　　　　　　　　　　　　　　　　　　　　　　Manchester
Private and Confidential

Dear Mr Churchill,

I have noticed recently in the press, references to the scheme framed by the Board of Trade for the establishment of an Arbitration Court.

As the provision of such a Court has been the subject of my anxious consideration for many years, I think it well that I should send you copies of two letters dealing with the matter which I wrote to Mr A. Wilson Fox in the Spring of last year.

The present dispute in the Cotton Industry is the third which has arisen since the first of these letters was written, and the successive disputes show that what I said was probable, has actually happened.

[1] Report on Unemployment in the United Kingdom in September 1908.
[2] Charles Wright Macara (1845–1929), Manchester cotton manufacturer; President, English Federation of Master Cotton Spinners' Association 1894–1914; promoter of sliding-scale and short-time agreements and industrial arbitration; baronet 1911.

Had there existed an Arbitration Court, composed of men holding the highest official positions, representing the organizations of Capital and Labour, in, say, half a dozen of our principal industries, the Board of Trade might, in my opinion, have justly asked that the present dispute should be submitted to such a Court. Of course I could not vouch for even this meeting with approval, the feeling against intervention being so strong in the Cotton Trade; but I could hardly imagine that, if the Arbitration Court were composed as I suggested, it could be ignored without the risk of incurring hostile criticism.

I must ask you, considering the personal references made, to treat these letters as private and confidential.

I am Yours faithfully
C. W. MACARA

WSC to Lord Crewe
(*Crewe Papers*)

30 October 1908   Board of Trade

My dear Crewe,

I have a plan for our Cabinet Committee on Sunday wh I trust will commend itself to you. Lloyd George is coming down for the day to my Mother's house near St Albans, & Birrell will come too. Can you not manage to join us? It is only fifty minutes in a motor car. We can lunch, sniff the country air, and solve the Irish problem, in quick succession. It would give my Mother so much pleasure if you were able to come.

Yours very sincerely
WINSTON S. CHURCHILL

Lord Northcliffe to WSC

31 October 1908   Hotel St Regis
                                                         New York

My dear Churchill,

I am glad to see that your speeches are being well reported by a certain ancient institution, and that the speeches themselves are extremely good. But what I am writing about now is something that Mr Crawshay Williams will speak about more fully when you see him. I know what your political ambitions are, and it seems to me very desirable that, being as they are, you should not allow *that portion of the Empire which must most certainly dominate the Imperial situation* to regard you as they do.

I remember speaking to you on this subject on the occasion of my last visit to Canada, a country with which I am well acquainted, and I feel now that you could immensely increase your reputation and force both there and at home, if you were to embrace the opportunity of taking Mrs Churchill to Canada and of speaking before the wonderfully organized chain of Canadian Clubs, one of which exists in every city of any importance; keeping clear, however, of your damnable Free Trade, which most of the people there loathe.

During the fifteen years that I have known Canada it has developed much more rapidly than you can imagine, but so far as its connection with the Old Country is concerned, it is, owing to our great neglect, (as Lord Milner remarked to me the other day in Toronto, and as I have heard every one say) a matter of 'touch and go' in the next thirty years. I wish you could urge some of your colleagues to go there.

You may have noticed a special article in *The Times* of October 17th on the Canadian question.

Yours vy sincerely
NORTHCLIFFE

Emmanuel Joseph[1] *to WSC*

2 November 1908   48a Charing Cross Road

Mr Joseph begs to enclose a rough memorandum of the books he had from Mr Churchill.

Mr Joseph regrets to say he has ascertained the *War of the Rebellion* 28 vols is of no commercial value, will Mr Churchill kindly let Mr Joseph know what he shall do with them.

List of Books sold to Mr Joseph

Newman's Sermons	9 vols	Small edition
Smith *Wealth of Nations*	3 vols	
[?D'Abrantes] *Memoires*	10 vols	do
Macaulay's *History of England*	5 vols	
Macaulay's Works	6 vols	
Locke's Works	10 vols	
Gibbon's Rome	8 vols	2 *sets*

---

[1] Emmanuel Joseph (1857–1930), bookseller; began his career with a barrow of books in Aldgate; moved to the Strand, and in 1902 to the Charing Cross Road; descended from a bookseller who was charged with murder in 1516; his son is still active at the same address.

Lamb's Works	4 vols	
Hume & Smollett *England*	13 vols	
Austen's Works	10 vols	
Froude's *England*	12 vols	Small Edition
Buckle's *Civilization*	3 vols	do
Carlyle's Works	6 vols	
Novels etc	50 vols	
Official Books etc	20 vols	
War of the Rebellion	28 vols	

Duplicate	*Remarks by Edward Marsh*
La Fontaine's *Fables*	keep both
Miss Austen	sell old
Thackeray	do
Pepys Diary	The new one (from A. Lyttelton) is written in, & is better bound, but not such a good or complete edition.
H. Walpole	The one I gave you is the new & best edition – & has bookplate. Runciman's is vy nicely bound – it is not written in.
Mme de Borgue	You had 2 volumes out of four, one was burnt at Burley; sell first volume.
Fielding	Keep your old one, it is nicer & has bookplate. Keep also 1st edn of *Tom Jones*.
Ruskin	Sell the new *Munera Pulveris, Sesame & Lilies, Crown of Wild Olive* – Keep *Unto This Last*. Also you have a *little* old set.
Sterne	You have 2 copies sell the modern one.

Cabinet Minute by WSC

2 November 1908   Board of Trade

I circulate to my colleagues the Memorandum of the Board of Trade upon the state of Employment and Trade during the first nine months of 1908.

The depression has affected, in successive degrees of intensity, the United States, the United Kingdom, Germany and France; and in the first three cases it has been attended by much industrial dislocation and sharp and unusual increases in unemployment. These conditions have been aggravated in the United States by financial insecurity, and in the United Kingdom by protracted labour disputes.

Although there are some slight evidences of better trade in the spring, there are no grounds for expecting any improvement in the immediate future. On the contrary, the winter season, especially if severe, added to the progressive impoverishment of the urban labouring population, and the exhaustion of municipal and benevolent funds, may steadily aggravate the distress.

The influence upon this situation of a prolonged stoppage in the cotton trade, *which may not be averted*, cannot be measured.

WSC

WSC to C. W. Macara and others

13 November 1908

Copy   [Board of Trade]

Dear Sir,

As you are aware, I followed with the utmost concern from day to day the various phases of the recent dispute in the cotton spinning trade – I greatly rejoiced that an end to the conflict had been reached a week ago, and I congratulate both sides that they were able to arrive at a settlement by direct negotiations with each other.

It has already been officially declared by both employers and operatives that strikes and lock-outs are disastrous and ought to be avoided. The Brooklands[1] agreement appears to have worked admirably – so far as it goes – and hitherto under its provisions many disputes have been amicably settled. But the Brooklands agreement is in itself incomplete. A supplementary scheme for ascertaining the actual state of trade – such as is generally known as the 'sliding scale' or 'conciliation scheme' is its necessary counterpart.

I am aware that during recent years much thought and consideration have been given on the part both of the employers' and of the operatives' organizations to the elaboration of some equitable and practical scheme for attaining this object, and the Board of Trade are in possession of certain proposals which they understand have formed the basis of discussion. While,

[1] The Brooklands Agreement in the cotton spinning industry was drawn up in 1893; it provided for annual adjustment for wage-rates of not more than five per cent.

however, the general principle of such a scheme does not appear to be contested, I understand that it has not been found possible so far to overcome altogether the difficulties of detail which stand in the way of the completion of a generally acceptable arrangement.

Feeling that the time has come when an earnest and determined effort ought in the public interest to be made to arrive at a mutually satisfactory agreement for the prevention of future disputes as to wages in the cotton trade, I have decided to invite representatives from all parties concerned to meet me in conference at the offices of the Board of Trade. It would be desirable for both employers and operatives to bring their own accountants. I should propose that the expense of any inquiry that may result from the conference should be borne by the State. Any scheme agreed upon under the auspices of the Board of Trade, while of course in no way binding on the various parties represented, might be confidently submitted for adoption by the several organizations concerned.

I should be glad to learn whether your Federation [or] Amalgamation would be prepared to send representatives to the proposed Conference. I am addressing similar invitations to the:

1 Federation of Master Cotton Spinners' Associations Ltd
2 Amalgamated Association of Operative Cotton Spinners
3 Amalgamated Association of Card and Blowing Room Operatives
4 Amalgamated Weavers' Association

and on receiving favourable replies I will at once advise the various parties as to the date of the Conference and the number of suggested representatives.

* * * * *

Cecil Grenfell to WSC

27 November 1908   28 Throgmorton Street

Private

My dear Winston,

A company I know all about, the Lake Superior Corporation, being in need of money, has to borrow the same as best it can, its affairs having been mismanaged. Many leading Financiers, both here, in New York and Canada are interested in its affairs. Briefly I have taken an interest of £5,000 for myself and £1,000 for you in the advance. We shall receive adequate security and 6% on our money. The Company will be reorganised, and we should be repaid our advance, with I hope a handsome bonus in stock: the worst that can happen to us is that we receive 6% and most probably we shall more than double our money: I certainly hope for £5,000 profit on my share.

My office have paid £1,000 for your account to the Canadian Agency. I hold the receipt for the same. Later we will receive the securities and further data which I will let you have. If you do not want the other £500 you have here I think I should put that in too – unless you like me to keep it for a favourable gamble.

European politics have kept me 'quiet' lately, but I hear today that a loan has been made to the Turk of £1,500,000 by England, France and *Germany;* Sir E. Cassel taking the English share of £500,000 – I don't suppose they would do this if an European Conflagration was imminent.

I want you both to dine and meet Uncle Francis[1] December 3rd.

Yours

CECIL GRENFELL

Cabinet Minute by WSC

9 December 1908 [Board of Trade]

Confidential

I circulate to my colleagues a Memorandum dealing with the work of the new London Traffic Branch of the Board of Trade, and suggesting certain developments. It is clear from the representations recently received by the Prime Minister, both from the dominant party in the London County Council and also from the Progressive members, that a moderate extension on the lines suggested would meet with general approval, and in the absence of legislation constituting an independent statutory Traffic Board a development of the existing Traffic Branch seems necessary and desirable. In the circumstances, the expenses of the branch must be defrayed out of public funds, as no local contributions could be made from rates without legislation. The additional cost, however, will not for the present exceed 3,000*l.* a year,

---

[1] Francis Wallace Grenfell, 1st Baron Grenfell (1841–1925), Field Marshal 1908. Governor and Commander-in-Chief, Malta 1899–1903; commanded 4th Army Corps 1903–4; Commander-in-Chief, Ireland 1904–8.

and I hope by enlisting the assistance of certain members of the staff of the Light Railways Commission to reduce even this amount.

Unless my colleagues object, I propose forthwith to make arrangements on the lines indicated in the Memorandum.

WSC

WSC to Lord Salisbury
(*Hatfield Papers*)

10 December 1908   Board of Trade

Private

My dear Salisbury,

I am anxious that the Port of London Bill should have a smooth passage. It is an absolutely non-party Bill. The only opposition consists of sections who made their case before the Joint Committee (a vy strong body) & whose case was not admitted by that Committee after exhaustive examination. The purchase terms being 'by agreement' constitute in their interest a bargain wh we have no power to vary without reopening the whole of a vast & intricate series of compromises. Postponement would involve past the death, for the bargain is off unless confirmed by Dec 31. The state of the Port of London in the event of such a collapse would be worse than ever.

I am pretty sure that if the H of Lords were fully apprised of the whole agreement for the Bill there would be no difficulty. But the subject is dull, tangled, and almost interminable: & time is short!

If you have any doubts or incipient criticisms, if there are any points upon wh you desire information I should be vy glad to ask Llewellyn-Smith (who has the whole thing at his finger ends, & whose quality you know) to come to see you tomorrow or Saturday for the purpose of assisting you to form a fair judgment. He will I am sure gladly submit himself to your examination. Will you let me know your wishes.

Yours vy sincerely
WINSTON S CHURCHILL

Mrs H. H. Asquith to WSC

11 December [1908]   Archerfield House
                                                                              Dirleton

Dear Winston,

I want you to do me a service. You told me in Scotland and indeed several times that the *Manchester Guardian* was a *most* important Liberal paper worth taking in in London – and not only you told me but several of our men when I sigh over the Tory press say Oh! you don't know the influence of the Liberal Press in the Country! The *Manchester Guardian* etc. Now lately the *Manchester Guardian* has been decrying my husband as leader and saying that they will take care that there is no future Asquith régime and all possible odious and *disloyal* things about their Prime Minister. Do you think a hint from you to the editor wd be a good thing?

When this Govt falls neither you nor I will be very well off! I don't care for myself so much but I do care for the children. Life is not easy without money. I don't however think the *Manchester Guardian* will make or mar any Ministry but it makes my blood boil that it shd choose this time when the Prime Minister has worked magnificently against fearful odds and has not quite succeeded to yap at him like a cur. Even the *Scotsman* has praised him! Talked of his courage and patience and remarkable tact; this from our strongest enemy is a strange contrast to what one of our few great organs writes. Do write and tell the editor that you and others of influence will not support and praise him if he tries to make mischief in a great party. I set no store by the Press but when some of its organs are supposed to represent a large section of our men like the *M Guardian* and it is pointed out to me as a sign of disloyalty, discontent and decadence in our ranks this naturally makes me unhappy.

I know you wd do *anything* for your chief and that you have power with the Press. So I confide my sorrows to you. My husband doesn't even see the *M Guardian* and tho' he cares what his colleagues and supporters think of him he doesn't care what the papers say of him at all. *I* do I confess. Write one line to cheer me up and tear this letter up.

Yrs

MARGOT ASQUITH

Mrs H. H. Asquith to WSC

11 December [1908]   Archerfield House

Dear Winston,

I wrote enclosed in bed in early morning when I was dead out of spirits but feel better after a cheering post. Edward Grey writes that H is in great form tho' he looks tired & that he has done magnificently & only shines out bigger in contrast to the curs that yap at his heels & AJB told Ly Betty[1] & Ly Frances that the higher he was tried the bigger he was so I feel a good deal cheered. The rawest occupant of a back bench is quite prepared to

---

[1] Lady Elizabeth Balfour (1867–1942), daughter of 1st Earl of Lytton, married 1887, Gerald, A. J. Balfour's brother, later 2nd Earl of Balfour.

teach Henry how to be Prime Minister! One of the reasons I felt low was I heard from my brother Edward that he had a horrid cough & looked fagged to death.

Write me one line, Yours with love to Clementine

MARGOT ASQUITH

Ly Frances is very amusing on the Lloyd George's Meeting! I rather hope no Cabinet Minister will speak for the ladies again.

Mrs H. H. Asquith to WSC

13 December 1908   Archerfield House

Thank you dear Winston for your letter. I daresay you are right – papers had better be left alone. I know [C. P.] Scott, I met him at Mentmore in old days.

I have had some interesting letters since I wrote to you wh have cheered me. Henry is in good form and tho' he has a cough is not the *least* depressed wh is always cheering.

I agree 'concerted action' is the thing: this is always the hardest part of a Gov and above *all* not to undertake such a lot at a time, it bores and fatigues.

You cd perhaps tell Lloyd George to tell Henry not to go on with the Welsh Church – it won't hurt Wales to go on a little longer and we have got more than enough to do. However you had better not! as it may be urged all the more. Lloyd George is charming and full of tact but he has not much judgement. I know many good critics but few good judges.

Do your best dear Winston to promote what you so truly say is wanted 'fuller consultation' and 'more concerted action'. Edward Grey is full of enthusiasm for H's conduct of affairs. He has the greatest of all qualities patience and insight but I wish he cd have a turn of luck in trade. Wishing you and Clementine all good luck I am

Yours ever

MARGOT ASQUITH

Memorandum by WSC

EXTRACT

11 December 1908   Board of Trade

. . . a system of public Labour Exchanges stands at the gateway to industrial security. It opens the way to all immediate practical reforms. It prevents no extension hereafter. We do not know what is the extent of unemployment, in what trades or in what places it is acute. We cannot trace its seasonal and cyclical variations. We cannot distinguish between the unemployed and the under-employed, between the worker and the loafer, between permanent contraction and passing depression. These Exchanges should be the Intelligence Department of labour. In constant touch with the employers on the one hand, and with the elementary and technical schools on the other, they should be able to 'place' numbers of boys in trades which offer a steady livelihood. Properly co-ordinated with the Statistical Department of the Board of Trade, the Labour Exchanges would furnish information over the whole field of material labour to workmen, employers, parents, Parliament, and the public at large, and the joint Advisory Committees of masters and workmen, by which they must be guided, would form another social link between capital and labour. . . .

Unemployment is primarily a question for the employers. Their responsibility is undoubted, their co-operation indispensable. There already exists all over the country a great recognition on the part of the employing class of their duties towards their workmen, and legislation is not required for the purpose of inculcating any new doctrine, but only to give concrete embodiment and scientific expression to a powerful impulse of just and humane endeavour. A system of compulsory contributory Unemployment Insurance associates directly for the first time the practical interest of the employer and the unemployed workmen. Both contribute to a common fund; both are concerned in its maintenance and its thrifty administration. Such a system will afford a powerful motive for the voluntary support of Labour Exchanges. It is in its wake, however, and as a direct consequence of it, that we may expect to see a more general adoption of those methods of collective regulation of labour hours which have already given a comforting element of security to the collier and the cotton operative. The admission of apprentices or the engagement of new workmen would, in the interests of the common fund, be scrutinized with far closer regard to the permanent average needs of the trade than at present. And in all the arrangements of business contracts some attention would always be paid to the possibility of sudden, wholesale discharges draining the fund or increasing the levy. On the other hand, the improved position of the workmen while employed in the insured trade would seem to give the employer increased power to exact efficient service. . . .

The two measures here proposed are intimately connected. The establishment of Labour Exchanges meets fluctuations and changes in the demand for labour with the minimum of delay and waste showing itself as unemployment. The insurance scheme maintains men when unemployment is inevitable, and involving as it does contributions from employers and workmen alike, supplies a direct motive for both parties to reduce unemployment by all the minor shifts and adjustments of daily life. The establishment of Labour Exchanges is necessary for the efficient working of the insurance scheme; for all foreign experiments have shown that a fund for insurance against unemployment needs to be protected against unnecessary or fraudulent claims by the power of notifying situations to men in receipt of benefit so soon as any situations become vacant. The insurance scheme, on the other hand, will be a lever of the most valuable kind to bring the Exchanges into successful operation; for the employers, interested in reducing friction in the passage of workmen from job to job, and in not drawing fresh men into a trade while any man already insured in it is standing idle, will turn naturally to the use of a Labour Exchange. The administration of the twin measures must become increasingly interwoven, as the draft Bill provides. Together they organize in due proportions the mobility and stability of labour.

WSC

Memorandum by Sidney Webb

EXTRACT

13 December 1908

. . . my wife and I had come to the conclusion that Compulsory Insurance was impracticable unless we had a Compulsory Labour Exchange; and that, along with a Compulsory Labour Exchange, Compulsory Insurance was unnecessary. It is, of course, no objection to the present scheme, that it makes provision only for a part – indeed, only a small part – of the Unemployed. But it is very relevant to consider that, even if it were adopted, *there would still have to be some public provision for at least half the men now on the Distress Registers.* Of the four classes into which we divide the Unemployed, the Compulsory Insurance Scheme provides only for one (Class II); and only partially for that. A merely Voluntary Labour Exchange is (as I argue above) insufficient even as a protection for the Insurance Scheme; and useless for Class III (The Underemployed). With a Compulsory Labour Exchange it would be possible to take in hand the decasualization of the Underemployed; and incidentally so facilitate the discovery of employment by Classes I and II as greatly to help their case. With a subsidy to Trade Unions (the Ghent system, now spreading so widely on the Continent), we think that Insurance may be left voluntary, and in Trade Union hands. *This gets over practically all the difficulties enumerated above.* The Trade Union can look after its own members. On the other hand, it compels the State to organize a system of Maintenance for those in destitution. This we have got already, first in the Poor Law, and now under the Unemployed Workman Act, *which cannot be dropped.* But it is so bad that it cannot be left as it is. Moreover it is indispensable (we think) to any grappling with the problem of Class III (the Underemployed); and the addition made to it by providing for the uninsured men of Class I (men of Discontinuous Employment) is not great.

Hence our proposal is: –

1 National Labour Exchange compulsory on Employers of casual labour as defined.

2 Trade Union Insurance, voluntary and optional, but encouraged by subvention of 50 per cent of the Out-of-Work payments the preceding year.

3 Decasualization of Labour by 'dovetailing' all short jobs and discontinuous employments.

4 Maintenance for such men as are in distress, and for whom the Labour Exchange cannot discover places; but under carefully graduated conditions.

5 For such men, who have not insured or saved, theirs will be

   (a) Compulsion to register at Labour Exchange, and accept jobs offered;

   (b) Home aliment for wife and family (superseding school-feeding)

   (c) Meals for the men; who must be compulsorily in attendance for *Training*; either

      (i) at Central Labour Depot (for labour at call); or

      (ii) Training Depots – day only; or

      (iii) Farm Colonies of various sorts; or

      (iv) Detention settlement; or

      (v) Employment Colony for crippled, defective or infirm Unemployable.

We cannot help thinking that the Compulsory Labour Exchange, plus subsidized Voluntary Insurance, and Maintenance under disciplinary Training for uninsured men in distress, solves more difficulties than Compulsory Insurance, plus a Voluntary Labour Exchange. And we cannot help believing that it will prove more difficult to get the employers and the Trade Unions to consent to Compulsory Insurance than to a Compulsory Labour Exchange.

WSC to Theodore Lumley

12 December 1908   Board of Trade

Copy

Dear Mr Lumley,

I enclose you my income tax return. Will you explain to me the basis on which the property tax is computed? I do not remember to have paid this in previous years.

My income for the year should be calculated as follows: – 1/3 of £7,400, i.e. £2,466 – being the last instalment of the profits arising from my *Life of Lord Randolph Churchill*.

This year, I have made as the result of my articles and book on *My African Journey* a profit of £2,000, from which must be deducted £800 which were the necessary expenses of my journey to Africa and an essential condition of the production of the work. This £1200 I propose to spread over 3 years, making £400 income taxable in the present year.

There is also a sum of £225 arising from a reprint of my novel *Savrola*. This I shd propose to pay wholly in the current year.

The total income is therefore £3,091, from which shd however be deducted the payments wh I have made of premium on my life policy; of these Messrs Nicholl Manisty can furnish you an account. They are about £200.

The assessment wd therefore appear to be approximately correct, and need not be disputed; but the Surveyor of Taxes shd be certified of two facts. 1) that the last instalment of my profits on my Father's Life is now completed; and 2) that the profits of *My African Journey* will be spread over 3 years at the rate of £400 a year.

Yours very truly
WSC

Sch A. Ppty Tax	250.		12 10 0	
D.			150 0 0	
House	@ 9d – 275		10 6 3	
Land Tax	@ 2d – 230		1 18 4	
			174 14 7	

Joseph Chamberlain to WSC

15 December 1908   Highbury

Dictated & private

My dear Churchill,

I have just received the copy of your book *My African Journey* and thank you for it. I have not yet had time to read it but I have no doubt I shall like it as I did very much the Life of your Father.

At the time I admired your decision to take a journey in some part or other of the possessions which were to come under your notice as Under Secretary for the Colonies.

The part you visited I also saw something of although I only spent some days in East Africa. At the time when I was at the Colonial Office East Africa was under the Foreign Office and I was not brought in close contact with this province. I saw, however, enough of it to be sure that there were many problems that deserved closer consideration and no doubt if I had remained I should have seen more of the country.

I was glad to hear of your promotion though I regret that you did not complete your work at the Colonial Office. I incline to think that our stay in these departments is shorter than it ought to be if the public good alone were considered. However, I hope your example of visiting the Colonies may be followed by others who may hereafter be in a responsible position at Downing Street.

I am, Yours truly
J. Chamberlain

WSC to Sir Edward Grey

24 December 1908   Board of Trade

Copy

My dear Grey,

You appear to have derived a completely false impression of my intentions, for which perhaps Marsh's note, (wh I have not seen) may be responsible. But I cannot believe that this is the kind of answer wh you would wish me to see as an expression of your views; for it would be entirely out of harmony with all that courtesy wh I have always valued so highly from you.

I am going to Paris on the 15th January for a week. I have some friends there & I shall use my own judgement as to who I see & what I say. Nothing

that I have ever said or done justifies in the slightest degree the assumption
that I should set myself up in competition with the Prime Minister & yourself
as 'an exponent of the views of HM Government in questions of foreign
policy', & the suggestion is in fact as in form not only undeserved but uncivil.

Yours sincly
WINSTON S. CHURCHILL

Sir Edward Grey to WSC

26 December 1908   Fallodon

Dear Churchill,

I saw a letter from Marsh, which I read at the time, but have not seen since.
My recollection is that you were going to Paris & wanted arrangements
made (through the Embassy I suppose) to see as many important people,
Ministers & Deputies, as possible while you were there.

I am told that Clemenceau[1] & Pichon,[2] who are the responsible men in
foreign politics in Paris, prefer not to discuss them except with 'the Prime
Ministers, Foreign Secretaries & Correspondents'. If this be so I think they
are right; to do otherwise adds greatly to the work & to the list of mis-
understandings.

For the rest you, especially you, cannot discuss politics with prominent
political people abroad as a private individual. Importance will be attached
to all you say, in such circumstances; it will certainly give rise to much talk
and probably to some reports in the French Press, which may be misleading.

I told Tyrrell[3] to say this to Marsh as my view.

You seem to have taken Tyrrell's letter as reflecting upon your *intentions*.
I see nothing of that in it.

I do see a warning about the unintentional, but in my view more than
probable, consequences of what it was understood that you proposed to do.

I think this still, but if we are to quarrel let it be about the substance &

---

[1] Georges Clemenceau (1841–1929), Prime Minister of France and Minister of the Interior
1906–9; Chamber of Deputies 1876–93 and 1902–29; Prime Minister and Minister of War
1917–20. In *Great Contemporaries* WSC wrote of him 'happy the nation which when its fate
quivers in the balance can find such a tyrant and such a champion'.

[2] Stephen Jean-Marie Pichon (1857–1933), French Foreign Minister 1906–11, and again
from November 1917 to January 1920; was French Minister in Peking at the time of the
Boxer rebellion.

[3] William George Tyrrell (1866–1947), Private Secretary to Sir Edward Grey 1907–15;
Permanent Under-Secretary of State for Foreign Affairs 1925–8; Ambassador in Paris 1928–
1934; President of the British Board of Film Censors 1935–41. Baron Tyrrell 1929; CB 1909;
KCMG 1913; KCVO 1919; GCMG 1925; PC 1928; GCB 1934.

not about the form of expression. Correspondence always leads to the latter; indeed there is a sentence in your letter, which I would take up as a challenge, if I thought it was intended.

So let us discuss the substance when we meet. I shall be in London on the 4th & 5th & perhaps again after that before you go to Paris.

Ys sincerely
E. GREY

WSC to Lord Crewe
(Crewe Papers)

25 December 1908   Blenheim

Secret

My dear Crewe,

Your 46715 of 23rd instant. Have you really made up your mind to have a delegation from South Africa over here to settle the Constitution? I confess at first sight I feel doubtful that you would find this a help. The delegates will come absolutely on their trial before S. Africa not to budge an inch to home pressure. Their pressure & that of the native delegations will triple Parliamentary interest & agitation, & will give the impression to all our wildest folk that HMG is the arbiter of the situation. We are not. We have great influence; but power has passed. I am quite ready to be convinced – but my feeling is strong on first reading the last papers that this change of venue will multiply the difficulties of a very complex affair.

My view is – have it all settled for good or ill in S. Africa for S. Africa by S. Africans: & then confront Parliament with a complete, imposing and irrevocable scheme to ratify or disown. There is the path of safety & simplicity.

Yours vy sincerely
WINSTON S. CHURCHILL

Lord Crewe to WSC
(Crewe Papers)

29 December 1908   Crewe Hall
Confidential

Copy

My dear Winston,

The SA position is one of some difficulty, and I should like you to realize how matters stand. The original idea was that the discussions on the spot would last all through 1909, and that the conclusion would be reached some time in the following year. But the wheels have been so much greased that it is by now contemplated that the SA Parliaments will ratify the resolutions of the Convention during the early summer of this next year, that a drafting Commission should then come over here to settle the terms of the Act, and that we should pass it in an autumn session – a delightful prospect for us. You will see what this means. Once the SA Parliaments have agreed to the terms, no modification of principle will be possible, and the drafting will be lawyers' work, nothing more. It is necessary, therefore, to settle beforehand what safeguards for the Protectorates, either for deferred inclusion, or in relation to restrictions on land-exploiting, importation of liquor etc, we regard as crucial. This could of course be done through Selborne, which is what he would like. But he is rather a dangerous plenipotentiary, with all his industry and enthusiasm. He is intensely obstinate, and his ideas run away with him. If you look carefully at the last papers you will see that we are approaching a position in which we might be made nominally liable for a breakdown of the whole project of Union. It may really go off on other questions, but the blame would be laid on us. We must not find ourselves in Lord Carnarvon's silly plight.[1] Now we have never adopted Selborne's plan of a permanent independent Commission, though we have authorized him to discuss it unofficially, and I believe it would be a good solution in itself. In a modified form the Convention have taken it, but rather grudgingly, and it does not look as if it would be commended *con amore* to the Parliaments. To drop it now would be to throw over Selborne entirely, with the possibility of his appearing as the defender of native rights against us, who are willing to throw them to the wolves. I can see an excellent Tory–Radical combination formed out of this. Consequently it seems to me the best thing to talk the matter over, if possible, with Selborne and the African Representatives, while I do not dread, but rather welcome, a certain pressure of English opinion being put on the latter. The black deputation must come in any case, as the Basutos have already formally asked to be allowed to lay their case before the King, and they cannot be refused.

Personally, though it is not necessary to say so now, I should not stand out for the Commission in the last resort, and shall be content if we can get the restrictive clauses into the constitution.

Forgive me for troubling you with this long letter, but I shall be glad if you will send me any further observations that occur to you.

With cordial good wishes for the New Year, for you both,

Ever yours
[CREWE]

---

[1] Lord Carnarvon, Disraeli's Colonial Secretary, made an unsuccessful attempt in the 1870s to encourage South African confederation.

WSC to H. H. Asquith

26 December 1908 [Blenheim]

Copy

Private

Dear Prime Minister,

I learn that Lansdowne in private utterly scouts the suggestion that the Lords will reject the Budget Bill, & this confirms Beach's interesting speech in Gloucestershire ten days ago. On this assumption you will I presume be making your plans for two more complete sessions.

After the Budget Statement Insurance schemes will be in the air. I don't think I could press my Unemployment Insurance plan until Lloyd George has found a way of dealing with infirmity or (wh is possible) has found that there is no way. The Insurance policy must I feel be presented as a whole; for it would never do to exact contributions from masters & men in successive layers. One shot must suffice. I therefore would desire to begin with a simple project of Labour Exchanges wh might be announced in the King's speech, & wh to prevent overlapping of machinery would be framed so as subsequently to support the Unemployment Insurance Scheme. The Bill would either be introduced in two parts, the second of wh (Unemployment Insurance) would have blank schedules & not be immediately proceeded with, or a memorandum would explain in general terms the second & complementary part. The negotiations & conferences with the interests affected, wh are essential to the smooth development of such a scheme could then take place during the autumn of 1909, and the whole policy could receive legislative form in 1910 either as one half of a big Infirmity Insurance Bill or (if that fails) as the second part of the Labour Exchange Bill. Nothing will in fact be lost by getting the Labour Exchanges under way & everything will be gained by the opportunities for discussion and bargaining with the trades and workmen specially concerned. This is the course of action wh Lloyd George and I after much debating think best, and I should like to know what view you take upon it.

The position of the Railways at the present moment requires attention. No less than six agreements of pooling or amalgamation have been announced & we must declare a policy in regard to them. There is no doubt that railway development has practically reached its conclusion in Great Britain; all the main lines have been constructed, doubled, or quadrupled. The network is complete. At the same time the old competition alike with its waste and its safeguards is going to stop short. In its place has come combination and what we have to do & do quickly is to devise some form of

State Control of these amalgamations wh will secure the interest of the trading public.

I am feeling my way towards a considerable policy in this, wh might possibly be ripe for presentation in the shape of a big Railway Bill during 1910. It would be of immense assistance to me if I could have some expression of your general views in these matters.

I feel we must look ahead and make bold concerted plans for the next two years. I look to the large measures of Finance and Unemployment wh are pending to dignify & justify our retention of office. I believe that there is an impressive social policy to be unfolded wh would pass ponderously through both Houses and leave an abiding mark on national history. I care personally and I think the country cares far more about these issues than about mere political change; & anyhow I am confident that there is a great work to be done & that we are the men to do it.

I shall be in London almost continuously from Jan 5 working at Labour Exchanges and Sweated Trades & I hope to have these two bills fit for the Cabinet when we meet again. Perhaps you will let me write to you later as these develop.

Ivor Guest (who is here) has finished his Afforestation Commission report. It is a first class document and will serve as an admirable basis for action. I have told him to send you an early copy. It will well repay a morning's study.

With good wishes for the New Year,

> I remain Yours vy sincerely
> WINSTON S. CHURCHILL

H. H. Asquith to WSC

27 December 1908   Archerfield House

Private

My Dear Winston,

I don't know what Kearley's decision will be, but in the event of his going from the Board of Trade I have been considering who would be his successor.

On the whole I think that Jack [H. J.] Tennant – my brother-in-law – is the right man. He deserves recognition having been 14 years in the House, and (as most people thought) rather hardly treated in being left out when the Govt was formed.

He has a very direct & intimate knowledge of labour questions. He has been Chairman of a number of Home Office departmental Committees, & in these matters has advanced views. His wife[1] is in my opinion far the most *capable* of the women who have given their brains and lives to industrial reform. He is further quite a reasonably good speaker, is on the Chairman's panel for Select Committees, & being a rich man, with business training & connections, would be *persona grata* (or *gratior* than some others) to the City & to Capital.

Masterman is young, with no special knowledge of these matters, & should for the present stay where he is. R. Rea[2] is an admirable economist but an unimpressive Parliamentary figure, and much junior in H of C standing to Tennant.

I do not believe you could do better, but I shall be glad to hear what you say.

Best wishes for all good things both to yourself & your wife.

Yrs always

H. H. ASQUITH

WSC to H. H. Asquith

29 December 1908　　　　　　　　　　　　　　　　　Board of Trade

Copy

My dear Prime Minister,

The appointment you have in mind seems to me to be a very good one. It will give me great pleasure to work with Tennant, whom I like & of whose ability, activity, & Parliamentary standing there can be no doubt. He has much more force than Russell Rea, & there are besides disadvantages in bestowing under-secretaryships upon men at the end of their careers, who are not likely to be able to use that invaluable experience in more responsible positions later on. A Privy Councillorship would seem more appropriate to Russell Rea, & I think that honour has been merited by his connection with two of the principal measures of the year.

Assuming that Kearley accepts (of which I think there can be little doubt) I should like to have Tennant as soon as possible. He ought certainly to be in the Board of Trade before the end of this month, if he is to get a good grip

---

[1] May Tennant (1869–1946), second wife of H. J. Tennant; Assistant Commissioner to Royal Commission on Labour; Inspector of Factories; Chief Adviser on Women's Welfare, Ministry of Munitions; Director of Women's Department National Service.

[2] Russell Rea (1846–1916), Liberal MP for Gloucester 1900–10; for South Shields 1910–1916; Chairman of Departmental Committee investigating Eight Hour Day for Miners; Chairman of Joint Committee on the Port of London Bill; PC 1909.

of the legislation upon which we are working. The Chairmanship of the Port of London could be announced whenever convenient.

I send you herewith the report of the Trade Unionists who went to Germany to study Insurance & Labour Exchanges. Shackleton gave it to me ten days ago in order that we might revise it from the point of view of accuracy.

I have been revolving many things during these few days of tranquillity & I feel impelled to state to you the conviction that has for a long time past been forming in my mind. There is a tremendous policy in Social Organisation. The need is urgent & the moment ripe. Germany with a harder climate and far less accumulated wealth has managed to establish tolerable basic conditions for her people. She is organised not only for war, but for peace. We are organised for nothing except party politics. The Minister who will apply to this country the successful experiences of Germany in social organisation may or may not be supported at the polls, but he will at least have left a memorial which time will not deface of his administration. It is impossible to under-pin the existing voluntary agencies by a comprehensive system – necessarily at a lower level – of state action. We have at least two years. We have the miseries which this winter is inflicting upon the poorer classes to back us. And oddly enough the very class of legislation which is required is just the kind the House of Lords will not dare to oppose. The expenditure of less than ten millions a year, not upon relief, but upon machinery, & thrift-stimuli would make England a different country for the poor. And I believe that once the nation begins to feel the momentum of these large designs, it will range itself at first with breathless interest & afterwards in solid support behind the shoulder of the Government. Here are the steps as I see them.

1. Labour Exchanges & Unemployed Insurance:
2. National Infirmity Insurance etc:
3. Special Expansive State Industries – Afforestation – Roads:
4. Modernised Poor Law i.e. classification:
5. Railway Amalgamation with State Control and guarantee:
6. Education compulsory till 17.

I believe there is not one of these things that cannot be carried & carried triumphantly & that they would not only benefit the state but fortify the party. But how much better to fail in such noble efforts, than to perish by slow paralysis or windy agitation.

I say – thrust a big slice of Bismarkianism over the whole underside of our industrial system, & await the consequences whatever they may be with a good conscience.

Pray forgive the vehemence and frankness of this letter. I would not write it to you did I not feel confident you would receive it in an equal mood of earnestness.

Yours vy sincerely
WINSTON S. CHURCHILL

Herbert Gladstone to WSC

18 December 1908   9 Buckingham Gate

Private

My dear Winston,

Last July I saw George Askwith KC[1] on the Sweating question. He knows more about the possibilities of a Wages Bd than any man alive in this country. I hope you will consult him. You will find that there is much emotional enthusiasm of no use for practical suggestion but wh is a great driving force – earnest, persuasive & determined – wh can be made use of as such. Askwith is a rare combination of enthusiasm & practical knowledge.

The creation of public opinion has been largely due to the anti-sweating League, headed by G. Cadbury[2] & Gardiner[3] of the D.N. [Daily News]. I venture to hope you will take them into council for all they are worth. The Sec[y] is a little man of energy who knows the ropes of the public movement & it will be worth your while to see him. On the other side is Ramsay MacDonald whose opposition to the minimum wage has long ago reached the personal stage. But he stands alone among his fellows.

Yrs always
H. J. GLADSTONE

I did not mislead you when I told you we were going to hold on to the Eight Hours Bill at a time when it had hardly a friend – not one in the Cabinet excepting yourself!

---

[1] George Ranken Askwith (1846–1942), Assistant Secretary Board of Trade (Railways) 1907; Comptroller General Commercial and Statistical Depts, Board of Trade 1909; Chief Industrial Commissioner 1911–19; Chairman of the Industrial Council 1912–13; Vice-President Federation of British Industries 1913; Chairman of Committee on Production under the Munitions of War Acts 1915–17; KC 1908; CB 1909; KCB 1911; Baron Askwith 1919. He was arbitrator in many trade disputes, was chairman of the Monotype Corporation, and author of *Industrial Problems and Disputes*, 1920, and *Lord James of Hereford*, 1930.

[2] George Cadbury (1839–1922), Quaker cocoa manufacturer and philanthropist; with his brother, took over their father's factory in 1860s which they moved to Bourneville in 1879, where Cadbury carried out his experiments in housing and town planning; bought the *Daily News* in 1900.

[3] Alfred George Gardiner (1865–1946), editor of *Daily News* 1902–19; in 1923 he published a biography of George Cadbury. A brilliant essayist, he published studies of WSC in both *Prophets, Priests and Kings* (1908), and *Pillars of Society* (1916).

WSC to Herbert Gladstone
(*Herbert Gladstone Papers*)

30 December 1908   Board of Trade

Private

My dear Herbert,

This is the first time I have been able to thank you for your letter about Sweated Trades. All your recommendations are being followed as to persons fit for consultation. I shall be working in London continuously from 5th Jany onwards, & hope to have definite proposals before Cabinets begin. Meanwhile we will keep in touch with HO so as to make adjustments & cooperation easy later.

The Mines 8 Hours Act is a vy substantial piece of work: & I heartily congratulate you on its achievement. I was glad indeed to be able to wind up the debate on the second reading of a Bill for wh my father always cared so much. I have just got a copy of my speech wh has been translated into French, & I must say it reads quite improvingly in that language. With all good wishes for the New Year from both of us to both of you.

WINSTON S CHURCHILL

WSC to Lord Crewe

3 January 1909   Board of Trade

Confidential

Copy

My dear Crewe,

I have never thought much of Selborne's plan of a Commission to stand between the Natives and a South African Parliament. I do not go so far as to say that a people can never protect itself against itself by delegation to a statutory body of its own creation; for I think they can to a very great extent especially when parties are healthily balanced. But a Commission imposed upon SA by outside pressure, unsupported by any party or section in the new legislature, cannot have any real resisting power, and must collapse in the face of any serious resolve on the part of the white population.

The only securities which the natives have are first of all our power to delay by a variety of methods the handing over of the Protectorates. I have always been in favour of this *Fabius Cunctator* game as simple, obvious, safe and practical; and I am still. In my view five or six years is a period of very great importance in S. African history just now; and a delay of five years would make many problems which now seem insoluble obsolete. Within that period two things will happen: the Government of United SA will take a broader and calmer view of native questions because it will be above local panics and conscious of its strength; secondly – and this is the real security – the natives are gaining in education, civilisation and influence so rapidly that they will be far more capable – apart from force altogether – of maintaining their rights, and making their own bargain. My view is therefore what it was when we met at Cabinet Committee, that we should assert our intention to hand over the Protectorates, should frame in general terms the necessary adhesion or inclusion clauses – the more SA will swallow the better for H of C – and should then play steadily for time with all the cards in our hand.

Now so far I do not see any divergence of view between us here, or between the Colonial Office and Selborne, except that he has hustled the Convention into accepting his Commission plan as a part of the inclusion clauses and has ruffled their feathers in doing so. There is not any great harm in this, indeed from some points of view it is an advantage. But I wonder what the local Parliaments will say to it; and I should not be surprised if all but that is ratified. I agree however with you that we cannot drop it now, and since it is to go to those local Parliaments upon the authority of the Convention and not directly from us, we do not run much risk ourselves.

But where I feel total misgiving is in the transference of this affair to British soil. Selborne will obey instructions however unpalatable like a soldier, as I know from past experience. No one else has the knowledge of or the influence upon South African politics and politicians which this very able and experienced Minister and Administrator has acquired in four stormy years. But further, any arrangement made in Africa will be made with real plenipotentiaries on the other side – Botha, Smuts, Merriman, Jameson, &c can in fact swing SA to their decisions. A mere delegation over here would be tied and powerless except within rigidly prescribed limits; and any arrangement come to over here would be suspect from one end of SA to the other. Therefore I feel that from the standpoint of trying to get as much as we can for the natives in the way of securities South Africa is the best place and Selborne is the best man to drive the bargain.

But on the other hand look at the H of C. There is only one way to steer this question through that assembly. No solution that SA can consent to on native affairs will be satisfactory to the H of C. On the other hand the Liberal party is much attracted by the idea of unification and reconciliation, and fully alive to the credit which we derive from its achievement. The horse will draw the cart, if both are tied together. But do not let them get separated. Confront Parliament with a complete scheme, majestic, beneficent, far-reaching. Prove to them that you have done your best for the natives. Console them by assurances that you have no immediate intention of handing over the Protectorates – on the contrary that you intend to wait and watch. Invite them to ratify or reject – and they will acclaim your settlement, although they cannot be any more a party to it *before* its announcement than they were to the Transvaal Constitution, or than they are to Foreign Treaties. It would be much better for you to go out yourself than to change the venue of these negotiations to London.

You are good enough to encourage this expression of my opinion which is given in all sincerity and with conviction, but with a full sense of the fallibility of one's own judgment, especially in regard to matters which one does not watch from day to day with direct personal responsibility.

Ever yours
WINSTON S. CHURCHILL

Sidney Webb to WSC

4 January 1909   41 Grosvenor Road

Dear Mr Churchill,

I am taking the liberty of sending you *in proof*, the two final chapters of Mrs Webb's *Minority Report for the Poor Law Commission* – as to which kindly preserve strict confidence for the next few weeks, because the Commission makes rather a fuss about it.

But as these chapters give, first our diagnosis of the Unemployed today, and secondly, our complete plan, I think you would like to see them at once.

Naturally, my wife has had the task of carrying with her, in the proposals, the two Labour Men on the Commission; & there *may* yet have to be modifications in detail.

On the whole, however, I think that the plan as now stated is one in which I thoroughly believe, both as an economist & as a politician.

Will you kindly *return* these proofs when you have looked at them?

Yours very truly
SIDNEY WEBB

A. P. Watt to WSC

5 January 1909   Hastings House

Dear Mr Churchill,

Thank you for your letter of the 2nd inst. Since writing to you the other day, I have heard from Messrs Hodder & Stoughton that they are about to open a branch in New York; to be more accurate, they have, I understand, acquired an interest in an American business which will be more or less affiliated with their own. They seem anxious to have the American rights of *My African Journey* and are prepared to offer us a royalty of 15% of the American nominal selling price rising to 20% after the sale of 5000 copies.

Taking all the circumstances into consideration, I am inclined to advise you to accept this offer: (it is, of course, rather better than that we have got from Messrs Appleton) especially as since last I wrote to you Messrs Scribner and Messrs Macmillan, to whom the book was then on offer, have written that they are unable to make me any proposal regarding it.

I am, dear Mr Churchill
Yours sincerely
A. P. WATT

Note by Edward Marsh:

Ansd; inclined to accept but thinks decidedly they shd make advance, if only £100.

A. P. Watt to WSC

8 January 1909   Hastings House

Dear Mr Churchill,

Since receiving your letter of the 6th, I have had another interview with Mr Hodder Williams but I regret to say that I was quite unable to get him to agree to pay any sum in advance and on account of royalties on the sales of the American edition of *My African Journey*. I don't think it likely that we shall now get a better offer than Messrs Hodder & Stoughton's, and under these circumstances I shall be glad in due course to hear that you have decided to accept it.

I am, dear Mr Churchill
Yours sincerely
A. P. WATT

*   *   *   *   *

Two controversies dominated the politics of 1909. The first was over the Naval Estimates. The Chancellor of the Exchequer, David Lloyd George, and Churchill were initially prepared to budget for four Dreadnoughts, but the Admiralty under Reginald McKenna asked for six. In early February Churchill and Lloyd George indicated their willingness to make preparations for the laying down of two ships at the start of the financial year 1910–11, but by that time the Board of Admiralty had come to the conclusion that six ships in 1909 would be needed in order to maintain British security. Accordingly, the Admiralty hinted at the desirability of having eight ships. In March the Cabinet finally decided to accept four ships unconditionally, and to allow preparations to be put in hand for four more. In the Naval Estimates the Government failed to make clear whether the extra ships would be part of 1909–10 Programme or would be laid down in subsequent years. This ambiguity, although it enabled Cabinet unity to be preserved in the critical days of February and March, also enabled the Conservatives, unashamedly informed by Fisher, to demand a programme of eight ships in the year. The 'We want eight and we won't wait' campaign, and the news that Austria-Hungary and Italy were each planning to build Dreadnoughts, finally forced the Cabinet's reluctant hand.

The second controversy was over Lloyd George's Finance Bill, introduced on April 29. It proposed an increase in Death Duties and increased taxation on spirits, tobacco, motor cars and petrol. But it was his new land taxes which were most vehemently opposed, particularly by the landed Peers. After considerable amendment, the Bill passed the House of Commons on November 5, but was thrown out by the House of Lords on November 30. The struggle between the Commons and Lords over the control of Government finances was not resolved until 1911 when the Parliament Bill was passed.

H. H. Asquith to WSC

11 January 1909   Archerfield House

Private

My dear Winston,

The changes at the Board of Trade appear to be well received.[1]

I have thought on your two letters, & took the opportunity of discussing their main points with Edward Grey, Haldane, & Gladstone, who were all here together last week.

I am heartily at one with you as to the supreme importance of pressing on with our social proposals, particularly as they affect the various aspects

[1] The appointment of H. J. Tennant as WSC's Parliamentary Secretary had just been announced.

of the problems of Unemployment – e.g. Labour Exchanges, Boy Labour, Insurance.

It may as you say, in view of the possibility of grappling with the much more complicated question of invalidity, become necessary to postpone Insurance to another session. I should regret this, but I quite see that it may be inevitable.

In the meantime I trust you will push on with all the schemes of which your department is the natural parent.

Yours always

HHA

I have not yet had time to read afforestation, but I have made some progress with the Poor Law Report.

WSC to H. H. Asquith

12 January 1909   Board of Trade

Private

Copy

My dear Prime Minister,

I am delighted to get your letter. The group of appointments announced on Mon have been extremely well received. I took a little trouble with the 'Keynote' press beforehand & it was adequately repaid.

Now I have had a vy fruitful week here. We have had repeated Conferences upon Sweating, Labour Exchange, Railway policy,[1] & Electric Supply. I shall be ready to bring sweating before the Cabinet whenever you wish. We have hammered out a plan wh we all think sound & workable & wh we expect will unite all favourable forces. I send you herewith the heads in a form prepared by Ll Smith. The mainspring consists in the 3 paid permanent members, common to all the Board in any trade – (& so far as they will go, over the whole area) who are to grip, guide & coordinate the operations of local Wages boards. The characteristic is the variety of treatment with wh it will be possible to meet the circs of different trades & the successive steps wh are necessary before actual compulsion is applied. You will see running through this organisn the same idea wh the Germans call 'Paritätisch' – joint & equal representn of masters & men plus the skilled permanent impartial element. This is the principle of the new Arbitrn

[1] The Railway Conference was convened by Lloyd George early in 1908, and reported in May 1909. It investigated the machinery for the adjudication of railway complaints, 'Owner's risk' traffic, siding agreements, and the organization of continental railways.

Court lately set up, & it will also be the root principle of the Labour Exchanges & Unemployed Insurance Committees. There is nothing new abt L Exchanges except that we are wondering whether the machinery of Wages Bds cannot be dovetailed into them in some sort of way for the sake of economy & unity.

I had a visit from Allerton, Claud Hamilton[1] & Alex Henderson[2] abt their amalgamation – (GNR – GER – GCR) a big thing – half England! They are prepared to give a good deal, & I have asked a no of questions wh they are now considering. Up to the present I think this is the best policy – Read their Bill a second time: send it to a Committee. Take power (if legally practicable) to have B T represented by counsel before Comee. Prescribe in general terms on 2nd Reading the condns wh we regard as necessary to secure an equitable division of advantages between the traders, the employees & the public.

In Committee try to stamp this Bill (the 1st & biggest of all the amalgamns to come to Parlt) with a model form applicable to the other pooling arrangements & potential amalgamns. Then if a satisfactory form is reached, squeeze, encourage & finally force the other amalgamns to seek Parlt sanction & submit themselves to the same safeguards.[3]

All this will in no way conflict with but will greatly aid larger & more general amalgamns later. But of that of course nothing need yet be said.

You will remember the Electric Bills last session. I am pledged to introduce a little tiny sweeping up bill in respect to the smaller group of Companies wh is generally agreed with all parties & follows naturally from what has been done. I propose now to finish the job of centralising all electrical supply in the LCC of 1931 [sic]; by including in this little bill a provision transferring at a stroke *sans phrase et sans dédommagement* all the existing Boro undertakings at the same time. This is most desirable, & will bring our own people squarely into line upon an issue in wh all the scientific & economic arguments are on our side.[4]

I have also two little twin Insurance bills – one to stop pure gambling in P.P.I. [Policy Proof of Interest] Insurance policies, the other to extend to Fire, Accident & Endowment Insurance the same provisions as regards £20,000 deposit & inspection of a/cs wh have proved so beneficial in regard

[1] Lord Claud Hamilton (1843–1925), second son of 1st Duke of Abercorn, Conservative MP for Londonderry 1865–8; King's Lynn 1869–80; Liverpool 1880–8; South Kensington 1910–18; Chairman of the Great Eastern Railway; PC 1917.

[2] Sir Alexander Henderson (1850–1934), Chairman Great Central Railway; Liberal Unionist MP 1898–1906, 1913–16; baronet 1902; Baron 1916; CH 1917.

[3] A Departmental Committee on Railway Amalgamations and Agreements was set up in June 1909.

[4] An Electric Lighting Act was passed in 1909, extending the powers of the Board of Trade to grant facilities to Local Authorities and Electricity Companies.

to Life Cos.[1] We are bringing the interests concerned along with us gently – but by the ear.

I trust you will be able to find a place for this numerous progeny. I plead on their behalf that many of them are small, & all are well behaved & have been brought up properly.

I am to speak at B'ham on Wed & at Leicester on Thurs & have taken a deal of pains to be at once suggestive & discreet. The general situation does not easily lend itself to a fighting speech. Yet we exist on controversy!

I hope the Cabinets will not fall on the 4th or 5th as I am bound to Newcastle. They are my only filled days, & were gone three months ago.

Yours vy sincerely
WSC

WSC to H. W. Massingham

22 January 1909   22 Carlton House Terrace

Private & Confidential

Copy

My dear Massingham,
Your argument will remain incomplete if you exclude unpleasant facts from its scope.

The Licensing Bill was unpopular throughout the English constituencies, and the Lords who always act upon excellent caucus information, gained strength with the Electorate by rejecting it.[2]

There is no strong feeling against the Lords at the present time outside the regular political classes upon our side. I understand that the Party agents which were lately consulted were only of one opinion – that it would be impossible to choose a worse issue or a worse time.

To attack the Lords upon the constitutional question alone is to court defeat. The constitutional attack, however vigorous, must be backed by some substantial political or social demand which the majority of the nation mean to have and which the Lords cannot or will not give. Unless or until that conjunction is created – and I am by no means sure it cannot be created – a Lords' Reform Bill would only be a forlorn prelude to a disastrous election.

The Education Bill of 1906 was not dissimilar in its circumstances. But

---

[1] Passed as the Marine Insurance (Gambling Policies) Act, and the Assurance Companies Act 1909.
[2] The Licensing Bill of 1908 was designed to reduce the number of licensed houses by basing them on a fixed ratio to local population.

there at least the constitutional issue was presented in all its strength – a new Parliament, a Government with unimpaired prestige, above all the practical certainty of a majority after an appeal. Both Lloyd George and I were willing to fight in January 1907, but the Cabinet and CB took another view; and I have always understood that you acquiesced in that view. Now the circumstances have vastly changed; and I do not perceive a single argument for that course except the Chinese – that you should commit suicide on the doorstep of the man who has wronged you.

I am where I was when I wrote you 'The Untrodden Paths of Politics'. For the first time some of those with whom for a long time you have liked to work, have got some power. Very large plans are being industriously and laboriously shaped. They will certainly be brought forward. They may even acquire a national momentum. Two complete Sessions will be needed to produce them and to finance them. They are worth doing for their own sake, whatever the upshot. I do not think the Lords will interfere with any of them. I am sure they cannot do so without coming near to creating that conjunction of forces which is most dangerous to them. Anyhow I would back them cheerfully with our political existence.

There is no reason why controversial political bills should not meanwhile move forward to the climax *together* – like a volley of grapeshot – in the last weeks of 1910. Then indeed – life or death, but with a chance of victory; and for something worthy of the effort and the risk.

You ought to be with us in all this.

[WINSTON S. CHURCHILL]

G. E. Buckle to WSC

EXTRACT

25 January 1909 Printing House Square

Private

My dear Churchill,

. . . If you contemplate making an important speech, dealing with fresh matter, we should be glad to give a good report such as we accorded to your last two speeches. But only you, not we, can tell.

If you do make a prepared speech, it wd help us if you were as on the last occasion to send me your notes.

Yours sincerely

G. E. BUCKLE

Cabinet Memorandum by WSC

EXTRACT

26 January 1909

Confidential

I propose, with the concurrence of my colleagues, to introduce a Bill during the coming Session for the establishment of Trade Boards for industries in which the evils known as 'sweating' largely prevail.[1]

I understand from the Home Secretary that the Home Office would prefer that any measure on this subject should be in charge of the Board of Trade, feeling that the establishment of Trade Boards is more akin to a development of the province of Boards of Arbitration than an extension of the Factory Acts, and that their existing machinery and inspecting staff are not adapted for the supervision of the working of such a measure.

The whole subject has been carefully considered by the Board of Trade, in consultation with the Home Office and other experts, and an outline of a proposed Bill has been prepared.

The Bill would extend both to factory workers and home workers engaged in specified 'sweated' trades or to particular classes of work-people engaged in such trades, with power to add to the list. It would set up Trade Boards, both central and local, including a representative element, consisting of employers and work-people in equal numbers, and three appointed paid members, who would be unconnected with the trade and whose presence on all the Boards in any one trade would secure uniformity of policy. The

[1] These proposals were originally recommended by Sir Thomas Whittaker's Select Committee on Homework in 1908.

Boards would be charged with a variety of duties in addition to the fixing of minimum wages, and I understand that the Home Office expect to derive much advantage from their assistance in respect to such matters as truck, particulars, out-workers, &c.

Decisions of the Trade Boards fixing minimum rates will at once become compulsory on holders of public contracts, and will be binding on other employers in the absence of an express agreement to the contrary. After a delay of a year, it would be open to a Trade Board to apply to the Board of Trade to make the decisions compulsory on all employers, but before making such an order, the Board will have to be satisfied that the decisions are in harmony with the predominant opinion in the trade, and only resisted by a comparatively small section of the less reasonable employers. . . .

The total cost of the scheme would have to be defrayed out of Imperial funds, there being no other source available. I do not, however, anticipate an annual expenditure of more than about £5,000 a-year during the first few years, including salaries of appointed members, allowances to representative members, travelling investigations, secretarial assistance, and central office, but not cost of local accommodation. Eventually the cost will of course depend on the success and extension of the scheme, but it is unlikely that the cost will ever rise above £10,000 a-year at the outside.

WSC to Herbert Gladstone
(*Herbert Gladstone Papers*)

28 January [1909]   Board of Trade

Private

My dear Herbert,
    Do *please* give Edgar Lafone the vacant Chief Constableship in the Metropolitan Police, & gladden the heart of

Yours vy sincerely
WINSTON S CHURCHILL

Memorandum by WSC

EXTRACT

3 February 1909   Board of Trade

    Employment and trade generally in the United Kingdom in 1908 suffered from a serious depression, and, except in coal and iron mining and the tinplate trade, the depression extended to all important branches of industry. The foreign trade of the country appears to have suffered to a less extent than the home trade, as, although imports and exports were considerably less in value than in 1907, they were about the same as in 1906, and greater than in any previous year. On the other hand, the proportion of trade unionists returned as unemployed was greater than in any year since 1886, and other evidences of depression are afforded by a decline in the goods receipts of the railways, and in the bankers' clearances through the London and provincial clearing houses, and increases in the amount of pauperism, and the number of failures of traders.

As is usual in a 'critical' year, i.e., a year immediately following a change in the general tendency of trade and employment, the number of persons involved in trade disputes was high. Wages generally declined, though not, except in the coal-mining industry, to any great extent.

With declining wages and diminished employment, the unfavourable circumstances of the working classes have been further aggravated by an increase in the retail prices of workmen's food.

Signs, however, are not wanting that the general depression has reached, or nearly reached, its worst, and that conditions may soon be expected to improve. An increase in the number of pig-iron furnaces in blast and a slight check to the decline in the imports of raw materials are among some of the indications of an improvement, which, however, are as yet slight and uncertain.

A similar depression has also been felt in Germany and the United States, though in the former country the amount of actual unemployment has been lessened and distress mitigated by the prosperity of German agriculture, which found employment for a certain number of persons previously engaged in manufacturing industries. The fact that United States exports declined less than those of the United Kingdom, which has caused some comment, is, of course, due mainly to the forced exports of the earlier part of the year, necessitated by the financial crisis of the previous autumn and the consequent demand for gold. . . .

Rates of wages at the end of 1907 stood at a higher level than at the end of any year since these statistics were first recorded by the Department (1893). Further advances in wages took place during January and February 1908, based in the majority of cases upon prices and conditions which had ruled in 1907, but since then the general movement has been downwards. Having regard, however, to the bad state of employment in most of the principal industries, the amount of the fall has not been so great as might have been expected, and a further fall is anticipated. The net result of all the changes in rates of wages taking effect during the year is a reduction computed at £61,897 per week, and the general level of wages remains higher than at the end of any of the years 1893–1907, with the exception of 1907.

The number of workpeople whose rates of wages were changed during 1908 was 908,627 of whom 63,802 received net advances amounting to £4,589 per week and 465,035 sustained net decreases amounting to £66,486 per week. The remaining 379,790 had upward and downward changes which left their wages at the same level at the end as at the beginning of the year. In 1907, 1,233,739 workpeople had their wages changed, the net result being an increase of £200,820 per week. The year 1906 was also a year of rising wages, but it was preceded by five years of falling wages, which again were preceded by five years of rising wages. For the whole period 1896–1908 the net result of all the changes in wages reported is an increase of about £397,000 per week. It should be understood that these figures relate to changes in rates of wages as distinct from changes in earnings caused by fluctuations of employment or altered conditions of work. The figures are also exclusive of changes in certain groups of trades, in which the numbers affected are not known, and also those affecting police and Government employees, the particulars respecting these two latter groups for 1908 not yet being available. The numbers employed in industries to which the statistics apply are about nine millions. . . .

The industry in which rates of wages are subject to by far the greatest fluctuations is coal mining. During 1908 the reduction in coal-miners' wages accounted for three-fourths of the amount of the total reduction in the year, and miners in every coal-field were affected, with the exception of those in South Wales. The changes resulted in net reductions in all the coal-fields affected except Lancashire, Yorkshire, and the Midlands, and Bristol and Radstock, where upward and downward changes left miners' wages at the same level at the end as at the beginning of the year. The total number in the coal-mining industry whose wages were changed was over 660,000, and the amount of the net reduction in weekly wages, £47,000.

As regards the other trades, the principal net decreases affected 40,000 workpeople in shipyards on the North-east Coast and the Clyde, 16,000 workpeople in engineering works on the North-east Coast, and 17,000 blast-furnacemen and 50,000 iron and steel workers in the principal centres.

*   *   *   *   *

H. H. Asquith to WSC

17 February 1909   10 Downing Street

Private

Dear Winston,

Barnes[1] is apparently to move his amendment to-day. Burns will of course be prepared to meet any criticisms on his department & on the general outlook. But I think it would be well that you shd be ready – without of course disclosing particulars – to dispel the impression that our future legislation is to be a hand to mouth affair, or to be confined to the Bills actually announced in the Speech.

Yrs

HHA

WSC to H. Llewellyn Smith

14 February 1909   Board of Trade

Labour Exchanges. An Inter-Departmental conference is to be held without delay between representatives of this department & the War Office upon the question of the cooperation of the two Departments in the working of Labour Exchanges. Mr Haldane is anxious that the Special Reserve should be recruited through the Labour Exchanges, that recruiting literature shd be exposed, & is willing to instruct the Army contractors to use the Exchanges as far as possible. He is anxious that the conference should take place.

Mr Beveridge[2] and Mr Rey[3] should represent the B of Trade in addition to the Comptroller.[4]

WSC

[1] George Nicoll Barnes (1859–1940), Labour MP for Blackfriars (later Gorbals) Division of Glasgow 1906–22; Minister of Pensions 1916–18; member of War Cabinet 1917; resigned from Labour party 1918; Founding member of ILO; Delegate to League of Nations 1920; PC 1916; CH 1920. Barnes moved an amendment declaring that the proposals in the King's Speech were inadequate for dealing with the causes or evils of unemployment. Labour Bureaux, he felt, would be of little use; he suggested in their place the taxation of land values, afforestation, the nationalization of the railways, and shorter working days.

[2] William Henry Beveridge (1879–1963), recently appointed to serve under G. S. Barnes in the Commercial Labour and Statistical Department of the Board of Trade; First Director of Labour Exchanges 1909; Assistant General Secretary to the Ministry of Munitions 1915–16; Director of the London School of Economics 1919–37; Master of University College, Oxford 1937–45; author of the report on 'Social Insurance and Allied Services' – *The Beveridge Report* – 1942; Liberal MP for Berwick 1944–5; KCB 1919; Baron Beveridge 1946.

[3] Charles Fernand Rey (1877–1968), General Manager of Labour Exchanges 1909 and of Unemployment Insurance 1912; Ministry of Munitions 1915–17; Director General of National Labour Supply 1918; Assistant Secretary, Ministry of Labour 1918; Resident Commissioner in Bechuanaland 1930–7; author of several works on Abyssinia; knighted 1938.

[4] The arrangements which Haldane requested were put into operation almost immediately.

H. H. Asquith to WSC

17 February 1909   10 Downing Street

My dear Winston,

The Chr of the Exr, whom I have just seen, is anxious – & rightly – that nothing shd be said as to future & further developments of Unempt policy which will commit *at this stage* the Treasury to expenditure. You will I am sure be careful of this.

Yrs

HHA

G. E. Buckle to WSC

9 March 1909   64 Warwick Square

My dear Churchill,

Thank you for your letter.

When you sink the partisan (it is your own word, otherwise I would avoid the impoliteness of using it) in the statesman, you will never find any reluctance to praise you on the part of *The Times*. While we differ strongly from the present Ministry on many of its policies, you will I am sure agree that we have not been slow to acknowledge good work done in the FO, IO, WO, your own department (under two chiefs) and several other offices.

I sincerely hope you may be able to bring to a peaceable & permanent working arrangement all the great trades of the country in succession. It is a very worthy ambition.

Yours sncly

G. E. BUCKLE

Cabinet Memorandum by WSC

12 March 1909   Board of Trade

I circulate the latest draft of the Trade Boards Bill. Four observations occur to me: –

1. These methods of regulating wages by law are only defensible as exceptional measures to deal with diseased and parasitic trades. A gulf must be fixed between trades subject to such control and ordinary economic industry. A clear definition of sweated trades must comprise (a) wages *exceptionally* low, and (b) conditions prejudicial to physical and social welfare.

Every further extension of the Act to trades not in the Schedule must obtain Parliamentary sanction. Thus there is no danger of such principles being unwittingly accepted as the normal basis of industry.

2. A minimum time rate is taken as the general basis. To this standard all minimum piece-rates are referred. Different piece-rates and possibly different time-rates will be necessary for home and factory work. To screw up the home wages without a proportionate movement of factory wages might only improve the home worker into extinction. All rates in any trade must be co-ordinated to hold the balance between one district and another. Great flexibility of procedure, treatment which varies with the complexities of each special case, a wide discretion entrusted to Boards of persons interested in the fortunes of each trade and each district, and the guidance, at every stage, of expert impartial officials, are the necessary features of the administrative machinery proposed.

3. Devolution from a central body is to be preferred in this subject to the federating of local bodies. A Trade Board, having been formed in any trade, establishes, as may be needed, District Trade Committees on which a proportion of its members sit, together with local trade representatives, to whom it delegates powers.

A District Trade Committee in session with its official members recommends minimum time and piece-rates. The Trade Board of the whole trade considers these in all their bearings from a central point of view, and, after an interval to hear objections, amends, approves, and finally prescribes them publicly. Thereupon they become obligatory upon Government and municipal contractors, and in all cases the wages specified are recoverable as a civil debt in the absence of a written contract to the contrary. The rates will be posted in manner similar to notices under the Factory Acts, and a 'White List', accessible to the public, will be formed of employers willing to be bound by them. By such methods it is hoped that a healthy trade opinion and a degree of organization among employers and workers will be promoted.

At any time not less than six months after the minimum rates have been 'prescribed' the Board of Trade may, on the application of a Trade Board, make an order making them obligatory by law upon all, and may then use any powers permitted by the Act which may seem likely to be most effective for enforcement.

4. The use of such powers must depend largely upon the state of opinion in each trade and district. They authorize entry of factories and workshops, but not of houses except with worker's consent. They comprise investigation upon complaint or detection, and inspection with prosecution of employers, but not of workers, before a Court of summary jurisdiction with pecuniary

penalties up to £20, &c. The Trade Board may, with the consent of the Board of Trade (and of course the Treasury), appoint what officers are necessary, and my advisers agree that a system of peripatetic inspection working under the Trade Board and with the District Trade Committee will probably be more effective than an addition to the duties and numbers of existing factory inspectors, who will however co-operate in several important ways. This opinion is shared by the Home Office. But it is important for the House of Commons that statutory powers should be taken in the Bill, if necessary at a later stage, to hand over the duty of enforcement in any particular trade, in whole or in part, to the Home Office by agreement between the Ministers responsible.

This Bill should be read a first time before the introduction of a similar measure by Mr Hills[1] on the 26th instant.

WSC to Alfred Lyttelton

3 April 1909   Board of Trade

Copy

Dear Lyttelton,

You are reported in *The Times* of this morning as having made the following statement in your speech at Brighton:

'The reason for that infirmity was that they (the Prime Minister & Sir Edward Grey) were encumbered by colleagues who were not anything like what they were, & *who had let the nation into the secrets of the Cabinet*. It was plain that Mr Lloyd George and Mr Churchill were influences in the Cabinet which militated strongly against the policy of Mr Asquith & Sir Edward Grey etc.'

Words I have underlined namely 'who have let the nation into the secrets of the Cabinet' contain a direct charge not only against my discretion but my honour. It is not true. I am astonished that you should have made it. I cannot believe that you would have done so on gossip & rumour; & I invite you to make public your authority for your allegations or to withdraw them absolutely.

Yours sincerely
WINSTON S. CHURCHILL

---

[1] John Walter Hills (1867–1938), Conservative MP for Durham City 1906–22, Ripon 1925–38; Financial Secretary to the Treasury 1922–3; PC 1929.

Alfred Lyttelton to WSC

5 April 1909

Dear Churchill,

The two sentences you quote from the necessarily abbreviated report in the *Times* of my speech at Brighton are substantially accurate, but they did not follow one upon the other, & any inference drawn from their juxtaposition in the report wd be therefore unfounded. The statement underlined by you & of wh you complain viz. 'They are encumbered with colleagues . . . who had let the nation into the secrets of the Cabinet,' is quite plain & speaks for itself. It is sufficient to cite one authority only in support of it.

In a recent public speech a very distinguished member of the present Cabinet who has personal experience of this Cabinet only, refers to a Cabinet 'as about the only place in the country where as far as he can see there are no secrets.' Your colleagues & yourself are in a better position than any outsider for allocating the blame for this state of things to the person or persons who ought quietly to bear it. I have not attempted, and shall not attempt, from a position of less advantage to interfere with your & their opportunities.

Your complaint – if I rightly understand your letter – relates only to the sentence with which I have dealt & it is perhaps superfluous to add more – but I shd like as a matter of courtesy to you, to say that in referring to your opinion & influence on the subject of armaments, of wh you have made no secret, & for wh you have received many tributes from the party of economy, I neither made nor intended to make any imputation on your personal honour, nor were the words I used unless twisted from their context susceptible in my opinion of the construction you have put upon them

Yours sincerely

A. LYTTELTON

WSC to Alfred Lyttelton

6 April 1909 Board of Trade

Copy

Dear Lyttelton,

I have waited to acknowledge your letter until I had the advantage of reading your speech at Brighton in a full account. I gladly recognise that it is susceptible of a perfectly harmless interpretation. And yet at the same time I think that most people reading it *in extenso* would have drawn the same inference that I did from its condensed form; and in view of this danger I cannot help thinking that your reply might, without the sacrifice of any argumentative advantage, have been couched in a more gracious style. Still since it clearly & specifically repudiates any intention to make a personal charge against the Ministers whose names you mentioned, I express my thanks for it, & my regrets to have put you to any trouble.

For the rest fancy is free & inexpensive & of course I do not in the least complain of any speculation you may care to make upon my opinions or influence in regard to any question of policy. Had it not been for the sentence to which I have referred I should certainly nòt have written to you about your speech. I know how hard it is sometimes to find things to say.

Yours sincerely

[Winston S. Churchill]

Memorandum by WSC

17 April 1909   Board of Trade

1. I now circulate to my colleagues the Memorandum which has been prepared during the last six months in the Board of Trade on Unemployment Insurance. This Scheme is the counterpart and companion of the national system of Labour Exchanges to which the Cabinet has already assented. Labour Exchanges are at the present moment supported by an imposing array of authorities and examples, and they will not be challenged so far as can now be foreseen by any political party. I am a strong believer in them, but I cannot disguise the possibility of their being inadequately supported by the higher class of working men, and gradually relapsing into the distress machinery from which they are now being extricated. The combination of a system of Unemployment Insurance with Labour Exchanges will make it certain that a very large proportion of the skilled and organized labour of the country, and some of its most powerful industries, will, from the outset, be associated with the Labour Exchanges; and, on the other hand, no scheme of Unemployment Insurance could be worked except in connection with an extensive apparatus for finding work, and testing willingness to work, like that afforded by national Labour Exchanges.

2. The proposals now made are important in character and scope; they embrace a compact group of industries mostly paid by the time wage, in which unemployment usually shows itself by dismissals rather than short time, and in which the rate of unemployment, both seasonal and cyclical is conspicuous. The number of adult workers comprised in these trades is 2,250,000, or one-third of all the males engaged in distinctly industrial

occupations (i.e. excluding the professional and commercial classes, domestic service, agriculture, fishing, &c). Of the remaining two-thirds nearly half are engaged in the railway service or the mercantile marine, or in the textile, mining, or other industries, which adopt short time or 'missing shifts' systems in place of discharging workmen. Consequently, the scheme may be said, broadly speaking, to cover half the whole field of unemployment, and that half the worse half.

3. The finance of the scheme has been most carefully examined. The estimates and calculations of the Board of Trade have been checked actuarially by Mr Thomas Ackland,[1] a Vice-President of the Institute of Actuaries, whose Report is appended to the Memorandum. It will be seen that he concurs in the Board of Trade estimate, that on the basis of contributions of 2d a week from employers and workmen respectively, and one-third of the total of such contributions, viz., 1⅓d a week from the State, unemployed benefit ranging from 7s. down to 5s. a-week payable for fifteen weeks can be paid to all persons in these trades falling out of employment.

The cost to the State, including administration, is estimated for the first year at under £800,000, and is not expected to exceed £1,000,000 during the first five years. In view, however, of the admitted incompleteness and uncertainty of the data on this subject, I have stated the sum at from £1,250,000 to £1,300,000 a year for the combined scheme of Insurance and Labour Exchanges. My advisers are confident that this is an extreme figure.

4. It will not, of course, be possible to carry a measure of Unemployment Insurance this year, and in my opinion the earliest date on which any charge should fall upon the Exchequer would be the 1st January, 1911. It is also undesirable that the full details of the finance of the scheme should be disclosed until the Bill is actually introduced next Session. With the consent of my colleagues, however, I should propose, on the introduction of the Labour Exchanges Bill, to state that the Government have prepared a scheme of Unemployment Insurance to be worked in connection with the Labour Exchanges, and to indicate the general principles on which that measure will be based.

5. Lastly, I may observe that these proposals are confined solely to the Organization section of the Poor Law Distress problem; that they are, so far as they go, complete in themselves; that they do not hamper in any way the treatment of other parts of that problem; that they have been conceived in close correspondence with the work of the Poor Law Commission, and

---

[1] Thomas Gans Ackland (1851–1916), Actuarial Adviser to the Board of Trade; appointed Manager of the Gresham Life Assurance Society 1888; lecturer, writer and actuarial consultant.

with a view throughout to that concerted and comprehensive treatment of the whole subject upon which the Government is engaged.

WSC

WSC to David Lloyd George

[?] April 1909   Board of Trade

Copy

The revised version that you have sent me certainly guards you in form and substance, though not in spirit, against the danger which I noticed in the original. There is, however, another danger against which you must protect yourself. You must not seem to be looking about for excuses to spend public money. The Chancellor of the Exchequer is the last man in the Country, and this the last Budget of modern times, for that. Most heavy burdens will be laid on many classes; some individuals may suffer very severely. The great schemes of Insurance which you will have already foreshadowed are so massive and necessary that I think they will forge ahead by their own weight, and that the House and the Country will soon begin to regard them as the principal work of next year. But your various items of Development, agricultural research, experimental farms, transport for agricultural produce, co-operation, agricultural instruction, afforestation, boy sailors, all excellent in themselves, but many of them not more excellent than a great many other public objects, seem to me likely to give the impression that they have not been thoroughly thought out, that they are not a precise and rigid catalogue but rather samples of the sort of thing you would propose to do with the Development Fund. It is a reversal of our financial practice to create a Fund and then look around for objects on which to spend it, and I think that such a reversal is not to be defended on the grounds of finance. Take the case of experimental farms, or boy sailors, or light railways, there is a great deal to be said for and against action in any of these spheres on their respective merits; there is a great deal more to be said when they are weighed with competing objects, the cure of tuberculosis, or Charlottenburg endowment, or even a national theatre. Afforestation is all right, that has been thoroughly explored and has a following in the country; motor roads too have their own argument and supporters; but I do confess to serious misgivings of the effect which will be produced upon the mind of the country by the recital of a catalogue of capriciously selected and vaguely outlined fads, good enough in themselves no doubt, but no better than hundreds of others which clamour for a share of Treasury favour. Besides, in the course of the year, I suppose, the Chancellor of the Exchequer does provide money for a great number of public objects just as worthy and just as interesting as those now selected, and I do not think that these minor State activities make a very congruous or imposing array at such a time as this.

My counsel to you, therefore, is to use very guarded language upon the details of your Development expenditure, not to commit yourself to any specific outline except upon afforestation and motor roads. You will have dealt with your intention to form a great Fund for Social Organisation. You will proceed to declare your intention to provide by another method a similar Fund for Economic Development. I do not think you should go beyond a very general statement of the objects to which your Fund will be applied.

[WINSTON S. CHURCHILL]

WSC to his wife
(CSC Papers)

27 April 1909   Board of Trade

My darling,

The debate last night was poisonous.[1] I was vy glad that I had adopted a course wh left me unassailable personally. The jealousy of the 'private member' for the 'front bench' was clamant. The division however was satisfactory, & now the bill will go up to a committee and have only 2 more stages in the House of Commons. There were general cheers when FE (who made an admirable little speech) said that he could not imagine that the House would be mean enough when assenting to the principle to exclude the existing holder. I think it is all right but a sinister element may be introduced by the Budget into the feeling of the House.

Eccleston marches famously. The 'soffit' of the window is the most successful thing we have done. The proportions of the window arch are fine. Practically all the woodwork will be done by tomorrow night. FE is going to put me up at his house after tonight. This will be vy convenient.

Hemmerde[2] is going to prepare a rejoinder, but it will not appear till next week's *Spectator*. The answer given this afternoon by McKenna on the Two Power Standard & US America is a complete vindication of my letter, and a consolation for much abuse.

My Unemployment Insurance plan encountered much opposition from

---

[1] The second reading of the Board of Trade Bill by which the Salary of the President of the Board of Trade was to be raised to £3,000 per annum.

[2] Edward George Hemmerde (1871–1948), Recorder of Liverpool 1909–48; Liberal MP for East Denbigh 1906–10, NW Norfolk 1912–18; Labour MP Crewe Division of Cheshire 1922–4; author of several plays and winner of the Diamond Sculls 1900.

that old ruffian Burns & that little goose Runciman, & I could not get any decision yesterday from the Cabinet. Asquith is however quite firm about it, & I do not doubt that in the end it will come safely through.

Tomorrow – Sweated Trades! Thursday – the deluge!!! Thus the world wags – good, bad, & indifferent intermingled or alternating, & only my sweet Pussy cat remains a constant darling.

Your devoted husband
W

WSC to his wife
(*CSC Papers*)

28 April [1909]   [House of Commons]

My darling,

I write this line from the Bench. The Trade Boards Bill has been beautifully received & will be passed without division. A. Balfour & Alfred Lyttelton were most friendly to it, & all opposition has faded away. But the House was tired & jaded and speaking to them was hard work.

You certainly have made a most judicious selection of carpets & I entirely approve it. I am not quite convinced upon the stained boards in the Library – but it does not press. The work is going on vy well. The book*shelves* are being put in the cases & the colour is being most attractively polished.

Tomorrow is the day of wrath! I feel this Budget will be kill or cure! Either we shall secure ample funds for great reforms next year, or the Lords will force a Dissolution in September.

I breakfasted yesterday with Cassel. He wants us both to come to his mountain villa. Post is just going so with best love & kisses, believe me ever your loving & devoted husband

W

Ivor Guest to WSC

4 May 1909   Wimborne House

Confidential

Dear Winston,

To illustrate the harshness with which the new rates of death duties may press and the effects of their retrospective character I have made some calculation as to how I personally am likely to be affected.

I may say that as my father has left a large portion of his fortune to my mother absolutely to be allotted by her to his sons and as he is not in a position now owing to his health to make other arrangements, that portion will be twice liable to death duties unless she survives him by five years.

I am bound to make allowance for this. It is also noticeable that houses and effects which do not represent revenue to their occupants are capitalised for death duties – and landed estates which, as the Chancellor himself admitted in his speech, are scarcely more remunerative are not only treated in the same way but the valuation of them has been very much increased by the late proposals.

I have taken 15% as the maximum death duty and where applicable 2% for settlement and 1% for succession.

On these figures I calculate that in a capital of £1,250,000 I shall have ultimately to pay £373,000 or just 30%.

It is true that a further £500,000 must be added to the capital upon which the sum is payable for landed property and houses but even so the duties amount to 21% of the whole.

Were it possible to realise this half million in land and invest it, matters would not be so serious, but under the old system everything is settled and I am not free to deal with my landed property – (or investments for the matter of that) as their absolute possessor.

The law will not permit me to sell Canford (defined as the principal mansion house) even with the consent of my trustees – and I can only convert other portions of the estate into trustee investments. The property would never find a purchaser without the house and in any case no such price could be obtained as it will be valued for death duties.

In view of this prospect, not to mention super taxes, land taxes, increment deductions and mineral taxations I don't think I can be described as 'shabby' if I protest the death duties are onerous, capricious and often assessed on non-existent wealth.

I suggest that the death duties should not be made retrospective but that past transactions carried out in good faith under the law and often embodied in marriage settlements should be respected.

I further hope that tenants for life will be allowed to set aside entails and strict settlements.

These arrangements belong to an age which has passed away and individuals should be allowed to make fair provisions to meet the claims of taxation and adapt their way of living to the new conditions.

I should be obliged if you would consider these suggestions and if you think fit urge them in the proper quarters.

Yours ever

Ivor Guest

WSC to his wife
(*CSC Papers*)

4 May 1909

My darling,
 It was dear of you to write to me. But I did not feel the least little bit reproachful. I think I was thoughtless to dwell upon the need of your resting so much before your mother. But I could not help feeling anxious when I pictured you surrounded by all that stir & bustle. It is only in *these* critical months that you will find me a tease. My sweet Clemmie I did not think the Kat was fretful at all: & if she had been, it would have given me so much pleasure to comfort her & bring her round, that I should not have minded a bit.
 I think the arrangements you are making at Eccleston are excellent & I am only anxious that you should not wear yourself out in them.
 I have put old Asquith off. He quite understood. Ivor Guest has just been to me in a great state. His father transferred his estates to him 2 years ago, in order to avoid death duties. The law allows this – if more than one year before the death. Now we make five years necessary to prevent this rather shabby kind of evasion: Ivor has only just realised that he will have to pay after all! Result – fury. Perhaps even he will resign his seat. This is a great worry to me. It would ruin his career – & cost me a friend & ally.
 The PM is quite scornful about the proceedings of the Grand Committee this morning. He says it can easily be put right on report in the House.

WSC

WSC to H. H. Asquith

5 May 1909   Board of Trade

Copy

My dear Prime Minister,
 Last year Mr Barnes, the head of the Companies Department of the Office, wd have been recommended for a CB but I was obliged to set his unquestioned claim aside in order to obtain that honour for Mr Evans[1] who was retiring from the service, & whose last chance was reached. I now venture to submit Mr Barnes's name to you & to express my hope that the King may be advised to confer a Companionship of the Bath upon him.
 Mr Askwith, the Comptroller of the Labour Commercial & Statistical Dept, is charged with the most important duties of any BT officer, & has

[1] William Evans (1841–1919), Inspector General of Official Receivers 1906–7.

come into much public notice lately in connection with questions of Conciliation & Sweating. It wd be an advantage to the work of the BT, if the head of this branch, wh is so often concerned in matters wh attract wide attention, cd receive a similar distinction. Had Mr Wilson Fox lived, I shd most earnestly have pressed you to recommend him for a KCB. That alas is a debt wh will never be paid. But the importance of the post filled by his successor, esp at the present time, not less than personal claims, makes me anxious that Mr A shd be given the 1st step on this occasion in the order of the Bath.

If however this is impossible, I shd like to know soon, for in that case I shd ask Grey to include his name in the FO List of CMG's for his work on the Copyright Convention. I hope however that you will be able to grant my request.

Mr Carlaw Martin,[1] the Editor of the *Dundee Advertiser*, has been brought to my notice by the Master of Elibank & I will only say that a Kthood conferred upon him wd be from every point of view justified, & wd be vy widely welcomed in Scotland.

Mr Cater Scott[2] lately Manager of the London Docks, who rendered services in connection with the P of L [Port of London] Bill wh cd not well have been dispensed with, has asked me to bring his wish to receive a baronetcy before you. I do so with pleasure, but I cannot attempt to measure his claims against those of others whom you will have to consider. I shd also like to add my support to those who have made recommendations on behalf of Edgar Speyer.[3]

May I remind you finally of the promise wh was made to Kearley of a PCship, & of the important services both upon the Mines 8 hrs & P of L Commees last year wh I am bound to say wd seem to me to entitle Russell Rea to similar recognition.

Your v sincerely
WSC

Memorandum by WSC

17 May 1909   Board of Trade

I circulate to my colleagues the Memorandum of the Board of Trade on the state of employment and trade during the first quarter of 1909.

---

[1] T. Carlaw Martin (d. 1920), editor of several newspapers including the *Dundee Advertiser* 1890–1910; Director, Royal Scottish Museum 1911–16; knighted 1909.

[2] Charles James Cater Scott, Chairman of London and India Docks Companies; leading witness before Royal Commission on Port of London 1900–2.

[3] Edgar Speyer (1862–1932), partner in family firm of Speyer Brothers, London; one of founders of Whitechapel Art Gallery; baronet 1906.

Though employment was on the whole worse than during the corresponding period of 1908, there has been an improvement in the last month of the quarter, and the 'significant indications of a slightly improved prospect for the coming spring', to which I drew attention in my note of the 1st February covering a similar Memorandum, have to some extent been confirmed.

The following are some of the encouraging features in the industrial outlook: –

1. The unemployed percentage has dropped from 8·7 in January to 8·4 in February and 8·2 in March. In the linen, tinplate, worsted, lace, and hosiery trades there has been an actual improvement on the first quarter of 1908.

2. Though the value of imports and exports for the whole quarter has been considerably less than in the first quarter of 1908, the decline in March has been less than in the two previous months. If imports and exports had been entered at prices of 1908, no falling off would have been shown in the March returns.

3. The decline in the railway traffic receipts for March 1909, as compared with March 1908, is less than the decline shown for the two previous months.

4. The bankers' clearings in London show some increase in the first quarter of the year over the corresponding period of 1908.

5. There are at the moment no serious labour troubles.

In Germany during the first two months of the quarter there was on the whole no indication of general improvement in industrial and commercial conditions. The outlook at the end of March, however, is distinctly better. In the United States the conditions generally compare favourably with those obtaining in the first quarter of 1908, when the depression was exceptionally severe as compared with other countries.

Lord Crewe to WSC

28 May 1909   Colonial Office

Confidential

My dear Winston,

You have taken so much interest in E. Africa that I write to tell you that I have as good as decided to send Girouard there. Apart from the well known difficulties, I am getting uneasy at the economic stagnation which seems to prevail, and it is this in particular which has influenced my choice, as I consider Girouard the most likely man in or out of the service to set things going.

I am sorry not to have been able to follow your original advice, for your man is in many respects admirably qualified.

Ever yours

C

WSC to Lord Crewe
(*Crewe Papers*)

30 May 1909   Board of Trade

Private

My dear Crewe,

It is an excellent appointment. No man would do it better. But what about Nigeria or the Buro-Kano Railway? I was responsible in fact both for the railway & for sending Girouard to build it. He *personally* guaranteed the cheapness of construction, & on his estimates and assurances all the calculations & statements to Parliament were made.

I can well believe that the progress already made may be sufficient to govern the character & the cost of the enterprise. But you will need a thoroughly capable fellow to succeed Girouard, & a clear understanding that the 'pioneer' character of the Railway is not to be abandoned. The greatest discredit was done to all these colonial lines by the alterations in the estimates & character of the Uganda Ry. I had much difficulty to overcome this with CB & with Asquith when he was Ch of the Exch.

This is my only anxiety about your new appointment, tho' of course I am sorry that in Edward Cecil[1] you have not added another first class man – like Girouard – to the Colonial Service.

I do not think Cecil would possess the same qualifications for Nigeria as in my judgment he possessed for E. Africa. But perhaps Machell[2] would fit that place.

Yours sincerely
WINSTON S. CHURCHILL

[1] Lord Edward Cecil (1867–1918), fourth son of 3rd Marquis of Salisbury; Agent-General Sudan Government and Director of Intelligence in Cairo; served in Grenadier Guards in Dongola, Abyssinia, Egypt and in South African war; Financial Adviser to Egyptian Government 1912; Egyptian Under-Secretary for War and Finance 1915.

[2] Percy Wilfred Machell (1862–1916), Adviser to Egyptian Ministry of Interior 1898–1908; Brigade major, retired; Alderman, LCC, 1912–13.

WSC to his wife
(CSC Papers)

30 May 1909   Camp Goring

My darling sweet,

I am sorry it was too wet for you to come. I sent the motor as soon as I could get it, for here there was scarcely any rain – only warm damp drizzle, & I did not think that with proper precautions there was any risk wetting the Kat's fur: and I thought she would be disappointed if she had to put off her visit. But I think on the whole it will have been better for her to go straight to Stoke Poges – & thither I send this.

Did you get my wire before you started! I hope so – for otherwise you will be wondering what I am doing.

I daresay you read in the papers about the Field day. My poor face was roasted like a chestnut and burns dreadfully. We had an amusing day. There were lots of soldiers & pseudo soldiers galloping about, & the 8 regiments of yeomanry made a brave show. But the field day was not in my judgment well carried out – for on one side the infantry force was so widely extended that it could not have been used with any real effect, & on the other the mounted men failed to profit by this dangerous error. These military men vy often fail altogether to see the simple truths underlying the relationships of all armed forces, & how the levers of power can be used upon them. Do you know I would greatly like to have some practice in the handling of large forces. I have much confidence in my judgment on things, when I see clearly, but on nothing do I seem to *feel* the truth more than in tactical combinations. It is a vain and foolish thing to say – but *you* will not laugh at it. I am sure I have the root of the matter in me – but never I fear in this state of existence will it have a chance of flowering – in bright red blossom.

So Jack and Goonie have their P.K.![1] Jack like a little turkey-cock with satisfaction. 'Alone I did it' sort of air.

It seems to have been a most smooth & successful affair. Goonie dined out, walked home slept soundly till 2. Then felt the premonitory sensations wh precede the act of destiny. And at 4 or 5 all was gloriously over – & another soul – escaping from its rest or unrest in the oceans of the spirit world crept timidly up on to a frail raft of consciousness & sense – there to float – for a while. She hardly had any pain & Philips was most skilful.

My dear Bird – this happy event will be a great help to you & will encourage you. *I* rather shrink from it—because I don't like your having to bear pain & face this ordeal. But we are in the grip of circumstances, & out of pain joy will spring & from passing weakness new strength arise.

Bourke Cockran – a great friend of mine – has just arrived in England

[1] John George Spencer-Churchill (born 1909), artist.

from U.S.A. He is a remarkable fellow – perhaps the finest orator in America, with a gigantic C. J. Fox head – & a mind that has influenced my thought in more than one important direction. I have asked him to lunch on Friday at H of C & shall go to London that day to get my Money Resolution on the Trade Boards Bill.

But what do you say to coming up too & giving us both (& his pretty young wife) lunch at Eccleston? We could settle up lots of things & see each other. Reynolds would 'hand over' etc. Do think about this; & let me know whether it is feasible.

Now it is pouring here, but I am going to take my whole squadron out for a gallop over the Downs. Tomorrow there is a field day against the Berkshires. So that Thursday must be the day for Pussy to come to luncheon, if she thinks it worth while, & if the skies are clear: & Friday we will meet in London (D.V.)

Goodbye my beloved Clemmie I would so much like to kiss your dear lips & to curl up snugly in your arms, but I am glad you have found a nice refuge from paint & worries for these few days. Goodbye my darling, write & send by the bearer – a line of news & love to your loving husband

W

WSC to the Editor of the People's Journal

17 June 1909   7 Whitehall Gardens

Copy

My dear Sir,

I have read with interest and appreciation the article on 'Friendly Societies and State Insurance' which you have been good enough to send me. The article deals naturally only with those forms of collective thrift, provision for sickness and invalidity, and for widows and orphans, which are typical of Friendly Societies, and upon which the Chancellor of the Exchequer is now at work, and it does not touch directly upon that other and distinct form of collective thrift insurance against unemployment – which is now largely confined to Trade Unions and falls within the scope of the Board of Trade. Nevertheless your article appears to me to suggest one or two considerations of great importance, affecting both branches of the subject. The present position is this: that against certain admitted and inevitable evils of industrial life – sickness, premature infirmity, death of the breadwinner, irregularity of employment – one part of the people make their own provision thriftily and in advance by subscription to a Friendly Society or Trade

Union, while another part, making no provision at all, have to be cared for wholly by the State or by charity. The State now pays nothing in some cases, and the individual pays nothing in other cases. Provision is made beforehand in some cases; in others – this is particularly true of unemployment – no provision is made beforehand even by the State, but each crisis is dealt with in a panic and a muddle as it comes. The question arises whether the time has not now come to generalize, for the State and the individual, the principle of providence represented by the Trade Unions and Friendly Societies; to see that provision is made in advance in all cases and that in all cases the burden is shared by the individual and the State. That is the meaning of State-aided insurance. No individual, as you point out, need fear that he will lose anything by such a process; he can only gain in security of benefits, not lose. No association conducted on sound lines need fear that it will lose by the process; such associations will be regarded by the State as among its most valuable instruments for securing the good administration of its insurance schemes. Certain changes and adjustments of machinery will no doubt be necessary to make existing limited associations into parts of a larger whole. The central principle of these associations, the principle of provident and collective provision, will remain, and with it I trust all the ceremonies and regalia in which it is now enshrined, and the spirit of brotherhood by which it is inspired.

Yours faithfully
WINSTON S. CHURCHILL

WSC to David Lloyd George

20 June 1909   Board of Trade

Secret

Copy

My dear Lloyd George,

We have not properly clamped together the various plans for counteracting trade depressions by Government and Municipal work. You have your Development Grant and Development Commission schemes; there is the great field of Army, Navy and Public works contracts; there are all Burns' municipal relief works; there are special schemes, like the Forth-Clyde Canal, now being examined by the Committee of Imperial Defence; there are Afforestation and Road-making under the Development Commission; there is the Traffic Branch of the Board of Trade, with considerable possibilities of indicating useful work on the outskirts of London.

Now, all these things require to be brought into relation and reduced to order. The functions of the Board of Trade over the whole of this field seem to me to bear the closest resemblance to those of the Intelligence Department of the Army. The Intelligence Department does not govern military policy, it does not command the troops, it does not organise the commissariat, or purchase the supplies, or execute the field works, or select the Staff Officers, or pay the bill. It studies war from every possible point of view; it accumulates, sifts and examines information; it prepares plans, it criticises plans; it estimates the numbers and dispositions of the enemy; it computes the resources needed to overcome him. Now, applying this example to the unemployment problem, it seems to me that the Board of Trade ought, each year, to endeavour to forecast, from all the information at its disposal, the relative degree of unemployment which will be reached. I do not think it would be possible to forecast the exact percentage, but I think we ought to be able to classify winters in advance as Very Good, Good, Medium, Bad, and Very Bad, and each of these terms would mean something which could be expressed in figures of great detail. We ought, further, to be able to indicate, within general limits, in advance, the trades and localities most likely to be affected. The information thus afforded should go at once to all the great contracting departments, to the Treasury, and to the Development Commission. So far as ordinary contracts are concerned, they ought originally to be considered in the light of this information, and with the view to counteracting unemployment so far as possible; and they ought, secondly, to be considered by an Inter-departmental Committee, comprising representatives of the spending Departments themselves, of the Treasury, Local Government Board and the Board of Trade. Could you assign any degree of control to this Committee, or should its functions be purely advisory?

It is clear that all the forthcoming Government work ought to be registered in some central *dossier;* and we ought to know beforehand, within as narrow limits as are possible, how much Government work will be being done in any particular month: that certainly could be arranged without interference with anybody. But could we not go a step further, and say that if the Board of Trade estimates show that the forthcoming distribution of work does not correspond in any helpful way with the approach of unemployment as respects localities or periods, readjustments and redistribution of all these contracts should be made within certain limits, and, if so, within what limits? You cannot go very far, I fear, without affecting the economy of public contracts. But I feel convinced that if five or six of the principal contracting officers of the State sat round a table with Treasury, Board of Trade, and Local Government Board representatives, they would, without any loss of public economy, or at any rate without any sensible increase in expense, be able to make a much more reasonable and useful disposition than is made at the present time. And my first point is that we should try to call into existence some such Inter-departmental Committee as I have indicated.

I think, in the second place, that when the Board of Trade forecast of the approach of unemployment is received, and when from that total has been subtracted any relief afforded by a judicious distribution of Government contracts, the net should be considered by the Treasury. I do not think the Treasury ought to become itself a constructive department in this sphere. All constructive work ought to be discharged either by the special department concerned, or by the new Development Commission, and just as the functions of the Board of Trade are limited to Intelligence, so those of the Treasury seem to me to be comprised in control. After the forecast of the Board of Trade, less any subtraction for Government contracts, has been considered by the Treasury, it should be brought before the Cabinet, and the Cabinet should decide what they are going to do to relieve the approaching unemployment. This decision can obviously be expressed only in terms of money. When the total sum, having regard to the whole situation, which the Cabinet are prepared to spend has been settled, the question of its distribution between the various enterprises on hand arises, and must be faced. How would you propose to deal with this? Estimates would have to be prepared by all the different competing enterprises, showing the amount of employment that would follow from their respective expenditures, and these estimates again would have to be framed in some relation to the forecast of the Board of Trade as to periods and localities of the impending unemployment, so that you would help the right districts and help them at the right time. This process is, no doubt, difficult, but I do not think it need be more complex than the Famine Relief policies of the Government of India.

Again, however, there must be joint consultations between the Departments affected, and again I come to some sort of Inter-departmental Committee in this as in the Contracts branch of the subject. And, if that be so, of course the two Committees would be merged into one, and the whole process of counteracting unemployment, and of constructive development, be carried out at once. What, then, are to be the relations of such a Committee to the Departments charged with the actual execution of public works and with the Development Commissioners? How far have you thought this out? It is clear the whole business of forecasting the degree of unemployment, of distributing the funds provided by the Treasury between the different development bodies, of deciding on the respective merits of various development processes, must be conducted from a single Inter-departmental point of view, and with high authority in control.

And now I come to my main conclusion, which swallows up all provisional conclusions. It is this: That we should reproduce for the defence of this country against poverty and unemployment, the sort of machinery that we have in existence in the Committee of Imperial Defence to protect us against foreign aggression. There should be formed a Committee of National Organisation (call it what you will) analagous in many respects to the Committee of Imperial Defence. The Chancellor of the Exchequer should *ex officio* preside over the new Committee, just as the Prime Minister presides over the old; and the Presidents of the Board of Trade and Local Government Board should be *ex officio* Members of the one just as the War Office and Admiralty Chiefs are Members of the other. A certain number of Permanent Officials should be regular Members of the Committee, including, of course, the First Development Commissioner, but as in the Committee of Imperial Defence, any other person who might be thought useful, should be invited to attend from time to time; and Sub-Committees could be formed whenever required to deal with special questions.

I believe that this is the only way of properly co-ordinating and combining the study of these problems and securing the easy, smooth, speedy transaction of a succession of questions, each involving three or four Departments, or different groups of Departments, of preventing over-lapping, waste, friction, and omission, and of securing a continuous policy in spite of the numerous interests and Departments affected. It seems to me to be in complete harmony with your Budget Speech, and with the idea of war against poverty.

Pray think these reflections over, and let us have a talk.

I enclose you my first thoughts on the Budget agitation; we are going to talk this over at 5 o'clock on Monday. Let me know how you think they can be expanded, and what other ideas you have.

Yrs Ever
W

*   *   *   *   *

WSC to H. H. Asquith
(*Asquith Papers*)

19 July 1909   Board of Trade

My dear Asquith,

I am really vy sorry to get your letter, wh comes to me as a complete surprise.

In the first place my statement [at Edinburgh], so far as it referred to Dissolution was not & could not be the announcement of a decision; for the

Act of Dissolution rests with the Crown & not with Ministers; but it was rather a forecast of what is in my judgment an inevitable sequence of events.

In the second place I did not say that 'if the Lords seek to amend the Budget, Parliament will be dissolved': but on the contrary I made it perfectly plain that it would only be if the Lords insisted on their amendments that the ultimate consequences would ensue.

Nothing in my words is inconsistent with any amount of preliminary negotiation & conflict between the two Houses, or with a delay including perhaps a prorogation before a Dissolution, or even with the resignation of your Government & a dissolution upon the advice of another Government – though I can hardly imagine that this last course would be adopted.

The statement for wh I take full responsibility is that the necessary outcome of a constitutional deadlock consequent upon the Lords insisting on their amendments to the Budget must be Dissolution & an appeal to the constituencies. That is a truism so obvious that it requires no argument.

In the third place however I was certainly under the impression that the Cabinet contemplates a Dissolution in the event referred to & nothing else. We have on several occasions discussed the matter, once on my initiative, and no one has ever mentioned any other alternative as being ultimately possible, whatever manoeuvring might occur in the meantime: and when at Cabinet I said that I presumed that no amendment to the Budget by the Peers would be accepted by us, your answer was according to my recollection 'That goes without saying'.

In these circumstances while I have not in any case compromised future action, I certainly believed till I got your letter, that I was speaking in the fullest harmony with your views.

There is however one aspect of the incident which troubles me. The peculiar significance & importance wh seems to have been attached to my words, & your reference to them, makes me feel that you may perhaps reproach me with having adopted a tone of undue authority.

If that be so I should greatly regret it. I have had no other intention or thought than to exert myself to the utmost for the continued success of your Government.

Yours vy sincerely
WSC

PS I am dining at Roehampton, but I shall be in the House by ten.

WSC to H. H. Asquith
(*Asquith Papers*)

20 July 1909   Board of Trade

My dear Asquith,
    Here is what I said in Birmingham six months ago. (*Times* January 14).
I asked you when you returned to town whether you dissented from or
objected to anything I had said in that speech & you said you were quite
satisfied.
    Nothing in my speech at Edinburgh goes beyond this. Indeed it seems to
me to be a mere restatement.

Yours vy sincerely
WINSTON S. CHURCHILL

Speech by WSC

14 January 1909   *The Times*

    I do not, of course, ignore the fact that the House of Lords has the power,
though not, I think, the constitutional right, to bring the government of
the country to a standstill by rejecting the provision which the Commons
make for the financial service of the year. That is a matter which does not
rest with us, it rests with them. If they want a speedy dissolution, they know
where to find one. (Cheers). If they really believe, as they so loudly proclaim,
that the country will hail them as its saviours, they can put it to the proof.
If they are ambitious to play for stakes as high as any Second Chamber
has ever risked, we shall not be wanting. And, for my part, I should be quite
content to see the battle joined as speedily as possible (cheers) upon the plain
simple issue of aristocratic rule against representative government (cheers),
between the reversion to protection and the maintenance of free trade
(cheers), between a tax on bread and a tax on – well, never mind. (Cheers
and laughter). And if they do not choose, or do not dare to use the powers
they most injuriously possess, if fear, I say, or tactics, or prudence, or some
lingering sense of constitutional decency, restrains them, then for Heaven's
sake let us hear no more of these taunts, that we, the Liberal party, are
afraid to go to the country, that we do not possess its confidence, and that we
are impotent to give effect to the essential purposes of our policy. (Cheers).

Sir Edward Grey to WSC
(*CSC Papers*)

31 July 1909   3 Queen Anne's Gate

Dear Churchill,

I must send one line to congratulate you on the settlement of the coal dispute. However much good sense the two parties showed in the long run, as far as I can judge it needed your own firmness, trust & insight to bring about a settlement. It is a success for which everybody will be grateful & which must give the greatest pleasure to all your colleagues – certainly it does to me – ; it is a real public service of the very best kind.

Yours sincerely

E. GREY

Don't trouble to answer – have a free glorious & happy weekend.

WSC to Lady Randolph

4 August 1909   Board of Trade

My dear Mamma,

I am so glad to hear of your excellent stroke of business. The utility of most things can be measured in terms of money. I do not believe in writing books which do not sell, or plays which do not pay. The only exceptions to the rule are productions which can really claim to be high art, appreciated only by the very few. Apart from that money value is a great test. And I think it very creditable indeed that you should be able after two or three months work, which you greatly enjoyed, to turn over as large a sum of money as a Cabinet Minister can earn in a year. There is no reason why the experiment should not be repeated. There are lots of other houses in London, and you will have learned a great deal more than you knew before of the latest methods of furnishing. I really think it would be well worth your while to look about for another venture of the same kind. Your knowledge and taste are so good and your eye for comfort and elegance so well trained, that with a little capital you ought to be able to make a lot of money and if you sell a few more houses, you will be able, very nearly, to afford to produce another play. I am sure George admires your great cleverness over this house as much as I do. I hope the china cock has not passed into the Mott maw. Has the unfortunate Walden gone under the hammer, or is he still your servant? Here I get on so well without a man, I do not think I shall ever have one again.

I had a great triumph over the Coal Strike. We had 20 hours negotiations in the last two days; and I do not think a satisfactory result would have been obtained unless I had personally played my part effectually. I had a nice telegram from the King, and letters from Asquith and Grey all very eulogistic. It was a great coup, most useful and timely.

The baby [Diana] is going to be christened on Monday; Sunny is to be God-father. We shall look forward to receiving the coral rattle; I remember it well.

On Tuesday Clemmie hopes to be well enough to go to Blenheim, where I shall soon join her. Jack and Goonie are going too, and we shall, no doubt, have a very pleasant fortnight or three weeks.

The information from the country is very good. The meetings of the Budget Protest League have proved a lamentable failure. Whereas, on the other hand, our proposals gain in popularity and support every day. The Conservative Leaders have received reports from their agents all over the country, that the country is not with the Conservative Party in opposing the Budget, and that a fight on that issue would be disastrous. Northcliffe had formed the same impression from his many journalistic sources. I think it very unlikely that the Lords will throw out the Budget now. If it is done, it will only be because the Tariff Reform Peers take the bit between their teeth and bolt. And I firmly believe that if they do so the consequences will be disastrous to them. I never saw people make such fools of themselves as all these Dukes and Duchesses are doing. One after another they come up threatening to cut down charities and pensions, sack old labourers and retainers, and howling and whining because they are asked to pay their share, as if they were being ruined. The latest recruit is the Duke of Portland. You must read what he has said in the papers – the Liberal papers give great prominence to it. Every line of it is worth a hundred votes in the country to us.

I do not agree with you about the Spanish business. I think the King is, no doubt, plucky; but he is playing the fool. What on earth he wanted to go and get mixed up in this row in Morocco for, I cannot imagine.[1] And why Spain wants to build a Navy when it has no Colonies at all to protect, and when no one is likely to attack it, is equally difficult to understand. He is wasting the resources of his State on a tin-pot attempt to appear a great Power, and on military and naval playthings which are dangerous as well as being expensive. No nation has ever shown more patriotism and a higher

[1] In July 1909 Spanish workmen building a railway near Melilla in Spanish N. Africa were attacked by native tribesmen. The government decided to send reinforcements and called up the reservists. This led to demonstrations in many towns and in Barcelona actual revolution broke out, which was suppressed by the army with unbending severity.

sense of honour than the Spaniards did in resisting Napoleon. I am bound to say they show a great deal of good sense in not wishing their sons to be taken by compulsion to go and perish in Africa trying to steal the country away from the Moors.

I hope you will enjoy yourself at Aix. It must be very pleasant there. Have a thoroughly good cure, and go through it religiously. Everyone wants a thorough scrubbing after the gourmandising of the season.

The German Emperor has invited me to the Manoeuvres as his guest, and I am to be at Wurzburg, in Franconia, on the 14th September. Clemmie will come too, and I hope we shall have a good time.

Once more let me tell you how wise you are to prefer a mind free from money troubles and petty vexations to the mere possession of a particular house; not being a snail you can get on quite well without it.

Your loving son
WINSTON S.C.

Memorandum by WSC

4 August 1909   Board of Trade

I circulate to my colleagues the memorandum of the Board of Trade on the state of employment and trade since the beginning of the present year.

Except in the iron and steel trades and the textile trades there is, so far as our returns go, practically no increase in the amount of employment, and the changes in rates of wages which came into operation in June were chiefly in a downward direction. Similarly, the statistics of the foreign trade yield little sign of expansion. High and rising food prices continue to prevail. Pauperism reaches its maximum for ten years.

On the other hand, the coal dispute is now settled; the activity on the Stock Exchange, shown by the increase in the clearings at the London Bankers' Clearing House, indicates at any rate an expectation of an approaching trade revival; and the traffic receipts of the railway companies also show in the last three months a considerable improvement as compared with the preceding three months. We should, I think, continue to regard the recovery in the United States as the most potent and hopeful factor. The financial crisis in that country was one of the first causes of the general depression. The wounds were too deep to heal quickly. But the process is now at work over a very wide area, and the recovery as it progresses cannot fail to fortify us here.

WSC

WSC to David Lloyd George

13 August 1909

Private

Copy

My dear Lloyd George,

I have been turning over in my mind the question we touched upon yesterday, about allowing land-owners the option of paying Death Duties in land. The more I think about it the more it appeals to my sense of justice and to my notions of policy. It may be in the public interest, and certainly it is in the public mood, that great estates should be broken up; but it cannot be in anybody's interest that they should merely be encumbered. The reduction, paring off, or division of large landed properties may easily be attended with an increase of population and prosperity in the district affected. But to have great landed estates strictly entailed, drifting about in a sort of waterlogged condition, only kept afloat by grinding economies and starvation of development, must be attended in this country, as in Ireland, with severe evils to the rural population. That population is indeed deprived of any benefits resulting from either system of land tenure. They do not get the support and stimulation of the old system; they do not have the freedom and enterprise of the new.

On the other hand, we must, I take it, view with favour all transferences of land to the state. We shall require as the years go by a continued supply of land, spread about all over the country, for the purposes of small holdings, village gardens, and public purposes generally. It is a deep-rooted conception among our supporters, that the peculiar attributes of land which enable its successive owners so often in the course of a few generations to sell it over and over again to short-lived leaseholders and so secure a continuing and recurring right, are such as to make its possession by private people undesirable. All comes back to the land, and in proportion as the State is the owner of the land, so in the passage of years all will come back to the State.

When we have a complete valuation of the whole land of the country, the fact that land could be used for the paying of Death Duties, at the option of the owner, would be a protection to the owner against unduly high estate assessments; and, on the other hand, though to a less extent, it would be a protection to the State against the owner endeavouring unduly to lower his assessments. As the Death Duty is a charge upon capital, as it is essentially a part of the *corpus* of the estate, which is taken away, it is surely much more logical as well as economic to lop off a complete branch than to drain the sap from the whole tree.

The effect upon the revenue should not be large. I see that last year agricultural land was responsible for only 7% of the yield of the Death Duties. The great majority of land owners would much prefer to keep their land, however mortgaged, the permanent and recreative character of that security being well-known to them. At the outside I should judge that one-seventh part of the Death Duties on agricultural properties might be paid in land – that is to say 1% of the total. Yet for that very small consideration you would not only be advancing the general policy of the State ownership to it, not only introducing a valuable and real check upon arbitrary assessments, not only averting to some extent the evils which come upon particular districts through encumbered estates, but also relieving, to some extent at least, the undoubted inequality of sacrifice which follows the working of the present system upon agricultural properties as against personality.

Please consider this; and after we have had a talk I think I will bring it up in the Cabinet.

[WINSTON S. CHURCHILL]

J. C. Horsfall[1] to WSC

25 August 1909   Hayfield
                                                    Near Keighley

Dear Sir,

I have noticed with considerable pleasure that the Budget League which has been formed under your Chairmanship & the Presidency of Mr Haldane is energetically expounding and advocating the Budget up & down the country.

I believe that the financial proposals of Mr Lloyd George are not only just but also that their enactment is of vital consequence to the Liberal Party. Moreover I am convinced that this method of taxation is the real alternative to Tariff Reform to which I am strongly opposed.

I have pleasure therefore in contributing £15,000 to the Campaign Fund for which I enclose my cheque. Kindly ackn receipt.

I have the honour to be
                                        Your most Obedient Servant
                                        JOHN A. HORSFALL

[1] John Cousin Horsfall (1846–1920), worsted spinner; three months after his contribution to the Budget League he was created a baronet.

Lord Hugh Cecil to WSC

27 August 1909   Eastbourne

My dear Winston,

Tho' I have spiritually & intellectually cut you off with a shilling, I take up my pen to urge on you that it is your duty as a Christian & a patriot to interfere at Preston on behalf of Harold Cox.[1] As a Christian because you should do as you would have been done by six years ago: think what a letter from Austen supporting you at Oldham would have meant. As a patriot because the tendency to drive independent men out of Parlt is becoming a serious public mischief.

Sit down therefore & write to H. Cox expressing your regret at the attacks made upon him & your earnest hope that all Liberals will unite to send him again to the House. Moreover this will make you appear in a very generous & amiable light & give a much needed touch of whitewash to your character.

Yrs ever

HUGH CECIL

WSC to Lord Hugh Cecil

30 August [1909]   Board of Trade

[Copy]

My dear Linky,

Together with most Liberals I have a keen sympathy for you. Together with most Conservatives you have a keen sympathy for Cox. And I am inclined to think that this kind of sympathy flows more naturally across than along the ordinary party lines. If that be true I cd scarcely expect to win the reputation of a Christian & a patriot by an act wh wd seem to diverge from the usual harmonies of political life.

If the budget is passed, Cox will be safe by the time the general Election arrives. If the Budget is rejected by the Lords, there can be no quarter in the Election wh will swiftly follow that event: & Cox may easily be swept away in an avalanche wh will overwhelm even venerable things.

In either case my intervention wd be valueless.

Yrs ever

WSC

---

[1] Cox opposed many of the new taxes in Lloyd George's Budget, particularly the licensing and land taxes. His stand alienated many of his own supporters in Preston and he was decisively defeated in the General Election of January 1910.

WSC to his wife
(*CSC Papers*)

31 August 1909   Board of Trade

Beloved,

I shall come to you by the 1.40 tomorrow afternoon – arriving at 3.19 at Southwater.

It is allright about the Crewe's. I have explained to him that I will go on Saty & you will not go at all. I have had no letter from you today – but only one from Nellie. Please thank her for me. I do trust dearest that you are making steady progress. Do send me a telegram in the morning – in case you have not written.

The P.K. is vy well – but the nurse is rather inclined to glower at me as if I was a tiresome interloper. I missed seeing her (the P.K.) take her bath this morning. But tomorrow I propose to officiate!

If you read the *Daily Mail* of today you will see a vy sad case – Mrs Whitley – the wife of one of the Whips[1] – stealing potted meat! poor thing she went off her head. He is broken by it & has fled to Italy with her. Mind my sweet pussie cat not to steal potted meat.

The news about the Lords is flickering but seems to harden towards rejection. 'Those whom the gods wish to destroy, first they make mad.'

Please telegraph early, & whether I can bring anything down for you. & with best love I remain

Your loving and devoted
W

WSC to his wife
(*CSC Papers*)

12 September 1909   Strassburg

My darling Clemmie,

A year to-day my lovely white pussy-cat came to me, & I hope & pray she may find on this September morning no cause – however vague or secret – for regrets. The bells of this old city are ringing now & they recall to my mind the chimes which saluted our wedding & the crowds of cheering

---

[1] John Henry Whitley (1866–1935), Liberal MP for Halifax 1900–28; Junior Lord of the Treasury 1907–10; Chairman of Ways and Means and Deputy Speaker 1911–21; Speaker of the House of Commons 1921–8; Chairman of the BBC 1930–5; PC 1911. In 1917 he presided over a committee which resulted in the setting up of 'Whitley Councils' aimed at improving relations between employer and employed. His first wife was Marguerita, daughter of Guilio Marchetti, one of Garibaldi's officers. She died in 1925.

people. A year has gone – & if it has not brought you all the glowing & perfect joy which fancy paints, still it has brought a clear bright light of happiness & some great things. My precious & beloved Clemmie my earnest desire is to enter still more completely into your dear heart & nature & to curl myself up in your darling arms. I feel so safe with you & I do not keep the slightest disguise. You have been so sweet & good to me that I cannot say how grateful I feel to you for your dear nature, & matchless beauty. Not please disdain the caresses of your devoted pug. Kiss especially the beautiful P.K. for me. I wonder what she will grow into, & whether she will be lucky or unlucky to have been dragged out of chaos. She ought to have some rare qualities both of mind & body. But these do not always mean happiness or peace. Still I think a bright star shines for her.

We reached this place last night after motoring from Metz. The Grave-lotte[1] battlefield was well worth seeing. All the graves of the soldiers are dotted about in hundreds just where they fell – all are vy carefully kept, so that one can follow the phases of the battle by the movements of the fallen. I must tell you more about this.

Thereafter we motored 120 miles through the Vosges Mountains to Strassburg. Here Herr Councillor Dominicus is anxious to take us constantly to Museums, Cathedrals, picture galleries, & old musty houses.

I have had more than enough but am to be dragged off now to a chateau of the Emperor 40 kilometers off in the mountains. (They are clamouring for me and I am abusing them back).

These Germans are alarmingly efficient – yet when I talk to them about subjects wh I begin to understand, I don't feel their instinct carries them vy far. They just work it all out & practise often – so they advance by great effort. We move more slowly but by bigger steps.

Rosebery's speech has come in this morning's *Times*. What poor stuff! & so inaccurate in fact. Over & over again he betrays an almost childish unacquaintance with the common details of the Budget. He does not urge the Lords to reject it. On the other hand he warns them against it. But the execution of the speech, its argument, its phrasing, seem to me feeble beyond words.

The most extraordinary thing in *The Times* is Lord Knollys' letter about my Leicester speech. He & the King must really have gone mad. The Royal prerogative is always exercised on the advice of Ministers, & Ministers & not the Crown are responsible; & criticism of all debateable acts of policy should be directed to Ministers – not to the Crown.

This looks to me like a rather remarkable Royal intervention, & shows

---

[1] The French, under Marshal Bazaine, were defeated in a fierce battle here in 1870 during the Franco-Prussian War.

the bitterness wh is felt in those circles. I shall take no notice of it. It will defeat itself.

Consul-General Oppenheimer of Frankfurt has invited us to stay with him tomorrow, I have accepted. We have no servant & in spite of my portmanteau & its excellent arrangements there is a regular whirlpool of linen & clothes all over my room, Alack Freddie & Eddie are quite well – & I am getting a complete change of mind & occupation. I will write again from Frankfurt.

Always my own darling Clem-puss-bird

Your loving husband

W

WSC to his wife
(*CSC Papers*)

14 September 1909   Frankfurt

Dearest,

We reached here late last night after a vy long motor drive of 220 kilometres – the last 3 hours of wh were in darkness & rain. It is queer that one should like this sort of thing – yet there is such a sense of independence about motoring that I should never think of going by train, if the choice offered. The country is like a garden. For a hundred miles the whole countryside was covered with small patches of high cultivation – vegetables & vineyards, & the roadsides lined with avenues of fruit trees. I did not see a single park wall or country seat. Nothing but the simple planting of a strong population. The villages and small towns are all becoming the centres of manufacture. Everywhere new walls of all kinds are built or building: & their artisans nourish & in their turn are nourished by the prosperous agriculture that surrounds them. Forests of timber scientifically regulated intervene continually. All this picture makes one feel what a dreadful blight & burden our poor people have to put up with – with the parks & palaces of country families almost touching one another & smothering the villages & the industry.

Here we are stay[ing] with Consul-General Oppenheimer, who is the British rept of Trade in Frankfurt: a young Jew, of high ability, & great wealth who enjoys this honorary appointment. He has an enormous house, more like an official residence than that of a private person, & is quite an interesting man. Of course owing to the rain, & puncture, & a mistake in the road, we arrived 2 hours late for dinner!

But I did not worry much about that because I found your letter of 11th showing me the delicious Kat sheltering the P.K. in its encircling tail.

It was clever of you to hit me off here. I was not expecting any letters till Wurzburg tonight. I am so glad you are happy & peaceful with the Alderney cows. They are nice folk – & I admire their undaunted, unrewarded Radicalism. I have telegraphed to you today to tell you to communicate with Henry Norman[1] about tickets for Asquith's meeting. If it *can* be done it will be.

All reports seem to confirm my view of Rosebery's speech – tedious, undistinguished, inconclusive. You criticise it vy severely & shrewdly. He really reminds me of a rich selfish old woman grumbling about her nephew's extravagance.

I have to go over to the Town Hall where Mayor Adicker is to receive me & show me the Labour Exchange. There is no doubt I have got hold of a tremendous thing in these Exchanges. The honour of introducing them into England would be in itself a rich reward.

Tonight we arrive at Wurzburg & I shall be almost constantly out at the manoeuvres – so do not expect much more than my daily telegrams.

With fondest love & many kisses to you & darling P.K.

Your own
W

WSC to his wife
(*CSC Papers*)

15 September 1909   Kronprinz Hotel
                                                         Wurzburg

My darling,

We have been out all day watching these great manoeuvres. There are no less than 5 Army corps & 3 cavalry divisions engaged. Today however has not been vy interesting, as the armies are still approaching, & effective contact has only just begun on the extreme flank. I have a vy nice horse from the Emperor's stables, & am able to ride about wherever I choose with a suitable retinue. As I am supposed to be an 'Excellency' I get a vy good place. Freddie on the other hand is ill-used. These people are so amazingly *routinière* that anything at least out of the ordinary – anything they have not considered officially & for months – upsets them dreadfully. They magnify difficulties & are really disquieted in their souls when others are unable to worship the prearranged thing. But I hope to put matters all right tomorrow. I saw the Emperor today & had a few minutes talk with him. He introduced me to Lonsdale with elaborate precautions to guard against 'disagreements on party politics' & chaffed about 'Socialists' in a

[1] Henry Norman (1858–1939), Honorary Secretary of the Budget League 1909; Liberal MP 1900–23; Assistant PMG 1910; Chairman of Imperial Wireless Telegraphy Committee 1920; and of other communications committees and societies; knighted 1906; baronet 1915; PC 1918.

good-humoured way. He is vy sallow – but otherwise looks quite well. I don't expect to see anything of him as his Headquarters are 30 miles away from this town & we shall only meet in the field.

It would not have been a good trip for you. There is no court – no arrangements for ladies – no facilities for seeing the manoeuvres – in fact a vy different business from the Silesian manoeuvres of 3 years ago. We have not yet even got leave for Freddie's car to go *privately* into the manoeuvre area. (It has just come.) I get good days in the open air, and see fine soldiers & country. *Voilà tout.*

We have had a banquet tonight at the Bavarian palace. A crowd of princes & princelets & the foreign officers of various countries. It began at 6 p.m. & was extremely dull. I sat between General von Lindquist & the Bavarian War Minister – & conversation proceeded formally & fitfully in broken French.

Eddie has gone on to Munich despising military pomp & pageantry. We shall pick him up at Nuremberg. I have not yet made up my mind whether I shall return for 2 days of the British manoeuvres or go on to Nuremberg & Munich, & then motor home. I will wire you when I decide. I am rather inclined to do the whole trip by motor. It is so jolly cruising about the land on one's own – with never a guard or a station master to tease you.

What a battle you had with the Bear. You must mind he does not give you a good hug. Such is the habit of these vy intelligent animals!

I wired to H. Norman today about your tickets for the B'ham meeting. I hope it will be allright.

The old palace where we dined tonight is quite worth seeing – beautiful big rooms with ceilings by Tiepolo (so I was told) – do you admire him or not? It appears to me to belong to the whipped cream & sponge cake style of painting. All was lighted by thousands of candles. In such a scene Napoleon used to hold his military levees when he roamed about Germany as its Lord & conqueror. What revolutions 100 years have seen. I suppose it was a toss up whether Bavaria, Saxony & the Rhine provinces were definitely *French* or Prussian. They are quite digested now however.

This army is a terrible engine. It marches sometimes 35 miles in a day. It is in number as the sands of the sea – & with all the modern conveniences. There is a complete divorce between the two sides of German life – the Imperialists & the Socialists. Nothing unites them. They are two different nations.

With us there are so many shades. Here it is all black & white (the Prussian colours). I think another 50 years will see a wiser & a gentler world. But we shall not be spectators of it. Only the P.K. will glitter in a happier scene. How easily men could make things much better than they are – if they only all tried together! Much as war attracts me & fascinates my mind with its tremendous situations – I feel more deeply every year – & can measure the feeling here in the midst of arms – what vile & wicked folly & barbarism it all is.

Sweet cat – I kiss your vision as it rises before my mind. Your dear heart throbs often in my own. God bless you darling & keep you safe & sound. Kiss the P.K. for me all over.

With fondest love
W

[and drawing]
this is the galloping pug – for European travel.

WSC to his wife
(*CSC Papers*)

[? 19 September 1909] Hotel Russischer Hof
Ulm

My darling,

I am returning & will be with you on Wednesday morning early. How shall I find you? I do hope you will have made good progress during this fortnight & that the Alderney cows have nourished & cherished you both. It is really very kind indeed of them to have made you so welcome. A cat may perhaps easily be accommodated, but a P.K. is a vy formidable undertaking. Anyway you will be glad to get back to your own basket. I too. We have scurried about with great rapidity – never once using the train & have seen a lot of fine country. We arrived here last night at 10 after a long wet drive through the storm. Today we are going to try to get to Nancy through Strassbourg. Tomorrow to Paris & Tuesday to Calais. But these are long laps – & we may take the train earlier.

Yesterday we visited the battlefield of Blenheim. It is not difficult to follow the positions of the armies. In the village of Blenheim we found an amiable curate & an intelligent postman, both of whom knew about the battle & were able to point out the features of the field. There is a little commemorative cross & an inscription on the church wall. But the village has been entirely rebuilt – even the church is since the battle. The Danube too has changed its bed – or rather has been confined by civilisation to a regular channel instead of meandering from side to side as its floods led it. But the old bank of the river – wh was the right of the French position – can be clearly seen; & the Nebel stream which the Allied army had to cross, & the ground of the great cavalry charge, & the wooded hills through wh Prince Eugene fought his way – all are recognisable. Sunny ought to make this pilgrimage.

The manoeuvres finished with a tremendous cannonade in a fog. I had only two minutes speech with the Emperor – just to say goodbye & thank him for letting me come. He was vy friendly – 'My dear Winston' & so on – but I saw nothing of him. Perhaps it was just as well. I rather dreaded the responsibility of a talk on politics. It is so easy to say something misunderstandable – & Foreign affairs are not – after all – my show. I met however Enver Bey[1] *the* Young Turk who made the revolution. A charming fellow – vy good looking & thoroughly capable. We made friends at once. He is a great power in Turkey – though behind the Throne. I had a vy useful talk with him about Baghdad railway – of wh I must tell Grey when I get home.

Now my sweet Clemmie I must finish – For we are to start out. I hope to find a letter from you at Paris if not at Nancy. It is 4 days since I had *signe de vie*. The Pug is therefore disconsolate.

Your ever loving
W

PS I hope you heard Asquith! He seems from the telegrams to have said what was necessary.

WSC to Lord St Davids[2]

22 September 1909 Board of Trade

Private

My dear St Davids,

Many thanks for your letter of the 16th, which I find here on my return. I was very disappointed in Rosebery's speech from a purely artistic point of view; so much inaccuracy, so much irrelevance, so little real grip or real purpose: it was more like a rich old woman scolding her steward, than a Liberal Statesman. After all, if he were not going to urge the rejection of the Bill by the House of Lords, there was no reason to have made a speech. '*Il a manqué une belle occasion de se taire*'. I read with great interest your letter to Lloyd George about opinion in the Lords. How do you think it has moved in the last few weeks?

Yours sincerely
WINSTON S. CHURCHILL

[1] Enver Pasha (1881–1922), Turkish politician and leader of the 'Young Turks'; at the time Turkish military attaché in Berlin; became war minister in 1914 and was virtual ruler of Turkey during the First World War. After the collapse of Turkey he was condemned to death but had already fled the country; he was killed near Stalinabad in 1922.

[2] John Wynford Philipps (1860–1938), Liberal MP for Lanark 1888–94, for Pembroke 1898–1908; created Baron St Davids 1908, Viscount 1918; succeeded father as 13th Baronet 1912; PC 1914.

WSC to his wife
(*CSC Papers*)

17 October 1909   Queen's Hotel
                                               Dundee

My darling,

This hotel is a great trial to me. Yesterday morning I had half-eaten a kipper when a huge maggot crept out & flashed his teeth at me! To-day I could find nothing nourishing for lunch but pancakes. Such are the trials wh great & good men endure in the service of their country!

The meeting yesterday passed off vy well. I made a dull but solid speech wh was received most respectfully by a large audience who had gathered at this tiny village among the hills from all parts of Perth & Fifeshire. The suffragettes arrived in a motor-car and were much pelted with mud by angry ploughmen – within the meeting all was still.

I find everyone here in high spirits & full of fight. I am endeavouring to restrain them from running a second Liberal candidate to turn out the Labour man. It is too soon to decide now. There are many inquiries after you, & I have tactfully explained that you are recuperating.

You must read Wells's new book *Ann Veronica*. Massingham tells me (this is most secret) that Wells has been behaving very badly with a young Girton girl of the new emancipated school – & that vy serious consequences have followed. The book apparently is suggested by the intrigue. These literary gents!!

The PM writes me that the King got nothing out of the Tory leaders except that they had not yet made up their minds: which was just the answer he might have expected. (This is even more secret though less libellous than the Wells item.)

I hope the Burgundy has reached you safely & that you are lapping it with judicious determination.

I slept in the train without any veronal like a top. Really that must be considered a good sign of nerves & health.

I am vy glad the P.K.'s vaccination has taken. Poor little wow. I expect she will have a lot of discomfort in the next few days.

My sweet cat – devote yourself to the accumulation of health. Dullness is salutary in certain circumstances. I wish you were here, but I am sure you will not afterwards regret this period of repose.

The post goes early, & I want to have a walk before it gets dark, so I will end now with fondest love & many kisses from your devoted & loving husband

W

WSC to his wife
(CSC Papers)

18 October 1909

My darling,

I write you this in gt haste between two meetings & in the midst of a scrambled dinner.

I hope you will not be very angry with me for having answered the suffragettes sternly. I shall never try to crush your convictions. I must claim an equal liberty for myself. I have told them that I cannot help them while the present tactics are continued. I am sorry for them. The feeling here is vy hot against them. The woman's meeting I addressed later – 1500 – absolutely orderly & enthusiastic – was unanimous against the rowdyism. The Woman's Lib Association has doubled its membership in the last 12 months. They were full of solicitude for you: & I told them you would be at their head on the day of battle.

My sweet cat – my heart goes out to you tonight. I feel a vivid realisation of all you are to me: & of the good & comforting influence you have brought into my life. It is a much better life now. Then too I think of this beautiful pussy cat, that purrs & prinks itself before me, & I feel as proud & conceited as three peacocks to possess it.

Your letter has arrived all right. I am glad you liked the speech. The *D.T.* was the best report.

I am terribly hard up for something to say tonight & tomorrow.

Ever my darling your loving husband

W

Kiss the P.K. for me.

WSC to his wife
(CSC Papers)

25 October 1909   Board of Trade

My darling,

A line to tell you that I find all well here. I am working vy hard at the Speech book wh I want to get published as soon as possible.[1] I am going to give B.B. [Basil Blackwood] the appointment. I *did* enjoy my Sunday

---

[1] *Liberalism and the Social Problem*, published by Hodder and Stoughton 26 November 1909. It contained twenty-one speeches made between 1906 and 1909, and had an introduction by H. W. Massingham. Over 5,000 copies were sold. It was published in the United States in 1910.

with you. And you rode so well this morning. As soon as you come back to London you must order a habit & then riding lessons in earnest.

I wish you were not tied by the leg to Crowboro all this week. I would like so much to take you to my arms all cold & gleaming from your bath. Embrace the P.K. I never did say good bye.

She progresses famously & is not only the best, but far and away the best, I have ever seen.

The stupid Mclaren dinner is *Frid. 29th*!

Sweet Kat – I kiss your soul.

Your own loving husband
W

[And drawing]

WSC to Lord Crewe
(*Crewe Papers*)

26 October 1909   Board of Trade

My dear Crewe,

Basil Blackwood has asked me to consider his name for employment in the Labour Exchanges; & upon the merits of his career & qualities I should – if you consent – be prepared to offer him the post of Assistant General Manager. I should be vy glad if you could spare him to me. We want one man at least who will be thoroughly attractive to the employers. And he is a vy clever fellow. I talked to Hopwood about this & he led me to hope that you would not object to my offering him the post.

But will you let me know as soon as possible?

Yours vy sincerely
WINSTON S. CHURCHILL

Note by WSC

He wants to be at home after so many years abroad. I can give him a permanent & pensionable post £450–600 pa.

WSC to his wife
(*CSC Papers*)

[2 November 1909]   35 Eccleston Square
Tuesd night

My beloved,

This day has been on the whole propitious – but my work literally crushing.

The Assurance Bill difficulty is partly solved, after all sorts of struggles & risky compromises. The Suez Canal affair is yielding under my pressure. Perhaps after all it will fall through. I do not think it is a good plan. All day I have been at conferences & interviews. I now write this to salute you with my fondest love & to tell you that in all sorts of work I find it soothing & vivifying to think of my dear sweet Pussy Kat, & her angel kitten.

I have missed the country post & am keeping the messenger waiting to take this to Mount Pleasant – whence there is a special delivery.

F.E. tells me Hemmerde's affairs are still desperate. He feels quite sure that before a man would humiliate himself by going round begging, he must have gone to the Jews & borrowed on ruinous terms: So that probably the crash is only postponed. Bottomley undertook the collection of the £10,000 which was gathered in a few hours from Conservatives & Liberals. What a curious place the House of Commons is! Fancy Bottomley whom we were all trying to put in prison this time last year acting as delivering angel & philanthropic organiser, dealing with all sorts of members on the most confidential terms – with the PM etc; & men of all parties joining together to help a not vy attractive fellow of a peculiarly aggressive type! This is all for the most secret Kat.

I was not overjoyed when Lulu asked me what truth there was in the rumour that McKenna would go to India; but I never turned a hair. The other choice is Beauchamp.

Such are the moods of the powers that be. I shall accept the event – whatever it may be – with much composure. It is evident that I must play a far more calculated game than hitherto.

I have seen Lloyd George on business repeatedly, & have made him feel a sensible difference in my attitude – without emphasis of any kind.

Dearest Clemmie to you my heart opens in a confidence which is perfect & sweet.

Your own loving husband
W

WSC to his wife
(*CSC Papers*)

10 November 1909   Board of Trade

My darling,

The PM was evidently much pleased by my consulting him on my speech. He has authorised me to make what will be a most memorable pronounce- ment upon the consequences of rejection. See his letter enclosed.

This telephone message has also arrived from Margot. I propose to go – as I think you would wish to me to. I am to see Lord Morley who has telegraphed to me tomorrow morning at the India Office on my constitutional memorandum. I am therefore arranging for a motor car to meet me at 2.25 at Three Bridges, so as to get down to Crowborough about 3 for our game.

My interview with Abe [Bailey] was satisfactory. The investment has already grown to £2500 & a much greater yield is probable. He begged me to hold on: & I shall for the present – & as long as I can.

Dearest, it worries me vy much that you should seem to nurse such absolutely wild suspicions wh are so dishonouring to all the love & loyalty I bear you & will please god bear you while I breathe. They are unworthy of you & me. And they fill my mind with feelings of embarrassment to wh I have been a stranger since I was a schoolboy. I know that they originate in the fond love you have for me, and therefore they make me feel tenderly towards you & anxious always to deserve that most precious possession of my life. But at the same time they depress me & vex me – & without reason.

We do not live in a world of small intrigues, but of serious & important affairs. I could not conceive myself forming any other attachment than that to which I have fastened the happiness of my life here below.

And it offends my best nature that you should – against your true instinct – indulge small emotions & wounding doubts. You ought to trust me for I do not love & will never love any woman in the world but you and my chief desire is to link myself to you week by week by bonds which shall ever become more intimate & profound.

Beloved I kiss your memory—your sweetness & beauty have cast a glory upon my life.

You will find me always your loving & devoted husband
W

H. H. Asquith to WSC
(*CSC Papers*)

10 November 1909   10 Downing Street

Secret

My dear Winston,

I think you might also dwell on the length of time & amount of patient care – both unprecedented – which for 6 months, without any holiday worth the name, the House of Commons has given to perfecting the details & improving the mechanism of the Budget, & to providing safeguards against all suggested or imaginable cases of injustice or hardship. All this is to be water thrown upon the sand! (a variant of my old 'ploughing' metaphor).

I am sure that your attitude would be one of grave & dignified regret – more in sorrow than in anger – opening out in a serious spirit the most serious political issue that has been presented in our time.

Yrs always
HHA

WSC to H. H. Asquith
(*Asquith Papers*)

10 November 1909   Board of Trade

My dear Prime Minister,

Thank you vy much for your letter. I think I see my way to making just the sort of speech you will consider useful.

The argument against rejection is so overwhelming that it can be stated with ferocious moderation.

I send you a note I have dictated on House of Lords reform.[1] I have not circulated yet, nor shown it to anyone except Morley & Haldane. The difficulty is that wise proposals are not good electioneering. I would therefore avoid if possible any showing of one hand in detail before the election & fight on the general phrase of 'smash the veto' or any more sober variant of that. But will it be possible to remain in the clouds, if this question becomes as it is bound to do the cardinal issue?

Yours vy sincerely
WINSTON S. CHURCHILL

*   *   *   *   *

Memorandum by WSC

8 November 1909   Board of Trade

I shall be glad if the Commercial Department will prepare me a short memorandum on 'Taxing the Foreigner'. I am discontented with Mill's chapter 4, Book V. The theory appears to me to be much too fine-spun for practical effects. Please see page 453, last paragraph. First disadvantage 'the equilibrium of trade would be disturbed.' Second disadvantage, the consumption of the taxed import would be diminished. Third disadvantage, 'As

[1] Probably WSC's statement of the arguments for the total abolition of the House of Lords circulated to the Cabinet in February 1910.

the tax is levied at our own Custom House, the German exporter only receives the same price as formerly, though *the English consumer pays a higher one.*' Fifth disadvantage, 'Prices will rise in England.' Sixth disadvantage, 'Cloth (for export) will rise in the English market.'

Are not these arguments a refutation of the theory advanced? If it be assumed that the rise in the price of linen, due to the import duty, diminishes the consumption of linen in the English market, why should it not equally be assumed that the rise in the price of cloth, resulting from the disturbance in the equilibrium of trade, will diminish German consumption of cloth, or divert German purchases of cloth to other markets. Thus the balance of trade would be at once restored, and that condition would be reached indicated in the second paragraph of page 454, namely, that the whole of the tax will be paid by the home consumer. See also page 453, the last line, 'the Germans will pay a higher price for cloth.' If the argument had been stated justly it should have read 'English Cloth'. The fallacy would then be apparent. Why should the Germans pay a higher price for English cloth? They might buy French or Flemish, or they might buy less English cloth. 'The quantity of cloth consumed' in Germany might be diminished, would certainly be diminished, or, leaving the special instance, the quantity of British exports consumed in Germany would be diminished. All the reactions described in the paragraph will now recoil from Germany to Britain. A smaller sum of money will be due from Germany to England. This sum will no longer be equivalent, &c., &c. In short, the fault in the argument appears to me to consist in tracing with great precision all the consequences which follow a rise in the price of German exports in the English market, and omitting to trace the similar consequences which would follow upon a rise in the price of British exports in the German market.

It may be admitted that the immediate effect of the import duty would cause a disturbance of the equilibrium which would involve a money payment from Germany to England; but this money payment will necessarily be returned so soon as the drag of increased prices makes itself felt upon British export trade. Thus the balance of trade will be restored, but at a lower level owing to the new impediment to commercial intercourse between the countries. And while the British will pay the whole of their own tax plus the cost of collection, both nations will suffer in a diminished interchange of commodities. The effect of enhanced prices in the British market would, further, detrimentally affect our competing power in all other markets beside the German.

Please have this note examined, and show, if it is fallacious, wherein the fallacy of my argument resides.

WSC

Memorandum by WSC

15 November 1909

EXTRACT

Though industrial and commercial conditions are improving, the upward movement is very slow, and does not appear to have been accelerated in any marked degree during the quarter just ended.

The general condition of the working classes during the first nine months of 1909 was, on the whole, about the same as in the corresponding period of 1908. There was, however, an improvement in employment during the last three months, and at the end of the period the position was considerably better than at the end of September, 1908. The fact that the percentage of unemployed members of trade unions, which ordinarily increases at this season of the year, has shown a continued decline in 1909, must be regarded as a favourable sign, in spite of the relatively high level at which that percentage still stands, namely 7·4 per cent. The depression in the building and shipbuilding trades continues very marked, and the high price of raw material is adversely affecting the position in the cotton trade. Retail prices of food are now somewhat lower than a year ago, and the decline in rates of wages has slackened considerably.

No large general disputes between employers and employed are in progress and none are threatened.

The statistics of pauperism are still indicative of the existence of a large amount of distress and compare unfavourably with those of a year ago, and still more with the figures for the corresponding dates in every one of the last ten years except 1905.

The statistics of clearings at the London Bankers' Clearing House and those of bankruptcies are both more favourable than for the first nine months of last year. The receipts of railway companies, on the other hand, have been smaller than last year.

The value of the exports of United Kingdom produce has in each month since June been in excess of the figures for the corresponding months of last year, though the aggregate for the first nine months of 1909 is still less than that for the first nine months of 1908. The deficiency of about 3 per cent is, however, wholly due to the lower range of average prices in 1909 as compared with 1908. The imports have exceeded in value those of the first nine months of 1908 by £14,000,000, about one-half of which was accounted for by food, drink, and tobacco. The lower prices of raw materials generally being taken into account, imports of this class have increased in quantity by about 9 per cent, and, deducting re-exports, the net imports have increased in quantity by about 6 per cent.

The improvement of conditions in the United States is a favourable indication in the outlook for the near future. . . . The figures of imports and exports reflect not only changes in the volume of trade, but also changes in the prices of the merchandise dealt with. In the first nine months of the year the net imports of raw materials decreased from £114,100,000 in 1908 to £112,700,000 in the current year. An examination of the principal items, including nearly 90 per cent of the total, shows that, had the prices of 1908 remained unchanged in 1909, the quantities of the raw materials imported this year, after deduction of re-exports, would have been valued at about £121,000,000, or about 6 per cent more than in 1908. A similar calculation for the manufactured goods exported, covering over 70 per cent of their total value, shows that instead of the decrease from £227,000,000 in 1908 to £219,000,000 in 1909 there would have been shown for 1909, had the prices prevailing in 1908 remained unchanged, a value of about £230,000,000 of manufactured goods exported, or a small increase instead of the decrease of over 3 per cent actually recorded. It thus appears that, over the nine months, there has been, as compared with last year, a substantial reduction of the average prices at which the goods which form two important divisions of our foreign trade are valued, and that the prices of raw materials have fallen more than those of manufactured goods. . . .

General Trade Conditions. – Industrial and commercial conditions generally are improving, but the upward movement is very slow, and it does not appear to have been accelerated – at any rate, as regards the United Kingdom – in any marked degree during the quarter just ended; the inertia shown by the cotton and the iron and steel trades has to be overcome before any decided advance can be made. Iron and steel works and machinery makers record some slight improvement; the satisfactory recovery of the United States iron and steel trade is beginning to react on British markets, and American purchases of British pig iron are re-commencing. Steel and engineering works are not fully occupied, but the demand for shipbuilding material appears to be increasing. As regards textiles, the Manchester Chamber of Commerce reports that the cotton trade is gradually becoming more active, but is handicapped by the enormous capacity for output and the high prices of raw material. Such improvement as has occurred, however, seems to be almost entirely confined to the weaving section, and spinners propose to continue organised short time for another six weeks. The woollen and worsted trades have continued to improve and general activity is reported; the heavy woollen industry of Dewsbury, the Bradford piece goods trade, and the Rochdale flannel trade, are all busy, and overtime is worked in some cases. Manufacturers of linen goods in Belfast and Scotland report a very fair degree of activity and the continuance of an improved demand. Conditions in the jute trade are fairly satisfactory. Conditions in the leather and boot and shoe industry and the leather trade generally are not discouraging.

J. A. Pease[1] to WSC

25 November 1909   12 Downing Street

My dear Winston,

Norman tells me that the Budget League has only about £3,000 left in its coffers.

Having regard to the enormous demands made upon my purse and the fact that I have advanced the Budget League more than this sum already, I do think that the money ought to be repaid to me. It is no use the Budget League trying to run on without financial resources and, in my opinion, it cannot make anything of a splash to help us as a separate Organization during our Election Campaign and I do want the money badly.

I am, Yours ever
JOSEPH A. PEASE

PS I have suggested to Norman that we should have a Committee Meeting on Thursday next when the matter may be discussed by a full Committee.

WSC to J. A. Pease

26 November 1909   Board of Trade

Secret

Copy

My dear Pease,

You had better come yourself to the Committee on Thursday & take part in the discussion. There was a very clear opinion expressed last time that it would be a great pity to destroy one of the very few outside organisations available for by-election purposes on our side – that, I know, is the view of the Chancellor of the Exchequer, & I certainly share it. So far as the

[1] Joseph Albert Pease (1860–1943), Chief Whip of Liberal Party 1908–10; MP for Tyneside 1892–1900; Saffron Walden 1901–10; Rotherham 1910–16; President of Board of Education 1911–15; Postmaster-General 1916; Chairman of BBC 1922–6; Baron Gainford 1917.

remaining £3000 is concerned, that can only be disposed of upon the authority of the Executive Committee. I thought myself that you had only advanced in actual cash some £1,500. It is quite true that you have no doubt paid expenses for speakers, but it should be borne in mind that the whole of this propaganda work, though no doubt on a smaller scale, would have had to have been defrayed from your central fund; & there is no doubt whatever that the activities of the Budget League during the six months of its existence have greatly relieved you of expenditure which you would otherwise have had to incur. Considering the great activity & success of the agitation which has been maintained all over the country, I think it not extravagant to say that the £1,500 you have advanced us is far & away the best investment of any party funds in political agitation which any human being has ever been fortunate enough to make. Had there been no Budget League, your expenses would far have exceeded it. You must also remember that we have spent our money freely in outside work at by-elections, & this again has directly contributed to the objects for which your central fund is maintained.

In these circumstances I should rather deprecate the casting up of balances in any narrow spirit, & I have no doubt that such is far from your intention.

Yours vy sincerely
WINSTON S. CHURCHILL

WSC to Lord Morley

27 November 1909   Board of Trade

Confidential

Copy

My dear Lord Morley,

I enclose you two notes, which have been prepared in the Commercial Department, for what they are worth. Upon Revelstoke's point, it is true to say that the fall in the value of securities which has taken place during the tenure of the present Government is far less heavy than that which took place under the late Government; that there has been a recovery of over 225 millions in the value of the 387 representative securities since October, 1907, and that there has been no fall in the value of these securities, but, on the contrary, a slight increase since the Budget was introduced. It is also true to state that since the introduction of the Budget the proportion of unemployment has progressively improved in spite of adverse seasonal tendencies to the contrary; that the recovery in the Trade Returns has, during the last four months, become pronounced; and that the imports of bullion show a large excess – 6 or 7 millions – over the exports. The argument that British securities are being sent out of the country is absurd. It would imply that we were decreasing the sum total of our foreign investments; whereas in common with Germany, France, and other highly developed modern communities, we are actively and profitably increasing them. It cannot be maintained upon any basis of facts and figures that the production and discussion of the Budget during the last six months has been injurious to trade, credit or employment. The uncertainty and acute political excitement inseparable from the constitutional crisis which the Lords' action will now provoke, conjoined with the financial disturbance necessarily involved, may, however, be expected to react unfavourably upon all three.

Milner's statement that 'the accumulated wealth of the nation is not remarkably progressive. It is alarmingly stationary', is altogether contrary to the facts. Sir Robert Giffen[1] estimated some years ago that the addition to the capital wealth of the nation was at least between two and three millions a year. The paid-up capital of registered companies alone, which was 1,013 millions sterling in 1893, had grown naturally up to 2,123 millions sterling in 1908. The gross amount of income which comes under the view of the Income Tax Commissioners was 762 millions in the year 1898–9, and it had risen to 980 millions in the year 1908–9. That is to say by 218 millions in 10 years. No doubt a substantial deduction must be made from this for more efficient methods of collection. Even if this were taken to be a half (which the Treasury tell me would be a handsome allowance) the increased annual income of the classes paying income tax (only 1,100,000 all told) is therefore 109 millions in rents, dividends, interest and profits. It is true that the valuation of estates paying estate duty does not keep step with this, the increase being only 6% as against rather more than 12% net increase of income assessable to income tax. The increase in the number of estates liable to estate duty has, however, increased by nearly 9%. There can be no doubt about the income tax figures; and the fact that the death duty figures do not fully sustain them, or go all the way with them, is probably due to an increase of gifts *inter vivos* and to other methods of evading what is unquestionably, in many cases, an onerous tax.

It is melancholy to turn from these gigantic accumulations and augmentations of the wealth of the income tax-paying & propertied classes to the condition of the wage earners. The wages of 10 million persons (the

---

[1] Robert Giffen (1837–1910), economist and statistician; Assistant Secretary Board of Trade 1882–97; Editor of *Journal of Royal Statistical Society* 1876–91, and author of *Essays in Finance* etc; a Unionist free-trader; knighted 1895.

aristocracy of labour) are comprised in the annual Board of Trade Returns. In the last 10 years the increased annual wage has only been about 10 millions, and nearly the whole of that has only been attained during the last four years. A steady increase in rents, and latterly an unfavourable movement in food prices, must be set against this. When we consider that the alternatives before us for raising the money required by the State are to draw upon the overflowing fund of wealth or upon the almost stationary wages of labour, the general policy and substantial justice of the Budget are alike conclusively vindicated.

All the facts set out in this letter came either from the Treasury or the Board of Trade, and are I believe unimpeachable. For the purposes of composing your argument, I think you may rely upon them fully; but to guard against any possibility of error, I am sending a copy of this to Sir George Murray[1] and asking him to check them for me on Monday.

Yours vy sincerely
WINSTON S. CHURCHILL

J. E. Hodder-Williams[2] to WSC

16 December 1909 St Paul's House
Warwick Square

Dear Sir,

I have pleasure in sending you herewith agreement in duplicate for the publication of 'The People's Rights Defended',[3] together with cheque for £100. If you will be so good as to sign both copies, returning one to us and keeping the other for your own personal use, I shall be much obliged to you.

As you suggested, we are making up the book into page form. The printers have been most careful, and have suggested various deletions of repeated matter, so I think you can safely leave it in our hands, but of course I am sending you page proofs as fast as possible.

I remain, Your obedient servant
J. E. HODDER WILLIAMS

---

[1] George Herbert Murray (1849–1936), Permanent Secretary to the Treasury 1903–11; Chairman of Board of Inland Revenue 1897–9; Secretary to Post Office 1899–1903; knighted 1899.

[2] John Ernest Hodder-Williams (1876–1927). Chairman of Hodder & Stoughton Limited, publishers; knighted 1919.

[3] Published in 1910 as *The People's Rights*. It contains extracts from WSC's Lancashire speeches, and appeared on the bookstalls in the second week of January, price one shilling. In 1969 a good copy was worth about £50.

Agreement between WSC and Messrs Hodder and Stoughton

Memorandum of Agreement made this sixteenth day of December, 1909 between The Right Hon Winston Leonard Spencer Churchill, MP of 33 Eccleston Square, W hereinafter called the Author, on the one part, and Messrs Hodder & Stoughton, of St Paul's House, Warwick Square, London, EC, hereinafter called the Publishers, on the other part, whereby it is mutually agreed:—

1. The Author shall assign to the Publishers during the legal term of copyright, the exclusive right of producing and publishing in book form in all countries, subject to the conditions following, the literary work at present entitled 'THE PEOPLE'S RIGHTS DEFENDED'.

2. The work shall be issued at the nominal prices of 1/– net & 2/– net and the Publishers shall pay the Author a Royalty upon the published price of every copy sold, (subject to the exceptions hereinafter named), of ten per cent on the 1/– net edition and fifteen per cent on the 2/– net edition. One Hundred Pounds (£100) to be paid in advance and on account of the foregoing royalty on signing the agreement.

WSC to Lord Morley

23 December 1909   Board of Trade

Private & Confidential

Copy

My dear Lord Morley,

The enclosed cutting from the usually well-informed *DT* [*Daily Telegraph*] makes me write to you.

I have no intention of going to the LGB, and I do not want it to be offered to me. The PM pressed it upon me strongly nearly 2 years ago. I then accepted it. At that time there were Pensions, Labour Exchanges, Unemployed Insurance, all within its scope. Now the Poor Law only remains, and I have not been studying the Poor Law. Secondly when I went at the last minute when the government was reformed to the Board of Trade, it was assigned to me as an office equal in all respects to a Secretary-ship of State. It has not been possible for me to benefit by this promise in any way – had I done so, I could not have been of any use at this crisis. I make no complaint: but I see no reason why I should a second time be placed in an embarrassing position. No statutory authority accords the new President of LGB the higher status. It would be a simple act of the Executive – of wh I am a member. The same arguments which led me to refuse the advantage offered to me at the B of Trade would apply in this case again. I should not in any circumstances expose myself to the taunts which would be directed upon me. It would be said that a mere shuffle of offices had been arranged to get round the definite decision of the House of Commons last session & for my personal benefit! I will not participate in that transaction.

If I am to be moved from the Board of Trade, there is no doubt in my mind where I should go. Two years ago when the P. Minister was forming his Government he spoke to me about the Admiralty as an office which 'would suit me very well'. I felt a great difficulty then in pressing for it.

Tweedmouth was a relation and a dear friend. His fate hung in the balance. Further I did not then realise what a tremendous part these warlike matters played in the inner life of a Liberal Cabinet. I let the moment pass without a clear expression of choice. I have deeply regretted this since. The only troubles that have come to us have come from this quarter. The only menace to our continued unity lies there. How serious it is you well know.

I believe we are about to gain a substantial victory at the polls. But the House of Commons which will meet will be one in which the Radicals, Labour & Irish will hold the balance. What such a Parliament will say to Navy Estimates of over 40 millions coupled with an exposed & derided scare, is a queer question to answer. We agreed at the last Cabinet that the issue should be postponed till after the elections – but no one blinked at the fact that it might then determine the life or at any rate the composition of the Government.

A resolute effort *must* be made to curb Naval expenditure. This means hard fighting inside & outside at the same time. It is an ugly & thankless job. Still I think I could do it – without a smash in any direction – Westminster – Downing Street – Whitehall – the North Sea!

There is much to be said against this plan on the surface – it would raise a Tory outcry & so on. But if you look at it fixedly in its relation to the party, the Parliamentary, and the Cabinet situation, I venture to think its merits will grow upon you.

McKenna & I were great friends before this miserable difference arose. I stood out of his way when he wanted the Financial Secretaryship to the Treasury and took a lower post. He offered when the Government was reformed to ask the Prime Minister to let me go to the Admiralty instead of him. Therefore I feel I can discuss the question upon a level altogether above personal claims & personal feelings. It will be much better for him to go to the Home Office which is a promotion & to leave the Admiralty at this juncture. It will be better for us all.

I write all this to you as there is no one else to whom I could write it. Pray forgive the intrusion upon your holiday. Use the information as you think best in your judgment & believe me

Yours very sincerely
WSC

Lord Morley to WSC

27 December 1909

Secret

My dear Winston,

I have read and pondered your letter, as its importance deserved; and it is very important both for what it says, and for the vista that it opens into the future of the Party.

The para from the *DT* sets out a scheme of which I had heard before in the floating gossip of high places. I regard it with profound incredulity and indifference, as a practical plan. The PM is the last man in the world to think seriously of details of reconstruction, until he knows more about his majority.

I won't write you now, as I should like, for these matters are not well adapted to foreign post offices, and *I shall be at home by Sunday* or Monday. Then we might meet, if you chance to be in town.

Meanwhile, I only drop a couple of hints for you to know and weigh:

(1) In the bosoms of our two colleagues concerned, what is desired is a *chassez-croisez* in Parliament Street between Admty and WO. They discussed it much when we were at Windsor – and I know that one of them at any rate is keen for it.

(2) The FO would warmly concur in the above, and from his own point of view, for good reasons. I much suspect that he would actively dislike such an arrangement at the Admty as you now mention.

The old Lib League confederacy still subsists (minus Ld R and the PM), and for reasons not at all to their dishonour.

They will not deny the hugely improved position that your Lancashire Campaign has made for you. They will urge you to go to HO. But I have been told that the PM wants a lawyer there – e.g. Robson.

Ever your friend
M

*   *   *   *   *

Sir John Fisher to WSC[1]

27 April 1907   Admiralty

Dear Winston,

St Lucia quite splendid! Dog eat dog! You are using niggers to fight niggers! For God's sake don't send British Bluejackets inland amongst sugar canes on this job or we shall have to set up a War Office inside the Admiralty & goodness knows *one* War Office is enough! I enclose a very secret paper. *Dont let anyone see it.* The best thing ever written in the English language bar the Bible & Robertson's Sermons & letters from a Competition Wallah. Kindly return the print with your improvements in the margin— study it closely.

                                                    Ever yours
                                                    J. A. FISHER

Remember wht I told you 'History is a record of exploded ideas'.

Sir John Fisher to WSC

18 January 1908   Admiralty

My dear Winston,

Here are the '*Sancta Sanctissima*' papers – Please be careful of them and return to me – *you did me great good today.*

                                                Yours till a cinder
                                                    JF

Now mind you read all these 3 prints

WSC to Sir John Fisher
(*Lennoxlove Papers*)

EXTRACT

19 January 1908

Secret

My dear Fisher,

I return you herewith the papers you sent me, having read them with great interest. The historical argument is most reassuring and makes very good reading besides.

[1] This is the first letter from Sir John Fisher to WSC that survives. In it he refers to the sugar strikes and riots that were taking place in St Lucia at that time. The first seven letters which WSC received from Fisher have been collected here for the reader's convenience.

I am very glad to see the unhesitating acceptance and even assertion by the Admiralty of what I have always considered the fundamental proposition of home defence, *viz* that the land force need only be sufficient to compel the enemy to employ more than 150,000 men. This premise I have always regarded as establishing (a) real function for the Volunteers, Militia and Yeomanry and (b) removing the contention that we require a large *regular* army for home defence.

I understand of course that your Memorandum is selective and not comprehensive in its treatment of the subject. I think, however, you should face more squarely the one unique operation which falls in the third or intermediate category of half-raid half-invasion attack. Would it or would it not be worth while to sacrifice 60,000 men for the pleasure of burning London to the ground? Would it or would it not be possible to accomplish this, if it were thought worth while? This is to my mind the only doubtful point and all other descents in the United Kingdom remote from the capital would be purely irrelevant operations from a military point of view and would only confer upon the British Government an immense accession of resisting power through the resulting infuriation of the whole people.

I do not suggest that the destruction of London would be decisive; but it would be a staggering blow at the commencement of a long war. I would hang the people who did it. . . .

Sir John Fisher to WSC

13 February 1908   Admiralty

Secret

Beloved Winston,

I've kept clear of you & Lloyd George (you might tell him) as it got wind I had been with you both and further odium resulted; however I've worked like a nigger & hope the best has been done but yesterday I found another crisis here which by a Machiavellian subterfuge I got round – (you remember you gave me *The Prince*[1]) but I hope Lloyd George will lend us a hand by boldly proclaiming himself in debate *à la* Cobden that he will give a hundred millions to the Navy to keep our Maritime Supremacy.

Our 3 Horatii don't 'catch on' but you & Lloyd George would! One day I thought I had my demission – it was a near thing *but* this *is private*.

Esher has sent me the enclosed as specimens he says 'of *dozens* of letters

---

[1] WSC also sent a copy of *The Prince* to Max Aitken, later Lord Beaverbrook, around 1911.

like them' also a retired Lieut sent me a bit of his Father's journal he had just read – his Father was Second Sea Lord –

Yours till a cinder!

JF

Dont bother to answer or to read enclosed till some other time. *Private* I dont think it was quite nice of Lulu [Harcourt] to threaten me with Beresford coming here, *it nearly made me go!*

Sir John Fisher to WSC

8 July 1908

My beloved Winston,

It would be delightful if you could come the following trip in Admiralty Yacht & it would be so good for you & would you like to bring someone with you? Would Lloyd George for instance? Leave Waterloo next Tuesday at 5 pm for Portsmouth – for Admiralty Yacht – Next day – Wednesday – for over *Indomitable* – *well worth your seeing*. See the Prince of Wales start off at noon for Canada & then we go in Admiralty Yacht to Osborne – go over Osborne that afternoon and at midnight sail for Dartmouth arrive there Thursday morning – go over Dartmouth – & leave Dartmouth by train 8.30 *am* on Friday & get to London at 1.30 *pm* & lunch on train. The others who are going are my colleagues – Adl Winsloe,[1] Sir H. Jackson[2] The Controller & Macnamara. McKenna is not going. Do try & come. Send me a line,

Ever yours

J. A. FISHER

In regard to this Beresford agitation I suppose I may say '*An Enemy hath done this*' The Bishop of St Asaph told a friend of mine yesterday that he witnessed the Levée incident and that the interest was unmistakable I mention this as I know you have an idea Beresford could wriggle out of it – A. H. Lee MP a snake in the grass professing immortal friendship but his letter the worst service he could have done me! Dont bother to answer & tell Marsh to let me know yes or no whether you can come. It will do you good.

[1] Alfred Leigh Winsloe (1852–1931), 4th Sea Lord 1906–10; knighted 1909.

[2] Henry Bradwardine Jackson (1855–1929), Controller of the Navy 1905–8; commanded 6th Cruiser Squadron, Mediterranean, 1908–10; in command of Royal Naval War College 1911–13; Chief of War Staff 1912–14; First Sea Lord 1915–16; President of Royal Naval College at Greenwich 1916–19; knighted 1906; Admiral of the Fleet 1919

Sir John Fisher to WSC

11 July 1908   Admiralty

My beloved Winston,

The King spotted the two of us together last night! A good thing for both of us I think! but that is not why I write: – I had an urgent message from Arnold-Forster & saw him and listened to 'drivel' for an age about the Army and I think he meditates a secret alliance with you! He seems to have got hold of something in your line but I expect you'll boom him off as a harmful friend! Anyhow I thought I'd warn you in case you see a way to use him as he is indefatigable in his virulent hate of the Soldiery as represented by the Army Council

Ever yours
J. A. FISHER

I did not see Lloyd George. I called but he had left for Henley last night. What do you think of this from Pascal:

Pensèes Chap IX.19

'Le Coeur a ses raisons que la raison ne connait point'

I think it's exquisite!

Sir John Fisher to WSC

Sunday 8.30 pm

12 July 1908

Secret

Beloved Winston,

I am greatly pressed for time excuse haste & pencil & *burn this* when read. Today I was pressed against the grain to lunch with Spender. I was very busy but I went. It began by Mrs Spender saying confidentially to me that you & Lloyd George (*but you especially*) were in a very dangerous position ('*more so than you thought*'). I did 'Simple Simon' & said 'Oh! Really but what about' – then she said you were running against the whole Cabinet & would fall like your Father!! – that was what was expected – Later on Spender himself said to me 'are you a friend of Haldane's' – 'Yes,' I said, 'I hope so – I went & saw him yesterday & he was very cordial' – Then he said 'The Army would turn and rend him as they would anyone who ventured such a step as Winston Churchill'. I said 'What rot! those very words were used to me by Selborne when we started 4 years ago and we have not altered one comma of everything then decided on'. He was glum & silent & then I added – 'I can't of course know what you know but I can tell you this much that the sacred fire burns brightly in Winston & you'll no more stop the Great Reformation in the Army than you can stop a glacier' He *then* grunted & nodded & then after a pause said 'Yes but *very very* dangerous' So I rather suspect myself but it's only my own imagination that they are all going for you but of course if you sit tight & carry out those maxims you enunciated to me for my guidance also I cant see how they can touch you but they have been d——d fools to put it in the *Yorkshire Post* & *DT* as the heather has caught fire & they won't be able to put it out

Burn this please – Yours

JF

WSC to Reginald McKenna

September 1908   [Baveno]

Secret

[Copy]

My dear Reggie,

I must confess myself a little disappointed by the result of your correspondence with Lloyd George and I am afraid that your suspicions have prevented you from doing justice either to the proposal or to the anxiety of your colleagues which has given rise to it.

The situation in the Shipbuilding and Engineering trades is most unsatisfactory; more than one third of the engineers are out of work irrespective of those affected by the strike. The distress on the Tyne and on the Clyde cannot fail to be exceptionally acute during the whole of the coming winter and will produce a grave unrest among the artisan classes greatly to the prejudice of all the most essential interests of the Government. As the result of conferences held last week, the engineering strike is now practically settled; for I have reason to believe the ballot will ratify the decision come to. There will therefore be a prospect of placing several contracts very advantageously in these districts because of the keen desire of both masters and men to resume activity after so long a stoppage. The idea of turning to the Admiralty for some help in these circumstances was mine. It originated at the Board of Trade and not from the Treasury. I have been strongly impressed by the complaints which leading people in shipbuilding circles make of the uneven and indeed spasmodic manner in which naval construction is regulated.

If events take their usual course, I suppose we shall have to face a winter of starvation and stress on the Clyde and Tyne, with great numbers of respectable Trade Unionists reduced to the gutter, and then after infinite misery has been caused and widespread discontent created, next year upon a reviving trade, the Admiralty will crack a very large ship building programme drawn up to an artificial level not to be sustained by ordinary market demand, and have everybody working under unsatisfactory conditions of overtime.

It was with the object of avoiding this that I was anxious to have a discussion between you and Lloyd George. I never contemplated the laying down of Dreadnoughts – even as a basis for discussion – but I know you have about twenty smaller ships which have to be constructed every year, and I should have thought that nothing would be more easy than to have placed seven or eight of these during the period when work is so much needed. The difficulties you raise about supplementary estimates I cannot discuss within the scope of a letter, because it is obvious that such matters cannot be examined by correspondence but that personal consultation between departmental chiefs is necessary. It is enough for me to say that the proposals which I had wished to lay before you in general outline would not have involved any supplementary estimates or any departure from the recognized, financial practice. In view of your letter, however, I feel that the matter must drop, and the responsibility cannot in any degree rest with the Board of Trade. We have done our best to signal the injurious situation which will be created, and more than that it is not in my power to do when the Cabinet is not sitting.

It really is hardly necessary, I should suppose, for me to say that neither I nor the Chancellor of the Exchequer, whom I had the greatest difficulty in persuading, ever contemplated action being taken without first consulting with the Prime Minister, but I thought then and still think that it will be only respectful for his colleagues to present any case for action in a complete form so far as inter-departmental discussion can go. There would not be much use in taking up his time with the examination of a proposal which perhaps a little preliminary enquiry would have shown to be wholly impracticable; and on the other hand you would have had great reason to complain if Lloyd George and I had addressed ourselves to the Prime Minister in the first instance without appealing to you, or even informing you of our action.

[WSC]

Reginald McKenna to WSC

24 September 1908   Admiralty

My dear Winston,

Your letter from Baveno, which has just reached me, gives me the impression that my letter to Lloyd George was misunderstood by you and him. I was asked to attend a discussion between us three on the subject of expediting the laying down of warships, and being unable to attend I endeavoured to explain that in view of what I had done already such a discussion could serve no good purpose.

You must do penance for having misunderstood me by submitting to be told what you know already.

Our shipbuilding estimates for the year are framed upon the basis that each ship shall be laid down at a particular date. Should this date be anticipated or delayed there would be an over- or an under-expenditure. In the former case application would have to be made to Parliament for a supplementary estimate, and in the latter the surplus would be surrendered to the Exchequer at the end of the financial year leaving the naval programme short of its proper completion. It follows therefore that in ordinary circumstances nothing of the kind that you suggested as the subject of discussion could be undertaken without having a supplementary estimate in view. It so happens, however, that this year owing to the engineer's strike our full estimated expenditure up to date has not been made, and a margin is therefore left me with which I can expedite my programme.

Forecasting early last July that this would be the case I gave instructions for preparations to be made for anticipating our programme dates and since then the designs have been pushed on with the utmost rapidity.

Our programme for the year outside Dreadnoughts consists of six protected Cruisers and sixteen destroyers. Of these one cruiser is already laid down at Pembroke, and I saw a fortnight ago when I was inspecting the Dockyards that substantial progress is being made with her. As regards the destroyers, the invitations to tender were issued some time ago and the tenders are now actually in: we have been working double shifts and overtime to complete the necessary preparations. For the cruisers I hope to be able to invite tenders by the first of next month. Thus you will see that not seven or eight, as you suggest in your letter, but twenty-one ships will be in course of construction in the very minimum of time.

I had not overlooked the terrible state of unemployment on the Clyde and Tyne, which I fear must be a cause of the gravest anxiety to you, and you may be perfectly sure that I should do everything possible in the way of placing my contracts early, up to the point at which a supplementary estimate would become necessary.

In mentioning the Prime Minister I did not mean to imply that you or Lloyd George contemplated *action* being taken without first consulting him, but I wished to make it clear that every matter which we could *discuss* had already been dealt with so far as it could be without referring to him.

If my letter conveyed more than this, and I honestly cannot see that it does, I must plead the haste with which it was written and if Lloyd George shares your feelings I hope you will send this letter on to him.

It is very hard on you to have the double worry of Tyne and Clyde un-employment and the Cotton Strike at the present moment, but I hope all the same that you are enjoying yourself and that Italy is rising to the occasion.

Yours ever
REGINALD McKENNA

David Lloyd George to WSC

21 December 1908   Treasury Chambers

My dear Winston,

I cannot go away without expressing to you my deep obligation for the assistance you rendered me in smashing McKenna's fatuous estimates & my warm admiration for the splendid way in which you tore them up.

I am a Celt & you will forgive me for telling you that the whole time you were raking McK's squadron I had a vivid idea in my mind that your father looked on with pride at the skilful & plucky way in which his brilliant son was achieving victory in a cause for which he had sacrificed his career & his life.

Wishing Mrs Winston Churchill & yourself a merry Xmas & a very happy New Year.

I remain Ever yours sincerely
D. LLOYD GEORGE

Starting Friday for the South of France. Should anything occur to you on which you would like to communicate with me write me Prince de Galles Hotel, Cannes.

David Lloyd George to WSC

EXTRACT

Hotel Prince de Galles

3 January [1909]   Cannes

My dear Winston,

The Admiralty mean to get their 6 Dreadnoughts. Murray sent me a message through Clark that the Admiralty have had very serious news from their Naval attaché in Germany *since our last Cabinet Committee* & that McK is now convinced we may have to lay down *8* Dreadnoughts next year!!!

I feared all along this would happen. Fisher is a very clever person & when he found his programme was in danger he wired to Davidson for something more panicky—& of course he got it.

Can we not secure *reliable* information on this through the Foreign Office —or even through the German Embassy as to what the Germans are really doing.

Frankly I believe the Admirals are procuring false information to frighten us. McK feels his personal position & prestige is at stake. He has postponed his visit to the South of France in order to organise the intelligence for the next fight. The [Admiralty Yacht] *Enchantress* is waiting outside Monte Carlo for him!

Could you not get Grey to write to the Embassy or see Metternich? I do not believe the Germans are at all anxious to hurry up their building pro-gramme, quite the reverse. Their financial difficulties are already great. Why should they increase them? . . .

David Lloyd George to WSC

[Postcard]   House of Commons

[Undated]

Dear Winston,

Can you come to my room soon? I have gone farther into the figures. They are much more serious than even your ingenious computations would suggest.

D.LL.G.

Cabinet Paper by WSC

2 February 1909

Secret

THE following observations are addressed *solely* to the question of whether public security will be endangered by German naval armaments during the period April to September 1912.

1. Assume no further acceleration of the German programme than is *now* ascertained; assume that we lay down 4 and not 6 Dreadnoughts this financial year; assume that a British Dreadnought takes two years to build after three months' notice.

2. There are now 47 first-class British battleships in commission against 24 German. There are 12 British Dreadnoughts, 7 built, 5 building, against 13 building, German. The number of first-class battleships which we can keep in commission is limited by *personnel*, plant, harbours, expenses, &c. Therefore for every new ship added an old ship more or less must be struck off. In April 1912, as the result of this process, the British sea-going fleet (apart from older vessels laid up) will probably consist of 48 battleships, of which 16 will be Dreadnoughts.

3. The revised German Navy Law authorizes the following naval credits for maintenance and construction:—

GERMAN ESTIMATES.*

Financial Year	Recurring Expenses	Shipbuilding and Armaments	Other Non-recurring Expenses	Total	Remarks
	£	£	£	£	
1908	6,541,096	8,365,949	1,687,867	16,594,912	Projected Estimates
1909	7,030,333	11,095,890	1,712,329	19,838,552	
1910	7,519,570	12,333,659	1,712,329	21,565,558	
1911	8,106,654	12,769,079	1,712,329	22,588,062	Maximum Estimates
1912	8,693,738	11,810,176	1,467,710	21,971,624	
1913	9,280,822	10,303,327	1,467,710	21,051,859	
1914	9,867,906	9,050,881	1,467,710	20,386,497	
1915	10,259,296	8,170,254	1,223,092	19,652,642	
1916	10,650,685	8,170,254	1,223,092	20,044,031	
1917	11,042,074	8,170,254	1,223,092	20,435,420	

* Admiralty figures.

The amounts are only shown to the nearest 100,000 marks (roughly, 5,000*l*).

This programme may, and no doubt does, admit of acceleration, but it also fixes limits. Navies cannot be built without money, and money, even in small sums, must ultimately be obtained from Parliament. The larger the amount the sooner must recourse be had to Parliament. It is therefore submitted that these limits, if not rigid, are nevertheless real, and that any substantial or prolonged transgression of them must be followed by an increased vote by the Reichstag. This would be notorious, and would create an entirely new situation.

4. In the year 1909 the Germans provide no less than 11 millions for new construction out of Estimates of 19¾ millions. The British Estimates now asked for by the Admiralty provide 9 millions for new construction out of a total of 35¼ millions. The Germans maintain their whole Navy, apart from new construction, for 8¼ millions a year. The British Estimates, exclusive of new construction, are 26¼ millions a year. These figures are amazing, in view of the fact that we are told that the new construction of capital ships is the vital and essential point upon which British national security depends. They force the conclusion, after every allowance has been made, that the British Admiralty have over a long period of years failed to exercise that severe discrimination between essentials and non-essentials which has characterized German naval finance, and have found it easier to obtain fresh money from Parliament than to effect economies within their own existing charges.

5. But these figures also support the more comfortable conclusion that existing German Estimates for the Navy are so narrowly cut that they do not admit of further reductions in cost without equal reductions in strength; that consequently any considerable increase not provided for in the Estimates of the new construction charges must affect the number of ships maintained in commission, and the general efficiency and size of the sea-going fleet; and that conversely any great expansion of the number of ships maintained in permanent commission would necessitate a slackening of the building programme. It is therefore submitted that the same considerations which lead us to strike off an old ship when a new one is added will operate in Germany, and that the regular German Navy of 1912 will not, apart from quality, be greatly in *numerical* excess of the existing German Navy.

6. If no ships were discarded by either Navy, and all existing vessels were maintained in commission, the following would be the relative strength in battleships in April, 1912:—

GREAT BRITAIN	GERMANY
16 Dreadnoughts.	17 Dreadnoughts.

GREAT BRITAIN	GERMANY
2 Lord Nelsons.	5 Deutschlands.
8 King Edwards.	5 Braunschweigs.
5 Duncans.	5 Wittelsbachs.
8 Formidables.	5 Kaiser Barbarossas.
6 Canopus.	—
9 Majestics.	37
2 Swiftsures.	
—	
56	

7. I gathered from the First Lord of the Admiralty that before April 1912 is reached, the 6 Canopus and the 2 Swiftsures will have been laid up by Great Britain. I suggest that by that date Germany will have laid up 5 Kaiser Barbarossas certainly, 5 Wittelsbachs probably, 5 Braunschweigs possibly. Assuming, however, that only the 5 Kaiser Barbarossas and the 5 Wittelsbachs are laid up, the German sea-going fleet in 1912 – *the danger point* – will consist of 27 first-class battleships, of which 17 will be Dreadnoughts.

8. Let these two fleets now be compared with each other. The Germans will have 17 Dreadnoughts and 10 other battleships. The British will have 16 Dreadnoughts and 32 other battleships. Cancel like with like. The British preponderance will be 21 first-class battleships; the German preponderance will be 1 Dreadnought. Assume (a large assumption) that this odd Dreadnought is equal to any two of the remaining British battleships, which, be it remembered, include among them the 2 Lord Nelsons, and the net preponderance in British battleships will be 19 – *against nothing*, or a clear majority nearly equal to the whole existing German battleship fleet.

9. This does not exhaust the comparison. We have now (April 1, 1909) 35 first-class armoured cruisers. The Germans have 8, a majority of 27. The British superiority in class is greater even than in number, for the first 9 British cruisers are almost up to battleship class, and the Germans have only 3 vessels to match these. Speed is a vital point in cruisers; and it is in speed most of all that we are superior. We have *now* 29 cruisers of 23 knots or over. The Germans even in 1912 will only have 3. Similar, and even greater superiority, can be traced through the smaller types of war-ships. It is assumed that these proportions will be substantially maintained.

10. Therefore at the danger point, April 1912, the absolute British margin of safety as against Germany will be 19 battleships and about 27 armoured cruisers, all of the first class. This enormous advantage will be still further

increased in September 1912 by the arrival of the first 2 Dreadnoughts of the 1910–1911 programme, securing as a plurality in every class as well as on the whole. Both Powers will have numbers of serviceable ships laid up available to replace casualties. The far greater scale of British *personnel* would enable us much more easily than Germany to make effective use of this reserve.

11. It cannot therefore be argued that national security is involved in the question of whether 4 or 6 Dreadnoughts should be laid down this financial year. No justification has in my view been shown for 6, and still less for the Cabinet being committed to 6 so long before the last 2 are wanted. My conclusion therefore is that 4 Dreadnoughts should be announced to Parliament as the programme for 1909–10.

WSC

NOTE. – I have done my best to obtain exact figures, and I am confident that no accidental minor error will affect the general argument. But I must ask for some indulgence from my colleagues in attempting to deal with technical details.

WSC

WSC to H. H. Asquith

3 February 1909   Board of Trade

Private

[Copy]

My dear Prime Minister,

The figures wh we worked out at the last Cabinet before the holidays & wh I copied as you read them to us are these:—

Dreadnought Construction

March 1911	Gt Britain	12	Germany	9
July 1911	,,	14	,,	9
Nov 1911	,,	16	,,	13

This wd appear to result naturally from laying down 2 ships in June and 2 in Oct, on wh we are all agreed. So we seem to be all square in 1911 & it is only after Ap 1912 that any ground for difference may be reached. Your speech refers exclusively to 1911, & yr pledge will be fully made good by a programme of 4 ships.

But I shd certainly not risk our naval policy upon an accidental margin on this side or that of one or two ships of a particular class at a given moment. Such a basis is in my judgement altogether too narrow, too uncertain, & in any case too easily disputable for decisions of such immense consequence. The general expansion of German naval armaments as embodied in the revised Navy law, irrespective of anticipations of a doubtful, indefinite & as I hold non-vital character, calls for the adoption of an equally comprehensive scheme on our part.

We ought not to build from year to year & from hand to mouth in panic spurts upon rumour and espionage information, probably false, certainly interested and exaggerated. We did match the German programme over a measured period of years with an adequate Naval Defence Act. Instead of jerky construction in response to the gossip of naval attachés & the whisper of Krupp's backyard, & after recurring friction between the Admiralty & the Cabinet, we shd make our plans with something of the precision & foresight of our German rivals. Naval policy wd then pass out of its present nervous and superheated atmosphere into a mood of sober & solid confidence. We shd be able to show *first* that if the Germans by anticipation are at any moment a few ships ahead in new construction, that advantage is only temporary, & that our margin of safety in other classes is overwhelming; & secondly that when both evolutions are complete, when the German Navy Law & a Br Naval Defence Laws both run their course, Br superiority at all points will remain unimpaired.

In the absence of such a policy I am quite willing to agree to Grey's formula of 4 ships declared now, & 2 others later if in Oct circumstances require them – yrs vy sincerely

WSC

PS L [Lewellyn] Smith is *delighted* with Tennant who is most helpful.

Cabinet Paper by Reginald McKenna
(with marginal comments by WSC)

8 February 1909

Confidential

A REPLY TO MR CHURCHILL'S NOTE
ON NAVY ESTIMATES, 1909–10.

I venture to submit to the Cabinet these notes upon the First Lord's Memorandum in a form which renders reference easy.	Mr Churchill has addressed some observations to the question of whether public security will be endangered by German naval armaments during the period April to September 1912.

WSC

I propose to reply to these observations, following the arguments paragraph by paragraph:—

1. For the purposes of the argument, I accept the assumptions stated in the first paragraph.

2. In seagoing commission there are at this moment 39 first-class British battleships, and 2 'Indomitables.' Two more battleships are in dockyard hands preparing for seagoing commission, and 3 more 'Dreadnoughts' and 1 'Indomitable' will be commissioned in the spring. On the occurrence, however, of such commissioning, 5 'Canopuses' will pass into special reserve – leaving a total of 39 battleships in commission, with full or nucleus crews, and 3 'Indomitables' (a).

The earliest group of the battleships were launched in 1894, 1895, and 1896.

In April 1912, on the assumption in Mr Churchill's paper, 8 more 'Dreadnoughts' and 1 more 'Indomitable,' will be in commission. At that date 5 'Majestics' and 2 'Swiftsures' will have been put into special reserve, and all the 'Canopuses' will be on the Motherbank (b) – leaving a total in commission of 39 battleships, of which the earliest will date from 1894–6, and 4 'Indomitables' (c).

3. The German estimates laid down in the Navy Law are not precisely the same as those presented year by year to the

2. (a) No difference is disclosed by this paragraph. My figure was 47 first-class battleships, based on a complete table of battleships on April 1, 1909, furnished me by the First Lord of the Admiralty in December (Appendix (A)).

We have always been accustomed, for purposes of discussion, to treat 'Indomitables' as if they were 'Dreadnoughts,' and they are so treated in paragraph 7 of his Memorandum. The total, therefore, stands at 42+5 'Canopuses' (whose impending disappearance my note assumed)=47. WSC

(b) I presume if these vessels are thus treated, while German battleships of equal or inferior strength are retained in sea-going commission, it is because they are not needed to maintain public security during the period April–September 1912 – the margin on other later types being already sufficient. I print as a foot-note figures from Admiralty Tables comparing these 12 battleships with the 5 'Wittelsbachs' and the 5 'Kaisers.'*

(c) The discrepancy is only apparent; 39 battleships+4 'Indomitables'=43. I had assumed 5 'Majestics' not then put into reserve= 48 as I stated. But I am quite content to accept instead Mr McKenna's figure of 43 battleships and 7 in special reserve=50. WSC

---

* See the table on pages 951–3 below.

3. It would be of great advantage if the Chancellor of the Exchequer could institute an expert inquiry into the financial aspects of the German naval programme. At present we have to rely upon the Admiralty in financial matters quite outside their *expert* authority.

I append a Table furnished me by the Admiralty of the relative proportions of revenue and loan expenditure in the German Estimates (B). It will be seen that the loan expenditure steadily and rapidly diminishes after 1911. It is submitted that no serious anticipations even of loan funds can take place without Reichstag sanctions; that what is overdrawn one year must be defrayed the next; and that the anticipation of any part of the programme brings with it in natural course an acceleration of its end. My view is still that the money to build the German fleet, whether by loan or taxes, must be voted by Parliament within a reasonable time after its expenditure. What is the Admiralty theory of its origin? W S C

4. (*a*) I agree that the figure should be 10,300,000*l*.
(*b*) No. I compare like with like, *viz*, the use proposed to be made of the funds entrusted to them by the German and British Admiralties respectively in the year 1909. W S C

Reichstag; but as the difference has not been very large in any case, the Navy Law figures may be accepted for purposes of discussion. Mr Churchill's argument in this paragraph is vitiated by two circumstances: (i) the limits laid down by the Law have already been exceeded without recourse to the Reichstag; (ii) the cost of the German Navy is defrayed partly by loan. Thus, of the total of 19,830,000*l* in the year 1909–10, a sum of 5,760,000*l* is charged to loan.

Apparently no application to the Reichstag is needed in respect of any excess on the loan charge. Notwithstanding the fact of the existing serious advance on the programme and the consequent creation of the entirely new situation which Mr Churchill recognizes as possible, there has been no notoriety.

4. Mr Churchill's figures in this paragraph are not quite correct. The German figure of 11 millions includes shipbuilding and armaments, and the corresponding British figure is not 9 millions, but 10,300,000*l*. (*a*). The comparison, even as it stands, is moreover faulty in another respect. The amount spent on construction this year is in respect of a navy which will come into being and have to be maintained in 1912 (*b*). The true cost of maintenance of that navy according to the German law will be 10,160,000*l*.

(c) The amended figures should stand 8¼ millions in Germany as against 25 millions in Great Britain.
The basis of my argument is not in any respect affected. WSC

(d) A much more detailed comparison than a mere statement of total figures would be needed to enable us to form a useful judgment of the different scales of pay and victualling. WSC

I do not anticipate any material increase in the cost of maintaining the British navy.

If this anticipation be justified, the figures which ought properly to be compared are not 8¼ millions in Germany as against 26¼ millions in England, but 10,160,000*l* in Germany against 24,900,000*l* in England (c).

Mr Churchill has overlooked the fact that pensions, reserve, half and retired pay, and the charge for loans for great works, are not borne by the German naval votes.

On a comparison of the estimates of the two countries for the coming year, it will be found that on the two items of Pay and Victualling together the cost to the British exchequer is greater by 9,680,000*l*. (d). If to this be added the loan charge, it will be seen that British naval estimates have to bear on these items alone, an excess of 11 millions over and above the charge on German estimates.

I have shown that the true difference between the cost of maintenance of the two navies was 14¾ millions. If the excess charge for the items already named be deducted, it will be seen that the balance against the British navy is 3¾ millions.

I do not know what are the essentials and non-essentials, the severe discrimination between which, he tells us, has charac-

(*e*) I presume the *numbers* of the personnel whether 'our bluejackets' or more highly paid ranks, are occasionally a subject of review.

          WSC

(*f*) The brutal fact remains that with an expenditure of 35 millions a year we are, *it is alleged*, being outbuilt in the essential units of naval strength by a Power whose expenditure is scarcely more than 20 millions. WSC

5. (*a*) My paragraph 5 was based on the following answer which the First Lord gave me in writing to the following question:—
Q. How many first-class battleships will Germany have in April 1912?
A. If she keeps all her ships in commission she will have 24+17=41. But the cost of maintaining 9 or 14 of the earlier ships would not in my judgment justify them being retained. Germany has, however, added 7,000 men to her personnel in the last two years, and is at this moment adding more officers to the executive than we are per annum.
(*b*) The *Navy List*, February 1909, gives the names of the following first-class battleships not included in the 47 aforesaid. 8 'Royal Sovereigns,' 1 'Renown,' 2 'Centurions,' 2

terised German naval finance; but unless he considers that a reduction should be made in the rate of pay or the scale of food for our bluejackets, there is no other item on which a reduction could be made (*e*).

The British Admiralty are responsible for maintaining large cruiser squadrons in China, the Cape, East Indies, Australia, and the West Indies; this is a question of policy upon which it has never been suggested that the Admiralty have taken an extravagant course at their own discretion. When our naval responsibilities all over the world in respect of docks and harbours, as well as the maintenance of ships, are taken into account, I do not think any serious critic could be found to charge the Admiralty with being less discriminating than the German naval administrators (*f*).

5. I regret to say that the comfortable conclusion suggested in paragraph 5 is also without warrant (*a*). It is based upon the erroneous belief that the 24 German battleships referred to in paragraph 2 are the only battleships which Germany now keeps in commission. Behind the first-class battleships Germany has a considerable number of second and third-class battleships – 12 in all (*b*). The Scheme of the Fleet Law is to replace each of these, as well as some smaller armoured ships, by a 'Dreadnought' – the

'Trafalgars.' I ask whether these 13 vessels may not be considered an offset against the German battleships of the second and third-class. 11 of these 13 battleships are included in the Special Service Division of the Home Fleet. I have not counted them in any calculations. W S C

6. There surely cannot be any dispute about paragraph 6 of my Memorandum. It is a plain list of 1st-class battleships as they would be in 1912, if no old ones were laid up. It is taken bodily from the Admiralty Tables (appended). The First Lord wrote it out for me himself on Monday last. W S C

8. This is an extraordinary calculation. In point of fact a 'Dreadnought' is not equal to any two other battleships, and is not so reckoned by the Admiralty. To express naval strength in terms of 'Dreadnoughts' is an unsound and arbitrary method in any case. But, where the principle of cancelling like with like has been adopted, it is positively irrational to express the surplus battleships in terms of 'Dreadnoughts'. When the 'Dreadnoughts' have been cancelled out from both sides the remaining vessels become the most powerful ships left, and it is meaningless to express them in terms of a vanished standard. When like has been matched with like the resultant margin of safety is absolute, not relative. The king is as good as the ace, when the ace is out.

But the calculation also proves too much. The First Lord proves that, in terms of 'Dreadnoughts,' Great Britain will, if only 4 are laid down this year, have in 1912 33 and Germany

ultimate intention under the Law being to maintain in commission 39 battleships, of which 22 will be 'Dreadnoughts,' and 17 of earlier types, viz., 5 'Deutschlands,' 5 'Braunschweigs,' 5 'Wittelsbachs,' and 2 'Kaisers,' together with 19 armoured cruisers, of which 11 will be 'Indomitables'. Of this whole programme, no less than 17 'Dreadnoughts' and 6 'Indomitables' represent substitute ships, and do not entail such a serious increase to the charge for maintenance as would be the case if they were newly added to the total of the existing German navy.

6. I have said enough in the last and in the first paragraphs to show that the comparison of battleships set out in paragraph 6 of Mr Churchill's Memorandum, has no serious foundation.

7. In accordance with the German Law, the German sea-going Fleet in 1912, including the 'Indomitables' as 'Dreadnoughts', will consist of 17 'Dreadnoughts', 5 'Deutschlands', 5 'Braunschweigs,' 5 'Wittelsbachs,' and 2 'Kaisers'.

8. In April 1912, the Germans will have 17 'Dreadnoughts' and 17 other first-class battleships. The British will have 16 'Dreadnoughts' and 27 other battleships in commission, with 7 more in special reserve. Adopting Mr Churchill's method of cancelling like with like, the British pre-

25½, or just over 5 to 4 in favour of Great Britain *against Germany only*. To avert this grave conjuncture he asks that not 4, but 6 'Dreadnoughts' should be laid down this year. That is to say, if all that is asked for were conceded, the result would be Great Britain 35 'Dreadnoughts,' Germany 25½ 'Dreadnoughts,' or a balance in British favour not of over 5 to 4, but of under 7 to 5. It is submitted that the difference between these two scales is too small to be material. Yet according to the First Lord's contention, it revolutionises the whole situation. If we lay down 4 'Dreadnoughts' this year, we can as we are assured, scarcely face Germany alone in 1912. If we lay down 6, then we can not only face Germany in 1912, but shall have a fleet equal to the two next strongest Powers. Result through laying down two extra battleships in March instead of in May! The contention is absurd.

Reverting to the figures in dispute, there is no real difference between us. My surplus of battleships was 19 (it should have been 20, but for a clerical error). The Admiralty figure is 15, with 7 more including 5 'Majestics' in the special reserve, total 22. I had counted the 5 'Majestics' as if in sea-going commission. If they are placed in reserve during 1912, it will not be because they are not available, but because they are not needed.

I assert that the basis of my argument and the substantial accuracy of my figures have not been affected. W S C

9. I agree that allowance must be made for the dispersion of some of our cruisers on foreign stations. If the whole 13 so detailed by the Admiralty were deducted the relative strength would be as follows: Great Britain, 22; Germany, 9; a preponderance of nearly 2½ to 1. The British cruisers in home waters available for mobilization comprise all the most powerful vessels, including the 'Minotaur' and 'Warrior' classes.

It is worth while to notice destroyers and submarines. Great Britain: Destroyers, 147 (of which 62 since 1899); Germany, 72 (all since 1899). Building: Great Britain, 21; Germany, 12. (20 new destroyers proposed in this year's British programme.) Submarines: Great Britain, 45; Germany, 4; building: Great Britain, 23; Germany, 2. W S C

10. *Personnel.* – The strength of British personnel is 128,000 officers and men of all ranks

ponderance will be 17 first-class battleships: the German preponderance will be one 'Dreadnought'.

Again, accepting for the purpose of the argument Mr Churchill's assumption as to the value of the 'Dreadnought', the net preponderance of British battleships will be 15 – equal to 7½ 'Dreadnoughts'. Granting this superiority to Great Britain, the total comparison between the two fleets in terms of 'Dreadnoughts', will be: Great Britain, 33 'Dreadnoughts'; Germany, 25½ 'Dreadnoughts' – or just over 5 to 4 in favour of Great Britain.

9. Of first-class armoured cruisers we have 35, Germany has 9. Our superiority in this class of cruiser is needed for commerce protection all over the world, and 13 of our ships are, in fact, distributed over our remote naval stations or are engaged on special service. Unless we withdraw them from their present positions and leave our commerce to look after itself in war, it would be improper to reckon them as being all available in any comparison of British and German naval strength in home waters.

10. I have said enough to show that Mr Churchill's conclusion in paragraph 10 cannot be relied upon.

As regards September 1912, there can be no doubt that even if 4 more German 'Dreadnoughts' and branches (Navy Estimates, 1907–8), maintained under long service conditions at a cost of over 9½ millions a-year above the German charges. Whether it is 'misleading' to claim for them a superiority in quality over the German personnel is a question upon which different opinions may no doubt be formed. About numbers there can be no dispute. My contention was that we have laid up a large reserve of vessels which, when newer types had been disabled, would be of service in naval war, and that, to man and handle such vessels, we had a far greater accumulation of professional training and seafaring skill than Germany.

Let me, in conclusion, remind the Cabinet that I have throughout assumed, for the purposes of the argument, that Germany will have 17 'Dreadnoughts' in commission in 1912. I do not believe this will be so, and no evidence worthy of the name has been furnished us to support the suggestion. But even upon this unreal hypothesis the British fleet will, during the period April-September 1912, exhibit a superiority in battleships, cruisers, destroyers, and submarines which, taken as a whole, is not less than 2 to 1.

The Admiralty are, at any rate, prepared to prove that this superiority is so great that it will meet the whole Two-Power standard formula with 10 per cent. to spare – *if 2 more battleships are added*. W S C

be not completed at that date, they will certainly be launched and approaching completion.

The reference made to the far greater scale of British personnel is also misleading. The German navy is recruited on a 3 years' short service system, with 16 years in the reserve, divided into 3 successive periods of 4, 5, and 7 years. The reservists serving in the first period are now about 40,000, and can be instantly called upon to man the German fleet, in addition to the 50,000 men already on active service.

German personnel has been increased by 7,000 in the last two years; German executive officers are now entering the service at a greater rate than British. At this moment the proportion of officers in the two countries is as 1 to 14.

When it is remembered how many of our officers and men are necessarily detached for commerce protection on remote foreign stations, it will be seen that, even in personnel, British superiority is not of the kind Mr Churchill suggests.

R McK

APPENDIX (A)

The following Tables were supplied by the First Lord of the Admiralty, in December, as the result of a request I made during the discussions of the Cabinet Committee on Estimates:—

GREAT BRITAIN

First-class Battleships completed 1st April, 1909—(47).

	Launched	Displacement	Maximum Speed	Armaments
		Tons.	Knots.	
Superb	1907	18,600	20·75	10—12-in, 16—4-in Q.F., 5 machine, 3 S.T.
Temeraire	1907	18,600	20·75	
Bellerophon	1907	18,600	20·75	
Dreadnought	1906	17,900	21·6	10—12-in, 27—12-pr Q.F., 5 machine, 5 S.T.
Lord Nelson	1906	16,500	18·5	4—12-in, 24 12-pr Q.F., 10—9·2-in, 5 machine, 5 S.T.
Agamemnon	1906	16,500	18·5	
Invincible			25·0	8—12-in, 16—4-in Q.F., 5 machine, 5 S.T.
Inflexible	1907	17,250	(estimated) 26·5	
Indomitable			26·1	
Hibernia	1905			
Africa	1905			
Britannia	1904			
New Zealand	1904	16,350	18·9	4—12-in, 4—9·2-in, 10—6-in, 14—12-pr Q.F., 12—3-pr Q.F., 5 machine, 4 S.T.
King Edward VII ...	1903			
Commonwealth ...	1903			
Dominion	1903			
Hindustan	1903			
Swiftsure	1903	11,800	19·6	4—10-in, 14—14-pr Q.F., 4—6-pr Q.F., 14—7·5-in, 2—12-pr Q.F., 4 machine, 2 S.T.
Triumph		11,985		
Duncan				
Cornwallis				
Exmouth	1901	14,000	19·1	4—12-in, 12—6-in, 12—12-pr Q.F., 6—3-pr Q.F., 2 machine, 4 S.T.
Russell				
Albemarle				
Prince of Wales ...	1902			
Queen	1902			
Formidable	1898			
Implacable	1899			4—12-in, 12—6-in, 18—12-pr Q.F.,
Irresistible	1898	15,000	18·2	6—3-pr Q.F., 2 machine, 4 S.T.
Bulwark	1899			
London	1899			
Venerable	1899			
Canopus	1897			
Goliath	1898			
Ocean	1898			4—12-in, 12—6-in Q.F., 12—12-pr
Albion	1898	12,950	18·3	Q.F., 6—3-pr Q.F., 2 machine, 4 S.T.
Glory	1899			
Vengeance	1899			
Majestic	1895			
Magnificent	1894			
Prince George ...	1895			
Victorious	1895			4—12-in, 12—6-in Q.F., 18—12-pr
Mars	1896	14,900	17·0	Q.F., 4—3-pr Q.F., 2 machine, 4 S.T.,
Jupiter	1895			1 T.
Hannibal	1896			
Cæsar	1896			
Illustrious	1896			

GERMANY

Battleships completed 1st April, 1909—(20).

	Launched	Displacement	Maximum Speed	Armament
		Tons.	Knots.	
Schleswig-Holstein	1906	13,040	18·0	4—11-in Q.F., 20—3·4-in Q.F.,
Schlesien ...	1906	13,040	18·0	14—6·8-in Q.E., 8 machine, 6 S.T.
Hannover	1905	13,040	18·5	4—11-in Q.F., 22—3·4-in Q.F., 1 light,
Pommern	1905	13,040	18·7	14—6·8-in Q.F., 8 machine, 6 S.T.
Deutschland	1904	13,040	18·5	
Lothringen	1904		18·5	
Hessen	1903		18·2	4—11-in Q.F., 8 machine, 14—6·8-in
Preussen	1903	12,988	18·0	Q.F., 1 light, 29—3·8-in Q.F., 6 S.T.
Elsass	1903		18·0	
Braunschweig	1902		18·4	
Schwaben	1901		18·0	
Mecklenburg	1901		18·1	4—9·4-in Q.F., 20 machine, 18—6-in
Wettin	1901	11,611	18·1	Q.F., 12—3·4-in Q.F., 6 S.T.
Zähringen	1901		17·7	
Wittelsbach	1900		18·0	
Kaiser Barbarossa ...	1900	10,474	17·5	4—9·4-in Q.F., 14—6-in Q.F., 12—3·4-in Q.F., 10 machine, 5 S.T.
Kaiser Karl der Grosse	1899	10,974	17·5	4—9·4-in Q.F., 18—6-in Q.F., 12—3·4-in Q.F., 20 machine, 5 S.T.
Kaiser Wilhelm de Grosse	1899	10,974	17·5	4—9·4-in Q.F., 12—3·4-in Q.F., 14—6-in Q.F., 10 machine, 5 S.T.
Kaiser Wilhelm II ...	1897	10,974	17·5	
Kaiser Friedrich III ...	1896	10,974	17·5	

APPENDIX (B)

GERMAN NAVAL ESTIMATES

Table showing how Expenses are to be met.

Financial Year	Out of Ordinary Revenue	By Loan	Increase on Previous Year of Claims on Ordinary Revenue
	£	£	£
1908	12,186,889	4,408,023	1,374,755
1909	14,075,342	5,763,210	1,888,453
1910	15,352,251	6,213,307	1,276,909
1911	16,497,064	6,090,998	1,144,813
1912	17,108,610	4,863,014	611,546
1913	17,548,924	3,502,935	440,314
1914	18,023,484	2,363,014	474,560
1915	18,317,026	1,335,616	293,542
1916	18,953,034	1,090,998	636,008
1917	19,540,117	895,303	587,083

* A Comparison of Battleships to be laid up by Great Britain before 1912 with others that, according to the First Lord's Memorandum, will be retained by Germany in sea-going Commission.

To be laid up by Great Britain

	Launched	Displacement (Tons)	Max. Speed (Knots)	Principal Armament
Swiftsure ..	1903	11,800	19·6	{ 4—10″ guns
Triumph ..	1903	11,215	19·6	{ 14—7·5″ guns
6 'Canopuses' ..	1897–1899	12,200	18·3	{ 4—12″ guns / 12—6″ guns
5 'Majestics' ..	1894, 5, 6	14,900	17	{ 4—12″ guns / 12—6″ guns
Total—13				

To be retained by Germany

	Launched	Displacement (Tons)	Max Speed (Knots)	Principal Armament
Kaiser Friedrich III ..	1896	10,974	17·5	{ 4—9·4″ guns / 14—6″ guns
Kaiser Wilhelm II ..	1897	10,974	17·5	{ 4—9·4″ guns / 14—6″ guns
Kaiser Wilhelm der Grosse ..	1899	10,974	17·5	{ 4—9·4″ guns
Kaiser Karl der Grosse ..	1899	10,474	17·5	{ 14 or 18—6″ guns
Kaiser Barbarossa ..	1900			
5 'Wittelsbachs' ..	1900–1901	11,611	18	{ 4—9·4″ guns / 18—6″ guns
Total—10				

It will be seen that the 13 British battleships to be laid up are, upon the whole, superior in date of launching, in speed, in size, and, above all, in weight of metal to the 10 German ships, which are, we are told, to be retained. In primary armament especially we have 8—10-inch and 44—12-inch guns, against 40—9·4-inch German guns. (The Cabinet will appreciate the enormous difference between a 12-inch and a 9·4-inch gun, especially when of equal date.)

I do not at all quarrel with the policy of laying up ships, and believe it essential to the economy of the Navy in time of peace. But there could scarcely be a greater measure of the superiority of the British fleet than the high class of the ships they do not think it worth while to maintain in seagoing commission. And, of course, by declaring that so many perfectly good ships will be laid up by us at a particular date, and declaring that at the same time so many inferior ships will be retained by Germany, the Admiralty are able to produce almost any paper result of relative strengths which they may feel disposed to show.

7 *February* 1909   WSC

Sir John Fisher to J. L. Garvin[1]
(Garvin Papers)
EXTRACT

11 February 1909

My beloved Garvin,

BURN!!!

When your letter came just now I was on the point of writing to tell you of a 'Nicodemus' visit by Esher . . . to report Cabinet Secrets! . . . Winston & Lloyd George having failed to get hold of me they implored Esher to meet them privately . . . I cannot tell you what passed but these were his concluding words to them both: 'If the Admiral was to go back on the six he would be irretrievably damned.' (N.B. the Beauty of it is that though SIX are sufficient I am going for *eight!!!* and if the Germans . . . should have made the progress that is possible though not probable *we shall have the eight!* but don't allude to this as it will utterly humbug Asquith in playing his game with his Brunner[2] party) – So they – Winston & Lloyd George said 'very well, then out we go'!

(NB They are not such d——d fools!!!). . . .

WSC to Sir Edward Grey
(Foreign Office Papers)

16 February 1909

My dear Grey,

You used two quite separate arguments to me last night – public safety and public opinion. Upon the first there really is no immediate difference. We are *all* agreed that 2 ships shall be laid down in June and 2 in October. If the facts are what McKenna thinks we shall all equally be agreed in October that 2 more shall be laid down in March. And the facts can be proved in the interval. Nothing therefore of material security will be impaired or affected by the delay which your colleagues asked you to give. You cannot plead that the safety of this country or the strength of the Fleet is involved in the slightest degree. There is no difference between us which

[1] James Louis Garvin (1868–1947), Editor of *The Observer* 1908–42, *Pall Mall Gazette* 1912–15; in his youth he had been an ardent Parnellite and his earliest appearances in print were letters written in Hull to the *Eastern Morning News* in support of Home Rule. His support for WSC's retention of the Ministry of Defence in 1942 contributed to his disagreement with Lord Astor which led to his resignation.

[2] John Tomlinson Brunner (1842–1919), Liberal MP for Northwich 1885–6 and 1887–1909; Chairman of Brunner, Mond & Co, Alkali manufacturers; member of Royal Commission on Canals and Waterways 1906; leader of a radical parliamentary group which advocated public investment in scientific and economic development; Baronet 1895; PC 1906.

would – if the facts are proved – prevent McKenna laying down every ship exactly as he plans it now – to the very hour.

Upon the second argument we do differ seriously. I do not think [it] right to concede to force what we will not give to reason. The fear of a naval panic, the apprehension of the resignation of the Sea Lords may or may not be well grounded, (I do not think they are); but they do not justify the catastrophe we may conceivably involve the Government and the Party. Only public safety *could* justify that. Rather than compromise naval security, I agree a Government had better be broken. But panic and intimidation should be resisted fearlessly.

And remember you yourself were prepared after much examination to propose a policy of 4 now and 2 later if necessary. Are you really prepared to drive out colleagues who accept the basis you yourself laid down, when no scrap of public security is compromised, simply because you fear a naval panic? Are you willing to see the Government broken irretrievably rather than postpone for a few months during wh the facts may be proved – the announcement of two vessels wh are not in any case to be begun for more than a year? These are the questions wh I put and they are upon you and not upon us in their responsibility.

Yours very sincerely,
WINSTON S. CHURCHILL

Sir John Fisher to J. L. Garvin
(*Garvin Papers*)
EXTRACT

17 February 1909

Private & Secret

My dear Garvin,

Winston Churchill told McKenna yesterday that he was being advised by Custance[1] & Sir W. White[2] in only having 4 Dreadnoughts and they have supplied him with all his arguments technical & otherwise!

The baseness of this is that they Custance & White know that only 4 Dreadnoughts would compel my resignation! *That is the object & not the safety of the country* . . . Of course Winston Churchill may be a liar but I don't think so as the technicalities in his memoranda to the Cabinet are beyond him . . .

[1] Reginald Neville Custance (1847–1935), 2nd in Command of Channel Fleet 1907–8; ADC to Queen Victoria 1897; Director of Naval Intelligence 1899–1902; Rear-Admiral Mediterranean Fleet 1902–4; knighted 1904.

[2] William Henry White (1845–1913), naval architect; was responsible for designs of many British ships from 1885–1902; consulting Naval Architect to Cunard Lines 1904–7; knighted 1895.

Sir John Fisher to WSC

Sunday   Admiralty

28 February 1909

Private & Secret

My dear Winston,

I appreciate your kind motive in writing me your long letter of today's date – I confess I never expected you to turn against the Navy after all you had said in public & private – (*Et tu Brute!*) – I am sure you wont expect me to enter into any discussion with you as there can be only one exponent of the Admiralty case – the First Lord.

As to want of foresight on part of the Admiralty, the Sea Lords expressed their grave anxiety in a memorandum presented to the First Lord in Dec 1908. The Cabinet ignored that anxiety & cut down the Estimates. You want to do the same again!. We can take no risks this year – last year we did! We felt then there would be time to pull up – that margin is now exhausted.

I reciprocate your grief at our separation – I retain the memory of many pleasant duets!

Ever yours truly

J. A. FISHER

Count Metternich to WSC

2 March 1909   Kaiserlich Deutsche Botschaft
                                                        9 Carlton House Terrace

My dear Churchill,

The Chancellor Prince Bülow said in a speech delivered in the Reichstag on the 10th of December last:

'Our naval armaments have been laid down by legislation, merely with a view to protecting our coast and our trade. It is absolutely out of question – and I know that the administration of our Navy agrees with me in this respect – that we should go in our shipbuilding programme beyond the limits necessary for our defence and, for this reason, laid down by legislation. It is out of question on one hand because of our geographical situation which shows that our safety will always depend upon a strong army; on the other hand it is out of the question, because our economic and financial resources are naturally limited and already heavily called upon by expenses for the army and for our social politics, which are much in advance to those of other countries.'

Sincerely yours

O. METTERNICH

WSC to Sir John Fisher

4 March 1909   Board of Trade

Private & Personal

My dear Fisher,

I think you ought to know that McKenna referred in Cabinet yesterday to my private conversation with you at our chance meeting in the Athenaeum Club on Sat & that he appeared desirous of suggesting that I had been guilty of improper behaviour. I dealt with this aspersion at once in the manner wh the circs required & with results wh I regard as entirely satisfactory. But I do not think that a perfectly informal conversation between friends wh you expressly desired shd be treated as strictly private ought to have become the subject of serious Cabinet discussion. On my part I have carefully refrained from imparting to my colleagues the infn wh you gave me abt your holding a written pledge from McK that 8 & not 6 Dreadnoughts were in fact to be laid down, or that you had had a private interview with Grey; I do not think you were discreet in giving McK any a/c however fragmentary of my remarks.

But I am sure you did not mean him to make the use of the infn wh he has done, and wh produced a vy unpleasant effect so far as he was concerned upon those who heard him.

My object in seeking a copy of my letter to you was to lay it before my colleagues, but as it has been burned that course is now impossible.

Yrs v Sincerely, *sans rancune*

WSC

Sir John Fisher to WSC

4 March 1909   Admiralty

Private & Personal

My dear Winston,

Thanks for your letter just come and more especially its concluding French words of unaltered feelings towards me. It's kind of you to send me these Cabinet revelations – It's too sad and most deplorable! Let us write the word

'*Finis*'. The Apostle is right! The tongue is the very devil! (*NB* Yours is slung amidships and wags at both ends!)

Yours till the Angels smile on us (four more Dreadnoughts!!!)

JF

I told Marsh I had burnt your previous letter. No eye had seen it. I have burned this one just come for the same reason – *Amantium irae amoris intergratio est!*[1] Have you got the same cook as you had at Bolton Street?

I think it would be lovely to call the four extra Dreadnoughts

No 1 – *Winston*

No 2 – *Churchill*

No 3 – *Lloyd*

No 4 – *George*

How they would fight!

Uncircumventable!

Read this out at the Cabinet!

WSC to Sir Edward Grey

9 September 1909

Copy

I send you the enclosed note I have made of a talk I had with Metternich last Saturday week, i.e., before the Cabinet at which we discussed these matters. You will see that the conversation was quite banal in its character; but I send it to you in order that you may let me know whether this is the sort of line which you think I ought to take in case any of these subjects should be broached to me when I am at Wurzburg. I may add that, as you know, I am going to Germany only to amuse myself at the Manoeuvres and to see some Labour Exchanges and some Battlefields: I do not propose to talk politics or to be interviewed by any newspaper. I do not expect to see anybody of political consequence except the Emperor. I should certainly make no effort to engage him on any of these matters in conversation, but if he himself raised them, I should propose to reply with simplicity and candour in this sort of strain.

Many thanks for helping me about Sedan.

[WINSTON S. CHURCHILL]

---

[1] Love's quarrels are the renewal of Love. (Terence, *Andria* l.555.)

Note by WSC

Count Metternich lunched with me last Saturday week, and we talked over my plans for going to Germany and the arrangements he had made for me to see the Labour Exchanges and to attend the Manoeuvres.

We had some conversation on things in general in the course of which I told him what I thought about the existing situation between the Government and the House of Lords, the chances and prospects of a General Election and the increasing possibilities, as I discern them, of the present Government being in power for several years. We then got on to the old subject of the Navy, and I said, as I felt that there had been a *détente* on this subject and that the position was unquestionably easier than it had been some months ago; I said there was no doubt that the original German Navy Law in itself was a very formidable fact for British eyes to contemplate; that the revised Navy Law was still more serious; but that the prospects of an acceleration even upon that had been the cause of the deep disquiet which had spread among all parties and all classes in this country at the beginning of the year. I told him that in December last, when we were considering the question of the Navy Estimates, we were confronted with the fact that whereas according to the paper programme of the Second Navy Law we should have expected to find the Germans at work upon nine Dreadnought vessels, they were, in fact, at work upon eleven; that although this was explainable by reasons which I had always believed were perfectly innocent, the fact remained, and it was to that fact that I attributed the public anxiety which had been expressed, no doubt in some cases, with much exaggeration, in Parliament and in the press. I said that a good many months had gone by since then and that, as far as I knew, the exaggeration which we had noticed seems to have stopped, and that so far as I could follow the figures (of course I had no special information) the Germans were at present two behind their paper programme, instead of being two in front as they were in December last. I told him that if, and in proportion as, these facts gradually became established and recognised as indisputable, there would be a great feeling of relief which would be very beneficial to Anglo-German friendship. After making what you call the usual parade movement, he said, in effect, there was certainly a feeling in Germany about the Navy, that the pressure upon the Government towards Naval expansion had been very greatly reduced, and that he did not think it at all likely there would be any movement of German public opinion towards acceleration or expansion of the Navy programme; on the contrary, the pressure was growing stronger the other way, and that there had been a sensible change in that respect. I said that it was no good shutting ones eyes to facts, and that however hard Governments and individuals worked to make a spirit of real trust and confidence between the two countries they would make very little headway while there was a continually booming naval policy in Germany; but that if ever for purely German reasons the German Government decided upon a policy of slackening off and generally of Naval *détente* they would have incidentally a very rich harvest to reap in England; that of course they would naturally judge this question entirely for themselves; but it would be a great pity if in judging it they undervalued the results which might be reached here if the real cause of recent anxieties were abated. He said he did not think there was anything very considerable to be gained. He showed by what he said that he clearly thought that the whole of this Navy scare had been part of a deep policy to rally the British Empire together, to obtain contributions from the Colonies towards the Navy, and to act upon Parliamentary and public opinion to obtain the necessary estimates for a forward building programme. I told him he was quite wrong in this. I had not myself shared all the anxieties which many of my colleagues felt on this subject, but I knew enough of their minds to know that they were absolutely certain in their anxieties, and that no such ulterior motive had the slightest influence upon their minds in deciding what should be the measure of our provision for this year. I told him that the Liberal Government was quite simple in these matters, and never played any game at all, that a policy of strong armaments was not popular with the political forces by which we were supported, and that whether as a party or as a Government we had nothing whatever to gain by, and much to lose by, creating a sensational atmosphere. I said, of course, a case had to be made in the House of Commons for the great Estimates presented, and the objections which so many of our Radical supporters entertained to high Naval Estimates had to be met by a full statement of the facts as we believed them; that these facts were disquieting in themselves, and that no doubt they had produced an unexpected effect in the country and in the Colonies, and also, no doubt, they had been much exaggerated by the newspapers and by the Opposition.

He then said, after some intervening conversation of no consequence, that arrangements on armaments were only possible between friends and where there was a spirit of trust, and that it was no good trying to make them between Powers who regarded each other as likely antagonists, or words to that effect. I said there was no reason why we should be antagonists, we had nothing whatever to quarrel about, and no alliances to involve us in any way. He said there were understandings and arrangements which amounted to alliances, and that the German Government knew perfectly well that the closest plans had been concerted between the French and British War Offices for joint action. I said I knew nothing of it, and that I did not believe it was true. He then pointed out the fact that General French was the only foreign Officer at the French Manoeuvres, and he said that the significance of that was understood all over the Continent. I repeated that I was sure there was no truth in it; but even if soldiers did talk to one another professionally, no one knew better than a German how little that bore to the commitments of Governments. He said that up to a very few years ago the German Government had had plans for war prepared by their Intelligence Department against every country with whom they could come in contact except England; that they had had no plans whatever made against England until the discovery of the close military relations between England and France had rendered it necessary for them to make such plans, and that they had since been occupied in making them, although they were quite certain the contingency would never occur. I said I supposed every decent Intelligence Department made plans for all sorts of contingencies however remote and improbable, and anyone who had the smallest knowledge of the military profession understood how purely professional such arrangements were.

The only other subject I touched on with him was the Bagdad Railway. I said, abruptly 'What about the Bagdad Railway, how are you getting along with that?' He said, in reply, that it was 'going very slowly', that there were 'great difficulties in getting the money,' and that there had been 'rather a falling off of German interest in this respect'. I said we had great and old-established interests in the Persian Gulf, which we were bound to watch over. He said 'Yes', and that 'they would be greatly aided by the arrival of a Turkish Railway, built with German capital, on which goods could be carried on equal terms.' I smiled at this, and said that I had often thought it a great pity myself that we had not been able to work together in that enterprise on fair terms, and that it would be much easier and better for both; that we should get on ever so much quicker in an enterprise, which in itself was a great 'culture' work. He said 'Well, it may come to that', and then he repeated 'It may very easily come to that'.

At this point my wife came into the room and we talked about other matters.

Memorandum by WSC on Germany

3 November 1909   Board of Trade

Believing that there are practically no checks upon German naval expansion except those imposed by the increasing difficulties of getting money, I have had the enclosed report prepared with a view to showing how far those limitations are becoming effective. It is clear that they are becoming terribly effective. The overflowing expenditure of the German Empire strains and threatens every dyke by which the social and political unity of Germany is maintained. The high customs duties have been largely rendered inelastic through commercial treaties, and cannot meet the demand. The heavy duties upon food-stuffs, from which the main proportion of the customs revenue is raised, have produced a deep cleavage between the agrarians and the industrials, and the latter deem themselves quite uncompensated for the high price of food-stuffs by the most elaborate devices of protection for manufactures. The splendid possession of the State railways is, under pressure, being continually degraded to a mere instrument of taxation. The field of direct taxation is already largely occupied by State and local systems. The prospective inroad by the universal suffrage Parliament of the Empire upon this depleted field unites the propertied classes, whether Imperialists or State-right men, in a common apprehension, with which the governing authorities are not unsympathetic. On the other hand, the new or increased taxation on every form of popular indulgence powerfully strengthens the parties of the Left, who are themselves the opponents of expenditure on armaments and much else besides.

Meanwhile the German Imperial debt has more than doubled in the last thirteen years of unbroken peace, has risen since the foundation of the Empire to about 220,000,000*l*, has increased in the last ten years by 105,000,000*l*, and practically no attempt to reduce it has been made between 1880 and the present year. The effect of recurrent borrowings to meet ordinary annual expenditure has checked the beneficial process of foreign investment, and dissipated the illusion cherished during the South African War that Berlin might supplant London as the lending centre of the world. The credit of the German Empire has fallen to the level of that of Italy. It is unlikely that the new taxes which have been imposed with so much difficulty this year will meet the annual deficit.

These circumstances force the conclusion that a period of severe internal strain approaches in Germany. Will the tension be relieved by moderation or snapped by calculated violence? Will the policy of the German Government be to soothe the internal situation or to find an escape from it in external adventure? There can be no doubt that both courses are open. Low as the credit of Germany has fallen, her borrowing powers are practically unlimited. But one of the two courses must be taken soon, and from that point of view it is of the greatest importance to gauge the spirit of the new administration from the outset.[1] If it be pacific, it must soon become markedly pacific, and conversely.

WSC

[1] Bethmann Hollweg had replaced Bülow as German Chancellor in June 1909.

13

Parliament 1910

(See Main Volume Chapter 10)

POLLING in the first General Election of 1910 began on
15 January and ended on 14 February. The Liberal Party
won only two more seats than the Conservatives and depended
upon Labour and Irish Nationalist support in the House. In
Dundee the result was as follows:

Rt Hon W. S. Churchill (Liberal)	10,747
A. Wilkie[1] (Labour)	10,365
J. S. Lloyd (Conservative)	4,552
J. Glass (Conservative)	4,339
E. Scrymgeour[2] (Prohibitionist)	1,512
Liberal majority over Conservative	6,195
Labour majority over Conservative	5,813

[1] Alexander Wilkie (1850–1928) formed in 1882 the forerunner of the Ship-constructors'
and Shipwrights' Association; Labour MP for Dundee 1906–22; according to *Who Was Who*
'never missed a single meeting' of the TUC; CH 1917.

[2] Edwin Scrymgeour (1866–1947), Prohibitionist MP for Dundee 1922–31. He opposed
WSC at six elections between 1908 and 1922, gradually increasing his votes from 300 to over
32,000, when he defeated WSC in 1922. WSC described him in *Thoughts and Adventures* as 'a
quaint and dim figure . . . who pleaded for the kingdom of God upon earth with special
reference to the evils of alcohol'. When he was elected in 1922 'Ephesian' remarked that 'It
is understood that his constituents easily reconcile themselves to his absence at Westminster'.
His father, James Scrymgeour, was a pioneer of the Scottish Temperance Movement and the
subject of a poem by William McGonagall which contained the lines:

> Fellow-citizens of Dundee
> Isn't it really very nice
> To think of James Scrymgeour trying
> To rescue fallen creatures from the paths of vice?
>
> He is a man of noble principles
> As far as I can think
> And the noblest principle he has got
> Is, he abhors the demon drink.

H. H. Asquith to WSC

1 January 1910   Archerfield House

My dear Winston,

My people in East Fife – many of whom pass their working days in Dundee – are hoping that you may be able to come & give them a speech in our contest. The 20th or 24th are suggested as the most appropriate days. Of course I should be very grateful for your help.

All good luck for always

HHA

I go South on Monday

John E. Gorst to WSC

19 January 1910   84 Campden Hill Court

My dear Winston,

It was awfully good of you to send me a telegram of condolence in the middle of your own election. It was a great pleasure to see your magnificent majority, which is the best answer to all your detractors. Preston was a surprise and a disappointment. I was looking forward to be in the fight with the Lords. I think the Tariff Reform propaganda had made more progress amongst the poorer electors than we supposed, and that was the main cause of the turn-over of those who voted Liberal in '06. It appears that Preston was the only Lancashire Town in which this took place: I feel a little ashamed of the want of shrewdness in my native place. Calvert, who took Cox up, is one of the richest mill-owners in Preston, and he worked very hard. He injured us more by what he did to depress us, than by what he did to exalt Cox, whose case was always hopeless. The Labour party played quite straight: the difference between Macpherson[1] and me was accounted for by Roman Catholic splits on Cox.

You are now going to make history: good luck to you!

Ever Yours

JOHN E. GORST

---

[1] J. T. Macpherson (who had been Labour MP 1906–10) came third of the five candidates at Preston; Gorst and Cox were fourth and fifth.

Cabinet Memorandum by WSC

January 1910   [Board of Trade]

Everything now tends towards a battle. Can we find the right battle-ground? Can we lead the army to it? In this light all questions must be viewed. It is more important at this juncture to keep the confidence & enthusiasm of our own supporters than to remain in office. I fear most a charge of having failed to keep our pledges. However unjust, it would be fatally damaging. We should have to fight an election on an apology. I would rather put the Unionists in for a year, & take all the chances of their queering the pitch, than be thrown out on the Budget by the Irish party on the allegation that we had broken our word. In the former case we could keep together & win. In the latter we should be destroyed. Everything depends upon the election. Everything not involving material interests must be secondary to entering upon that struggle in the best possible posture.

Two courses present themselves.

First: – To announce in the King's Speech or as early as possible that measures will be brought forward to secure the undivided authority of the H of C over money Bills, to define the relations of the two Houses (so that the will of the people as expressed by their representatives shall prevail within the lifetime of a single Parliament), & to establish an elective second Chamber based upon the Parliamentary franchise.

To pass the Budget etc under drastic guillotine.

To adjourn at Easter to prepare the Bill.

To bring the Bill to the Lords in July.

To advise a dissolution upon its rejection, & *then* the bill having been definitely tabled, passed by the Commons, rejected by the Lords and become the subject of a special appeal to the electors to ask for guarantees for a creation of peers to pass it in the event of a majority being returned.

This is perhaps the best & safest plan, because it is orderly, because it enables us to keep the reins of power, & to unfold our policy with all the authority of a Government. But we may not have the power to carry it out. Unless we are sure that we can carry it out, we should adopt the second course – namely resignation. We should interpret our pledges in the narrow-est & most literal sense. The PM should formally ask the King whether he would be prepared to create peers sufficient to pass the defeated CB [Campbell-Bannerman] Bill & on his certain & natural refusal, we should resign – saying that we did not at all complain of the King's action, but that the constitution as it stands is so unfair that we cannot be responsible for the conduct of affairs. We can raise the anti-hereditary issue in opposition.

Both of these roads lead to an election in a few months. Either course will bring us honourably before our constituents with a perfectly clear straightforward policy. We ought not to shrink from resignation. Redmond should be confronted with the plain alternative. I think he will give way, make the best of the King's Speech declarations and promise to support the Budget. But if he or any large section of our majority choose to interpret the Albert Hall pledge in the sense that we are debarred from continuing to hold office without guarantees, we ought not to resist their view. Anything is better than a charge of breach of faith. Nothing could more surely ruin the democratic cause, than an election at wh we should be forced on every platform to apologise for & explain our retention of office without guarantees until we were ignominiously defeated in H of C. I would then let Redmond know that unless he promises to support the Budget we will not go on at all.

There is only one question: – How to bring the party into a general election against the House of Lords on the best possible grounds. Everything else is secondary. The Budget is secondary.

Altho' no doubt it would be very nice to be able to pass the Budget without the change of a comma, it would be mere vanity to risk the main issue for that. Each House of Comms has a right to its own opinion about the best way of raising money for the service of the year. Every Government ought to make proposals for defraying the expense which it believes the H of C will accept. If concessions are useless let us make none. Unless concessions are necessary, let us make none. But if we can get 4/5th of the Budget, including Land, Mineral Royalties, Supertax, Licences & Death Duties, by giving up 1/5 (for wh we have no majority & wh brings no revenue) obviously we ought not to stand on any false pride. We want the Budget out of the way. We want a clear & naked issue with the Lords. If we have to choose between dropping the Veto policy, or dropping the Whisky tax, can anyone doubt which is the more important. I would therefore run all risks (if necessary) of opening the Budget again in order to make it possible for the Irish to vote for it. I would not propose a Budget wh the Irish cd not vote for. The pinch is then over.

On the Lords – I agree with Grey. The CB resolution does not go far enough. No election can be fought with enthusiasm except upon the abolition of the principle of hereditary legislators. No one can Un-Radical the man who means that. On the merits certainly therefore, I am for our adopting the policy of the CB resolution plus an elective second chamber with consequent modifications.

But what will our friends say? I believe they will throw up their hats. I am firmly convinced that this note once struck will dominate. But we ought to test their mood & feel our way. Time is vital. We must at all costs find the true line on the Lords question. And we must not hesitate to sacrifice our triumph on the Budget for the sake of getting the necessary time.

The composition of H of C may legitimately affect the character of the Budget. If there is a majority *for* 4/5ths of it, & a majority *against* 1/5th of it, the Government may be forced to shape their policy accordingly. There are no doubt many objections to making any change. But the whisky duty is not a vital point, & we have to reason for trying to make it one. At such a moment subsidiary propositions may have to be sacrificed to secure success on the main lines. It is the duty of a Government to make proposals to Parlt for meeting the charges of the year which the present House of Commons will accept. We should not be justified in insisting upon a particular set of proposals simply because they commended themselves to the late House of Commons. If we carry Land, Licences, Supertax, Death duties, & Mineral Royalties we shall have succeeded in all the main points of contention, & all the substantial sources of revenue. In the last ditch therefore to secure the Irish support I would run all the risks of reopening the Budget in order to modify or leave out the whisky tax.

[WSC]

Mrs H. H. Asquith to WSC

10 February 1910   10 Downing Street

Private – Burn

Dear Winston,
    One line to say I am glad you are going to H[ome] Office. I also want to say that the King sent Knollys to me Friday last to say he (the K) was no longer vexed at our not going Windsor as he understood how tired & over-tired H was – he also told me that if it was true a rumour he heard of yr going to H Office he (the King) wanted me to tell H that if you wd just keep up that moderation of language wh had struck so many in this election you wd not be at all unappreciated. You must take this as it is meant in kindness. The fact is dear Winston (I am the most genuine woman in the world & I know from our talk you will xcuse my frankness) you have a *unique* opportunity of Selling all yr enemies but not only this – of improving yr position in the eyes of the best element both in politics & society. Believe me cheap scores, hen-roost phrases & all oratorical want of dignity is out of date. You have only to say to yrself 'Margot Asquith is a little boring & over-earnest but she is right. Loyalty, reserve & *character* pays more than all the squibs & crackers. I have got a beautiful young wife, an affectionate heart & a love of amusement. I will make the Court, the Colonies, the West

and the East end of London change their whole views of me. I wont see a Press man & I wont have my name coupled with anyone's & I shall thrive on being liked instead of loving abusive notice & rotten notoriety.'

I have never said anything of you that I was not prepared to say *to* you & I hope you will never feel that I am not *absolutely* trustworthy & true. I have a great feeling for Clemmy; she is *so* rare not to be vain of her marvellous beauty.

Yrs
M.A.

Cabinet Memorandum by WSC

14 February 1910   [Board of Trade]

1. We are not committed to the method of the CB plan, but only to its object and its general scope. We are free to adopt any reasonable variant, or equivalent, and still more to make any extension beyond it.

2. The CB plan, convenient though it has proved in the preliminary phase, does not go far enough, and is not sufficiently based on principle for a pitched battle on it alone. If we are to aim at winning another general election in July against the Lords, we must not deprive ourselves of the right to develop the full argument against the principle of hereditary legislators.

3. The time has come for the total abolition of the House of Lords. Powerful sections of the Conservative party are now engaged in cutting that Assembly to ribbons. Many Conservatives have frankly abandoned the hereditary principle. Scarcely a voice in any party is raised on behalf of the existing institution. We cannot as a Liberal party stand outside this spontaneous repudiation of hereditary and aristocratic privilege. Still less can we stand by and watch inertly the attempt to replace hereditary privilege by other and more objectionable forms of securing Conservative predominance.

4. Since we are agreed in opposing the principle of a hereditary legislative Assembly, the only fundamental question open is – one Chamber or two?

I would not myself be frightened by having only one. The stability of this country does not depend upon its form of Government, but upon the general balance of the nation, the diversity of interests, the ever-widening diffusion of property, and the intelligence and strong character of the British people. The masses of wage-earners have only to vote once or twice with some approach to solidarity to do anything they like with our Parliamentary machinery. It is not the existence of a Second Chamber – ancient or modern – but causes far more intimate and powerful that prevent their combination.

5. But I recognize the convenience and utility of a properly constituted and duly subordinated Second Chamber, to revise legislation, to revise it so far as possible from a non-party point of view, or at least from a differently constituted party point of view, and to interpose the potent safeguard of delay. I recognize also its soothing effect upon large classes, who fear that their special interests may be ill-treated by the modern House of Commons. Moreover, we could not now agree upon a single-Chamber system, and at this juncture unity is vital.

I am therefore prepared to support a two-Chamber system at the present time both on merits and tactics.

6. If this conclusion be accepted, we cannot rest content with it. We must go further. We must face the labour and the peril of construction. No one can be contented with a policy which, while it recognizes the need of a Second Chamber, reduces the existing Assembly to a sham, and proclaims its impotence to create a new one. It would be highly dangerous to leave the void unfilled. The CB plan will not by itself command intellectual assent nor excite enthusiasm. But even if by a dead-lift effort we succeeded in carrying it – which I gravely doubt – the work would remain unfinished. On the first return of the Conservative party to power the Lords would be reformed in the Conservative interest and their veto restored to them. To make any victory permanent in this field the captured ground must be strongly occupied by a new institution erected upon the ruins of the old. It is a matter for argument whether a sudden or a gradual declaration of such an intention would be most likely to command the assent of our supporters. That is a question of tactics, and must be weighed carefully. But in thought, apart from action, the issue is actually upon us. What shall be the constitution of the Second Chamber?

7. There are any number of good plans, all of which would work more or less well, and any of which could be speedily established by the agreement of the great parties. But there is no chance of agreement. There are no means of compromise. The contrariety of interests is absolute. When we speak of a reformed Second Chamber, what we mean is a Second Chamber which will enable us to pass Home Rule, Welsh Disestablishment, Plural Voting, and other Party Bills. What the Conservatives mean is a Chamber which will enable them more effectually to resist these measures. There can, in the nature of things, be no agreement.

8. No plan for a Second Chamber can be carried in the absence of agreement that is not based on broad and simple principles. When it comes to a great controversy to be maintained before the whole country – no arbitrary scheme, however well intended, however practical, could compete with a symmetrical and logical system. What we have to do is to find a plan based

on broad principles, and also producing the right results in practice; surely this is not impossible?

9. There are three essentials to any Second Chamber we could touch: –

(i) It must be subordinate. The undivided authority of the House of Commons over Money Bills, and its due predominance in general legislation must be established.

(ii) It must be democratic. The Second Chamber must be based upon the votes of the whole body of the Parliamentary electors, though a different grouping should be sought.

(iii) It must be fair. It must give all parties an equal chance.

Other important conditions are: –

(iv) It must be in numbers less than one-quarter of the House of Commons, and consequently chosen by very large constituencies.

(v) It must consist of persons of experience and public service.

(vi) It should not all be elected at one time.

(vii) It should afford means of entry to a certain number of distinguished men not suited by health or temperament to popular election.

10 These conditions would appear to be satisfied by the following heads of a plan (for which I do not claim authorship): –

One hundred members elected upon Parliamentary franchise by fifty great two-member constituencies;

To sit for eight years, retiring by halves;

To be chosen from a panel of public service automatically recruited: –

Ten years in either House of Parliament;

Special municipal services of long duration;

Certain great offices, &c.

The one hundred Members when elected to co-opt by a system of voting which enables the strict party proportion to be preserved, and consequently secures that the complexion of the Chamber as settled by the electors shall not be altered – fifty more members from the same panel (like the Aldermen of the L.C.C.).

The Chamber thus constituted would have no power to touch Bills certified by the Speaker of the House of Commons to be Money Bills, and consequently no power to make or unmake Governments.

It would possess a suspensory Veto upon all legislation to the third year, when in the event of disagreement between Houses continuing a Joint Session of the two bodies should, upon the demand of the House of Commons, be held, whereat the Members of both should sit together, debate together, vote together, and a simple majority decide.

11. Other points of a consequential nature are suggested: –

(i) A Quinquennial Act for the House of Commons.

(ii) Ministers to have the right to speak in both Houses.

(iii) Two representatives of each of the great Dominions to have the right to speak but not vote in the Second Chamber.

(iv) Peers to be eligible to sit in the House of Commons.

(v) The creation of a Supreme Court of Appeal for the British Empire.

12. The sentence in the King's Speech might run: –

'Measures will be laid before you with all convenient speed to define the relations between the Houses of Parliament, so as to secure the undivided authority of the House of Commons over finance and[1] its due predominance in legislation, and to establish an elective Second Chamber based upon the Parliamentary franchise.'

13. It is suggested that, if provisional agreement can be reached on this declaration, the other points should be referred to a Cabinet Committee.

WSC

WSC to H. H. Asquith

18 February [1910]   Board of Trade

[Copy]

Prime Minister,

We are becoming involved in a perfectly unreal dispute with our own supporters. The Irish, the Labour party & I daresay half our own men say 'Veto before Budget', because they think (or pretend to think) that withholding the Budget means putting pressure on the Lords to pass the Veto. Surely a triumph of absurdity! It is the refusal of the necessary votes in supply that alone could embarrass a new Government – & about these there is no dispute & no danger. On the other hand we say 'Budget before Veto' because we feel that our duty as Ministers obliges us to safeguard the national finances.

But the situation has changed.

When 'Veto first' meant 'Veto *Bill* first' there would have been real injury to the Finances owing to the delay involved. Now that 'Veto first' means

---

[1] Alternative conclusion noted in the margin by WSC: 'to provide that the House should be so constituted and empowered as to exercise impartially in regard to proposed legislation the function of revision, and under proper safeguards of delay.'

nothing more than 'Veto *Resolutions* first' & only a week or ten days is in question – no injury to public interests can occur.

One has only to realise how artificial the point in debate has become, to feel reassured about the outcome.

Your own statements are perfectly compatible with either course. If the Budget is to be 'the first act' that means the first completed controversial business of the new Parliament. Nothing prevents 'the first *step*' being taken to lay the Veto policy before Parliament at any time or in any form you may consider convenient.

I write this note – because I hope our full freedom to take the best path – agreeably to our public declarations, & the national interest – will not be restricted by the false points of dispute around wh our discussions have revolved.

WSC

WSC to the King
(*Royal Archives*)

21 February 1910　　　　　　　　　　　　House of Commons

Mr Churchill with his humble duty to your Majesty has the honour to state that the course of events in the House of Commons this afternoon has been productive of some grave features. After some preliminary talk about the standing orders, the Prime Minister in reply to a moderate speech from Mr Balfour unfolded the policy of the Government at this juncture: to wit – to proceed with the indispensable financial business, to lay the proposal for the reform of the relations between the Two Houses before Parliament in the shape of resolutions, and to pass the Budget unamended into Law. The Prime Minister further laid stress upon the fact that the Government were resolved not to allow Your Majesty's Sovereign position to become involved in the strife of parties. 'We have not' he said 'received guarantees. We have not asked for any.'

Mr Redmond followed and in an adroit but at the same time vy menacing speech indicated the position of the Irish party. He did not commit himself to final action. But he seemed anxious to force the Government to a decisive issue at the earliest possible moment, and the general tenor of his demand pointed to the early resignation of Your Majesty's Ministers as a protest against the present unfair balance of the Constitution involved in the existing relations of the Two Houses. His remarks received a great deal of support from the more advanced members of the Ministerial majority.

After his speech the House adjourned, all parties being inclined to reflect and sleep upon the situation.

That situation indeed presents many elements of instability; but Mr Churchill believes that a policy of simplicity and determination upon the part of Your Majesty's Ministers will result in the direction of affairs remaining in their hands for the next few weeks. If these are surmounted it is possible that the Parliamentary position will improve.

Mr Churchill trusts that Your Majesty was satisfied with the reasons he gave to Lord Knollys for allowing the Law to take its course in the Capital case to which Your Majesty's attention has been drawn.

And with his humble duty remains, Your Majesty's obedient servant

WINSTON S. CHURCHILL

Mrs H. H. Asquith to WSC

21 February 1910   10 Downing Street

Dear Winston,

I myself am delighted at what has happened – We stand to gain more than we lose by being unthreatenable by Irish or anyone else & surely the Labour men wont let the Tories score off us. As you & I said it was a great misfortune that my husband misled his own men & I think a quicker hint might have been given to our newspapers of his real meaning – legislative safeguards & not putting the King into the fighting line but we are all in the same boat & if we all stand close – tight – brave & confident – I think we shall win – We have *all the brains* on our side & the country doesn't care for Tariff Reform – You are a good fighter – let us all keep our tails up & perhaps because our Prime Minister *has* made a mistake – of wh he was quite unconscious – let us rally round him.

Yrs affecly

MARGOT ASQUITH

WSC to the King
(*Royal Archives*)

22 February 1910   House of Commons

Mr Churchill with his humble duty to Your Majesty has the honour to report that the situation in the House of Commons, though not clear or satisfactory, has become distinctly less critical than last night.

The debate upon the Address to Your Majesty in reply to the gracious speech was resumed by Mr Barnes, the Leader – or it would be more accurate to say – the spokesman of the Labour Party. This gentleman voiced strong opinions upon the various topics of the hour with a considerable flavour of Scotch good sense; and the tenor and purport of his remarks was evidently to strengthen the position of the Government and under guise of vehement counsel to support sober action.

Mr F. E. Smith who as Your Majesty knows is a vy good speaker upon the Conservative side followed him with a smart general attack upon the Government which Mr Churchill is informed – for he had to leave for a Cabinet Council – was a successful Parliamentary performance. The Debate hereafter became Hibernian in its character. Mr O'Brien[1] expressed his detestation of the Budget and of Mr Redmond's policy and person with eloquence, and Mr Moore[2] from Belfast – a strong Conservative – delivered a long and sarcastic diatribe against the Irish Nationalist Party, the Government and the supposed relations of the two. Mr Churchill had been deputed by the Cabinet to make a further statement in the Debate. He therefore followed Mr Moore and while adhering to the policy declared yesterday by the Prime Minister, endeavoured to make it clear to the House that the Government had no intention of delaying the issue which must soon arise when the proposals for dealing with the House of Lords and the relations between the two Houses are laid before Parliament.

The House listened with a very apparent sense of anxiety and oppression to the speech and every word was attended to with severe concentration. Upon the whole, however Mr Churchill feels that an easier and friendlier feeling towards the Government was created among its own supporters, and Your Majesty will be glad to hear that Mr Walter Long who followed commented favourably upon the 'improvement' in Mr Churchill's 'manners' towards the Opposition which appeared to have resulted from his transference to the Home Office.

No developments of any real interest are expected tonight, and Mr Churchill feels that it is improbable that any will take place during the next fortnight.

The fiscal amendment of the Opposition is to be the first business tomorrow.

[1] William O'Brien (1852–1928), journalist; Irish Nationalist MP Cork City 1910–18; prosecuted several times and imprisoned for political offences; elected for various Irish seats 1883–92.
[2] William Moore (1864–1944), Barrister; Conservative MP North Armagh 1906–17; MP County Antrim 1899–1906; Lord Justice of Appeal Supreme Court of Northern Ireland 1921–5; Lord Chief Justice of Northern Ireland 1925–37; PC Ireland 1921; Baronet 1932.

WSC to the King
(Royal Archives)

23 February 1910   [House of Commons]

Mr Churchill with his humble duty to Your Majesty has the honour to state that after his letter was written last night a dreary succession of attacks upon the Government from the more extreme of their supporters occupied the sitting. No doubt considerable dissatisfaction exists among the rank and file of the Ministerial party, but Mr Churchill has talked to several of these malcontents without being able to learn from them what they really wish the Government to do. It is vy easy to be discontented with the facts of daily life and of the political structure, and very hard to suggest a cure for them. On the other hand a great number of our supporters are disposed to await with patience the disclosure of the Government's policy. It would be imprudent, however, of Your Majesty's Ministers not to realise to the full the insecurity and complexity of the position which must soon be reached.

Today the Fiscal Amendment of the Official Opposition has been moved by Mr Austen Chamberlain in a reasoned speech. Your Majesty will be familiar with the arguments – the evils of unemployment and their certain remedy, the swifter proportionate progress of other countries, the satisfactory social conditions of the German working man. This is ground upon which the two parties meet with tireless zeal. Mr Churchill remembers to have heard the late Lord Northbrook observe of the controversy between Free Trade and Protection 'that it was a vy good subject for gentlemen to differ about'. Mr Sydney Buxton replied for the Government, having been heavily armed with the voluminous statistics of the Board of Trade. The debate will not be concluded until tomorrow night, and as the Irish members propose to abstain, the Government majority will present a sad contrast to the massive preponderances of the last Parliament.

Mr Churchill hopes that if Your Majesty desires him in his letters to touch on any other points than those with which he has been dealing, Lord Knollys may be instructed to advise him.

WSC to the King

24 February 1910   House of Commons

Copy

Mr Churchill with his humble duty to Your Majesty has the honour to report that the fiscal debate has been resumed today. Mr Mond[1] a Liberal

---

[1] Alfred Moritz Mond (1868–1930), wealthy industrialist; Liberal MP Chester 1906–10, Swansea 1910–23, Carmarthen 1924–8; First Commissioner of Works 1916–21; Minister of Health 1921–2; Baronet 1910; Baron Melchett 1928. Among his companies were the Imperial Chemical Industries, the Mond Nickel Company and Amalgamated Anthracite Collieries; he was also a Director of the Westminster Bank.

member of very wide commercial experience made an excellent speech on Free Trade to a large and appreciative House. He was followed by Mr Samuel Storey[1] who as Your Majesty will recollect is a unique Parliamentary figure being a Radical-Tariff Reformer. This veteran who has been returned triumphantly from Sunderland asserted his unalterable Liberalism and his sincere faith that in Protection alone could the prosperity of our country be secured. Mr Crawshay-Williams, the Liberal member for Leicester, a young man who was formerly an Artillery Officer, made a maiden speech which was a creditable performance.

Everyone had expected that Mr Balfour would speak early in the debate; but he reserved himself until after six o'clock and in consequence the Government arrangements for the debate have had to be somewhat altered – Mr Runciman is to follow him, and the Chancellor of the Exchequer will wind up after dinner. Mr Balfour has certainly made a perfectly unmistakeable Protectionist speech; and Mr Churchill thinks that his party must have been extremely well satisfied with his utterance. Mr Churchill feels however that while the opinion of Lancashire and Yorkshire – the main centres of our industrial strength – remains unconverted to the new doctrines, it will be very difficult for any Conservative Government to take any very decided steps in actual policy.

The division tonight will be narrow. The Government Whips place their majority at between 21 and 31. This result must be regarded as a depressing factor in the general position of the Administration. Mr Churchill feels most deeply the difficulties and burden of the situation, and the hard task of Ministers in bearing up against so many menaces, and in endeavouring with weak forces to carry forward the tremendous constitutional changes to which they are absolutely committed and bound by conviction and honour.

Tomorrow the debate on the Address will be concluded after an amendment relating to the sad case of the hop industry. There seems no reason to suppose that any difficulty will arise. On Monday however when the Prime Minister will propose to take all Private Members' time till Easter, a challenge will be made from the Radical benches to disclose a part at least of his proposals for dealing with the Veto of the House of Lords. It is proposed to meet this, if it is persisted in, by the bluntest methods. The Government can only adhere to their declared policy and carry forward meanwhile the necessary financial business of the country.

---

[1] Samuel Storey (1840–1925), Radical MP for Sunderland 1881–95; 1910 as Independent Tariff Reformer; Mayor of Sunderland 1876, 1877, 1880.

C. P. Scott to WSC

24 February 1910   The Firs
                                       Manchester

My dear Churchill,

It was good of you to write to me in the midst of your preoccupations – I hope none of us will refuse to keep an open mind for the proposals of the Government, but you can have little idea of the confusion & almost despair which has spread through the party as the result of the announcements so far made. Men go about declaiming loudly that they have been betrayed and that seats have been won on false pretences. There has been a double disillusion – first the discovery that the Albert Hall declaration was not meant in the sense in which it was universally understood & that there is no question of asking for guarantees from the King at this stage or of refusing office in case they are not forthcoming; then the suggestion of a complete change of policy on the question of the Lords' Veto – the abandonment of the simple policy of the CB resolutions dealing with the power of the H of L and the substitution or addition of an elaborate scheme for constituting a new Second Chamber. People simply won't listen to it – for three years they have had the other policy placed authoritatively before them, they have just fought & won an election on it and to be asked when the very moment for action has arrived to sit still & wait till a quite different policy has been contrived & presented is more than they can stand.

I report this to you quite frankly. The fighting spirit of the party is still strong, but if they are not strongly led & speedily it will evaporate & we may whistle for our North of England majorities.

Thank you for suggesting that I shd come to see you shortly. It wd be a great help.

Believe me, Yours sincerely
C. P. SCOTT

William Royle[1] to WSC

24 February 1910   Elmwood
                                       Rusholme

Dear Mr Churchill,

You will I am sure excuse me sending you the enclosed but it is only a type of *scores* of communications I am receiving every day. There is a regular

[1] William Royle (1854–1923), Chairman of the Executive of the Manchester Liberal Federation 1903–23. He twice refused a knighthood.

'slump' in Liberal feeling & there will be a revolt unless the Cabinet give us relief in a few days. It may be that when you are able to publish the terms of your resolutions & bill concerning the House of Lords these may bring about a change of feeling but at present *everyone* is dead against any reform of the House of Lords. 'Give us the veto & leave reform to the Tories'. Let me suggest that next week the House begin to deal with finance & the Budget & later before the Budget leaves the Commons introduce a short measure dealing with the veto of the Lords on lines you have no doubt determined. Send the Budget to the Lords & then ram the Veto bill thro' the Commons. This will bring immense enthusiasm to our party & all the past will be forgotten. A reform bill would take until July/August to pass Commons & then would be rejected by the Lords & all the Session wasted.

But do at once relieve the present tension which is *most* damaging to us. Hosts of your friends here ask me daily to write you on these matters.

With kind regards, Sincerely yrs
WM ROYLE
Chairman MLF

If you wish to make me a medium to send us a message of hope I shall be delighted.

WSC to the King

25 February 1910   Home Office

Copy

Mr Churchill with his humble duty to Your Majesty has the honour to report that the debate today in the House of Commons was not productive of any features of significance or general interest. Mr Courthope[1] moved from the Conservative benches an Amendment relating to the Hop industry and the question of its advancement by a protective duty was discussed. The Government majority of 31 last night was this afternoon improved to 43. The Irish Nationalists continued to abstain.

Reviewing the events of the week Mr Churchill feels that the position of the Government has become one of the utmost weakness. There can be no doubt that their supporters in the House and still more in the country are thoroughly disheartened and deeply angered by two grave disillusionments: first that Your Majesty's Ministers are remaining in office without any real

---

[1] George Lloyd Courthope (1877–1955), Unionist MP, Rye Division Sussex 1906–45; Baronet 1925; created Baron 1945.

prospect of carrying their Legislation upon the Lords' Veto; and secondly that the simple question (to them) of the limitation of the Veto according to Sir Henry Campbell-Bannerman's plan should have been clouded by the intention to deal with the constitution of the Second House. It is impossible that the wide and almost universal feeling which now exists should not make its effect upon the policy which it will be open to Ministers to pursue.

Monday will be a climacteric in the existence of this short-lived Parliament. Mr Churchill does not mean to suggest to Your Majesty that the Government will be defeated. He thinks that even if Mr Redmond votes against them with their discontented followers as he has formally announced his intention to do, it is improbable that the Opposition will wish to turn out Ministers upon a question like taking the time of the House – a matter that is to say which would be absolutely vital to them (the Opposition) should Your Majesty recur to them for the conduct of public affairs. But unless the Prime Minister is able to make a statement which will reassure his supporters as to the simple issue of a limitation of the Veto being adhered to, and as to the resolution of the Government upon that point, the general situation must degenerate rapidly.

If however such a statement could be made a very sensible and marked improvement would be produced, and the necessary financial business, including the great estimates of nearly 41 millions for the Navy might be expeditiously transacted.

Mr Churchill has ventured to place the absolute facts of the situation in the House of Commons, as he sees them, before Your Majesty.

C. P. Scott to WSC

27 February 1910   The *Guardian* Office
Manchester

Dear Churchill,

Very many thanks. I had heard of the proposal and you may have seen that we had already supported it in Friday's paper. It wd be a fine thing if it cd be done but I'm afraid the Irish will be dead against it fearing its application to a Home Rule Bill.

Whatever happens I hope we shall hold the anti-Lords combination together and, if we have to fight again, fight with the same forces.

Yours very sincerely
C. P. SCOTT

WSC to the King

28 February 1910   House of Commons

Copy

Mr Churchill with his humble duty to Your Majesty has the honour to report that the situation in the House of Commons has been effectively relieved by the statement of the Prime Minister this afternoon. That statement makes it clear that the collision between the two Houses will not be reached before the 15th of April; but will in all probability occur in the weeks which immediately follow. The gravity of the situation is not diminished, but its decision is postponed. The Irish Nationalists and the Radical supporters of the Government are in the main content. No division was taken in the House, upon an issue which many had thought would be fatal. An air of *détente* was very apparent towards the conclusion of the debate. The unexpected plays such a prominent part in our Parliamentary affairs, that Mr Churchill hesitates to forecast the course of events, but – with all deductions made – he is strongly inclined to think that no Ministerial crisis or change of Government will occur before the month of May, as the result of House of Commons business. He hopes this will be agreeable to Your Majesty and will secure Your Majesty's plans against any inconvenient interruption.

After the Prime Minister had spoken Mr Balfour made a very clever speech picking out on the spur of the moment all the points about which Mr Churchill felt uncomfortable. Then Mr Redmond came forward in the *rôle* of arbiter of national destinies, but with less success than he achieved this day week, and without any of the support which he then received from the Radical benches. Lord Hugh Cecil who was listened to with much consideration on his return to the House followed with a speech of historic flavour. He reminded the House of the various precedents which exist for the extraordinary use of the Royal Prerogative in the creation of Peers, – to show that they were very bad precedents and applied to very evil circumstances and occasions. Mr Churchill has always felt that the destruction of the Whig majority in 1711, and the squandering of the fruits of all the Duke of Marlborough's victories by the Treaty of Utrecht, through the creation of 12 new peers, is a singularly unsatisfactory example from the history of the past. Lord Hugh Cecil quoted at length the fierce terms in which the Hanoverian House of Commons impeached the responsible author of these transactions.[1] But the practical issues of the 28th of February, 1910 were already decided. The subsequent speeches, though constituting an excellent debate, did not impair the renewed stability of the situation and Mr

[1] Lord Hugh Cecil was referring to the impeachment of Robert Harley, Earl of Oxford, in 1715.

Churchill feels that Your Majesty may be assured of the speedy settlement of the urgent business of supply, on which the security and economy of the public service depends.

C. P. Scott to WSC

1 March 1910

Dear Churchill,

The situation was saved as by a miracle last night and I put a lot of the working of the operation to your account. Now I hope we shall go right ahead. I see no reason why we shd not hold the Govt for years & years if we make the war against the Lords hot enough and all the while go on building up the great wall of free-trade interests in the great industrial districts of the North.

Yours very sincerely
C. P. Scott

Edwin Montagu[1] to WSC

28 February 1910

My dear Churchill,

I am unhappy to think that I should have caused you or the Govt or be thought to have caused any difficulty to you or any one else when my one anxiety is to endeavour to help you all to win through the difficulties through which you are steering us.[2]

After warning constituents for seven years that they should contemplate unexpected dissolutions and be prepared for them it is startling to find so much importance attached to a repetition of this platitudinous warning at a private lunch. I was face to face with a committee the which had been and

[1] Edwin Samuel Montagu (1879–1924), Liberal MP Chesterton Division of Cambridgeshire; Parliamentary Secretary to Chancellor of Exchequer 1906–8, to Prime Minister 1908–10; Parliamentary Under Secretary of State, India 1910–14; Chancellor Duchy of Lancaster 1915; Financial Secretary to Treasury 1914–16; Minister of Munitions 1916. Married Hon Venetia Stanley 1915. PC 1914.

[2] Montagu had been reported as saying: 'The result of the last Election, despite its revelation of local loyalty, has been a bitter disappointment to those who believed that this Parliament would see the end of the veto of the House of Lords. It was equally certain that no Radical could refuse to attack the hereditary principle, provided that it did not delay the limitation of the veto. The last few days had proved that the majority that the Government could rely on was small. Under these circumstances an early General Election was irresistible.'

was even then advising the Cabinet and the PM how to govern. My sarcasms were directed at interrupting teaching of egg-sucking to the PM.

But I've learnt to learn that I must never say anything again that can possibly have the slightest meaning.

I am going to speak at St George's tonight. At that meeting I will say nothing of any interest. I will certainly however make some reference to the misreading of my speech. Otherwise I had better let it slide and be forgotten.

Yrs

ED S. MONTAGU

WSC to the King

1 March 1910   Home Office

Copy

Mr Secretary Churchill with his humble duty to Your Majesty has the honour to report that all is quiet in the House of Commons. The necessary financial business is being transacted with smoothness and rapidity. This afternoon the Report Stage of the Borrowing Powers Bill has first been agreed to. It is a well-argued question whether a Government ought to pay off its old debts with one hand while it contracts new debts with the other. Mr Pitt has been quoted against us as the Minister who even in the shock of the Napoleonic struggle when credit was almost exhausted and when colossal loans formed the staple of British finance, nevertheless religiously continued out of borrowed money to repay the outstanding debts of the State. This has always been regarded by financial purists of every school as a blemish on his reputation as an economist. The Prime Minister in reply to criticism based on the Pitt example, cited Canning who said in a speech which, I am assured, is well worth reading, that to pick out this point in Mr Pitt's finance and to hold it up as a model is like the behaviour of savage tribes who when the sun is in its noonday splendour remain unimpressed and unmoved, but who bow themselves in adoration when that luminary suffers a temporary eclipse.

For the rest the sitting has been apathetic. The War Loan Bill has been advanced a stage, and Irish supplementary Estimates and some other minor business have been disposed of. The House concluded its affairs at about 8 o'clock and its members dispersed after an uneventful but fertile day.

Mr Churchill feels that for the time being the critical condition of affairs to which he felt it his duty to draw Your Majesty's attention is at an end. The situation is however none the less acute, and the passage of six or seven weeks must lead to a decision.

It would not do justice to the Government to attribute to them a weak surrender to [the] Irish faction. If Mr Redmond's words have carried weight, it is not because he held the power of altering the balance of voting strength in the House of Commons but because the counsels which he urged were in full harmony with the views of by far the greater part of the Ministerial majority. 'In a representative system it is sometimes necessary to defer to the wishes of other people.' Mr Churchill thinks that in supreme matters a rigid attitude is often alone in accordance with policy and honour. But in such questions as whether a week should be spent upon the discussion of this question before that, or whether a particular Administration should or should not hold office after a certain period, the House of Commons is fully entitled to be the judge. That is the way the Constitution works; and Mr Churchill rejoices to think that in its working, it has year after year conduced to the strength, the unity and the tranquillity of the State, and has resulted in the association year by year of new forces with the great institutions of the realm, and the direction of all those forces towards the maintenance of the Throne and of the Empire.

C. P. Scott to WSC

3 March 1910

Dear Churchill,

Thank you very much for your letter. I fully realise the value of the Party's taking up early a definite line against the hereditary basis of the Second Chamber provided that does not confuse the immediate and vital Veto Issue, and in writing on Asquith's Monday night statement we took care to emphasise that. I expect to be in London at the week-end & could call on you on Monday if you had a few minutes to spare – But as you say the course seems clear for the moment and the difficulties are a little further ahead.

Yours very sincerely
C. P. SCOTT

WSC to the King

3 March 1910   House of Commons

Copy

Mr Secretary Churchill with his humble duty to Your Majesty has the honour to report that the House of Commons has this day resumed the discussion of the borrowing powers of the Treasury. Upon this Mr Horatio

Bottomley intervened with an appeal to the Government to legalise at once by resolution the collection of the Income Tax. This lead – albeit from a somewhat doubtful quarter – was promptly followed by Lord Hugh Cecil, who certainly seems inclined to take a very active and prominent part in this Parliament, and by Sir Robert Finlay and generally by the Conservative Opposition.

The Government, whose policy was defended by the Chancellor of the Exchequer and by Mr McKenna and the Solicitor-General, replied decisively that they could not agree to break up the Budget and thus recognise the claim of the House of Lords to pick and choose between different classes of taxation – the whole of which field must remain exclusively within the control of this House: that a resolution would only acquire validity – from the practical certainty of its being followed by a Bill to confirm it; and that unless the Opposition could undertake to allow the Budget as a whole to pass *sub silentio*, they could not depart from the programme of business which has been already amassed. This last innocent suggestion met however with no favourable welcome from the Conservative party, who then proceeded to suggest and even to urge that we should revert to the old practice of introducing different Bills for the different taxes and passing them separately through the House instead of combining them in a single measure. As Your Majesty is well aware this method was finally abandoned by Mr Gladstone in the reign of the Late Queen, for the direct and avowed purpose of excluding the House of Lords more effectually from the region of finance. It was thought in those days that there never could be any question of the Lords rejecting the whole provision of the year. Modern experience has disconcerted this conclusion, and has shown how insecure even the strongest safeguards of the past have become in the severe contentions of the great political parties. But it could not be expected that the Government should at this moment of all others make such a dangerous concession to the claims of the Peers over Finance. Your Majesty will perceive how closely this debate – though conducted in a thin House, but with some vivacity and feeling – played around the main questions of the day.

Your Majesty is no doubt anxious to learn of the prospects of the Budget. The Government and especially the Chancellor of the Exchequer are steadfast in their intention to pass that measure into law. The difficulties and uncertainties of the situation cannot well be exaggerated. Yet Mr Churchill does not write without knowledge when he declares that his colleagues have confidence that the chances of the Budget being carried have by no means disappeared. The complete failure of the Whisky tax as a revenue producing instrument clearly indicates that the future of this tax in another year will require consideration.

Mr Churchill ventures to express to Your Majesty the great pleasure with which he has read of the barony which has been graciously conferred on his cousin, Mr Ivor Guest[1] and of Your Majesty's intention to have him sworn a member of the Privy Council.

The House is now discussing peacefully the supplementary Estimates of the Navy. Tomorrow it will be Mr Churchill's duty on behalf of the Colonial Office to make a statement about Somaliland, of which he will not fail to transmit a full account.

WSC to the King

3 March 1910   Home Office

Copy

Mr Churchill with his humble duty to Your Majesty has the honour to report that the House of Commons after dealing with the further stages of the two financial Bills – Temporary Borrowings and War Loan – proceeded to the discussion of Colonial Office Estimates. The vote of £96,000 extra for the Somaliland Protectorate gave rise to a languid discussion. Mr Churchill who had charge of this business was pressed to make some statement of the policy which General Manning[2] is seeking to execute of withdrawing from our advanced posts in the interior and holding the coastal towns of Berbera, Bulhar and Seila. For this movement General Manning has been supported by a good battalion of Indian infantry and more troops will be sent him, if they are needed. The moment must however be carefully timed in order that it may be fully successful. Mr Churchill therefore confined himself to very vague generalities and did not unfold to the House any clear account of the operations which he understands are now in progress. The members were somewhat restive under this and asked a great many questions which it was awkward to leave unanswered and which it would have been still more awkward to answer. In the end however the subject dropped, and Mr Churchill was glad to feel that no one was any the wiser for the several speeches he was forced to make.

The policy of concentrating on the Somaliland coast is a wise one. It is on the coast that all the revenue is raised and it is there that the intercourse

---

[1] Ivor Guest was sworn of the Privy Council on 5 March 1910, and created Baron Ashby St Ledgers on 15 March.

[2] William Henry Manning (1863–1932), Commissioner and Commander-in-Chief Somaliland Protectorate 1910; held various military posts in Africa 1893–1910; Governor and C-in-C Nyasaland Protectorate 1910–13; Governor Jamaica 1913–18, Ceylon 1918–25; Created CB 1903; KCMG 1904; KBE 1918; GCMG 1921.

with the tribes of the Hinterland can best be conducted. The expense of holding these few isolated posts in the interior is heavy and cripples the Protectorate. The military risks are considerable; and the tribesmen themselves are not afforded any adequate protection. No other power will be able to trespass in the region from which we are withdrawing; and the retention of the coastline will secure us every advantage which could possibly be looked for in these unpromising deserts. Mr Churchill believes that the military officers on the spot are in full agreement with the policy; and certainly Captain Dawnay,[1] Lord Downe's son, who has just returned from being Chief Staff Officer in Somaliland, and who is now employed at the Colonial Office, is able to adduce the strongest reasons in support of it.

Thereafter the House adjourned early, the business of the day, although considerable, having been disposed of with singular despatch.

WSC to the King

4 March 1910   Home Office

Copy

Mr Secretary Churchill with his humble duty to Your Majesty has the honour to report that the Third Reading of the Treasury (Temporary Borrowings) Bill was the occasion for a further debate in the House of Commons today upon the general position of the Finances and the policy of the Government towards them.

The claim of the Opposition led with some acerbity by Lord Hugh Cecil – who seems inclined to set up a new edition of the 'Fourth Party' below the gangway, and is at present supported by Lord Castlereagh[2] as his lieutenant – was that the rapid progress made each day this week with Supply and the early risings of the House proved that there was plenty of Parliamentary time available to pass the Budget, or at any rate to deal with the Income tax, if only the Government would do their duty to the taxpayers, instead of standing obstinately on points of constitutional principle in the relations of the two Houses.

Mr Churchill has already explained to Your Majesty the view which the Government take of this argument. They cannot consent to divide the Budget into a series of separate Bills heralded by separate Resolutions: for that would surrender the whole advantage which the House of Commons has

---

[1] Hugh Dawnay (1875–1914), 2nd Life Guards and Rifle Brigade; ADC to FM Lord Roberts 1901–4; served Somaliland 1908–10; son of 8th Viscount Downe; married his cousin Lady Susan de la Poer Beresford; killed in action 6 November 1914.

[2] Charles Stewart Henry Vane-Tempest-Stewart, Viscount Castlereagh (1878–1949), Conservative MP Maidstone 1906–15; succeeded father as 7th Marquess of Londonderry 1915; first cousin of WSC; Under-Secretary of State to WSC at Air Ministry 1920–1; Secretary of State for Air 1931–5; KG 1919; PC 1925.

enjoyed for fifty years in sending forward the provision for the public service in one single Budget Bill. They have already announced their course of business to the House viz the necessary Supply, the Lords' Resolutions, and thirdly the Budget: and this course has been approved by the responsible leaders of all parties, and agreed to by the House last Monday without a division – and practically without dissent. On the faith of their arrangement Members of every party – including the Leader of the Opposition – have scattered to their homes or gone abroad for a needed holiday. Suddenly to turn round and introduce with scanty notice the question which is vital to the life of the Ministry, would be a breach of faith of the plainest character. Your Majesty ought to know – though the Government have not mentioned it in debate – that a definite request was made by the Opposition Whips as a condition of their agreement to last Monday's arrangement – that the Budget should not be taken till after Easter. To this stipulation the Government formally but privately agreed. It could not be departed from in any circumstances. And no doubt it was a respect for this understanding that induced every ex-Minister on the Conservative front bench of Cabinet rank to absent himself from the debate, and to take no part in proceedings which are clearly of an irresponsible and factious character.

The debate was favourable to the Government. The Opposition speakers pleaded that the Budget should be taken forthwith in order 'to relieve the financial confusion'. But even if they had been met, they would have voted against the Budget, and if the Budget had been defeated – as no doubt it would be at the present time – the financial confusion so far from being relieved would have been terribly aggravated. The defeat of the Budget – apart from the consequences to the Ministry – would involve the actual repayment of many millions of taxes already collected; and if this event took place before the necessary Supply votes for the fighting services had been secured – a condition of financial and political confusion of the very gravest character would be created.

Mr Churchill ventures to write at some length on this point, because he is deeply concerned to assure Your Majesty that your advisers are earnestly striving with slender forces and unstable support in the face of great difficulties to secure that the public service shall be carried forward through these critical times with the minimum of friction and loss. He would regard the loss of the Budget as a catastrophe. He believes that with wise and judicious management that catastrophe may be avoided. The future is no doubt uncertain, but Mr Churchill has very good hopes that at the right moment and in the right way the necessary taxes will be assented to by the House of Commons before the final dispute between the two Houses is reached, and before Parliament separates for the Spring Recess.

Mr Churchill ventures to express his hope that Your Majesty's visit to Biarritz may prove a pleasant interlude in these political complications and that that delightful place may once again be found highly beneficial to Your Majesty's health. He will of course continue to report fully upon the situation in the House of Commons as it unrolls from day to day.

Lord Fisher to WSC

2 March 1910   Kilverstone Hall

Private

My dear Winston,

Now that I am absolutely free of the Admiralty I suppose I may venture to ask to be welcomed once more into your arms unless in the meanwhile you've got to hate me! My only official attachment now is the Defence Committee (on which as I told you *long ago* you ought to be & I've said it again lately behind your back!) but on the Defence Committee I only survey the Admiralty from an Olympian height and its right perspective! How is the beloved Marsh? is he still with you? I hope so. What an awful hash you have made of your stunning majority of 124? I am no politician but if from the first you had walked straight for the Lords your progress would have been irresistible! Now it's all vacillation! I hope I am not kicking your shins! but I do detest cowardice whatever party it is! The Budget was nothing as everyone had got to see that through!

I hope I may send my best love to Mrs Winston.

Ever yours
FISHER

I'm told the Government is sure to be kicked out in June – if so it will be the Government's own doing! What would Dizzy have said with a majority of 124?

WSC to Lord Fisher
(Lennoxlove Papers)

3 March 1910   Home Office

Private

My dear Fisher,

I am truly *delighted* to get your letter. I stretched out several feeble paws of amity – but in vain. I like you vy much indeed – & I am only sorry that the drift of events did not enable us to work together. Your elevation to the

Peerage was a source of real pleasure to me; & was a partial recognition of the great services you have rendered to British Naval supremacy.

I have deeply regretted since that I did not press for the Admiralty in 1908. I think it would have been easily possible for me to obtain it. I believe it would have been better for us all.

But my best wishes will always go with *you*, & I do hope we shall be able to meet & have a good talk before long.

Yours vy sinly
WINSTON S. CHURCHILL

We shall pull through all right

Lord Fisher to WSC

7 March 1910   Kilverstone Hall

Private

My dear Winston,

You've sent me a very nice letter!
'To my faults a little blind'
'To my virtues more than kind'
I belong to no party and am no politician! only a patriot! I said to Rosebery
'Sworn to no party – of no sect am I'
'I can't be silent – and I will not lie!'
So what I now say to you is purely disinterested: Say to T. P. O'Connor[1] who I always think so sensible 'It's the only chance that ever will offer for Ireland' and it's the only chance that ever will offer for England to get unity so let the 124 be solid for 2 years definite – you can't do with less! If the Government go out in the next 18 months they wont come in again for 20 years! *That's sure!* If the 124 are solid for 2 years or more then you stay in for 20 years! I'm no prophet only an outsider but before the Election I said the majority would be 120 and wrote it to a friend. I was only 4 out! Kindly burn this letter.

You'll all be d——d idiots if you lose this splendid opportunity!

Ever yours
F.

---

[1] Thomas Power O'Connor (1848–1929), journalist and Irish Nationalist; Nationalist MP Galway 1880–5; Liverpool (Scotland division) 1885–1929.

WSC to the King

8 March 1910   Home Office

Copy

Mr Secretary Churchill with his humble duty to Your Majesty has the honour to report that the Army Estimates have occupied the House of Commons during the last two days. There is an increase of £325,000 in the cost of the land forces; but that is explainable and excusable by the satisfactory fact of the success of the Territorial Army whose numbers are already in excess of what we had thought it prudent to expect or necessary to provide for a few years ago. The Estimates which were introduced by Mr Haldane in a speech of comparatively moderate length have been well received in all quarters of the House. Deep peace has brooded over the debates; and Mr Churchill looks back with some complacency to the stormy days of 1903 and 1904, when the Army was the centre of such fierce controversies and when such strong rifts of opinion were manifest among its leaders and between those leaders and their political chiefs.

Indeed Your Majesty has reason to regard the present administrative position of this great service with a certain measure of contentment. The excellent relations which Mr Haldane has maintained with the principal military officers have enabled him to achieve a large number of reforms after which his predecessors laboured in vain. The improvements in the organisation of the forces, whether for Home Defence or Foreign Expedition, have been real and constant. The improvement in the life, character, and efficiency of the individual soldier has been no less remarkable. Crime has diminished, punishment has diminished, disease and wastage have diminished. The private soldier is more and more coming to be looked on by the population as an honoured and valued citizen and the old idea of his being a bad character in peace, however brave in war, has passed almost entirely away. Mr Churchill is also led to believe that the officers of the Army are at the present time more keenly devoted to the technical details of their profession than has ever before been the case during a period of peace. Although no doubt it would be foolish to attempt to compare the British Army in strength with the vast conscript forces of the continent, the House has been generally inclined to adopt the view that the best use is made of the available resources, and the Committee of Imperial Defence believe that those resources are not inadequate to our special needs – so long as the unquestioned supremacy of the Navy is maintained.

A debate of a cool but not uninstructive character has taken place. Mr Wyndham has spoken for the Opposition. Mr Churchill thinks that the prominence assigned to him in this sphere may perhaps not be without significance as bearing on the composition of some future Conservative Government. Lord Tullibardine[1] has made a maiden speech – in a nice modest manner but with some real knowledge of his subject. Mr Arthur Lee has offered a few criticisms; and so of course has Sir Charles Dilke.

The only difficulty arose from a question of the non-payment of trade Union rates of wages in Government shops under the War Office. The Labour Party moved an Amendment, and although the Conservative front bench refused to support it, a good deal of backing was found on the back Opposition benches, and below our own Gangway. The division in the present uncertain situation was viewed with some anxiety. In the end however the Government, who were supported by many of the Labour party, and – a noticeable fact – by some of the Irish nationalists, obtained a majority of 67. The debate will be continued tomorrow.

WSC to the King

9 March 1910   Home Office

Copy

Mr Secretary Churchill with his humble duty to Your Majesty has the honour to report that the debate on Army Estimates was resumed today. The Prime Minister had asked Mr Churchill to continue it, and he therefore offered to the Supply Committee a general survey of the progress of military policy during the last four or five years in organisation, in administration, and in the social position of the soldier, which was on the whole very kindly received by both sides. Mr Churchill addressed himself in conclusion to the question of whether our land forces were adequate to our needs. It may be justly asserted that they are adequate to our immediate and primary needs. The argument to support this rests on three main propositions which Mr Churchill thinks are accepted by the responsible leaders of both great parties:—first: that no sudden descent could be made by *surprise* upon this country by any foreign force large enough to achieve decisive results: if the force were large it would be discovered and intercepted; if it were small it would be useless. Secondly, that no descent that was not sudden could be made at all, provided we retain the command of the sea. Thirdly, that the whole regular army would not be sent out of the country until complete naval supremacy had been established, and that in any case the mere process

---

[1] John George Murray, Marquess of Tullibardine (1871–1942), Unionist MP West Perthshire 1910–17; son of 7th Duke of Atholl whom he succeeded 1917; served Royal Horse Guards, South Africa 1899–1902; served World War 1914–19. WSC had been at Omdurman with Tullibardine, and with him had taken water to the wounded dervishes after the battle.

of despatching the Expeditionary Army would afford an invaluable training period to the Territorial Army.

Mr Wyndham followed and in a rather good debating speech twitted Mr Churchill with his part in former army discussions which Your Majesty may remember was sometimes of a critical and even controversial character. Mr Crawshay-Williams is now engaged from the Liberal benches in vindicating the efficiency of the Territorial artillery – no doubt the weak spot in the second line. The House is thin and apathetic. The reductions of the Estimates which were moved last night have not been renewed to-day and have consequently lapsed. Mr Churchill thinks it unlikely that any division will take place, but if one should occur no unexpected results need be feared. The Navy Estimates next week will perhaps produce more striking features, but an air of suspended animation hangs over Parliament and Mr Churchill would be surprised if it were dissipated until the Lords Resolutions are brought forward after the Easter recess.

Nothing has occurred which would lead Mr Churchill to wish to modify the account of the general situation which he has had the honour to transmit to Your Majesty in his earlier letters. He may however perhaps be permitted to express the hope that Your Majesty has made the journey to Biarritz without undue fatigue and that that journey has been rewarded by bright sunshine and fine waves.

WSC to the King

11 March 1910   Home Office

Copy

Mr Secretary Churchill with his humble duty to Your Majesty has the honour to dwell with some emphasis and significance upon the fact that the Vote on Account which was moved yesterday in the House of Commons provides supply for no longer than six weeks. There are very good precedents for this in similar circumstances which Mr Churchill will not now specifically adduce. It is sufficient to draw Your Majesty's attention to the fact that up to the year 1896 it was the invariable practice of both great parties to ask for Votes on account for no more than a month or two months at a time. The Vote on account is the most powerful and the most simple Parliamentary engine by which the House of Commons is assured of its influence upon the Executive Government.

Mr Churchill has publicly expressed his opinion that a refusal on the part of the House of Commons to vote the main and necessary supply of the year would be attended with swift disaster to the party responsible. And no such intention exists in the present House of Commons. Still it is right that in the present strange tangle of affairs when Your Majesty's Ministers cannot feel any security except for the immediate future, that the Government of the day should ask for no more supply by the Vote on Account than is sufficient to carry them forward over the period for which they may reasonably expect to be responsible; nor should they ask for an amount of supply which would be out of all proportion to any taxes which the House of Commons has shown itself disposed to vote. At any time in the next few weeks another Vote may renew and extend the necessary supply after half a day's discussion. But of course the retention of this power in the hands of the House of Commons would make it impossible for a Government which could not command a majority to remain indefinitely in office without an appeal to Your Majesty for a Dissolution.

The announcement of the Government's decision was received with some excitement in the House of Commons and with an explosion of wrath on the Conservative Benches. Mr Austen Chamberlain, Mr F. E. Smith and Lord Hugh Cecil immediately attacked Ministers in unmeasured terms. They were replied to by the Chancellor of the Exchequer and later Mr Gibson Bowles came to the support of the Government with an amusing and combative speech. Upon a division being taken on a motion to report progress the Government secured a majority of 71 – the largest of the new Parliament. There is no doubt that this step, which causes not the slightest public inconvenience, but which is at the same time an effective assertion of the financial powers of the House of Commons, has consolidated and strengthened the forces upon which the Government must count. As certain speakers in the Debate and the Conservative press generally have alleged that the action taken was part of a bargain with the Nationalist party, Mr Churchill thinks it right to tell Your Majesty, that there is not the slightest foundation for such a suggestion. The decision was taken by the Government alone and the Cabinet were unanimous upon it.

During the rest of Thursday the discussion of Estimates proceeded uneventfully. Sir Edward Grey made a statement upon the Congo annexation which defines the policy of the Foreign Office at the present time.[1] But the carefully turned phrases and periods of such a speech do not lend themselves to any epitome. The general effect was that Great Britain would not recognize the Belgian annexation without receiving reports from our own consuls to show that the long and often promised reforms were actually being carried out.

[1] The British Government had still not recognized the annexation of the Congo by Belgium in 1908.

Friday was consumed in a very thin discussion of the remaining Army Estimates required at the present. The House assumed that listless air which indicated that the questions of interest lay outside the debates. Captains and Majors talked mildly to each other and the other Members took refuge in the smoking rooms.

The Navy Estimates are the staple of next week's Parliamentary business. The provision and programme of the year are unexampled. In December 1908 when Mr McKenna brought Estimates before the Cabinet, he asked for 6 Dreadnoughts to meet the alleged accelerations of the German programme. He got 8 Dreadnoughts. He got further the 2 Colonial Battleships and now this year 5 more are to be begun, or 15 of these tremendous vessels undertaken in scarcely 12 months. At the same time the German acceleration in Dreadnoughts has ceased. They are carrying out their very serious naval programme – but no more: and the utmost Dreadnought fleet which they can have ready in April 1912 will be not 17 as we were led to expect, not 21 as we were told might happen, not 25 as Mr Balfour suggested, but 13 only, and perhaps only 11. Against this the British Admiralty will possess at least 20.

In ordinary circumstances these Estimates would have led to vehement debates in the House of Commons, and the Government would have had to face the attack of a very large number of their own supporters. Mr Churchill anticipates however – so far as can be seen – that no difficulty will arise. The political issues between the two Houses dominate the situation. The resistance to expenditure of all kinds was never at a more feeble ebb; and the only check upon the ever-growing charges of the public service, consists in the general disinclination of all parties to vote the necessary taxation.

Mr Churchill is now sending his letters whenever there is a messenger instead of writing separately of each sitting. He trusts that this course will be satisfactory to Your Majesty.

Edwin Montagu to WSC

EXTRACT

14 March 1910　　　　　　　　　　　　House of Commons

My dear Churchill,

I am not one of those who are honoured either by your confidence or often by your discussion but I am prompted to ask you to read a word or two of my handwriting because I find myself in the most detached of offices, obsessed by views for which I can find no effective target.

I heard your words of condemnation at the Speaker's on Friday when you were accosting Sir Thomas Elliott.[1] How true they were! The country hates impotence. We might have abandoned all attempt to democratise and Liberalise agricultural England. But we were brave or foolhardy and attacked the most potent of vested interests – those that are rural. . . .

May I remind you that SW Norfolk and West Cambridgeshire were conspicuous for the success of the Small Holdings Acts and *therefore* remained true to Liberalism. We were able to translate paper acts into living achievements and gave those who were with difficulty Liberals some reason for their faith. Why can't the Board of Agriculture be spurred into activity? They have now, trusting perhaps that no agitators are left, been drawing in (Ye Gods!) such activities as they had and limiting their temporary staff – but keeping of course the Tory agriculturalists.

Then again the act might be so much easier to work if you compensated farmers who suffer for the Commonwealth. Why can't they be compensated either out of the Small Holdings Act or by 6d an acre addition to small-holders' rent?

But it is only my duty now to urge you to materialise your vehement attack, not to argue the case. If you wish I will make detailed suggestions later, if you can find time to urge the matter through.

On another subject, I fear the policy of the Government is shaping towards *resignation*. Can you agree with me that this is fatal? It postpones submitting your detailed schemes to the country. It admits half the battle by admitting the end of Liberal administration. It makes way for a new Ministry of men with fresh certificates unendorsed and with a new shop-window programme including a *naval loan*. It does not obviate differences of opinion, which, beginning at the top, cleave downwards to the root, and it postpones achievement while it paves the way for an evildoing Conservative government. Remember that you belong to that part of the party which is too well represented in the Cabinet to be driven out, and go for dissolution rather than resignation. And, above all, forgive all this.

Yours, &c
Ed S. Montagu

WSC to the King
(Royal Archives)

14 March 1910   Home Office

Mr Secretary Churchill with his humble duty to Your Majesty. At Question Time today the Prime Minister was asked by Lord Hugh Cecil

[1] Thomas Henry Elliott (1854–1926), Secretary to Board of Agriculture and Fisheries 1892–1913; Deputy-Master and Comptroller of the Mint 1913–17; CB 1897; KCB 1902; Baronet 1917.

whether the Government intended to pass the Budget through *all* its stages before the House adjourned for the Spring Recess. The question was devised in order to place the Government in the position of abruptly confronting the Irish party with the certainty of having to vote upon the Budget, without reference to the treatment by the House of Lords of the Veto Resolutions. The answer was plain. The Government do intend if they have the power to carry the Budget completely through all its stages before the adjournment for any holiday (other than the four days at Easter).

It cannot yet be seen how this declaration will be taken by Mr Redmond and his friends. It must have been extremely disquieting to them, and they have been making many requests in private ways to be spared the ordeal of so dangerous and critical a vote. Mr Churchill is however strongly of opinion that nothing but the pressure of events will resolve the situation, and to that pressure the Irish leaders must now be exposed. The result will for some time remain uncertain. But Mr Churchill still feels – and he gathered that this is also Your Majesty's view – that it will be vy difficult for Mr Redmond at the last minute to turn the Government out. It is unsatisfactory from many points of view that so large an element of instability should enter into the political situation and that Your Majesty's Ministers should live from day to day under the shadow of the axe. He has however passed the Sunday in the fascinating task of reading the volume of the letters of the late Queen and the correspondence relating to the Ministries of Lord John Russell and Lord Palmerston with their precarious majorities and their swiftly changing constructions; and he finds it comforting to reflect that all came out right in the end, that the Queen's Government was faithfully carried on in spite of the utmost party confusion and many personal rivalries which now happily do not exist.

The First Lord of the Admiralty is now reading his annual statement. A year ago this was the subject that electrified Parliament. Today the naval issues are no less important and the expense far greater. Yet so fickle is the House of Commons, so ready always to discard the old love for the new, that the Chamber is but half filled, and the members (including Your Majesty's servant) are off to the House of Lords to hear Lord Rosebery move the first of his Resolutions. There does not seem any danger of difficulty arising upon the Naval programme or the money votes.

All of which is humbly submitted by Your Majesty's faithful subject and servant

WSC

WSC to the King
(*Royal Archives*)

17 March 1910   Home Office

Mr Secretary Churchill with his humble duty to Your Majesty. The debates upon the Naval Estimates have followed the course which Mr Churchill indicated in his letters last week as probable. The discussions have been lifeless, and enormous sums of money and vast programmes of reconstruction have been agreed to with an almost cataleptic apathy. The central feature of these important but sluggish proceedings has been the collapse of Lord Charles Beresford. Mr Churchill has rarely been more impressed with the efficiency of the House of Commons in reducing outside reputations to a more modest compass, than in this case. Lord Charles has spoken with good manners and good humour. He showed to advantage all the personal qualities of his family in genial and breezy modes of speech. He was received with great respect and sturdy cheers by the Conservative party. His opponents heard him without the slightest dislike. He failed utterly to make any impression in any quarter of the House. As a Fleet commander he may deserve his widespread popularity, as an election orator he may return it, but as a naval statesman his hour has struck.

One of his arguments to wh Mr Churchill was forced to listen, was to the effect that although Great Britain might be three times as strong as Germany, that fact proved nothing because we had 'so much more to guard'. This theory carried to its full extent would seem to require us to have a supreme fleet in every part of the globe at once: whereas the sea is all one, the command of the sea wherever gained is effective everywhere, and the whole fortunes of the war pass into the hands of the power that secures victorious decisions from the great naval engagements – upon which all our preparations should be concentrated.

The tremendous expenditure has caused much heart searching among the supporters of the Government. Mr Churchill himself can only hope that the Germans will dislike it as much as he does. But when the Division took place last night upon a small reduction, only 34 members recorded their votes against the Government, who secured a majority of 191, – a figure reminiscent of happier days!

The general situation remains unaltered and obscure. Divergencies of view in the Cabinet add their perplexities to those of the House of Commons. Mr Churchill still nourishes a hope which certainly does not weaken, that the Veto and Budget Resolutions will all be carried before the end of April.

He greatly regrets the bad weather which has descended upon Your

Majesty and trusts that the indisposition of which the newspapers speak is of the most trifling character.

WSC to the King
(*Royal Archives*)

18 March 1910

Mr Secretary Churchill with his humble duty to Your Majesty. Nothing has happened in the House of Commons during the last two days, except the uneventful passage of the various groups of the Estimates. Yesterday the Report stage of the Navy votes was concluded, and today an almost empty House has discussed the grievances of Ireland in respect of Old Age Pensions – which most people were inclined to consider not grievances at all but exactly the contrary – and now we are concluding with some discussion on Labour Exchanges. Your Majesty will be glad to learn that although the new machinery is still vy imperfect and has not got properly to work, we are already actually finding situations for nearly 5000 persons every week.

The interest of Parliament has this week been shifted to the House of Lords where a long, distinguished and vy curious debate was yesterday terminated by Lord Lansdowne's declaration that he would vote for Lord Rosebery's third Resolution which clearly disowns the hereditary principle. Mr Churchill thinks that this is an astonishing position. The two parties in their conflict seem to be almost exchanging weapons – like in the duel between Hamlet and Laertes – the orthodox Liberals all wishing to concentrate upon the limitation of the Veto which was proposed by Sir Henry Campbell-Bannerman, the unbending Conservatives wishing to boast that they are not supporters of a hereditary Assembly.

Mr Redmond's speeches have been minatory in their character and the general outlook has not improved.

WSC to the King

30 March 1910   Home Office

Copy

Mr Secretary Churchill with his humble duty to Your Majesty.

The Prime Minister made a magnificent speech yesterday in introducing the motion to go into committee upon the Vote Resolutions. Not in this Parliament nor in the last has Mr Asquith been heard to such advantage. The strategy of the speech, its phrasing and general arrangement were

admired by all – by none so much as by those best informed upon the difficulties of the situation. Mr Churchill was very disappointed with Mr
Balfour's reply. He hopes that he is able to judge Parliamentary performances
with an eye not wholly influenced by partisanship. He has often enjoyed
listening to a brilliant attack upon his own friends and opinions. He has
often listened with delight to the Leader of the Opposition. But he could not
help feeling that Mr Balfour's speech yesterday was quite inadequate; and he
noticed with much regret that there seemed to be considerable evidences of
physical weakness as well as of weariness.

Mr Redmond followed and was heard by a thin House which had melted
steadily from the moment the Prime Minister sat down. He approved and
supported the resolutions, for which we should no doubt be grateful, but he
finished by suggesting that the Budget should not be allowed to pass unless
or until Ministers had received from Your Majesty some assurance as to a
future use of the Royal prerogative to overcome the certain resistance of
the House of Lords. The Government on the other hand feel that their
policy in respect to the Veto, and particularly to the financial Veto, will be
vitiated and stultified, so long as it can be said with some show of truth that
the electors have approved the rejection of the Budget by the Lords. Everything therefore tends towards a climax. The only new fact of a modifying
and hopeful character is the change in the attitude of Mr O'Brien and his
group, which has become much more friendly to the Government and is a
circumstance of some significance.

Important as was the occasion, the House was still oppressed by the coma
and even stupor which has been the extraordinary feature of this session.
Nothing seems capable of arousing it. Your Majesty's new Parliament has
been born in a trance. Two prevailing impressions are in everyone's mind –
that its hours are numbered, and that in the pass to which we are come,
speeches are but empty words. Yet in the country the party organizations
are strong and militant. There can be little doubt that the Liberals would
maintain and possibly improve their position in any appeal to the electorate.
Mr Churchill is drawn increasingly to the conclusion that nothing but Your
Majesty's intervention in some exceptional form or manner which cannot as
yet be defined will relieve a constitutional deadlock which if prolonged
indefinitely must prove injurious to the public welfare and to the structure of
British institutions. The action of the House of Lords in the last Parliament
has made it impossible – unless it be corrected – for Liberal Ministries to
govern with credit however large be the majorities which they may command among the elected representatives of the Commons.

Today the debate has been excellently well maintained. First an amusing
and indeed a masterly speech by Mr F. E. Smith, who has now become one

of the principal figures upon the Opposition benches; then a rejoinder very apt in point and argument by Mr Simon,[1] also a young King's Counsel of distinguished ability; thirdly Lord Hugh Cecil who was vehement and surprising in manner and matter; and now Mr Birrell is replying generally on behalf of the Government. Tomorrow the official amendment of the Opposition will be moved by Sir R. Finlay, and the debate will be concluded on Monday. Mr Churchill expects that the Veto Resolutions will be disposed of by the 14th and the Budget will then immediately be proceeded with.

All of which is now humbly submitted by Your Majesty's faithful servant and subject

H. H. Asquith to WSC

31 March 1910   10 Downing Street

Midnight

Private

My dear Winston,

You made a most admirable speech: one of your best. The only thing I regret is the last sentence – associating 'the Crown' & the people: which I hope may be ignored. Otherwise – I have not a word of criticism.

Yrs always
H.H.A.

WSC to the King

2 April 1910   Home Office

Copy

Mr Secretary Churchill with his humble duty to Your Majesty.

The debate upon the motion to go into Committee upon the Veto Resolutions was continued yesterday. Sir Robert Finlay moved an Amendment on behalf of the Opposition refusing to consider the relations between the two Houses till after the Reform of the House of Lords had been undertaken. The speech which he delivered in support of this was a very long, a

[1] John Allsebrook Simon (1873–1954), Liberal MP Walthamstow 1906–18, Spen Valley 1922–31; Liberal National MP Spen Valley 1931–40; Solicitor-General 1910–13; Attorney General 1913–15; Home Secretary 1915–16; Foreign Secretary 1931–5; Home Secretary 1935–7; Chancellor of the Exchequer 1937–40; Lord Chancellor 1940–5; knighted 1910; PC 1912; created Viscount 1940.

very serious examination of the legal aspects of the situation. It occupied an hour and a half and was listened to with praiseworthy diligence by a half-filled House. The Attorney-General replied at once and gave satisfaction to the supporters of the Government. He made one point which touched a sensitive chord in the heart of every member, when he complained that the House of Lords – itself indissoluble – had by asserting its claims over finance, impinged upon the prerogative of dissolution and acquired the power to fine every member of the House of Commons nearly one thousand pounds for an election whenever they might choose. It must be remembered that the average member of Parliament is not a rich man, and that the increasingly severe service at Westminster is unpaid. The suggestions thrown out from the Unionist benches in the Debate that there would be *two more* general elections in this year, is thus profoundly resented as an attempt to strike at political opponents by ruining them financially. Mr Churchill draws Your Majesty's attention to this aspect, because it will explain in part the darkening mood which the continuance of the constitutional deadlock is drawing over British politics.

The rest of the debate was composed mostly of maiden speeches: Mr Arnold Ward,[1] the son of Mrs Humphrey Ward – fantastic; Mr Spencer Leigh Hughes[2] – bright and amusing; and Mr Valentine Fleming,[3] a very nice young gentleman, who is a subaltern in the Oxfordshire Yeomanry and the Conservative Member for Henley – good and simple – but a trifle too long. Mr Churchill spoke for the Government at 10. He trusts Your Majesty will not attach any importance to the crude and strained interpretations which the Opposition's newspapers have placed upon his concluding remarks. They meant and were intended to mean, in themselves and in their context, that the existing Constitutional difficulty will not be relieved by any mere continuance of the breach and warfare between the Lords and Commons, but will require – at a time, in a manner, and under circumstances which cannot now be foreseen – the intervention of the Crown. This is the truth, and Mr Churchill with deepest respect accepts the fullest responsibility for its expression.

Today upon a private member's Bill the House has been engaged in debating the evils of Plural Voting and the possibilities of having all elections on one day. It would not be fair or reasonable to expect that the basis of the franchise should be altered before the next election – unless indeed this

[1] Arnold Sandwith Ward (1876–1950), Unionist MP West Hertfordshire 1910–18; special correspondent of *The Times* in Egypt, Sudan and India 1899–1902; son of Mrs Humphry Ward, the authoress.

[2] Spencer Leigh Hughes (d. 1920), journalist; Liberal MP for Stockport 1910–20.

[3] Valentine Fleming (1882–1917), Conservative MP for Henley Division of Oxfordshire 1910–17; barrister; a friend of WSC and father of Peter and Ian Fleming.

Parliament should live its normal term. But the commercial classes are indignant at the prospect of the revival in trade being checked by the prolonged tumult and agitation of another general election following so soon upon the last, and there is a very strong opinion that if Your Majesty should at any time in the near future grant a Dissolution to Your Ministers, at least steps should be taken to hold all the elections simultaneously, instead of sprawling them out through the protracted disturbances of five weeks.

The Government have now announced their intentions in respect to business. The Veto Resolutions, which are after all only the basic principles of a Bill which must pass through all its stages in the ordinary way, are to be disposed of by the 14th instant. The Budget will then immediately be brought forward under a rapid procedure which will carry it through the House of Commons by the end of April. There is not at present any settlement with the Irish, and it cannot be said that the main uncertainty of the situation has been removed. There are still however reasons to believe that at the last moment a rupture fatal to the Government – and to the finances – may be avoided.

Viscount Morley to WSC

5 April 1910   India Office

Private

My dear Winston,

I am really very grateful for your excellent note. Crewe will take the labouring over, but he wants me to be ready for possible supplementary purposes.

It cut me to the heart to come into collision with you yesterday. But I have an old-fashioned prejudice against a Cabinet being committed on points of vital importance and the utmost delicacy, without abundant consultation. Why did you keep the unhappy phrase dark when we broke bread together a few hours before it was launched? But let it pass. The curtain is slowly descending: I only wish it did not creak so damnably.

Yrs
M

'There is no loss of friends', cried Fox to Burke, when they fell asunder about the Revolution.

WSC to the King
(*Royal Archives*)

6 April 1910   Home Office

Mr Secretary Churchill with his humble duty to Your Majesty.

The debate on the motion preliminary to the Veto Resolutions was concluded on Monday by the speech of the Chancellor of the Exchequer. Mr Lloyd George addressed to the House a long and soberly reasoned argument. It was designed to show how very unfair the existing system and the use of the Lords Veto were to the Liberal Party. It set forth how at each General Election the country chooses broadly between two opposing programmes. When the Conservatives are returned they can and do carry their controversial party bills, like the Education Act of 1902 and the Licensing Act of 1904. When the Liberals are returned they are only allowed to carry so much of their policy as the Conservative Opposition approve of, or as they do not judge it expedient to disapprove. In 1906 every Liberal candidate pledged himself to deal with Education, Licensing, Land Values, Plural Voting. Every one of these measures was actively discussed in every constituency. Every single one was rejected by the House of Lords although sent to them by enormous majorities. The speech which was neither exciting nor amusing brought home to the House in a powerful yet unpretentious way the grievance which lies at the heart of the present discontent, the essential inequality and unfairness of the Constitution to more than half of Your Majesty's loyal subjects. What struck Mr Churchill as curious was that the speaker was more successful in stirring Conservative consciences than in rousing Liberal enthusiasm. There are some vy deep and strong points of resemblance between the present Chancellor of the Exchequer and Mr [Joseph] Chamberlain. Mr Churchill has often been powerfully struck with them. They appear in manner, in view, in mood and expression. Mr Churchill has seen a photograph of Mr Lloyd George taken about ten years ago without his moustache, which really presented an extraordinary resemblance in type to the Chamberlain of the early eighties. And certain it is that both, though strong radicals by temperament have possessed in a peculiar degree the power of pressing the springs which actuate the ordinary Conservative mind.

The division – the first real shock of the session upon the vital question of the Parliament – afforded Ministers a majority of 106. The Irish Party voted with the Government, though not in their full strength. Mr Healy[1]

[1] Timothy Michael Healy (1855–1931), MP Wexford 1880–3, Co Monaghan 1883–5, South Londonderry 1885–6, North Longford 1887–92, North Louth 1892–1910, North East Cork 1910–18. He had been expelled from the Irish Nationalist Party for the second time in 1910. From 1922–8 he was Governor-General of the Irish Free State.

also voted in the majority. This is deserving of attention as it shows what Mr Churchill has already indicated – the change in the attitude of the O'Brienite group and its comparative friendliness to the Government. Since this first good division the Government have enjoyed very respectable majorities. Yesterday upon the 'Guillotine' Resolutions to allocate the time upon the Veto discussions, there have been nearly a dozen trials of strength, yielding the Government majorities which ranged from 85 to over 150. The effect of these repeated votes is of course to engender a spirit of confidence in the immediate future, which Mr Churchill hopes may be well-founded. While nothing can be counted on, it appears increasingly probable that the Veto and Budget will be disposed of in the House of Commons before the end of April. Should these results be obtained, an interval of at least four weeks might it is hoped be allowed to intervene for reflection upon a situation of unexampled perplexity and some real gravity, and for repose after Parliamentary and electioneering activities which have proceeded without intermission for upwards of fourteen months.

All of which is humbly submitted by Your Majesty's faithful subject and servant

WINSTON S. CHURCHILL

WSC to the King

9 April 1910   Home Office

Copy

Mr Secretary Churchill with his humble duty to Your Majesty.

This week in the House of Commons has produced no new developments affecting the general situation. The Resolution abolishing the financial Veto of the House of Lords has been fully debated and was carried without amendment on Thursday night by the respectable majority of 102. The discussion was not very lively. Mr Haldane who moved dwelt much on precedents and constitutional maxims which appear to abound on both sides of most important questions. He concluded by emphasizing the need of adding the policy of Reform to that of limiting the Veto. Mr Haldane favours a measure of a far-reaching and drastic character, which could certainly not be objected to on democratic grounds. It is curious however that the advanced Radicals take very little interest in, and are even extremely distrustful of any attempt to alter the constitution of the House of Lords, and seem quite content so long as the Veto is restricted to leave that body untouched. Mr Haldane's sincere and able speech was therefore somewhat coldly received.

Mr Churchill learns that in the general opinion Mr Austen Chamberlain made an extremely good reply. The last Parliament was prejudiced against him by the fact that he had been too rapidly advanced to the great office of Chancellor of the Exchequer and that his personality had not seemed adequate to his employment. But since the introduction of last year's Budget, his Parliamentary position has strengthened steadily, and his speech on Tuesday certainly leaves him by general consent in the first rank as a debater and as a leader.

On Thursday a really delicious speech from Mr Balfour was the feature. Two years ago the Leader of the Opposition speaking at Dumfries said 'It is the House of Commons, not the House of Lords which settles *uncontrolled* our financial system.' This and other similar utterances were expected to place Mr Balfour in a position of some difficulty in the present circumstances. His answer was conclusive. One must assume some knowledge in one's audience. The fact that the House of Lords has full powers to reject Budgets was so obvious that it did not need to be stated. The suggestion that his words conflicted with this power of rejection was too absurd even to be discussed. If he had said 'the plain is perfectly flat', it would have been understood all the time that the statement was without prejudice to the fact that the world was round. He would never have expected to be reproached for not having mentioned specifically *the normal curvature of the earth's surface*. So when he said the Lords could not touch Money Bills, he never meant that they could not reject all the Money Bills of the year singly or at a stroke! That of course went without saying.

Mr Churchill thinks this doctrine of 'curvature' may be found very convenient by others besides Mr Balfour, who have from time to time to explain away past speeches or phrases, and he feels that the Leader of the Opposition has placed the House under a real obligation by the brilliant audacity with which he has laid it before them.

The division on the Tariff Reform motion on Wednesday night produced only the meagre majority of 33 for Ministers. The Irish Nationalists abstained. The Irish Unionists voted. Hence the slender margin which stands between the country and the tremendous economic change involved in the abandonment of Free Trade.

WSC to the King
(*Royal Archives*)

13 April 1910   10 Downing Street

Mr Secretary Churchill with his humble duty to Your Majesty.

The House of Commons has this week entered upon and pursued the discussion of the Resolution which is designed to restrict to a period of two years the Veto of the House of Lords upon ordinary legislation. The debates have been well sustained though devoid of any strong feeling of excitement or passion. The Prime Minister who opened on Monday referred in his speech to the preamble of the Veto Bill (a draft of which has, I understand been already submitted to Your Majesty) which makes it clear that the reform of the House of Lords is a secondary but essential step in the policy of the Government. It was to be apprehended that the reference to this preamble would create a good deal of disquiet among the Radical members who are so anxious that the Veto proposals shall not be complicated by the introduction of this great new topic, upon which such wide divergencies of opinion may be opened up. The announcement has however been taken vy calmly and whether from inadvertence or indifference has not figured at all in the subsequent debates.

Mr Neil Primrose made an excellent first speech, wh created a pleasant impression on both sides of the House. Lord Rosebery making a vy rare appearance in the Peers' gallery heard his son's maiden effort: and Her Majesty the Queen who was present in the Speaker's Gallery also listened to the Debate.

On Tuesday the discussion was continued. Mr Balfour spoke at six o'clock. His tone was moderate, his argument serious, and his manner conciliatory. He acknowledged that very great powers would still be left to the House of Lords after the Veto Resolutions had passed into law; but he argued that these powers – increased as they well might be – would be employed not to improve legislation but to aggravate and multiply the causes of disagreement between the Houses, and would at the same time afford no check against a grave constitutional change.

It was Mr Churchill's duty to follow the Leader of the Opposition, and he naturally used Mr Balfour's admission of the great powers which the House of Lords would retain, as a proof that the policy of the Government could not be fairly described as the establishment of a Single Chamber system. The general debate lapsed at the dinner hour, and one amendment was moved exempting constitutional changes from the scope of the new procedure. This was resisted by the Government who upon a division were found in possession of a majority of 109.

William Royle to WSC

13 April 1910   Elmwood
                                                         Rusholme

Dear Mr Churchill,

I must send you a line of congratulation on the great speech you made in the House last night. You seem to revel in constitutional subjects & I have no hesitation in saying it was the greatest speech we have had since the Veto question was mentioned. You have laid us all once more under great obligations & you put new heart into the rank & file. The Liberal party is now in good heart waiting for the decisive moment when the clash will come with the House of Lords. Reading between the lines of your last speech *here* & the speech of the Chief Whip we are confident that when the resolutions are rejected the Prime Minister will ask for guarantees & if refused then we are to fight at the polls. *This is* the policy to adopt & I have no fear as to the future.

> With kindest regards, Sincerely yrs
> WM ROYLE

WSC to the King

15 April 1910   Home Office

Copy

Mr Secretary Churchill with his humble duty to Your Majesty.

Since writing yesterday afternoon from the House of Commons events have occurred which render a further report to Your Majesty necessary. The amendment respecting the exclusion of measures affecting the rights, powers and prerogatives of the Crown from the scope of the Veto Resolutions, having been disposed of at about 6 o'clock, after a debate marked by expressions of the utmost loyalty and respect to Your Majesty's Throne and Person from all quarters of the House, including the Labour and Nationalist benches, a further amendment seeking to prevent Home Rule being carried under the new procedure was moved. It was very maladroit of the Conservative party to raise this issue on the verge of the vital division on Monday next on the Budget. It of course brought the Irish and Liberal parties together upon common ground, and in united opposition to the Conservatives. In a few minutes the House became crowded and excited as it was known that the Prime Minister intended to make a statement and a spectacle of lively stir and throng presented itself. Mr Churchill made it plain that the Government would certainly not debar themselves from using the new powers they are seeking for the House of Commons to carry a Home Rule Bill and thus effect a national settlement with Ireland, subject to the supremacy of the Imperial Parliament. But when the Prime Minister rose at a quarter past seven to end the debate, and began to refer to the advice which it would be his duty to tender to Your Majesty if the Resolutions were rejected by the Lords, Mr Balfour objected to the statement being made on the grounds nominally that it was not relevant to the amendment (which was no doubt true) and actually because the fall of the guillotine would not have left him any opportunity for making the disagreeable comments which were expected of him in the circumstances. This successful attempt to prevent the Prime Minister from saying what everyone was on tenterhooks to hear roused the growing feeling of the assembly to a fierce pitch; and Members separated under the influence of strong emotions of anger and of expectations.

All this of course tended to enhance the effect of the declaration when it was eventually made at 11 o'clock on the motion for the Adjournment. The House then presented a scene of animation and almost of violence. Mr Churchill is reminded of his father's description of House of Commons life – 'months of dullness, moments of passion'. It is very rarely that such moments occur. This is the first time this Parliament has really breathed and lived; and certainly it sprang at an instant into an ebullition of energy and conflict which revealed the depths of the quarrels of our time. Amid a tremendous storm of cheering and counter-cries, the Prime Minister walked up the floor of the House bearing his fateful bill, while his whole party stood erect or even on the benches and waved their hats. Even after the Speaker had left the chair the parties remained standing in the Chamber facing each other, and an insulting cry from the Tory benches almost provoked an actual collision between them and the Irish Nationalist members.

No agreement or bargain of any kind has been made with Mr Redmond's party. The decision of the Government has been taken in fulfilment of their own pledges, and with the support and insistence of their own followers. Mr Churchill feels however that the current of events is now flowing so strongly that Mr Redmond will be compelled to vote for the Budget in all its stages.

All of which is humbly submitted by Your Majesty's faithful subject and servant

WINSTON S. CHURCHILL

WSC to the King

20 April 1910   Home Office

Copy

Mr Secretary Churchill with his humble duty to Your Majesty.

The position of the Government has been vastly improved by the events of the last week. All the Parliamentary forces upon which they depend have been combined and united into a powerful majority. The Budget, failure to pass which must have utterly discredited their whole complaint against the House of Lords, is passing swiftly and smoothly through the House of Commons. It is substantially unaltered. It has yielded, in spite of all the disturbance of the year and the extraordinary strain to which the finances have been put, results which, when the collection of the taxes is complete, will realize a surplus of almost £3,000,000 – a surplus which it may be found very convenient to devote to the needs of the Naval programme. These are considerable events. They do not indeed decide the grave issues which hang in the balance: but they ensure that the utmost force which lies in the democratic parties will be effectually developed at the next trial of strength: and they secure in the meanwhile the safety and material well-being of the country.

The statement of the Chancellor of the Exchequer has produced a very marked impression in all quarters. The figures, unfolded without any ostentation, told their own tale. Parties rise and fall and governments flow by; but the vast solid financial strength of the British taxpayer and of British fiscal methods stands like the rock of Gibraltar, unbroken by any siege. There is not another State in Europe that could have produced a surplus upon so great an expenditure in circumstances of similar difficulty. German finance certainly compares unfavourably in every respect with the most sombre view of British wealth and credit.

The debate on Monday was occupied largely with the explanations and recriminations of Mr O'Brien and the Chancellor of the Exchequer. There was only one opinion in the House – *viz* – that the matter took up much more time than its importance warranted. Mr O'Brien spoke in public with a want of discretion which was certainly unfair and unusual in Parliamentary manners, about the conversations which he had had with Mr Lloyd-George. These conversations were perfectly proper and natural in every respect: but for one party to them to give a one-sided and grossly inaccurate account to the world, was outrageous. On the other hand Mr O'Brien is a good-hearted, single-minded man and Mr Churchill thought he got quite as much censure as he deserved – and more. The O'Brienite group which as Your Majesty knows had drawn very near to the Government in the hopes of securing concessions upon the Budget, has now swung violently back into rancorous Opposition: and they are consequently much admired for their patriotism by the Conservative Party.

No change in the situation is now likely for the next six or seven weeks.

WSC to the King

22 April 1910   Home Office

Copy

Mr Secretary Churchill with his humble duty to Your Majesty.

The Committee and Report stages of the Vote on Account have occupied the last two Parliamentary days, and have served principally as a vehicle for the discussion of the conduct of Sir Robert Anderson[1] and the bygone story of the Parnell Commission.

Sir Robert Anderson has behaved very badly. The series of articles he is contributing to *Blackwood's Magazine* deal with a great many confidential matters of which he became cognizant through his official position. They are interlarded with disagreeable remarks and personalities about his former comrades and superiors. They are finally both scrappy and dull. The feeling in the House of Commons was very hot against him. The Irish Nationalists of course thirsted for his blood – or at least his pension. The Conservative Party offered no word of defence. Mr Balfour joined in the general censure.

Mr Churchill has not however been able to bring himself to the decision of depriving this old policeman of his sole means of support, as a punishment for his indiscretions and his bad taste. It would have been a harsh step to take, and although due cause could have been shown for it, there is no public interest which will necessarily be endangered by leniency. The House was therefore informed that his pension would not be taken away. They accepted the decision with reluctance. The supporters of the Government were much divided in opinion: and at 10 o'clock on Thursday night the Government was confronted with the prospect of a very awkward division. Mr Churchill was in charge of the debate and he was much pressed to alter the policy or at least to allow members to vote freely without Government Whips. Neither of these requests could be entertained.

While matters were in this uncomfortable situation, Mr Campbell,[2] the ex-Attorney General for Ireland, meaning to make an unprovocative speech, dropped a most unfortunate and ill-timed observation. He treated or affected to treat Mr Parnell's complicity with the Phoenix Park murders as if it were an open question; whereas after the Pigott forgery it was absolutely disproved by the Special Commission in 1890. This created a great

---

[1] Robert Anderson (1841–1918); Barrister; adviser to Home Office on political crime 1868–1901; Assistant Commissioner of Metropolitan Police and head of Criminal Investigation Department 1888–1901; KCB 1901.

[2] James Henry Mussen Campbell (1851–1931), Unionist MP Dublin University 1903–16; MP St Stephen's Green division of Dublin 1898–1900; Solicitor-General, Ireland 1901–5; Attorney-General, Ireland 1905 and 1916; Lord Chancellor, Ireland 1918–21; Chairman Irish Free State Senate 1922–8. Baronet 1916; created Baron Glenavy 1921.

storm. For twenty minutes the House was in complete disorder. Not a word could be heard except in agitated intervals. The Irish were resolute that Mr Campbell should not continue unless he would withdraw. The Chairman of Committees did not feel justified in actually compelling him to withdraw. Uproar continued to reign, and threatened to develop a dangerous excitement. Mr Churchill thought that it was best to terminate the scene by the Closure and he therefore made a Motion which the Chairman was very glad to accept. The divisions were exciting, especially the second, which was full of uncertainty: but in the end the Government came off safe with adequate majorities. The House is to rise on Thursday next for the welcome and needed holiday of a month.

All of which is humbly submitted by Your Majesty's faithful subject and servant

WINSTON S. CHURCHILL

WSC to the King

[15 April 1910]   Home Office

Copy

Mr Secretary Churchill with his humble duty to Your Majesty.

For the last two days the House of Commons has debated the various Amendments to the second Veto Resolution which the Opposition have placed upon the notice paper. These amendments have all sought to exclude from the scope of the new procedure measures involving changes in the constitution, in the new procedure itself, in the electoral system and lastly in the rights, powers and prerogatives of the Crown. It has been Mr Churchill's duty on behalf of the Government to resist all these amendments – and with good reason at the present juncture. There would indeed be great difficulty in giving effect to them by the words of any statute, since it is clear that the amending words could themselves be deleted from the Act, by subsequent legislation. Still Mr Churchill feels the force of the argument which has been urged with so much iteration from the Conservative benches, that there is a plain distinction between bills designed to alter the machinery by which laws are made, and ordinary legislation; and that the instrument of government should have a stability of a special and extraordinary order. Before this constitutional quarrel is finally settled it seems very likely that these complaints and criticisms of the Conservative party will have to be met in some effective manner.

This evening the Prime Minister is to conclude these debates by making the important statement as to the course which will be taken by the Government, if the House of Lords should reject or refuse to discuss the Veto Resolutions, of which Your Majesty has already been informed.

WSC to the King

27 April 1910   Home Office

Copy

Mr Secretary Churchill with his humble duty to Your Majesty.

The Budget of 1909–10 has passed the House of Commons for the second time. The discussions upon it during this week have been cool. It is recognized that it is substantially the same Budget, that there has been no material alteration, and that there is an effective British majority (apart from the Irish members) of over 60 resulting from the late election. The chagrin which the Opposition have naturally felt has been expressed by their general attitude rather than by speeches. Mr Bonar Law and Captain Pretyman[1] have been their spokesmen today; but neither has said anything that has not been repeated many times in the interminable debates of last year. The most interesting feature was provided by the speech of Mr Devlin[2] – the Nationalist member for Belfast. This gentleman is a figure in Irish politics deserving of increasing attention. He belongs to a new type of Irish politician – progressive, democratic and radical; and he is of course in the closest sympathy with advanced opinions in Great Britain. He made a really fine speech – full of courage and of a high order of eloquence. He declared himself a whole-hearted supporter of the Budget on its merits. Most Irish Members have attempted a sort of apology for supporting it. Mr Devlin made a bold and able defence of it as a good Budget for Ireland. His effort, which was really a very fine one, drew loud cheers from the supporters of the Government.

The passage of the Budget makes it easy now to see how very unwise the House of Lords were to reject it last year. Had matters taken the ordinary course the old Parliament would be smoothly and gradually declining to its normal end, through peaceful sessions of Workmen's Insurance and Poor Law Reform: and it is probable that in the full maturity of the Government,

[1] Ernest George Pretyman (1860–1931), Conservative MP Chelmsford Division of Essex 1908–23; MP Woodbridge Division of Suffolk 1895–1906; Civil Lord of Admiralty 1900–3; Secretary to Admiralty 1903–6; Parliamentary Secretary to Board of Trade 1915–16; Civil Lord of Admiralty 1916–19. PC 1917.

[2] Joseph Devlin (1872–1934); Nationalist MP West Belfast 1906–18; MP Kilkenny North 1902–6; Falls Division, Belfast 1918–22; Fermanagh and Tyrone 1929–34.

the ordinary causes would have operated to place another party in power by an adequate majority – whereas a far more difficult and uncertain prospect is now opening out before us, and we are moving steadily forward to grave and novel situations.

The Prime Minister concluded the debate in one of his brief and clear cut statements. He reviewed the long course of this conflict. It is almost exactly a year since the Chancellor of the Exchequer made his Budget speech. He justified the general structure of the scheme. He pointed out that its financial success could not be disputed. He stated that in the course of this exceptional year, in spite of the high expenditure and financial disturbance, no less than 12 millions of the capital of the National Debt had been repaid, 6 of which had been actually provided from the revenues of the Budget. The crowded House listened with attention but without excitement. Everyone is tired out by the unceasing strain, and the holiday of a month is the dearest wish of most Members of the House of Commons.

In the division the Government carried the Budget by a majority of 93.

WSC to the King

28 April 1910   Home Office

Copy

Mr Secretary Churchill with his humble duty to Your Majesty.

In an almost empty House the motion for the adjournment for the holidays has been debated. The usual discursive discussion has trickled over the broad expanse of external affairs. The arrest of Arabindo Ghose[1] and the evacuation of Somaliland have been the principal features. Upon the latter Colonel Seely made a full explanation of the policy and situation. Mr Churchill has already in his letters made Your Majesty acquainted with some of the main arguments which justify a withdrawal of the British military posts from their insecure position in the interior to the three coastal towns whence they can effectively maintain all necessary hold upon the country. The operation is being satisfactorily carried out by General Manning. The friendly tribes having organised themselves have met the Dervishes with spirit and have given the Mullah a taste of their quality. It is probable that raiding and counter-raiding will continue for some time. But there seems no

---

[1] Arabindo Ghose was an Indian journalist, arrested for what was considered to be an inflammatory article in the periodical *Karmayogin*. Charges against him were later withdrawn.

reason to doubt that the friendly tribes will be able to make themselves respected by the Dervishes.

The House adjourned at 6.15; and Mr Churchill must offer to Your Majesty this apology for writing so brief an account – namely that a longer description of its proceedings would convey a disproportionate idea of their importance.

WSC to King George V

10 May 1910   10 Downing Street

Mr Secretary Churchill with his humble duty to Your Majesty has the honour to submit the enclosed draft of a Gracious Message from your Majesty to both Houses of Parliament tomorrow & would be glad to know whether it obtains Your Majesty's approval.

It has been framed in accordance with precedent.

Draft Message by WSC

10 May 1910   Home Office

The King knows that the House of {Lords shares in the profound and {Commons sudden sorrow which has fallen upon His Majesty by the death of his Majesty's father, the late King; and that the House entertains a true sense of the loss which His Majesty and the Nation have sustained from this mournful event.

King Edward's care for the welfare of His country and His people, His skilled and prudent guidance of affairs, His unwearying devotion to public duty during His illustrious reign, His simple courage in pain and danger, will long be held in honour by His subjects at home and beyond the seas.

WSC to the King
(*Royal Archives*)

EXTRACT

4 June 1910   Home Office

Mr Secretary Churchill with his humble duty to Your Majesty:
Immediately after questions today the Home Secretary introduced under the Ten Minutes Rule the Shop Hours Bill. This measure was prepared last year by Lord Gladstone, but in the throng of events it was crowded out. It seeks to limit the hours of shop assistants to 60 hours a week exclusive of meals; to prevent their being employed after 8 o'clock (except in special trades & circumstances) on more than three nights in the week; to secure a universal half holiday & some lesser things. There are about a million shop assistants & half a million shop keepers, of the shop keepers nine-tenths serve their own little shops themselves, & only one-tenth employ assistants. No restriction is placed by the Bill on the little shops who in fact get a certain advantageous preference thereby: but the shop assistants who are an intelligent – deserving class – very loyal, vy well behaved, but hard pressed & defenceless, will be secured – if the bill passes – a certain amount of leisure to enable them to have some share however small in the pleasures & enjoyments of life, – in the fruits of their toil. It must be remembered that shop keeping is not a matter of *producing* anything but only of *distributing;* & there is no reason why the distribution should be inconsistently sprawled out over the whole week, instead of taking place within reasonable hours. Many exceptions must however be granted to meet the special conditions of particular trades.

The House thence resumed its discussions upon the Budget. Mr Austen Chamberlain made a long, moderate, but distinctly good speech, criticising the financial proposals in detail, & taking the Chancellor of the Exchequer to task for his references to naval expenditure, wh were stigmatized as disrespectful to that subject. Mr Dillon[1] followed and in another long speech scolded Your Majesty's ministers for having consented to reach great expenditure, especially as so he contended, there was no German acceleration & no Austrian Dreadnought. Between these opposing fires the Government remained serene.

Mr Whittaker[2] a Liberal member for the Spen Valley continued the

[1] John Dillon (1851–1927), Irish Nationalist MP County Mayo 1885–1918; Member Royal College of Surgeons, Ireland; MP County Tipperary 1880–3; Chairman Irish Nationalist Party 1918.

[2] Thomas Palmer Whittaker (1850–1919), Liberal MP Spen Valley Division, Yorkshire 1892–1919; played an active part in Temperance movement; member of Royal Commission on Licensing 1896–9.

debate & expressed his pleasure at the removal of the whisky tax & its effects on national habits.

Tomorrow the Regency bill will be advanced a stage, & as the Prime Minister will have to attend another Conference in his room, Mr Churchill is to take charge of the measure. All of which is now humbly submitted to Your Majesty.

WINSTON S. CHURCHILL

WSC to the King
(*Royal Archives*)

14 July 1910   Home Office

Mr Secretary Churchill with his humble duty to Your Majesty:

Naval Estimates occupied the House today. Mr Dillon moved a reduction of the vote for Shipbuilding of £2,000,000. He attacked the Government & the Opposition for the alarmist statements of last year. He asserted that these were now found to be without basis. He deplored the suspicion & ill-will fomented between Great Britain & Germany by irresponsible people. He inveighed against the cruel & burdensome expenditure. His speech was heard with approbation by many of the supporters of the Government.

The Prime Minister replied at once. Your Majesty would find it advantageous to read his statement in full. He surveyed the relative state of naval construction in England & Germany. Now we have 10 Dreadnoughts ready for battle: Germany has 5. We have 6 launched: Germany has 5. We have 4 on the slips: Germany has 3 – total 20 against 13 available in March 1912.

By the end of 1913 Germany will have 4 more ships already ordered = 17. We shall have the 5 ships of this year's programme = 25. In addition to this there are the two colonial ships making – unless they are sent away = 27 British Dreadnoughts in 1913. These figures do not include the *Nelson* & *Agamemnon* which as Your Majesty is well aware are equal to the earlier French Dantons, classed as Dreadnoughts for the purposes of comparison. Neither do they include any ships which we may decide to lay down in 1911–12 ready for the fleet during 1913–14.

Assuming that 4 ships were laid down in 1911 as the programme for the year our total strength available for an emergency in 1913 would reach the astonishing figure of 33 British Dreadnoughts to 17 German. The preponderance in all other classes (except Mr Churchill believes in torpedo boat destroyers) is of course even greater.

Mr Churchill would only add that he personally does not believe that the Germans will have more than 11 ships of this class ready in April 1912 & that Admiral Tirpitz's[1] statement last year that 13 will not be ready until the autumn will be strictly borne out by events.

Mr Balfour followed the Prime Minister & now Lord Charles Beresford is addressing the House at length, but with effect. The Division will not be dangerous. Mr Churchill hopes that Your Majesty will find time to glance at his reply tomorrow to the very unfair statements attributed to Lord Lytton in todays *Times*.

WSC to the King
(*Royal Archives*)

22 July 1910   Home Office

Mr Secretary Churchill with his humble duty to Your Majesty:

Upon the 2nd Reading of the Appropriations Bill Mr Balfour reviewed the whole position in which Colonial Preference now stands. He said it was the last opportunity for discussion of the question before the Imperial Conference of 1911. He insisted on the growing necessity for 'mutual good offices' between the naturally linked communities of the Empire. All nations are entering into agreements which by their peculiar character whittle away any advantage we may have had from the most favoured nation clause: we stand in 'stolid isolation', immoveable because of 'doctrinaire prejudice'; the outlook is dark.

On this challenge the Prime Minister rose at once and a brisk & animated debate began upon the well trampled battlefield of Tariff Reform. The Free Traders propounded their old questions. What do you mean by Preference. On what articles would you accord it. Will you give it on corn! If so where do South Africa & Australia profit? Will you give it on wool? How then is Canada served. Will you give it on timber – Is not this the taxation both of food & raw materials? Again what do you mean by Reciprocity? Do you mean that in return for preference the Colonies should give us an equally free entry in their markets? Do you mean that there shall be Free Trade within the Empire? But there is no chance of it; & so on. Mr Mackinder,[2]

---

[1] Alfred Peter Friedrich von Tirpitz (1849–1930), German Grand-Admiral; Secretary of State for the Navy 1897–1915; in 1898 he presented to the Reichstag his first Navy Bill, the beginning of the serious growth of the German Navy; his second Bill, in 1900, started the naval arms race.

[2] Halford John Mackinder (1861–1947), economist; Conservative MP Camlachie Division, Glasgow 1910–22; served on a number of Royal Commissions; KT 1920; PC 1926.

Captain Tryon,[1] Sir Joseph Walton[2] & afterwards Mr Chaplin (in a vy good speech) continued the debate; & it was concluded by Colonel Seely, shortly before dinner. Egypt & Foreign Office questions were dealt with after dinner & Sir Edward Grey replied to various criticisms.

Your Majesty will have noticed with pleasure the collapse of the threatening North Eastern Railway Strike. The firmness of the Trade Union leaders in boldly telling their men they were entirely in the wrong is a remarkable instance of the great improvement in the character of these organisations in the last 20 years.

WSC to the King
(*Royal Archives*)

22 July 1910   Home Office

Mr Secretary Churchill with his humble duty to Your Majesty:

There was a vy good temper in the House during the discussion of the Civil List Resolutions. The Labour Party made their protest, but they said the vy least they could to support their positions. The Irish Nationalists abstained altogether. The opposition voted with the Government & the division lists showed overwhelming majorities. The Chancellor of the Exchequer conducted the debate with his usual skill. Only a single sentence of Mr Keir Hardie's seemed to offend the House; & that sentence he repeated in a modified form & without desire to provoke. Mr Churchill thinks the proceedings may be regarded as quite satisfactory. No trouble need be anticipated at later stages.

After the Civil List the Regency Bill was passed through the Report & Third Reading stages. Mr Churchill left the House free to vote as it pleased on a vy trivial point connected with Protestantism in Scotland & the division resulted in a tie. This is vy rare & Mr Speaker's casting vote was invoked to settle the matter. He gave it to restore the Bill to its original form. All of which is humbly submitted, by Your Majesty's faithful servant & subject

WINSTON S. CHURCHILL

---

[1] George Clement Tryon (1871–1940), Unionist MP Brighton 1910–40; served Grenadier Guards 1890–1902, 1914–18; Minister of Pensions 1922–9, 1931–5; Postmaster-General 1935–40; Chancellor of Duchy of Lancaster, First Commissioner of Works 1940; PC 1922; Baron 1940.

[2] Joseph Walton (1849–1923), Liberal MP Barnsley Division, Yorkshire 1897–1918, Borough of Barnsley 1918–23; Baronet 1910.

WSC to the King
(*Royal Archives*)

25 July 1910   Home Office

Mr Secretary Churchill with his humble duty to Your Majesty:

This day on the Report stage of the Budget Resolutions Mr Hope[1] & Lord Ronaldshay[2] proposed to reduce the duty on tea grown within the Empire from 5d to 4d: the thin end of the wedge of Imperial Preference. Many members spoke, nearly all wandering beyond the rules of order to discuss Tariff Reform generally, whereupon Mr Speaker invited them 'to come back to tea'. Colonel Seely speaking for the Government said the proposal would mean a loss to the revenue of £1,000,000, which the Chancellor of the Exchequer was not prepared to face: this country has deliberately rejected preference because the losses are greater than the gains. It may be mentioned that nearly all the tea consumed in this country already comes from British Colonies.

Mr Hobhouse, the financial Secretary to the Treasury added to these arguments the fact that a reduction of 1d in tea does not affect prices. 2d must be taken off before any real benefit is experienced by the consumer.

The Labour Party is supporting the Government.

WSC to the King
(*Royal Archives*)

26 July 1910   Home Office

Mr Secretary Churchill with his humble duty to Your Majesty:

Today on the Motion that Mr Speaker do now leave the chair the Indian Budget has been discussed.

Mr Montagu the Under Secretary made a masterly statement, covering the whole range of Indian policy & affairs & occupying nearly two hours in delivery. His chief Lord Morley watched him from the gallery. It was a vy creditable effort & indicated high intellectual qualities.

Mr Wyndham followed & among other things paid a warm well-deserved

---

[1] James Fitzalan Hope (1870–1938), Conservative MP Brightside Division, Sheffield 1900–6, Central Division 1908–29; Financial Secretary to Ministry of Munitions 1919–21; Chairman of Committees and Deputy Speaker in the House of Commons 1921–9. Created Baron Rankeillour 1932; PC 1922.

[2] Lawrence John Lumley Dundas, Earl of Ronaldshay (1876–1961), Unionist MP Hornsey Division, Middlesex 1907–16; Governor of Bengal 1917–22; Secretary of State for India 1935–40; for Burma 1937–40; succeeded father as 2nd Marquess of Zetland 1929; GCIE 1917; PC and GCSI 1922; KG 1942; Biographer of Lord Curzon.

tribute to the memory of the late Earl Percy who used always to shine on these occasions, & who is mourned in all quarters of the House.

The Conference is sitting again this afternoon, & is perhaps entering upon a fateful phase in its history.

The Declaration Bill tomorrow gives rise to some anxiety; but the Whips believe that all will be well. It is vy important to get it cleared out of the political arena, as the agitation against it tends to grow.

WSC to the King
(*Royal Archives*)

27 July 1910   House of Commons

Mr Secretary Churchill with his humble duty to Your Majesty:

The Prime Minister's speech this afternoon on the Royal Declaration Bill produced a highly beneficial effect upon the House. He indicated that the Government would be willing to accept a rather simpler form of words than those of the Schedule as it stands today. The speech deserves to be read in full as it is a masterly & conclusive statement on the whole question. The new words – omitting as they do, all reference to the 'Church as by law established' – meet the principal objections of Scottish members & English & Welsh Nonconformists without offending the Roman Catholics. There could be no doubt of the good temper of the House.

Mr Agar-Robartes[1] rose pluckily to oppose the Bill & to move its rejection. He spoke well & sincerely: but he does not carry vy heavy metal. Mr Mitchell-Thomson[2] & Mr Moore from the Unionist benches opposed the bill – the latter in a better speech. Lord Hugh Cecil generally supported it.

The debate is still proceeding. Mr Churchill does not anticipate any serious difficulty, & looks forward to a good majority in the Lobby.

The Conference[3] seems still to make progress.

---

[1] Thomas Charles Reginald Agar-Robartes (1880–1916), MP Bodmin Division, Cornwall 1906–8, St Austell Division 1908–15; served World War I; died of wounds received in action; eldest son and heir of 6th Viscount Clifden.

[2] William Mitchell-Thomson (1877–1938), Conservative MP North West Lanark 1906–1910, North Down 1910–18; Conservative Unionist, Maryhill Division of Glasgow 1918–22; Conservative, South Croydon 1923–32. Postmaster-General and Chief Civil Commissioner 1924–9; succeeded as 2nd Baronet 1918; KBE 1918; PC 1924; created Baron Selsdon 1932.

[3] The inter-party Conference on House of Lords Reform.

WSC to Edward Marsh
(*Longleat Papers*)

8 August 1910

My dear Eddie,

We have a pleasant journey so far, though we had one rough night, and I was very sea-sick. I am now better, and am, I think, getting accustomed to the less devilish forms of motion attendant upon marine adventure. You will be glad to hear that I visited the Monte Carlo Gambling Hell on four occasions and took away from them altogether upwards of £160.

I shall not expect to get any more letters till we reach Athens, when you will send a bag, or bags, by the Messenger who leaves on the . . . th instant. I will, however, cable you my telegraph address as it becomes fixed.

Yours ever
W

Lord Knollys to Lord Crewe
(*Crewe Papers*)

8 August 1910   Marlborough House
Private

My dear Crewe,

I am glad to say that the King has consented to ask Lloyd George to Balmoral.

I suppose it does not signify his not inviting Winston Churchill there as well. He would be *very* reluctant to do so.

Would you kindly send me a line to Balmoral.

Yrs ever
KNOLLYS

Lord Crewe to Lord Knollys
(*Crewe Papers*)

9 August 1910   Crewe Hall
Copy

My dear Francis,

I am very glad that the K has asked Lloyd George to Balmoral: he & his friends will regard it as a real compliment & he has shown such good feeling that it is a compliment well deserved. I see no reason why HM should invite W. Churchill on this particular occasion: I think it has always been the usage for the Sovereign to select Ministers in attendance for particular times & places without including the whole number: for instance though the late K often honoured me with invitations I was never in attendance on HM until I went to Berlin last year, and it certainly never occurred to me that I was left out: so this would surely apply to any Ministers.

Ever yrs

C

WSC to Sir Edward Grey

9 September 1910   Mytilene

My dear Grey,

I am vy much obliged to you for taking my work & for your kind letter. I know you must have felt keenly the painful duties wh I put upon you. There was however no doubt as to the course to pursue. The only capital decision with wh I have been dissatisfied during my tenure was about a man I reprieved just before I started on grounds wh I do not feel wholly convinced were adequate. He has since committed suicide! To most men – including all the best – a life sentence is worse than a death sentence.

I am glad that no other serious business came upon you on my account. I have received three substantial mails with departmental work & have chewed up a good many tough bits I had put aside for leisure days. Such days I have had in abundance. I cannot remember ever to have had such a restful holiday. We have visited all the most beautiful places in the most luxurious manner – Monte Carlo (where I won £160), Elba, Naples (Vesuvius & Pompeii), Messina still utterly in ruins, Syracuse, Ithaca, Corinth, Athens, Delos, Santorin (a wonderful volcanic island), Crete, Rhodes – the fortress of the knights is still perfect – the best & largest specimens of 14th century fortifications I have ever seen – then to the coast of Asia minor – Marmarice, Boudrum, Smyrna. At Smyrna we took a special train & with a seat fitted up on the cow catcher & a proper escort against brigands we travelled the whole length of the British Aidin railway 260 miles into the interior. There is no better way of seeing a country in a flash. We hope to have escaped without fever – but it is a fine fertile province. The Governor Mahmoud Muktar[1] a thoroughly able & Europeanised Turk – of whom you have heard a great deal – was well worth meeting. And in spite of mosquitos the expedition fully repaid the time & exertion it required.

Then de Forest in wantonness shot a seagull by an unusually good shot

[1] Mahmut Muhtar Pasha (1867–1935), Governor of Aidin 1908–10; Minister for the Navy 1910 and 1912; Turkish Ambassador in Berlin 1913.

from a Mauser pistol. In consequence the next day we were stranded in the narrow unbuoyed entrance of a Mytilene bay & for the last four days we have been struggling in a circle of competing tugs to free ourselves. At last we are afloat again & undamaged & in two days I shall be at Constantinople whence I return by train.

The days have passed by rapidly – reading, bathing & bridge their only occupations – & I am astonished to find six weeks already flown. I have made some extensive plans for prison & punishment reform which I want you to view with a friendly eye – but otherwise politics have not entered my head – much.

The only view I have formed about this part of the world of ruined civilisations & systems, & harshly jumbled races is this – why can't England & Germany come together in strong action & for general advantage?

Hoping that you have had some real refreshment & relaxation – believe me

Yours vy sincerely
WINSTON S. CHURCHILL

David Lloyd George to WSC

25 September 1910   Brynawelon
                                                       Criccieth

Private and Personal

My dear Winston,

I am delighted to find that Mrs Winston Churchill and yourself will be able to spend a few days with us here. I think I can guarantee you an enjoyable time, weather permitting.

I hope you will bring your golf clubs with you. We can arrange an excellent 'foursome'. My big boy,[1] who has just finished his Cambridge career, plays much better golf than either you or I used to play at Walton Heath, and he and Mrs Winston Churchill, with a couple of biscs, will more than hold their own against us. The motor-runs around here are very fine; and if you care for sea-fishing, there is plenty of it in the Bay. But I hope we shall be able to squeeze in some serious talk about the future.

I have never known a time when things were as uncertain as they seem to be now: our real danger is that the Government will drift along without any clear definite policy or purpose. I am perfectly certain that our more important associates have no plan of operations in their minds. This aimlessness,

[1] Richard Lloyd George (1889–1967), 2nd Earl Lloyd George of Dwyfor. He had taken an Honours degree at Christ's College, Cambridge in 1910. He wrote a biography of his father, published in 1960.

if persevered in, means utter disaster. It is not too late to pull ourselves together: on the contrary I think it is just the time when we ought to be thinking out our next step (a) if Conference succeeds, (b) if it fails. I have some ideas, and I think they are winning ones; in fact, I have two alternative sets of ideas.

These are the things I am most anxious to talk over with you; in fact, I think it is a matter of urgent moment to the Party that we should meet without any further delay to talk things over.

I would have written you weeks ago to thank you for that most beautiful and extremely useful present that you were so kind as to send me. I found, however, that you had already sailed from England before I received it. I shall always treasure it, not merely for its value; but for the great admiration I have always had for the giver ever since I first met him.

One word as to trains: my earnest advice is, do not travel by the night mail; there is no sleeper and you have two or three changes. There is an excellent train leaving Euston at 11 in the morning and arriving here at 5.33; you have a through carriage, a restaurant car and a comfortable journey.

Ever sincerely
D. LLOYD GEORGE

WSC to David Lloyd George
(Lloyd George Papers)

6 October 1910 Levishie
Private Inverness-shire

My dear David,

We enjoyed our visit to your beautiful country and house very much indeed. My wife and I will always remember your kindness and hospitality; and Wales in sunshine, shadow and sunset did the honours by sea and land not less agreeably. I hope we may some day be asked again.

I have just read Balfour's speech. Knollys must have said something to him. If so his utterance is all the more significant. On Land too he marches in step with you.

My own opinion has not departed from our conversations. It is not for me to take the lead. I cannot tell how such an arrangement might ultimately affect democratic political organisations. But if we stood together we ought to be strong enough either to impart a progressive character to policy, or by withdrawal to terminate an administration which had failed in its purpose. Let us dine on Tuesday and talk to Grey about it all.

I am sorry for the poor little King. I am told that the mass of the Portuguese people are opposed to the corrupt politicians of the capital.[1] I wish we could have been together when this news arrived. We might have found something to work with Germany upon. The Kaiser will be rampant.

I have spent my days walking after horned beasts, and my nights in recovering from the effects of such exertions. With many thanks and all good wishes to you and Mrs Lloyd George – I remain

Yours ever
WSC

WSC to David Lloyd George
(*Lloyd George Papers*)

14 October 1910   Home Office

Secret

Dear David,

How can they stick to Home Rule so far as the immediate Constitutional Settlement is concerned?

The condition that the new machinery is only to work after another election, means a fresh appeal to the people anyhow on a disagreed Home Rule scheme and makes it necessary for us to have three general elections running in order to carry it. To say that even after the next election has been won on H.R. by a majority big enough for a joint session, there is to be yet another election – the Fourth – won running by the Liberals cannot conceivably be maintained by any people who wish to act fairly.

I put the point to you for what it may be worth. A messenger has orders to come to you about 12 or 1, and to bring any note you may send me straight down to me. Do not then wire.

Yours always
WSC

[1] On October 4 republican revolutionaries had seized power in Portugal. King Manoel fled from Lisbon and took refuge in Gibraltar whence he was conveyed to England in the royal yacht of King George V. The republic was declared at once.

WSC to H. H. Asquith

22 October 1910   Home Office

Copy

Secret

My dear Asquith,

It is with some diffidence that I write to you on a matter which you may consider outside my province.

I had a talk with Morley yesterday and found a distinct undercurrent of feeling in his mind that he had been somewhat easily let go.[1] He would of course be vy vexed with me for coming to such a conclusion, still more for repeating it to you. But I do so because I am strongly of opinion that Morley's complete detachment from the Govt at this stage might prove vy disadvantageous to us, and secondly because I have a deep personal affection for him and am proud to sit in council by his side.

From what he said yesterday I am convinced that you could even now retain his services in some great office without administrative duties. Such an office is vacant at the present time; for Crewe is not only Col Secretary but Privy Seal. I wd therefore venture respectfully and earnestly to suggest to you to invite Morley to stay with us in a post which wd relieve him from the administrative burden he has found so heavy, and wd at the same time associate him with your Govt in an effective and distinguished manner. The Cabinet will be spared a very heavy loss in counsel and distinction, if you find yourself able to make this offer.

I may add that the C. of E. whom I saw this morning authorised me to say on his behalf to you that 'he saw great danger in Morley's being separated from us entirely at the present time'.

Please do not be offended by my addressing you on such a subject. Only its importance and my wish to see your administration successful has prompted me. In no case let Morley know I have written.

Yours vy sincerely
WSC

[1] John Morley was just about to leave the India Office to become Lord President of the Council.

WSC to the King
(*Royal Archives*)

EXTRACT

22 November 1910

Mr Secretary Churchill with his humble duty to Your Majesty: The Prime Minister's statement upon Friday last effectually extinguished the pallid flickering life of this House of Commons. It has never really lived, & now it is to die. No one cares about it any more. The members are hurrying to their constituencies & the routine business incidental to the winding up of the session is being attended to with admirable despatch. Today the guillotine Resolutions providing for the passage of all the taxes of the year practically without debate were assented to by large majorities before the dinner hour was reached. Mr Austen Chamberlain & Lord Hugh Cecil delivered fiery speeches to a thin House. Everyone is looking to the country & the first pollings are the predominant thought in the minds of every politician.

Mr Churchill trusts that Your Majesty will excuse a brief report. He does not remember having been so hard-pressed before. The general situation, the South Wales Strike, & no fewer than eight capital cases wh have descended from the summer assizes have been a great burden in the last few days. . . .

Sir Joseph Lawrence[1] to J. S. Sandars
(*Balfour Papers*)

20 November 1910   11 Old Court Mansions
Copy

Dear Mr Sandars,

Perhaps it may interest Mr Balfour or you to know of a little bet I made with Lloyd George & Winston Churchill on the Walton Heath Golf Links yesterday afternoon.

They hallo'ed out to me the conversation retailed in the next page.

Last year Lloyd George made a similar bet of £1 each with Sir T. Lipton,[2]

[1] Joseph Lawrence (1848–1919), businessman; Conservative MP Monmouth Boroughs 1901–6; Baronet 1918.
[2] Thomas Johnstone Lipton (1850–1931), tea merchant and yachtsman; knighted 1898; KCVO 1901; Baronet 1902. A friend of King Edward VII, and known popularly as the King's 'grocer'.

Kennedy Jones, Sir T. Dewar,[1] myself, & Mr Henry MP[2] – that they would win by 90 excluding the Irish!

My bet this time may not be good betting (as the odds against our winning on the Stock Exchange were on Saturday £60 to £40 – taken) but it was *good politics* to put up a big bluff on the biggest bluffer of modern times!

Yours very truly

JOSEPH LAWRENCE

Conversation on Links

L. George: Hello Lawrence why aren't you electioneering?
Lawrence: I am waiting for you.
L. George: What's the betting?
Lawrence: Two to one on us!
L. George: I'll take you.
Lawrence: In Sovereigns?
L. George: All right!
Lawrence: Agreed.
Winston: Will you lay me the same odds?
Lawrence: Yes – in Sovereigns.
Winston: Right!

*   *   *   *   *

The second General Election of 1910 was held between 2 and 19 December. The Liberals and Conservatives each won 272 seats, and the balance of power was held by Irish Nationalist and Labour MPs.

The result in Dundee was as follows:

Rt Hon. W. S. Churchill (Liberal)	9,240
A. Wilkie (Labour)	8,957
Sir G. W. Baxter[3] (Conservative)	5,685
J. S. Lloyd (Conservative)	4,914
E. Scrymgeour (Prohibitionist)	1,825
Liberal majority over Conservative	3,555
Labour majority over Conservative	3,272

[1] Thomas Robert Dewar (1864–1930), whisky distiller; Conservative MP St George's Tower Hamlets 1900–6; London County Councillor 1892–5; Sheriff of City of London 1897–8; knighted 1902; Baronet 1917; Baron 1919.

[2] Charles Solomon Henry (1860–1919), Liberal MP Wellington Division, Shropshire 1906–18, Wrekin 1918–19; Baronet 1911.

[3] George Washington Baxter (1853–1926), Chairman Dundee and District Liberal Association 1886–1910; Chairman Dundee Unionist Association 1910–19; knighted 1904; Baronet 1918.

WSC to Lord Robert Cecil
(*Cecil Papers*)

16 December 1910   Home Office

My dear Robert Cecil,

I am vy much obliged to you for sending me a copy of *The Round Table*.
It seems an admirable publication in every way & I should like to become a
regular subscriber to it. Perhaps you will kindly tell the publishers to send
it regularly & to bill me accordingly.

While I must prefer the [Neil] Primrose, I am vy sorry indeed that this
new & important Parliament is not to be the richer for your presence. I hope
that your return may not be long delayed.

Whatever else the election may or may not have proved, it has at any rate
shown that the Conservative party regard Tariff Reform as a burden & not
a stimulus, & that they are right in this view.

Yours sincerely
WINSTON S. CHURCHILL

Richard Lambert[1] to WSC

23 December 1910   1 Essex Court

Dear Mr Churchill,

I have to thank you for your very kind telegram of congratulation on the
N. Wilts result, and also for the magnificent speech you delivered at Swindon
on the eve of the Poll.

I have no hesitation in saying that it was your speech which mainly brought
about our success. I have personally come across several Tories who were
influenced by it, and eventually voted for me, and yesterday I heard of one
of the assistant managers in the Swindon works, who told a Liberal friend that
he had to leave halfway through your speech, because, if he had stayed, he
would have had to vote Liberal. I feel therefore that the Liberals of Swindon
and I owe you a very special debt of gratitude for all that you have done for
us, and, though I am unable to express adequately what we really feel, I
desire to thank you most sincerely in their name and in my own for the
splendid and unselfish efforts you put forth on their and my own behalf.

Yours sincerely
RICHARD C. LAMBERT

[1] Richard Cornthwaite Lambert (d. 1939), Liberal MP North Wiltshire 1910–18;
barrister.

14

Parliament 1911

(See Main Volume Chapter 10)

WSC to H. H. Asquith

3 January 1911   Blenheim Palace

Secret

Copy

My dear Asquith,

I have been pondering ever since the election was decided over the general position of our affairs, and as my view has not changed at all with reflection I write it to you for what it is worth. But first let me tell you what everyone feels – that yr leadership was the main & conspicuous feature of the whole fight. It is not always that a leader's personal force can be felt amid all that turmoil. You seemed to be far more effectively master of the situation & in the arguments than at the January Election, & yr speeches stood out in massive preeminence whether in relation to colleagues or opponents. Balfour made heroic exertions, considering his health, but you fairly beat him all along the line, & I noticed that Liberal audiences responded to yr name with increasing enthusiasm as the days wore on. The result was decidedly a victory, & decidedly your victory.

The course now seems to me to be quite plain and smooth and safe. We cannot parley with the Tories on any question until we can meet them on fair and equal terms. We cannot resume discussions when we argue & they decide, when we propose and they pronounce. The veto must be restricted as an indispensable preliminary to any cooperation between parties on the reform of the Lords, Ireland, or any other subject.

We ought to go straight ahead with the Parliament Bill & carry it to the Lords at the earliest date compatible with full discussion. We are I conceive perfectly free to accept any amendments not affecting the principle, wh appear useful in themselves or likely to conciliate opposition. It wd be disrespectful to H of C to suggest that we were not. Among such amendments are those wh wd seek to impart stability and permanence (unless changed by consent) to the important safeguards left to the Lords under the new procedure; & those wh wd secure that at each passage through H of C a bill shall be set down first in order for debate upon an adequate number of days. I wd myself like to add to these a provision enabling Peers to stand for the H of C on renunciation of their privileges, & its counterpoise, ministers to be allowed to speak in both Houses.

We should state at the proper time that after the Veto has been restricted we shall be quite ready to discuss the future composition of the Lords with the Conservative leaders in the true spirit of the Conference: & that we do not now attempt to prejudge what arrangements for adjusting differences wd be appropriate in regard to an assembly wh was not onesided in its character.

We ought as early as possible to make it clear that we are not a bit afraid of creating 500 Peers – if necessary: that we believe ourselves beyond doubt possessed of the power, & will not shrink from using it. Such a creation wd be in fact for the interest of the Liberal party, & a disaster to the Conservative party. It wd be possible to make a list of men whose local & civic reputations stood so high with both parties in cities & counties that all attempts to ridicule their character or to compare them unfavourably with the present nobility wd fall vy flat. We shd at a stroke gain a great addition of influence in the country. The wealth & importance of British Society cd easily maintain 1000 notables – much more easily than 300 a century ago. The enlarged Peerage wd serve as an admirable panel from wh a working body of 200 to 400 cd be chosen. As we shd have a majority in the panel, we shd obtain a majority in the chambers; & our representatives wd be far more capable & determined politicians than the Tory nobles. We shd then at any rate for some years be able to dispense through the agreement between the Liberal majorities in both Houses with any of the inconveniences (to us) of the two years delay & the three sessions procedure. All these considerations are obvious to the Tories. Without the provocation we shd not be justified in taking such an extreme step. But let us make our Tory friends realize at the outset that we regard such a creation coolly & in a matter of fact mood, that we shall make no bones about it, if the need arises, & that we have no doubt who wd suffer from the event.

I do not believe we shall get the chance – the Parliament Bill ought to receive the Royal Assent before the Coronation. Two months for the discussion in both houses will be ample for such a short & simple measure. One thing we must not put up with is any dilatory vapourings in the Lords about constitutions in general. If the Bill does not make proper progress we should clink the coronets in their scabbards! Until the Veto is out of the way there can be no peace between parties and no demonstration of national unity. The quicker & the more firmly this business is put through, the better for all.

After the Veto has been restricted, I hope we may be able to pursue *une politique d'apaisement*. The circumstances of the year & the questions wh have to be settled are favourable to such a policy. I trust that some of the disappointment of defeat may be mitigated by a liberal grant of Honours (following the precedent of the last Coronation) to prominent members of the Opposition. Privy Councillorships for Bonar Law & FE: the Order of Merit for Joe [Chamberlain]; a proportion of Tory Peers & Baronets; something for the Tory Press. If you cd find a little place for Neil [Primrose] it wd please Rosebery in spite of himself.

Then on policy. We shd offer to confer with the Conservatives not only on the Reform of the Lords but on Ireland. On the Poor Law, Boy Labour & Insurance there is already common ground. I should like to come to an understanding with Balfour about the Navy, if necessary letting him & Cawdor[1] have full access to all Admiralty information. We should not hesitate to make a good arrangement with Portugal & France about the wine scale merely because that involves an incidental preference to the Colonies. The sharp edge might be taken off the License duties where they are really cutting too deep. Death duties ought not to fall on landed estates more than once in 25 years. We ought to pursue a national & not a sectional policy: & to try to make our prolonged tenure of power as agreeable as possible to the other half of our fellow countrymen. You will have the power to do all this because of the unshakeable confidence which the Liberal masses will give to the leader who restricts the veto of the Lords by strong & fearless action. You will be strong enough to pursue a sober & earnest policy without the stimulus of undue partisanship; & it is my hope that after triumphing in the storm of faction Liberalism may enjoy that measure of national approval which is due to those who have not merely been successful but right upon many of the greatest questions of the day. All this may lead us further still.

These are my feelings at the present juncture, wh I put before you in all sincerity, knowing that you will share many of them, & that you will not resent the expression of any.

I was interrupted in copying out this letter by the Stepney affair from

---

[1] Frederick Archibald Vaughan Campbell (1847–1911), 3rd Earl of Cawdor; MP Carmarthenshire 1874–8; Chairman Great Western Railway 1895–1905; First Lord of the Admiralty 1905; succeeded father 1898.

wh I have just returned. It was a striking scene in a London street – firing from every window, bullets chipping the brickwork, police & Scots Guards armed with loaded weapons, artillery jingling up &c. I thought it better to let the house burn down rather than spend good British lives in rescuing these ferocious rascals. I think I shall have to stiffen the Admin^n of the Aliens Act a little, & more effective measures must be taken by the police to supervise the dangerous classes of aliens in our midst.

The King is well pleased with the proceedings against Mylius wh are taking a normal course.

Yr vy sly
WSC

WSC to Arthur Elliot
(Elliot Papers)

27 January 1911   Home Office

My dear Elliot,

The letter seems quite suitable for publication & I shall look forward to reading the book on wh I am vy glad to hear you are engaged.[1]

I daresay our Conservative friends will begin soon to get tired of their wild excursion into fiscal improprieties. At least then the despised 'Free Fooders' will have been justified by events.

Yours sincerely
WINSTON S. CHURCHILL

WSC to King George V
(Royal Archives)

[7 February 1911]   House of Commons

Mr Secretary Churchill with his humble duty to Your Majesty:

The first Parliament of Your Majesty's reign has met in circumstances of unusual tranquillity as far as House of Commons proceedings are concerned. Mr Churchill's experience only extends to four Parliaments, but he cannot remember any debate upon the Address wh has opened as calmly & even so tamely. What a contrast is presented by the first days work in this Parliament & in the last! Then His late Majesty's advisers felt themselves without any adequate support & exposed to the most harsh and damaging reproaches from their opponents & still more from their friends. Now although our

---

[1] Arthur Elliot was writing a biography of George Goschen. This was published the same year.

majority is no larger all seems to be smooth weather. The Government supporters are confident & united: the Opposition do not appear vy indignant or very perturbed. There can be no doubt that two general elections in a single year with all their expense & exhaustion have produced sensible effects upon the *personnel* of the House of Commons.

The mover & seconder of the Address in reply to Your Majesty's gracious speech acquitted themselves well & even in the case of Mr Harold Baker[1] with distinction. Mr Balfour appeared to be in restored health & spoke with his usual easy good humour. He made various humorous allusions to the episodes of Home Office administration wh have lately attracted public notice; & the battle of Stepney & the case of the Old Shepherd of Dartmoor or old swineherd of Dartmoor[2] received their mead of merriment. Mr Balfour touched rather injudiciously on the Canadian Reciprocity Treaty which has after all not yet been discussed by the Canadian Parliament. To this the Prime Minister replied in one of his admirable speeches which would well repay Your Majesty's perusal. He cast his aegis over the Home Office & explained to the House his intention to take the time of private members and to press the Parliament Bill up to the House of Lords so that the constitutional question may be disposed of before Your Majesty's Coronation. His statement was well received.

Tomorrow there is to be an Irish debate on the motion of the Ulster Orangemen. Tonight all is quiet and Mr Ramsay Macdonald (the new leader of the Labour party) and Mr George Wyndham have both made interesting though not exciting speeches.

Your Majesty's faithful servant
WINSTON S. CHURCHILL

WSC to the King
(*Royal Archives*)

EXTRACT

8 February 1911 Home Office

Mr Secretary Churchill with his humble duty to Your Majesty: The House of Commons was yesterday found vy well disposed to support the Government in taking all private members' time till Easter. The Parliament

---

[1] Harold Trevor Baker (1877–1960), Liberal MP Accrington Division of Lancs. 1910–18; Financial Secretary to War Office 1912–13; PC 1915.
[2] A convict whose sentence WSC had partially remitted. (See Main Volume II, p. 391.)

Bill occupies all minds and the majority behind Ministers are willing to make every sacrifice to carry it swiftly forward. An inroad on the remaining rights of private members, wh is usually most unpopular, became on this occasion extremely popular. The divisions showed majorities of 99 & 109.

Thereafter Mr Campbell raised what is known as the Belfast mixed marriage case, in a long & fierce speech. Mr Birrell pointed out that the law allowed civil marriage and indicated the remedy; but Mr Devlin, who is the one new figure of distinction in the Irish party, made a powerful reply and showed that the whole case wh was an ordinary tale of a private quarrel had been deliberately used on the eve of the Belfast election as a means of exciting partisanship. This speech practically settled the incident. . . .

. . . All of wh is herewith submitted to Your Majesty's faithful subject & servant.

WINSTON S. CHURCHILL

WSC to the King
(*Royal Archives*)

8 February 1911   House of Commons

Mr Secretary Churchill with his humble duty to Your Majesty: Today the House of Commons has discussed the Tariff question. As this topic now closely involves the Canadian Reciprocity Treaty the opposition were forced to discuss it under considerable restraint, the observance of which did them credit, in spite of some lapses. Mr Austen Chamberlain delivered an excellent speech in support of his Amendment and his friends were highly pleased with its substance & delivery.

The President of the Board of Trade replied with the plentiful ammunition of that redoubtable department. The issue between parties was broadly this: the opposition declared that the refusal of the Liberal party to meet with reciprocal treatment the preferences accorded by Canada was the fatal cause of driving the Dominion into the arms of the United States. The Government replied that Imperial Unity could never be advanced by an artificial arrangement wh sought to preclude India from doing the best for herself in consideration of Great Britain imposing a tax on corn. This sort of bargain of reciprocal deprivation & disadvantage could never have any other result than to array natural forces & predominant interests against the union of the British Empire. These points of view are sufficiently familiar: and vy few opinions are likely to be altered at this time of day.

Mr Ormsby-Gore[1] – a young Conservative of promise – he is only 25 – made a good speech for Tariff Reform, & Mr Mond on the Liberal side delivered a long oration which gave great satisfaction to the Government supporters, & was in fact a luminous and profound examination of the whole subject. With every drawback in manner & appearance this vy able man held the House in interest and activity for upwards of 45 minutes. Sir Gilbert Parker is now replying in a speech of much knowledge carefully assembled.

Your Majesty should notice the answer given by the Prime Minister at Question time on the subject of Mr Justice Grantham[2] & the extraordinary extra-judicial utterances in which he conceives himself entitled to indulge.

The Irish party propose to vote with the Government in the division tomorrow night, so that the ministerial majority will be substantial.

WSC to the King

10 February 1911

Copy

Mr Secretary Churchill with his humble duty to Your Majesty: Today has been occupied in the House of Commons by a debate on an amendment moved by the Labour Party on what is called for want of a more satisfactory description The Right to Work Bill. Mr O'Grady,[3] an advanced Labour politician from Leeds, put his party's point of view in a moderate and per-suasive speech: that even in times of booming trade there was a surplus of labour: that increases in the technical skill of workmen could not remedy this: that if work could not be found, maintenance ought to be provided. He was seconded by Mr Clynes,[4] a Manchester Labour man and one of the best of them, a quiet intelligent hard working member. The President of the Local Govt Board replied. Mr Burns as usual dealt faithfully with his former colleagues. He opposed the Motion on the grounds that it would discourage

[1] William George Arthur Ormsby-Gore (1885–1964), Conservative MP for Denbigh 1910–18, Stafford 1918–38; Under Secretary of State for Colonies 1922–4, 1924–9; Post-master-General 1931; First Commissioner of Works 1931–6; Secretary of State for Colonies 1936–8; married in 1913 Beatrice Edith Mildred Gascoyne-Cecil, eldest daughter of 4th Marquess of Salisbury; PC 1927; succeeded father as 4th Baron Harlech 1938; KG 1948.

[2] In 1906 Mr Justice Grantham was among the judges appointed to try election petitions and was subsequently criticized in the House of Commons for alleged bias towards the Conservatives. In a speech of 7 February 1911 he revived the controversy and was rebuked by Asquith.

[3] James O'Grady (1866–1934), Labour MP Leeds 1906–24; Governor of Tasmania 1924–30; Falkland Islands 1931–4; KCMG 1924.

[4] John Robert Clynes (1869–1949), Labour MP Platting Division of Manchester 1906–31 and 1935–45; Lord Privy Seal 1924; Home Secretary 1929–31. PC 1918.

thrift and would prevent employers from keeping on good men in times of trouble as they now often do and he pointed out with force that only 24 out of 2600 Municipal Corporations had agreed to the principle of the Bill. He finally quoted the long list of remedial measures passed by the Govt for the relief of unemployed labour.

The subject is a very great one and cuts down to the foundation of things. Mr Churchill has always felt that it ought to be possible with our present science and civilisation to mitigate the violent fluctuation of trade by some recourse to public works of a reproductive character which could be carried on placidly in good times and actively in bad.

As for tramps and wastrels there ought to be proper Labour Colonies where they could be sent for considerable periods and made to realise their duty to the State. Such institutions are now being considered at the Home Office. It must not however be forgotten that there are idlers and wastrels at both ends of the social scale.

In the division all parties including the Nationalists voted with the Govt who had a majority of 224 to 39. So ends the first week of the new Parliament and certainly no more successful opening could be wished for by any Administration.

[WINSTON S. CHURCHILL]

Lord Knollys to Vaughan Nash
(*Asquith Papers*)

11 February 1911   Buckingham Palace

My dear Nash,

The King thinks that Mr Churchill's views, as contained in the enclosed, are very socialistic. What he advocates is nothing more than workshops which have been tried in France & have turned out a complete failure. In 1849 Louis Blanc[1] introduced them in Paris and we all know what was the result: they were in reality the forerunner of the street fighting in June of that year when so many thousands lost their lives.

HM considers it quite superfluous for Churchill in a letter of the description he was writing to him, to bring in about 'idlers and wastrels at both ends of the social ladder.'

Yours sincerely
KNOLLYS

[1] Jean Joseph Charles Louis Blanc (1811–82), French politician and historian. After the revolution of 1848 he presided over a government commission on labour problems and advocated the establishment of national workshops. Charged with complicity in the disturbances which ensued he fled to England. He returned to France in 1871 and became a member of the National Assembly.

WSC to the King
(*Royal Archives*)

[13 February 1911] Home Office

Mr Secretary Churchill with his humble duty to Your Majesty: The debate on the Address has this day been resumed. Mr Hayes Fisher[1] moved an amendment on the subject of the relations between Local & Imperial taxation, in order as he declared to elicit information about the immediate instructions of the Government. This amendment was seconded by Mr Griffith-Boscawen[2] who also asked for some relief of the burdens of the rate-payers. Mr Wedgwood[3] replied that the proper source for such relief was to be looked for in the further taxation of Land Values. Mr Runciman rose to meet the charge that the recent action of the Board of Education had seriously increased the burden of the rates in London. Sir William Anson reviewed the situation described by Mr Runciman & dwelt upon the difficulties of the average local authority. Mr Lough[4] pointed out how much Imperial burdens had increased with the result as he described it that the Treasury was between the devil & the deep sea. The debate is still proceeding in a half filled House. All of which is hereby submitted by Your Majesty's faithful servant & subject

WINSTON S. CHURCHILL

WSC to the King

13 February 1911

[Copy]

Mr Secretary Churchill with his humble duty to YM. He has received with deep regret the expressions of YM Displeasure wh have reached him through the PM upon a phrase wh occurred in his Parly letter of Friday last. Mr Churchill has never been offered any guidance as to the form wh such letters shd take and he consequently pursued the course he had been accustomed to follow when His late Majesty was on the Throne, namely

[1] W. Hayes Fisher (1853–1916), barrister; Junior Lord of the Treasury 1895–1902; Financial Secretary to the Treasury 1902–3; leader of Municipal Reform Party in London County Council; Conservative MP Fulham 1885–1906, 1910–16.

[2] Arthur Sackville Trevor Griffith-Boscawen (1865–1946), Conservative MP Tonbridge 1892–1906, Dudley 1910–21, Taunton 1921–2; Minister of Agriculture and Fisheries 1921–2; Minister of Health 1922–3; knighted 1911; PC 1920.

[3] Josiah Clement Wedgwood (1872–1943). Liberal (later Labour) MP for Newcastle-under-Lyme 1906–42; served at Antwerp 1914 and Gallipoli 1915; Vice-Chairman of Labour Party 1921–4; Chancellor of Duchy of Lancaster 1924; Mayor of Newcastle 1930–32. Member of famous Staffordshire pottery family. Created Baron Wedgwood of Barlaston 1942.

[4] Thomas Lough (1850–1922), Liberal MP for Islington W. 1892–1918; Parliamentary Secretary to the Board of Education 1905–8.

with deep respect to write freely and frankly upon the events, issues and feelings of the debates in the H of C. His late M on several occasions conveyed to the Home Secy His approval of the form and style of these letters, wh were frequently of a discursive character and frequently contained expressions of personal opinion upon the subjects under discussion. Mr Ch now gathers that YM desires that he shd confine himself to a narrative of the debates. He is of course most anxious to meet YM wishes in every respect: and in this case the result will be a lightening of his labours wh at this season are severe. He ventures however to point out that very excellent summaries of the debates, far better than any that he could write in the time and space available appear in all the newspapers, and that the use of the Parly letter has greatly diminished from this modern cause. YM is also apprised before the letter is despatched by telegram of the actual course of business. If the letter is merely to repeat at slightly greater length than the telegrams a summary of the debate wh has at the same time been published verbatim in the newspapers, its usefulness in informing YM of facts and issues in the H of C will not be great. Mr Ch will also feel a serious difficulty in writing these letters in the future after what has occurred, for fear that in a moment of inadvertence or fatigue some phrase or expression may escape him wh will produce an unfavourable impression on YM. He therefore wd earnestly desire that YM wd give commands that the duty shd be transferred to some other Minister who wd be able to write with the feelings of confidence in YM gracious and indulgent favour, wh Mr Ch deeply regrets to have lost.

With regard to the particular phrase wh has caused YM's displeasure, wh Mr Ch understands is 'It should be remembered that there are idlers at both ends of the social scale' Mr Ch cannot understand why this shd be thought to be Socialistic in its character. The Govt contemplate measures to deal with vagrancy and the punishment and reform of tramps and incorrigible loafers by means of labour colonies on the continental system, and the HO is already studying the subject with a view to drafting a bill. It is a national difficulty wh stands in the way of such measures that the reproach may be uttered that even-handed justice wd require that all persons shd render some service to the State whether rich or poor. To say this is not to attack the wealthy classes, most of whom as Mr Ch knows well have done their duty in many ways: but only to point to those particular persons whose idle and frivolous conduct and lack of public spirit brings a reproach to the meritorious class to wh they belong. Mr Ch therefore adheres most respectfully to the truth and sincerity of the opinion wh he expressed in endeavouring in a few sentences to give YM a correct impression of the issue in the H of C on Friday last.

All of which is submitted with great respect by YM faithful servant

WSC

Lord Knollys to WSC

14 February 1911   Buckingham Palace

My dear Churchill,

The King desires me to acknowledge the receipt of your letter of yesterday – he regrets that your feelings should have been hurt by anything which the Prime Minister may have said to you in consequence of HM having taken exception to two passages in your House of Commons Letter of the 10th Instant.

In one of those passages you appeared to advocate the, what is called, 'Right of Work' scheme, although in the division on the debate the Government voted against it.

You then implied that a comparison could be fairly drawn between 'Tramps and Wastrels' whom you would relegate to 'Labour Colonies', and 'idlers and wastrels' at the other end of the social scale.

I cannot conceal from you that the King would have preferred it, had you seen your way to suppress this remark, to which moreover an obvious answer might be offered that the cost of support in one case falls on the State and does not do so in the other.

These personal views were of course your own, but they were contained in a communication from a Cabinet Minister to the King.

HM feels that in certain contingencies, difficulties and embarrassments would inevitably arise were individual Ministers to express in official, though private letters, written daily during some months of the year to the Sovereign, their own views on important questions, which opinions might not be in agreement with those of their colleagues.

The King directs me to add that your letters are always instructive and interesting and he would be sorry if he were to receive no further ones from you in the future. At the same time he would not wish you to continue them if you feel disinclined to do so.

I ought to mention that I know King Edward took the same view of your 'House of Commons letters' as the present King does, but he also did not always appear pleased with certain occasional passages in them.

With reference to your statement that you 'have never been offered any guidance in the form' of your letters, I hope you will forgive my saying that you have never asked for any, or else it would of course have been most cheerfully given. It would give me great pleasure to show you some 'House of Commons letters' from Lord Palmerston, Lord Beaconsfield and Mr Gladstone, which are bound up and are in my room, if you would care to see them.

Yrs sincerely
KNOLLYS

WSC to the King
(*Royal Archives*)

14 February 1911 Home Office

Mr Secretary Churchill with his humble duty to Your Majesty:

After questions today the debate on the Address was resumed by Lord Helmsley,[1] who moved an amendment on the administration of the taxation of Land Values. He complained that provisional valuations had been fixed far too low in order to show an increment in later years when land changed hands, & quoted numerous instances in support of this statement. He remarked that land taxation though a good electioneering cry was a dishonest cry, because, as he alleged, it was only successful where the electors were ignorant of the details of the policy. Mr Churchill is informed that his speech which was long was also effective.

Mr Cave[2] who followed said that though the valuers were all able honest men, they were not all properly qualified, & could not appreciate the full consequences to the owners when land was underrated at the first valuation under the late Finance Act. He argued that the whole system of valuation needed over-hauling, as only those who could afford good expert advice were in a position effectively to defend their own interests & appeals were too costly to constitute a proper safeguard. The Attorney General is now replying to these speeches.

All of which is submitted by Your Majesty's faithful servant

WINSTON S. CHURCHILL

WSC to David Lloyd George
(*Lloyd George Papers*)

14 February 1911 Home Office

Secret

My dear David,

The Cabinet Committee did nothing this morning. Crewe was unable to be present except for a very few minutes. I brought the *Daily Mail* article to the notice of the Committee. McKenna declared the Admiralty had nothing to do with it. It is not accurate in all respects. There never has been

---

[1] Charles William Reginald Duncombe (1879–1916), Unionist MP for Thirsk and Malton 1906–15; married, in 1904, Marjorie Greville, eldest daughter of 5th Earl of Warwick; succeeded grandfather as 2nd Earl of Feversham 1915. Killed in action 1916.

[2] George Cave (1856–1928), Unionist MP for Kingston 1906–18; Solicitor-General 1915–16; Home Secretary 1916–19; a Lord of Appeal 1919–22; Attorney-General to Prince of Wales 1914–15; PC 1915; knighted 1915; created Viscount Cave of Richmond 1918.

any talk of six. And our discussion has mainly turned on the Colonial ships. I send you a memorandum which I circulated to the Cabinet Committee only, in the hopes of coming to an arrangement with McKenna which would be helpful and which would enable us all to come in. He did, however, nothing but raise difficulties and resist. The Committee will, I think report in favour of four ships contingent upon an arrangement being made to retain one or both of the Colonial Dreadnoughts during the period 1914–15. If two ships could be built, namely four this year and four next year, instead of two fives, you would get a reduction of nearly a million-and-a-half each year from that cause alone. McKenna announced this morning that as the result of pressure he would build two fewer unarmoured cruisers, effecting a saving next year of £450,000, and the year after of about £300,000. The Cabinet Committee were dead against increasing the expenditure this year artificially, and the Estimates are being provisionally printed on the basis of an increase of £3,800,000. McKenna also told us this morning that the cost of the foreign fleets of this country, the Mediterranean, Atlantic, Pacific, &c, was £5,000,000 a year. I believe myself that there is a great field for reduction here, as, after all, the sea is all one, and naval supremacy must be settled at the central point.

Runciman has not yet been before us, and I doubt very much whether there is much use in our seeing him in your absence.

Owing to the Prime Minister having promised our fellows two days' debates on Army and Navy Estimates together, it is now said that the Naval Estimates must go to press in the course of the next two or three days. We shall discuss this further at the Cabinet tomorrow, and if necessary we shall have to ask you to come up for a meeting of the Estimates Committee on Thursday afternoon, and probably there will have to be a special Cabinet on Friday.

I send you also a note which I dictated this morning, which I have shown nobody, on the inconvenient method by which we are always committed nearly a year ahead to ships which are not wanted until long after we have been bound, and which cost nothing in the year in which they have been sanctioned and millions of money in the years which follow.

I think on the whole Crewe is inclined to recommend that something may be done about the Colonial vessels. There are no other prospects of relief as far as I can see.

Unless you have to come up on Thursday, I will meet you at Walton Heath at 11 o'clock on Friday.

Yours always
W

WSC to Lord Crewe
(*Lloyd George Papers*)

14 February 1911 [Home Office]

[Copy]

Secret

My dear Crewe,

I suggest to you that the Estimates Committee might be asked to consider the following conclusions in order to produce some result from our impotent discussions.

1. That Haldane's estimates have increased by £750,000 during the last three years, and that this must be regarded as an increase in the permanent cost of the Army.

2. That an arrangement should be made with NZ and if possible with Australia which will secure us one or both of the Colonial ships in the North Sea in the period 1914–16; and that we should therefore sanction 4 new ships this year and (if both the Colonials are secured) 4 next year.

3. That we do not recommend any artificial inflation of this year's Estimates to those of next year.

4. That we report that McKenna has reduced the protected cruiser programme by two, with consequent savings.

5. That a Cabinet Committee assisted where necessary by experts, should overhaul the whole question of British fleets abroad.

6. That we invite the favourable attention of the Cabinet to the recommendations of the Committee on Public Expenditure 1903 in regard to an Estimates Committee of Members of the House of Commons.

As to Runciman, we have not heard him; but I really do not see where the money is to come from, however good his case. The PM seems to think that Lloyd George will have to come up. Thursday afternoon is the only time I have free this week. I hope we shall be able to agree upon that at any rate!

Yours sincerely
WSC

Lord Knollys to Vaughan Nash
(*Asquith Papers*)

15 February 1911   Buckingham Palace

My dear Nash,

I think Mr Asquith may like to see W. Churchill's letter to the King with reference to the PM lecture to him.

I don't think the tone of the letter is quite a proper one nor has he taken the matter in the right way.

So far (7.30 pm) he has not answered me, but if he does I will send you on his letter. Of course the matter will end here unless he says he does not want to write any further 'House of Commons letters' to the King, & then we must think of someone else.

Yrs sincerely
KNOLLYS

WSC to the King
(*Royal Archives*)

16 February 1911   House of Commons

Mr Secretary Churchill with his humble duty to Your Majesty:

The debate yesterday upon Mr Malcolm's Amendment to the Address turned upon the question of Home Rule & was in its character important & so far as the supporters of the Government were concerned highly satisfactory. The Prime Minister's announcement that after the Parliament Bill has been passed into law the Government would proceed to confer upon Ireland a Parliament and an executive of their own was received with great satisfaction by the Irish party, & accepted with goodwill by all classes of ministerialists. Mr Churchill has had some private talk with Mr Redmond & is not without the expectation that the Irish members will find it possible to participate in the Coronation ceremonies. This would be a memorable and auspicious event & would mark the first stage in a reconciliation between the English & Irish peoples and would unite Your Majesty's Irish subjects to the Throne by bonds which have for generations been broken. Mr Redmond's speech was admirable in its tone and substance and would repay Your Majesty's perusal in the verbatim reports. The divisions which closed the debate on the Address resulted in majorities of 113 and 114 for the Government.

Today the Prime Minister has asked the House to consent to the sacrifice by private members of all their time till the 13th of April in order that the

Parliament Bill may reach the House of Lords early in May. A languid debate is proceeding and the Government is secure in the support of its friends.

All of which is hereby submitted to Your Majesty by Your Majesty's faithful servant & subject

WINSTON S. CHURCHILL

WSC to Lord Knollys

16 February 1911   Home Office

Copy

My dear Knollys,

I have to thank you for your letter which reached me yesterday, and for the kind expressions which it contains. I now feel that I ought either to have written much more, or nothing at all, on the general question to which I alluded in my letter of last Friday to the King. Nothing in what I wrote was intended to suggest I was in favour of the 'Right to Work' bill. On the contrary I have always voted and spoken against it; and in my Friday's letter I carefully stated the principal arguments on the other side adduced by the President of the L.G.B. [Local Government Board]. The principle of affording special aid by public works to unemployed persons in times of depression is however already embodied in the Unemployed Workmen's Act passed by the Conservative Govt in 1905. The principle of continuous and State-managed public works is embodied in the Development Act of 1909; and a clause in that Act specially empowers the Devlt Commrs to vary the progress of their enterprises, having regard to the conditions of the labour market. There is little doubt that these principles will be carried further when the question of the reform of the Poor Law is dealt with; and in advocating a more scientific application of this form of public relief in place of the haphazard method and useless and wasteful employment now so lavishly afforded in times of distress, I was not going in any respects beyond the limits of practical and reasonable policy as they are recognised by the supporters of the Govt or by my colleagues; or even to a considerable extent by many members of the Conservative Party.

Between advocating a continuous effort by the State to mitigate and average the extraordinary fluctuations in employment wh are the result of world wide trade on the one hand, and affirming the right of every person to be provided with State employment in the last resort, there is a great gulf fixed, which I have never had the slightest intention of bridging. This, together with what I wrote to HM on the particular sentence abt 'idlers and wastrels at both ends of the social scale', is my explanation of the merits and propriety of the opinion wh I ventured to express.

I own to you that I was surprised and grieved to receive through the PM a formal notification of the King's displeasure. I have greatly valued the privilege and honour of conducting the Parly correspondence with HM. I have always endeavoured to place HM in possession of the best infn of the H of C situation at my command. In writing these daily letters and trying to make them interesting and readable, it is always possible that some sentiment or opinion may occur wh has not received the severe and deliberate scrutiny and reconsn wh should attach to a State Paper. In these circs a Minister would wish that the most favourable construction wd be placed upon his words and sincerity, or that if the case were to require it some friendly suggestion or guidance might be conveyed to him from some person like yourself near to the King. The slightest indication of HM wishes and feelings wd always be studied by me with the most prompt and earnest attention. But I felt and feel that the serious and exceptional step of a formal significn to the Home Sec through the PM of the King's displeasure was utterly undeserved on this occasion, and bore no proportion to any error unconsciously committed. It was this that led me to express the pain I felt, and to ask to be relieved of a duty wh I felt might expose me to further possibilities of forfeiting HM favour.

In view of your letter and of the fuller information which you give me upon HM views and wishes, I will be glad to continue to keep the King informed of what passes in the H of C.

May I ask you also at the same time to express to the King my regret and sympathy for the anxiety wh is caused Him at the present time through the illness wh the P. of W.[1] and Prince [Albert][2] have contracted while doing their duty at the Naval College.

I may add that the great pressure of my work prevented my writing the H. of C. letter last night, and that I propose to combine the two sittings in the one wh I shall dispatch this evening.

Yours very truly
[WINSTON S. CHURCHILL]

[1] Now HRH Duke of Windsor (born 1894), who succeeded his father, King George V, as King Edward VIII, 20 January 1936. Abdicated 11 December 1936.
[2] Later King George VI (1895-1952), who succeeded his brother, King Edward VIII.

Lord Knollys to Vaughan Nash
(*Asquith Papers*)

17 February 1911   Buckingham Palace

My dear Nash,

I enclose you Churchill's reply. He means it to be conciliatory I imagine, but he is rather like 'A Bull in a China Shop'.

I have merely thanked him for his letter & told him that the King is glad to hear he is going on with his 'House of Commons' letters.

I could have added, but I did not, that he is quite wrong in what he intimates would have been the right way of finding fault with him. At least I imagine so as surely the PM is the proper medium for conveying a reproof from the King to a member of the Cabinet.

Queen Victoria used always to send remonstrances to Lord Palmerston through Lord John Russell.

Yrs sincerely
KNOLLYS

Lord Knollys to WSC

17 February 1911   Buckingham Palace

My dear Churchill,

I have shown your letter of yesterday to the King, and he desires me to thank you for continuing your 'House of Commons letters' which are always very interesting.

HM is much obliged to you for asking after the two young Princes – Nothing could be better than the accounts which he receives about them.

Yours sincerely
KNOLLYS

WSC to the King
(*Royal Archives*)

[17 February 1911]   Home Office

Mr Secretary Churchill with his humble duty to Your Majesty: The House today has continued the discussion of Supplementary Estimates & especially one connected with the improvement of horse breeding, the Report stage of the Budget Resolutions having been disposed of. The business of the Government has been most tiresomely deranged by the adjournment motion yesterday; & Mr Churchill is vy apprehensive that the Friday which he had secured for the Shop Hours Bill in which Your Majesty took an interest last session, & which has many friends on both sides of the House may be taken from him. Nothing is however to interfere with the progress of the main business of the session.

All of which is humbly submitted by Your Majesty's faithful subject

WINSTON S. CHURCHILL

WSC to the King
(Royal Archives)

18 February 1911   Home Office

Mr Secretary Churchill with his humble duty to Your Majesty:

The House of Commons was surprised yesterday by the breach of privilege committed by Mr Wedgwood & Mr Ginnell[1] in reflecting upon the impartiality of the chair. The Speaker has the full confidence of every section of the House & a vy unfavourable impression was created by the fact that Mr Wedgwood did not attempt to apologise. Mr Ginnell's offence appears however the more serious, because he not only committed the breach of privilege but seems to have violated private confidence as well.

The rest of the sitting was occupied with Supplementary Estimates, on wh the Government secured the handsome majority of 266. The result of the Horncastle election was also a subject of much satisfaction in ministerial circles as indicating that the Government is even stronger upon the new register than the old.

WSC to the King
(Royal Archives)

21 February 1911   Home Office

Mr Secretary Churchill with his humble duty to Your Majesty:

The feeling in the House of Commons yesterday on the question of the Speaker's impartiality was disturbed by the irritation wh the back bench members feel at not being able to speak more frequently; & some disagreeable expression was given to their views. The division showed 102 members who voted against the motion to suspend Mr Ginnell, who was quite unrepentant, and made the most of his opportunity. Mr Speaker did not expect that the debate would be prolonged & so did not offer the whole

[1] Laurence Ginnell (1854–1923), Irish Nationalist MP North Westmeath 1906–23.

strength of his argument for the existing practice of . . . [?] speakers to the House. Had he done so members would more readily have understood the strong & good reasons wh guided him. All the cranks had their chance of raising their voices & did not miss it.

The Chancellor of the Exchequer took his seat & made a short speech upon the Budget resolutions. His voice was weak, but his welcome cordial.

WSC to the King
(*Royal Archives*)

21 February 1911   Home Office

Mr Secretary Churchill with his humble duty to Your Majesty:

The Parliament Bill was introduced by the Prime Minister today in one of his vy best speeches which was so compendious & lucid that it defies summary. Mr Balfour was depressed & weary & his not unconciliatory remarks were received in a gloomy silence by the Unionist party. The House was vy orderly & there was a complete absence of excitement. When is the conflict going to begin? Every week it seems to recede a stage. There is not any real anger that is apparent in any quarter of the House. No passion, no threats, no defiance – only a sort of sulky acquiescence under the form of refusal. Sir Robert Finlay is to take up the discussion before dinner & Mr F. E. Smith begins tomorrow. But peace broods sluggishly over the Assembly and considerable events drift or flow steadily forward.

Mr Churchill will try tomorrow night when he winds up to show the Conservative party the great safeguards wh will be retained in the constitution after the veto of the Lords has ceased to be absolute and become suspensory, and how strong are the natural & social guarantees of stability wh exist in England apart altogether from political institutions.

It is a curious feature of the situation wh appears to be developing that the Radical & Labour members are as little inclined to abolish the House of Lords as are the majority of peers themselves. It is the veto only wh is the object of their attack.

WSC to the King
(*Royal Archives*)

23 February 1911   Home Office

Mr Secretary Churchill with his humble duty to Your Majesty:

The Parliament Bill was read a first time last night in a scene of much animation after a division which gave the Government a majority of 124.

Mr F. E. Smith's speech was the best for the Opposition & he was listened to by a full House for an hour with the greatest attention. Mr Wyndham also spoke well & in a conciliatory tone. But there can be no question of a Conference at the present time. After the Veto Bill has passed into law, it may by vy necessary for the two great parties to undertake the work of reforming the second chamber which neither will be able to do satisfactorily alone. It is curious that the Conservatives were to be so much more anxious to abolish the legislative functions of the Peers than the Radicals, the greater number of whom will be quite content to leave them everything except their absolute veto. Mr Ramsay Macdonald, the able leader (for the time being) of the Labour party, even pleaded for a hereditary second chamber to advise & check, but not to rule.

The Conservatives seem to be vy doubtful about the Referendum, & Mr Churchill tried to show them some of its perils from the point of view of property. It would be a dangerous thing to put a great measure of a confiscatory character to the direct vote of millions of people, the vast majority of whom have only what they earn each week by constant toil. Yet that would certainly happen under the system sooner or later.

The Irish members have decided with great regret that they cannot participate in the Coronation ceremonies. Mr Redmond told Mr Churchill privately that this decision would give them much more power to secure Your Majesty a hearty welcome from all classes in Ireland on the occasion of the Royal visit. The explanation of their reasons for abstaining is marked by good feeling.

There is a genuine & spontaneous loyalty for the Monarchy in the Irish character, & some day Your Majesty will find the Irish people among the most faithful subjects of the Crown.

All of which is humbly submitted by Your Majesty's devoted servant & subject

WINSTON S. CHURCHILL

WSC to the King
(*Royal Archives*)

24 February 1911   Home Office

Mr Secretary Churchill with his humble duty to Your Majesty:

The House of Commons was yesterday engaged in financial business connected with the Budget of last year. The whole financial situation is good. Alone among European nations Great Britain is in the enjoyment of revenues wh not only enable her to pay her way in these expensive times, but to redeem debt continually. The success or of the Chancellor of the Exchequer's finance from the point of view of revenue is now undisputed, whatever may be the differences of opinion upon its other aspects.

The adjournment of the House was moved from the Liberal benches to censure the Home Secretary for not insisting upon the dismissal of the super-intendent of the Akbar Nautical School for certain irregular floggings & other punishments wh he had been responsible for. This unpleasant case has attracted a great deal of public attention & knowing beforehand the strong views of the House of Commons on corporal punishment, Mr Churchill had taken the precaution to have a special enquiry made by Mr Masterman the Under-Secretary of State. Mr Masterman is an extremely able minister and is greatly esteemed in the House for his high personal character, & remark-able for an unusual combination of being a strong churchman and an ad-mired Radical. He carried a great many guns for the purposes of this debate, & his striking report & earnest and effective speech broke the back of the attack. In any case Mr Churchill would not have been prepared to sacrifice the Superintendent who though guilty of irregularities is a thorough-ly good man and has worked wonders with the school. Although criticisms came from both sides of the House, the opinion of the majority was never in doubt & on a division the Home Office was supported by 244 to 67.

Many Conservatives voted with the majority. This was satisfactory, but through the debate Government business has been retarded one day & the Prime Minister was extremely displeased with Mr Atherley-Jones[1] the Liberal member who moved the Adjournment.

Mr Churchill received with great pleasure last night a kind letter from Sir A. Bigge[2] containing some vy gracious expressions wh Your Majesty had been pleased to use about the ceremony yesterday. Mr Churchill could not help thinking what a remarkable instance these honours accorded to policemen, miners, firemen & ordinary folk for acts of civil bravery, is of the deep wisdom of the late King. The idea of raising the simple acts of heroism wh occur in times of peace to the level of the noblest feat of arms,

[1] Llewellyn Archer Atherley-Jones (1851–1929), Liberal MP for Durham NW, 1885–1914; a judge, writer on legal questions and author of a number of novels, among them *The Fall of Lord Paddockslea.*

[2] Arthur John Bigge (1849–1931); Extra Equerry and Private Secretary to King George V 1910–31; Groom-in-Waiting to Queen Victoria and Assistant Private Secretary 1880; Equerry in Ordinary 1891; Private Secretary to Queen Victoria 1895–1901; Extra Equerry to King Edward VII and Private Secretary to the Prince of Wales 1901–10; created Baron Stamfordham 20 June 1911. Lord Stamfordham owed his career at Court to his friendship with the French Prince Imperial, who was slain in the Zulu War, for Queen Victoria sent for him to give her particulars of the Prince's death. He so impressed the Queen that she made him a Groom-in-Waiting and he served her and her successors for 50 years. CB 1885; CMG 1887; KCB 1895; GCVO and KCMG 1901; KCSI 1906; GCIE 1911; GCB 1916.

was in full harmony with the peace loving inspiration of King Edward: and the circulation of these medals among classes whence the sunlight of royal honour had never previously reached – is pregnant alike with political consequence & moral value. The stories of gallantry were splendid to read & are to the honour of the British race.

All of which is humbly submitted by Your Majesty's faithful & devoted servant

WINSTON S. CHURCHILL

WSC to the King
(*Royal Archives*)

28 February [1911]   Home Office

Mr Secretary Churchill with his humble duty to Your Majesty: The 2nd Reading debate on the Parliament Bill began yesterday. Mr Austen Chamberlain moved the rejection in a good speech, but a thin House. Mr Haldane replied for the government & showed how impossible any negotiation with the Conservatives was until the government was armed with the powers of the Parliament Bill and could meet them on even terms. The vy idea of any further conference when the government would argue and the Opposition decide is odious to all sections of those who support the Ministry. Afterwards however when & if the question of reform has to be considered a vy different set of considerations will apply.

The House was curiously listless and for the most part vy empty. Private members, however loudly they assert their rights to speak, cannot command audiences. The chamber was for hours occupied only by fifty or sixty gentlemen most of whom were there not to listen, but in the hopes of speaking. At one time only one member of the Opposition was present; & the House would have been counted out but for the rule wh protects the dinner hour from such a process. There is a total absence of excitement or passion: & no one would believe that business of fierce controversial importance was proceeding.

The opinion of the Conservative party seems to be much divided on the question of the Reform of the House of Lords. The younger men are clamorous for the complete abolition of the hereditary principle & the substitution of a sort of senate of elected persons. The deep sagacity of Sir Henry Campbell Bannerman in not interfering with the composition of the Lords but dealing only with relations does not become less apparent as the days pass by.

WSC to the King
(*Royal Archives*)

1 March 1911

Mr Secretary Churchill with his humble duty to Your Majesty: The Parliament Bill proceeds steadily on its way. The House remains half filled, but troops of members, more eager to speak than to listen rise on any occasion in the hopes of catching the Speaker's eye.

Mr Lyttelton spoke yesterday, as usual in a quiet & unassuming manner, & Colonel Seely made a creditable reply. Young Mr Waldorf Astor[1] made a maiden speech wh was well received: & Mr Ryland Adkins[2] for the Government delivered an exceptionally good statement. Today the Ministry will be represented by Sir Rufus Isaacs[3] & Mr Runciman, while Lord Hugh Cecil will speak for the Opposition. Great pressure obliges Mr Churchill to crave Your Majesty's indulgence for not sending a fuller report. But all is tranquil & there is nothing of consequence to relate.

Mr Churchill's answer about the suffragette allegations against the police was extremely well received by all parties. Mr Snowden[4] did not even venture to put the usually inevitable supplementary question.

WSC to the King
(*Royal Archives*)

3 March 1911　　　　　　　　　　　　　　　　　　　　　　Home Office

Mr Secretary Churchill with his humble duty to Your Majesty: The 2nd Reading of the Parliament Bill was carried last night by 125 after a debate wh on its concluding day was marked both by interest & excitement. The speeches of Mr Balfour, of the Prime Minister & of Lord Hugh Cecil were all valuable & well-received contributions. Mr Balfour's use of the word 'fraud' provoked a storm wh did not easily subside. Still the House of Commons must not be mealy-mouthed, & such an accusation when not personal in its

---

[1] Waldorf Astor (1879–1952), eldest son of first Viscount Astor; Conservative MP Plymouth 1910–19; Chairman Royal Institute of International Affairs 1935–49; succeeded father 1919; husband of Nancy Astor.

[2] William Ryland Dent Adkins (1862–1925), Liberal MP Middleton Lancashire 1906–23; knighted 1911.

[3] Rufus Daniel Isaacs (1860–1935), Attorney-General 1910–13; called to Bar 1887; Liberal MP for Reading 1905–13; Lord Chief Justice 1913–21; Viceroy of India 1921–6; Foreign Secretary 1931; knighted 1910; PC 1911; created Baron Reading 1914; Viscount Erleigh 1917; Earl of Reading 1917; Marquess of Reading 1926; GCB 1915; GCIE 1921; GCSI 1921; GCVO 1922.

[4] Philip Snowden (1864–1937), Labour MP 1906–18, 1922–31; Chairman of Independent Labour Party 1903–6, 1917–20; Chancellor of the Exchequer 1924, 1929–31; Lord Privy Seal 1931–2; PC 1924; created Viscount Snowden of Ickornshaw 1931.

character but referring generally to election issues ought not to be considered as going beyond the limits of debate. The Prime Minister's reply was effective and spirited. Mr Samuel who wound up the debate acquitted himself well.

Mr Churchill begs to express to Your Majesty the great pleasure with wh he received Your Majesty's most gracious commendation of the draft replies to . . . [?] wh he had the honour to submit.

There is no part of the Home Secretary's duties wh he regards as more honourable or important than that of advising Your Majesty in regard to the text & tenor of the messages wh are sent from the Throne to the people. Mr Churchill knows that no labour in such a matter can be thrown away in an endeavour to express the proper sentiments without touching upon controversy, and degenerating into platitude.

WSC to the King
(*Royal Archives*)

4 March 1911 Home Office

Mr Secretary Churchill with his humble duty to your Majesty: Supplementary Estimates occupied the House of Commons yesterday. There was a clear disposition on the part of the opponents of the Government to discuss them at length; & for nearly two hours an expenditure of £20 was debated. As the number of supplementary estimates this year is unusually large, it seems probable that the House will have to sit up all Tuesday night to get through them. Yesterday there were nearly a dozen divisions & the Government majorities varied between 110 & 130.

Last night, at the Lord President's dinner to prepare the list of sheriffs wh Mr Churchill attended, Lord Crewe was suddenly struck down by a fainting fit of some kind. Mr Churchill deeply regrets to tell your Majesty that he may be ill for some time. The dinner was just over and he had been talking quite cheerfully & well, when on coming out of the dining room at Claridge's he fell on the floor as if he had been struck by lightning. Doctors were hastily obtained & after half an hour consciousness or semi-consciousness slowly returned. Your Majesty will no doubt soon receive a medical report. The spectacle was vy painful and Lord Morley & the Prime Minister were much distressed.

Overwork & anxieties of several kinds have told upon Lord Crewe during the last few months, & he has not been looking well for some days. Everything possible was promptly done & Lord Rosebery reached the hotel before Mr Churchill left. Lord Crewe is such a charming man and so trusted by all who work with him, that the deepest concern is felt at his illness, & his colleagues must earnestly hope for his speedy recovery. At first however so alarming were the symptoms that it was feared that his life was in danger. This was happily unfounded.

It is curious that the number at dinner was 13.

WSC to the King
(*Royal Archives*)

7 March 1911   Home Office

Mr Secretary Churchill with his humble duty to Your Majesty: Supplementary Estimates continue to make their way through the House of Commons in the face of a good deal of discussion. An arrangement has been reached between the Whips that they shall all be disposed of by Friday morning. The unfortunate Shops Bill has been postponed to a later date!

Last night Mr Keir Hardie returned to the charge about Tonypandy, & opened up a debate in which two perfectly opposite attacks were delivered on the Home Secretary. Mr Churchill refused to grant any inquiry – except with specific cases of injury, concerning wh no facts have been submitted to him in spite of the invitation. He also had the assistance of Mr Haldane in repelling the criticism that the troops should have been sent earlier. The debate was lively: & Mr Keir Hardie was so nettled at being attacked by another Labour member, Mr Clem Edwards,[1] who dealt vy faithfully with him, that he described him as a 'reptile of the viper kind'. This expression he was compelled to withdraw.

At half past twelve came the division but the Conservatives, although loud in criticism of the Home Office, would not & could not press their views in the division lobby: & the Home Office secured a majority of 238 to only 23 wh followed Mr Keir Hardie. This was satisfactory. All of wh is humbly submitted by Your Majesty's faithful & devoted servant

WINSTON S. CHURCHILL

WSC to the King
(*Royal Archives*)

8 March 1911

Mr Secretary Churchill with his humble duty to Your Majesty: The 2nd Reading of the old Finance Bill was concluded yesterday after a wrangling debate. The absence of the Chancellor of the Exchequer left a gap in the defences of the Government wh was not filled completely by those who took his place. No one but the Chancellor of the Exchequer is able to do full justice to this controversy of wh he alone knows all the details & forces.

---

[1] Allen Clement Edwards (1869–1938), Liberal MP for Denbigh Borough 1906–10; Labour MP for East Glamorgan 1910–18, East Ham South 1918–22; author and journalist.

The Government majority of 71 was a little below the average of recent divisions.

Today the House has been occupied by a discussion on the question of the issue of the writ for North Louth, wh has been vacated by the result of the recent election petition. The Orangemen moved to postpone the issue for 4 months, & the eminent lawyers on both sides of the House have expressed their opinions with fluency & precision. Sir Edward Carson,[1] the Attorney General, Mr F. E. Smith & the Attorney-General for Ireland followed each other in quick succession. The Government left the question to the House, but in accordance with their previous practice in the Worcester petition voted in favour of the issue of the writ, wh was sanctioned by 254–150.

Mr Churchill hopes Your Majesty will excuse his not having written yesterday; but a slight indisposition forced him to go home to bed at an early hour before dinner & he was not fully apprised of the course of events.

All of wh is humbly submitted by Your Majesty's faithful subject & servant

WINSTON S. CHURCHILL

Sir Arthur Bigge to WSC

8 March 1911　　　　　　　　　　　　　　　　Buckingham Palace

My dear Churchill,

The King has just read your H of C letter of today and desires me to say how sorry he is to hear of your being unwell yesterday and obliged to leave the House and go home; but HM hopes you are better today.

Yrs very truly
ARTHUR BIGGE

WSC to the King
(Royal Archives)

[9 March 1911]　　　　　　　　　　　　　　　　Home Office

Mr Secretary Churchill with his humble duty to Your Majesty: The Committee Stage of the Revenue Bill (apart from the new clauses) was finished this evening. The Opposition have definitely refused to come to any arrangement in regard to its further stages, & a guillotine motion will in consequence be prepared on Monday in order to secure the passage of the measure within the limits required by the law.

All of which is humbly submitted by Your Majesty's faithful servant & subject

WINSTON S. CHURCHILL

[1] Sir Edward CARSON.

WSC to the King
(*Royal Archives*)

6 a.m.   House of Commons
10 March 1911

Mr Secretary Churchill with his humble duty to Your Majesty: The House has sat all night upon the Budget Bill. In the absence of the Prime Minister Mr Churchill has had charge of the business; wh is advancing steadily to its proper conclusion. There has been á certain amount of ill-feeling during this prolonged debate, but the temperature is now again normal and the discussion is good. The Government is well supported. The House is likely to sit continuously till 10 or even 11 o'clock. Your Majesty's faithful servant dutifully submits the above.

8.45 *am* The debate is still proceeding in a lively fashion & Mr Churchill proposes to persevere in the hopes of securing the Committee stage of the Revenue Bill but without the new clauses, of wh there are no less than 22 pages.

Mr Churchill desires also to express to Your Majesty his sincere thanks for the gracious inquiries wh Your Majesty made through Sir Arthur Bigge about his health. The indisposition wh was but slight has yielded to treatment, and has not returned under the strain of this arduous night.

WSC to the King
(*Royal Archives*)

11 March 1911   Home Office

Mr Secretary Churchill with his humble duty to your Majesty: The House yesterday disposed finally of the Supplementary Estimates, after a debate which in spite of the fatigues of the all-night sitting threatened occasionally to become turbulent.

The Master of Elibank is addressing a letter to the newspapers vindicating the course adopted by Ministers, to wh Mr Churchill would with great respect draw your Majesty's attention when it appears.

The debate on Monday on expenditure is likely to cause considerable misgivings to the supporters of the Government who are pledged to economy. Sir Edward Grey has however undertaken to make an important speech covering the whole international field.

All of wh is submitted humbly by Your Majesty's faithful servant
WINSTON S. CHURCHILL

WSC to the King
(*Royal Archives*)

EXTRACT

14 March 1911   Home Office

Mr Secretary Churchill with his humble duty to Your Majesty: The House of Commons yesterday discussed Mr Murray MacDonald's[1] motion wh criticised the general growth of the cost of British armaments. The debate was memorable for the speech with wh Sir Edward Grey concluded it. The far reaching & suggestive arguments wh he employed greatly impressed the House, & the idea of a Treaty of Unlimited Arbitration between the United States & ourselves glittered with splendid hopes. Mr McKenna spoke well in his own defence; but many of his supporters will not forgive him for the figures wh they regard as the basis of the panic of 1909. The division at the end was most satisfactory to the Government. Only 56 members voted against the enormous expenditure to wh we have now been put. . . .

WSC to the King
(*Royal Archives*)

[15 March 1911]   House of Commons

Mr Secretary Churchill with his humble duty to Your Majesty: Mr Haldane made his annual statement on The Army yesterday afternoon in a quiet, attentive but moderately filled House. He devoted special attention to the questions of horse supply & aeronautics; & a good businesslike discussion occupied the afternoon & evening.

The debate has been resumed today & is continuing without incident or accident & Mr Churchill will send Your Majesty a later report either tonight or tomorrow morning. He has been almost continuously occupied in trying to secure the passage of the Mines Bill on Friday afternoon. This depends entirely on good-will, wh cannot always be obtained in the House of Commons. Still the omens are not unfavourable.

All of which is humbly submitted by Your Majesty's faithful & devoted servant

WINSTON S. CHURCHILL

[1] John Archibald Murray MacDonald (1854–1939), Liberal MP for Bow and Bromley 1892–5, Falkirk Burghs 1906–18, Stirling and Falkirk Burghs 1918–22; PC 1916.

WSC to the King
(Royal Archives)

16 March 1911   Home Office

Mr Secretary Churchill with his humble duty to Your Majesty: The debate on Army Estimates continued yesterday was again marked by good and painstaking speeches & a thin & listless House. The Government have promised to give a further opportunity for an Army discussion later in the year.

Sir Reginald Pole Carew's[1] attack on his old brother aide-de-camp Sir Ian Hamilton was the least pleasing feature.

The effects of Sir Edward Grey's speech are vy considerable among the Liberal & Labour members. He has never before appealed so effectively to the deep sentiments of peace by which they are inspired. As a result the debates on the Naval estimates will be smoother for the 1st Lord of the Admiralty. The House sat up talking placidly about the army till after two.

WSC to the King
(Royal Archives)

17 March 1911   House of Commons

Mr Secretary Churchill with his humble duty to Your Majesty: After Supplementary Estimates had been disposed of this afternoon the House entered upon the 2nd Reading of the Coal Mines Bill: & Mr Churchill is vy glad to be able to inform Your Majesty that, after a debate of only two hours, & despite the fact that it was in the power of any individual member to talk it out, it passed its 2nd Reading with unanimous consent. Considering that it was only published yesterday morning it is a great vote of faith & good will on the part of all parties to have allowed it to go so swiftly on its way.

Mr F. E. Smith welcomed it on behalf of the Conservatives, Sir Clifford Cory[2] on the part of the coal owners, & Mr Enoch Edwards[3] the miners' leader spoke of it as especially appropriate to the Coronation year and specially satisfactory to the miners from that cause.

There will be a great deal of discussion in committee no doubt, but on the general principle of grappling with the death roll all parties & both capital & labour are able in this country to join hands in friendship.

Now that the Prime Minister has returned Mr Churchill terminates his

[1] Reginald Pole Carew (1849–1924), Unionist MP Bodmin 1910–16; served 37 years in Army; retired as Lieutenant-General 1906; knighted 1900.

[2] Clifford John Cory (1859–1941), Liberal MP for St Ives 1906–1924; chairman of Cory Brothers, colliery proprietors; Baronet 1907.

[3] Enoch Edwards (1852–1912), Labour MP for Hanley 1906–12; secretary of North Staffs Miners' Association from 1877.

discharge of the temporary duty of leading the House, & he is vy glad to think that this is in circumstances much less controversial than when he assumed it a week ago.

All of which is humbly submitted by Your Majesty's faithful & devoted servant

WINSTON S. CHURCHILL

WSC to the King
(*Royal Archives*)

[22 March 1911]   Home Office

Mr Secretary Churchill with his humble duty to Your Majesty: The debate yesterday upon the vote on account was at first vy placid. The miners asked for more inspectors and Mr Masterman proposed on behalf of the Home Office that the appointment of the whole thirty announced in Novr should take place within the current year. After some discursive conversation on Persia, Mr Hoare[1] a young Conservative member raised the question of an Education circular wh was open to considerable objections as unduly favouring persons who came from Oxford & Cambridge Universities. Mr Runciman was indignant at the use of a confidential document, & accused Mr Hoare of being a receiver of stolen goods. On this there was a disagreeable debate, in which the Board of Education was attacked from various quarters, Mr Balfour concluding with an animated speech. The report of the vote was agreed to without a division.

There are some signs of restlessness among the supporters of the Government at the lengthy interval of financial business wh interrupts the progress of the Parliament Bill. Next week it will be necessary to dispose of the last years Budget Bill and late sittings and stormy weather must be looked for. The general outline of government business seems now to contemplate the month of April being occupied in the discussion of the Parliament Bill.

Mr Churchill hopes to secure Friday 31st for the Shop Hours: but the expectation is not vy confident.

Mr Churchill is vy glad that Your Majesty was satisfied with the draft reply he ventured to submit on the subject of the Bible tercentenary. It will please Your Majesty's Protestant subjects, without offending the Catholics.

All of which is humbly submitted by Your Majesty's faithful & devoted servant

WINSTON S. CHURCHILL

[1] Samuel John Gurney Hoare (1880–1959), Conservative MP Chelsea 1910–44; succeeded to baronetcy 1915; Secretary for Air 1922–4, 1924–9; Secretary for India 1931–5; Foreign Secretary 1935; First Lord of Admiralty 1936–7; Home Secretary 1937–9; Lord Privy Seal 1939–40; Secretary for Air 1940; Ambassador to Spain 1940–4; created Viscount Templewood 1944.

WSC to the King
(*Royal Archives*)

29 March 1911   Home Office

Mr Secretary Churchill with his humble duty to Your Majesty: The Committee stage of the Revenue Bill was yesterday concluded under the Closure. The debate was good & in it, as in other Budget discussions this year, the Government suffered somewhat from the absence of the Chancellor of the Exchequer. Towards its close there were some symptoms of good tempered noisiness on both sides of the House; but all finished quite quietly. Mr Churchill had the opportunity yesterday of hearing for the first time Mr Eyres-Monsell,[1] a young Conservative formerly a naval officer. He speaks extremely well – with knowledge, fluency, ease & an engaging appearance & a pleasant voice. He is the only new one that this Parliament has yet produced.

The collapse of the Referendum policy in the House of Lords was the subject of comment in the Lobbies yesterday. It always seemed to Mr Churchill impossible that this strange device so full of menace to the interest of property & good government could ever bear the pressure of sustained Parliamentary scrutiny. The Reform Bill is also postponed, so that on Monday when the Parliament Bill is debated in committee of the House of Commons, it will be the sole solution wh holds the field.

WSC to the King
(*Royal Archives*)

30 March 1911   Home Office

Mr Secretary Churchill with his humble duty to Your Majesty: The debate on the Revenue Bill was continued yesterday & will be concluded to-day. It was ragged & dull, but the House was moderately filled throughout, & there were occasional breezes.

On the adjournment Colonel Seely was attacked from all sides of the House on the subject of the new Army sash for Officers. The Conservatives were especially forward in condemning this increased charge upon officers; but they were supported from the Liberal & Labour benches. The unanimity of the hostile criticism was unbroken. It seems quite impossible that this proposal should be persisted in, & a pledge was given that it should be

---

[1] Bolton Meredith Eyres-Monsell (1881–   ), Unionist MP South Worcestershire 1910–1935; Whip 1911; Chief Whip 1923–31; Parliamentary Secretary to WSC at the Treasury 1924–9; First Lord of the Admiralty 1931–6; PC 1923; knighted 1929; created Viscount Monsell of Evesham 1935.

reconsidered from the beginning. An optional arrangement would seem to combine the disadvantages of all courses.

The House rose at 12.15 *pm* [*am*].

Submitted by Your Majesty's faithful servant

WINSTON S. CHURCHILL

WSC to the King
(*Royal Archives*)

31 March 1911   Home Office

Mr Secretary Churchill with his humble duty to Your Majesty: The Revenue Bill passed yesterday evening under the closure in a sulky but tranquil House, & was thereafter carried by the Lords through *all* its stages in less than a minute.

After dinner the Commons were occupied in discussing the report of Army votes. To-day the Shops Bill is to be read a second time.

Submitted by Your Majesty's faithful subject & servant

WINSTON S. CHURCHILL

WSC to the King
(*Royal Archives*)

1 April 1911   Home Office

Mr Secretary Churchill with his humble duty to Your Majesty: The House of Commons yesterday gave unanimous assent to the 2nd Reading of the Shops Bill; and a motion to refer it to a select committee (wh would have delayed it) was rejected by 264 to 21. The great bulk of the Conservative party voted with the Government for the Bill, & a vy pleasing feature of the debate was the sincere support accorded to the measure by the younger representatives of 'Tory Democracy'.

WSC to the King
(*Royal Archives*)

4 April 1911   Home Office

Mr Secretary Churchill with his humble duty to Your Majesty: The debate yesterday was loose, discursive, & distinctly obstructive, & if continued on these lines the Committee Stage of the Parliament Bill would be a vy long & vy dull experience to those whose duty it is to take part in it.

The preamble is the difficulty. The supporters of the Government are entirely against it in the proportion of four or five to one. They are willing to consent to its inclusion only in order that the general form of the Bill would remain unchanged. They do not seem inclined at all to support any constructive plan.

The Opposition, curiously enough, appear to be anxious above all things to sweep away the House of Lords & put something or anything in its place. They assail the Government with reproaches for not proceeding at once to say what form the reconstituted House should ultimately take. They declare it impossible to proceed with the effective discussion of the Parliament Bill while these details are unknown. The Government reply that the abolition of the Veto is the essential preliminary to any reconstitution of the House of Lords.

Mr Churchill thinks that in the end it will vy possibly be found that there are only 2 solutions: First, the Parliament Bill pure & simple, with the Lords left untouched: and secondly – a reform of the Lords after the Veto has gone agreed on by both parties. He thinks the Opposition make a mistake in worrying too much about Reform. It would be better for them to wait for better times & make their own Reform. Some of them are beginning to see this.

The Government have been well supported in all divisions and the current of opinion in the ministerial ranks is running strong.

All of which is humbly submitted to Your Majesty by Your Majesty's faithful servant

WINSTON S. CHURCHILL

WSC to the King
(*Royal Archives*)

4 April 1911   Home Office

Mr Secretary Churchill with his humble duty to your Majesty: The debate on the Preamble & with it the Committee stage were concluded yesterday. The Labour party made their protest, but only 47 members of all parties (including a few irresponsible Conservatives) followed them into the Lobby on the single-chamber principle. The supporters of the Government stood firmly by the Preamble as an integral part of the measure for wh the electors have voted at the polls. Thus this point wh threatened at one moment to involve the Government in serious difficulties was safely & smoothly passed. The Bill was reported to the House by a majority of 118. In 18 divisions on Tuesday the Ministerial majorities averaged 126. Members generally seem much puzzled at the sudden break down of resistance to the Parliament Bill, & there were many rumours yesterday that some arrangement had been made. These are of course denied to be of the slightest basis.

Today the Chancellor of the Exchequer will explain the long promised Insurance scheme. Mr Churchill believes that this is far more important to the prosperity contentment & security of Your Majesty's Kingdom, than any other measure of our times; and it will ever be associated as a noble act of social reconstruction with Your Majesty's reign & with the Coronation Year. Henceforward everyone will have 'a stake in the country' in the remarkable rewards wh scientific organisation & the strange power of averages can confer on thrift.

Humbly submitted by Your Majesty's faithful & devoted servant

WINSTON S. CHURCHILL

WSC to the King
(Royal Archives)

5 April 1911   Home Office

Mr Secretary Churchill with his humble duty to Your Majesty: The feature of yesterday's debate was Mr Balfour's remarkable speech in reply to Lord Hugh Cecil & against his proposal that members should vote by Ballot in the House of Commons. No more profound & brilliant vindication of the House of Commons system has been delivered for many years. The House was deeply interested & the supporters of the Government hailed the pronouncement with enthusiastic, if astonished cheers.

84 members of the Conservative party voted against their leader; the rest either abstained or voted with the Government. Vote by Ballot was rejected by nearly a 300 majority.

Progress is vy slow & much obstructed. The last hour last night was the only good & lively debate which has arisen in the Parliament Bill. There is great apathy & boredom, & the Committee drags dully along.

Humbly submitted by Your Majesty's faithful servant

WINSTON S. CHURCHILL

WSC to the King
(Royal Archives)

6 April 1911   Home Office

Mr Secretary Churchill with his humble duty to Your Majesty: Four lines of the Parliament Bill have passed through Committee in the week's discussion given to it. It is clear that other methods must be adopted next week.

The debates are dull enough in the afternoon, but an air of genial rowdiness pervades the House after dinner; & last night Mr Clough[1] (the Liberal Member who figured so ridiculously in a recent libel case) was subjected to a vy unseemly & disorderly hustling & jeering, to wh Mr Churchill thought it necessary to call the immediate attention of the Speaker.

Humbly submitted by Your Majesty's faithful & devoted servant

WINSTON S. CHURCHILL

WSC to the King
(Royal Archives)

8 April 1911   Home Office

Mr Secretary Churchill with his humble duty to Your Majesty: The House of Commons read the Copyright Bill a second time yesterday, after a careful explanation by Mr Buxton and interesting speeches from Mr Birrell & Mr Balfour. All the authors are vy pleased at the extension of the period of copyright. The Bill should certainly pass.

Mr Churchill trusts Your Majesty will excuse him for not having made a report of Thursday's debate, in wh the Archer-Schee[2] case was satisfactorily disposed of; but vy great pressure of work yesterday morning overwhelmed him.

On Monday the Government will apply what is called the 'Kangaroo' closure to the Parliament Bill, which means that the Chairman will be empowered to select the amendments to be discussed down to a certain point in the clauses.

All of which is humbly submitted by Your Majesty's faithful servant

WINSTON S. CHURCHILL

WSC to the King
(Royal Archives)

11 April 1911   Home Office

Mr Secretary Churchill with his humble duty to Your Majesty: The Prime Minister was absent from the conclusion of the debate last night

[1] William Clough (1862–1937), Liberal MP for Skipton 1906–18.

[2] In October 1908 a naval cadet, George Archer-Schee, was compulsorily withdrawn from Osborne after being accused of stealing a postal order worth 5s. His innocence was subsequently established. On 6 April 1911 Mr Cave complained that Archer-Schee had been given no opportunity to defend himself and said that the Admiralty should have paid a substantial compensation. The First Lord, Mr McKenna, expressed his regret to the boy and his father and agreed to refer the question of compensation to arbitration. £7,120 was awarded when the case was decided in August. The case forms the basis of Terence Rattigan's play *The Winslow Boy*.

through his cold, but the Government were nevertheless able to come to a good arrangement with the Opposition over the immediate progress of the Parliament Bill. After a long negotiation across the floor it was agreed not to sit up late, but that the Government should have the whole of clause 1 except the proviso & the question 'that the clause stand fast' by the end of to-night's sitting. This greatly improves the position of Government business, & enables the House to separate for Easter with more than 1/3rd of the Committee stage behind them, in place of the three lines wh alone had been achieved last week. A good tempered settlement is always to be preferred to a fierce fight, tho not always to be obtained without one.

Humbly submitted by Your Majesty's faithful servant

WINSTON S. CHURCHILL

WSC to the King
(*Royal Archives*)

19 April 1911   Home Office

Mr Secretary Churchill with his humble duty to Your Majesty: The House sat till nearly five this morning on Clause 1 of the Parliament Bill, but disposed of that finally before reporting progress. The debate was excessively dull & wearisome, being largely occupied with foolish & obstructive amendments, but there was no heat or ill-feeling on either side. Nearly 20 divisions took place in wh the Government, many of whose supporters are still on their holidays, had to be content with majorities of little over 50. These however were well maintained throughout.

Mr Churchill introduced yesterday under the 10 minutes rule a Bill to deal more effectually with the Alien Criminal. Your Majesty was pleased earlier in the year to take some interest in this question, and Mr Churchill has endeavoured to profit by the expression of Your Majesty's wishes wh then reached him. He ventures to send (in another box) a copy of the Bill. Sir Edward Henry[1] thinks it will be vy useful. Some of the supporters of the Government are not however vy pleased about it, and the Minister must walk warily lest the flock rebuke him.

Today the Army Account & tomorrow the Parliament Bill Clause 2.

Submitted by Your Majesty's faithful servant & subject

WINSTON S. CHURCHILL

[1] Sir Edward Richard Henry (1850–1931), Commissioner Metropolitan Police 1903–18; Inspector-General of Police, Bengal 1891; Assistant-Commissioner Metropolitan Police 1901–1903; KCB 1910; GCVO 1911; Baronet 1918.

WSC to the King
(*Royal Archives*)

19 April 1911   Home Office

Mr Secretary Churchill with his humble duty to Your Majesty: Another arrangement was come to late last night with Mr Balfour by wh the first nine words of Clause 2 of the Parliament Bill are to be concluded before we separate on Monday. This is much more substantial than it sounds, and no less than 9 pages of amendments wh might well have occupied a weeks debating will disappear at a stroke. Mr Churchill had not expected that such a large forward step could be made without much outcry & that it should be acquiesced in is satisfactory & significant.

The debate was throughout the sitting dull & decorous, but at the vy end after everything was settled there was a little ill-temper and Lord Winterton[1] became conspicuous. Lord Hugh Cecil has been much more conciliatory lately and used his influence last night to promote an agreement. The progress made is so good that the immediate use of the 'guillotine' may be postponed.

All of which is submitted by Your Majesty's humble servant

WINSTON S. CHURCHILL

WSC to the King
(*Royal Archives*)

[20 April 1911]   Home Office

Mr Secretary Churchill with his humble duty to Your Majesty: The Army (Annual) Bill was yesterday carried through the House of Commons, and in the evening a private member's motion relating to the association of the Colonial Prime Ministers with the Foreign policy of Great Britain was discussed. Mr Mackinnon Wood[2] dealt with this satisfactorily & Mr Harcourt afterwards gave the assurance that the Colonial representatives would be invited to attend meetings of the Committee of Imperial Defence. The motion was then withdrawn.

[1] Edward Turnour (1883–1963), 6th Earl Winterton, Conservative MP Horsham 1904–51; Under-Secretary for India 1922–4, November 1924–9; Chancellor of the Duchy of Lancaster 1937–9; Paymaster-General 1939.
[2] Thomas Mackinnon Wood (1855–1927), Liberal MP St Rollox Glasgow 1906–18; Financial Secretary to the Treasury 1911–12, 1916; Secretary for Scotland 1912–16; Chancellor of Duchy of Lancaster 1916; PC 1911.

This pause in the progress of The Parliament Bill gave those in charge of it an opportunity of taking a more general survey of its prospects than has lately been possible. The rate of advance has hitherto been much too slow. There has been a great deal of obstruction and many absurd & frivolous amendments. Unless the rate of advance is sensibly improved in the next two or three days, a motion must be made to regulate the various stages, it being important that the measure should reach the House of Lords early in May & certainly not later than the 18th.

All of wh is humbly submitted by Your Majesty's faithful & devoted servant

WINSTON S. CHURCHILL

WSC to the King
(Royal Archives)

22 April 1911   Home Office

Mr Secretary Churchill with his humble duty to Your Majesty: Nothing worthy of report happened on Friday in the House of Commons. The Exeter election petition having resulted in the return of Mr Duke[1] by one vote, after a curious judgment, he was allowed to take his seat in spite of certain protests by members who desired to debate the conduct of the judges; but who were not allowed to do so.

Thereafter the House debated small private members' Bills – the first to improve the pensions of policemen outside London, who are injured on duty: the second to give a 60 hours week to the attendants in the Lunatic Asylums. Both these proposals are good in themselves, but they have the defect of being measures by which the House of Commons gives away the ratepayers money without consulting the local authorities who have been given the responsibility. They were prepared by the Young Conservative Members who take an interest in social reform. They were both read a second time, but will not it is to be expected go much further this session.

All of which is humbly submitted by Your Majesty's faithful servant

WINSTON S. CHURCHILL

---

[1] Henry Edward Duke (1855–1939), Conservative MP Plymouth 1900–6, for Exeter 1910–18; Lord Justice of Appeal 1918–19; President of Probate, Divorce and Admiralty Division of High Court of Justice 1919–33. Privy Councillor 1915; created Baron Merrivale 1925.

WSC to his wife

22 April 1911   [Blenheim]

My beloved,

You will see from the enclosed *Hansard* what a little pig Winterton made of himself. I ought not to have called out his name in my position – but the House was thoroughly good tempered & I did not expect him to take such a nasty line. I have done with him. He showed real malignity – wh I never forget. No evil consequence has arisen – & no one attached any importance to the incident except myself.

Our party to the Gaiety was vy amusing. 'Peggy' is so good. I must take you to see it. There are some poisonous allusions; but the piece is lively & sensuous. George Grossmith[1] asked me to come & see him & I went behind to see a stage full of pretty cats in all their warpaint! There is a good song 'What has become of the girls I used to know' 'Many said No but some said Yes' etc. Vy amusing – you wd laugh.

Lloyd George has practically taken Unemployment Insurance to his own bosom, & I am I think effectively elbowed out of this large field in wh I consumed so much thought & effort. Never mind! There are many good fish in the sea.

On Thursday night the PM was vy bad: & I squirmed with embarrassment. He could hardly speak: & many people noticed his condition. He continues most friendly & benevolent, & entrusts me with everything after dinner. Up till that time he is at his best – but thereafter! It is an awful pity, & only the persistent free-masonry of the House of Commons prevents a scandal. I like the old boy and admire both his intellect & his character. But what risks to run. We only got him away the other night just before Balfour began the negotiations wh I conducted but wh otherwise wd have fallen to him – with disastrous consequences. The next day he was serene, efficient, undisturbed.

There is a vy nice & remarkable party here. All clever patriotic young Empire Builders out of work. Practically the whole of Milner's 'Kindergarten'. These young men whom he gathered from the Universities to govern SA after the war. They all regard me as the devil incarnate, & are only just beginning to realise that I am not so bad as they have always thought. You might have been amused. I played golf better this afternoon – & slept 10 hours last night. We shall be up all night Monday – & I am going to put the screw on the Parliament Bill as it has never been put before in the next few days. We must get on. No peace till after the shock.

[1] George Grossmith (1847–1912), actor; co-author with his brother Walter Weedon Grossmith of *The Diary of a Nobody*.

Lansdowne is seriously ill, & Wernher[1] dying.

Wire me when you return & bring your PK & CB with you my sweet darling Clem pussie bird –

Your loving & devoted husband
W.

WSC to the King
(*Royal Archives*)

25 April 1911   Home Office

Mr Secretary Churchill with his humble duty to Your Majesty: Good progress was made yesterday without any closure owing to the agreement reached last Thursday. Amendments dealing with the exclusion from the provisions of the Parliament Bill, of Home Rule, disestablishment, the prerogatives & rights; the Crown & the Parliament Bill itself were necessarily negatived by majorities of between 90 & 95. Mr Moreton Frewen[2] made a maiden speech wh is also probably a swan song. He pleased the House both in matter & manner. Mr Waring[3] has returned to his allegiance, his constituents being much perturbed by his divagations. Three more Parliamentary weeks ought to conclude the Bill in the Commons.

All of which is humbly submitted by Your Majesty's faithful & devoted servant

WINSTON S. CHURCHILL

WSC to the King
(*Royal Archives*)

26 April 1911   Home Office

Mr Churchill with his humble duty to Your Majesty: There is a remarkable collapse in the opposition to the Parliament Bill & the fight seems practically over so far as the House of Commons is concerned. The dullness of the debates has led to vy small attendances, though the Government

[1] Julius Charles Wernher (1850–1912), member of Wernher, Beit and Company; created Baronet 1905.

[2] Moreton Frewen (1853–1924); son of Thomas Frewen MP, of Northiam, Sussex, and Helen Louisa, daughter of Frederick Homan of County Kildare; married 1881 Clara, eldest daughter of Leonard Jerome. A knowledgeable if unlucky student of economic affairs, he was the author of a number of works on bi-metallism. MP for North-East Cork, 1910–11.

[3] Walter Waring (1876–1930), served in South Africa 1899–1900; Liberal and later Coalition Liberal MP Banffshire 1907–18, and Playdon Division of Durham 1918–22; National Liberal MP East Lothian and Berwick 1922–3; Parliamentary Private Secretary to Secretary for War 1919–22.

majorities have been well maintained. A complete absence of anything like bitterness or passion has characterised the whole proceedings.

Today the House will discuss the Referendum, & after that there only remain the question of identity – *ie* whether a Bill is the same Bill or not if it be amended in a second or third session – & the Preamble. Mr Churchill expects that the Bill will be out of the Commons & read a 3rd time on the 11th of May. It should be considered by the Lords in the week of the 15th. *Thus there will be ample time for the solution of the crisis* before Your Majesty's Coronation, unless delaying tactics – the utility of wh is not obvious – are adopted. Lord Lansdowne's regrettable ill-health has led to some unavoidable delay in the production of the Reform Bill.

All of which is humbly submitted by Your Majesty's faithful servant

WINSTON S. CHURCHILL

WSC to the King
(*Royal Archives*)

27 April 1911　　　　　　　　　　　　　　　　　Home Office

Mr Secretary Churchill with his humble duty to Your Majesty: The Referendum was debated yesterday in the House of Commons and was rejected by a majority of 122. There is no doubt that a great many Conservatives view this expedient with distrust. It would certainly be most dangerous as applied to property questions: & on ordinary matters of general politics it would lead to complete irresponsibility in both members & ministers. A Referendum is not compatible with an effective 2nd chamber, to wh indeed it is an alternative. Mr Cave who proposed the amendment was convicted of having condemned the system out-spokenly a year ago in the debates on the Resolutions of this vy Bill: & the Prime Minister replied to Mr Balfour with a strong and well expressed defence of representative institutions.

The introduction of the Insurance Bill is postponed till Monday 8 May. This will perhaps introduce a new factor into a situation wh so far as the House of Commons is concerned is worn threadbare.

WINSTON S. CHURCHILL

WSC to the King
(*Royal Archives*)

28 April 1911   Home Office

Mr Secretary Churchill with his humble duty to Your Majesty: The House of Commons yesterday proceeded to 'get the Speaker out of the Chair' on Civil Service Estimates, when the Labour party raised a debate on the question of the administration of the Poor Law. The attendance was small, most of the members being glad to take a rest after the long sittings on the Parliament Bill. Later in the evening the appointment of Sir E. Soares[1] to the National Debt Office was the subject of unfavourable criticism wh was well answered by Mr Hobhouse. The Prime Minister has postponed his answer about the Justices appointments till Monday.

All of which is humbly submitted by Your Majesty's faithful & devoted servant

WINSTON S. CHURCHILL

WSC to the King
(*Royal Archives*)

[29 April 1911]   Home Office

Mr Secretary Churchill with his humble duty to Your Majesty: The Aliens Bill introduced by Mr Goulding[2] was read a second time yesterday. It is not a good bill as it stands, but it is capable of unlimited amendment; & as the prospects of securing Government time for the Bill on the same subject which has official authority, are vy small, Mr Churchill induced the House to pass this Bill on to the Grand Committee with the intention of altering it there to meet ministerial views. The Young Conservatives who are pressing the Bill quite understand this plan and are glad to have a chance of legislating albeit on a modest scale. The great bulk of the supporters of the Government voted against the 2nd Reading, but enough followed Mr Churchill's advice to secure its acceptance. The further conduct of this measure will require careful management but Mr Churchill is not without hopes that a useful Bill may eventually emerge from the manoeuvring.

Mr Churchill had no intention of suggesting to Your Majesty in his letter

---

[1] Ernest Joseph Soares (1864–1926), Liberal MP for Barnstaple 1900–11; Parliamentary Private Secretary to the Home Secretary 1906–7; Charity Commissioner 1908–10; Junior Lord of the Treasury 1910–11; knighted 1911.

[2] Edward Alfred Goulding (1862–1936), Conservative MP Devizes 1895–1906; Unionist MP Worcestershire 1908–22; sometime Chairman Rolls Royce Limited; PC 1918; Baronet 1915; created Baron Wargrave of Wargrave 1922.

of last Thursday that a crisis would necessarily arise on the Parliament Bill during the next few weeks; but only that it might arise either from rejection or counter proposals, & that in any case delay will lead to considerable unrest. But the course of events cannot in any respect be forecasted.

All of which is submitted humbly by Your Majesty's faithful servant

WINSTON S. CHURCHILL

Lord Knollys to WSC

29 April 1911   Buckingham Palace

My dear Churchill,

I spoke to the King today about his giving Mrs Churchill a ticket for his Box in Westminster Abbey on the occasion of the Coronation. He said he should have much pleasure in giving her one, and you may like to know that he was very nice about it.

Yours sincerely
KNOLLYS

I explained to him what you meant when you alluded in your letter to the 'crisis'.

WSC to the King
(*Royal Archives*)

2 May 1911   Home Office

Mr Secretary Churchill with his humble duty to Your Majesty: The Government time table is well maintained & the Bill made good progress yesterday. The Committee stage including the Preamble should be finished tomorrow. The debate was languid and thinly attended. The points discussed were not important and dealt chiefly with the question of identity of measures repeated in a second or third session. The House adjourned at 11 o'clock having completed Clause 2 except the general question that the clause stand fast wh will be disposed of today.

The Prime Minister's reply about the appointment of magistrates has not satisfied the discontents wh exist among Ministerial supporters, & these will probably be expressed more loudly after the main work of the session has been completed.

The Insurance Bill is fixed for Thursday.

The above is humbly submitted by Your Majesty's faithful & devoted servant

WINSTON S. CHURCHILL

WSC to the King
(*Royal Archives*)

3 May 1911   Home Office

Mr Secretary Churchill with his humble duty to Your Majesty: Clause 2, Clauses 3, 4, 5 & 6, & all the new clauses comprising the whole of the Committee stage (except the Preamble) were carried or disposed of last night by large majorities rising at one time to 149. The Conservative party in many divisions did not number 100. The debate was tranquil & in spite of much trifling progress was fully in accord with the most optimistic expectations of the Government. The Committee stage will thus have been disposed of, without any guillotine resolution. The collapse of any effective resistance to the Parliament Bill in the House of Commons is complete.

The Insurance Bill today, & Lord Lansdowne's Reform Bill tomorrow are new factors in the situation. Mr Churchill endeavoured yesterday to indicate that the Reform proposals of the Opposition might be viewed without unnecessary hostility.

All of which is humbly submitted by Your Majesty's faithful servant

WINSTON S. CHURCHILL

Max Aitken[1] to WSC

[Undated]

Private

Dear Mr Churchill,

About Canada. If you go you will have a great reception and if properly looked after it might easily be a turning point. Chamberlain intended to go to Canada but illness interfered. Had he gone it's my belief the Country would have been aroused and Imperial Preference forced on England. You would have regarded that as disastrous, and I am only illustrating the possibilities in Canada, which is like America, and can be swayed by the right person. I was Secy to the Nova Scotia Committee which was making the Chamberlain arrangements.

I don't think any other person can arrange your reception as efficiently

---

[1] William Maxwell Aitken (1879–1964), son of Reverend William Aitken of Newcastle, New Brunswick. In 1907 he became a Montreal stockbroker and made a fortune by amalgamating cement mills. He arrived in England in 1910 and was Conservative MP, Ashton-under-Lyme 1910–16; Chancellor Duchy of Lancaster and Minister of Information 1918; Minister for Aircraft Production 1940–1; Minister of State 1941; Minister of Supply 1941–2; Lord Privy Seal 1943–5; Proprietor of Beaverbrook Newspapers; knighted 1911; created Lord Beaverbrook 1917. His intimate friendship with WSC did not begin until 1916.

as I can. Please forgive the conceit. I know you won't do anything for Imperial Preference but you are aiming for the same end and your plan may be as efficient. I don't think so, but that makes no difference.

There is an objection to me you must know about. I created all the big trusts in Canada. None of them are bad trusts but the Western farmers attack me very often and sometimes very offensively. I don't care. But you might not like an intimate connection. I can best illustrate the position when I tell you that my relation to Canada was in a small way the same as Morgan's relation to America. I'm done now and in fact for eighteen months past I have steadily pulled out. But the trusts remain, and will and can remain with or without tariffs. In fact there are more efficient trusts in England than in Canada or America. If you don't think so I'll prove it to you. Transportation not tariff is the corner stone of the Trust.

If you don't mind the objection I would take care to relieve you from the incubus if it developed. And if you are to be my guest it won't so appear. Probably it doesn't make any difference at all, and I exaggerate it.

Another matter for your consideration is the Canadian political situation. To efficiently organise your reception I would have to use both liberals and conservatives. I couldn't get them together if Canada is then in the midst of an election. And you couldn't avoid political chairmen etc. I think this requires consideration.

On behalf of Mrs Aitken as well as myself I urge you to go with us on such date as you may fix via New York – because I have all the transportation I require by that route – If you would rather go West alone we will start you on your way and meet you on return.

Please don't tell anybody I admitted I organised any trusts, and please forgive me for this very long letter.

Yours faithfully
W. M. AITKEN

WSC to Max Aitken
(*Beaverbrook Papers*)

5 May 1911   Blenheim

My dear Aitken,
    It is with vy great reluctance that I have come to the conclusion that our Canadian project must stand over till next year. I am vy much indebted to you for the kindness with wh you have offered to smooth my path. I shall look forward to availing myself of your powerful aid in the not distant future.

I hope you will come & dine on Tuesday night to meet Louis Botha.
I hope LG may be there too.

Yours sincerely
WINSTON S. CHURCHILL

WSC to the King
(*Royal Archives*)

6 May 1911   Home Office

Mr Secretary Churchill with his humble duty to Your Majesty: The
Chancellor of the Exchequer's Titanic proposals for National Insurance
have unquestionably introduced a new & healing factor into the political
situation. There is no doubt that the general character of the scheme is a
true and sincere expression of the principles & feelings which Mr Disraeli &
other Tory Democratic leaders inculcated. The two great parties hold each
other in such effective equipoise on most occasions, that when they appear
ready to join forces a feeling of enthusiasm & of irresistible strength is created.
Such an emotion pervades political circles at the present time and cannot fail
to mitigate the fierceness of other disputations. The moment has been
exceptionally well timed. There need be no anxiety about the substance &
details of the Bill. They will be found to improve & not to betray the impression which the first announcement has caused. Their discussion &
passage will at every stage appeal to all that is most generous & most truly
national in all parties. Their adoption in practice will confer upon the British
people material benefits & moral security almost immeasurable, & conduce
at every point to the stability of society, and to attachment to the Monarchy,
under which progress & prosperity are possible through State action on a
scale never attempted in any country before.

Mr Churchill desires to express to Your Majesty his earnest & heartfelt
congratulations on achieving the first year of a reign from which so much is
hoped & during which so much may easily be accomplished. The anniversary of Your Majesty's accession will be marked by sad memories of the loss
Your Majesty sustained a year ago. But apart from personal griefs, Your
Majesty cannot but feel fortified & encouraged by the auspicious beginning
of Your Majesty's reign in every sphere of national affairs. There is not a
single important political difficulty that does not present itself today in a less
menacing aspect than on Your Majesty's accession; and although a very
grave & imminent obstacle remains barring the way to national consolidation, there are many reasons for believing that it will be successfully surmounted and will lead to still better developments in the future. With the

removal of the Veto of the House of Lords a general settlement of out-standing & largely obsolete party controversies will be possible – if not inevitable – & the supreme questions connected with the social & industrial organisation of the people on modern & scientific lines, & with the unity & strength of the Empire at large may become the province of no one party in the state.

All of which is humbly submitted by Your Majesty's faithful servant & subject

WINSTON S. CHURCHILL

Mr Churchill shd not omit to add that the Women's Suffrage Bill was read again a 2nd time yesterday in a dull & flat House. Its immediate further progress is not very probable. But there will doubtless be a measure of disorder. The large majority will no doubt encourage the advocates of this change.

Lord Knollys to WSC

7 May 1911   Buckingham Palace

My dear Churchill,

The King desires me to thank you for your House of Commons letter of yesterday which interested him very much. He thanks you also for what you kindly say about him in connection with yesterday's anniversary.

He hopes that Mr Lloyd George's magnificent scheme on National Insurance (I have written to congratulate him on it from HM) will have the political effect you mention and he thinks it will up to a certain point, but he is afraid that feelings and interests are at the present moment too strong to make him believe that political passions will be softened beyond the moment, though undoubtedly the Bill ought to produce some good effect in that direction.

The scheme ought also to keep the Liberals in office for the next 15 years unless they come to grief over the Home Rule question.

I am lunching with Guest tomorrow to meet some of the promoters of the proposed new Club, about which you wrote to me.[1]

Yrs sincerely
KNOLLYS

---

[1] The Other Club, of which WSC and F. E. Smith were the founders.

WSC to the King
(Royal Archives)

8 [9] May 1911   Home Office

Mr Secretary Churchill with his humble duty to Your Majesty: The Closure Resolutions for concluding the debates on the Parliament Bill were passed yesterday in the House of Commons. The Bill will be read a third time on Monday next. This delay of three days was agreed to between Report & Third Reading to meet the wishes of Mr Balfour & the Opposition.

The interest yesterday lay in the Lords. Mr Churchill has not yet been able to measure opinion on Lord Lansdowne's Bill. He is making some inquiries. The first impression appears to be that the scheme is fantastic: but there is no doubt that it is a vy substantial advance from any position yet occupied by the Conservative leaders. Some of the Peers will doubtless prefer the veto Bill which leaves them all where they are.

Humbly submitted by Your Majesty's faithful servant

WINSTON S. CHURCHILL

WSC to the King
(Royal Archives)

10 May 1911   Home Office

Mr Secretary Churchill with his humble duty to Your Majesty: The opposition to the Parliament Bill reached its lowest ebb last night. At one moment only seven Conservative members were in their places to stem the tide of revolution, & of these, two were deep in the pages of the Insurance Bill just issued. On the Government side Mr Churchill at one moment found himself absolutely alone. The divisions although occurring on trivial points yielded majorities of between 100 & 120 to Ministers. There is a total absence of heat or even interest.

The Lansdowne Bill may be helpful if the Conservative party are insistent upon Reform after the Parliament Bill has passed. But probably many of them will wish to leave things alone. Mr Churchill is vy doubtful whether the Government would have the strength to carry a Reform of the House of Lords Bill unless the Conservatives co-operated. The main feeling on the Liberal benches is adverse to any change in the character of the Lords; & although the supporters of the Government would no doubt acquiesce in a drastic Reform Bill, there would never be the enthusiasm & energy necessary to carry it in the teeth of Conservative opposition. Such a change could scarcely come about except by general consent.

All of which is humbly submitted by Your Majesty's faithful servant

WINSTON S. CHURCHILL

WSC to the King
(*Royal Archives*)

12 [11] May 1911   Home Office

Mr Secretary Churchill with his humble duty to Your Majesty: The Report Stage of the Parliament Bill was brought to an end last night after a loose debate – a little more lively than on Tuesday night. The third Reading will take place on Monday. The opposition have confided the duty of moving the rejection to Mr F. E. Smith.

Today the salary of the Chancellor of the Exchequer will be under discussion.

Submitted by Your Majesty's humble & faithful servant
                                    WINSTON S. CHURCHILL

WSC to the King
(*Royal Archives*)

[13 May 1911]   Home Office

Mr Secretary Churchill with his humble duty to Your Majesty: The House being occupied with private members' Bills yesterday only a vy small attendance was secured. Mr Remnant's[1] Bill to prohibit the importation of sweated goods could not command the necessary 100 members required for Closure & was consequently adjourned at 5 *pm* the matter remaining undecided. Mr Churchill thinks that Your Majesty's references on Tuesday next to the German Emperor will be very warmly welcomed by the Peace party in the country; & will do a lot of good to public sentiment here & in Germany.

Humbly submitted by Your Majesty's faithful servant
                                    WINSTON S. CHURCHILL

WSC to the King
(*Royal Archives*)

[16 May 1911]   Home Office

Mr Secretary Churchill with his humble duty to Your Majesty: Last night in the House of Commons the Parliament Bill passed its 3rd Reading by a majority of 121.

The debate was not well attended except just before the division, when of course the House was crowded. Mr F. E. Smith moved the rejection of the

[1] James Farquharson Remnant (1863–1933), Conservative MP Holborn 1900–28; created Baron Remnant of Wenhaston 1928.

Bill in a speech of much power and full of a real spirit of conciliation. The Prime Minister and Mr Balfour both spoke in the afternoon, & it was left to the Home Secretary to conclude the discussion. Mr Churchill laid down three propositions: that the Bill must be passed before any further steps could be considered: that once the two great parties could meet on even terms the constitution of the 2nd Chamber should be considered between them: & that if a satisfactory agreement was reached it would be open to the House to determine whether a better method of adjusting differences between the Houses could not be devised than the cumbrous machinery of the Parliament Bill: provided however that the Liberal party should be no worse off under the new rearrangement than under the present proposals. This last has not been accepted by the supporters of the Government before. They have always appeared indeed to insist on the Parliament Bill being permanent whatever the House of Lords may ultimately become. Last night they gave a vy friendly hearing to the suggestion that other equally good methods may be discovered in the future.

Mr Churchill ventures to express to Your Majesty what he is sure is the general view – that the ceremony this morning was one of the most impressive & well considered that can be remembered. Everyone was loud in praise of its splendour, interest & simplicity. The statue of Queen Victoria is certainly vy striking, the force and character of the features being so vividly portrayed.

All of which is humbly submitted by Your Majesty's faithful servant

WINSTON S. CHURCHILL

WSC to the King
(*Royal Archives*)

17 May [1911]   Home Office

Mr Secretary Churchill with his humble duty to Your Majesty: The Budget statement of the Chancellor of the Exchequer was of so satisfactory a character that it was accepted with general approval, the only criticisms being directed towards the provision made for the payment of members. On this no doubt much division of opinion prevails.

The general finance of the country has however responded wonderfully to the demands made upon it in these years of exceptional strain, & every month indicates the efficiency of the Budget of 1909 as a financial instrument.

The Government in their tenure of office have reduced the liabilities of the state by upwards of 70 millions.

Humbly submitted by Your Majesty's faithful servant

WINSTON S. CHURCHILL

WSC to the King
(*Royal Archives*)

18 May 1911   House of Commons

Mr Secretary Churchill with his humble duty to Your Majesty: The consideration of the Finance Bill was resumed yesterday by the House of Commons and after a languid debate in a thin House the necessary resolutions were agreed to. The interest at Westminster yesterday centred in the House of Lords where Lords Curzon & Rosebery made important speeches. Complete tranquillity reigns in the Commons and does not seem likely to be disturbed in the immediate future. The Conciliation Committee on women's suffrage is pressing that facilities should be accorded to their Bill this session. This is however quite impossible & meets with so little support, that only 10 out of the 250 members who voted for the 2nd Reading attended the meeting of the Committee to decide on further steps.

All of which is humbly submitted by Your Majesty's faithful servant

WINSTON S. CHURCHILL

WSC to the King
(*Royal Archives*)

19 May 1911   Home Office

Mr Secretary Churchill with his humble duty to Your Majesty: the Postmaster General yesterday made a vy interesting annual statement of the work & projects of his Department. Mr Herbert Samuel is a most efficient Minister who works with mechanical regularity from morning till midnight and whose health appears quite unaffected by the most strenuous exertions. His proposals for cheap telephones for farmers, for cheaper foreign parcels post, for reducing the cost of foreign cables and telephones & for issuing 1d & ½d letter cards at their face value were well received by the House, & will be welcomed by the public. There seems to be no end to the wonderful work of the immense Postal machine, which in spite of the increasing pay of its servants & their demands, yields a handsome yearly income to the state, & discharges its vast & intricate duties with marvellous precision. It is greatly to be hoped that the telephone system will improve now that it is placed under the Postal department.

Submitted most respectfully by Your Majesty's faithful servant & subject

WINSTON S. CHURCHILL

WSC to the King
(*Royal Archives*)

21 May 1911   Home Office

Sir,

I venture to write to Your Majesty upon a private matter. It concerns my cousin the Duke of Marlborough. Owing to the fact that he and his wife are living apart neither is invited to the regular ceremonies of Your Majesty's Court. It is easy to see that this rule is necessary, and as it is general and affects a considerable number of persons, it does not impose special hardship in most cases. But the Duke of Marlborough is a knight of the Garter. He has been summoned to attend the Chapter of the Order to be held at Windsor on June 10. On the last occasion when he obeyed this summons he was alone excepted and excluded from the entertainment in the Castle which followed the Service. Your Majesty will I am sure see that an incident of that character is wholly different from the general exclusion from Court functions which is the rule, and that it inflicts a serious humiliation upon the Duke where he is only obeying an official summons which he receives as a Knight of the Garter. The Garter ceremonies are so rare, the membership of the order is so small that public attention is able to distinguish any incident. On the last occasion the base press of the United States was filled with insulting references to the Duke and highly coloured accounts of his treatment at the Castle and a great deal of unkind comment was excited in London.

The Duke has been unhappy in married life, but he is respected in his country and in his home. He has been three times chosen Mayor of Woodstock. He commands a regiment of Your Majesty's Yeomanry. He is a member of the Privy Council. He has served in the field. He has been Under Secretary of State for the Colonies and it is not at all improbable that he would receive office, subject to Your Majesty's approval, if a Conservative Government were returned to power.

Having regard to all this I would venture most respectfully to ask your Majesty whether the special circumstances of the Chapter of the Garter do not separate it from the regular Court function in such a way as to enable distinction to be drawn in the case of Knights attending the Chapter without any prejudice to the general rule.

Your Majesty has always been most kind and gracious to the Duke and I know well Sir what will be the wishes of Your Majesty's heart in the matter. If it were not for the fact that there seems to be very good grounds of principle for treating a Chapter of the Garter as standing on a different footing to regular Court ceremonies, I would not have presumed to trespass upon Your

Majesty's indulgence always extended with so much favour to Your Majesty's faithful and devoted servant and subject

WINSTON S. CHURCHILL

Lord Knollys to WSC
(Royal Archives)

22 May 1911   Buckingham Palace

Copy

My dear Churchill,

The King desires me to acknowledge the receipt of your letter of yesterday respecting the Duke of Marlborough.

He agrees with you in thinking that there is a difference between the Duke of Marlborough being invited to the Luncheon, which will be given at Windsor Castle to the Knights of the Garter on the 10th June, and to his being asked to an ordinary Court Function.

He has therefore told the Master of the Household to send the Duke of Marlborough an invitation to the Luncheon in question, but he is sure the Duke of Marlborough will understand that in taking this step it must not be supposed that his Majesty proposes to abrogate the general rule, which affects him in regard to his coming to Court.

Yours sincerely
KNOLLYS

WSC to the King
(Royal Archives)

23 May 1911   Home Office

Mr Secretary Churchill with his humble duty to Your Majesty: Yesterday the House of Commons discussed the Budget Resolutions. That relating to tea was the subject of the usual preferential amendment in favour of tea grown within the British Empire. As nearly all our tea comes already from within the British Empire any preference would involve a vy serious loss to the revenue, without a corresponding gain to the consumer. The amendment was negatived by a majority of 65. The House was small & good tempered. It disposed of the remaining financial business rapidly, and rose at 7.30, the Finance Bill having been formally brought in.

Mr Churchill desires to express to Your Majesty his sincere thanks for the gracious kindness with which Your Majesty has treated him in coming so promptly to a decision upon the case of the Duke of Marlborough. The Duke is vy grateful, & quite understands that the general rule which affects his coming to Court is in no way altered. Mr Churchill is vy deeply recognisant of the favour & patience which Your Majesty has shown to him in permitting him to bring such a matter to Your Majesty's notice.

Humbly submitted by Your Majesty's faithful & devoted servant & subject

WINSTON S. CHURCHILL

WSC to the King
(*Royal Archives*)

[? 24 May 1911]   Home Office

Mr Secretary Churchill with his humble duty to Your Majesty: the House yesterday discussed the Ordnance vote. An atmosphere of apathy prevailed and after a tame debate on Woolwich questions the House rose at 6.30.

The Insurance Bill is the only political topic now engaging the attention of members. The Conservative leaders are secretly hostile to this measure and the organised & persistent attacks directed upon it in the London newspapers are probably inspired. There is however a considerable body of Conservatives who are genuinely friendly to the Bill, & this may become manifest during the Committee stage. But for the present all politics are in abeyance.

Submitted by Your Majesty's faithful & devoted servant

WINSTON S. CHURCHILL

WSC to the King
(*Royal Archives*)

25 May 1911   Home Office

Mr Secretary Churchill with his humble duty to Your Majesty: There is so much general agreement between politicians upon the principle of compulsory Insurance that the opposition of the large but rather selfish interests wh has been aroused in the country is almost without a spokesman. No doubt this will make itself felt in Committee, but now upon the 2nd Reading there is an almost unbroken chorus of assent, approval, & finally suggestion. The best speech yesterday was made by young Mr Waldorf Astor, who confined himself to the provisions affecting the cure & prevention of tuberculosis, from wh he has at one time been a sufferer. The knowledge & distinction of the speech and the pleasant manner of delivery won great praise from all sides & quarters of the House.

The Attorney General made a long & full exposition of Invalidity & Sickness Insurance extending even into todays sitting. The President of the Board of Trade dealt with Unemployment. Mr Churchill proposed to deal further with this latter branch in the course of this afternoon's debate.

All of which is humbly submitted by Your Majestys faithful servant

WINSTON S. CHURCHILL

WSC to the King
(Royal Archives)

27 May 1911   Home Office

Mr Secretary Churchill with his humble duty to Your Majesty desires to offer his sincere congratulations to Your Majesty upon this auspicious day[1] & to express his heartfelt wish & hope that Your Majesty's life & health may be prolonged during many happy years of that Kingly service to the nation & the Empire which Your Majesty is proud to render.

The Insurance Bill was further debated on Thursday in the House of Commons. The Attorney General concluded his long & carefully considered exposition of the details of the Invalidity scheme; & Mr Churchill dealt at length with the Unemployment Section. The House continues overwhelmingly favourable. The interests in the country which are affected are restless, but the power of the two great parties when agreed upon a general principle is so complete, that minor grievances are scarcely articulate. The Chancellor of the Exchequer will speak on Monday when the debate will be completed.

Yesterday a private member's Bill dealing with Poor Law Administration in London was discussed, but after an appeal from Mr Burns that the House 'should not swap institutional horses when crossing the Insurance stream' the measure was talked out without a decision being taken.

All of which is humbly submitted to Your Majesty.

WSC to the King
(Royal Archives)

[31 May 1911]   Home Office

Mr Secretary Churchill with his humble duty to Your Majesty: The Insurance Bill was read a second time on Monday. The only difference apparent between the parties is that many of the Conservatives favour the

[1] The King's official birthday.

Bill being delayed till next year, while the Government is most anxious to proceed with it immediately.

Yesterday the Trade Union Bill of wh Mr Churchill has charge was debated. This Bill gives the Trade Unions the power to take part in politics if they decide to do so, but at the same time it provides effectively for those who do not agree with their politics being free not to subscribe to the political fund. The Opposition did not severely attack the measure, & on a division being forced at 11 o'clock only 18 members voted against the 2nd Reading to 219 in its favour. Considering how thorny this subject has proved in the past the reception of the Bill must be regarded as vy satisfactory.

Other business has also progressed. The Shops Bill is more than half through Grand Committee: and the Aerial Bill to regulate the movements of aircraft was passed through all its stages in the House last night & will be passed through the House of Lords on Thursday. It will thus have become law in less than a week from its first introduction.

All of which is humbly submitted by Your Majesty's faithful servant

WINSTON S. CHURCHILL

WSC to the King
(*Royal Archives*)

1 June 1911   Home Office

Mr Secretary Churchill with his humble duty to Your Majesty: The House yesterday discussed various topics in the motion for the Whitsuntide Adjournment. The deputy Chairman ruled that it was not competent to raise the question of Mr Churchill's remarks on the previous evening with reference to the disadvantages attaching to the connexion of the Courts with issues involving class & party feeling. Mr Churchill would have welcomed an opportunity of dealing further with the subject on which he had taken the opinion of the Cabinet in the morning. He hopes that if Your Majesty's attention should be drawn to the incident his words may be read in their actual text & context.

Colonel Morgan's appointment was sharply criticised from various quarters, but Colonel Seely with his usual ability & good manners defended the Secretary of State for War.[1]

Humbly submitted by Your Majesty's faithful servant

WINSTON S. CHURCHILL

[1] In 1905 a Committee of Inquiry set up to examine the relationship between contractors and the Army Service Corps in South Africa concluded that surplus war stores were being sold off at low prices to contractors, and then resold to the Army at a profit. Colonel Morgan, who had been Director of Supplies, was held responsible by the Committee for bringing this about. In May 1911 he was appointed messing adviser to the War Office and allowed to

WSC to his wife
(*CSC Papers*)

2 June 1911   Blenheim Camp

My sweet and beloved Clemmie,

The weather is gorgeous and the whole Park in gala glories. I have been out drilling all the morning & my poor face is already a sufferer from the sun. The air however is deliciously cool. We have 3 regiments here, two just outside the ornamental gardens, & the 3rd over by Bladon.

I have 104 men in the squadron & a vy nice new young officer – Valentine Fleming's younger brother – 'the lesser flamingo'. FE is here and everything promises to be vy pleasant. Many congratulations are offered me upon the son. With that lack of jealousy wh ennobles my nature, I lay them all at your feet.

My precious pussy cat, I do trust & hope that you are being good, & not sitting up or fussing yourself. Just get well & strong & enjoy the richness wh this new event will I know have brought into your life. The Chumbolly must do his duty and help you with your milk, you are to tell him so from me. At his age greediness & even swinishness at table are virtues.

We are all going to bathe in the lake this evening. The water is said to be quite warm. No cats allowed! How I wish you were here, it wd be such fun for you – there are lots of young men to [talk?] with & sounds of music, & beautiful trees & all sorts of things, including in a corner your ever loving & devoted Pug.

Always my darling your own loving Winston.

The Tories threaten to move a vote of censure on me after Whitsuntide. I hope they will. They are really too idiotic.

There are scores of precedents for the language I used about the Courts & including Mr Gladstone & many of the great Parliamentarians.

Two thousand kisses my sweet birdling

Your own for ever.

This goes to you by the King's messenger who is taking the box.

WSC to the King
(*Royal Archives*)

2 June 1911   Blenheim

Mr Secretary Churchill with his humble duty to Your Majesty: The House was yesterday abandoned to the Scottish members who discussed

---

retain at the same time a number of directorships. Colonel Seely declared that Colonel Morgan was best fitted for the job and had done nothing wrong in South Africa.

Scotch estimates with vigour. The Lord Advocate was fully equal to dealing with all the critics, but the whole sitting was occupied till 11 o'clock with the discussion, during which the absence of the English, Welsh & Irish members gave the House the air of a Scotch Parliament. Mr Churchill being on duty here with the Yeomanry in camp will not be able to send your Majesty any bulletin of todays proceedings, wh will however also be concerned with Scotch business.

Humbly submitted by Your Majesty's faithful servant

WINSTON S. CHURCHILL

WSC to his wife
(*CSC Papers*)

5 June 1911   Blenheim

Secret

Lock up or destroy

My dearest,

Both your letters have now arrived. You should address them Q.O.O.H. [Queen's Own Oxfordshire Hussars] Blenheim Camp, not Palace, (wh latter produces delay).

I am so glad you are both progressing so well. Ten ounces since last Tuesday is indeed good. I hope he is helping you as well as himself!

French[1] is away motoring & my letter will probably not reach him till tomorrow. This is late for our plans. Yesterday afternoon I went for a long drive and walk with the King [of Portugal][2]. He is really a vy charming boy – full of gravity & conviction, & yet in spite of his sorry plight – a boy brimful of life & spirits. He has a great air, natural and compulsive. He is extremely clever and accomplished. We made great friends. In harmony with my duty & British interests, I will do my best to help him. He wants to come & dine at [33] Eccleston [Square] to meet a few men. I am suggesting Friday 16th. You could receive him on a sofa in the library & then go up again to bed – if you felt well enough.

He told me much about his views of Portugal & his hopes of returning soon by a *coup d'etat*. I had to be extremely guarded so as not to raise false hopes, or encourage adventures in wh I shd not share the risks. I talked to

[1] John Denton Pinkstone French (1852–1925), CIGS 1911–14; Commander 1st Army Corps 1901–7; Field-Marshal 1913; C-in-C of the BEF 1914–15; C-in-C of U.K. troops 1915–18; Lord Lieutenant of Ireland 1918–21.

[2] Manoel II (1889–1932), King of Portugal 1908–10; succeeded his father Carlos I when he was assassinated; deposed October 1910, and lived in Twickenham.

him about the Church – such a strong ally, but demanding such a heavy price, & entailing so many powerful foes in a modern state. You will see the difficulty for yourself. It is his main prop. Yet priestly rule & ascendancy will always I trust encounter staunch resistance from free & enlightened men. He said nothing cd be achieved without religion. He began our talk by saying – Mr Ch I am not a leader of the democracy. I am a King and it is as a King I must manage my affairs.

I must say I do not see why we should be in a hurry to recognise this provisional Republic. Their leaders still condone & glorify the murder of King Carlos, & the State Museum exhibits the ghastly trophies of that event. The elections have been carried by force & terrorism. But on the other hand – the Catholic Church has ruined every country in wh it has been supreme, & worked the downfall of every dynasty that ruled in its name. How then to reconcile Past & Present – and to do this without sapping those stubborn forces upon wh the counter-revolution must rely. These are deeper problems than the inquiring mind of this intelligent, good Master & devout young exile has yet reached.

We all marched past this morning – walk, trot & gallop. Jack & I took our squadrons at the real pace and excited the spontaneous plaudits of the crowd. The Berkshires who followed cd not keep up & grumbled. After the march past I made the General form the whole Brigade into Brigade Mass and gallop 1200 strong the whole length of the park in one solid square of men & horses. It went awfully well. He was delighted. No news about the night march yet.

Yes Balfour has written to A. [Asquith] protesting agst FE being made a PC [Privy Councillor] & to FE to tell him so.

There is a lot of soft sawder about his great position & prospects and about Hayes Fisher's long services (as a wretched Whips' room hack & county council wirepuller) & his misfortunes (due entirely to AJB); but the main purpose is pretty plain. They want to keep him (FE) back.

The result is important either way. If FE does not get it, he will not forgive Balfour. If he does, Balfour will not forgive him. But what an insight into the fatuous & arrogant mind of the Hotel Cecil, wh even at its last gasp, would rather inflict any amount of injury upon the Tory party than share power with any able man of provincial origin. So may it long continue.

And now my sweet little darling with my fondest love I sign myself your devoted friend & husband

W

WSC to his wife
(*CSC Papers*)

7 June 1911   Blenheim

My dearest,
    I am going to come home tomorrow & will reach you before dinner. I
am longing to see you & the Ch B. again. He really seems a wonder to put
on weight. I will have dinner with you in your room my darling & tell you
all my news & give you lots of kisses on your dear cheeks & dearest lips.
    We have been out all day sham fighting, & as usual opinions differ about
the result. The party has gone and the Palace is solitary except the Goonie.
With much love
                                            Always your devoted husband
                                                                   W

WSC to the King
(*Royal Archives*)

21 June 1911   Home Office

    Mr Secretary Churchill with his humble duty to Your Majesty: The
passage of the Consolidated Fund Bill yesterday was the occasion of one
unpleasant little scene, when Mr Ketby-Fletcher[1] a new and rather ill-
mannered young member abused the Chancellor of the Exchequer as a
'country solicitor' & charged him with having used his influence to get one
of his former partners into a government situation. This charge being untrue,
a withdrawal was forced upon the offender by the House & recorded by the
Chair.
    It is not unlikely that after the festivities & rejoicings of the Coronation
are ended, there will be an ebullition of ill-temper as a reaction. Apparently
the Parliament Bill will be disposed of by the House of Lords early in July,
& the difficulties of a deadlock may then arise.
    The Honours List has been vy well received and the fact that recognition
has been accorded to both parties by Your Majesty is generally applauded.
    Mr Churchill was delighted that General Brabazon[2] should be included in
it. The general was deeply gratified by Your Majesty's kind words to him.
    The most interesting of the new Privy Councillors is undoubtedly Mr

---

[1] J. R. Ketby-Fletcher (1869–1918), a journalist and Liverpool merchant; Conservative
MP for Altrincham 1910–13 when he resigned his seat.
[2] John Palmer Brabazon (1843–1922), appointed to command 4th Hussars 1893; WSC's
first Commanding Officer; Commander of 2nd Cavalry Brigade, South African Field Force
1899–1900, and Imperial Yeomanry February to December 1900; knighted in the 1911
Coronation honours list.

F. E. Smith. This honour conferred upon him by Your Majesty will give great satisfaction to the Tory working men who regard him with the utmost favour. It will also add sensibly to his influence upon affairs. Humbly submitted by Your Majesty's faithful & devoted servant

WINSTON S. CHURCHILL

WSC to Sir Edward Grey

21 June 1911   Home Office

[Copy]

Private

My dear Grey,

I have just read Villiers'[1] telegram of 16th in ten sections. Surely this question of recognition cannot be made contingent on a small isolated incident like the application of the law of separation.[2] Very likely they are only being disagreeable in order to get what they want. I hope before you finally make up your mind you will let me have another talk with you. I am sure that the time has not yet come for recognizing the revolutionary Govt. The situation is not ordinary, & involves issues far more important than anything connected with S American republics. I know that your mind has been more turned to the first class questions connected with arbitration & the Japanese alliance than upon Portuguese affairs. Of course I know so little about these matters that I write with hesitation to you on them. But first have you any information about the Portuguese election? Has Villiers written despatches about them, or about the effect upon the country people of the law of separation? If so, could I, or could the Cabinet, see these reports?

Secondly, have you considered the Spanish aspect? Why is Spain leaning on Germany? Why has she been so stiff to France? Is it not clear that events in Portugal may be of profound consequence to the Sp monarchy? Braga[3] has declared that his Govt look forward to the establishment of republics in all the Latin countries. Deeply rooted in the hearts of the Spaniards is the desire to absorb Portugal. Can we not conceive circ^s arising wh wd

[1] Francis Hyde Villiers (1852–1925), Envoy Extraordinary and Minister Plenipotentiary to Portugal 1911–19; Assistant Under-Secretary of State for Foreign Affairs 1896–1905; to Belgium 1919–20; knighted 1906; PC 1919.

[2] The Portuguese Republic, proclaimed in 1910, had still not been recognized by the British Government.

[3] Dr Theophil Braga (1843–1924), became President of the Portuguese Republic when King Manoel was deposed in October 1910.

make it the vital interest of the Sp monarchy to place Sp patriotism and Portuguese republicanism in the sharpest antagonism, thus smothering Spanish republicanism? Can we not conceive the possibility of Spain receiving support at such a juncture from some powerful European monarchy with Colonial appetites? Has not Portugal got Colonial possessions of the highest consequence to us – and to Germany? I only open up this line of thought, without attempting to connect it with immediate policy.

Thirdly, what are the real wishes of the interested Powers? Does France like the Portuguese revolution[8] or is she secretly disquieted. The German Emperor must hate it – except for the chance of fishing in troubled waters. St Petersburg cannot like it – Italy cannot like it – and the King of Spain!

What will be the effect on the policy of these powers of our recognising the Republic? Our position as the 600 years ally of the Portuguese monarchy invests our action with peculiar significance. If we recognize, the others must follow, whatever their secret feelings. Yet the independence & stability of Portugal – which can I am sure only be secured under a limited monarchy – is a safeguard to us against the opening of vy grave questions. We have laboured from Blenheim to Toulouse to prevent the Peninsula and its oversea possessions from falling under the control of the greatest military power on the Continent. The fundamental antagonism wh naturally exists between the monarchical Govt of Spain & the republican Govt of Portugal may lead to conditions of deep insecurity in the not distant future. The decision of Gt Britain to take a step wh will be widely regarded & universally represented as a pronouncement in favour of the Republic & of the republican movement may determine the action of the Sp monarchy, wh after all holds the reins.

My feeling is that this situation shd be handled by the Powers in concert, & I was delighted to find you had this view also. But further I earnestly suggest to you that we shd ask them what they think in such a manner as to invite or at least encourage the answer that the time has not yet come for recognition. In this way we shd be able to await without risk the further developments in Portuguese internal affairs. We shd be acting in common with Spain & Germany. We shd not take sides against the Portuguese Monarchy. We shd I believe prevent the squalid course of events in Portugal from opening up any of the deep fissures wh undoubtedly exist beneath the crust of the Peninsula.

Pray do not take this letter amiss. It is written in no spirit of meddling.

Yours vy sincly

[WSC]

WSC to his wife
(*CSC Papers*)

25 June 1911   Hartsbourne Manor
                                                Herts

My darling Clemmie,
    It rained all the morning so I stayed in bed & ruminated amid my boxes.
At luncheon [JM] Barrie[1] arrived – but I am vy sorry to say that he went
off again unexpectedly this afternoon without my ever having a talk with
him. I am vexed at this because I am sure I like him – and always something
crops up to prevent my getting to know him.
    Curzon cd not come – ill. But Mamma is here and Muriel [Wilson] comes
to dinner. Maxine[2] [Elliott, his hostess] is so nice. She has a new bullfinch –
arrived only last night & already it sits on her shoulder and eats seeds out
of her mouth. See how much these innocent little birds know! I went for a
long walk in the rain with Alex Thynne[3] – and talked all the time. I like
him. He is just one of these young Tories who wd have followed my father
or me with perfect satisfaction. But now – without leaders or ideas or plan –
they drift off into all sorts of foolish backwaters of thought.
    Maxine sends you her best love. She & I spent a long time last night
singing your praises. Did the Cat's ear burn!
    The general turn-out on Friday made a great impression. Everyone
admired the cat, the carriage, the horses and the tiger – separately, but in
combination they fairly lifted the sultana. It really was great fun, & I am
sure you will long look back to our drive & will like to tell the PK & the
Chumbolly all about it [the Coronation] – so it will become a tradition in
the family & they will hand it on to others whom we shall not see. Dear
me, I have thought of you with tender love to-day. May all blessings be
yours & all good fortune.
    I did not tell you that I wrote at gt length to Grey about Portugal & made
out a vy strong case for non-recognition of those sanguinary swine.
    He has agreed to take the first step I advocated – i.e. to write to the other
Powers in such a way as to give them a strong lead to say that they think
the time is premature.
    I am sending this up by a special messenger who will find your address

[1] James Matthew Barrie (1860–1937), novelist and playwright.
[2] Maxine Elliott (1868–1940), born Jessie Dermot in Rockland, Maine, she adopted the
name 'Maxine Elliott' for her stage career. A famous hostess, she organized a Belgian Relief
Barge during the First World War from which, in fifteen months, she fed and clothed some
350,000 people.
[3] Alexander George Thynne (1873–1918), Conservative MP for Bath 1910–18; killed in
action; third son of 4th Marquess of Bath.

in London & will send it off to-night so that I hope it will reach you early tomorrow morning.

With fondest love, Your own ever loving Husband

W

Do ask Grey to be godfather – I am sure it is a vy good idea, & will give him great pleasure. I am always hearing nice things he has said about me. He likes and wistfully admires our little circle. What do you think?

WSC to the King
(*Royal Archives*)

27 June 1911   Home Office

Mr Secretary Churchill with his humble duty to Your Majesty: The Home Office vote being set down for debate yesterday, Mr Lyttelton made a speech raking up a lot of old stories about Sidney Street, Tonypandy & the Dartmoor Shepherd, to wh Mr Churchill endeavoured to reply – as was thought by his friends – not without some measure of success. Thereafter the debate produced a long discursive conversation on Factory legislation. This wide field affords no soil for controversy and many useful and well informed speeches occupied the time till dinner. The Opposition moved formally a reduction of £500 on the salary of the Home Secretary, and as the Irish members were away, half the Labour members absent, ministers at the gala and holiday moods in the air, this flagitious proposal was rejected only by a majority of 32.

All of which is humbly submitted by Your Majesty's faithful servant

WINSTON S. CHURCHILL

WSC to the King
(*Royal Archives*)

29 June 1911   Home Office

Mr Secretary Churchill with his humble duty to Your Majesty: Mr McKinnon Wood opened the debate yesterday on the Declaration of London with a full and lucid justification & explanation of its policy. The First Lord of the Admiralty who spoke after dinner was able to state that both Lord Fisher & Sir Arthur Wilson[1] were in favour of the Declaration. On

---

[1] Arthur Knyvet Wilson (1842–1921), First Sea Lord 1909–11; promoted upon his first retirement in 1907 to Admiral of the Fleet; knighted 1902; Order of Merit 1912; succeeded brother as 3rd Baronet 1919; won Victoria Cross for gallantry at El Teb 1884.

the other side there has been a great eagerness to attack it and the Government have now consented to allow the debate to continue on Monday. It seems a serious inroad in Parliamentary time, but the Ministers concerned feel bound to make their case good. The Admiralty view is that the declaration is of small practical significance, but on the whole beneficient.

Humbly submitted by Your Majesty's faithful servant

WINSTON S. CHURCHILL

WSC to his wife
(CSC Papers)

3 July 1911   [House of Commons]

My darling,

All is well here. Hull is peaceful and the strike has been settled. It is impossible to deny that violence has played its part in this – but that was not my fault. The House supported me warmly to-day on the sending of the police.

The German action in Morocco has caused a flutter. The French want us to send a *batiment* [*de guerre:* man-of-war] to Agadir. This would be a serious step on wh we shd not engage without being ready to go all lengths if necessary. There is to be a special Cabinet tomorrow on the question. I have written a letter to Tuttie [Baron de Forest] wh you will see in tomorrow's papers.

I am writing these lines to you on the bench while Grey is defending (vy ably) his Declaration of London. There is no news besides – except that Symes will probably get 12 months during wh his mind will get either better or worse.

My cold is pronounced but simple. What a bore to catch cold in July!

I enjoyed my Sunday so much. It was a wonderful thing to see the whole family rallied & marshalled under a single roof. I was so glad that you were making such good progress. It will be wise of you to stay for another fortnight. There is nothing like making a complete recovery. A set back is so disheartening. I fear it will seem a little dull – but it is worth it.

I am going to dine with Seely & then coming back to vote here in this important division.

Write to me regularly & think often of your own loving & devoted husband

W

WSC to the King
(*Royal Archives*)

4 July 1911   Home Office

Mr Secretary Churchill with his humble duty to Your Majesty: The Government is strongly of opinion that it emerged victorious from the long debate on the Declaration of London. Sir Edward Grey's speech yesterday was an admirably lucid & cogent exposition of the case for ratification. The Prime Minister wound up the debate vy vigorously and the chagrin of some members of the Opposition was such as to induce them to hail the result of the vote with cries of 'Traitors'. These expressions of opinion besides being unParliamentary, are unflattering to the Colonial Premiers who have unanimously approved the Declaration. The main points on wh Ministers rest are these: 1. We cannot stand outside the general movement of international agreements except for reasons of the utmost gravity. None such are involved in the Declaration. 2. As neutrals we gain clear advantages in the substitution of an International for a partisan Prize court, & on minor points. 3. As belligerents for our food supply we must rely not on any paper instrument, but on our own naval strength – but we gain considerable advantages in the general adoption by European powers of our views about Blockade.

While some of the misgivings of the Opposition were undoubtedly respectable & sincere, their case was spoiled by a great deal of mis-statement and misrepresentation.

Mr Churchill takes this opportunity of expressing his sincere hope that Your Majesty has not felt unduly fatigued by the great exertion of the last fortnight. He knows from his own experiences when driving with Your Majesty last Friday how very tiring long hours amid crowds & in the glare are. He feels that the strain upon both Your Majesty & the Queen must have been vy severe: and although the unquestionable success which has marked every step & every function is no doubt a strong stimulus, yet it must have been necessary for Your Majesty to draw upon the reserves of physical & nervous energy to meet such exceptional demands. He hopes that Your Majesty may find the Irish, Welsh & Scottish celebrations less onerous & exacting.

And with his humble duty submits the above

WINSTON S. CHURCHILL

WSC to his wife
(*CSC Papers*)

5 July 1911   Home Office

My darling,

I have got a vile cold in the head wh makes me thoroughly uncomfortable, & so far remedies have proved very inefficacious. This is the first summer cold I can remember. I wonder how I caught it.

I am sorry the nurserymaid is a hussy. 'Don't hesitate to sack', as Balfour wd have it. I hope to come down to you for the Sunday – but I wd much rather not dine out. Let us dine together quietly. We can go & lunch if you like with the B.B's and look at the garden afterwards.

I missed the post last night but I trust this will reach you during the day.

You will read the Symes case in the newspapers. Darling[1] of course cd not resist a chance of being funny. Six months is not a vy satisfactory ending. His friends are going to try to get him out of the country; & this if possible I shall facilitate.

LG, Grey, Haldane & I dined together last night and made good progress on the Home Rule problem. But I hope we may get some aid from the other side. Meanwhile the Lords go on tearing the Veto Bill to shreds. I shall be vy glad when the crisis actually comes.

We decided to use pretty plain language to Germany and to tell her that if she thinks Morocco can be divided up without John Bull, she is jolly well mistaken.

A gent (who wants a baronetcy) has sent me a most interesting correspondence with my father in *1892* in wh the latter absolutely repudiates Protection & predicts the ruin of the Tory Party if ever they go in for it. I will send you a copy. I wish I had known of it before.

Beauchamp the Doctor has just been. He thinks I am getting on vy well: but one feels so heavy & foolish with a congested nose.

With my fondest love (I am in no condition to offer kisses)

Your ever devoted husband
W

[1] Charles John Darling (1849–1936), Judge of the King's Bench Division of the High Court of Justice 1897–1923; QC 1885; Conservative MP Deptford 1888–97. Created Baron Darling of Langham 1924. Biography by Sir Derek Walker-Smith: *The Life of Lord Darling* 1938.

WSC to the King
(*Royal Archives*)

10 July 1911   Home Office

Mr Secretary Churchill with his humble duty to Your Majesty: The Insurance Bill is making good progress and the Chancellor of the Exchequer is patiently & skilfully disarming opposition and compacting differences. In the first six days of the discussion the Government will probably have succeeded in getting almost as far without any form of closure as they would have got under a regular guillotine time table. The general aspect of the House is painstaking but weary.

The result of the West Ham election[1] is much commented on. Baron de Forest's large majority was quite unexpected by friends & foes – of which latter are there not a few. It is vy welcome to the government and comes most opportunely. Four new members took their seats this afternoon – two for each party to cheer – but the West Ham representative received the best ovation.

Mr Churchill is vy glad indeed to tell Your Majesty that the Manchester strike difficulty has been settled. The men have received large and justifiable concessions in regard to their wages. All the troops & extra policemen have been withdrawn. General Macready[2] is returning tonight. The Greys have already gone North for Edinburgh.

Mr Churchill is glad to be able to inform your Majesty that all difficulties in regard to Sir Edward Henry's accompanying Your Majesty to India have been successfully overcome. That officer will also be on the spot at Carnarvon.

The hearty welcome wh your Majesty has received from the Irish people is vy gratifying to all parties here & not the least to those who look forward to a complete national reconciliation being effected between the two peoples under the aegis of the Crown during Your Majesty's reign.

Humbly submitted by Your Majesty's faithful & devoted servant & subject

WINSTON S. CHURCHILL

[1] At the West Ham by-election on 8 July Baron de Forest, standing as Liberal candidate, beat his Conservative opponent by 6,087 votes to 5,776. The by-election had been caused by the unseating on petition of Masterman.

[2] Cecil Frederick Nevil Macready (1862–1946), Director of Personnel Services 1910–14; served in Egypt and South Africa 1898–1902; Colonel 1903; Major-General 1910; Adjutant-General, B.E.F., 1914–16; Lt-General 1916; Adjutant-General to the Forces 1916–18; General 1918; GOC Forces in Ireland 1920–2.

WSC to his wife
(*CSC Papers*)

14 July 1911   [Penrhos]

My darling Clemmie,

It was indeed a beautiful and moving ceremony wh I witnessed yesterday.[1] The little prince looked & spoke as well as it was possible for anyone to do. The enthusiasm was sincere & unbounded. The great radical crowds gave the King & his son the best of welcomes. It was a most happy event & will long live in the memories of all who took part in it.

My reading of the Patent was much praised & I thought went well. I returned after the ceremony to the Yacht & dined again on board. The PM was also bidden. He had a good & useful talk with the King. I am vy glad I suggested this meeting. Things are clearly tending to a pretty sharp crisis. What are you to do with men whose obstinacy & pride have blinded them to their interests and to every counsel of reason. It would not be surprising if we actually have to create the 500. We shall not boggle about it when it comes to the pinch.

I decided to spend last night & tonight at Penrhos and not to go to Criccieth till Saturday. It is vy pleasant here. The weather perfect: the garden delicious. We all bathe each morning and lie & bask on the hot rocks. How I wish you were here my dearest, & how glorious you wd look in your thinnest Venetian bathing dress!

The PM is in great form – apparently without a care in the world quite happy talking to the young. Sylvia[2] is here as well as Blanche[3] and Mrs Goodenough. Eddie [Marsh] leaves tonight. I shall be in London early Monday morning.

This afternoon we motored to a large sandy bay & paddled about placidly. I was not vy much amused by this. My cold still hangs in a feeble way about me. I don't think the bathing does it any harm. Though the sun is vy hot there is a fresh cool breeze. It is a good holiday – I have scarcely even opened my boxes to-day.

I shall find you all gathered at Eccleston on Monday I trust to receive the Head of the Family, on his return. I hope you got the money all right.

With fondest love Ever your devoted

W

[1] The investiture of the Prince of Wales at Carnarvon Castle. As Home Secretary WSC read out the Letters Patent instructing the investiture.

[2] Sylvia Laura Stanley, daughter of the fourth baron Stanley. She married in 1906 Brigadier-General Hon Anthony Morton Henley.

[3] Blanche Florence Daphne Stanley, Sylvia Stanley's sister. She married in 1912 Brigadier-General Eric Pearce-Serocold.

PS Much chaff by Violet[1] & the PM of Venetia[2] – who is alleged to have flirted with McKenna to the effect that on his saying to her at Golf 'Come along my little mascot' she replied (she denies this) 'I wish I were – & then I could hang on your watch chain.' Wrath of Venetia. Do not spread this. It is a good joke for a few people only.

WSC to the King
(*Royal Archives*)
17 July 1911   Home Office

Mr Secretary Churchill with his humble duty to Your Majesty: The Insurance Bill has again occupied the House of Commons today. The principal point of discussion has been whether the payment of sick benefit should begin immediately or not until the 4th day. The Chancellor of the Exchequer strongly urged the latter course. It is vy desirable to prevent malingering that all the little ailments should be cleared out of the benefit area. The extra cost involved in running the 4th day safeguard is £560,000 a year. The Conservatives and the Labour party however joined together in pressing the more profuse course upon the Government, and on a division the Government majority fell to 40. This was however one of the awkward corners of the Bill. It is so easy to advocate generosity when other people have to find the money. The debate is proceeding.

Submitted by Your Majesty's faithful & devoted servant

WINSTON S. CHURCHILL

WSC to the King
(*Royal Archives*)
19 July 1911   Home Office

Mr Secretary Churchill with his humble duty to Your Majesty: Yesterday after the debate had passed the point at wh the letter was written to Your Majesty a vy remarkable incident occurred. Certain effective safeguards against malingering are provided in the Insurance Bill and are necessary to secure the soundness of the finance & the solvency of the Friendly Societies. The Labour Party & the Conservative party in unbroken chorus condemned these provisions as reflections upon the character of the working classes, and a lot of maudlin and disingenuous language was used to the effect that workmen never do wrong and never malinger and so forth. The Liberal supporters of the Government were very uneasy and apprehended a campaign of

---

[1] Violet Asquith (1887–1969), daughter of H. H. Asquith; married 1915 Sir Maurice Bonham Carter (1880–1960); created Baroness Asquith of Yarnbury (Life peerage) 1964.
[2] Beatrice Venetia Stanley, sister of Sylvia and Blanche. She married in 1915 Rt Hon Edwin Montagu.

prejudice being directed against them in the constituencies. In nearly 3 hours debate the Ministry had only one articulate supporter.

Up got the Chancellor of the Exchequer just before 8 o'clock & in a vy short but vy courageous speech, delivered with great earnestness & air of command, swept away all this nonsense, declared that malingering was a real danger, that everyone knew workmen were often guilty of it, that the working classes did not respect mere flatterers, that the financial soundness of the scheme was the real road to public credit, & that temporary obloquy should not be feared for the sake of good permanent arrangements. All delivered with great spirit. The effect on the House was most impressive. The Conservatives who in their hearts agreed with every word sat as openly ashamed as has ever been seen. The Liberals rallied to the Government & the Labour party actually split, half voting for the Conservative amendment & the others standing by the Chancellor of the Exchequer, who to universal surprise was triumphant in the division by 74 votes.

Mr Churchill never remembers to have seen the House so suddenly changed in its mood, or so swiftly recalled to a high sense of its dignity & duty.

Clause X is now being discussed.

With his humble duty the above is submitted by Your Majesty's faithful servant

WINSTON S. CHURCHILL

WSC to the King
(*Royal Archives*)

24 July 1911

Mr Secretary Churchill with his humble duty to Your Majesty: The Prime Minister was this afternoon subjected to prolonged organised insult & interruption from a section of the Conservative party, among whom Lord Hugh Cecil & Mr Goulding were the most prominent. For more than 25 minutes he attempted to deliver his speech, but in spite of the Speaker's appeals the Conservatives continued their rowdy and unreasonable disorder. He therefore confined himself to stating the course wh the Government would adopt without further argument or explanation.

It was therefore a great triumph of restraint on the part of the majority of the House, including as it does the Labour & Irish parties that they listened patiently and politely to a long & controversial speech from Mr Balfour, who acknowledged their courtesy & expressed regret for the behaviour of his friends.

Sir Edward Grey then rose and in a few impressive sentences told the Opposition that the Prime Minister would be the only spokesman of the Government and its supporters, & that if they would not listen to argument from him, 'no one on these benches will take his place.' Action would however follow on the lines wh the Prime Minister had marked out.

Mr F. E. Smith who had been himself vy disorderly attempted to continue the debate; but of course the House would not listen to him & the Speaker after some further clamour had arisen, held that a condition of grave disorder had been reached, & adjourned the House under the special rules.

The feeling on the Government side is one of sober resolve. The violence of the Opposition was limited to a section only of their party. The irritation of the Conservatives is no doubt natural: but their claim to govern the country whether in office or opposition and to resort to disorder because they cannot have their way will not in any circumstances be acquiesced in by the majority of the House of Commons.

Mr Churchill should add that Mr Balfour pointedly asked the Prime Minister *when* he had received the 'guarantees', & the Prime Minister refused to answer. This will however probably be pressed.

All of wh is humbly submitted by Your Majesty's faithful & devoted servant

WINSTON S. CHURCHILL

WSC to Sir Edward Grey

25 July 1911   Home Office
[Copy]

My dear Grey,

This is what I want to press upon yr consideration: – The conjunction of Spain & Germany is vy unfavourable for us. Germany can use Spain to create indefinite trouble in Morocco. She can also push her into an attack on the Portuguese Republic (wh wd suit the internal situation in Spain in certain circumstances); & the break-up of Portugal leads to the operation of the Secret Treaty, wh again is vy advantageous to Germany, & vy harmful to us. We ought therefore to try hard to win back Sp, to make good friends with her, & to promote friendly dealing betw Sp & France. It is not I think too late yet. The K of Sp[1] comes here next week & he ought not to be personally disinclined to the closest relations with England. But these

---

[1] Alfonso XIII (1886–1941), posthumous son of King Alfonso XII. He married in 1906 Princess Victoria Eugénie of Battenberg, niece of Edward VII. He abdicated in 1931.

will be impossible if we take any line in regard to Portugal wh ranges us as supporters of the Repub^n movement in the Peninsula. The main preoccupation of the Sp Govt is the security of the Monarchy, & any countenance given to the Port republic must throw Sp increasingly into the arms of Germany wh as the greatest monarchical power wd be the only support left. I trust that this aspect may be well thought over before any question of recognising the Port republic is decided.

I am vy glad that no step on this road has been taken yet. Some assurance of this kind to the K of Sp wd do much to facilitate friendly relations with that power, & they wd feel a confidence that we were not indifferent to the character of their institution.

Yrs vy sy
WSC

WSC to the King
(*Royal Archives*)

26 July 1911   Home Office

Mr Secretary Churchill with his humble duty to Your Majesty: There was some recrudescence of disorderly conduct at Question time yesterday owing partly to the irritation of the supporters of the Government at the events of Monday & mainly to the provocative attitude of Lord Hugh Cecil and his friends. A large section of the Conservative party deeply & sincerely regrets the shameful scene wh was then created. The ugliest feature was the absence of any real passion or spontaneous feeling. It was a squalid frigid organised attempt to insult the Prime Minister & to prevent debate. The ringleaders are however making themselves a distinct force as against Mr Balfour & there is no doubt that a great many Unionists in the country who are dissatisfied with his leadership will take the opportunity of supporting the rebels. It is noticeable that Mr Goulding & others acting with him did not rise from their seats to welcome their leader with the rest of the party, & no doubt had he appealed to them to desist from disorder they would have vy bluntly refused him. The spectacle of Lord Hugh Cecil, Mr F. E. Smith & Mr Worthington-Evans[1] now all concentrated below the gangway revives something of the old force of the Fourth Party in the eighties: & this should

---

[1] Laming Worthington-Evans (1868–1931), Conservative MP Colchester 1910–29, St George's 1929–31. Assumed prefix surname Worthington by Royal Licence, 1916; Minister of Blockade 1918; Minister of Pensions 1919–20; Minister without Portfolio 1920–1; Secretary for War 1921–2, 1924–9; Postmaster-General 1923–4; Baronet 1916; PC 1918.

be carefully watched if it develops as it may lead to considerable changes within the Unionist party itself.

The rest of the sitting was occupied in the peaceful discussion of the revenue Bill when the methods of valuation were debated.

Submitted by Your Majesty's faithful servant

WINSTON S. CHURCHILL

WSC to the King
(Royal Archives)

27 July 1911   Home Office

Mr Secretary Churchill with his humble duty to Your Majesty: A great moment in the House of Commons, showing at its very best the power & dignity of this country.[1] The Prime Minister made his statement – careful, & friendly in form & feeling, but strong & firm in substance. Then Mr Balfour – admirable, also vy short. No party dissensions even at their worst could affect national unity in great issues. Lastly Mr Ramsay Macdonald – restrained, sombre but perfectly correct. The whole three speeches together occupying less than half an hour – in a dead hush with occasional deep murmurs of assent.

No one else rose – the whole subject dropped & after a long pause a young Conservative member began to talk about Persia. It may well be that this episode following upon the speech of the Chancellor of the Exchequer will have exercised a decisive effect upon the peace of Europe. It is certain that it redounds to the credit of British public life.

Mr Churchill thought Your Majesty would like to have an immediate account. He has not attempted to reproduce the speeches wh can be read in a few minutes.

Humbly submitted by Your Majesty's faithful servant

WINSTON S. CHURCHILL

Lord Knollys to WSC

27 July 1911   Buckingham Palace

My dear Churchill,

I am desired by the King to thank you for having so promptly sent him an account of what took place in the House of Commons this afternoon on the German-Morocco question.

HM thinks it is very satisfactory that in the middle of the angry and excited

---

[1] The House was discussing the Agadir Crisis. Lloyd George had already warned Germany not to underestimate Britain's support for France when he spoke at the Mansion House.

passions aroused by the Constitutional crisis, all parties have united in supporting the Foreign policy of the Government.

Yours sincerely
KNOLLYS

Memorandum by WSC

[Undated]   Home Office

It is true G has some (minor) claims about Morocco wh if amicably stated we should be glad to see adjusted either there or elsewhere – subject to Brit int being safeguarded – wh ought not to be difficult.

Her action at Agadir has put her in the wrong & forced us to consider her claims in the light of her policy & methods.

We are bound to give diplomatic support to F in any discussion about Morocco: but are entitled to tell France if necessary & to make public fact that this is only diplomatic if we think she is unreasonable.

If no settlement is reached between F and G & dead lock results we must secure Brit interests independently. This again ought not to be impossible.

If Germany makes war on France in the course of the discussion or dead-lock (unless F has meanwhile after full warning from us taken unjustifiable ground) we shd join with France.

Germany should be told this now.

[WSC]

WSC to the King
(Royal Archives)

31 July 1911   House of Commons

Midnight

Mr Secretary Churchill with his humble duty to Your Majesty: The Insurance Bill again occupies the House of Commons. There appears to be no obstruction – so far – consequent upon the veto crisis. But the volume of the business wh must be transacted is vy considerable, & the Prime Minister seems adamant against an autumn session. If the House will stand it, it looks as if we shall sit to the middle of September. These are hard prospects!

The negotiations between France & Germany occupy the minds of Ministers.

Mr Churchill has felt it his duty to take more effective measures to ensure the safety of the great naval magazines, now under the guard of the Metro-politan Police. Chattenden & Lodge Hill alone hold 3/5ths of the cordite ammunition of the Fleet. Two companies of infantry have this night been sent to Chattenden – Lodge Hill – and one company to Marchwood. These especially the former are vital spots & it is high time to make absolutely sure of their safety. It is possible that some report of this may leak out & Mr Churchill thinks it right to apprise Your Majesty.

And with his humble duty submits the above.

WINSTON S. CHURCHILL

WSC to his wife
(CSC Papers)

2 August 1911   Home Office

My dearest,

I received with great pleasure your telegram. I hope the journey did not tire you too much.

The situation here develops well. The MPs kick so sensibly against sitting through August that the PM will be forced to yield. Parlt will be up probably by the 17th: & we shall all come back Nov 15. I will come out to you at once unless some vy serious troubles threaten here, & we will go to Cassel's Villa till the end of August. I am telegraphing him to-day and will let you know more tomorrow. We can potter home in time for the manœuvres. Blenheim is off. Let me know if you can make plans for bridging the interval between Garmisch and my coming. Bâle is evidently the rendezvous.

If I can get away sooner I will come sooner.

The Lords crisis is comical & complicated. The 'diehards' are about 100 (with the whole party at their back). Lansdowne has 324 abstainers: of whom 50 to 60 will follow Cromer & St Aldwyns into the Government Lobby. We have 75 wh with stray bishops & Court Officials may be 85. *But* at least 20 perhaps more of Lansdowne's abstainers say that if any Unionists follow Cromer and vote with the Government, they will hold themselves freed from their pledge to Lansdowne and vote against the Government.

Thus a creation wd be necessary or at least it is a damned near thing! And if one single peer is made Lansdowne & his gang will all vote against the Govt. What a whirlpool!

The split in the Tory Party is deep & bitter. We are going to take strong action: & it looks as if at least 300 will have to be made – if any are made.

To-day the news about the big thing is that the bully is climbing down & it looks as if all would come out smooth and triumphant.[1]

---

[1] A reference to the Kaiser's attitude following Lloyd George's Mansion House speech on Morocco.

I sent on Monday plenty of soldiers to both points I told you of: and all is safe now.[1]

I swam with Grey this morning, & the dinner last night (12 we were) was vy good.

> With fondest love Your devoted husband
> W

*WSC Note of conversations between the German Emperor and
Sir John French*

10 August [1911]

Secret

The Emperor arrived at Alton Grabow to inspect troops at 6 am on Wed Aug 2nd.

He rode at once on parade, & after riding down the line & speaking to the German Officers, he sent for me to speak to him.

He began by giving me a vy hearty welcome, & said that he wished me to see everything that there was to be seen. He added these words: 'Remember the French are now yr allies, & whatever you may tell your own people I trust to yr honour to see that nothing that transpires here is reported through you to France.'

At luncheon I was placed on HM's right, & he spoke vy freely on the political situation & military affairs generally.

The Emperor strongly deprecated Mr Lloyd George's [speech] at the Mansion House, describing it as provocative, encouraging France to resist him, & dangerous to the peace of Europe. He said he was the more surprised at our attitude on the Morocco question, because he had himself told the King (when in England in May) the action he had intended to take, & wh he actually did take. He gave me to understand that the Br Govt also knew long beforehand that he intended to send a warship to Agadir.

The Emperor told me that in his opinion the action of the French in Morocco had completely wiped out the Treaty of Algeciras, & had left the signatory Powers an absolutely free hand.

He said that he personally deplored the differences between Germany & England, but that they were none of his making & that if we interfered in the affairs of Germany, we must take the consequences.

He said we had always fought shoulder to shoulder, & were natural allies.

He further expressed the opinion that great wars of the future wd be

---

[1] See preceding letter (pp. 1105–6).

'racial', hence his reason for wishing all Europe to be as strong as possible against such possible contingencies as the 'Yellow Peril'.

I talked a good deal to him on technical military subjects, & took notes of what he said. They are not of importance from a political point of view, & so I am not including them in this précis.

On Thursday Aug 3rd I sat opposite the Emperor at luncheon, & he talked quite freely to me across the table. He had previously presented me with his photograph, saying in a jocular manner: – 'Here is your arch enemy, here is the disturber of the peace of Europe!'

HM said he considered his Army was as efficient a machine of war as any army cd possibly be made, & implied that it was superior to any in the world. He explained the system by wh the army is under his sole command & control. The War Minister has only to provide the money & deal with certain details of administration. He said that all officers' reports came direct to him, & were dealt with altogether in his Military Cabinet. Thus every officer understands that his future prospects depend upon the Emperor alone.

HM further remarked upon the necessity for being able to 'support one's politics with the sword' & of keeping the 'sword sharp'. He told me that I had seen how sharp the sword of Germany was in my experiences at Alton Grabow, & assured me that each separate arm was just as efficient as the Cavalry.

He added words to the effect: – 'Remember, those who run up against that sword will find it very sharp indeed'; & further: – 'I don't mean to interfere with you, nor do I mean you to interfere with me; & if you do, you will find how sharp the sword is.'

(Note. I cannot vouch that every word is accurate, but the sense is absolutely as stated).

Speaking of France, the Emperor said he had no fear but that he cd overrun her whenever he liked. He said her soldiers were brave & good, but he did not think the French Army was well led, or that their discipline was high. He said he did not think France wd ever fight him unless egged on and supported by us & our press. He particularly mentioned Harmsworth & the *Daily Mail*, also the late Moberly Bell[1] of *The Times*, as being most hostile to Germany & doing much harm.

The Emperor said his policy was not understood in England. That he had made proposals to Ld Rosebery when Foreign Minister 13 or 14 years ago, to occupy coaling stations conjointly with England, but that he had met with nothing but rebuffs. He said that he had afterwards concluded similar arrangements with Russia.

[1] Charles Frederick Moberly Bell (1847–1911), Managing Director, *The Times*, from 1908 until his death on 5 April 1911.

WSC to his wife
(*CSC Papers*)

6 August 1911   Blenheim

My dearest one,

I am staying in this quiet Sunday morning to make up my speech for tomorrow night. It is quite likely that the Tories will be so angry & excited after dinner that they will not let me be heard. But still I must have something ready on the 'wretched-man-I-do-not-wish-by-any-words-of-mine-to-add-to-the-anguish-which-you-no-doubt-feel' tack. All the indications now are that the Bill will be carried by about 80 Liberals, 4 Bishops, 4 King's friends (Knollys, Bigge etc) & 25 to 40 Independent Unionists against 70 to 80 diehards. If anything goes wrong we make 350 Peers at once. Sunny is going to speak on both the Vote of Censure & the Lord's Amendts. He is in the best of tempers & spirits.

They have all gone off to hear Dickson's first sermon. Ivor who has been reconnoitring says there are thirteen pages of it!

Blandford has a bad cough & is upstairs. He has been neglected at Eton & has come back looking vy poor & skinny.

There is no doubt the Germans are going to settle with the French on a friendly basis. They sent their *Panther* to Agadir & we sent our little Panther [Lloyd George] to the Mansion House: with the best results.

The War Office have behaved well about my squadron & will pay everything. It looks as if we should have 90 men at least & 6 or 7 good officers.

Write or wire & tell me what you will do in the interval between Garmisch & Villa Cassel. I don't think it is worth while to come home, but whatever you like. Perhaps you might join Violet [Asquith] as she proposed.

Edward Grey wants us to stay a night or so with him on our journey north by motor car. See quite nice plans unfolding for the dear love bird.

Always your own devoted husband

WINSTON S. CHURCHILL

Give my love to Venetia & the others

WSC to the King
(*Royal Archives*)

8 August 1911   Home Office

Mr Secretary Churchill with his humble duty to Your Majesty: Yesterday's debate was a great triumph for the Government. The Prime Minister's speech was magnificent. The Ministerial reply was throughout the debate superior at every point to the attack. The Opposition appeared deeply dispirited. Order was well maintained. There is no doubt that the full statement of the relations & communications of Ministers with the Crown, sensibly cleared the air. The published account shows an absolutely impeccable constitutional procedure. It was an enormous advantage to have nothing concealed, especially when everything was so far above reproach. The majority of 119 realised the full strength of parties.

The Prime Minister is unhappily voiceless today and Mr Churchill will it appears have to make the statement about the Lords Amendments. The Government will accept several that are not vital so as to make the submission of conscientious & honourable men as little galling as possible. Humbly submitted by Your Majesty's faithful servant

WINSTON S. CHURCHILL

WSC to the King
(*Royal Archives*)

9 August 1911   Home Office

Mr Secretary Churchill with his humble duty to Your Majesty: In a House charged with much excitement the Lords Amendments were disposed of yesterday. The debating was good & fierce, the general level of the discussion being well maintained. The principal trial of strength was taken upon a proposal to postpone consideration for 3 months: & on this the Government had a majority of 139. Lord Hugh Cecil spoke well as did Sir Edward Carson; but threats of riot & violence are not suited to the occasion nor to the position of those who used them. Mr Bonar Law was the spokesman of the Opposition. All these speeches would deserve Your Majesty's attention.

In order not to appear discourteous to the House of Lords at this final moment the Government accepted every amendment which did not strike at the heart of the Bill. Mr Speaker was also satisfied by the new arrangement for advising the Chair.

All has now been done to render the passage of the Bill easy, & it will only be by some unforeseen and untoward conjunction that it can be rejected today.

Mr Churchill took occasion yesterday again to make clear Your Majesty's complete detachment from political parties & controversial party questions. The opinion in the House is not really so much stirred upon the passage of the Bill as would appear.

Extremely good personal relations are maintained by persons most strongly opposed to one another. Everything points to a characteristically British solution of this great crisis wh has imposed such serious and unusual anxieties upon Your Majesty.

Humbly submitted by Your Majesty's faithful servant

WINSTON S. CHURCHILL

Lord Knollys to WSC[1]

9 August 1911   Sandringham

My dear Churchill,

In *The Times* report of your speech in the House of Commons yesterday you said that 'His Majesty was fully acquainted in November with the true facts of the political situation and of all the matters at issue between the various parties in the State, among which Home Rule was unquestionably one of the most important.'

Now people will imply from these words that the Home Rule question formed part of the conversation which took place between the King, and the Prime Minister and Lord Crewe – this however would be an entirely erroneous impression as no reference to Home Rule was made either by His Majesty to the Prime Minister and Lord Crewe, or by them to the King. But your words will lead people to suppose that his consent to the creation of Peers under hypothetical circumstances, was given, not only for the purpose of enabling the Parliament Bill to be passed, but likewise for the Home Rule Bill.

In a great political crisis like that which is now going on, the King stands in a very helpless and peculiar position, as he is unable to defend himself; and the point in question is he thinks so important a one for him, that he would be glad if you would take steps to explain that nothing, relating to Home Rule, passed at the audience on 16th of November.

I return to London tomorrow morning.

Yours sincerely
KNOLLYS

[1] The reader will find this letter repeated on p. 1379 as it also concerns Home Rule.

WSC to Lord Knollys

[Draft][1]

10 August 1911   Home Office

My dear Knollys,

The statement to which you refer was made in the House in answer to a direct question, which could not be left unanswered in the circumstances. Before making it, I consulted, in the absence of the Prime Minister, the Chancellor of the Exchequer, and for greater security committed the actual words to writing. Two versions of the statement have appeared. That of the *Daily Mail* and some other newspapers is a gross travesty. The correct account is given in *The Times*, and is accurately quoted by you in your letter. Some absurd comments have been made in a section of the press, which apparently bases itself on the inaccurate version, suggesting that my words implied that the King was prepared to grant a creation of Peers not only to carry the Parliament Bill, but also if necessary a separate creation to carry Home Rule. Neither the true version nor the travesty afford any grounds for this, and I cannot think that it is credited in any responsible quarter. My own feeling is strongly that it should be dismissed as one of the extravagances of partisanship to which a crisis like this must necessarily give rise. Contradiction would only create an importance which it never possessed, and revive it now that it is passing from public notice.

With regard to the actual words used by me, I do not think they could be improved upon.

His Majesty was of course fully seized with all the facts of the political situation, including those which led to the breakdown of the Conference, aud those connected with the debate, to which I referred in my speech on the subject of Home Rule on April 10th 1910; and the Prime Minister has stated that the King's decision was given after full consideration of all the facts of the situation. This last is no less than what I said. I am quite sure there is no real misunderstanding, and that the importance of the whole matter is dwarfed by other events.

The Prime Minister will not be back until tomorrow, and I could not in his absence make any statement as to the conversation of November 16th. I am forwarding him a copy of your letter by special messenger, together with this answer; and he will no doubt at onoe give the most earnest attention to His Majesty's wishes.

Yours very sincerely

WSC

[1] The letter was not sent. Mr Asquith to whom it was submitted wrote to Vaughan Nash 10 August 1911:

'. . . I return Winston's communications. I think he had better see Knollys rather than reply by letter.' WSC took this advice.

WSC to the King
(*Royal Archives*)

11 August 1911 Home Office

Mr Secretary Churchill with his humble duty to Your Majesty: The proceedings in the House of Commons yesterday were completely over-shadowed by the memorable and dramatic events in the Lords. The Chancellor of the Exchequer moved the resolution affirming the principle of payment of members in a speech of much good-humoured skill which was extremely well received by the Conservative party. The speech & its arguments would deserve Your Majesty's attention.

Mr Churchill ventures to offer to Your Majesty his respectful congratulations upon the conclusion of this long drawn & anxious constitutional crisis. When the keen feelings of the moment have passed away, the singular moderation of the change that has been effected will be apparent and will gradually be admitted with relief by the Conservatives & with regret by many of the supporters of the Government. It was a shocking thing that the tremendous issues of last night's division should have depended on the votes of a few score of persons quite unversed in public affairs, quite irresponsible & undistinguished who refused to accept guidance from all the most notable leaders of every political party in the State. But though the margin of safety was so small it was sufficient to reach a final decision. Mr Churchill feels certain that the course taken by Your Majesty in circumstances of such unusual gravity & difficulty was the only one wh could have averted vy evil consequences, & that history will approve & justify all that has been done by those responsible.

It is to be hoped that a period of co-operation between the two branches of the Legislature may now set in & that the settlement of several out of date quarrels may lead to a truer sense of national unity. The strike in London yesterday absorbed Mr Churchill's attention. It was decided to await the result of the Board of Trade's negotiations. If these are abortive extraordinary measures will have to be taken to secure the food supply of London wh must at all costs be maintained. Twenty-five thousand soldiers are being held in readiness & can be in the capital in six hours from the order being given.

Humbly submitted by Your Majesty's faithful servant

WINSTON S. CHURCHILL

WSC to the King
(Royal Archives)

12 August 1911   The Home Office

Mr Secretary Churchill with his humble duty to Your Majesty: The House of Commons yesterday dealt only with minor bills – the most important of which was the Telephone Transfer Bill – & adjourned after only two hours sitting having transacted all the prescribed business.

The conclusion of the London Strike was a great relief. The Board of Trade have done vy well. The men had a real grievance and the large additions to their wages wh they have secured must promote the health & contentment of an unduly strained class of workers, charged as has been realised, with vital functions in our civilisation. The intention of the government to use very large bodies of troops to maintain order & the food supply if the strike was not settled promptly had a potent influence on the men's decision. They knew that they had reached the psychological moment to make their bargain, & that to go on was to risk all that they had within their grasp.

Liverpool is less satisfactory & it is possible that the military force available there will have to be strengthened.

Mr Churchill encloses a circular wh he has issued to Chief Constables for their guidance in dealing with the laws relating to Trade Disputes, with a view to preventing intimidation & other unlawful evils.

And with his humble duty submits the above to Your Majesty.

Sir Max Aitken[1] to WSC

[? August 1911]   Grand Hotel
Eastbourne

Dear Mr Churchill,

I know you have more letters than you can read but I plead special circumstances *from my standpoint.*

I want to tell you how much I appreciated the dinner party. You said that evening you would pay £10 to dine with Balfour any night & I said to myself I would pay £20 to dine with you.

Then you seated me next to Lloyd George. He didn't arrive but that does not change things. Every other person at the dinner wanted that place since Botha sat next to you.

I've finished your South African book.

Yours faithfully
W. M. AITKEN

---

[1] Aitken received a knighthood in the Coronation honours list of June 1911.

WSC to Sir Max Aitken
(*Beaverbrook Papers*)

12 August 1911 Home Office

My dear Aitkin [*sic*],

Thank you so much for your letter. We must make another plan for you to meet the Chancellor of the Exchequer.

This has been an exceptionally interesting week for me. So many things in & out of politics – not all moving forward.

Yours sinly
WINSTON S. CHURCHILL

WSC to the King
(*Royal Archives*)

15 August 1911 Home Office

Mr Secretary Churchill with his humble duty to Your Majesty: It was his duty to make a statement upon the disorders in Liverpool yesterday couched in pretty stiff terms & fully reported in *The Times*. This was well received by the House in general, & of course applauded by the Conservative party. The subject will be debated tomorrow on the Appropriation Bill. It is necessary in times like the present to make it clear that the police will be supported effectually & to warn persons in crowds not to take liberties with the soldiers. There is no doubt that the House of Commons will assent to all necessary measures to maintain order.

The debate on the Payment of Members came to a close, the Government securing a majority of 109. Thereafter the outstanding votes in supply were disposed of in seven divisions in which the Government were supported by majorities of about 120.

It is a vy fortunate thing for this country that the political & social currents of strife have been kept quite separate & have not flowed into one channel. The power of a Liberal Government to deal with riots is very great because large numbers of persons who might easily be led into disorder are the party & political supporters of the Administration & are thus enlisted effectively upon the side of law & order. In addition the whole influence of the Conservative party can be counted on. The Government can then rely on double forces.

Humbly submitted by Your Majesty's faithful servant
WINSTON S. CHURCHILL

WSC to the King
(*Royal Archives*)

[18 August 1911] Home Office

Mr Secretary Churchill with his humble duty to Your Majesty: Good progress was made yesterday with the Insurance Bill and many important points were decided. The first claim was passed and an inroad made upon the second. The Chancellor of the Exchequer was at his best – cool, business-like, conciliatory. No one could succeed in imparting any unfriendly colour to the debate.

Mr Churchill has had to authorise the despatch to Manchester of the Scots Greys & an infantry battalion: but 250 Metropolitan Police have been sent as well and General Macready who has been placed in general control will not use the military unless & until all other means have been exhausted. It is an anxious time as at any moment a collision resulting in loss of life may occur. But order must be maintained & ample force has been provided.

It is greatly to be hoped that the Board of Trade who are on the spot may arrive at another settlement. The strikers are vy poor, miserably paid & now nearly starving.

Humbly submitted by Your Majesty's faithful & devoted servant

WINSTON S. CHURCHILL

WSC to Sir Edward Grey

30 August 1911 [Home Office]

Copy

Perhaps the time is coming when decisive action will be necessary. Please consider the following policy for use if and when the Morocco negotiations fail.

Propose to France and Russia triple alliance to safeguard (*inter alia*) the independence of Belgium, Holland and Denmark.

Tell Belgium that, if her neutrality is violated, we are prepared to come to her aid and to make an alliance with France and Russia to guarantee her independence. Tell her that we will take whatever military steps will be most effective for that purpose. But the Belgian Army must take the field in concert with the British and French Armies, and Belgium must immediately garrison properly Liège and Namur. Otherwise we cannot be responsible for her fate.

Offer the same guarantee both to Holland and to Denmark contingent upon their making the utmost exertions.

We should, if necessary, aid Belgium to defend Antwerp and to feed that fortress and any army based on it. We should be prepared at the proper moment to put extreme pressure on the Dutch to keep the Scheldt open for *all* purposes. If the Dutch close the Scheldt, we should retaliate by a blockade of the Rhine.

It is very important to us to be able to blockade the Rhine, and it gets more important as the war goes on. On the other hand, if the Germans do not use the 'Maestricht Appendix' in the first days of the war, they will not want it at all.

Let me add that I am not at all convinced about the wisdom of a close blockade, and I did not like the Admiralty statement. If the French send cruisers to Mogador and Saffi, I am of opinion that we should (for our part) move our main fleet to the north of Scotland into its war station. Our interests are European, and not Moroccan. The significance of the movement would be just as great as if we sent our two ships with the French.

Please let me know when you will be in London; and will you kindly send this letter on to the Prime Minister.

WSC

Sir Edward Grey to WSC
(*Lloyd George Papers*)

30 August 1911   Fallodon

Copy

Dear Churchill,

Russia's assurance to France is categorical. What Iswolsky[1] said he was instructed to say '*officiellement*'.

What I shd like to think is what the Russians *can* do, & on that we must take the opinion of our military authorities. But I think the latter might when talking to the French Generals get their opinion also as to what Russia can do.

Things have moved in Portugal. France has recognised; Germany has instructed her representatives to do it, & we cannot postpone the decision any more.

I am going to be in London on Monday & Tuesday. If you or Lloyd

[1] Alexander Izwolsky (1856–1919), Russian Minister for Foreign Affairs 1906–10; Ambassador in Paris 1910–17.

George are there I shall be glad, but I can't ask you to come up on purpose unless there is some decision to be taken.

Jules Cambon[1] is not to see Kiderlen[2] till the 3rd or 4th.

Yours sincerely

E. GREY

WSC to David Lloyd George
(Lloyd George Papers)

31 August 1911   Home Secretary

Secret

My dear David,

I hope you will now have received from me my letter enclosing Gen Wilson's[3] private note. I now send you a copy of a letter which after much reflection I have sent to Grey, & also Grey's note to me covering his return of your letter.

I have had a talk with Wilson today. He entirely agrees that great strategic advantages wd be immediately derived from our being able to move into a friendly Belgium, and from our being able to threaten the German flank in conjunction with the Belgian army. He also concurs fully in the policy of my letter to Grey. He tells me however that Sir W. Nicholson is much more doubtful abt the utility of the Belgian army. Will you tell me what you think abt my letter? I hope we shall be in pretty close accord. I think there is no doubt yr view is sound – that we shd get hold of the Belgians; and I think yr phrase 'pivoting on Antwerp' is much more correct than 'based on Antwerp', wh I had rather loosely employed.

Meanwhile, according to the newspapers, the Belgians are taking steps to hold the Liège-Namur line, either of their own accord or at French prompting. This is excellent. We are bound by treaty to protect Belgian neutrality. Its violation wd be an undoubted *casus belli*, independently of other 'griefs'. The Belgians must however be made to defend themselves. How do we know what their secret relations with Germany are? All their

[1] Jules Martin Cambon (1845–1935), French diplomat; Ambassador in Washington 1897–1902; in Berlin 1907–14; Secretary-General to the foreign ministry 1915; a signatory to the Versailles treaty.

[2] Alfred von Kiderlen-Wächter (1852–1912), German Minister for Foreign Affairs 1910–12.

[3] Henry Hughes Wilson (1864–1922), Director of Military Operations at Army HQ 1910–14; Major-General 1913; Chief liaison officer with the French Army 1915; commanded IV Army Corps 1915–16; head of mission to Russia 1916–17; Lieutenant-General 1917; commanded Eastern District 1917; Field Marshal 1919; CIGS 1918–22; created baronet 1919; assassinated by Sinn Feiners 1922.

interests are with the French; but it is possible that British neglect & German activities may have led to some subterranean understanding – for instance, that the Germans shd not go above the Namur-Liège line, & that the Belgians, in consideration of this, should forbid either British or French troops to come to their aid. This wd deprive us at once of the Belgian army and of the strategic position on the German flank, as well as of a *casus belli* wh everyone here wd understand. Wilson said in conversation that Anglo-Belgian co-operation, promptly applied to the German flank, might mean the subtraction of as much as 10 or 12 divisions from the decisive battle front. But I have grave misgivings lest we may be too late, and that the Belgians are got at already.

I hope also that you will think well of the idea of meeting any fresh German move at Agadir, not by sending ships in concert with the French, but by moving the fleet to its Scottish station, where it wd be at once the most effective & least provocative support to France, & a real security to this country. It is not for Morocco, nor indeed for Belgium, that I wd take part in this terrible business. One cause alone cd justify our participation – to prevent France from being trampled down & looted by the Prussian junkers – a disaster ruinous to the world, & swiftly fatal to our country. My wife & I are hoping to go to Dieppe from the 5th to the 12th. It wd indeed be nice if you cd come too.

Yours ever
W

Sir Charles Ottley[1] to WSC
(*Lloyd George papers*)

2 September 1911   Coruanan Lodge
Secret: destroy   Inverness

Dear Mr Churchill,

I sent a copy of the secret print – 'Military needs of the Empire' to the Chancellor of the Exchequer at Criccieth.

I am still anxious regarding the international situation and think we should not relax our vigilance for a moment. You will notice that the entire German High Sea Fleet (25 modern battleships, 5 armoured cruisers, 11 smaller cruisers and about 80 torpedo craft) will be concentrated at Kiel

---

[1] Charles Langdale Ottley (1858–1932), Secretary of CID 1907–11; Naval Attaché to the Maritime Courts 1899–1904, serving in the US, Japan, Italy, Russia and France; director of Naval Intelligence 1905–7; Rear-Admiral; knighted 1907.

next Tuesday. This imposing force would call for no remark if we could feel sure that the sky was clear, but that is just what I don't feel certain about!

Yours very truly

C. L. OTTLEY

PS I believe the passage of the fleet through the Kiel Canal to Brunstuttel can be effected in about 6 or 8 hours.

C.L.O.

WSC to David Lloyd George
(*Lloyd George Papers*)

4 September 1911   Home Office

Secret

My dear David,

You do not tell me in yr letter whether you agree with what I wrote to Grey about Belgium; & I shd greatly like to know yr view. General Wilson tells me that his information now shows that the Belgians have hurried as many as 4000 infantry into Liège, & it is probable that a similar number are in Namur. This looks as if they had a serious intention of holding this line.

Wilson further tells me that a British officer (French by birth) was sent by him along the Belgian frontier & was stopped by the Germans from crossing into German territory and entering Malmedy. He made two attempts, once on a bicycle & once in a motor car, but was prevented both times. This is very peculiar as it is quite unusual to interfere with ordinary people crossing the frontier in time of peace. The inhabitants of the Belgian village of Stavelote, opposite to Malmedy, told him that 12 regiments of German cavalry were concentrated in Malmedy. If this proves to be true, it will be a fact of deep significance. Malmedy is perhaps the best starting point for a cavalry dash into Belgium.

There are no cavalry there in ordinary times, & such a large force as 12 regiments cd not have been massed without drawing on the Rhine garrisons.

Capt Kell[1] of the WO secret service has reported to us this afternoon that the price of flour has risen today by 6/- on large German purchases in 'floating bottoms' otherwise destined for this country. He reported two days ago that one small firm of the name of Schultz purchased as much as 30,000

---

[1] Vernon George Waldegrave Kell (1873–1942), Imperial Defence Committee 1907–9; War Office 1909–14; Directorate of Military Intelligence 1914–24; War Office 1924–40; KBE 1919; Major-General 1924.

bags and refused to resell at a higher price. I send you this for what it is worth.

Yours ever
W

PS I think you ought to keep a cipher with you.

WSC to David Lloyd George
(Lloyd George Papers)

5 September 1911   Home Office

My dear David,
The enclosed (from a British officer of German origin) is interesting.
The flour news was all wrong. There has been a rise but it is not significant specially of anything except bad harvest in Europe & elsewhere.
The German naval reservists in England have received special summonses to be ready to return the moment mobilisation is ordered.
The news from Berlin is quite indeterminate. Grey made the same suggestion about Taft[1] as you do. I entirely agree. The Russians are better today. [?] is the weakling.
I am off to Dieppe tonight for a week. I have the Cabinet cipher (K) so do not hesitate to wire me.
I enclose a letter from Ottley. I hope that McKenna is not as full of cocksureness, as his Admiral is deficient in imagination.
I shall be vy glad of a letter from you. Send anything here. I shall have a messenger at short intervals.

Yours always
W

David Lloyd George to WSC

5 September 1911   Brynawelon
Secret   Criccieth

My dear Winston,
I thought I made it quite clear that I approved the general idea which you discussed in your letter – that I would take no steps to approach either Belgium, Denmark or Holland just yet. I think it much too risky. If it came to the ears of Germany, it might even precipitate war.

[1] William Howard Taft (1857–1930), President of the United States 1909–13; Secretary of War 1904–8. He was defeated in the Presidential Election of 1912 by Woodrow Wilson.

I am not at all disquieted by the news you send me about the frontier. Even if the Germans did not mean mischief, the situation is such as to compel them to take precautions.

I received your telegram. How am I to get a cipher?

Ever yours

D. LLOYD GEORGE

Edward Marsh to David Lloyd George
(Lloyd George Papers)

13 September 1911   Home Office

Dear Mr Lloyd George,

I don't know what can have gone wrong with Winston's telegram, which I sent you in 'G' with the utmost care this morning. I have just sent a duplicate, in case it was corrupted in transmission – but in case there is still any difficulty, here is the text: 'Further details of German proposals to hand this morning emphasize at several points its unsatisfactory character. Of these the most important is that Germany has struck out in Art: 1 of the Fr draft the words 'Germany has only economic interests in Morocco'.

Will you please burn the figures of the telegrams at once as a measure of precaution!

Yours vy truly

E. MARSH

WSC to Reginald McKenna

13 September 1911   Home Office

[Copy: Incomplete]

Confidential

My dear McKenna,

The maintenance of the food supply in time of war and the prices resulting from its insecurity, touch public order very closely. I had a long talk with Sir Frederick Bolton[1] the other day, and he spontaneously and most earnestly confirmed the impression which I had begun to form in my mind, that on the outbreak of war the British Government should guarantee to pay full indemnity for all British or neutral ships sunk or captured by the enemy in the course of bringing necessaries of life and manufacture to this country.

[1] Frederick Bolton (1851–1920), Insurance broker and shipowner; knighted 1908.

I believe this not to be a substitute for but a necessary counterpart of a supreme and effective naval defence. If the naval defence is perfect the additional cost of paying indemnity would be nominal, but its advantage in preventing artificial enhancement of insurance rates will be none the less real. Even if only one ship in a hundred were sunk or captured the rise in insurance would be enormous and the consequent effect upon food prices, and thereafter on public order, very serious. On the other hand, in this case the full cost of insurance to the Government would only be one per cent. It seems to me that the sound and dignified policy, equally agreeable to the Naval prestige and practical interests of this country, would be for us to say, on a declaration of war, that Great Britain is prepared to maintain the complete security of the seas for all vessels trading with the United Kingdom which conform to certain conditions, and that if and in so far as we fail to make this good by naval force we will pay full compensation for all loss resulting. The result would seem to be that we should continue to get our food and raw material at world prices, although no doubt the prevalence of war would tend to some unavoidable enhancement of these. I asked Sir Frederick Bolton to write me out a statement of his views and of his plan, and I send it to you herewith together with some other papers on the subject, hoping that you will let me know the opinion you have formed, for you have no doubt had many other opportunities of studying the subject.

You asked me the other day at the CID about the maintenance of order in this country in time of war. I am sure that it depends almost exclusively upon the poorer people being able to purchase a certain minimum amount of the staple foods, especially bread, at prices which they can afford; and the Government will be forced to secure them this ration at all costs, paying themselves the difference in some form or another between the normal and war prices. The method indicated by Sir Frederick Bolton seems to me to be much the best way of effecting this purpose.

[WSC]

WSC to H. H. Asquith

13 September 1911   Home Office

Copy

My dear Asquith,

The enclosed deserves yr attention: I have sent a copy to Grey.

Are you sure that the ships we have at Cromarty are strong enough to defeat the whole German High Sea fleet? If not they shd be reinforced without delay. Are 2 div^{ns} of the Home Fleet enough? This appears to be a vital matter.

I cannot measure the forces, but the principle is clear that the fleet concentrated in the North Sea shd be strong enough without further aid to fight a decisive battle with the German Navy.

And something must be allowed for losses through a torpedo surprise.

Are you sure that the Admty realise the serious situation of Europe? I am told they are nearly all on leave at the present time. After his revelations the other day, I cannot feel implicit confidence in Wilson. No man of real power cd have answered so foolishly.

The Admy have ample strength at their disposal. They have only to be ready & to employ it wisely. But one lapse, as stupid as that revealed at our meeting, & it will be the defence of England rather than that of France which will engage us.

Excuse plainness. Clemmie & I are much looking forward to our visit to you on the 27th.

Yr vy sincly

WSC

WSC to David Lloyd George
(*Lloyd George Papers*)

14 September 1911 Home Office

Secret & Personal

My dear David,

Seely tells me that having to make some official enquiries at the Admiralty today he found that practically everybody of importance & authority is away on his holidays, except Wilson himself who goes tomorrow. The War Office cannot understand this at such a time, & Sir William Nicholson expressed his surprise to Admiral Wilson last night that he shd find it possible to leave the office so denuded. He was told in reply that everything was ready, & that all that was necessary was to press the button, which could as well be done by a clerk as by anyone else. I can only say I hope this may be so.

Sir Arthur Nicolson[1] saw Cambon[2] this morning, who repeated what we already know about the French reply to the German amendments, and

[1] Arthur Nicolson (1849–1928), Diplomat; Ambassador to St Petersburg 1906; Under-Secretary of State for Foreign Affairs 1910–16; knighted 1905; created Baron Carnock 1916.

[2] Pierre-Paul Cambon (1843–1924), French Ambassador in London 1900–20; brother of Jules Cambon.

also said that he still believed in his own mind that Germany wd give way, & that everything wd be settled. Cambon said he had no reasons for this view, except that it was his own feeling & that of M de Selves. Certainly there is not much confirmation of it in the papers we have seen.

While waiting to see Nicolson at the FO, I had a talk with Kitchener. He was much more respectful about French chances & military qualities, & he told me that Huguet[1] the French military attaché, had told him that the winter was the best time for Germany because at that season Russia cd not move. According to the WO there is no truth in this. The bad months for Russia are the spring & summer, when there is a great deal of rain & slush in Poland. The good months are from September to the end of February.

The City is bad this afternoon, but there is no other news. I am going to spend Sunday with Grey on my way north to Freddie Guest. Write to keep them progged up through any method that is open to you.

Keep this letter to yourself.

Yours ever
WINSTON S. CHURCHILL

David Lloyd George to WSC

15 September 1911   Balmoral

My dear Winston,

Rothstein's[2] letter makes no new discovery but it confirms one or two we had already made:

(a) that the Socialists are striving to maintain peace,

(b) that the Lord Chancellor [Lord Loreburn] is engaged in an active campaign in the course of which he does not hesitate to reveal Cabinet secrets.

I had a long talk with Balfour. He is very much worried – as you are – about the Navy. He is by no means happy about the Admiralty. He has no confidence in Wilson's capacity for direction and leadership. He thinks the Admirals too cocksure.

If there is war he will support us.

Benckendorff[3] is here. He told the King that if Germany attacked France Russia would certainly throw herself into the conflict. Of that he had no doubt.

Have you heard from the War Office that owing to the drought there is

---

[1] General C. J. Huguet, French Military Attaché in London 1904–16.

[2] Theodore Rothstein, socialist writer and theorist; author of *Egypt's Ruin* and other anti-imperial works.

[3] Count Benckendorff (1849–1917), Russian Ambassador in London 1903–17.

no water in that part of Belgium which the Germans must march through? That *may* have something to do with the delay.

Knollys does not believe in war. Benckendorff also says the Germans played the same with them over Persia as they are engaged in playing over Morocco with France. They made vital alterations in the draft then pleaded they were merely verbal. Eventually they gave in when they realised that Russia meant to be firm. Who can tell? I am not sure they know themselves. I think the chances are still against war.

I have promised to meet Grey in London on the 25th. Are you likely to be back? Will you please tell Grey that I shall try to arrange my tour so as to get to Fallodon on Saturday night. Write me to – Skibo, Sutherland-shire.

Ever yours
D. LLOYD GEORGE

WSC to Viscount Northcliffe

[Draft]   [Home Office]

13 September 1911

I shall be very much obliged to you if you will tell *The Times* to report me when I speak at Dundee on the 3rd, 4th and 5th of October. These are the only meetings I am undertaking in the Parliamentary Recess, and I shall have to deal with one or two difficult questions. I am notifying the Press Association so that they can arrange for a verbatim report, and the meetings will be held early enough for these to be telegraphed in time.

Far more important than anything that is happening or has happened in this country is the grave development of the European situation. I wish you were accessible or near London so that we could have a talk about it. I motored quite close to Sutton Place a fortnight ago, when I was staying at Reigate, and would have looked in upon you had I not heard you were on the Continent. I think that both *The Times* and the *Daily Mail* have taken a very good line, and no one can justly say that they have been at all provocative.

Viscount Northcliffe to WSC

18 September 1911   Newcastle
                                                                                              Co Down

My dear Churchill,

I have written to Printing House Square & Carmelite House about yr speeches.

I was sorry to miss you at Broadstairs. I was there during August & saw that you had gone there, most wisely, with Madame & Bébé doubtless to the benefit of all three as well as to the fame of that most invigorating corner of this menaced island of ours.

Many of the speeches of yr colleagues about international politics look supremely foolish in view of the present no-doubt-to-be-smoothed-over situation. Few of them apparently ever *go* to Germany & France. If they did they would know two things:

(1) That Germany, short of capital & with an army hampered by numbers, red tape & out-of-date tradition is bluffing her way into a position that will bring about a considerable reduction in the size of her lead &

(2) That the France of 1911 is not the France of 1870 or of 1875. Our Cabinet seems neither to *go* nor to *send* for information.

If they had a good service of information they would know that the Germans are as much afraid of the French Army of today as they are of our ships. They will try, but will not succeed in separating these forces.

My newspapers have never been provocative abt Germany. Germany resents my printing the facts about her forces & intentions.

V sincerely
NORTHCLIFFE

WSC to his wife
(*CSC Papers*)

24 September 1911   Balmoral

Secret

My dearest,

Here I am in the traditional 'Ministers' room' with all the portraits of departed Premiers & other political worthies on the walls around me. The party in the House is unexciting: principally Connaughts,[1] Soveral & Sir

[1] Arthur William Patrick Albert, Duke of Connaught and Strathearn (1850–1942); third son of Queen Victoria; created Duke of Connaught and Strathearn 1874; Field-Marshal 1902; Inspector-General of the Forces 1907; C-in-C Mediterranean 1907–9; Governor-General of Canada 1911–16. He married in 1879 Princess Louise Margaret Alexandra (1849–1917), third daughter of Prince Frederick Charles of Prussia.

Francis Hopwood. Also Dr Laking[1] who informed me that he brought you into the world some years ago. This morning we attended church where a considerable sermon was preached us, & then lunched at Mar Lodge with the Fifes.[2]

The King talks much to me about affairs. LG when here seems to have made a less good impression than last year. He electrified their Majesties by observing that he thought it wd be a great pity if war did not come now. They are of course repeating this statement somewhat freely. I shall practise caution. The King at first even put on a shocked air – but this soon wore off.

However the Germans are still adopting with most unChristian feelings the attitude of turning all their successive cheeks to the smiters.

I have made up my mind to try to stop the Wells-Johnson[3] contest. The terms are utterly unsporting & unfair.

Everyone is most civil & friendly & life is vy quiet & easy. I wish you were here. It would be jolly. This is vy little formality and much comfort.

Give my respects to your Grandmamma. I am going to bring the motor up here, & shall hope to reach you in it for luncheon on Wednesday.

Your ever loving husband,

W

I enclose you a cutting less poisonous than usual.

[1] Francis Henry Laking (1847–1914), Physician in Ordinary and Surgeon Apothecary to Queen Victoria, Edward VII and George V. Kt 1893; baronet 1909.

[2] Alexander William George Bannerman Carnegie (1849–1912), First Duke of Fife. He married HRH Princess Louise Victoria Alexandra Dagmar (1867–1931), eldest daughter of King Edward VII.

[3] The *Annual Register* for 1911 records:

A boxing contest was announced in September to take place at the Empress Hall, Earl's Court, on October 2, between an Englishman, Bombardier Wells, and the negro pugilist, Jack Johnson, whose victory over another white antagonist at Reno, Nevada, in 1910 (AR 1910, p.[449]), had set up race-riots in the United States, and angry feeling between the white and coloured races in various British colonies; and it was maintained, not only that the contest would be a prize-fight, and therefore brutalising to the spectators (a view contested by many leading sportsmen), but that if Johnson won, as was expected, there would be trouble wherever white and coloured men lived together, even if cinematograph pictures of the fight were not exhibited; and it was understood that the profit from these formed a large part of the expected gain. A movement to prevent the fight arose, chiefly under the influence of the Free Churches and a well-known minister, the Rev F. B. Meyer; a proposal to purchase its abandonment by compensating the promoters was dropped when it was found that over £12,000 would be needed; and the Home Secretary, who was at Balmoral, was memorialised to interfere. He anticipated the receipt of the memorial by intimating that, having obtained legal advice, he would take proceedings; and the principals and accessories were summoned at Bow Street Police Court on September 25. The case, however, was cut short by the grant of an injunction next day, at the instance of the Metropolitan District Railway, the freeholder of the Earl's Court site, restraining the lessee from permitting the fight. The Chairman of the London County Council had warned the lessee some time earlier that the licence might be affected if the project were persisted in.

WSC to Master of Elibank

TELEGRAM

14 October 1911   Home Office

Please tell PM of our conversation. I cannot feel that delay would be advantageous from public point of view. The Estimates should be brought before Cabinet in November & the minister who is to be responsible for defending them ought to have a fair chance to shape them & to master the subject. Naval estimates particularly govern both finance and policy but not only for 2 or 3 years ahead. There is no time to be lost if this duty is to be effectually discharged this year. Chancellor of Exchequer authorises me to say that he feels this very strongly. Much inconvenience will result further from keeping two departments hanging in the wind and I should have thought the delay would be equally unpleasant and unsatisfactory for both ministers.

I have been holding up appointments & decisions which ought fairly to be left for my successor & I should deprecate seriously new appointments at the Admiralty which might encumber the future and add to the difficulties of creating a war staff. If there is a long delay something is sure to leak out and this would be a real cause of mortification and be detrimental from every point of view. Such a change especially in times like these cannot be made too promptly once it is resolved on & parties affected know. I hope the Prime Minister will consider these facts.

There is no difficulty about Home Office Bills. I am quite willing to conduct Shops Bill to its end; there are only three Parliamentary days of it left & the task is practically completed. I have managed this Bill personally all through and it would not be right for me to withdraw from it. McKenna is himself engaged this autumn with Insurance and nothing wd be more natural than for me to finish Shops. The Mines Bill has always been in Masterman's charge who knows it thoroughly. There is nothing else this year worth speaking of. On the other hand surely the Minister who is to take charge of the Welsh bill ought now to be preparing that & other Home Office legislation for next year.

I feel deeply for the Prime Minister in his difficulty & it is painful for me to have to press these points but I am sure that it is not only in the public interest but in McKenna's personal interest that change should take place before Parliament meets and that it shd be accepted as a change agreeable to both Ministers.

Let me add that it would suit me not to move into Admiralty House till after Christmas as there are numerous small matters to be settled here and anyhow McKenna's convenience on such a point would be decisive for me but I darent even put this house into the hands of Agents for fear of starting rumours which would open a flood of spiteful gossip and canvassing odious to all concerned.

CHURCHILL

15

Home Office 1910

(See Main Volume Chapter 11)

———

ON 14 February 1910 Churchill was appointed Home
Secretary.

Viscount Morley to WSC

20 January 1910 　　　　　　　　　　　　　　　Flowermead
　　　　　　　　　　　　　　　　　　　　　　Wimbledon

Confidential

My dear Winston,

It was the greatest pleasure to me to hear from you. Nobody is more
heartily glad than I am, at the triumphant course of your affairs. It has been
really splendid. And your majority at Dundee was a proper crown of it all.
You promised me what the figures would be. Your position has now risen
to the first order. Those are the moments that most demand circumspection.

I had a long talk – two in fact – with RBH [Haldane]. The chassez-
croisez is dropped. The First Lord could not be changed – they think –
without being slighted. But if you cared for HO, no doubt it would be at
your disposal. RBH himself thought the LGB [Local Government Board]
the place with finest opening. I ought to say that he had seen the PM, but
how far he represented any views of the PM, I don't know. I gathered that
the PM had not yet at all considered the line of future transmutations.

Your figures seem probable. RBH gave the enemy 96 gains. 'Not one
above 80.' said I. My crude idea is after due closure of address, to move that
the Finance Bill be passed thro' all its stages without division or debate.
The resolution would be debated, of course, but after the 'voice of the people',

it could be pretty immediately smothered. Then a Declaratory Bill [?] affirming exclusive rights of H of C in finance. The voice of the people has said so. This would bring us to Easter. On re-assembling after holiday, either Budget 1910–11 (a terrible set of estimates preceding) or a Bill dealing with general powers of H of L would come first. Forgive these crudities. They may set your nimble brain to work.

Let us meet as soon as may be after your return.

Ever yours
M.

WSC to R. B. Haldane
(Haldane Papers)

24 January 1910   Board of Trade

Private

My dear Haldane,

I did not realise you ran any danger of permanent injury to your eyesight! How awful! I am indeed thankful you are preserved.[1]

You work too hard, & have done so for many years. I do trust your recovery is going to be complete. My wife sends her best wishes. Our victory although substantial is clearly Wagram not Austerlitz.

Yours always
WINSTON S. CHURCHILL

H. H. Asquith to WSC

1 February 1910   Chateau de Thorenc
Cannes

Secret

My dear Winston,

I must first offer you my warmest thanks & best congratulations on your work during this election. Your speeches from first to last have reached high-water mark, and will live in history.

There must be a certain amount of Cabinet reconstruction.

It has occurred to me that, in view of the character & composition of

---

[1] 'I had an attack of iritis in one eye, so serious that the doctors despaired of saving it. It did in the end recover, though I can hardly see with it now.' *Richard Burdon Haldane, An Autobiography:* Hodder and Stoughton 1929.

our re-arranged forces, you might see your way to take what is bound to be one of our most delicate & difficult posts – the Irish Office.

Twice in my experience, it has been held, under not more arduous conditions, by men (on each side) of the weightiest calibre – Balfour & Morley.

I don't press it on you, for I know well how keen you are on your great projects at the Board of Trade. And I should quite understand & appreciate a negative answer.

But it seems to me to offer, in existing circumstances, an avenue of great possibilities.

Yours always
H. H. ASQUITH

I am here till the end of the week

WSC to H. H. Asquith[1]

5 February 1910　　　　　　　　　　　　　　　　　Board of Trade

Secret

My dear Prime Minister,

Your letter only reached me last night.

I am sensible of the compliment you pay to my personal qualities in suggesting that I should go to Ireland at this juncture, & I realise the peculiar importance to the Government of the successful conduct of that post. I am the more grateful to you for not pressing me to undertake it. The office does not attract me now. There are many circumstances connected with it which repel me. Except for the express purpose of preparing & passing a Home Rule Bill I do not wish to become responsible for Irish administration. And before that situation can be reached, we must – it seems to me – fight another victorious battle in the constituencies.

Three years or four years ago I would have gone; but now I am sure that it would be more in the interests of the Government that Birrell should stand to his post. The Nationalists respect him & trust him. He has all the threads in his hands. He has been through the unpleasant process of being disillusioned.

I do not know what other reconstruction you contemplate, but for myself I should like to go either to the Admiralty (assuming that place to become vacant) or to the Home Office. It is fitting, if you will allow me to say so – that Ministers should occupy positions in the Government which correspond to some extent with their influence in the country. No minister holding an

[1] This letter underwent two drafts.

office of the second class can play a large part without producing awkward and doubtful relations with some of his colleagues in more important positions; & this in spite of much personal good will. It is convenient and it is fair that a true balance should be established. At a time so critical & with struggles so grave impending, there should be a generous appreciation of the real forces which contribute to the strength of the party & of your government.

One word more. Two years have passed since you offered me the Board of Trade as a Secretaryship-of-State. It has not been possible – for reasons wh I have loyally recognised – to make that offer good; but the fact that it was made will I am sure weigh with you at the present time – sufficiently at any rate to justify me in writing openly.

Let me finally thank you for the kindness of your letter. It gives me the greatest pleasure to know that you are satisfied with my work.

Believe me, Yours vy sincerely
WINSTON S. CHURCHILL

Mrs H. H. Asquith to WSC

12 February 1910   10 Downing Street

Sat morning

Dear Winston,

You may be as sure of me never whispering to any colleague even when one knows that the other has talked to me. I have known every detail of our cabinet since Henry was PM & never told or talked to a living soul. Henry thinks well of Grey's scheme (or all of your schemes) but I dont know that he is tremendously hopeful.

It is I confess a real deep grief to me – & I am *no funk* – to see how want of moderation & self control has smashed our splendid majority – a little imagination & knowledge of the wiser sort of voter – a stronger navy, less violence in the Budget, a little dignity & silence this horrible crisis wd *never* have come. We've lost the confidence of a large body of wise opinion & the question is can we go slowly bravely & *above all* silently forward to win it again. I dont mind owning to you & Clemmy I am a very *very* sad woman watching Henry with his loyal kind splendid nature drowning slowly.

Yours in perfect sincerity
MARGOT ASQUITH

Shane Leslie[1] to WSC

[15 February 1910]   Mt St Benedict
                                               Co Wexford

Private

My dear Winston,

Many congratulations on your well deserved promotion. Meantime do not worry about my seat, I am lecturing about the country and everybody seems anxious to put me in at the next by-election.

Needless to say I receive hundreds of applications for your favours but I only care to send on the enclosed – Alexander is a good Protestant Liberal of the type who are likely to make peace in Ireland.

He was staunch to me, but he has qualifications that would fit him for a Resident Magistracy.

I wish you could manage to put his name to Birrell, or as likely as not the others will push in a reactionary.

                                      Your affec cousin
                                      SHANE LESLIE

William Royle to WSC

EXTRACT

15 February 1910   Elmwood
                                                Rusholme

Dear Mr Churchill,

Your elevation to the rank of 'Secretary of State' has given very great satisfaction to your many friends here and we all rejoice in this well deserved honour. I sincerely hope however this position at the Home Office will not prevent you taking in hand those schemes of insurance against invalidity and unemployment which you have done so much to foster and make popular.

                          With kind regards, Sincerely yours
                          WILLIAM ROYLE

---

[1] John Randolph Shane Leslie (b. 1885), a first cousin of WSC. Author and Professor. Succeeded his father as 3rd Baronet 1944. In the General Election of January 1910 he fought Derry City as an Irish Nationalist but was defeated.

Lord Curzon to WSC

15 February 1910   Hackwood

My dear Winston,

Will you allow me to congratulate you on your promotion to so high and fine an office. It seems to me to be a fitting recognition of your very remarkable Lancashire campaign, of which, having followed *con longo intervallo* I am perhaps in a position to offer a modest opinion.

Yours sincerely
CURZON

Sir John Gorst to WSC

15 February 1910   84 Campden Hill Court

My dear Winston,

I am very glad to see in the papers this morning your appointment as Home Secretary. The Office will give you immense opportunities of promoting the cause of social reform, and carrying into practical effect the ideas of your father in former days.

Believe me, Yours ever
JOHN E. GORST

Sir John Gorst to WSC

15 February 1910   84 Campden Hill Court

My dear Winston,

I wrote you a line this morning to congratulate you on your appointment to the Home Office. I did not like to obtrude in such a letter any personal matter of my own. But as there is likely now to be a creation of Peers I hope you will if you have the opportunity remind the Prime Minister of me. My hope of getting back into the H of C is extinguished. But I think I could be a great help to the Govt in the H of Lords, both in the Constitutional struggle and in the discussion of social questions: and after the experience of the election I feel fit and anxious for political work.[1]

Believe me, Yours ever
JOHN E. GORST

---

[1] Gorst received no further political honours, and died in 1916.

Wilfrid Scawen Blunt to WSC

15 February 1910   37 Chapel Street

Dear Churchill,

A line of congratulation on your having got the Home Office for however long or short a tenure it may be.

You told me, I think, last autumn that if you ever were Home Secretary you wd bring about a thorough reform of prison discipline. As soon as you have time to think seriously of this I will, if you will allow me, draw you up a memorandum of what I, as an ex-convict,[1] think ought to be done, especially in regard to political offenders. In the meanwhile it would probably save you persecution at the hands of the suffragettes if you were to let it be known that the idea of such reform was in your mind.

Wishing you luck, I am yours very truly

WILFRID SCAWEN BLUNT

F. W. Hirst[2] to WSC

15 February 1910   *The Economist*
                                              Strand

Dear Mr Churchill,

Pray allow me to offer my congratulations as well as my regret that you are leaving the Board of Trade. I hope the Government will not resign, but will pass the Budget and the Bill, and then (if necessary) go to the country in the summer. The Brewers will not work nearly so hard after they have paid the new licence duties.

Yours sincerely

F. W. HIRST

Sir Francis Hopwood to WSC

17 February 1910   [Colonial Office]

My dear Churchill,

I was delighted to know that you were to move to a place of greater dignity because it marked in conspicuous fashion your unrivalled services

---

[1] Blunt was imprisoned in Ireland in 1888 for calling a meeting in a proclaimed district.

[2] Francis W. Hirst (1873–1953), Editor *The Economist* 1907–16; historian and advocate of Liberalism.

to the Cabinet and Party during the elections. It also satisfies the ambition of those of your friends who stand and mark your natural approach to the summit of political life.

For the rest I am sorry that you have to leave my old office for one which you will find in many ways less congenial.

Do try to innoculate it with something of the 'quality of mercy'. Keep an eye on the sentences passed by fat headed people and reduce them fearlessly whether they emanate from the Ermine or only the 'great unpaid'. – If you feel such interest in the 'prisoner' as you felt in the wrongs of the 'personal case' when with us you have a most beneficent period of service before you.

Yours v sincerely
FRANCIS S. HOPWOOD

Robert Harcourt[1] *to WSC*

19 February [1910]   Malwood
                                                     Lyndhurst

My dear Churchill,

I must write you one line to express the real personal pleasure that I feel in the proper consolidation of your great position in the country. A Secretaryship of State is the outward and visible sign and though (if HMG *are* going to last) I should have liked to see you at the LGBd 'sapping self-reliance' as G. Hamilton says, by a Poor Law Revolution, I suppose the HO looks better. For purely selfish reasons no one wishes to see you right on top more than I do. I certainly hold *my* seat on condition that things are shoved along and *you* are most satisfactory guarantee.

I shall never forget your kindness in coming to Arbroath for me in the midst of your colossal efforts.

Ever yours sincerely
ROBERT HARCOURT

Viscount Gladstone[2] *to WSC*

EXTRACT

19 February 1910

My dear Winston,

I desire to put on record a few observations and suggestions with regard to the Home Office. . . .

[1] Robert Vernon Harcourt (1878–1962), Liberal MP Montrose Burghs 1908–18; served Diplomatic Service; World War I, Lieutenant RNVR; married 1911 Marjorie Cunard.

[2] Herbert Gladstone was created Viscount Gladstone on 10 February 1910, when Churchill succeeded him as Home Secretary.

Staff Generally

There is an unpleasantness between Robertson[1] and More[2] of the Reformatory Department which is now under Blackwell's[3] investigation. I do not know the details of the matter, but I wish to put on record that I have always found Robertson an indefatigable and most reliable official. I appointed him after careful consideration in succession to Legge,[4] who had an extremely high opinion of him and his work. I have little doubt that the result of the enquiry will be to show that though Robertson may have been to some extent indiscreet in the handling of his subordinate, the charges against him are unfounded.

I wish to draw your attention to Branthwaite,[5] the head of the Inebriate Institutions. He is a very valuable man. I have strongly recommended him to the Lord Chancellor for appointment as Assistant Lunacy Commissioner, for which post he is eminently qualified.

Troup[6] is an admirable official. The closeness and accuracy of his work can always be relied upon, and there is no greater authority in the country on all matters relating to criminal administration.

Cunynghame[7] is a very interesting person. If you want to get the best out of him, give him his head. He is perhaps the ablest man in the office, but his mind runs on scientific rather than on official matters. His time is running out, and I have found it best to use him freely for scientific investigations bearing on the work of the office.

Blackwell has hitherto devoted himself to criminal work. His appointment greatly strengthened the department. He is devoted to his work, and you can implicitly rely on his accuracy and the soundness of his law.

Simpson[8] is a man of brilliancy, and it is always well on difficult questions with his department to have his opinion. But his judgment is occasionally flighty.

Byrne[9] has a good deal of the Irishman in him, is a Roman Catholic, and a very excellent and useful official.

[1] T. D. M. T. Robertson, Chief Inspector, Reformatory and Industrial Schools.

[2] T. J. M. More, Inspector, Reformatory and Industrial Schools.

[3] Ernley Robertson Hay Blackwell (1868–1941), Assistant Under-Secretary of State, Home Office 1906–1933; Legal Assistant Under Secretary 1913–33. Knighted 1916.

[4] T. M. Legge, Medical Inspector, HO Factory Department.

[5] R. W. Branthwaite, Inspector under the Inebriates Act.

[6] Charles Edward Troup (1857–1941), Permanent Under-secretary of State, Home Office 1908–22. Entered Home Office 1880. Created KCB 1909; KCVO 1918.

[7] Henry Hardinge Cunynghame (1848–1935), Assistant Under-Secretary Home Office 1894–1913; knighted 1908.

[8] Harry Butler Simpson (1861–1940), Home Office 1884–1925; Assistant Secretary.

[9] William Patrick Byrne (1859–1935), Assistant Under-Secretary, Home Office 1908–13; Chairman, Home Office Board of Control 1913–19; Registrar of the Baronetage 1910–14; KCVO 1011.

Delevingne[1] is par excellence an official; extraordinarily accurate and zealous, and quite invaluable. He thinks, however, in Home Office papers, and has not seen quite enough of the world. He is an official of first class merit.

Pedder[2] is a man of strong ability; somewhat dogmatic and aggressive; but his work is excellent.

Whitelegge's[3] work is always excellent. He has suffered somewhat from want of capacity to devolve business, and he is inclined to overwork himself. He has done a mass of excellent work, and is devoted to his duties.

Redmayne[4] I appointed as Chief Inspector of Mines two years ago. He is admirably qualified in the practical and theoretical side of his work, and he is very skilful in managing men. He is a great acquisition.

You will have to consider a good many important mining questions, and I think you will find that the organization of a Mines department in the Home Office is desirable. When I appointed Redmayne I directed his attention to this, and I have no doubt he has formed views now.

Legislation

My four last Bills – Shops, Inebriates, Check Weighing, Building and Engineering, were blocked by the Budget. I consider the Shops question of quite first rate importance. About a million and a half people are employed, and a great mass of them work excessively long, wasteful, uneconomic hours. The remedy is only to be found by State action, and it is a case where limitation of hours would be secured without any loss to the business to be done, and to a great saving of time, expense and health. Samuel and I went ino the minutes, and there is a mass of information in the office. The Bill, however, is undoubtedly a difficult one, and will necessitate a great deal of trouble.

The Inebriates Bill is a matter of real urgency, so far as the existing machinery is concerned. But there is not public opinion at its back, for it is a subject only known to those who are more or less experts.

The other two Bills are both needed, will prove useful, and should not cause much trouble. The Check Weighing Bill is *15 years* overdue.

---

[1] Malcolm Delevingne (1868–1950), Assistant Under-Secretary of State Home Office; eventually attained rank of Deputy Permanent Under-Secretary of State. Served in Home Office from 1892–1932. Knighted 1919.

[2] John Pedder (1869–1956), Principal Assistant Secretary Home Office; served in the War Office in various capacities 1895–1932; knighted 1919.

[3] Arthur Whitelegge (1852–1933), HM Chief Inspector of Factories and Workshops 1896–1917; KCB 1911.

[4] Richard Augustine Studder Redmayne (1865–1955), HM Chief Inspector of Mines 1908–20; Assistant to Controller of Coal Mines 1916–20; knighted 1914.

In the Factory Department there is always immense work to be done. I attach the greatest importance to administrative work, and in particular to questions of ventilation, which affect the work and health of masses of people.

As regards Prisons it won't be a bad thing to give a harassed department some rest. But there are changes about which I have recorded my opinion on various papers which can be effected I think very profitably, without much trouble or difficulty. The 1898 Act requires amendment. But this can't be done hastily, and no doubt the department will direct attention to this in course.

I wish I could have cleaned up the work of the Royal Commission on Mines, but the end came too quickly. The Commission has virtually completed its main work, but the Chairman died a short time ago. I suggest that you should appoint Cunynghame as Chairman of the Commission for the purpose of winding it up. I have a pledge that after the enquiry into Coal Mines was finished it should be diverted to Metalliferous Mines and Quarries. I suggest that after the Coal Mines Commission is wound up a new Royal Commission should be appointed for the further enquiry, composed mainly of masters and men who are interested. I suggest also that you should ask Ratcliffe Ellis[1] to serve on it. He is the Secretary of the Mining Association, and I understand would be willing to serve again. I commend him to your notice when any mining question arises. He is absolutely in the confidence of mine owners, and is the greatest authority on mining law and practice. He is further a most reasonable man, and he can be thoroughly trusted to act on any engagement and to work for peace. The ultimate passage of the Eight Hours Act was due chiefly to his good sense, and to the counsel he gave to the mine-owners.

I venture to make one suggestion in conclusion. The most responsible work which falls to the Home Secretary is the supervision of sentences. The final judgment subject to the law, is in his hands. Many cases are interesting enough, but the mass mean a great deal of irksome and minute examination. The office presents, as a rule, the traditional view of treatment, which in most cases is quite right. But they cannot bring to bear the outside, impartial view of human nature and human society which necessarily belongs to the Home Secretary. It very often happens that examination of the sordid affairs of rather discreditable and useless people involves a great deal of time. But you will find that if you give this generously you will be repaid by

---

[1] Thomas Ratcliffe Ellis (1842–1925), clerk to Wigan Borough Justices 1874–1900. Member of the Royal Commission on Mines 1906; of Board of Trade Railway Conference 1909; of Industrial Council 1911.

being able to lift up not a few miserable creatures out of trouble and disgrace. All good wishes,

Yours sincerely
H. GLADSTONE

WSC to Lord Knollys
(*Royal Archives*)

21 February 1910   Home Office

My dear Lord Knollys,

Mr Gladstone gave full consideration to the case of . . . . . .[1] He ordered a special statutory enquiry to be made into his sanity. The results of that enquiry were to dispose completely of the suggestion that he is insane at the present time, or was insane when he committed the murder. No doubt the harsh conditions of his life and the hopelessness of his outlook roused him, and prompted him to commit a terrible act as an expression of the spite and hatred with which suffering had filled his heart, and as a ferocious demonstration similar in its character to anarchistic crimes against Society in general. To this the life of a helpless child was sacrificed.

The previous character of the convict had not been good. When discharged from the Royal Navy he became possessed of £75 which properly used might have given him a fair start. Unfortunate as were his circumstances, his own evil nature aggravated them. The jury, who knew nothing of his past record, made no recommendation to mercy. Nor did the Judge. Mr Gladstone decided not to interfere with the due course of the law. I have thought it my duty, although this matter was decided before I received the Seals, to give a fresh and independent consideration to the case; and in the result I have no doubts in concurring in Mr Gladstone's decision. Will you kindly explain the position to the King?

Yours vy sincerely
WSC

Lord Hamilton of Dalzell[2] *to WSC*

23 February 1910   31 Curzon Street

My dear Churchill,

Very many thanks for your most kind letter. I am sure that everyone connected with the Board of Trade will regret as much as I do the loss of

[1] In accordance with custom, the name of the convict has been withheld.
[2] Gavin George Hamilton 2nd Baron Hamilton of Dalzell (1872–1952), Lord in waiting to Edward VII 1905–1910; and to George V 1910–11; served Scots Guards 1892–8; Imperial Yeomanry, South Africa 1900; succeeded father 1900; CVO 1908; KT 1909; MC 1917.

your brilliant leadership, but will at the same time be as pleased as I am at your well earned promotion.

It has been a very great interest to me to have charge of the Board of Trade work in the House of Lords and in particular I shall always be proud to have had a part – however small – in the passing of the Trade Boards and Labour Exchanges Bills.

I have an hereditary connexion with what was perhaps the beginning of modern ideas regarding the questions with which those bills deal, as my grandfather was closely connected with the establishment of the Orbiston Community – the first attempt to put Robert Owen's theories into practice.[1]

I hope that I have inherited the instincts which prompted my grandfather to embark on that enterprise, though the disastrous end to which it came would certainly deter me from attempting to proceed in that particular direction.

As the subject may interest you I am sending you a book which has just been published by a neighbour of mine – Mr Cullen[2] – and which gives a short account of the Orbiston experiment and of the better known and much more practical work done by Owen himself at New Lanark.

I am Yours very sincerely
HAMILTON OF DALZELL

Sir Charles Darling to WSC

24 February [1910]   Judge's Lodgings
                                          Derby

My Dear Churchill,

I have today written to you an official letter – to which I could hardly add this as a postcript.

But I must take the occasion to tell you how glad I am to see you in your present position, and to felicitate you on your brilliant success as a minister.

Besides this, may I say that should you at any time care to have my opinion on any point where that of a lawyer may be of assistance to you, as a mere matter of friendship I shall be glad to give you any help I may.

Let me say how greatly I admire – for its skill and tact – your speech of

---

[1] Robert Owen (1771–1858), Social reformer; finished education at nine years of age; mill manager in Manchester at nineteen; devoted himself to improving the lot of mill workers, particularly children. Founded Orbiston Community near Glasgow 1825 which, like many other similar communistic experiments, was a complete failure. The latter part of his life was devoted to the forming of the Co-operative movement.

[2] Alexander Cullen, a writer on socialism. The book referred to was called *Adventures in Socialism*.

Tuesday last. Very few could have made it and only a statesman in the larger sense would have done so. It put me in mind of Blake's sketch of 'Pitt guiding Behemoth'. You I trust may be able to lead the brute innocuously along but I fear he has been overfed and spurred into dangerous activity. Keep your hook firmly in his nose – or he will destroy you, along with some others, on his way to suicide.

We may I trust meet in London after the 'Spring Recess' when I hope I may have the pleasure of making Mrs Churchill's acquaintance.

Believe me Yours sincerely
CHARLES DARLING

Note by WSC:
Nice letter. Ansd.

Wilfred Scawen Blunt to WSC

25 February 1910   37 Chapel Street

Dear Churchill,
Here is my prison memorandum which I hope may be of use to you. Don't leave it too long in your pigeon holes, for I feel that your official soul may be required of you at any moment.

Yours very truly
WILFRED SCAWEN BLUNT

Memorandum by Wilfrid Scawen Blunt

EXTRACT

24 February 1910   Newbuildings Place
                                              Southwater

As the question of prison reform has become one of urgency in connection with the suffragette movement and the many women who have recently undergone detention for offences more or less political, I offer these remarks founded on an experience of some years ago, which I think may be of use.

In the early months of 1888 I served a sentence under the Crimes Act in Ireland of two months in Galway and Kilmainham gaols. My treatment was that of an ordinary prisoner with hard labour, though hard labour was not named in the sentence – that is to say, I was made to wear prison dress, sleep on a plank bed, pick oakum and perform the other duties assigned to hard labour prisoners. I was forbidden to receive visits or write letters or to have any books to read but a bible and a prayer book except during the last week of my confinement, which was strictly silent and separate during the whole two months. With the exception of the plank bed, which prevented sleep for more than a very short portion of the long winter nights passed in darkness, I found little to complain of in the way of physical hardship. The cells were clean and fairly well aired, the food sufficient, and the exercise, a dull round in the prison yard, more than I needed.

The oakum picking was so little a trouble to me that I came to be glad to secrete a piece of the tarred rope on Saturday nights so as to have it to pick on Sundays. It gave an occupation to the hands and slightly to the brain of the kind that knitting gives. It was pleasant to the sense of smell and to the eye.

The life under these physical heads was hardly worse than one has to put up with on a sea voyage and may pass without special comment. The suffering inflicted on prisoners under the present system I found to be of a different kind, moral, not physical. But this was severe.

The silent and separate system in the treatment of prisoners was, I believe, introduced as a humanitarian reform with the idea of preventing the less depraved among these from contamination with companions wholly vicious. Some reform of this sort no doubt was needed. But I doubt if those who devised it either understood its full effects or intended that it should be pushed as far as has been the case. Carried out as we see it under the present regulations it is a punishment in addition to the loss of liberty which I do not think society has any right to inflict for less than the most serious crimes, while its effect on the sufferers is wholly evil. Judges who pass long sentences on comparatively innocent breakers of the law and visiting justices who go the round of cells periodically and find all neat and clean, do not understand the severity of the suffering inflicted by leaving the minds of prisoners for long periods of months and years deprived of any spiritual sustenance whatever. It is starvation of a kind quite as real as the cutting off of meat and drink, and more enduringly pernicious. . . .

. . . Apart from crimes of violence which need to be treated penally – and for my part I should be quite prepared to see corporal punishment of the severest kind inflicted in cases of rape, wife-beating, cruelty to children and the like, with capital punishment still for murder – I do not see any advantage in severity of treatment, for crime unattended by violence, more than is necessary to keep loafers out of our gaols. The loss of liberty is in itself sufficient penalty to deter all but the most hardened, and for these hard labour is probably the only cure. Yet, even with the habitual thief, though he should be made to dig till he sweats and be put to labour of the least lenient kind, I see no reason that his taskmaster, the prison warder, should deny him a cheerful word or look upon him sourly. Nor do I understand that the prison dress which he is forced to wear should be made the obvious garb of infamy it is. The Spanish Inquisition in its day clothed the heretics it burned in fantastic robes with the object of robbing its victims of all human sympathy. Our 20th Century prisons should make an end of this barbarity. It is an infamy to clothe a grown man, used to decent dress, in a boy's jacket and knickerbockers and deny him skirt enough to cover his loins. I felt the indignity of this so strongly at the outset of my prison life that I rebelled (it was my only rebellion) and made appeal to the visiting justices, and with the result that a skirted coat was ordered me, as may be seen in the annexed photograph. Why should not all the convicts be thus provided? It should be no part of the prison system to degrade, even while it punishes the most severely.

Beyond and above this class of the hardened criminal, there need, I think, be two classes only—the one which should be in the nature of a reformatory rather than of what are now the second and third divisions, and the other identical with what is now the first division.

My second class, which is by far the most important, should be treated in some sort as a school, of which the warders should be the teachers, as well as guardians. This would, of course, require a quite different class of guardian from that from which our present warders are drawn, and one much more highly paid. The kind of men for the work should be that which is found in Scotland Yard, and the result, I am convinced, would be well worth the cost. These should control the working shops by day, and preside over the common midday meal, and the common recreation hour in the evening. The men would still be locked up in their separate cells at night, and also for one whole day in the week so as to give the warders their Sunday holiday, but it should be with books, writing materials, and some solitary game to play, a cup and ball, a box of wooden bricks or one of moveable letters.

With regard to the hour of recreation I have just mentioned nothing struck me more strongly in prison than the immense waste of opportunity displayed – an opportunity of good, whether religious or of instruction, which nobody made use of. It has been said that 'a prison is a convent without God' – and such is the fact. Gaol life has the austerity without the sanctifying motive. Yet it might easily be made, at least in Ireland, into a nursery of Saints. In England, where we do not ask for Saints, it might be turned to intellectual profit by any zealous humanitarian who would give his evening hours to the work of penny reading and lecturing. At present the English prison is a school without a teacher. I throw out this idea, believing that devoted men would not be wanting for the work of instruction, were it officially encouraged.

My first and highest class of all would be what is now the first division of misdeméanants. This should include with others already enjoying it all who for their opinion's sake have disobeyed the law. The prisoners under this head should be treated more or less as prisoners of war are treated, honourably that is, and as opponents whom the law has captured. England, I believe, is the only country of Europe where no distinction is made between political and ordinary offenders. It is time the two classes should be recognised as separate and the distinction legally drawn. The absence of it brings the law into contempt through the impossibility of persuading the public that a conscientious breaker of the law is a real criminal. And this leads me to what is the most important part of what I set myself to write, the position of the Government where it finds itself, as now, determinedly opposed by a small party of religious or political reformers who persist in infractions of the law to further their opinions.

As the law at present stands, it is probably impossible to deal satisfactorily with cases where assaults are committed or damage done to property so as to draw public attention to a public grievance; and until the magistrates who judge such cases are empowered to decide upon the motive of the act, whether it is public or private, there will always be confusion. A man resists the police in the execution of their duty, he breaks a plate glass window, or he strikes a Prime Minister with a cane. He is arrested. His motive may be anything. It may be political, or it may be a personal grievance, or that he is hungry and wants to be lodged in prison, or merely that he is a drunken rowdy. The magistrate already possesses a certain option in these cases; but I think it should be obligatory on him, where the evidence is that the motive is honestly a public one, that he should send the prisoner to the first division. The argument put forward in recent cases by the Government, that political propaganda should not be allowed to be carried on in prison and therefore that the second division should be enforced seems to me an unwise one and one which has defeated its own end. The Government cannot stop the advertisement and would do better in its own interests to give it full scope by allowing all the privileges accorded to first division prisoners. The public would not for more than a very short time interest itself in letters or interviews written in prison, unless indeed the political grievance was a just one, in which case it ought to be attended to and remedied. The Government has no right to order the seclusion of the second division merely to save itself from inconvenience.

As to more serious political cases which amount to crime, assassination, armed assault and the rest, they need not be considered here. The magistrate would refer the accused to the Assizes as untried prisoners. I am of opinion all the same that the nature of the sentences imposed requires special legislation. The Government has every right to inflict death on political assassins or to detain them for life or for shorter periods in prison so as to prevent a recurrence of their acts, but not I think to confound them with ordinary criminals under penal servitude. They should be confined as State prisoners or prisoners of war under special conditions not personally degrading.

There remains the question of how to treat those prisoners who for political or other reasons refuse to conform to prison rules. With the mass of prisoners under the reformatory system I have proposed it would, I think, be found that refusals would seldom occur and, if they did, that they could be dealt with by deprivation of privileges and relegation to a separate class for punishment. I do not believe in the continuation of the hunger strike to the point of death or permanent injury to health by any but political or religious fanatics. I would however risk that rather than continue the practise of forcible feeding, which is a form of torture no civilized Government has a right to inflict. As applied to political prisoners, it seems to realize the ideal of the medieval tortures, that of inflicting the maximum of pain without touching any vital organ and with the least risk to life or health. For the case of the suffragette ladies, I consider that the proper treatment would be to give them the fullest privileges of the first division with leave to see their friends daily and to provide their own food and their own medical attendance. If under those circumstances they continued to refuse food the Government would be free of responsibility.

WILFRED SCAWEN BLUNT

John Galsworthy[1] *to WSC*

[February 1910]   14 Addison Road

Dear Mr Churchill,

I write to offer you my best wishes in your new post, and to tell you how glad I am that you have been appointed to that department of Government which most requires a man, not only of judgment and decision, but of sympathy and imagination.

I am loth to ask you, while you are picking up the reins of office, to devote some little of your attention to a special point, but I feel that I must do so, and trust to your understanding and forgiveness of my unbecoming haste. I want you to spare the time somehow, some when, to read the enclosed

---

[1] John Galsworthy (1867–1933), novelist and dramatist. In 1909 Churchill had been to see Galsworthy's new play *Strife*, and greatly admired it. They exchanged several letters on the subject of prison reform in the first half of 1910.

writings on the 'closed cell' confinement of convicts. They are short, and contain the pith of the matter.

The upshot of them acting on the predisposition of Lord Gladstone and Sir Evelyn Ruggles-Brise[1] towards a change, has been a new order which comes into force on April 1st to the effect that convicts of all classes shall serve three months' separate confinement instead of nine, six, and three according to the class – recidivist, intermediate, or star – as they do at present.

This change is a great step in the right direction. But I want especially to draw your attention to the late Home Secretary's deliberate opinion, stated in the minute confirming this new order and repeated to myself, that separate confinement must be held to have broken down as a deterrent (deterrence being admittedly the only reason for its continuance, besides that of convenience and expense); and to the fact that he would have done away with it altogether (except for the purposes of classification) but for *administrative* difficulties.

I feel certain that you will come to the same conclusion. And I would urge you to consider (1) whether difficulty or expense (it cannot be very great) should be allowed by the most civilized State in the world to be responsible for what is seen to be a really appalling amount of unnecessary suffering, when the hours are added together in the lives of a thousand men and women, every year, each undergoing three months of almost complete solitude; and (2) whether it would not be possible to make such arrangements or to raise such money as would obviate this unnecessary suffering.

Superfluous suffering deliberately inflicted on a free man or woman rouses Society at once to the greatest indignation, and rarely goes unremedied; but in the case of prisoners it is unfortunately not so – they are too far out of the line of the Public's sight, and there is no hope, but in men at the helm who can see and feel.

Though personally convinced that separate confinement as a system is against common humanity and commonsense and should be abolished, except in rare cases, one would not have such a load on one's conscience if the three months were served, not in closed cells, but in the cubicles of what is called the 'shed system.' Unfortunately, though Sir Evelyn Ruggles-Brise told me that he much preferred the shed system, there are not at present sheds enough available, and – failing initiative and money – are not likely to be.

I need not say to you that, in prison as in life, men can only be reformed by kindness, by calling out the best that's in them; nor need I say that torture is not confined to the body. The whole tendency nowadays is to paint the

[1] Evelyn John Ruggles-Brise (1857–1935), Chairman Prison Commission 1895–1921; Private Secretary to successive Home Secretaries 1883–1891; knighted 1902.

outside of the house, and leave the inside to rot. Closed cell confinement is an illustration of that lamentable fact. I beg you to strike a crushing blow at a custom which continues to darken our humanity and good sense.

Once more, forgive me for my haste, and believe me,

Sincerely yours
JOHN GALSWORTHY

WSC to John Galsworthy

24 February 1910   Home Office

Private

Copy

My dear Mr Galsworthy,

I thank you for your letter, and I greatly admire the keen and vigorous way in which you are driving forward a good cause. I am in entire sympathy with your general mood. I have not yet had time to examine the question, but I have given instructions for it to be brought before me with the least possible delay; and as soon as I have acquainted myself with the facts, I shall welcome an opportunity of discussing the subject with you. My time may be short, so that if action is practically possible, it is essential that it should be prompt.

Yours very truly
[WINSTON S. CHURCHILL]

John Galsworthy to WSC

8 March 1910   14 Addison Road

Dear Mr Churchill,

I proceed almost at once to abuse the privilege of writing to you.

Your point about not leaving on the mind of the victim of crime a sense of aggrievement was extremely sound; and as to that my only point really was that in removing this sense of aggrievement the *Law* must do it not in the spirit of revenge, but in the spirit of protection, and the revenge which may be a justifiable individual emotion is not a justifiable official or State emotion. So far as I can see one must have fixed sentences of detention. I was not advocating rosewater prisons, I was advocating strict disciplinary schools, which would at once be infinitely irksome to the usual run of criminal, by reason of hard and steady work, celibacy, absence of drink and tobacco, monotony of diet, *loss of liberty*; but which should be so contrived as to give, in your own words, 'some kind of natural life' to the person thus restrained. I pitch on solitary confinement and the *perpetual* silence as the two features most hostile to that end. And I cannot see why education, mental, moral, and physical, should be confined to Borstal establishments; anything that stimulates competition and self-respect must surely be to the good. I feel certain that the habitual criminal, too, besides being improved, would be more deterred under a system that required him to make mental and moral effort than he is under the present regime. It was apropos of mental effort and self-expression that I suggested a copybook, with numbered pages, in the cells. They have it in Berlin, and the Governor said it was not abused.

Two other points: (1) If reformation is aimed at prisoners ought surely to be allowed to see the sky. I know they're trying to replace the thick glass, but very slowly (for lack of money, I suppose), and they're only putting in, as far as I have seen, quite small panes of clear glass. (2) Should prisoners not be allowed more chance of keeping in touch with their wives, husbands, mothers, and children? One letter in three months! With discretion, surely they might be allowed one a month. This, of course, would be an unpopular change, because, for one reason, it would entail thrice the amount of reading through of letters on the part of prison staffs. For all that, it seems to me an essential point, if there's to be any attempt to keep prisoners human.

If any period of separate confinement is to be retained for any class of prisoner, convicts or no, which, as you know, I personally trust will not be the case, will it not be found possible to split their time of exercise into two portions, morning and afternoon? Here again you are met with the difficulty of extra labour to the staff; but it surely might be got over.

You spoke of the importance of help to the prisoner when he gets out. Could not prisoners' aid societies be linked up into a sort of prisoners' labour exchange, and aided by the Home or Colonial Governments providing certain classes of work (on the ground that it is more economical to employ the discharged prisoner than to have him coming back to gaol for want of employment)?

I have been very sorry to hear that the Home Office generally thinks my Prison act [in his play *Justice*] unfair. I strove to be scrupulously fair. If each particular act is regarded in the light of the whole play, as it is meant to be, and should be in a work of art, I don't think this charge can be brought. In my limited experience I certainly saw convicts under separate confinement looking every bit as bad as Falder. I also saw men undergoing penal servitude whose record boards showed no previous offence. And it must be remembered that the appearance of an actor depends on the position of the seat from which you see him. Solitary confinement is a dumb thing; it cannot speak for itself; it is a long slow dragging misery, whose worst moments are necessarily and utterly hidden from all eyes. I have given it a tongue *for once* – surely that is not unfair. For it is my conviction that it is only because this thing is dumb that it has been kept on as part of our penal system.

Forgive my telling you a tale.

A man (who had served a term of imprisonment) was employed out of charity at the theatre, and after the first night of *Justice* the manager, going his round, came across him sweeping out the theatre. The man stopped sweeping and said: 'Thank you, Sir, for putting on that play.'

The manager looked at him hard – knowing of his past, but never having heard him say a word about it – and asked:

'Well, is it true?'

'Every word.'

This play was not written by me in any wanton spirit. It has been nothing but pain from beginning to end. It has cost me much peace of mind. I have written it, believing that what I have seen and thought and felt ought to be made known, and that I should not be true to myself or my art, and cowardly into the bargain, if I had turned my back on the task. I believe with every bit of me in the *essential* truth of my presentation. I've never dreamed of doubting the good faith and conscience with which justice is administered, and solitary confinement as a feature of justice persisted in; nor have I dreamed of doubting the humanity of the administration. As a whole my play was designed to show the immense and, if you like, natural dispropor-tion that exists between criminality and punishment in a great number of cases, so that all might be spurred to devise, so far as is humanly possible, machinery of justice that will minimize to the utmost this disproportion. What I have written has been written under the spur of conscience and con-viction, and with profound regret if I am causing pain to those who have been kind and courteous to myself. It would be in the nature of a relief to my mind if you would convey these words or the sense of them to Sir Evelyn Ruggles-Brise, and to those of his colleagues who feel that I have been unfair.

I am, dear Mr Churchill, sincerely yours

JOHN GALSWORTHY

WSC to John Galsworthy

11 March 1910   Home Office

Copy

Dear Mr Galsworthy,

I am sure I shall be able, with the aid of your courteous letter, to remove any feeling of vexation which may rest in the minds of my Officers. The whole process of punishment is an ugly business at the best. The prisoners are un-happy, and are meant to be much less happy than others outside in this not too happy world. The conditions in jail must necessarily be squalid, the cost of maintenance narrowly scrutinized, since it is raised from the taxation drawn, in part, from the poorest of the poor; and the process of meting out measure for measure according to human standards must be crude, im-perfect, and full of harsh discordances. But in Sir E. Ruggles-Brise we have a man who for 10 or 12 years has stood forward at the head of the movement for Prison Reform. It is to his personal exertions, and largely through his own contributions in money and subscriptions raised by him from his personal friends, that the noble institution of the Borstal System has been erected, is being expanded, and must ultimately cover practically the whole ground. I well remember how, at a time when a current of reaction seemed to be threatened, and when the 'No Pampering for Convicts' cry made itself heard, he cheerfully faced the prospect of abruptly terminating an official career full of achievement and high promise. I think he quite realizes the value to all the movement with which he has been associated, of the external driving-power which your thought and actions provide. At the same time the man who is laboriously dealing with intractable facts and small resources may be pardoned a temporary feeling of irritation when he is overtaken and surrounded on all sides by the airy and tenuous clouds of sentiment and opinion.

No one would ever question your perfect sincerity and good faith.

Amid the many cross-currents of the present situation I am trying to use what lights I have to explore the whole subject of prison administration, and if I have the time I daresay I shall get to one or two conclusions of my own. We must not expect much regeneration from a system largely devoid of sympathy; but it seems to me that effort, spontaneous, constant, increasing, and increasingly rewarded, is perhaps one of the most hopeful themes for reflection.

By all means write to me when you will

Yours very sincerely
[WINSTON S. CHURCHILL]

Minute by WSC for Sir E. Troup

28 February 1910   Home Office

I am anxious to prescribe a special code of regulations dealing with the treatment of political prisoners in His Majesty's Prisons. A political prisoner should, in my judgment, be defined as a person who has committed an offence, involving no moral turpitude, with a distinct political object. It should be in the power of the Secretary of State, either directly or upon the advice of some independent judicial authority, to classify any person as a political prisoner. The regulations for the treatment of such prisoners must be framed in precise detail. Their object should be to restrain the liberty of the prisoner, and by restraining his liberty to punish him, without the enforcement of conditions calculated to degrade or humiliate his dignity and self-respect. I am not sufficiently acquainted with the details of prison administration to be able to develop this idea with any thoroughness; but it seems to me that food might be obtained from outside on payment, that the prisoner should wear his own clothes, that no compulsory work should be executed, that no cutting of hair or any unnecessary interference with usual habits should be practised. A political prisoner should be allowed access to all books of the type which are found in a good public library, and without restriction to number, subject only to reasonable convenience. A political prisoner should not be allowed to receive daily or weekly newspapers, or contemporary publications dealing with political affairs. The question of the correspondence of a political prisoner and of his receiving visits from friends must be governed entirely by State policy, and the regulations should provide for its being extended or contracted to any extent from day to day as the Secretary of State may order.

Please let me have a memorandum upon this minute, showing how you would give effect to the views it contains, whether legislation would be necessary and how much could be done by administrative action.

Minute by Sir E. Troup

4 March 1910   Home Office

I should agree with Sir E. Ruggles-Brise in deprecating a distinction in prison treatment being made to depend on the political motive of the offender. If political motive is admitted in extenuation of a minor offence, it is difficult to resist the application of the same principle to graver offences, and even to political murders which are, from the public standpoint, the worst of all murders.

Further, I do not think that, the Prison Act having settled the classes of prisoners, we can by rule introduce a new class *eo nomine*.

But I think the same result can be obtained by other means. I think it may be put in the way Sir E. R. Brise suggests, in the shape of a power for the Secretary of State, or the Prison Commission, with his approval, to grant ameliorations or privileges to a particular description of prisoners (i.e. to individuals coming within the description). In the description of prisoners to whom the privileges are to be granted I think we should avoid any reference to political or to any sort of motive, and should describe them as 'prisoners (in the Second Division) who are persons of good antecedents, and who have been convicted of offences which do not involve dishonesty, cruelty, indecency, or serious violence'.

This would, I think, cover the class of prisoners you have in view. As regards the privileges to be given, I think it is a good suggestion that they should 'not be in excess of any privilege conferred on the First Division', but I think (if merely for Parliamentary purposes) they ought to be enumerated in the Rule 'any amelioration of treatment in regard to food, the wearing of prison clothing, hair-cutting, cleaning of cells, employment, books, visits and letters (and otherwise) provided, etc'.

If the Secretary of State agrees, a draft rule on these lines can be prepared for his consideration. It has to lie on draft before Parliament for thirty days.

Minute by WSC

EXTRACT

7 March 1910　　　　　　　　　　　　　　　　　　　Home Office

I have read with pleasure and interest the minutes of my predecessor, and am glad to see how closely our opinions, formed under entirely different conditions, coincide in this matter. I am much obliged to both you and Sir E. Ruggles-Brise for the manner in which you have laboured to give effect to my general view. I have re-considered the question in the light of the arguments you adduce. I agree that a distinction based on motive would be dangerous and undesirable. The Courts alone must judge of that. I like the plan of proceeding by Parliamentary rule. I think the definition of the class of prisoners as persons of good antecedents, not convicted of crimes involving 'dishonesty, cruelty, indecency, and serious violence', is very good. Certainly in any draft rule the exemptions should be stated fully as proposed by Sir Edward Troup, and not merely specified by reference to particular articles in the present code. I consider it of high importance that visits and correspondence in this class should be absolutely at the discretion of the Prison Commissioners acting under instructions from the Secretary of State. Complete isolation from the outside world is an essential point in regard to any prisoner who commits an offence with a political object. Let a rule be drafted forthwith on the lines proposed.

But how about *ultra vires*? This part of the case must be thoroughly explored. It would never do to run up against a dead wall. Any failure of that description would produce the worst possible effects and destroy all advantageous effect of the action proposed. I must have a positive opinion upon the subject. If necessary ask the Law Officers. I do not require an overwhelming or unquestionable case as a basis for action. As long as there is a certain good arguable ground for House of Commons purposes, and no danger of interference from the courts, I should be quite prepared to go on. But it is necessary to know exactly where we are at the outset. Please prepare a short memorandum on this special point which I can show myself to the Law Officers on Tuesday. If it is put in my question box, I will get the opinion from them before night. . . .

WSC

W. T. Stead to WSC

14 March 1910   *The Review of Reviews*
                                                           Kingsway

Dear Mr Winston Churchill,

In the new number of the *Review of Reviews,* a copy of which I send you herewith, I make a suggestion as to the Home Office and its Prison Officials, which possibly you have already acted upon so far as you yourself are concerned. But I do wish you could get your prison people to see Mr Galsworthy's play. There is a constant tendency on the part of all Prison Officials to forget that they are dealing with human beings. You, fortunately, have been in gaol, although only as a prisoner of war, but still you must have something of the feeling which binds us convicts all in a bond of brotherhood.[1]

I am, Yours sincerely
W. T. STEAD

Viscount Gladstone to WSC

16 March 1910   7 Grosvenor Place

Dear Churchill,

I am glad you are acting on my proposals as regards prison rules, though personally I doubt whether the extension of the changes to the 3rd division is necessary.

[1] Stead went to prison for three months in 1889, after his sensational exposure of criminal vice in England, for a lack of precaution in securing the evidence requisite for his purpose.

The form of your announcement in the House of Commons, however, to me is a matter of rather more than surprise. Apart from the merits of the proposal two deductions will inevitably be made – first that you initiated the changes and I did not; secondly that you have done the obviously right thing, and that I from foolishness and inhumanity did not. Whereas as you know I asked Brise a long time ago to draw up proposals for consideration. In the thick of the difficulties which fell to my lot I was unable to act. But the moment the women had ceased their folly I discharged remaining Suffragette prisoners, sent for the file, and drew up myself what I gather from your answer you are carrying into effect.

C'est tout.
Yours truly
H. GLADSTONE

WSC to Viscount Gladstone
(Herbert Gladstone Papers)

17 March 1910   Home Office

Private

Dear Gladstone,
I am sorry you consider that you have reason to complain. The fault – if any there be – lies with the newspapers which have commented upon the change, & not with my answer which clearly associated you with it. As, however, you feel that you have been insufficiently referred to, I will arrange to have a question put me in order to make your position clear. I have asked Troup to frame this & I enclose his suggestion for your information.

I may add that I decided to make a special code for political offenders as soon as I was appointed Home Secretary, & I dictated a memorandum on the subject in the first two or three days I was here. It was not until the matter had reached its final stage that I learned with pleasure from the official files how nearly we were in accord.

It has vy often happened to me when I left the Colonial Office to find much of the work wh I had quarried out laboriously, used with advantage by my successors. And I have always been vy glad that they should do so.

In this case however I acted in entire independence of your views & gave instructions upon my own initiative for a reform wh I have felt vy strongly should have been carried out three years ago, & might have been carried out at any time.

Yours truly
WINSTON S. CHURCHILL

Viscount Gladstone to WSC

18 March 1910   7 Grosvenor Place

Private

Dear Churchill,

Thanks for your letter. But I did not see any reference to 'my predecessor' in your answer as reported in *The Times*. I assumed the report to be verbatim. The answer, I take it, was as usual supplied.

Two things struck me. First that you declined to admit *political* motive as ground for interfering with sentences. I do not therefore understand that part of your letter in wh you say that you decided as soon as you became HS to make a special 'Code' for 'political offenders'. I have not seen the text of the new rules, but I imagine that you propose, as I did, to go far beyond 'political offenders' whatever that term may mean.

Secondly, the alterations seemed to follow my minutes in detail, and were based on the same principles.

I don't in the least agree that these changes could have been properly made in the midst of disorderly actions designed to defy the administrations of the law. Nor do I think that you or any one else would or could have made a concession to disorder which would have been as weak as it would certainly have been fruitless – at the time. During the past 3 years the Suff[ragette] question came frequently before the Cabinet. The concession was never suggested by any one, not even by you. In fact the only suggestion you made to me – last Dec – was that to safeguard Cabt Ministers & their meetings, I should proceed to lock up the Suff[ragette]s wholesale. I don't remember on that occasion any advocacy for the improvement of their prison treatment.

As regards Troup's suggestion I have only to say that the subject had been under consideration for a long time, & that I brought it to a head as soon as the opportunity came. Chiefly out of courtesy to yourself I did not make an official decision. But all this is a small matter, & I am sorry to have troubled you.

I am very glad that you acted & it is not my intention to claim credit which rightly belongs to the responsible man. Perhaps however if you had been through 3 years of a vexatious & nasty movement I faced with a minimum of public support from my colleagues* you would understand that I felt nettled at the invidious comparisons drawn at my expense in consequence of the form of your answer as reported in *The Times*.

Yours truly

H. GLADSTONE

[Note by Gladstone]:

* I have not forgotten *your* Dundee reference. That in fact so far as I remember was the solitary instance of 'colleagual' support!

Wilfrid Scawen Blunt to WSC

19 March 1910   Newbuildings Place

Dear Churchill,

I have had an interesting letter from Hyndman[1] about prison life apropos of your announcement. Would you by any chance like to meet him here the Sunday you are to spend here? If so I would ask him. He knew & was, he tells me, rather friends with your father, & is a man of ideas – a kind of William Morris,[2] but without Morris' literary & artistic side. Or wd you rather have a *relâche* from politics?

Yrs very tly
WILFRID SCAWEN BLUNT

Wilfred Scawen Blunt to WSC

23 March 1910   Newbuildings Place

Dear Churchill

Though I had written to Hyndman I fortunately kept the letter unposted till I shd hear more, & so have not sent it. Perhaps we may get Redmond instead. I was much pleased abt Somaliland.

Yours vy truly
WILFRED SCAWEN BLUNT

*   *   *   *   *

WSC to the King
(*Royal Archives*)

16 March 1910   Home Office

Mr Secretary Churchill with his humble duty to Your Majesty. Archbishop Bourne[3] proposes to include in the ceremonial of consecrating

---

[1] Henry Mayers Hyndman (1842–1921), Well-known Socialist, Marxist and social reformer of his day; member of the International Socialist Bureau 1900–10.

[2] William Morris (1834–1896), poet, artist and designer; founder of the Kelmscott Press.

[3] Francis Bourne (1861–1935), Roman Catholic Archbishop of Westminster 1903–35; Bishop of Southwark 1896; Cardinal 1911.

Westminster Cathedral on June 29th, a procession of his clergy in their vestments around the building for the purpose of blessing and sprinkling with holy water the external walls. There is no doubt that as this procession will pass through a public street for a short distance, it may be said to be technically an infraction of the law. The Protestant Societies have already begun to stir, and Mr Churchill apprehends that they will endeavour to arouse considerable feeling – perhaps with success. He feels, however, strongly that this is not a case in which the Attorney-General should be urged to move, and still less that police protection should be refused. The great and beautiful Cathedral which has been raised by the Catholic subjects of Your Majesty in all parts of the United Kingdom is a noble ornament to London. The procession is a necessary part of its consecration to divine service. For three quarters of the distance that procession will move upon private ground, and on the fourth side, it will still be contiguous to the external walls of the Cathedral. The Host will not be carried; but even if it were, Mr Churchill would not have felt justified in interfering with a celebration so unaggressive and so well deserved. Knowing however the interest wh Your Majesty feels in such questions, and in view of the agitation which may possibly be inflamed, he lays the facts before Your Majesty at the earliest moment in order that an expression of Your Royal pleasure may reach him if Your Majesty desires.

Mr Churchill has obtained the concurrence of the Prime Minister in his proposed course.

WINSTON S. CHURCHILL

Sir Arthur Davidson to WSC
(Royal Archives)

19 March 1910   Biarritz

Sir Arthur Davidson is commanded by The King to acknowledge Mr Churchill's Memorandum, relative to the Consecration of the new Roman Catholic Cathedral at Westminster.

Mr Churchill's view, that the Procession should be allowed to circulate in the streets adjoining the Cathedral, for the purpose of sprinkling its walls, puts The King in the same difficulty as that in which he was placed at the time of the Eucharistic Procession eighteen months ago.

It was then represented to The King, that the procession (as constituted) would be illegal, if it could be shewn that its progress through the streets would cause a breach of the peace: but this view was apparently so involved and obscured in legal and other issues, that no direct action was taken until a few hours before the Procession was to have taken place – The Procession with its illegal features was then prohibited.

In the meantime, Letters and Petitions from various quarters were sent to The King, appealing to him to maintain the Law, and prohibit the Procession.

The proposed ceremony of Consecration presents, in some ways, many of the same features – the chief differences being:—

(1). The Host is not carried in Procession.

(2). The Streets through which the Procession is to pass, all adjoin the Cathedral and are contiguous to it.

(3). The object of the Procession is a feature of the Consecration Ceremony, and is not a demonstration through streets not contiguous to the Cathedral.

The main feature as to whether the Procession, *per se*, is legal or not, remains the same.

If The King assents to Mr Churchill's suggestion, he will receive the same protests and petitions from those whose contentions are more or less justified by Law.

The King feels that the surrender of a principle (which would be involved by permitting the Procession to take place) is a very grave one, and it should be justified by some legal or other process.

The King fully appreciates Mr Churchill's opinion that the concession is one which will be valued by the Roman Catholic Community; but he is bound to respect the prejudices of those who hold contrary views with regard to the Procession, and before giving a definite opinion, therefore, The King would like the legal and constitutional aspect of the case to be clearly defined, in order to avoid the repetition of what was an extremely disagreeable period of discord eighteen months ago.

The King would, of course, be glad if there could be any friendly intermediation on the subject, and if any representation could be made in this sense to Archbishop Bourne.

Perhaps Mr Churchill might sound Lord Granard[1] as to whether this is feasible.

The King wishes full latitude to be given to his Roman Catholic subjects in all their religious questions, but he wishes the Law to be maintained, and in this view he feels sure he will be supported by Mr Churchill, both in opinion and action.

With regard to the Eucharistic Procession The King's view was perfectly

---

[1] Bernard Arthur William Patrick Hastings Forbes (1874–1948), succeeded father as 8th Earl of Granard 1889; Lord-in-Waiting to King Edward VII, 1905–7; Master of the Horse 1907–15 and 1924–36, Assistant Postmaster-General 1906–9; PC 1907.

simple, that if it was illegal it should be prohibited; and in this opinion His Majesty was entirely supported by the two Members of the Cabinet who happened to be on the spot when his views were being dispatched to the Prime Minister.

[A. DAVIDSON]

WSC to the King
(*Royal Archives*)

22 March 1910   Home Office

Mr Secretary Churchill with his humble duty to Your Majesty has the honour to submit the enclosed memorandum which he has prepared upon the question of the consecration ceremonies of June 29 at the Westminster Cathedral. Your Majesty will see that the Law Officers of the Crown have been consulted and that the Attorney General has expressed a vy clear opinion as to the powers possessed by the Home Office to prohibit the procession. The police arrangements present no features of difficulty, and Mr Churchill is convinced that both on grounds of law and policy the course he ventured to recommend is the only one which can with advantage be adopted.

[WINSTON S. CHURCHILL]

Sir Arthur Davidson to WSC
(*Royal Archives*)

25 March 1910   Biarritz

Dear Mr Churchill,
    The King would like to see the correspondence which passed between Mr Asquith and Archbishop Bourne, on the subject of the Eucharistic Procession.
    Will you kindly send the printed, or newspaper files if you have them at the Home Office.
    They shall be returned.

ARTHUR DAVIDSON

The King to WSC
(*Royal Archives*)

25 March 1910　　　　　　　　　　　　　　　　　　Biarritz

Sir Arthur Davidson is commanded by The King to acknowledge Mr Churchill's Minute and Memorandum regarding the Consecration Ceremonies of the Westminster Cathedral.

As it appears,

(1) that the Procession cannot be regarded as any violation of the spirit of the prohibition

(2) that the Attorney General would not be justified in taking proceedings to stop the Procession

(3) that the Home Office has no power to prohibit the proceedings.

The King says that in these somewhat anomalous circumstances it is evident that the Ceremonies must be allowed to take place.

WSC to the King
(*Royal Archives*)

30 March 1910　　　　　　　　　　　　　　　　　　Home Office

Mr Secretary Churchill with his humble duty to Your Majesty acknowledges gratefully the full and reasoned expression of Your Majesty's wishes in respect to the ceremonies of consecration of Westminster Cathedral, wh has reached him through Colonel Davidson. Mr Churchill is sure the position thus adopted will prove unimpugnable in argument and policy. He is hopeful however that no violent agitation will be fomented. The Protestant associations had a marked and not unjustified success in the case of the 1908 Procession. They would commit a serious error if they were to engage themselves now upon such an unfavourable occasion, wh. might render public opinion unsympathetic to their views.

The correspondence for wh. Colonel Davidson has asked is herewith submitted to Your Majesty.

*　　*　　*　　*　　*

While Churchill was considering his proposals for prison reform, a major industrial crisis broke in South Wales.

Shipping Federation to Home Office
(*Home Office Papers*)

TELEGRAM

19 May [1910]

Copy

Men employed by owners to load steamer *Indian Transport* at Newport Monmouthshire have been attacked, assaulted and grossly intimidated by other labourers on strike and are consequently unable work. Owners are suffering great loss from detention of vessels. Local authorities are unable provide adequate police protection without strong reinforcements from outside. Respectfully request that you will take necessary steps maintain law and order and afford such protection as will enable men engaged to pursue their lawful occupation: matter is urgent. Trust that immediate action may be taken.

SHIPPING FEDERATION

Sir Edward Troup to WSC[1]
(*Home Office Papers*)

TELEGRAM

19 May 1910   Home Office

Three representatives of Empire Transport Company called this morning to represent that, in connection with strike of stevedores loading vessel, serious disturbances have occurred, that police failed to give adequate protection and that their free workmen have been assaulted and intimidated. They ask Home Secretary to intervene. I have told them local police are entirely responsible, and if numbers insufficient should obtain assistance from other forces.

I have also communicated with Board of Trade who had not heard of dispute but Mitchell[2] is now communicating with firm and they will watch the case and give help if possible. Meantime may I telegraph to local police to remind them of their responsibility to maintain order and prevent outrage or intimidation?

TROUP

---

[1] WSC was staying at Canford Manor, Wimborne at the time.
[2] I. H. Mitchell belonged to the Investigators and Labour Correspondent section of the Board of Trade.

WSC to Sir Edward Troup
(*Home Office Papers*)

TELEGRAM

19 May 1910   Canford

You are authorized to telegraph as you propose but if any public announcement is made it should be stated that I have asked the Board of Trade to intervene and that Mitchell had already proceeded to Newport. The Empire Transport Company should be made to realize that employing large droves of men from London to break the strike is a very strong order. Do not on any account give them or the public the impression that we approve their action

CHURCHILL

Sir Edward Troup to Mayor of Newport[1]
(*Home Office Papers*)

TELEGRAM

19 May [1910]   [Home Office]
Copy

It has been represented to Secretary of State that police have not been able to preserve order in connection with strike of stevedores. He desires to remind you that police and magistrates are responsible for maintenance of order and prevention of outrage or intimidation and that if local police are insufficient immediate steps should be taken to obtain assistance from other police forces.

TROUP

Mayor of Newport to Home Office
(*Home Office Papers*)

TELEGRAM

19 May [1910]   [Newport]
Copy

Labour dispute at Newport Docks. Watch Committee to-day authorized Head Constable to take all necessary steps for preservation of the peace. Committee will meet again to-morrow to further consider matter.

MAYOR OF NEWPORT

[1] Councillor W. M. Blackburn.

Chief Constable of Newport[1] to Home Office
(*Home Office Papers*)

TELEGRAM

20 May [1910]

Copy

Watch Committee alive to situation and will require 500 men and 20 mounted officers to afford adequate protection if any further labour imported. Can only get 250 from neighbouring forces. Do not propose to provide additional assistance until informed further importation of labour certain and date. Can Committee obtain adequate notice of this and what men can be sent them? Wire reply.

HEAD CONSTABLE

Sir Edward Troup to WSC
(*Home Office Papers*)

TELEGRAM

? 21 May 1910   Home Office

Chief Constable of Newport in telegram which missed yours asks for 250 Metropolitan Police tomorrow. Henry is replying that he will send men if conditions mentioned in your telegram are accepted and he is getting his men ready.

TROUP

WSC to Sir Edward Troup
(*Home Office Papers*)

TELEGRAM

21 May 1910   Folkestone

Action approved. If they want more they must have more. My address for telegrams all tomorrow is Hotel du Palais Lucerne.

CHURCHILL

---

[1] Mr A. I. Sinclair.

Sir Edward Troup to Mayor of Newport
(*Home Office Papers*)

TELEGRAM

21 May [1910]   [Home Office]

Copy

In reply to Head Constable's telegram of yesterday, the Secretary of State desired me to say that he is confident that you with Watch Committee and Head Constable will take all necessary steps to maintain order and protect life and property. Every effort should be made to obtain ample force of police from other boroughs and from counties. Only in the last resort and when all other efforts to obtain neighbouring police have proved insufficient should application for assistance be made to the Commissioner of Metropolitan Police. He will be ready to send two hundred foot and fifty mounted constables if applied to, but as this measure must be reserved for grave emergency Secretary of State would not be prepared to authorize the despatch of any smaller body. You will of course understand that pay and allowances and all cost of transport must be met by Newport and that borough is fully liable in respect of men or horses injured. Secretary of State would recommend you further to use every effort to dissuade owners from taking action which would provoke conflict. Good offices of Board of Trade should be invoked in the hope of promoting a settlement.

TROUP

Chief Constable Newport to Home Office

TELEGRAM

21 May 1910   Newport

My telegram yesterday informing you of our additional police requirements to protect life and property is unanswered. Imported labour arrives tomorrow. It is essential we should have 250 Metropolitan Police to reach here by two o'clock Sunday afternoon. We have wired the Commissioner requesting these men to be sent. Please wire if we can rely upon your co-operation.

SINCLAIR

Sir Edward Troup to Chief Constable Newport

TELEGRAM

21 May 1910 [Home Office]

Your telegram of yesterday fully answered in Home Secretary's telegram to Mayor sent this morning. If all local resources are exhausted Home Secretary will sanction despatch of Metropolitan Police on terms mentioned in his telegram.

TROUP

Mayor of Newport to Sir Edward Troup

TELEGRAM

21 May 1910 [Town Hall Newport]

I am in receipt of your wire, and Head Constable now shown me your telegram just received. All local resources exhausted and am promised tomorrow sixty men from Bristol and forty from Merthyr, and am hoping to get forty from Glamorgan County and like number from Monmouthshire County: but these latter eighty are doubtful as demonstration is to be made in Cardiff tomorrow and Cardiff City can render no assistance. Imported labour arrives in two sections tomorrow, one by rail, the other by water. In these circumstances shall require 250 Metropolitan foot and 50 mounted policemen. Am providing accommodation for these. Please wire that I can rely upon their being sent in terms of your telegram.

MAYOR OF NEWPORT

Sir Edward Troup to Mayor of Newport

TELEGRAM

21 May 1910

Your telegram received. Commissioner of Police has been authorized to supply the force for which you ask.

TROUP

Shipping Federation to Home Office
(*Home Office Papers*)

TELEGRAM

21 May [1910]

Copy

Fifty five labourers for *Indian Transport* will arrive Newport Sunday evening nine o'clock. Owners have warned Mayor necessity for military protection as attitude and large numbers of strikers threaten very serious danger to persons carrying on work at this steamer. Trust you will take all possible steps assist owners to obtain protection from violence.

SHIPPING FEDERATION

Mayor of Newport to Home Office

TELEGRAM

21 May 1910   Town Hall
                                                   Newport

Serious riots anticipated here in consequence of dock strikes. At meeting of borough magistrates here this morning it was unanimously resolved that the War Office be requested to hold in readiness two hundred infantrymen and one hundred mounted men to assist the local police and five hundred imported police. Duplicate of this telegram sent Secretary of State for War.

MAYOR

Sir Edward Troup to Sir Edward Ward

21 May 1910   [Home Office]

Copy

Dear Ward,

I understand that the Newport Magistrates have telegraphed to the War Office asking you to hold troops in readiness.

The state of things at Newport is serious, and Mr Churchill, before he left, had considered the possibility of their applying for troops. He is most anxious to avoid their being used, and is doing all he can by offering to supply Metropolitan Police and otherwise to avoid the necessity; but of course if the Mayor or Magistrates requisition them, they must be ready to go. Mr Churchill asked me specially to impress on the War Office that *mounted troops* should be sent. They are far more effective than infantry in dealing with a riot, and the risk of their employment leading to loss of life is much less.

Yours sincerely
EDWARD TROUP

Sir Edward Troup to WSC

21 May 1910   Home Office

Dear Mr Churchill,
    The enclosed will show you what has passed since you left up to 6.30.
    I have not yet however got into touch with the WO No one was there or could be reached by telephone or messenger. If the 'possible invader' lands on Saturday afternoon, the WO will read the telegrams announcing his landing on Monday morning!
    I daresay I shall get at someone in time – the troops can hardly be wanted before Monday even at the worst.
    I have written fully to Haldane & explained your views about mounted troops, and of course said that you were doing all you could to avoid the necessity of being there at all.

Yours sincerely
EDWARD TROUP

Your telegram from Folkestone was most useful. They asked for 300: and 300 are being sent (including 50 mounted).

Sir Edward Ward to Mayor of Newport
(*Home Office Papers*)

21 May 1910   War Office

Copy

    Your telegram received. GOC in C Chester has been communicated with and will comply with such requisition as may be found necessary.

Mayor of Newport to Home Office

TELEGRAM

22 May 1910　　　　　　　　　　　　　　　　　　　　[Newport]

Further to telegrams of today, Newport labour dispute just been settled in conference with Mayor and representatives of masters and men, and with assistance of Board of Trade. Police and military assistance not now required. Have communicated direct with Scotland Yard and officer commanding troops at Chester to this effect.

I. H. Mitchell to Home Office

TELEGRAM

10.36 am
22 May 1910

My arrival very opportune. Both parties agreed to Board of Trade arbitration. All men resume work tomorrow morning.

MITCHELL

Sir Edward Troup to WSC

22 May 1910

Dear Mr Churchill,

I have the enclosed telegram from the Mayor of Newport between 2 and 3 o'clock this morning announcing that the Newport Strike had been settled.

I feel sure that this satisfactory result comes directly from your policy of supporting the authorities on the one hand and on the other insisting on conciliation.

I enclose a note of an interview I had last night with Mr Houlder[1] which was disturbing at the moment but is now unimportant. If Mr Houlder bullied his stevedores as he tried to bully me, it is no wonder there was a strike!

---

[1] F. H. Houlder (1867–1935), Chairman of Houlder Brothers, Shipping Company.

I had previously got into communication with Sir G. Ward, and cavalry were ready to go if the Mayor had requisitioned them – but the responsibility for calling them in if required was left entirely to the local authority. The Mayor cancelled all the arrangement for military and police but I made sure last night (or rather at 3 this morning) that the Metropolitan Police detachment was stopped.

Since beginning this note I have a telegram from Mitchell of which I enclose a copy.

Yours sincerely
EDWARD TROUP

Enclosure

Sir Edward Troup's report of his interview with Mr Houlder on evening 21 May 1910.

About 10.45 pm last night Mr Houlder called at my house about the Newport disturbances. He seemed to have dined and was much excited. He said that he had received a telephone message from the master of his ship at Newport, that it was incoherent, and that he made out that 500 strikers were assembled on the dock; that there were only three police on duty; and that his men were trying to save the vessel from attack by getting her off to a buoy in the river. On this Mr Houlder founded a statement that 40 of his men were at that moment being murdered, and he demanded that I should instantly take steps to save them. He said he held the Government responsible; that I was the Government, and that I must stop it! I explained that the local authorities, and not the Government, were responsible, but that the Government were ready to help, and ask him what he wanted me to do. He said 'send police'. I said we were sending 300 police by special train tomorrow. He said that was no use; they must be there tonight and stop the murder. I asked him how I could send men from London to be in the dock at Newport that night; pointed out that his proposal was impossible: told him that the Chief Constable at Newport was making every effort to secure assistance, and that I was certain he would do everything possible to maintain order and prevent outrage.

He said that in the Argentine they managed these things better; they would send artillery and machine guns, and give proper protection to their subjects. He claimed his rights as a British Citizen, and said the Government must give him the protection to which he was entitled *by law*. I again pointed out that *by law* it was the local authorities who were bound to protect him; in this case the Government were giving all the help they could by sending police and otherwise, but that the local authorities were responsible.

He again said that the police were doing nothing, and that there were only three policemen to protect them from 500 rioters. I expressed much doubt as to the accuracy of the information which he had received, but said that, even if it were true, it was clearly for the men on the spot to deal with the immediate crisis, and that directions from the Home Office would only confuse matters and add to the difficulty.

He had, about this time, been joined by his Secretary who assumed the same offensive and bullying manner as his chief. They finally left saying that they were going to the Admiralty to demand assistance from them.

After they had left I sent the following telegram to the Head Constable at Newport:

Representatives of Empire Transport Company state that strikers are attacking their ship tonight and that police protection is inadequate. Secretary of State is confident you are taking and will take all steps necessary to prevent outrage, and restore order. Under Secretary, Home Office.

and in the course of an hour or two received a wire from him assuring me that the statements which had been made were much exaggerated; that the strikers on the dock were few and the police force adequate, and that a conference was then in progress which he hoped would lead to a settlement.

WSC to Sir Edward Troup
(*Home Office Papers*)

TELEGRAM

22 May 1910   Lucerne

Am very glad to hear of settlement. Please send official letter to Board of Trade expressing satisfaction also appreciation of Mr Mitchell's excellent work. Telegraph to Houlder Brothers as follows: Begins: I desire to thank you personally for the assistance you have rendered in the friendly settlement of a dangerous dispute and for the consideration with which you have treated me throughout. I trust your difficulties will not recur. CHURCHILL. Ends. Also send civil letters to Mayor of Newport and Head Constable. Telegrams tomorrow will find me till 5 oclock at Grand Hotel Goeschenen, Switzerland. Shall not reach Venice till Wednesday. Wire full details. Foregoing complimentary messages are not to be sent if you see any serious reason not known to me against them in any case.

CHURCHILL

Sir Edward Troup to WSC

EXTRACT

23 May 1910   Home Office

Dear Mr Churchill,

You may be interested to see Mr Mitchell's report on the Newport Settlement – and copies of the letters of thanks I sent in accordance with your instructions. The terms of the latter were settled after I had heard from Mitchell what part each had taken in the affair.

I hear from Mitchell that there may be a hitch with Houlder who wants to repudiate the settlement but he relies on Macauley[1] (who represented them at then coference) to pull the thing through.

I shall probably telegraph to you about this to Lugano. . . .

Yours sincerely
EDWARD TROUP

Shipping Federation Newport to Home Office
(*Home Office Papers*)

TELEGRAM

2.52 pm   [Newport]
23 May 1910

Copy

At request Houlder Brothers, Shipping Federation have engaged fifty men load their vessel *Indian Transport* at Newport. These men are now on their way to Newport. Chairman Watch Committee and Mayor were advised this proceeding yesterday and this afternoon and requested provide protection. Reply has been received from Chairman Watch Committee that protection will not be granted. Men are due arrive this evening about eight o'clock. Request you will point out to Local Authorities their duty. Their

---

[1] Macauley was the docks manager at Newport.

refusal provide protection is based upon result of some negotiations between certain officials of Union and General Manager of Dock Company to which owners of vessel were not parties and by which they decline to be bound.

TRAFFIC

Sir Edward Troup to Shipping Federation
(*Home Office Papers*)

TELEGRAM

[23 May 1910]　　　　　　　　　　　　　　[Home Office]

Copy

Secretary of State thinks you should at once stop the sending to Newport of men mentioned in your telegram. You will incur grave responsibility if, in disregard of agreement by representatives you import unnecessary labour into Newport.

UNDER SECRETARY OF STATE HOME OFFICE

Shipping Federation to Sir Edward Troup
(*Home Office Papers*)

TELEGRAM

[23 May 1910]　　　　　　　　　　　　　Home Office

Received 7.14 pm

Copy

Telegram received. Secretary of State is misinformed. Owners had no representatives at meeting between Trade Union officials dock manager and Mayor which drew up so-called agreement which is not signed by owners nor anyone purporting to sign on their behalf nor by anyone authorized by them to treat on their behalf. Vessel remains blocked and suffering ruinous delay. Position apparently is that local authorities are averse from giving protection and are seeking pretext for disregarding their duty. Too late now stop men. Respectfully submit they are entitled to be safeguarded in pursuit of their lawful calling. Beg you will do what lies in your power to save them from the violence of Trade Unionists at Newport.

TRAFFIC

Sir Edward Troup to Shipping Federation
(*Home Office Papers*)

TELEGRAM

[23 May 1910]   Home Office

Copy

Secretary of State can only repeat that if you land men at Newport or bring them into docks in present circumstances you will incur very grave responsibility.

UNDER SECRETARY HOME OFFICE

Shipping Federation to Sir Edward Troup
(*Home Office Papers*)

TELEGRAM

[23 May 1910]

Received 9.7 pm

Copy

Reference previous telegram. Have been able arrange stop men en route but you will understand they cannot be indefinitely held back in this way. Local authorities have refused protection pending interview with you tomorrow.

TRAFFIC

Second Report by I. H. Mitchell

DOCK WORKERS, NEWPORT

24 May 1910

[Copy]

I received a telegram yesterday afternoon from Mr Tillett[1] to the effect that Messrs Houlder Bros, Shipowners, Newport, the originators of the trouble at the docks, had repudiated the agreement signed by Mr Macauley,

---

[1] Benjamin Tillett (1860–1943), Trades Union organizer and socialist; Secretary, Dock, Wharf, Riverside and General Workers' Union 1887–1922; Labour MP Salford N 1917–24, 1929–31.

Dock Manager, Newport, on their behalf. This was confirmed by the Chief Constable, Newport, by telephone, who also informed me that Mr Macauley and the Mayor of Newport were journeying to town to see the principals of Messrs Houlder Bros. They were expected to arrive at 4.20 p.m. and I thought it wise to meet them. They urged me to accompany them, which I did, and found the Brothers Houlder in company with Mr Laws of the Shipping Federation. We were informed that the Shipping Federation had had a meeting early in the day and decided not to recognise the agreement. Mr Houlder stated that their local manager denied giving Macauley any authority to act for the firm and that even if he did give such authority he had no power to do so. The local manager told the Mayor by telephone that he *had* given this authority. It was evident that the firm had put itself entirely under the control of Mr Laws, who made no secret of his intentions to importing men to load Messrs Houlder's boat on his conditions. He demanded police protection from the Mayor and altogether made any prospect of settlement impossible.

The position now is that a recurrence of all the trouble is threatened by the action of this one firm, all the men employed by the other firms being back at work. A ship's general cargo is lying at the docks ready to be loaded into one of Messrs Houlder's ships which is along side. If this could be got away Mr Macauley would, if he had power, decline to accept cargo at the dock for this firm and so save further trouble.

Mr Macauley and the Mayor of Newport will call today at Gwydyr House at 12 noon. The Dock Board meets in London at 2 pm.

Mr Laws is meanwhile pressing the Mayor for police protection for the new men he intends sending to Newport. If they are sent a general upheaval seems inevitable.

I.H.M.

Note by Sir Edward Troup

24 May 1910

This report was handed to me by Mr Askwith this morning.

The two telegrams I sent today to Lugano give the subsequent history of the matter so far as HO is concerned.

The conferences which B of T have been holding have not yet led to any definite result – but make it clear that Messrs Houlder are behaving very badly. On Sunday they or their agents so far accepted the agreement as to stop the bringing of 'free labourers' to Newport, & it was only on Monday they decided to repudiate.

Mr Macauley on behalf of the Docks Company offered, if they wd allow the loading of other ships to proceed on the old terms (& under proper inspection tonnage rates), that the Dock Company wd pay them any additional cost they might incur as compared with paying by time – but they would have none of it.

In the interview mentioned by Mr Mitchell they were so violent that he feared they would come to blows with Macauley.

The Mayor, whom I saw today, was vy much disturbed by their conduct. I told him that it was his duty to do his utmost to maintain order: but that he was clearly entitled to tell Messrs Houlder that he could not perform impossibilities, & that if they imported 'free labour' in circs which must necessarily give rise to uncontrollable disorder, their responsibility would be very grave.

24 May 1910

I have acted throughout in consultation with B of T & had a telegram from Mr Haldane approving generally of our line of action.

* * * * *

Sir Hubert Llewellyn Smith to WSC

13 May 1910   Board of Trade

My dear Home Secretary,

I have been thinking very carefully over the idea suggested in your letter of bringing up delegates of the great Trade Unions & possibly Friendly Societies to see the Funeral procession. If anything of the kind were done the Cooperative Societies should also be included. The suggestion is extremely attractive, but I am sorry to say that the more I think it over the more I feel that it would be a mistake. There are I fear absolutely no means of arranging a really representative delegation without causing endless heartburnings & jealousies. As you know there are over a thousand Trade Unions, each of which considers itself important, & though there are Federations & Parliamentary Committees &c, no single Congress or Committee appears on investigation sufficiently inclusive to be recognised as representing them all. Thus we should be forced to select, and I am afraid that this is an impossible task. The jealousies & cross currents are very strong within the Trade Union world, to say nothing of the antagonisms between Trade Unions & non-Unionists or Employers' combinations.

If the intention were to erect a large number of stands to be filled with representative delegations standing for all the principal sides of the national life, & including Trade & Manufacture, Shipping &c, as well as labour, of course Trade Unions & other classes of Workmen's Association should have a prominent place.

But I understand that there are to be no official stands & that the Trade Union stand would therefore be a unique exception. I do not think that in these circumstances it would be wise to proceed with the matter, though I am bound to say that at first I was greatly taken with the idea.

Yours sincerely
H. LLEWELLYN SMITH

Sir Evelyn Ruggles-Brise to Sir Edward Troup
(*Home Office Papers*)

3 June 1910   Prison Commission
                                               Home Office

Sir,

I have the honour to recommend, for the approval of the Secretary of State, that the services of Warders Robert R. Page and Edward V. Lowdell of Warwick Prison be dispensed with, with a month's pay in lieu of notice in each case, for scandalous conduct. On separate occasions these officers while escorting a prisoner to the Police Court made a detour and went to a Public House and drank with him. The officers admit the charge.

I am, Sir, Your obedient Servant
E. RUGGLES-BRISE

WSC Memorandum
(*Home Office Papers*)

9 June [1910]   Home Office

This conduct was grossly improper. Still there is a great distinction between it & any offence like cruelty to a prisoner, false evidence, corruption or open insubordination. Could not a less severe punishment be imposed?
WSC

Sir Evelyn Ruggles-Brise to WSC
(*Home Office Papers*)

10 June 1910   [Home Office]

These Officers were not dismissed, but their services were dispensed with, with a month's pay in lieu of notice, which technically according to Departmental practice, is a much less severe penalty. Dismissal follows immediately upon any of the graver offences referred to by the S of S.

These were very bad cases & the Governor, in submitting them, reported that they had brought great discredit on the Prison Staff, the circumstances having been reported to him by the Police, & the affair had caused much local scandal, the landlord of the Inn himself telling the Officers that they had no business to behave as they did. The prisoner was a notorious character, an habitual drunkard & a violent man, & awaiting trial on a charge of unlawful wounding & larceny. The inn was not even on the way to the Court & the Officers on each occasion arrived late with their charge. The prisoner addressed the Officers in very familiar way, & is stated to have paid for their drinks. Drastic & exemplary action must be taken in these cases if the high character of the Service is to be maintained. It is well known to officers & is laid down peremptorily in Rules & Standing Orders that dismissal will follow upon any action, showing that a Prison Officer betrays the confidence placed in him: that he frequents public houses: that he is unduly familiar with prisoners, etc.

It is & must be a very strict service & this is known & even appreciated by the officers, who take pride in the maintenance of a high standard of discipline.

The Commissioners would fail in their duty if they did not maintain this high standard, even in cases where their compassionate instincts might tempt them to take a more lenient view; but where scandal arises, as in this case, & the general reputation of the Service suffers, they cannot do this; and they feel sure that the S of S will support them in this view of their duty.

ERB

Note by Sir Edward Troup:
    I agree

ET
17.6.10

Note by WSC:
    Action appears to have been taken already.
    If so – what is the use of submitting the case to me?
    Please explain how the matter stands.

WSC
18/6

Memorandum by Sir Evelyn Ruggles-Brise

20 June 1910   [Home Office]

It has been the practice since the passing of the Prison Act, 1877 for the Commissioners to appoint and therefore to dismiss *subordinate* officers (Section 9 of the Prison Act), this, of course being in every case 'subject to the approval of the Secretary of State' as all executive action in Prisons must be (Section 5.2). There is no record of a case where the Secretary of State has called in question disciplinary action taken by the Commissioners in the case of subordinate officers but his formal approval is asked for in order to give the necessary legal sanction to the action of the Commissioners, as every officer of a Prison holds his office during the pleasure of the Secretary of State (Rule 99).

ERB

Memorandum by Sir Edward Troup
(*Home Office Papers*)

23 June 1910   Home Office

I think this is right. It would be a serious hindrance to administration if the Prison Commissioners had to come to S of S for *previous* sanction to the numerous appointments, promotions &c among subordinate officers.

ET

WSC to Sir Edward Troup
(*Home Office Papers*)

24 June 1910   Home Office

I cannot think that this is a satisfactory procedure. In cases where it is not intended to impose a severer punishment than a reprimand, suspension, deprivation of pay &c, I am quite content that my authority should be presumed. But where the final discharge from the service of an officer is thought to be necessary, and where my decision may easily be challenged in the House of Commons, no action other than temporary suspension should be taken until I have had an opportunity of considering the case. In the present case I think the period of suspension coupled with a severe reprimand, and possibly reduction to a lower rank, would have been sufficient. In view of the previous practice I confirm the action taken in this case.

WSC

Memorandum by Sir Evelyn Ruggles-Brise
(*Home Office Papers*)

29 June 1910   Home Office

The Commissioners greatly regret that the S of S is not able to support their decision in this case. Misbehaviour on escort is one of the most serious of Prison offences, & is, I understand, always dealt with in the Army & Navy with great severity. In the Prison Service, where the relations between officers & prisoners are guarded with such extreme care & strictness, any relaxation of discipline in this respect would, they fear, have most untoward results. Had they anticipated the opinion of the S of S, they would, of course, have submitted the case in the first instance, but in ordinary cases, they act by long custom & for administrative convenience as the interpreters of his pleasure, & they assumed that the pleasure would be that officers guilty of this particular offence should not remain in the Service. They were not dismissed, but (a far less dishonouring penalty) their services were dispensed with, with a month's pay in lieu of notice. This is the usual course when it is the pleasure of the S of S that the services of an officer are no longer required.

However, as the S of S is not able to agree with the action taken, the Commissioners feel that they have no alternative but to re-instate these officers with other punishment in lieu, and action has been taken accordingly.

ERB

WSC Note:
I am obliged to the Commrs for the course they have adopted.

Augustine Birrell to WSC
(*Home Office Papers*)

17 June 1910

My dear Churchill,

I am enclosing the memorandum on *Revolvers* & Firing Outrages which I circulated some time ago. It is a serious matter in Ireland & personally I am very sorry that the Peace Preservation Act Ireland 1881 was allowed to lapse some three years ago. It would be impossible *to re-enact* a purely Irish measure but I think you are disposed to favour the consideration of a *general* measure for the whole country, for undoubtedly the evil is spreading everywhere.

I am being pressed about the matter in Ireland & have in answer to

Questions indicated my own desire to see some steps taken. Perhaps you may mention the matter to me in conversation some day soon.

Yours sincy
A. J. BIRRELL

WSC to Augustine Birrell
(Home Office Papers)

19 June 1910   Home Office

Copy

I have sent your memorandum on Revolvers to my Department and have asked them to make me proposals upon it. I still think, however, that it is the Chancellor of the Exchequer who ought to deal with firearms in his next Budget: and I see no reason why persons who cannot obtain a dispensing order from the Home Office, showing that they have need owing to their lonely situation or other circumstances to have revolvers and pistols in their possession, should not be made to pay £1 a year for the privilege.

[WINSTON S. CHURCHILL]

Charles Hobhouse[1] to WSC

June 1910

My dear Churchill,

I have been looking into Ruggles-Brise's proposals for further assistance to convicts on release, and in considering the question I have been struck by the very large (and in many items disproportionate) increase in the cost of prisons that has taken place in the last ten years.

Taking the Estimates for 1900–1 and 1910–11, I see that the estimated prison populations provided for in those two years have been:

1900–1	1910–11	Increase
18,500	22,755	23%

whereas the money provision has been: –

In Prisons Vote (net)	1900–1	1910–11	Increase
	£618,964	£783,077	
In other votes „	103,582	159,479	
	722,546	942,556	30%

---

[1] Charles Edward Henry Hobhouse (1862–1941), Liberal MP East Wiltshire 1892–5, Bristol East 1900–18; Parliamentary Under-Secretary for India 1907–8; Financial Secretary to the Treasury 1908–11; Chancellor of the Duchy of Lancaster 1911–14; Postmaster General 1914–15; PC 1909; succeeded father as 4th Baronet 1916.

The increase on some of the subheads has been quite remarkable. For instance 'Victualling' has gone up by £49,420, or 66%, 'Clothing' by 53% 'Escort &c' by 48% 'New Buildings' (notwithstanding all that has been done in the meantime) by 28%: and the last-named subhead for 1910–11 includes a portion only of the large expenditure of over £100,000 to which we have recently committed ourselves for new schemes in the way of Borstal Institutions and Preventive detention at Camp Hill.

The particular subhead now concerned, viz 'Gratuities to Prisoners and Charities', has already gone up from £10,000 to £16,500, i.e. 65% and supposing we put the net additional cost of the new arrangements at only £7000 (i.e., eliminating the £3000 for Borstal cases, and supposing that you succeed in keeping within your Estimate) we get a total of £23,500, or an increase of 135%.

In view of the foregoing figures, present financial circumstances, and recent expensive departures in prison administration, I think we should have a very good case for criticising very closely the scheme and for asking you at least to postpone it to a more convenient season.

As I know that you are personally interested in this question, I do not want to adopt such a course. I think, however, you might fairly ask the Prison Commissioners to look very carefully into the expenditure under the subheads mentioned above which show such disproportionate increases, and into any others which may also repay attention. They may thus be able to suggest savings which can be utilised towards meeting the irreducible minimum cost of your new proposal, while we, on our part, will contribute towards the cost of a workable scheme and thus enable you substantially to realise your views.

Yours sincerely
C. HOBHOUSE

WSC to Charles Hobhouse

25 June 1910   Home Office

Confidential

Copy

My dear Hobhouse,

I am very much obliged to you for your letter. Let me, first of all, assure you how much I recognise the necessity for the efforts which you make to enforce an effective economy in all branches of the public service, and to secure thorough criticism and canvassing of all new items of expenditure.

At the same time, I cannot say that the inquiries I have made into the general cost of the Prison services have wholly borne out the conclusions of your letter. We very frequently do not spend our estimates. For last year we shall return £25,000 to the Treasury, largely owing to our realizing far more than we anticipated from the proceeds of prison industries. This year the prison population, up to date, is considerably lower than that estimated for, and if it remains at the present level we may be able to surrender a yet larger sum.

The estimates of the years you have selected are particularly misleading. The estimate for the year 1910–11 includes £25,000 for the purchase of Feltham, a quite abnormal and unusual item in an annual estimate; while the estimate for 1900–1 shows a reduced estimate of £25,000 consequent upon the receipt of that sum from the Corporation of London for the purchase of Newgate Prison, which is accounted for under 'Appropriations-in-Aid'.

I do not think that a comparison of estimate with estimate is satisfactory.

I submit that the proper test of the expenditure of a Department is by comparison of actual expenditure and not of estimates. You will see from the enclosed Memorandum the extent to which all recent changes in policy and practice since 1895 have caused a growth in Prison expenditure. There has not yet been time to compile a comparison for 1909–10, but there will be no great difference in the general result. It will be seen from this statement that if the increase in expenditure for 'Victualling' is eliminated (due to the new dietary imposed by order of Parliament, and to increased cost of provisions) there would have been an actual saving if the prison population had remained the same.

Let me say, however, that I shall be very glad if the Treasury can indicate any special branch of Prison expenditure in which, in their opinion, reductions can be made without retrogression or inhumanity.

With regard to 'Gratuities', which seems to be that section of Prison expenditure most nearly related to the new proposals which I am submitting, it is quite true that there has been an increase since the year 1900, but this increase is not great; it is largely accounted for by an increase in the numbers discharged (36,000 more this year than in 1900), and the total cost of gratuities, as they stand today, is only £1,300 more than in the year 1880. I ought, further, to remind you that the Commissioners have a statutory right to give £2 to every prisoner discharged from a local prison, and if they exercised that right to the full without regard to an almost harsh economy, they would spend nearly half a million annually on discharged prisoners.

I cannot feel, therefore, when our actual expenditure is so enormously below our legal powers, that any just charge of profuseness can be sustained.

With regard to the actual proposals which I have submitted to you, and to which, as you rightly recognise, I attach special importance, I am very much obliged for the considerate attitude you have adopted. The awful fact which forces itself upon the attention of anyone who studies our prison statistics is the hopeless regularity with which convicts return to penal servitude. I have discovered that of the convicts discharged during the years 1903-4-5 three out of every four are already back in penal servitude. It is this terrible proportion of recidivism that I am anxious to break in upon. It is clear that the existing attempt at reform, aid-on-discharge, and police supervision, fail altogether to enable or encourage a convict to resume his place in honest industry. A supervision more individualised, more intimate, more carefully considered, more philanthropically inspired, is necessary; and for this purpose I propose to weave all the existing Prisoners' Aid Societies into one strong confederacy, to sustain them with funds on a larger scale than they have hitherto had at their disposal, to place them in contact with individual convicts long long before these are again thrown upon the world, and only to use the ordinary methods of police supervision in cases which are utterly refractory. Sir Evelyn Ruggles-Brise tells me that he is prepared, in order to meet the Treasury wishes, to advise the gradual discontinuance of the 'Gratuity' system to the extent of about £2,000 a year.

This will be a bold experiment, attended with some risk of discontent but he and I are very anxious to give the Treasury practical assurance of the importance which we attach to the new proposals. He cannot put the cost of the treatment of each convict, on discharge under the new system, at less than £6 a head. And when Preventive Institutions are full as they may be in two or three years, the cost of 'after-care' for the assistance of these cases will not be lower. For the present an addition of £7,000 will enable me to carry out the plan I have in view. But it would not be frank to conceal from you the fact that three years hence, should the Preventive Institutions begin to operate, this expenditure will rise to £10,000 a year.

If there are any other points with regard to these proposals on which you desire to receive further information or to offer further criticism, I shall be very glad to send Sir Evelyn Ruggles-Brise over to see you himself, or we can talk about the matter ourselves; but if, as I hope, the reduced request I am now putting forward meets with your approval, I would most earnestly press for a favourable reply without delay. Our time may be very short, and I am most anxious to begin my negotiations with the various Prisoners' Aid Societies concerned.

Yours very sincerely
WINSTON S. CHURCHILL

John Galsworthy to WSC

15 May 1910   Wingstone
                                                                Devon

Private

Dear Mr Churchill,

Justice is about to be published in America; and I would so much like to
add an author's note qualifying the Prison Act in regard to the matter of
separate confinement, if you have modified or are going to modify the
period. Can you find time to tell me whether any decision has been come to?
I heard from Masterman that you were contemplating some change, but
the terms of it I did not grasp. In some countries, of course, (though not in
America I believe) this form of punishment is still carried to the pitch of
excruciating torture, and I [am] hoping my play may reach them; but I
shouldn't like it to do so without (from my point of view) being just to my
own country.

With kindest regards, I am sincerely yours
JOHN GALSWORTHY

Note by WSC:
Tell him changes *are* in contemplation & will be announced shortly. wsc

John Galsworthy to WSC

18 June 1910   Wingstone

My dear Mr Churchill,

Will there be any chance of my being able to see you when I return to
London, about July 5th?

I must record, *à propos* of your proposed Miners Bill, my great admiration
of your efforts in so many directions. You have given a real example of what
can be done by a Minister who is truly stirred to a sense of national needs.

I was glad, too, to see your name backing the Shackleton Suffrage Bill.
For at this time of peace I do hope something will be done. I have always
deplored the militant suffragism which seems to me to negate the very
essence of this movement, which is one towards Gentleness and Justice, and
away from Force. And now there seems a chance, if only people would take
it. I contemplate with something approaching to horror what I seem to see
this country drifting into – men and women definitely set against each other,
and all the havoc that means to the secret nerves and sinews of chivalry, in

the best sense of that word, and to all mutual confidence between the sexes, and to the lowering that will mean to our love of freedom and humanity.

I may be imagining things here, but I don't think so. The use of the writer's temperament, if it's any use at all – which, I suppose, is open to doubt – lies in his being the feelers, nerves, and eyes of a people – the first part of the animal, so to speak, that receives the shock of impressions. You have much of that temperament yourself, and will understand.

If you can spare me a few minutes on Prisons when I come up, it will be good of you.

With best regards, yours sincerely
JOHN GALSWORTHY

WSC to John Galsworthy

21 June 1910　　　　　　　　　　　　　　　　　　　　　　Home Office

My dear Mr Galsworthy,

Very many thanks for your letter, which I have read with great pleasure. If you will let Marsh know when you are back in London I shall be delighted to make an appointment to see you.

Yours sincerely
WINSTON S. CHURCHILL

Lord Knollys to WSC

5 July 1910　　　　　　　　　　　　　　　　　　　　Marlborough House

My dear Churchill,

The King desires me to say he is very glad you have brought in your 'Shop Hours' Bill.

He is in entire sympathy with the object of it, & he hopes that it will be one of those measures which will be disposed of before the House of Commons adjourns.

Yrs sincerely
KNOLLYS

WSC to Walter Runciman
(*Runciman Papers*)

6 July 1910 House of Commons

My dear Walter,

I have read your Choice of Employment Bill with much interest and have discussed it with my Board of Trade friends. I hope it may be arranged that Local Authorities shall only use their powers in accordance with schemes to be approved by the Board of Education after consultation with the Board of Trade, as arranged in the special rules under the Labour Exchanges Act.

This would I think remove the possibility of duplication of machinery.

Yours vy sincly
WINSTON S. CHURCHILL

WSC to the King
(*Royal Archives*)

21 July 1910 Home Office

Mr Secretary Churchill with his humble duty to Your Majesty:

The House yesterday discussed the Home Office & Prisons Vote. On the latter Mr Churchill made a statement of policy & reform wh will he is confident appeal strongly to Your Majesty's mind.

A new effort is to be made to prevent people being sent to gaol for petty offences & thus familiarised with the degrading surroundings of Prison. The Probation of Offenders Act is to be strictly enjoined on magistrates all over the country. A bill is to be introduced to secure by law a period of grace for the payment of fines – (90,000 people go to prison each year in default of payment a third of whom could probably have found money if a few days grace were allowed). Over 5000 lads between 16 & 21 are sent to prison every year for such offences as swearing, stone throwing, gaming, football in the streets. This is pure waste. Mr Churchill thinks a system of defaulters' drills might be instituted – not military (wh would reflect upon the possession of arms) but physical exercises, vy healthy, vy disagreeable; that this might be done at the Police Station; that the boy might do his ordinary work besides, & not be sent to prison unless incorrigible or really dishonest.

No lad between 16 & 21 ought to be sent to prison for mere punishment. Every sentence should be conceived with the object of pulling him together & bracing him for the world: it should be in fact disciplinary & educative rather than penal. The House was vy sympathetic to all this.

In the prisons themselves Mr Churchill proposes to reduce solitary confinements to 1 month (instead of 9) for all except 'old lags' or as they are more decorously called 'recidivists'. Power is taken to pamper the suffragettes & the passive resisters. Further every quarter there will be either a concert or a lecture in each convict prison. These wretched people must have something to think about, & to break the long monotony. Some months ago the Somersetshire Light Infantry quartered at the Verne asked leave to send their band in to play once to the Dartmoor convicts. The effect produced was amazing. These immunising influences must not be neglected. The more strictly discipline is maintained, the more indulgences may follow on good behaviour. There are to be special provisions & regulations for aged convicts & for weak-minded convicts. Lastly the whole system of Ticket of Leave is to be overhauled & reorganised.

The Treasury have given Mr Churchill £7500 a year for this purpose. All the existing Prisoners Aid Societies will be asked to send representatives to a Central Agency, wh will be semi-official (half charitable, half authoritative). This agency will study every convict's case separately: will distribute all the convicts between the different societies: will through these Societies endeavour to help them take their places again in honest life; & the police supervision will be entirely suspended except in refractory cases.

Mr Churchill regrets that fatigue & the late hour prevented him from writing to Your Majesty last night.

WSC to John Galsworthy

30 July 1910   Home Office

Private

[Copy]

My dear Mr Galsworthy,

I am very much obliged to you for your kind letter, and for the excellent valuable support you have given me in the public Press. There can be no question that your admirable play bore a most important part in creating that atmosphere of sympathy and interest which is so noticeable upon this subject at the present time. So far from feeling the slightest irritation at newspaper comments assigning to you the credit of prison reform, I have always felt uncomfortable at receiving the easily-won applauses which come to the heads of great departments whenever they have ploughed with borrowed oxen and reaped where they have not sown. In this case I can only claim a personal interest which has led me to seek the knowledge of others.

I am not quite sure whether I shall be able to carry all my plans through in the autumn. A good many of the administrative changes, however, require no legislation. All the machinery of prisoners' aid can be called into being at once, and I am hoping to make it operative from the 1st January. I expect to pass a little Bill securing time to pay fines, in the autumn session. The legislative treatment of the youthful offender will, however, probably stand over till next year; but of course the Bill will be completed, and will require nothing but Parliamentary time and support.

I am now looking somewhat further afield and bringing the whole subject of imprisonment for debt under review. I shall welcome from you any suggestions you may care to make on any branch of prison and criminal reform. 'Pit Ponies' are being examined by the Royal Commission.

Yours very truly
[WINSTON S. CHURCHILL]

* * * * *

Lord Chief Justice Alverstone to WSC

[22 July 1910]

We disposed of [this man's] case today and in reality there is an overwhelming case against him. There is only one matter that I need point out to you. It is suggested in some of the petitions to you that neither of the pistols were sold to him. As a matter of fact there is no doubt that he did purchase one of the pistols in 1907 and that it would have been proved but for the fact that there was a technical objection because the gun-maker could not swear that the entry made was an entry of his own transaction but might have been an entry of a fact communicated to him by an assistant. This prevented the fact being proved but you can easily ascertain what the true facts are.

WSC to Sir Edward Troup and Mr Blackwell

[? July/August 1910]

1. The second pistol: was it ever sent back as requested to the gunsmith? Have they received it?

2. About how many people left the train [at the station]?

3. How many people were travelling in the first two carriages of the train?

4. How was it that the bag was not found at the foot of the [mine's] airshaft till June? Is the bottom of an airshaft frequently visited?

5. When was [the accused brother's] statement made? Is it a deposition on oath or merely a letter?

6. Was there in fact a carriage at the rear of the train with 'reserved' on one of the compartments? Who was it reserved for?

7. Mr Blackwell enquires by pencil comment 'Where is the brown coat'. Prisoner in his evidence states: 'I have it here.' (In court.) Is this so?

8. What is the time taken between [the two stations] (by train)?

9. LCJ suggests in appeal: bag thrown out of window – it appears to me very improbable – what are your views?

10. There is a story that about a fortnight before the murder passengers travelling in the same train heard shots fired and a bullet came through the window of one of the carriages?

WSC to Sir Edward Troup

The evidence against the prisoner may be considered in three sections. First, the evidence of [the four witnesses] fixing the position of the prisoner in the train. Secondly, the account given by the prisoner of his movements from the time he left [the station] at 11.10 till he returned to his [home station] by the 1.40. Thirdly, subsidiary contributory evidence bearing on pistols, bloodstains and his financial position.

It is upon the first and second sections that the full weight of the conviction must rest. Unless we can be satisfied that these two sets of circumstances are alone sufficient to justify the verdict, the extreme penalty ought not to be enforced. If we are so satisfied, the subsidiary evidence may be considered on its merits as additional proof.

I have considered in the first instance the prisoner's own account of his movements particularly between 11.10 and 1.40. His account of his illness is not necessarily absurd. Why should it be? He suffered from piles – he would know the symptoms. They are not impossible symptoms. On the other hand he could easily invent them. But the kind of things he says he did in view of this malady carry no belief. He cannot remember whether it was a hedge, a railing, a gate or a fence through which or over which he got into the field. He returned to [the station] so hurriedly that he was hot, although it was [a cold time of the year]. He had eased himself in the field by lying down. Yet on arrival at [the station] instead of lying down or resting in the Waiting room, he wandered off into the town. He says that he returned to [this station] rather than to [another nearer one] because there was a refreshment room at [the first]. He does not tell us that he went into the refreshment room.

His errand to the Colliery is of the most shadowy description. Even more unsubstantial is his reason for visiting the 'drift' between [the two stations]. The fact that he had paid similar visits to [the manager] exactly a fortnight previously, i.e. on pay day, cuts both ways and deeper against than for him.

His action on arriving at [the] station appears unreasonable. He had been carried on already beyond his intended destination. He proposed to travel back to [his home] by the 1.40. He had only therefore 2½ hours to walk 5⅛ miles, to find [the manager] at the Colliery and to transact his business with him. He could have got a train back by waiting 10 minutes. To explain his action he has to fall back upon his desire to visit the 'drift' between the [two stations]. Nothing could be less convincing than his statement on this point. His account of his movements and motives, whether in examination or cross-examination, cannot be believed. It is not reasonable. It is quite uncorroborated. If nothing else were known about the prisoner but his own account of his movements between 11.10 and 1.40, the gravest suspicions would be aroused.

The crux of the case is however his position in the train and in relation to [the murdered man]. Three witnesses saw him and [the murdered man] together. [One] saw them together as if in company. He knew them both. [Another] knew the prisoner well. [And the third] knew [the murdered man] well. The evidence of these three directly counters the prisoner's statement that he never was in company with [the murdered man] and that he took his seat in the rear of the train. [One of the witnesses'] evidence appears to be perfectly trustworthy, in spite of the improprieties connected with the identification at [the] gaol. Nothing shakes the combined evidence. It stands by itself, if [the murdered man's wife's] sensational recognition is entirely excluded [after leaving the box, where she had failed to recognise the prisoner, she saw him from another angle and recognised him instantly]. It is completed by the prisoner's own statement that he travelled in a carriage with four or five or six passengers, not one of whom he can recall, although his attention was drawn to the importance of the point within three or four days of the murder – not one of whom has come to corroborate him, widely as this case has been made public. If [the three witnesses'] evidence is believed, the prisoner must be disbelieved and the conclusion is of the utmost consequence.

Now here we have two perfectly separate sets of highly incriminating circumstances. Either, if the prisoner be disbelieved, goes far to establish his guilt; taken together they complete the case against him. There is no reason to doubt the evidence of [two of the witnesses]. Only the most extraordinary series of accidents could possibly have led to an error. How incredible is it that the man who was the victim of such an extraordinary series of accidents should be the same man who, by quite another series of occurrences, should be able to give such an untrustworthy account of his actions after leaving [the] Station. Just as the evidence of [the two witnesses] fits together like a bracelet, so do the two sets of circumstances, namely, those which fix the prisoner's position in the train and those by which he accounts for his movements after leaving [the station]. I have been unable, though I have searched for it, to find any ground for differing on all these points from the conclusions to which Judge, Jury, Court of Appeal and the Home Office experts have, from such different points of view, successively and independently arrived.

The third section of the evidence consists of various separate circumstances, most of which tend, though in very different degrees, to strengthen and confirm the case against the prisoner, not one of which discloses any fact out of harmony with his guilt. First, the bloodstains. Accepting fully that the medical evidence concerning their age is unsatisfactory and not to be relied on, the fact that they are there on the glove and in the trousers pocket remains for what it is worth. Second, the pistols. One pistol, the .250, was certainly in the possession of the prisoner before the crime. As to the [other] pistol, all that can be said is that the prisoner received it under an assumed name, and at a different address. It may well be that both sets of bullets, small and big, were fired by the one pistol; but that theory, or any conclusions drawn from it, do not affect the evidence of his possession of the pistols, so long as we do not attach undue importance to that possession. Third, the prisoner's financial position. No one can doubt that he was pressed for money. The statement of [the prisoner's brother] again taken for what it is worth, which is not much, throws some light upon the mood in which the prisoner would face such difficulties.

The fact that he was carried on beyond [one station to the next one] by mistake on this fateful day, when so many other strange circumstances affected him; the conflict of his story with the evidence of [one of the witnesses] and the method by which the bag could have been carried through a slit in the coat on the right-hand side, all fit in just where they would naturally fit in in the chain of evidence.

The following questions may be asked: Can the prisoner be believed when he says he travelled at the rear end of the train, in a compartment containing five or six other persons? Can his account of his actions between 11.10 and 1.40 at or near [the station] be believed? Can his statement that he was not in financial straits be believed? The answer to each and all of these questions is clearly, No. And that answer leads directly to the conclusion of his guilt.

It should be further remembered that all these questions of fact have been pronounced upon and decided by a Jury under the guidance of one of the most humane and able Judges on the Bench, and by three Judges sitting as

a Court of Appeal. The whole question of facts as well as of law was submitted to the Court of Appeal. All additional information which could tell
in the prisoner's favour was placed before the Court of Appeal. All information that could tell against him was withheld. The careful and trained investigations of Mr Blackwell and Sir Edward Troup have led them to endorse
the verdict of the Jury and the Judgement of the Court of Appeal. My own
conclusions are the same.

Home Office

The verdict must be upheld. The execution of the sentence follows on this
necessarily. The murder was one of the most cold-blooded, deliberately
planned and brutally executed crimes for sordid ends that can be cited. The
law must take its course.

WSC

Sir Edward Grey to WSC

31 July 1910

Dear Churchill,

I return these papers. Unless there were a rule never to confirm a sentence
on circumstantial evidence I do not see how you could do otherwise than
acquiesce in the decision of the jury, the Judge and the Court of Appeal.

I shall treat the case as settled unless something is brought before me
which has not been before the authorities including yourself who have dealt
with the case.

The impression made upon me by the prisoner's account of his own
doings is unfavourable, otherwise I should have felt reluctance to accept the
conclusion to which the circumstantial evidence points.

Yours sincerely
E. GREY

Sir Edward Grey to WSC

21 August 1910   Balmoral

Dear Churchill,

Since the execution of [the convicted murderer] the work from the HO
sent to me has been infinitesimal. One warrant to open letters from an ab-
sconded criminal and one flogging of 12 lashes to an incorrigible tramp, who
misbehaved in prison & when being removed to a punishment cell bashed

one warder in the face with a pair of loose handcuffs, bit a second, and pulled a third to the ground by the testicles.

Nothing new turned up about either of the capital cases, except one or two obviously bogus stories in the case of [the convicted murderer]: but the constant stream of letters pointing out the weak point of the evidence & ignoring the strong points was very uncomfortable. I think this part of the job is beastly & on the night before the two men were hung I kept meditating upon the sort of night they were having, till I felt as if I ought not to let them hang unless I went to be hung too.

I heard a good deal about the [convicted murderer] case in Northumberland all going to prove that he was guilty, but I didn't repeat any of this to the HO so that they should not be influenced adversely to him by anything outside the evidence, & in consequence be reluctant to give him the benefit of any new fact.

I hope you are having a good time; but you are always fresh & everything seems [well].

Y. sincerely
E. GREY

You:

Bliss was it in that dawn to be alive,
But to be young was very heaven.

*   *   *   *   *

Edward Marsh to WSC

23 August [1910]   Home Office

My dear Winston,

Ruggles' breath was rather taken away by your prisons minute and he burst into Homeric laughter when he read that it would be *easy* for the P. Commrs to classify into 20 groups: but on the whole he was enthusiastic, and said your grasp of the subject was marvellous, and that *if* you or a Home Secretary like you were to be here for the next five years, it could be done – but that it is a 5 years job.

Blackwell shook his head over parts of it – especially the idea of a revising board to get uniformity of sentences. He thinks the Courts would strike, as they are very jealous of the interference of the Executive. I pointed to your remark that your proposal seemed only an extension of the principle exemplified by your new rules for offenders not tarred with turpitude – he said that the Courts might now and then submit to what they might consider an encroachment, if they didn't happen to object to the actual reform which it brought about – but that any attempt to make the exception into a system would be desperately resisted. His other criticisms were 1) on the specialisation of prisons. He said it would be very hard on the prisoners to be sent where they could not be visited by their friends – which would be the case if mixed prisons were abolished – also that the difficulties which have always arisen about the transportation of prisoners would be greatly extended. 2) he thought that the circumstances were so different in different cases that there would be no middle course between a rough classification such as we now have, and a classification almost into units.

He was not of course crabbing the scheme, and merely made such comments as occurred to him while he read the minute in my presence – I sent it to Troup but he doesn't mention it in his letter to me which I now enclose –

It will be quite easy to fill up the days from the 25th to the 10th – especially if you go to Dartmoor, which Brise says will take 3 days!

Delevingne does not much want you to have Shop Hours Conferences without him. He simply must have a holiday if he is to survive, and he will only have a month altogether including Lugano. He says there are only minor points to settle, and that there will be heaps of time between the 15th and the introduction of the bill – also that the points are mostly such as might well be left to Charlie. However he is telling Bettany[1] to mug up the bill, which he knows pretty well already, so that if you want conferences before the 15th they can easily be arranged.

I will tell Henry to be prepared for the things you will want from him.

I suppose you will be here for a morning on your way to the manoeuvres, and if you then tell Harris[2] what you want he will have heaps of time to make the arrangements while you are galloping about with French.

I shall start for Italy on the 30th and come back about the 24th, then my plan is to go to Scotland or will you want me back at once?

I'm sending you two more Arnims[3] but I'm afraid you will be disappointed. *The Caravaners* is so much the best of her books that I've read. I'm now preparing my mind for Ravenna with Gibbon, he *is* good –

I'm so glad you're enjoying yourself so much. I envy you your moonlight

---

[1] T. E. Bettany, Junior Clerk Home Office.

[2] Sidney West Harris (1876–1964); Private Secretary to Home Secretaries 1909–19; Assistant Under-Secretary of State Home Office 1919–34; President British Board of Film Censors 1947–60; served also with League of Nations and United Nations; knighted 1946.

[3] Elizabeth Mary Arnim (1866–1941); Novelist; married first, Count Henning August Arnim (d. 1910); second, 2nd Earl Russell (d. 1931). Her books included *The April Baby's Book of Tunes* (1900), *The Caravaners* (1909) and *Elizabeth and her German Garden* (1898).

visit to the Acropolis more than your investigation of the Greek voting system.

Love from

E

You realise that I have no directions as to where to send anything after this occasion.

WSC to H. H. Asquith

26 September 1910   Home Office

[Copy]

As I am sure you will be busy with the Conference in October, I venture to write to you betimes about Home Office business for next year – if there is a next year, as I trust there may be. I have only two Bills of any consequence, neither of which is likely to be controversial, certainly not in any party sense. The Bill for consolidating and amending the Coal Mines Regulation Act is long due. The Royal Commission has now reported and indicated a large number of points on which the laws relating to safety may be improved. The Miners demand, and the Coalowners are prepared to concede, a large number of Amendments. The Bill is now being prepared by the Department, and it will be in complete- draft during November. I shall then go through the main points with the different parties interested, and hope that it may be presented practically as an agreed measure to the Session of 1911. The mass of technical details with which it abounds renders it peculiarly suitable to examination by Grand Committee. I think it will be worth while to mention it in the King's Speech.

The second Bill, (or perhaps group of Bills,) will deal with the punishment of offenders, and will perhaps be more interesting and certainly more extensive than its companion. I hope you will have been pleased by the general good-will with which the prison reforms I announced to Parliament at the end of the Session have been received.

I did not trouble you or the Cabinet with details beforehand as they were all practical matters of administration; but I have never yet launched anything which has commanded such cordial and almost unbroken approval from all sections of the press, in the most Tory and the most Radical papers, they have been equally friendly and favourable, and I have heard the same from members of all parties in the House. I am quite sure that an extensive field of activity is open here in which the Government may gain in a minor way a great deal of commendation. A scientific and benevolent measure, dealing with prisons and the punishment of offenders, would be well suited to the Coronation year, and I am anxious to enlist your sympathy for it and to secure it an adequate place in our general scheme as early as possible.

The main fact on which my attention has been concentrated has been the immense number of committals of petty offenders to prison on short sentences. Out of 205,000 committals last year 61% or nearly 125,000 were committed for a fortnight or less, and of these nearly half so far as is known went to prison for the first time. It is clear to me and to my advisers at the Home Office that there is a terrible and purposeless waste of public money and human character involved in all this. A few days imprisonment to a workman does him as much harm as a much longer sentence, & in the great majority of cases may cause him to lose his job. Large numbers of people are familiarised with the inside of our prisons. They cease to have the fear of them that they should and at the same time they come out at a considerable discount for ordinary industrial purposes.

The short sentence itself is no effective deterrent, as statistics abundantly show; and, on the other hand, as the business of receiving a prisoner is the same for a lad who is in for a week or a convict under a life sentence, this useless succession of short committals imposes a great strain on the prison staff and is the cause of unnecessary expenditure. I wish to break in upon this volume of petty sentences for trifling offences from several different directions with a view to effecting a substantial and permanent reduction in them.

I have not yet come to a final conclusion as to the method by which this reduction should be effected. But there are clearly four main lines of advance: First the treatment of Juvenile Adults. Six or seven thousand lads are sent to prison every year under these stupid, entirely non-curative, short sentences for offences which are not criminal but merely mischievous. That is a great disaster. I may propose to re-enforce the Probation of Offenders Act in regard to juvenile adults by a kind of disciplinary probation, in which some form of physical training, at once highly salutary and extremely disagreeable, will figure prominently. I believe there is no better cure for rowdyism than drill. I have grounds for believing that the obvious difficulties in making the necessary arrangements can, at any rate in the large centres, be satisfactorily overcome. Anyhow I am sure you will assent to the general proposition that it is very undesirable that any lad should be sent to jail unless he is incurable or has committed some serious offence.

My second line of advance is the abolition of imprisonment for debt. Considerably more than 10,000 persons were imprisoned last year on County Court Judgements, and there is no doubt that in the overwhelming majority of cases there was no actual contempt of Court, but a genuine deficiency of means, having regard to their daily needs. The Parliamentary Committee which reported last year, reported against the abolition of imprisonment for debt, but only owing to the fact that Mr Athelstan Rendall[1] voted with the Conservative members, and that Mr Pickersgill,[2] the Chairman, as Chairman had no vote. I do not, therefore, attach much importance to the adverse decision. All the Radicals present except Rendall voted for the Minority Report and total abolition. The Lord Chancellor is, as you know, a strong advocate of this course, and has written to me to that effect. Lord James, Lord Gorell[3] & Sidney Webb have from different points of view written me their opinions at my request. All are for abolition. There is nothing in the argument advanced in some Tory quarters that workmen without imprisonment for debt would not be able to get the necessary credit to tide them over strikes in bad times. It is not the business of the State to facilitate strikes on credit by insolvent workmen. The trade union leaders do not use the argument. They are practically unanimous in condemning the present system of imprisonment for debt. They say that the workman can get quite as much credit as is good for him without pledging his body. Imprisonment for debt is practically non-existent throughout the whole metropolitan area, only one per cent of judgement summonses being followed by committals. It has been completely abolished except in principle without any evil results, on the Durham Circuit by the action of the County Court Judge there since 1901.

It does not exist, either for personal or for trade debts, in France. The law at present is open to grave reproach of partiality as between rich and poor. Only workpeople are sent to prison for not paying their debts. Mr Hooley[4] thrives in opulent insolvency. A thoroughly vicious system of credit, based on no proper security, is spreading among the working classes throughout the country. Its consequences are injurious both to thrift and honesty. Touts and tallymen go round with ever greater frequency and press cheap jewelry, musical instruments, and many other non-necessary articles upon the workman, and still more upon the workman's wife in his absence. The weekly payments, enforceable by imprisonment, are a source of endless vexation and worry to the household, and often a cause of fierce quarrels; not infrequently the workman is taken from his work to prison (under our man-

[1] Athelstan Rendall (1871–1948), Liberal MP Thornbury 1906–22, 1923–4; member of Fabian Society from 1895; joined Labour party 1925.
[2] Edward Hare Pickersgill (1850–1914), a civil servant (Post Office); called to Bar 1884; Liberal MP Bethnal Green SW 1885–1900, 1906–14.
[3] John Gorell Barnes (1848–1913), son of Henry Barnes, Liverpool shipowner; QC 1888; judge of the Probate Divorce and Admiralty Division of the High Court of Justice 1892–1905; President 1905–8; PC 1905; created Baron Gorell 1909.
[4] Ernest Terah Hooley (1859–1947), a stockbroker who made a fortune in London between 1896 and 1898, and then went bankrupt. He emerged again but was sentenced in 1922 to three years' penal servitude, at the end of which he published his *Confessions*.

made laws) for his wife's debts, and often his family is kept by the parish while the State is revenging by imprisonment the injury of a private creditor. All these arguments, with which you are, of course, familiar, are found in the Reports of the Parliamentary Committee, and the Minutes of Evidence. I summarise them here only for the sake of completeness. No doubt certain exceptions should be made to a general abolition of imprisonment for debt – for instance where there is real evidence of wealthy contumacy & in respect of damages for torts or payments under affiliation or separation orders. No doubt the law will require to be somewhat strengthened in regard to the fraudulent obtaining of credit. Imprisonment would, of course, be continued in respect of all existing debts, and it has been suggested that a man with an outstanding judgement summons against him should be required to disclose the fact in the same way as an undischarged bankrupt is.

But in regard to the great bulk of these 10,000 and more annual committals of debtors, I hope it may be possible to make a clean sweep. The question is not without its urgency, as the evil is increasing. Although the conditions of imprisonment of debtors have been made far more stringent in the last two years, and they are now treated practically as if they were convicts, ever larger numbers come upon us every year to the expense of the State, their own injury and the disappointment of their creditors. I recognise, of course, that the question of principle would have to be decided by the Cabinet. I should also have to walk warily so as not to offend or frighten our numerous supporters among the small shop-keepers. I hope, however, to make friends with some of these through their organisations and trade societies during the passage of the Shop Hours Bill in the Autumn, and I am inclined to think that if they are properly consulted while the Bill is in preparation and, as it were, made parties to it beforehand, it will be possible to conciliate them.

The third line of advance by which these petty committals can be diminished is in regard to proper time being given to persons to pay the fine to which they are sentenced. I have had a short Bill drafted to secure by law a week's grace to any person sentenced to a fine less than 10s and a fortnight to any person fined more; but as I reflect upon the whole subject and learn more about it, I feel that what I call 'grace for fines' is really only a part of the large general question of the treatment of petty offenders. I venture to put my plan on this subject before you while it is still in an incomplete condition, and before I am finally satisfied that it is the best method of dealing with the evil.

There are two classes of petty offenders, the occasional and the habitual. No occasional offender ought to be sent to prison for a single trivial offence. Habitual petty offenders ought to be sent to suitable curative institutions for periods adequate to effect sensible improvement in their habits. Vagrancy, drunkenness, obstruction, and the whole category of minor delinquencies for which scores of thousands of persons are imprisoned every year ought to be dealt with in the series and not in the instance. My present idea is to this effect: When a person is sentenced to imprisonment for certain offences (not involving violence, cruelty or the wilful destruction of property), for any period of less than one month, the Court shall declare the sentence to be suspensory in its character. Proper means will be taken to secure the identification of the offender, and if he is convicted subsequently of a similar offence he will be compelled to serve his previous suspensory sentence or sentences, provided that these together with the new sentence aggregate more than one month. The rule-of-thumb principle which I am seeking to establish is prolonged admonition: no imprisonment under a month, and that month a very severe correction. This system, or any better variant of it that may be devised, would require to be, and easily could be, supplemented by a much greater severity in dealing with *habitual* drunkards, rogues and vagabonds. The Courts should be empowered to order a year's training in a suitable institution for any person convicted of these petty offences three times within a twelvemonth, and up to two years' detention if convicted six times within twenty-four months.

By all these various methods I hope to effect:

(a) An immediate and striking reduction in the number of persons annually committed to prison on short sentences. I hope to knock the statistics down by at least a third, perhaps much more;

(b) A certain net reduction, say 10% or 15% in the daily average number of the prison population, and consequently an easement in accommodation; and

(c) A sensible relief owing to the great diminution in the reception and discharge of prisoners, in the work of the prison staff, and also, to some extent, in the cost.

Having thus got something substantial in hand at every point in our prison system, I should then propose to make a complete administrative reorganisation. Classification is the essence of penology. We have already been led to create a number of specialist institutions: Parkhurst, Broadmoor, Aylesbury, Borstal, are instances which readily occur. We have already embarked upon, or are moving forward towards, many other specialised establishments; homes for inebriates, and for inebriate prostitutes, institutions for the criminal weak-minded, detention prisons for recidivist convicts, disciplinary training establishments for juvenile adults, labour colonies like Merxplatz for loafers and vagrants – all are coming *disconnectedly* into view. It would be far better not to make more exceptions from the dead-level of the general prison system. I should propose to survey them as a whole, and organise them (gradually, of course) into one complete series of carefully graded specialised institutions conveniently distributed throughout the country, and adapted to the suitable treatment of every conceivable variety of human weakness and misdemeanour. You will see that this would be only another application of the principles which you and Haldane have adopted in regard to the Poor Law. The general mixed prison should, as quickly as may be, accompany the general mixed workhouse into extinction.

There is only one other point. The Courts, particularly the Benches of Magistrates, are so numerous and so diverse that it is impossible to work any scientific uniform system through them by means of Home Office circulars. There must be hard and fast rules, either embodied in statutes or otherwise clothed with Parliamentary sanction. Much ignorance prevails, with most haphazard methods, throughout the Courts on the differences between imprisonment with hard labour and imprisonment without, and between first and second division offenders. You could not trust the Courts to make the special classification which must be the central feature of any modernised system of criminal jurisprudence. Parliament has already given the Home Secretary plenary powers with regard to the conditions of imprisonment of the various classes of offenders. I should propose to take, by Parliamentary rule (as I have treated the Suffragettes) authority to use these powers to the full. I should set up administratively a Board, (or system of co-ordinated Boards) of Classification, which would consider the cases of all offenders after being sentenced, and distribute them to receive their appropriate treatment throughout the different penal corrective and curative institutions of the prison system: due regard of course being paid to the decision of the Court and provided always that no such modification or variation of treatment shall be in excess or in aggravation of the original sentence of the Court.

These are the general outlines of the proposals upon which the Home Office is now at work, and I should be immensely encouraged to know that you like the look of them in their present crude and skeleton form.[1]

The only other Home Office measures of 1911 will be two or three quite small departmental bills which will be wholly non-controversial in their character, and which you will perhaps allow to take their chance with the rest of the small fry.

[WINSTON S. CHURCHILL]

---

[1] WSC drew up a confidential Cabinet Paper, entitled 'Abatement of Imprisonment', dated 25 October 1910, in which his ideas as expressed in this letter were incorporated practically verbatim.

H. H. Asquith to WSC

2 October 1910   Archerfield House
                                                                Dirleton

My dear Winston,

I am very glad that you are interesting yourself in penal reform. I started overhauling the prisons when I was at the Home Office 15 years ago, and though we had not time to accomplish much, I was able to leave behind me, in Ruggles-Brise, a most capable & large minded administrator, whose counsel you will I am sure find invaluable.

I am entirely with you in regard to the evil of short sentences, & generally in regard to a better classification of offences & offenders.

The abolition of imprisonment for debt is a more difficult matter. The theory of the law is that no man can be sent to prison for the non-payment of a civil debt unless he has the means to pay it, but refuses to do so. In practice, this often works very harshly, & undoubtedly the existence of such a remedy stimulates & encourages the worst forms of touting for credit orders. But a proposal to abolish it (which I am quite prepared to support) will be found to be a highly controversial measure.

                                                    Yours vy sincerely
                                                    H. H. ASQUITH

Earl Beauchamp[1] to WSC

31 October 1910   Privy Council Office

My dear Churchill,

I thought your earlier prison reforms excellent – and these new ones seem to me better still. They are *admirable*. I wish you every success.

                                                    Yours vy sincerely
                                                    BEAUCHAMP

C. P. Scott to WSC

2 November 1910   Fallowfield
                                                             Manchester

My dear Churchill,

Very many thanks for your letter. I've been thinking a lot about it. I confess I think it would be well worth while even to delay social reform for a

---

[1] William Lygon, 7th Earl Beauchamp (1872–1938), First Commissioner of Works 1910–14; Lord President of the Council 1910, 1914–15. Succeeded his father 1891. Married Lettice Mary Elizabeth Grosvenor, sister of 2nd Duke of Westminster, in 1902. Privy Councillor 1906; KG 1914.

year if the alternative were to teach people that they can commit follies and extravagances without paying for them. So far as I can see the only possible check on this kind of thing is the necessity of paying the bill and if we are going to remove that we shall go from bad to worse. A little loan would be cowardly and a big loan wd be preposterous. I can't see any way out except by the road of honest finance and rather than desert it I wd gladly see another twopence on the income tax. There wd be a howl, but we could stand it. The loan policy wd be the less defensible in the present instance because the Government itself deliberately created the scare the consequences of which it is now called upon to face. Forgive me if I appear to you unreasonable. You know one would not lightly oppose one's party on a vital matter like this.

Yours sincerely
C. P. SCOTT

* * * * *

Sir Arthur Bigge to WSC

[Wednesday] 9 November 1910 York Cottage
Sandringham

Dear Churchill,

The King is concerned at the accounts given in the newspapers about the Riots in S. Wales.

Possibly these may be exaggerated.

His Majesty would be glad if you could let him have a short report of the actual state of things & of the steps which have been taken to deal with the trouble.

It seems rather hard upon the metropolitan police that they have to be imported into the disturbed area!

Yours very truly
ARTHUR BIGGE

WSC to the King

[November 1910]

[Draft]

Reports to-day from the whole of the Rhondda Valley are satisfactory. Absolute order has been maintained around all the threatened collieries.

A few trifling incidents of window breaking have occurred in two of the villages. The 1,400 Police at the disposal of the Chief Constable will, it is expected, be able not merely to prevent attacks upon the collieries but to control the whole district and to deal promptly with any sign of a disorderly gathering large or small. No need for the employment of the military is likely to occur. They will be kept as far as possible out of touch with the population, while sufficiently near to the scene to be available if necessary.

With regard to the action taken by the Home Office on Tuesday, the following facts should be known:

The 400 Cavalry and Infantry which were sent for by the Chief Constable on Monday night were not started by the Secretary of State for War or by the Home Secretary, but were sent, pending superior instructions, by the General Officer Commanding of the Southern Command. Up to 10 o'clock on Tuesday morning the Home Office had no knowledge of this movement or of the necessity for it. At 11 o'clock Mr Churchill, after consulting with Mr Haldane and communicating by telephone with the Chief Constable of Glamorgan at Tonypandy, definitely decided to employ police instead of military to deal with disorder, and, while moving troops near to the scene of disturbance, to keep them in the background until it was certain that police methods had proved insufficient. From this policy there has been no change whatever. 300 Metropolitan Police, of whom 100 were mounted, were ordered to start for Pontypridd as fast as trains could be got to convey them. This force of picked constables experienced in the handling of crowds was for every purpose better suited to the needs of the situation than an equivalent body of military. Infantry soldiers can if attacked or stoned only reply by fire from long-range rifles which often kills foolish sightseers unconnected with the riot, or innocent people at some distance from it. The Chief Constable of Glamorgan concurred in the substitution of the Metropolitan Police for the Infantry, who were halted at Swindon, and the Cavalry were told to proceed no further than Cardiff and to await further instructions there. General Macready was specially selected to take charge of any military forces which might be required to support the police. He proceeded at once to Cardiff where it was intended the Cavalry should remain pending further developments. As, however, the special trains conveying the Metropolitan Police were not expected to reach the scene of the disorder until about 9 pm on Tuesday night, both General Macready and the Chief Constable were authorised to move the troops forward if they considered it necessary. The train conveying the Metropolitan Police was delayed for about an hour in reaching its destination. All the attacks of the rioters upon the Glamorgan Colliery were, however, successfully repulsed by the Chief Constable with the County Police at his disposal, and when the Metropolitan Police arrived the rioters had already been beaten from the collieries without the aid of any reinforcement either of London police or military. The insensate action of the rioters in wrecking shops in the town of Tonypandy, against which they had not the slightest cause for animosity, when they had been foiled in their attacks upon the colliery, was not foreseen by anyone on the spot, and would not have been prevented by the presence of soldiers at the colliery itself. There is no reason to believe that the first contingent of the Metropolitan Police with the local police forces already gathered was not and is not sufficient to deal with the situation in the district without additional help. With the view however of increasing the strength of the police force in the district to a point which will obviate all risk of having to use the military, two further contingents, aggregating 500 additional police, have been sent from London. The whole district is now in the effective control of the police, and there appears to be no reason at present why the policy of keeping the military out of direct contact with the rioters should be departed from.

The King to WSC

TELEGRAM

10 November 1910   Sandringham

Many thanks for your full report with regard to Riots in Wales. Glad you are satisfied with the latest news and I trust that matters will soon settle down. Trust that it is not true that all the horses have been lost in one of the mines.

GEORGE R. I.

The Master of Elibank to WSC

10 November 1910   12 Downing Street

Confidentially dictated

My dear Churchill,
    Please see accompanying articles in:

> Morning Leader
> Daily News
> Daily Chronicle
> Manchester Guardian and
> Liverpool Daily Post

from which you will see that the principal Liberal papers in the country are backing you. The Editors were very nice when I mentioned the matter to them.

Yrs always

ALICK MURRAY

Morning Leader

9 November [1910]

There have been some deplorable excesses in connection with the miners' strike in the Rhondda Valley, and the first intention was to send troops, mounted and unmounted, as requested by the Chief Constable, to repress disorder. The introduction of military force on a big scale into such a district is an expedient which no one can regard without apprehension. The country does not want another Featherstone,[1] and Mr Winston Churchill in consultation with Mr Haldane, has thought out a much better way. He is sending down a force promptly, not of soldiers, but of Metropolitan police to the Cambrian Collieries, to see whether, with their special aptitude in dealing with crowds, they cannot preserve public order. Meanwhile, the regulars are held in reserve. It is an experiment as interesting as it is humane, and, considering the demands made upon the police force by to-day's silly procession and the Guildhall banquet, bold. It is accompanied by an appeal to the miners, of which they will almost certainly feel the force, to put an end to rioting and to discuss their case with the Board of Trade. That is entirely the right line for a civilised Government to take. The appearance of soldiers is always likely to provoke the violent resistance their rifles afterwards quell, while they are necessarily without the London policeman's instinct for prevention instead of cure. . . .

Daily News

10 November [1910]

An evening paper yesterday blamed Mr Churchill for 'countermanding the orders for the troops to come out', and complained that with 'a couple

---

[1] Urban district in the West Riding of Yorkshire about 2½ miles from Pontefract, where, in 1893, some miners were shot dead during a riot. Lord Bowen's report on the Featherstone riots, dealing with the duty of soldiers called in in aid of the civil power, is the *locus classicus* on this point.

of hundred good cavalrymen last night's trouble would never have happened'. Observations of this sort are a gross injustice to Mr Churchill and what is very much more serious, they point to a sentiment which if allowed influence would convert a riot into a social disaster. It is the duty of a Government to preserve order, and it is the duty of the Government to preserve order without bloodshed. We have no doubt that had the Home Secretary launched soldiers with rifle and sword against the Welsh strikers the riots might be checked, just as they might be converted into a civil war. What is quite certain is that the rifles would go off and the sabres would cut, and many a family in Wales would be mourning its dead. 'Strong' action of that kind might satisfy the blood lust of perverted minds, but it would be a crime against society – one of those crimes for which society takes revenge. Mr Churchill has preferred a wiser and more humane, if less sensational, mode of restoring order. He has sent what should be sufficient police to restore order, and the military are not to be used save in an emergency grave enough to call for dangerous as well as drastic measures. We have little doubt that the police will succeed in preventing further outbreaks, and the action of the police will not result in bloodshed or leave behind a bitter sense of grievance.

Daily Chronicle

10 November 1910

If it is unhappily necessary to employ military force in order to restore order in the mining district of South Wales, the rioters will have nobody to blame but themselves. The Home Secretary has carried conciliatory methods to the last possible point, and has boldly taken upon himself a serious responsibility in holding back in reserve the troops for which he was asked. The Miners' Federation, 'while deeply regretting the disturbances which have arisen, consider that the civil forces are sufficient to deal with them'. Unhappily, the sufficiency was not very clearly proved in the events of Tuesday night. Still, no loss of life has occurred, and unquestionably it is better to rely upon the police alone, if such reliance is in any way adequate. To have employed the military at once might very probably have caused as much disturbance and destruction in one direction as it could have prevented in another. It might very possibly have led to loss of life, which so far has been avoided. But the rioters must remember that the primary duty of any Government is to enforce law and order, and to establish security of life and property. His Majesty's Ministers are not unmindful of this duty. . . .

The Editor of the Cambria Daily Leader *to WSC*

10 November 1910   Leader Buildings
                                                        Swansea

Dear Sir,

I trust you will not consider me presumptuous in addressing you but whilst you are being subjected to so much criticism in respect of Tonypandy I think you ought to know that there are many Welshmen who think that in delaying the military you acted better than you knew. The state of affairs was deplorable – no one can possibly palliate it – but it might have been infinitely worse. The wrecked property can be restored, the broken heads can be rested, but there would have been no possibility of recalling the sacrifice of life that would have resulted inevitably from a conflict between the infuriated miners and an armed body of men. Featherstone would have been completely eclipsed by Tonypandy had you acted with more precipitation and less wisdom.

I am yours faithfully
THOMAS REES

WSC to David Lloyd George

13 November 1910   [Home Office]

[Copy]

I am deeply concerned at the situation in South Wales. The tension has not at all diminished, and only the great force of police and military has prevented an outbreak. Unless the situation is relieved there will be a battle royal between the police and the rioters at no distant date. I believe the police will be found strong enough to beat all rioters without any recourse being had to the military. But you will see that I cannot keep this great number of Metropolitan Police indefinitely occupied there, and the time will come in the course of the next week or ten days when I shall have to leave the soldiers in much more naked contact with the population than is now necessary. If the strikers delay rioting until the police force has been reduced they may come right up against the rifles with consequences of the utmost gravity. It appears to me, though I have received no information from the Board of Trade, that their intervention has failed to arrive at any agreement. The correspondence which I enclose (my letter will not be sent until to-morrow at 12 noon) shows you the spirit in which the colliery owners are treating the whole question. I feel convinced that unless some stronger intervention than any we have had is afforded, disaster may easily occur. As the Minister responsible for maintaining order I shall be very much obliged if you will tender your services to the Cabinet. I am satisfied that your influence in Wales and your knowledge of the Welsh language fully justify the departure from ordinary departmental practice. Unless some real quality is put into this business we shall get into very deep water indeed.

WSC

G. R. Askwith to WSC

13 November [1910]   12 Hans Crescent

Dear Home Secretary,

At my meeting with the employers connected with the disturbed mines on Saturday at Cardiff, they unanimously considered that any present action by the Board of Trade would be premature and that they would do nothing unless the constitutional position was restored – I am inclined to think that the constitutional leaders more or less agree with this – Mitchell will be in Cardiff on Monday to see about the 'black leg' difficulty in the Rhondda Valley, and may effect an arrangement. Unless the men approach the employers in the way laid down by them, imported labour may be necessary both there and at other times to protect power houses and valuable property, which for the first time in Welsh strikes the miners are not allowing to work.

The employers particularly stated that they ought to have adequate protection for life and property.

I said I had no administrative power in the matter, but would convey their statement to the Home Office.

In my opinion the lock-out and strikes may last for some considerable time.

I have caught a severe chill and been ordered to go to bed at once. I hope it will not last. Hence this dictation.

Yours very sincerely
G. R. ASKWITH

Sidney Buxton to WSC

14 November 1910   Board of Trade

My dear Churchill,

I will certainly keep you informed in reference to the progress of negotiations in South Wales.

Askwith has already given you shortly an account of his proceedings. The impression left on his mind is that, for the moment, active intervention by the Board of Trade would be premature. The employers that he saw were unanimously of opinion that any action would be premature, as they could not settle until constitutional action was resumed, and, to obtain that, it was necessary to bring the unauthorised people into line, and their view was that the men's leaders were not averse to the same course.

The owners will continue to give us the information in their power, and they recognise the courtesy and tact shown by representatives of the Board of Trade, and would not scruple to communicate with us as to any assistance that might be thought desirable.

Askwith has already told you the information we have in regard to the blackleg difficulty, and I need not repeat it.

I hope Mitchell will be able to effect an arrangement.

Yours very truly
S. BUXTON

Sir Arthur Bigge to WSC

15 November 1910   York Cottage
                                                    Sandringham

Dear Churchill,

The King thanks you for your letter of today about the Welsh Riots. He is glad that you have confidence in General Macready, who seems to be doing very well, & that you are hopeful of a settlement.

His Majesty was interested in the enclosed Reports which I return.

The police must have behaved capitally & The King was much pleased to learn from the H of C telegram tonight that you had defended them against Mr Keir Hardie's attack.

Yours very truly
ARTHUR BIGGE

WSC to Mr J. A. Seddon[1]

16 November 1910

Copy

You must not consider that the Shops Bill is dropped or shelved. It has had to be postponed temporarily on account of the extraordinary political

[1] James Andrew Seddon (1868–1939), President of Shop Assistants Union; Labour MP for Newton division of Lancashire 1906–10; for Hanley 1918–22. Chairman British Trades Union Congress 1914. CH 1918.

crisis which has arisen. The Prime Minister authorises me to say that if we should continue to be responsible for the government of the country we shall carry it forward again when Parliament reassembles, and I shall then be ready to continue the process upon which the Home Office has been engaged for the last six weeks of endeavouring to shape and modify the Bill to reconcile the varying needs and interests of all classes affected by it. We have not put our hands to this plough without intending to drive it to the end of the furrow; but we must be supported.

WSC to the King
(Royal Archives)

EXTRACT

22 November 1910   Home Office

... There was a hard furious fight last night in Tonypandy. The police were quite strong enough to scatter the rioters & beat them out of the town. The military were at hand but did not have to fire. All is quiet now. Six policemen have been severely injured & many of the rioters. Mr Churchill is quite satisfied that sufficient forces are upon the spot. There is and will be a good deal of petty disorder in the district & constant patrolling would exhaust even the large police contingents now concentrated. But in any pitched battle between the rioters & the police, the latter will be swiftly victorious. If not the troops have full liberty to act. ...

WSC to the King
(Royal Archives)

23 November 1910   Home Office

Mr Secretary Churchill with his humble duty to Your Majesty:

The House of Commons separated yesterday after the close of questions, the stages of the Budget Bill having been agreed to without debate.

Later reports from Tonypandy show that the forces in the district are ample to cope with disorder. The rioters have had a good dusting from the police & it has still been possible to keep the military out of direct collision with the crowds. The tension is however acute. The owners are vy unreasonable as well as the men; & both sides are fighting one another regardless of human interests or the public welfare.

Mr Churchill was questioned in Parliament yesterday both from the Labour & Conservative benches. But no one has attempted to challenge the policy wh he is pursuing.

The suffragettes have also been behaving in a vy naughty manner. Mr Churchill proposes to prosecute today only those who are guilty of acts of serious violence or wanton damage, & not to press the charges against mere destructionists arrested for their own protection rather than for misconduct. The Prime Minister concurs. Further trivial disorders will probably occur today & tomorrow, & public opinion will be increasingly alienated from these foolish people.

WSC to the King
(*Royal Archives*)

25 November 1910   Home Office

Mr Secretary Churchill with his humble duty to Your Majesty: The House was crowded in every part this afternoon. The Chancellor of the Exchequer in the absence of the Prime Minister moved an immediate adjournment till Thursday and this was later altered to Friday to suit Mr Balfour & his friends. On that day the Prime Minister will make his statement.

Upon the motion for adjournment Mr Keir Hardie raised the Tonypandy riots, the impropriety of sending military & the harsh methods of the police. He & other Labour members demanded an inquiry. Mr Churchill made a non-provocative reply but gave no inquiry. The Labour party thereupon voted against the adjournment as a protest. The Conservatives did not support the cause of law & order in any strength and it was left to the supporters of the Government to resist the Labour demand. The division yielded a majority for the Government of 120.

Mr Churchill's conduct was not challenged in any quarter of the House except from the Labour benches.

Afterwards a tussle took place between Mr Pretyman & Mr Lloyd George about valuation. The House adjourned at six o'clock.

General Macready to WSC

EXTRACT

1 January 1911   New Inn Hotel
                                                             Pontypridd

My dear Mr Churchill,

I am very much obliged for the kind and flattering way in which you have expressed your appreciation on behalf of His Majesty's Government for any services I have been able to render while in the Strike District.

The success in carrying out your system of importing Metropolitan Police in addition to the Military, in order to quell disturbances, has been due to a very large extent to the loyal co-operation of the superintendents and inspectors in charge of the Metropolitans, and also to the manner in which my Staff and Intelligence officers have assimilated themselves to a condition of things rather foreign to their usual military duties. Without the excellent intelligence system that they have inaugurated, it would have been impossible to have kept one's finger on the pulse of the two 'belligerents'. For myself I can only say that though the work has at times been anxious, it has none the less been extremely interesting, and has given me an opportunity which I should have been very sorry to have missed.

I do not propose to leave before Wednesday, as there is an important meeting being held on Monday, and I hope that the engineers will then finally break away from the coalcutters, if so, a great step in advance will be taken. I am preparing a memorandum, giving shortly the results of my experiences here, which may be of use both to you and to the War Office when strikes occur in the future, and I will bring a copy of it with me when you are at liberty to see me on my return to London. . . .

Yours sincerely
C. F. N. MACREADY

WSC to the King
(*Royal Archives*)

EXTRACT

8 February 1911   Home Office

. . . After dinner the conduct of the police in the Welsh riots was discussed. Mr Keir Hardie repeated in a moderate form the malicious & offensive statements he has been disseminating during the election. No Unionist speaker took part in the debate to support Mr Balfour in his attack on Monday on the Home Secretary's alleged vacillation; so that instead of being blamed for not employing enough force, Your Majesty's servant was scolded for employing too much. Mr Churchill could not assent to an enquiry into the conduct of the police, who rendered excellent service and ought not in reward to be put upon their trial.

The House was pleased to view the reply with approbation; & Mr Churchill learned that all parties – Conservatives, Liberals & Labour men were satisfied & only Mr Keir Hardie was offended. . . .

*   *   *   *   *

16
Home Office 1911

(See Main Volume Chapter 11)

The *Annual Register* records:—

The preparations for the [Coronation, which took place in June 1911,] were accompanied by the final destruction of a baseless slander which had been circulated for years in all classes of society, and had persisted in spite of public and authoritative protests and contradictions during 1910. The story was that King George V, when a midshipman in the Mediterranean Fleet, had contracted a secret marriage with a daughter of Admiral Sir Michael Culme-Seymour,[1] its Commander-in-Chief. It had been formally contradicted in a speech by the Dean of Norwich in July 1910, and by Sir Arthur Bigge, one of His Majesty's private secretaries, in *Reynolds's News-paper* of October 30, 1910; but it had been repeated by one Edward F. Mylius in November and December in the *Liberator*, a paper published in English in Paris by William Holden James, for the promotion of Repub-licanism. Mylius had asserted that the marriage had taken place in 1890, and that the King's subsequent marriage in 1893 was sham, shameful, and bigamous, and an offence against the Church. He had become connected with the *Liberator* through Pandit Shiyamaji Krishnavarma,[2] now resident in Paris, and had distributed it in England. The parcel had been examined by the police at Newhaven.

---

[1] Michael Culme-Seymour (1836–1920), 3rd Baronet; Admiral 1893; Vice-Admiral of the United Kingdom 1901–20; Commander Mediterranean Squadron 1893–7; C-in-C Plymouth 1897–1900.

[2] Krishnavarma had founded the Herbert Spencer lectureship at Oxford in 1904. He was barred from the Inner Temple on 1 May 1910 for having written a letter to *The Times* which was said to condone Indian unrest.

WSC to the King
(Royal Archives)

24 November 1910   Home Office

Mr Secretary Churchill with his humble duty to Your Majesty herewith submits the opinion of the Law Officers of the Crown upon the *Liberator* libel.

Mr Churchill proposes now to ask them more precisely whether a double prosecution could not be simultaneously instituted: first – action by the Culme-Seymour family from which no conviction might follow but wh would conclusively demonstrate the falsity of the libel: & secondly prosecution for a seditious libel on Your Majesty which would effectively secure the punishment of the offender. He will put this to them today.

The general question of policy need not be considered till after the legal aspect has been disposed of.

WSC to H. H. Asquith

26 November 1910   In the train

[Copy]

My dear Prime Minister,

As the King is sure to speak to you while you are at Windsor upon the *Liberator* libel, I send you a note which I have dictated upon the present position, and the successive steps which should be taken. Provided that all the conditions are satisfied, I am strongly of opinion that action should be taken and The King's good name cleared from such cruel & widely circulated aspersions.

Yours very sincerely
WINSTON S. CHURCHILL

Note by WSC

26 November [1910]   Home Office

The Liberator

The Law Officers of the Crown have given their opinion as follows:—The paper undoubtedly contains a criminal libel on the King. An action by the Culme-Seymour family would demonstrate the falsity of the libel, but would probably fail to secure a conviction in the face of a defence that it was the King and not the Culme-Seymour family who was attacked. A prosecution for seditious libel on the other hand would secure a conviction, but would afford no occasion for demonstrating the falsity of the libel. Both these courses are therefore unsuitable. Procedure by a criminal information for criminal libel on the King in the Court of King's Bench would however not only secure a conviction, but enable the falsity of the libel to be demonstrated. It would not be necessary for the King to appear as witness. Action could be taken on his behalf by the Attorney General, as was done in the case of George III. It is this third course therefore which alone is suitable.

Measures are being taken by the police to secure evidence of the publication of the libel by some person of sufficient substance to warrant a prosecution. If this evidence is not now obtained it may be obtained later.

The Law Officers, either by themselves or in consultation with Sir Charles Mathews,[1] should collect the evidence and prepare the case by which the falsity of the libel would be demonstrated.

These matters being settled, it would be for HM to decide whether action should be taken, but Mr Churchill would feel bound to consult the Prime Minister before finally advising HM on a matter of such serious consequence.

WSC

Edward Marsh to Sir Arthur Bigge
(*Royal Archives*)

18 December 1910   Home Office

Dear Sir Arthur,

Mr Churchill is sending The King a letter to say that all is now ready for proceeding by criminal information in the Court of King's Bench against Mylius for the publication of the *Liberator* libel; and that subject to HM's personal wishes both he & the Prime Minister are prepared to advise this course.

If HM agrees to this Mr Churchill proposes to have a meeting for final discussion of the matter next Thursday at 3 o'clock at the Home Office. He will in that case ask the Law Officers, Sir Charles Mathews, Sir Edward Troup and Sir Edward Henry to come, and he hopes you may also be able to be present.

Yours very truly
E. MARSH

[1] Charles Mathews (1850–1920), Director of Public Prosecutions 1908–20; stepson of Charles James Mathews, the comedian; Recorder of Salisbury 1893–1908; knighted 1907.

WSC to the King
(*Royal Archives*)

18 December 1910   [Home Office]

Mr Secretary Churchill with his humble duty to Your Majesty:

It will be seen from the enclosed note by Sir Charles Mathews that full & effective evidence of the publication of the *Liberator* libel has now been obtained by the police against Mylius. The evidence of the Culme-Seymour family is also being collected & will be ready shortly. The procedure exists by which upon a criminal information in the King's Bench the falsity of the libel can be demonstrated & the offender convicted without any need for Your Majesty's personal intervention. There are therefore no obstacles in the way of action save such as may arise from public policy or Your Majesty's inclinations.

There is no absolute necessity for action to be taken as Your Majesty's good name is beyond reproach in the eyes of the overwhelming majority of the nation & the libel is only an obscure undercurrent circulating among the credulous & base. Still it is sufficiently widespread to be a source of vexation to Your Majesty and Mr Churchill learned that it was Your Majesty's wish that its falsity should be demonstrated & justice be done upon the libeller. If then it be desired to strike at the libel and sweep the falsehood out of existence once and for all, the opportunity has now presented itself & may not come again of dealing with it in a tangible form & in a person not quite of the lowest class.

Mr Churchill has brought these considerations before the Prime Minister who says that 'if the Law Officers advise that the tackle is in perfect order, & the King is agreeable, I think you would do well to take the opportunity of crushing this thing out.' Mr Churchill favours action himself & is prepared, subject to Your Majesty's personal wishes, to take full responsibility for advising it. He would be glad to have a final expression of Your Majesty's pleasure in this matter. The case is not free from urgency as the offender may at any moment become alarmed at the detention of his packet & may fly the country. In the event therefore of Your Majesty's decision being in the sense of action, Mr Churchill would arrange to confer with the Law Officers and with Sir Charles Mathews on Thursday next & he thinks that Sir Arthur Bigge ought to come too, in order that a final survey of the whole position may be taken before a decisive & irrevocable step.

Mr Churchill begs in conclusion to express to Your Majesty his sincere sympathy that Your Majesty should have been the object of such vile calumny & with his humble duty remains Your Majesty's

faithful & devoted servant
WINSTON S. CHURCHILL

Memorandum by Edward Marsh
(*Royal Archives*)

A police officer can prove that an envelope containing about 100 copies of the November number of the *Liberator*, & addressed by Mylius to a Communist Club in Charlotte St was opened by the police officer & its contents seen by him. The officer closed the envelope and marked it with a private mark, & on the same evening saw Mylius post it. Next morning the officer saw & examined the same envelope, which he identified by his own private mark, & its contents, at the Paddington district sorting office, where it now remains.

WSC to The King
(*Royal Archives*)

22 December 1910

Dictated

Mr Secretary Churchill with his humble duty to Your Majesty:

In further consultation with the Law Officers, Sir Charles Mathews and Sir Edward Henry, it has become clear that Mylius would be able, if he chose, to claim that the article in the *Liberator* should be read as a whole, not only that part which affects Your Majesty, but that which asperses the late King and the Prince Consort. The reading of this article in Court would of course give it a universal publicity, and it is possible that the prisoner might also put some offensive questions. All this would be irrelevant to the point to be decided, and would not affect, except perhaps to aggravate it, the sentence of the Court; but Mr Churchill feels that he must be precisely assured that Your Majesty has read the article in its entirety, and is indifferent to the possibility of a certain amount of scandalous and offensive imputations upon others besides Your Majesty obtaining incidentally public expression. Mr Churchill does not himself regard this possibility as any valid argument against action. No doubt a man like Mylius, with his back against the wall, will spatter any dirt he can in the course of his defence. But Mr Churchill feels it his duty to put all contingencies before Your Majesty, especially those of which Your Majesty is the sole judge.

In the meanwhile no action is being taken, the legal procedure is being tested from every point of view, and Mylius is being carefully watched. All of which is now humbly submitted by Your Majesty's faithful and devoted servant

WINSTON S. CHURCHILL

Sir Frederick Ponsonby to Edward Marsh

23 December 1910

Dear Marsh,

The King thought it would be best for Bigge to write about the *Liberator* case, so I am sending him the Home Secretary's letter and explaining what HM's wishes are.

This is in every way advisable as personally I am not in agreement with the view taken by him and the Home Secretary.

Yours sincerely
F. M. PONSONBY

S. W. Harris to WSC

TELEGRAM

Handed in at 5.17 [*pm*]

Received 5.52 Woodstock

24 December 1910

Telegram received from Bigge in reply to your message which I telegraphed to him at Warren House Thursley begins: King wishes you to proceed as previously settled you will hear from me this evening. Bigge. Thursday telegram ends. Guy Stephenson,[1] 41 Egerton Gardens, telephone 2575 Western is in charge of legal machinery in absence of Mathews and it may be as well for you to telegraph your instructions direct to him. I have warned him to expect to hear from you.

HARRIS

WSC to Sir Arthur Bigge
(*Royal Archives*)

24 December 1910   Blenheim

TELEGRAM

When shall I hear from you in reply to my latest communication? If you would like a Home Office messenger to bring me your answer will you wire directly to Harris Home Office to send you one? The legal tackle is now perfect and I can move at any time.

CHURCHILL

[1] Guy Stephenson (1865–1930), Assistant Director of Public Prosecutions 1908–30. Knighted 1923.

Sir Arthur Bigge to WSC

TELEGRAM

24 December 1910   OHMS Thursley

Wrote and wired you a few hours ago to proceed sorry for delay.

BIGGE

Sir Arthur Bigge to Edward Marsh

24 December 1910   Warren Lodge
Thursley
Godalming

Dear Marsh,

I will send you a copy of the S of State's letter to the King of 22nd. I have only just got the correspondence from Sandringham & am writing in haste to Mr Churchill.

ARTHUR BIGGE

Sir Arthur Bigge to WSC
(Royal Archives)

24 December 1910

Dear Churchill,

The King wishes me to answer your letter of the 22nd regarding Mylius. HM considers that even in the event of its being found necessary to read the whole *Liberator* article no harm will ultimately be done. HM at the same time appreciates your carefulness to provide for every eventuality in this delicate question.

But surely anything in the article which does not refer to the libel against the King would be deemed irrelevant & the judge would therefore stop its being read.

However, HM, after due consideration & admitting that the reading of the article in full would be unfortunate, sees no reason why the proceedings should be stopped. So you can let matters go on whenever you consider it expedient.

Yours
A. BIGGE

Sir Edward Henry to WSC

TELEGRAM

25 December 1910

Handed in: West Strand 1.10 *pm*

Received: Woodstock 8.9 *pm*

Will not take action until tomorrow by which time all necessary procedure will have been completed Have talked with Reading and this course approved as causing no possible embarrassment.

HENRY

Sir Edward Henry to WSC

25 December 1910   29 Campden House Court

Dear Mr Churchill,

I had made up my mind after consulting with the Attorney General to arrest this evening – but he subsequently rang me up to say that it is most desirable to keep the case altogether out of the Police Court and this being so, some risk might well be run to effect this object. I imagine that the King would be averse to the case getting, at any stage, into the Police Court if this can be prevented. So upon full consideration, I have deemed inadvisable to run such risk as there may be [in] such arrest until the Judge's warrant is obtained though I shall not hesitate to have him taken tomorrow to New Scotland Yard & practically detained until we can read over the warrant to him. We ought to get it by noon tomorrow. I have made arrangements which would, I hope, defeat any attempt he could make to escape – but, of course, some risk must be run.

Yrs sincerely
E. R. HENRY

Guy Stephenson to WSC

TELEGRAM

25 December 1910   [41 Egerton Gardens]

Handed in: 9.54 *am*

Received: Woodstock at 10.25 *am*

Telegram received all is in order for action today if necessary I am giving matter every attention.

STEPHENSON

Sir Rufus Isaacs to WSC

TELEGRAM

25 December 1910

Handed in: Reading 10.22 *am*

Received: Woodstock 10.36 *am*

Yes will telephone to Lodge document and apply Judge immediately Thank Marlborough will motor over tomorrow afternoon returning at night.

RUFUS ISAACS

Sir Edward Henry to WSC

TELEGRAM

26 December 1910   Parliament St

Received at Woodstock 1.21 *pm*

Arrest effected Judges process no embarrassment.

HENRY

Guy Stephenson to WSC

TELEGRAM

26 December 1910

Handed in: Parliament Street 1.5 *pm*

Received: Woodstock 1.35 *pm*

Arrest effected on warrant of judge.

STEPHENSON

Sir Frederick Ponsonby to WSC

TELEGRAM

26 December 1910

Handed in: Sandringham 6 *pm*

Received: Woodstock 6.25 *pm*

The King desires me to thank you for your telegram His Majesty is pleased to hear that action has been taken.

PONSONBY

WSC to the King
(*Royal Archives*)

28 December 1910   Blenheim

Mr Secretary Churchill with his humble duty to Your Majesty: Sir Edward Henry very wisely deferred making the actual arrest of Mylius until all the legal formalities necessary to avoid any proceedings at a Police Court had been complied with; but before the Judge's Warrant, upon the criminal information of the Attorney-General, had been signed, the Chief Commissioner was armed with a Magistrate's Warrant which could have been executed at any moment, had it appeared possible that the accused person would leave the country. Careful precautions were also taken to prevent this in any event, and, like so much of Sir Edward Henry's work, they proved thoroughly effective.

The Judge, in issuing his Warrant, fixed bail, by which Mylius might avoid arrest, but the amount, £10,000 and two sureties of £5,000 each, was prohibitive. A perfectly regular and normal course will be followed in every respect so as to avoid any suggestion that the prisoner has not received fair play, or that the law has been strained on any point. In pursuance of this Mylius will be brought up to-morrow morning before the Vacation Judge, Sir Samuel Evans,[1] and will have the whole matter carefully explained to him, so that he will know exactly what charge he will have to meet. Eight days will be allowed him to plead. He may attempt to justify, he may plead guilty, or, and this is the most probable, he may plead not guilty and show contrition. In this last event he would probably say that he was attacking a system and not an individual, that he only published a story which he had heard very widely circulated, and that he deeply regrets his conduct. Mr Churchill does not think that any of these pleas will make much difference, and he is able to assure Your Majesty positively that in all three eventualities it will be possible, not merely to proceed against the offender, but to demonstrate in open court the falsity of the libel. Mr Churchill was visited here to-day by the Attorney-General, and went with him step by step over the whole future of the case in order that nothing may have been overlooked. Sir Rufus Isaacs will attend at the court to-morrow, and he will himself conduct the prosecution at all stages. The proceedings to-morrow being before a Judge in Chambers will be private, and Mr Churchill thinks it very probable that nothing will appear in the newspapers. Gradually, however, the arrest may become known, and there is a possibility that some

---

[1] Samuel Thomas Evans (1859–1918); Liberal MP for mid-Glamorganshire 1890–1910; called to the Bar 1891; Solicitor-General 1908; President of Probate Divorce and Admiralty Division 1910; knighted 1908.

reference may be made to the case in gossiping weekly journals, but Mr Churchill does not think it likely that any of the leading newspapers in the country will make any reference, however guarded, to a matter which will be *sub judice*. Sir Rufus Isaacs informs Mr Churchill that the trial will probably take place about the 20th January, and, if all goes well, it should be disposed of in a single day. Thus it is probable that the attention of the public will not be directed to the matter at all until the whole case will be put before them with the Attorney-General's carefully considered statement, the full evidence of the falsity of the libel and, it is to be expected, the sentence of the court.

Mr Churchill would himself propose to attend the court on the 20th January in order that it may be apparent that Ministers accept full responsibility for the course which has been taken. All of which is hereby humbly submitted by Your Majesty's Faithful and Humble Servant

WINSTON S. CHURCHILL

Sir Rufus Isaacs to WSC

28 December 1910

My dear Winston,

Re Mylius

All in order this morning – The Prisoner was brought before the Judge – I explained in some detail the procedure for the prisoner's information. I have ordered a copy to be sent to him of indications to him of all the possible courses open to him & the number of days within which the various steps must be effected. We are pursuing the course of allowing the prisoner the maximum of time – so that he may have no grievance. A telegram was received from James telling Mylius to get good counsel for which he, James, would be responsible. Mylius told the Judge this morning he hoped and had some reason to hope he would obtain the two sureties – if he can & the police who are to have 48 hours notice for inquiries are satisfied with the names given – he will be released – but I do not think there is any chance of this happening & he will never find the sureties. When arrested he said nothing material – from documents found he knew the *Liberator* had been stopped at Customs & I gather was not surprised at his arrest (this information is not direct to me). I have seen letters from James at Mylius' showing a pre-arranged plan to attack the King in relation to the alleged marriage – the great object being apparently to bring out a 'Bigamy Coronation Number' for distribution at the Coronation. I considered whether we would add the charge of conspiracy – but decided agst its inclusion. We cant get James & the effect of adding the charge agst Mylius would be only to add to the possible punishment – but I prefer infinitely to stick to the plain charge of libel – with its Defence of Justification & for public benefit always open to the Prisoner. I told him today, in the presence of the Judge (shorthand note taken) that he could assert the truth etc which will enable us to say that at the earliest moment he was told of this possible course – No word has yet transpired in public about the arrest but doubtless it will soon be out – Mylius appears to give out that he has been arrested for a political offence or a political libel. If this should appear in the Press I suggest to you that no communique be made – let it be – for any answer or statement you make must I think if it refer at all to the King state the nature of the libel otherwise all kinds of suggestions might be made if it was left to conjecture the terms or substance of the libel. In any event great care should be taken when making any Press statement to await any possibility of application to commit the solicitor for contempt of court. If I am not in England Simon will be available. I am not sure whether I shall be able to go to Cap Martin. Assuming the maximum allowance of time to be taken by the prisoner we shall not be able to get to trial till near the end of January. Even then if the prisoner can make a reasonable case for further delay it would have to be cancelled by us – for we must not appear to put any obstacle in his way – but it could not be a long delay.

Mylius appears (from letters found) to have been introduced to James by Krishnavarma. Various other Indian names occur in the correspondence between James & Mylius. We have only the letters from James & three Indians known to be living 'in Paris'.

There is no other news at present.

Yours sincerely
RUFUS ISAACS

WSC to the King
(*Royal Archives*)

29 December 1910   Blenheim

Mr Secretary Churchill with his humble duty to Your Majesty: The Attorney-General reports that all was in order this morning. The prisoner was brought before the Judge, and Sir Rufus Isaacs explained in some detail the procedure for the prisoner's information. He has ordered a copy to be sent to him of his indications of all the possible courses open to him and of the number of days within which the various steps must be effected. The course is being pursued of allowing the prisoner the maximum of time, so that he may have no grievance. A telegram was received from James, author of the libels, in France, telling Mylius to get good counsel, for which he (James) would be responsible. There is no harm in this, as good and respectable counsel will be very careful to deal only with the points at issue, and while endeavouring to safeguard the interests of their clients will probably refrain from offensive references which would only be damaging to him.

Mylius told the Judge this morning that he hoped, and had some reason to hope, that he would obtain the two sureties. If he can, and the police, who are to have 48 hours notice, are satisfied, he will be released; but the Attorney-General does not think there is any chance of this happening. When arrested he said nothing material. From documents found it is clear that he knew the *Liberator* had been stopped at the Customs, and he did not appear greatly surprised at his arrest. The Attorney-General has seen letters from James, found in Mylius' rooms, showing a pre-arranged plan to attack Your Majesty in relation to the alleged marriage, the great object being, apparently, to bring out a 'Bigamy Coronation Number' for distribution at the Coronation. The Attorney-General has considered whether on this new material he can add a charge of conspiracy, but he has decided against this inclusion. He told the prisoner to-day in the presence of the Judge, and the statement is on record, that he (Mylius) could, if he chose, assert that the statements were true. This course would be the most convenient to the prosecution, as it would raise a direct issue on the truth of the libel, and the fact that the prisoner has been told at the earliest moment of this possible course will make it clear that the prosecution wished him to be fully informed of all his rights.

No word has yet transpired in public about the arrest, but the Attorney-General thinks that it will soon leak out. Mylius appears inclined to give out that he has been arrested for a political offence or a political libel. If this should become public through the newspapers, Mr Churchill thinks it will be better to pay no attention to it and to await the final disposal of the case at the trial. From what the Attorney-General writes to-day Mr Churchill is inclined to think that the date of the trial may be a little later than he had anticipated, but he still hopes it will be over before the end of January. It appears from the letters found at Mylius' rooms that he was introduced to James by Krishnavarma & various other Indian names occur in the correspondence between James and Mylius. These Indians are known to be living in Paris. All the foregoing information makes it clear that it was right to proceed against a man concerned in this atrocious conspiracy of sedition and calumny upon the first well chosen opportunity. All of which is humbly submitted by Your Majesty's Faithful and Devoted Servant and Subject

WINSTON S. CHURCHILL

WSC to the King
(Royal Archives)

29 December 1910   [Home Office]

Mr Secretary Churchill with his humble duty to Your Majesty has the honour to observe that since he last wrote to Your Majesty references have appeared in nearly all the newspapers to the prosecution of Mylius. These references appear to Mr Churchill to be quite harmless and satisfactory. They make no mention of the actual character of the libel and only refer in the vaguest terms to the charge against the defendant. Mr Churchill is quite convinced that no official statement of any kind should be made, and that matters should be allowed, if possible, to continue in this indefinite state until the whole case can be thrashed out in court.

WINSTON S. CHURCHILL

Sir Francis Knollys to Sir Arthur Bigge
(Royal Archives)

30 December 1910   Sandringham

My dear Bigge,
    Please thank Churchill for the enclosed & tell him that the King quite approves of no official statement being made.

Yr ever
FRANCIS KNOLLYS

Sir Arthur Bigge to WSC

31 December 1910   Buckingham Palace

My dear Churchill,
    The King is much obliged to you for keeping him *au courant* as to the progress of the *Liberator* affair – all you tell His Majesty confirms him in the opinion that the absolutely right thing has been done to go for these scoundrels. The King agrees with your advice that no official statement of any kind should be made – and that we let the case be thrashed out in Court in the ordinary way – His Majesty much appreciates your intention to be present in Court when the trial comes on.
    It is a revelation to know that Krishnavarma is mixed up with James, Mylius & Co.

Yours very truly
ARTHUR BIGGE

I go to Sandringham Tuesday.

WSC to the King
(*Royal Archives*)

4 January 1911   [Home Office]

Dictated

Mr Secretary Churchill with his humble duty to Your Majesty sends some of the newspaper notices dealing with the affair of Mylius, which appear to him not unsatisfactory. He also encloses a copy of a letter written by Mylius in prison, which shows the character of the man. He is of course not allowing it to be forwarded.

Mr Churchill is informed that Mr Newton,[1] who was Dr Crippen's[2] solicitor, is likely to be engaged for Mylius. As this gentleman's professional reputation is now under a cloud, he is in doubt whether he should allow this, & he will discuss the question with Sir Charles Mathews.

Sir Arthur Bigge to WSC

                                                                York Cottage
5 January 1911   Sandringham

My dear Churchill,

The King thanks you for your letter of yesterday enclosing newspaper cuttings about the *Liberator* and copy of Mylius' letter to the *New York American*. The latter is interesting reading – The *Evening Standard* of yesterday announced that Mr James was coming over from Paris to his friend Mylius: but we now hear from Scotland Yard where I telephoned that that gentleman has thought better of his proposed visit to London.

His Majesty is sorry to hear a bad account of the injured fireman. He hopes that these recent outrages by foreigners will lead you to consider whether the Aliens Act could not be amended so as to prevent London from being infested with men and women whose presence would not be tolerated in any other country.

                                                                Yours very truly
                                                                ARTHUR BIGGE

[1] Arthur John Edward Newton had been solicitor for the defence in the Crippen case. According to Gilbert Martin in *Doctor Crippen*, 'His objective in the Crippen case – as was clearly demonstrated by the aftermath – was to make as much money as possible.'
[2] Hawley Harvey Crippen (1862–1910). He was tried for murder at the Old Bailey and executed on 23 November 1910.

WSC to the King
(Royal Archives)

10 January 1911 [Home Office]

Dictated

Mr Secretary Churchill with his humble duty to Your Majesty.

Mr Churchill learns that the Judge on Friday granted Mylius fourteen days extension of his time to plead, not because he thought it was either deserved or necessary, but because he thought that no shadow of ground should be afforded for saying that ample opportunity had not been allowed for filing a plea of justification, if any material existed for it. This is in the Judge's opinion the most effective way of killing the lie outright.

The trial cannot now begin before January 30th, but even so it will be over before February 6th.

WSC to the King
(Royal Archives)

Home Office

Dictated

Mr Secretary Churchill with his humble duty to Your Majesty has the honour herewith to enclose two letters which have been sent to the defendant Mylius, in Brixton Prison, by James, the proprietor of the *Liberator*, from Paris. These letters are characterised by a good deal of bluff and much ignorance of the course which the legal proceedings will take. Although from some points of view they are not proper letters to be received by a prisoner, Mr Churchill has, after consultation with the Attorney-General, thought it advisable not to impound them, but to let them be delivered. It is of importance that Mylius should have no excuse for saying that he has been hampered in the preparation of his defence by executive action. Mr Churchill has shown the letters to the Attorney-General with whom he had a long talk yesterday morning. The Attorney-General considers the position satisfactory in every way. If Mylius pleads justification, as James urges him to do and as he at present seems inclined to do, it will be particularly convenient; for then the demonstration of the falsity of the libel can be made in reply to a specific charge preferred in court, instead of being merely brought forward after the charge has itself been withdrawn by the defendant. No difficulty will arise, in Sir Rufus Isaacs' opinion, if Mylius adopts the course of claiming that Your Majesty should appear in person as a witness to deny the truth of the libel. The first step when the court opens, after a plea of guilty has been returned, will be a statement by the Attorney-General of the whole case. That statement will include a full explanation of the law which prevents Your Majesty from appearing in person to testify, will show that such a step would invalidate the proceedings, and that it is therefore necessary for the prosecution to demonstrate the falsity of the libel by other evidence which though less direct is not less conclusive. After this opening statement any theatrical demand for Your Majesty's appearance by the prisoner will not command serious attention. The Attorney-General, who has seen Mylius, is inclined to doubt whether he is sufficiently brazen to follow the course marked out by his confederate. Mr Churchill is also informed that Mr Arthur Newton, the solicitor who has been requested to undertake the defence, has refused to do so on the grounds that he cannot undertake to enter a plea of justification where there is no evidence of any kind to support it. In order, however, that the defence shall have every facility which equity can suggest, the Marriage Registers which are being brought from Malta by the Crown Advocate will be made available for the inspection of the defence some days before the trial. As Your Majesty is aware, this trial is likely to take place about the first or second of February. All of which is now submitted by Your Majesty's faithful and devoted servant.

WINSTON S. CHURCHILL

Sir Arthur Bigge to WSC

18 January 1911　　　　　　　　　　　　　　York Cottage
　　　　　　　　　　　　　　　　　　　　　Sandringham

Dear Churchill,

The King thanks you for your letter received yesterday about Mylius and for copies of the two letters addressed to the latter by James. His Majesty is glad that Mylius was allowed to have these letters agreeing as HM does with you that M should have no excuse for complaining that he had not been given every possible facilities for preparing his defence.

I wonder if James really believes in the Malta Marriage. In any case he has given his friend a biggish task to prove that the King married Miss Seymour in Malta!

Yours very truly
ARTHUR BIGGE

Sir Arthur Bigge to WSC

22 January 1911   Windsor Castle

Dear Churchill,

The King thanks you for your letter enclosing Mylius' plea of justification. It seems to have been drawn with every favourable consideration for the prosecution! The King has heard from Mr Aldred asking him to attend as a witness. I have sent the letter to Mathews. Are you quite sure that a summons served upon the King personally or upon anyone on HM's behalf should be received?

It is not likely that anyone would ever get within reach of the King. But suppose a man handed me a summons would I not be justified in refusing to take what I should hold to be tantamount to an insult to the King?

With regard to the suggestion that a statement should be made by the Counsel for the prosecution that the King was anxious to appear as a witness but was debarred from doing so by constitutional usage, would it be possible to say, instead of giving the above reason, that the *Government* declined to allow His Majesty to appear?

This is not the King's idea but that of

Yours very truly
ARTHUR BIGGE

WSC to Sir Arthur Bigge
(*Royal Archives*)

24 January 1911   Home Office

My dear Sir Arthur Bigge,

I have again consulted Sir Charles Mathews on the point of what should be done in the event of an attempt being made to serve a summons, and he still thinks that should anyone try to hand a paper to you or to anyone else about the King, it will be better simply to take it without comment. He does not, however, consider it at all likely that any further step will be taken now that Mr Aldred has written His Majesty his letter.

We are now getting very near the moment of action, and I think it would be desirable to have a final conference one day this week at which you and the Law Officers should be present with others now concerned in the case. I do not myself see any reason to depart from the path along which we originally decided to move, namely, to convict the offender and to demonstrate the falsity of the libel without exposing His Majesty to the need of appearing as a witness. There are of course only two courses open (1) that the King should appear and testify; or (2) that we should absolutely refuse even to consider the question of his appearance, and fortify our refusal by all arguments which may be necessary. If the defendant had any prospect of making out a plausible case in support of his libellous statements, I should certainly not *at this hour* exclude the first alternative. Had there been any chance of this however we should not have embarked on the prosecution. But in the absence of the slightest shadow or vestige of evidence to justify the libel, the claim of the defendant that the King should appear is a mere piece of impudent buffoonery and should be brushed away with the contempt it deserves. This is my view, but I think, however, that every argument for a contrary case which may be put forward by others in this business who are devoted to the King's service should be fairly and finally considered.

Would to-morrow, Wednesday, at 5 pm suit you? Is there anyone else whom the King would desire to attend?

Yours sincerely
WINSTON S. CHURCHILL

WSC to the King
(*Royal Archives*)

25 January 1911   [Home Office]

Mr Secretary Churchill with his humble duty to Your Majesty.

Everything proceeds well & smoothly in the Mylius case. The trial is now fixed for Feb 1st at 10.30 and will probably be concluded early on the same day. The Law Officers are of opinion that it would be contrary both to the Law & the Constitution for Your Majesty to attend & give evidence. Such evidence is not necessary to the plain demonstration of the falsity of the libel. Mylius' demand for Your Majesty's presence has no moral weight behind it, apart altogether from questions of Law. No vestige of evidence has been adduced in support of his contention. Mr Churchill feels confident that the result of the process will be quite satisfactory & that the effect upon public opinion will be good. Perhaps a few anarchists may continue to repeat the libel in a different form. But Your Majesty's loyal subjects will be armed with the truth; & except among those whose political intention it is to attack the institution of monarchy wherever it exists – an insignificant & malignant band in this country at any rate, the hateful lie wh has caused Your Majesty vexation will be dead forever.

WSC to the King
(*Royal Archives*)

31 January 1911   [Home Office]

Dictated

Mr Secretary Churchill with his humble duty to Your Majesty: The Law Officers and the Public Prosecutor have come to the conclusion that a statement in the form herewith enclosed, or other similar words, should be made by the Attorney-General in Court tomorrow *after* the case against Mylius has been disposed of by the jury. No one could then contend that the interests of the prisoner had been prejudiced thereby, and on the other hand Your Majesty's declaration would set the seal upon the ample and abundant proofs of the falsity of the libel which will be presented to the Court. Mr Churchill concurs with the Law Officers on this point, and considers that no more suitable and impressive conclusion to the proceedings would be possible. If this proceeding meets with Your Majesty's approval, Mr Churchill would be glad to receive the paper back initialled or signed by Your Majesty. The Messenger has instructions to wait for Your Majesty's reply.

Mr Churchill takes this opportunity of assuring Your Majesty that everything is in order, that the strength of the case from all points of view inspires Your Majesty's servants with complete confidence, and that they have every hope and expectation that by tomorrow night the cruel and malicious falsehood which has so long offended Your Majesty will have been effectually disposed of for ever.

WINSTON S. CHURCHILL

The *Annual Register* records:—

The case took place in the King's Bench Division before the Lord Chief Justice and a special jury on February 1.... Sir Michael Culme-Seymour gave evidence that his wife and two daughters first came out to him in Malta in 1893; that his younger daughter, Laura Grace, died unmarried in 1895 without ever having even spoken to the King, and that his other daughter, Mrs Trevelyan Napier, had not met the King between 1879, when she was eight years old, and 1898. This was confirmed by Mrs Napier and her three brothers, and it was also proved that the King had not been at Malta between 1888 and 1901, and that there was no record of any such marriage in the registers of the island, which were produced for the inspection of the jury. Sir Arthur Bigge also testified to his contradiction of the rumour, mentioned above. The defendant, who was unrepresented by counsel, objected that if, as the Attorney-General had stated, he was being tried for defamatory libel, the King ought to have appeared in Court as a witness and made affidavits, failing which the case should be dismissed. On this objection being overruled, he refused to proceed further. He was convicted and sentenced to twelve months' imprisonment, the maximum if the three publications were not treated as separate libels. After sentence, the Attorney-General read a statement signed by the King for publication, to the effect that he was never married except to the Queen, and never went through any ceremony of marriage except with the Queen, and that he would have attended to give evidence to this effect had he not been advised by the Law Officers that it would be unconstitutional for him to do so.

WSC to the King
(*Royal Archives*)

1 February 1911   10 Downing Street

Sir,

I cannot add anything to the full reports wh appear in all the newspapers of the trial today of the defendant Mylius, or to the account wh Sir Arthur Bigge will doubtless give Your Majesty. But I should like to offer my respectful and sincere congratulations to Your Majesty upon the entirely successful & satisfactory character of the whole proceedings in Court. I am confident that their reception throughout the Kingdom & the Empire will indicate the wisdom & propriety of taking action; & that Your Majesty's subjects will admire the robust and manly courage with which Your Majesty has not shrunk from an ordeal wh could not but be painful and anxious, and has sought regardless of personal feelings to defend Your Majesty's personal honour. In the result the truth has been established on unchallengeable foundations, justice has been done upon a miscreant, & Your Majesty's royal dignity has been in no respect compromised or flouted.

I have the honour to remain Your Majesty's faithful servant & subject

WINSTON S. CHURCHILL

The King to WSC
(*CSC Papers*)

1 February 1911   Windsor Castle

My dear Churchill,

I have just received your kind letter, telling me the result of the trial of Mylius. Bigge has also given me an account of all that happened. I hasten to send you these lines to say how deeply I appreciate the very thorough manner in which you have carried through the most disagreeable case, which has caused both the Queen & myself much pain & anxiety, to a successful conclusion. I am afraid it must have given you a great deal of trouble & work & I desire to express my most grateful thanks to you for your valuable assistance in your position as Home Secretary, in carrying out my wishes to prove to the world at large the baseness of this cruel & abominable libel. Hoping to see you at Buckingham Palace at 3 o'clock tomorrow afternoon,

Believe me very sincerely yours
GEORGE R. I.

Lord Morley to WSC

1 February 1911   Privy Council Office

My dear Winston,
I have written to the PM, that I should wish to raise at the Cabinet the proceedings about the libel on the King. It seems to me to be a profound mistake – and in any case, as it affects the Sovereign personally, the Cabinet ought to have been consulted.

Yrs
M

Sir Arthur Bigge to WSC

6 February 1911   Buckingham Palace

My dear Churchill,
Many thanks for the second consignment of newspaper cuttings which I will give to the King. It is, as you say rather curious that Dundee should produce the only adverse opinion as to the propriety of the prosecution. Still I consider the whole thing has been a triumph and HM has received congratulations from all sorts and conditions of men.

Bad luck has given me a bad cold and kept me in the house so I have not heard what reception T. Ms [Their Majesties] got going to and returning from Westminster: but I hope that it was a really good one.

The Sunday papers were excellent. I wonder why the *Westminster Gazette* took such a dry philosophic view of the case!

I suppose you are by now hard at it in the H of C.

I earnestly trust that the Govt will be ready to come to some agreement and avert the disastrous and evil manufacture of Peers.

Yrs very sincerely
ARTHUR BIGGE

Sir Arthur Bigge to Edward Marsh

15 February 1911   Buckingham Palace

Private

Dear Marsh,

Without being vindictive I cannot help feeling after reading these papers that Mylius ought not to be released before the expiration of his sentence. Any leniency will produce no gratitude in him or his friends and might lead the public to think that the trial was a 'put up' affair.

Yours very truly
ARTHUR BIGGE

Note by Marsh: Bigge telephoned that this represents the King's wish.

E.M.

*   *   *   *   *

On 16 December 1910, a gang of foreign burglars, mostly Letts, had been disturbed by London police while attempting to break into a jeweller's shop in Houndsditch and had opened fire on them, killing one and fatally injuring two. One of the burglars was also mortally wounded, probably accidentally by a companion. The police had been searching for the criminals, one of whom was known as 'Peter the Painter', believed to be particularly dangerous. On 3 January 1911, police surrounded a house, No 100 Sidney Street, Mile End Road, where they believed two of the wanted men, known as Fritz Svaars and Joseph, were hiding. They were met by automatic pistol fire. WSC arrived at noon and conferred with the police. Horse Artillery was called upon to demolish the house but before this could be accomplished the house caught on fire and burned to the ground. The bodies of two men were found in the ruins.

Josiah Wedgwood to WSC

5 January 1911   Moddershall
                                                           Staffs

Dear Churchill,

Please do not be rushed into exceptional laws against anarchists. It is fatally easy to justify them but they lower the whole character of a nation.

You know as well as I do that human life does not matter a rap in comparison with the death of ideas and the betrayal of English traditions. Rebelling against civilisation and society will go on anyhow. It is only a new form of the disease of '48; so let us have English rule and not Bourbon.

Yours with apologies but frightened by *The Times.*

JOSIAH C. WEDGWOOD

WSC to the King

6 January 1911   Home Office

[Copy]

Mr Secretary Churchill with his humble duty to Your Majesty has the honour to state that he has already invited Sir Edward Henry to propose to him any useful & practical measures by wh the hands of the Police authorities may be strengthened in dealing with foreign criminals in this country.[1] Mr Churchill thinks that Parliament might be asked to give the police power to arrest any alien who has no visible lawful means of earning a living, & to bring him before a magistrate who should be empowered to make an expulsion order subject to an appeal to the Secretary of State. He thinks also that Aliens should be forbidden to possess firearms without a special license from the police authorities, and that the breach of this rule should render the alien liable to fine or imprisonment & deportation. Possibly a special right of search for arms might be given in the case of aliens.

Mr Churchill would however deprecate any legislation directed against anarchists as such, & he proposes to be guided by Sir Edward Henry's great experiences on this point. It would not be right also to brand the general alien population of the country with the crimes of this particular tribe of criminals from the Baltic provinces.

The bulk of the Alien population is industrious, sober & law abiding.

[1] See above, p. 1230, Sir Arthur Bigge's letter to WSC, 5 January 1911.

There are fewer aliens in this country than in any great country in Europe except Spain. The transit of Aliens through England on their way to the United States is a vy important feature in our shipping trade & is a source of monetary advantages to many of Your Majesty's subjects. The administration of the Aliens Act could under the existing law be made more strict, but that would only cause a great deal of friction at the ports, without affording any guarantee that the really dangerous brutes would be excluded. The Courts have already a power of adding expulsion to any sentence of imprisonment upon an alien, & Mr Churchill greatly regrets they do not use it more. Out of 2000 cases of convicted aliens only about 400 have been expelled this year. At least 4 times as many should have been so treated for their abuse of British hospitality.

The whole subject will however engage the attention of Your Majesty's faithful servant & subject

WINSTON S. CHURCHILL

WSC to The Coroner, London

10 January 1911   Home Office

Draft

Not sent

Sir,

In view of references to me which I have read in the newspaper accounts of the proceedings before you yesterday, I think it right to submit the following statement to you.

At about 10.45 am on Tuesday morning I received an urgent message from the Home Office stating that the authors of the Houndsditch murders had been surrounded in a house in Stepney, that a Police Officer had been mortally wounded in endeavouring to effect their arrest, that they were firing continuously from the house upon the Police, and asking my authority for the employment of twenty infantry soldiers. After consulting, by telephone, with my advisers at the Home Office, I gave this authority. The soldiers had, however, very properly proceeded in anticipation of it. I reached the Home Office at a quarter past eleven, where I could learn no details of what [was] proceeding except that a continuous fusillade was going on in Stepney. In these circumstances I thought it my duty to go and see for myself what was happening. I reached Sidney Street a few minutes before 12 o'clock. I asked who was the Senior Police Officer present. I was told that Major

Wodehouse[1] an Assistant Commissioner of the Metropolitan Police was, but that a few minutes before I arrived he had gone off to the War Office.

Superintendent Mulvany[2] was in control of the Metropolitan Police upon the spot and was directing the proceedings. I did not interfere in any way with any dispositions which had been made or which were at any time made.[3]

At 1 pm the premises caught fire. No one knew how the fire had originated. The criminals were still shooting frequently from the house and no one could approach it safely along Sidney Street. Shortly after this, about 5 minutes past one, the Fire Brigade arrived, and one of their subordinate officers came up and asked me whether they were right in following the instructions they had received from the police to stand by for the present and not attempt to put out the fire. I replied that they were quite right to stand by, and that I accepted full responsibility for the action which the police had taken in this respect; but that the Fire Brigade should make all preparations to deal with the fire effectively as soon as the police authorities told them it was safe for them to advance. About half an hour later I asked a higher officer of the Fire Brigade whether he was confident of his ability to check the flames as soon as the firing was stopped and he was permitted to advance. He replied that he was making all preparations, and had his hoses in readiness at three or four separate points, and that as a matter of greater precaution, he would order up four more steam fire engines. For the rest I was a spectator, and remained on the spot till about a quarter to three.

I should add that I am willing to attend your Court if anyone desires to ask me any questions.

Yours faithfully
WSC

---

[1] Edwin Frederick Wodehouse (1851–1934), after twenty years in the Royal Artillery he became Assistant Commissioner of the City of London Police 1890–1902; Metropolitan Police 1902–1918; KCB 1917.

[2] John Mulvany was superintendent of the Whitechapel Division of the Metropolitan Police.

[3] Paragraph deleted by WSC:·

I made it my business, however, after seeing what was going on in front to go round the back of the premises and satisfy myself that there was no chance of the criminals effecting their escape through the intricate area of walls and small houses at the back of No 100 Sidney Street. This took some time, and when I returned to the corner of Sidney Street I was told that the house had caught on fire, and I could see smoke coming out from the top-floor window.

Sydney Holland¹ to WSC

12 January 1911   Knebworth
                                                       Herts

Dear Mr Churchill,

I don't suppose for one moment you need anyone to corroborate what you have written to *The Times,* but if you do I am quite ready to bear witness to the same effect, and I was with you the whole time. The only possible excuse for anyone saying that you gave orders is that you did once and very rightly go forward and wave back the crowd at the far end of the road. If those miscreants had come out there would have been lots of people shot by the soldiers. And you did also give orders that you and I were not to be shot in our hindquarters by a policeman who was standing with a 12 bore behind you!

Is there no revolver which will fire slugs? It would be far more effective than a single bullet firing pistol – and even if the man escaped the shot wound would be a means of identification.

It riles me to see a fuss made about you being present. In such an abnormal state of affairs surely a H Secy is entitled to see that everything is being done that can be?

Yours sincerely
SYDNEY HOLLAND

Inquest Pamphlet on Sidney Street Case
(*Examined 18 January 1911*)

Winston Leonard Spencer Churchill, upon his oath saith:

I am Privy Councillor and Principal Secretary of State for the Home Department.

On Tuesday, 3rd January, I received a message from the Home Office about 11 am that the War Office was enquiring if authority could be given for 20 men of the Scots Guards to proceed to the aid of the police in Stepney. The message stated that the criminals believed to be implicated in the Houndsditch murders had been located and that they were firing on the police, and that one police officer had been mortally wounded. I communicated with my advisers at the Home Office on the telephone, and gave

¹ Sydney Holland (1855–1931), Director Underground Electric Railways Company, City and South London Railway, London & Scottish Life Assurance Co; succeeded father as 2nd Viscount Knutsford 1914; was noted long-distance swimmer in his youth.

the authority that was asked. I was at my house when I got the message. Then I went on to the Home Office and tried to get more information. I could get no more information by telephoning, except that there was a regular fusillade going on in Stepney. I could get no definite or exact informaton of what was happening. In my opinion the circumstances were extraordinary, and I thought it my duty to go and see for myself what was happening. I went in a motor car to Sidney Street. I reached there about 11.50 a.m. When I got there I heard that some Scots Guards had been there long before I received any application at all.

My sanction was not legally necessary. When I got to Sidney Street I enquired who was the Senior Officer in command. I was told that Major Wodehouse was so, but that he had gone to the War Office a few minutes before I arrived, and that Superintendent Mulvany was in charge of the Metropolitan Police. I saw Mr Mulvany and others, and when I got there firing was going on there from the house. There were crowds at all the approaches and police officers were keeping them away. I saw a few soldiers. I remained there, and a little before 1 pm it was noticed that smoke was coming from the premises. At that time firing was still proceeding at and from the house. At about 1.5 pm some representatives of the Fire Brigade arrived with their appliances. A junior officer of the Fire Brigade (Station Officer Edmonds) came up to me where I was standing and said that the Fire Brigade had arrived, and that he understood he was not to put out the fire at present. Was this right? or words to that effect. I said, 'Quite right; I accept full responsibility.' I wish to make it clear that these words refer to the specific question asked me, and that I confirmed and supported the police in their action. From what I saw, it would have meant loss of life and limb to any fire brigade officer who had gone within effective range of the building. Assistant Divisional Officer Morris, of the Fire Brigade, was there, and I asked him whether he could be sure of getting the fire under control when it became safe for the men to advance.

He said he was making all preparations with the hosery, but that for greater precaution he would order up 4 more steamers. I was there when the Brigade were able to go to the fire. I left about 2.40 or 2.45 pm. I did not see Major Wodehouse on the scene at any time that day to my recollection. I did not in any way direct or over-ride the arrangements that the police authorities had made. I gave no directions to alter arrangements already made by them. I think I did so to Mr Mulvany. It would be quite untrue to say that I took the direction out of the hands of the Executive Officers. I did not in any way interfere with the arrangements made by the police. I was only there to support them in any unusual difficulty as a covering authority.

So far as I am concerned, the police had a free hand. I heard that a Maxim gun had arrived (from persons around me). I never directed anyone to send for a Maxim gun, nor did I send at any time for any further military force. The artillery came up as I was driving away. I met them. I should like to put on record that among the police and plain clothes officers all round the building there was a general and perfect readiness to volunteer to rush the building at any moment, and that any request for volunteers would have met with an eager response. The request was not made, and if I may express an opinion I am certain that in all the circumstances it would have been wrong to throw away valuable lives, until at any rate all other practicable means had been exhausted.

The officers and men of the Fire Brigade were quite willing to act at any time, and I think the officers were quite right in coming to me to ask if it was with my consent that they were not allowed to advance. I said to Mr Morris, 'You had better send for more engines if you think it necessary,' and four engines, I believe, were sent for.

WINSTON S. CHURCHILL

Memorandum by WSC

19 January 1911   Home Office

It is not possible to prevent the entry or return to this country of undesirable individuals either under the existing Aliens Act, however administered, or under any other legislative machinery which would not cause more inconvenience than it is worth. No reasons exist which should lead us to abandon the general position which the Liberal party has occupied in reference to alien exclusion, or upon the right of asylum. On the other hand, the principle of expulsion for abuse of hospitality, which has always been recognised by Liberal speakers in all discussions of the alien question, and has been publicly approved by the Prime Minister in former years, appears capable of more effective development at the present time.

I circulate to my colleagues a draft of a Bill directed exclusively to the prevention of crime among aliens, and the expulsion of criminals. Two naughty principles are involved in it. First, a deliberate differentiation between the alien, and especially the unassimilated alien, and a British subject, and second, that an alien may, in certain circumstances, be deported before he has committed any offence. Both these principles can be effectively sustained. The Bill aims, however, at removing the great mass of non-naturalised alien population from the fear of being harshly used by the new provisions.

If an alien has lived here for five years free from crime, he will, except in respect of bearing arms, suffer no disability or risk of expulsion, although he may not be able to afford to become naturalised.

I do not believe the provisions of clause 1, section (2), are in any practical conflict with the right of asylum for political offenders; these would, in every bona fide case, be able to find the necessary sureties for good behaviour.

On the other hand, the law will undoubtedly be rendered far more effective for the purpose of ridding this country of common alien criminals of the most dangerous type.

WSC

Memorandum by WSC
(*Home Office Papers*)

3 February 1911   Home Office

Copy

The publication of the Criminal Statistics for 1909, including, as they do, Mr Simpson's Memorandum, is exceedingly ill-timed, and will not improbably cause me embarassment and trouble. I regret that none of those privy to my confidential plans of Prison Reform thought fit to consult me before making this inopportune and injudicious publication. It is, moreover, unsatisfactory that papers should be presented to me for approval and publication months before they are published. In this case I authorised the publication on the 15th November and fully expected that it would take place during the Autumn Session of the last Parliament. If it could not have been published then, it should have been referred back to me, as the season as well as the material of such publications must be considered together.

For the future I have decided that all Home Office publications are to be finally approved by the Parliamentary Under-Secretary to whom they will be sent *after* they have been placed before me, and who will settle the date of publication and take a final view of the substance.

WSC

Memorandum by WSC

3 February 1911   [Home Office]

Of the enclosed Bills the Shops Bill has already received in principle the approval of the Cabinet in two successive years, and the Coal Mines Bill, though embodying a great mass of technical detail, raises no question of principle. The Aliens (Prevention of Crime) Bill and the Pistols Bill have been modified as the result of their discussion by the Cabinet Committee on Home Office Bills, of which Lord Crewe, Lord Beauchamp, Mr Birrell, Mr Runciman, and Mr Samuel are members, and the draft clauses effecting the Abolition of Imprisonment for Debt are now circulated to the Cabinet in the form in which they were agreed to by that Committee.

WSC

Sir Herbert Samuel to WSC
(Home Office Papers)

6 February 1911

Dear Churchill,

I noticed in the new draft of the Aliens Bill a provision in Clause 2 (1) that a person who fails to find sureties may be kept in prison until the Secretary of State gives directions. I do not remember that this was in the previous draft or I should have mentioned it at our Conference the other day. The provision seems to me to be open to grave objection, and I doubt whether Parliament would sanction it. The more I think of it the more doubtful I am whether this Clause is worth including in the Bill.

Have you considered the suggestion in my previous letter that the Title of the Bill should be more restricted? As it stands you will probably have long debates and difficult divisions in Committee and on Report upon new Clauses designed to establish a more effective cordon round the Coast.

Yours very truly
HERBERT SAMUEL

Note on above letter by Home Office official:

The paragraph referred to was not in the previous draft but it is a *pure piece of machinery* necessary if the Secretary of State is to have power to expel aliens who can't find sureties. It follows the provision made in section 7 (3) of the existing act. It is obvious that if the alien were not sent to prison there would be no hold over him, and if it were left to the Court to fix a term of imprisonment it might be either *too short* or *too long* for Home Office purposes. There is no limit in the case of a person committed to prison in default of finding sureties for breach of peace. Troup thinks some limit (e.g. 14 days) might be inserted in the draft if you think necessary.

WSC to David Lloyd George

3 March 1911   [Home Office]

Secret

Copy

My dear David,

I really must ask you to help me to deal adequately with the situation in the mining world. I am sure the proposals which you were good enough to sanction last year for increasing the Inspectorate will not meet the needs of the time, and we shall lose a great chance of winning the confidence of the miners throughout Great Britain. It is an awful fact that last year was the very worst death roll ever recorded since mining statistics have been kept. This is not merely due to the two great explosions but to a very large number of other accidents, in checking which our present staff and regulations appear wholly ineffective. The feeling among the miners' leaders is thoroughly friendly to the Government, and very hopeful that effective action is going to be taken to stop this awful waste of human life. What the public feels about it can be judged from the fact that the subscriptions both for White-haven and Pretoria disasters amounted to nearly a quarter of a million, and vastly exceed the amount needed to relieve the survivors. I am certain that a really bold and sweeping policy would be immensely popular through-out the country and that the expense would not be judged in any quarter. But I hate adding to your difficulties at the Treasury, and I think it absolutely fair that the mining industry should be made to bear the main charge for what is after all for their especial benefit. It is no good scratching and picking at a thing like this. You have already agreed to an increase of the Inspectorate which will cost you £7,600 this year, ultimately £18,800.

This is burdensome to you; it is not enough for me. I propose to you a policy which is the direct application of the principle you yourself have taught me. Make it clear that the general taxpayer will not be charged more than he has paid in the present year for mines inspection. Let it be known that you regard the 1/–d royalty as the utmost contribution *we* shall exact during our present tenure from the royalty owner for general purposes. Levy a special surcharge of 3d upon mining royalties earmarked for the express purpose of the prevention of accidents, and give me the resulting £80,000 a year to spend upon experiment and inspection. I will then within these limits produce you a scheme which shall be subject to the strictest criticism on grounds of value for money. Keep the announcement for your Budget statement as the one new feature of your policy. I believe you will be astonished by the acclamation with which it will be received. This is not a matter for Departmental correspondence but between ourselves.

During the last two days Charlie [Masterman] and I have been receiving the miners' leaders in deputations, and I hope you will realize how much they expect we shall rise to the challenge of this frightful death roll, and come to the rescue of this great community of labouring men.

Yours always
WINSTON S. C.

WSC to the King
(Royal Archives)

EXTRACT

14 March 1911   Home Office

Mr Churchill ventures to send herewith for your Majesty's examination an early draft of the Coal Mines Regulations Bill. The loss of life was heavier last year than in any year of wh the statistics have been collected & it is necessary that a real effort should be made to grapple with the death roll. The sympathy & interest of the public in the danger of the mining population may be measured by the fact that nearly 3 times as much as was needed was subscribed for the sufferers from the last Pretoria [a coal mine near Bolton] explosion.

Besides the bill which as Your Majesty will see is vy thorough & comprehensive, Mr Churchill has obtained from the Chancellor of the Exchequer substantial financial assistance, wh will enable the inspection of mines to be tripled in each year, & will also provide for an experimental study of the causes of explosions & the means of preventing them.

Knowing the deep sympathy Your Majesty feels for the miners, & the desire of Your Majesty that the Factory & Mining legislation in this country shall be abreast of the best models in any other modern State, Mr Churchill with great respect humbly submits the draft of the new Bill. It will not be contentious, & the only difficulty is to find the time necessary for its passages, wh is however assured this year. . . .

Sir Edward Troup to WSC
(Home Office Papers)

8 April 1911   Home Office

Mr Churchill,

There were many details discussed with the representatives of the Gun Trade which may be left aside for the moment, but I require your instructions on the principal points before the matter can be carried further. Their principal proposals were as follows: –

(1) That the provisions in Clause 3 of the Bill with regard to automatic pistols (the requirement of a magistrate's certificate, etc) should apply to *all pistols*. This appears a great extension of the most stringent provision of the Bill, but it is qualified to some extent by their asking that only one magistrate should sign the permit and by the extended definition of antique pistols which they propose. [*WSC note in margin:* yes]

(2) They propose that all pistols should be regarded as antique except those which can be used with safety cartridges, 'safety cartridges' being defined in the Explosives Act, 1875, as 'cartridges for small arms of which the case can be extracted from the small arm after firing and which are so closed as to prevent any explosion in one cartridge being communicated to other cartridges.' [*WSC note:* for discussion with them. An effective pistol means a *pistol wh will kill a man.*]

(3) While leaving at £1 the fee for a licence to *carry or use* a pistol, they propose reduced fees of 5s. for the first year and 2s. 6d. afterwards for the mere possession of a pistol. [*WSC note:* 5/– a year for renewal is the lowest limit conceivable]

(4) They propose that the Gun dealers should themselves issue licences to the buyers of pistols, sending in each case a copy of the licence to the police. [*WSC note:* Admirable]

(5) They propose that Gun dealers when they sell a pistol should not hand it over to the purchaser but should deliver it to the address which he gives after giving 24 hours notice to the police. [*WSC note:* Admirable]

These proposals shew that the trade are willing to accept very considerable restrictions on the use of pistols, and the chief question is whether, even if accepted by the trade, we would be able to carry them.

It is clear that we shall have to have a further meeting of the trade before the Bill is redrafted. Before asking them to come here, I should be glad to have your instructions as to how the above proposals are to be dealt with. The chief point is, *whether you are prepared to entertain the suggestion that the restrictions in Clause 3 should extend to all pistols.*

If so, we might make the procedure easier by requiring a certificate of one magistrate only instead of two, and by allowing a certificate from the police officer as an alternative to that of a magistrate; and we might fit the proposal in to the Bill by substituting police registration for licences. We might, in fact, reduce the proposals in the Bill to a system by which all owners of pistols should, either directly or through the Gun dealers, register themselves with the police, who would have power either to refuse registration to an unsuitable person, (with an appeal against such refusal to a magistrate), or alternatively, while registering every applicant, might have power to apply to the magistrate to remove from the register the name of an unsuitable person.

If we can get them to agree to this (and it seems to me on the whole less onerous than what they propose), we might offer to reduce the fee for carrying a pistol as well as the fee for possession; and so have one registration fee of 20s. for the first registration and 2s. 6d. for annual renewal (existing owners of pistols might be allowed to register at the renewal fee).

We might further make the fees not taxation duties but police fees. This would make no difference to the Treasury, and it would make very little difference to the local authorities, as the fees would go in relief of the police rate instead of in relief of the general rates.

We could then accept the proposal that the Gun dealers should issue the licences – that is, should register – and the proposals as to the notification of sales of pistols to the police. We should, however, have to press for a definition which would bring within the Act other effective pistols besides those used with 'safety cartridges'.

As thus modified, the scheme proposed by the Gun-makers seems to me a good one. The only difficulty is, would the public object to the registration of all pistols with the police? The objection would be mitigated of course by their being able to register through the Gun dealers. It would not go much further in the way of police control than our present proposal, which provides for the registration of all dealers with the police, and requires magistrates' certificates for automatic pistols on police guarantee. In this shape, there will be no difficulty about introducing the Bill in the House of Lords.

E.T.

Note by WSC at top of letter:

All this seems very good & sensible & a great improvement upon the original plan. The practical registration through the gun trade itself is esp valuable & would no doubt work quite smoothly. The Bill should be redrafted as proposed. It will suit me well to introduce it to the Lords. In this case Lord Ashby St Ledgers should take up the negotiations with the gun trade.

WSC

Note by WSC on draft clauses of Alien Bill
(*Royal Archives*)

12 April 1911   Home Office

These draft clauses are the results of the Sub-Committee of the Committee of Imperial Defence, which has been sitting under my presidency to consider the treatment of aliens in time of war. The military authorities are very anxious that their provisions should become law, and I should propose, if my colleagues approve, to try to graft them on to the Aliens Bill while it is passing through Grand Committee.

WSC

Draft Clause as to Registration of Aliens in Fortified Places

(1) His Majesty may, by Order in Council, make provision for requiring any aliens entering or residing in any defence area to comply with such provisions and requirements as to registration as may be contained in the Order.

(2) An Order under this section may make different provisions as respects different classes of aliens, and may provide for the imposition of penalties (not exceeding for any one offence a fine of one hundred pounds and imprisonment with hard labour for six months) for failure to comply with or contravention of the Order, for the expulsion from a defence area of any alien who is convicted of an offence under the Order, and for any other matters for which it appears expedient to provide with a view to giving full effect to the Order.

(3) For the purpose of this section the expression 'defence area' means any of the places specified in the Schedule to this Act, or any place which His Majesty may by Order in Council declare to be a defence area for the purposes of this section.

(4) His Majesty may revoke, alter, or add to, any Order in Council made under this section as occasion requires.

(5) Every Order in Council made under this section shall be laid before Parliament within forty days next after it is made, if Parliament is then sitting, or, if not, within forty days after the commencement of the then next ensuing session, and if an address is presented to His Majesty by either House of Parliament within forty days after the Order is so laid praying that the Order may be annulled, His Majesty may thereupon by Order in Council annul the Order and it shall thenceforth become void and of no

effect but without prejudice to the validity of anything previously done thereunder.

Draft Clause as to Powers with Respect to Aliens in Case of National Emergency

(1) His Majesty may, at any time when a state of war exists between His Majesty and any foreign power, or when it appears that an occasion of imminent national danger or great emergency has arisen, by Order in Council impose restrictions on aliens, and provision may be made by the Order –

(*a*) for requiring any aliens within a time limited by the Order, to leave the British Islands; and

(*b*) for prohibiting any aliens from entering the British Islands, or from entering the British Islands except at the ports specified in the Order or subject to the conditions so specified; and

(*c*) for preventing any aliens leaving the British Islands; and

(*d*) for preventing any aliens from entering or being in any areas specified in the Order in Council; and

(*e*) for requiring any aliens to reside and remain within a certain area; and

(*f*) for requiring any aliens to comply with such provisions as to registration, passports, or licences for residence, change of abode, or travelling, as may be made by the Order; and

(*g*) for any other matters which appear necessary or expedient with a view to the safety of the realm; and

(*h*) for the temporary detention of aliens and any other ancillary matters for which it appears expedient to provide with a view to giving full effect to the Order.

(2) If any person acts in contravention of or fails to comply with any provisions of any such Order, he shall be liable on summary conviction to a fine not exceeding one hundred pounds or to imprisonment with or without hard labour for a term not exceeding six months, and the court before whom he is convicted may, either in addition to or in lieu of any such punishment, require that person to enter into recognizances with or without sureties to comply with the provisions of the Order in Council, or such provisions thereof as the court may direct.

If any person fails to comply with an order of the court requiring him to enter into recognizances the court or any court of summary jurisdiction sitting for the same place may order him to be imprisoned with or without hard labour for any term not exceeding six months.

(3) His Majesty may revoke, alter, or add to any Order in Council made under this section as occasion requires.

(4) Any powers given under this section, or under any Order in Council made under this section, shall be in addition to, and not in derogation of, any other powers with respect to the expulsion of aliens, or the prohibition of aliens from entering the United Kingdom.

David Lloyd George to WSC

15 April 1911   . Criccieth

My dear Winston,

It was a great disappointment to me not to have met you yesterday at Carnarvon. I brought my clubs along, and meant to have had a game on the Carnarvon links. They are a little rough, but they would have served.

I was also anxious to talk over the police arrangements for the Investiture with you on the spot. I am not sure that we may not have to ask for a small contingent of the Metropolitan Police accustomed to deal with great crowds.

If you would like to see the Castle, I could meet you there on Monday about noon. Send me a wire; and we could play golf in the afternoon.

Have you seen the *Economist* for this week? It very strongly urges our point of view (insurance of separate trades) on the question of Unemployment Insurance, and it quotes your speech in the House of Commons as a proof that you also are of their opinion. I have been thinking out this question at leisure down here. I am perfectly convinced that the Board of Trade proposals are hopelessly faulty and would never reach a Second Reading, except on the distinct understanding that they would be radically changed in Committee. I have suggestions to make, which I hope will meet the difficulty; but the more I reflect upon the problem, the more unhappy I become about it. Unemployment in the Building trade is a perfect quicksand, which might very well swallow up any fund; and I am quite convinced that any attempt to deal with it by fixing 2d and 3d limits of liability must end in insolvency and discredit. The Actuary, who impressed me as being a very able man, warned the Board of Trade of the perils lying in wait for them when they came to deal with the Building Industry.

Although I am very anxious to introduce my scheme at the earliest possible moment, I would rather postpone that introduction for a week, or even a fortnight, than see the Government committed to any plan which would be laughed out of court owing to the actuarial exposure to which it would be subjected as soon as it appeared.

What does Haldane's appointment[1] mean? Surely it does not involve his retirement!

What made you surrender to Balfour on the question of Local Taxation? The treatment of the question of local rates is one of the essentials of Imperial finance in the immediate future, and to give the Lords the power of rejecting two years in succession a measure, say, dealing with the relations of Local and Imperial finance is to equip them with greater powers than those with which they are endowed at the present moment. Apart from this distinct recognition of their right in the Parliament Bill they would never dream of interfering with a Liberal measure dealing with this problem.

I am returning to Town by the train arriving at Euston about 9 on Tuesday evening. When do you propose to return?

Yours ever
D. LLOYD GEORGE

Henry J. Wilson[2] to WSC

29 April 1911   Thackeray Hotel
                                                London

Dear Mr Churchill,

Will you allow me to say how much I regretted the line you took yesterday about the Aliens' Bill. I do not know whether you will have noticed the composition of the majority. Leaving out members of the Government, who of course were obliged to follow your lead, the majority for that odious Bill was made up of 76 Tories, 25 *Liberals,* one Labour man, one Nationalist;

---

[1] Haldane, who remained Secretary for War, was created Viscount Haldane of Cloan in March 1911. He was then appointed a member of the Judicial Committee of the Privy Council.

[2] Henry Joseph Wilson (1833–1914), Liberal MP Holmfirth division Yorkshire 1885–1912; Member of Royal Commission on Opium in India 1893–5; actively supported temperance legislation; opposed 'militarism' and Protection.

leaving the Minority 30 *Liberals,* 21 Labour men, 34 Nationalists, and 3 Tories.

It seems to me so entirely contrary to the practice of old fashioned Liberalism to get into panics and manifest this hostility to foreigners, that I cannot help expressing the hope that you will reconsider your attitude towards the whole question, and will avoid as far as possible compelling sound Liberals to vote against the Government when it takes up these novel and objectionable proposals.

Yours faithfully
HENRY J. WILSON

WSC to Henry J. Wilson

2 May 1911   Home Office

Copy

Dear Mr Wilson,

I think your letter to me has been written under some misapprehension. There was no obligation on any member of our party to vote for the second reading of the Aliens' Bill last Friday, and I was careful to explain this. I am glad myself that the Bill has got a second reading, not because I agree with the Bill and with its clauses, but because I see a prospect of using it as a vehicle to carry the provisions of the Government Bill on the same subject into law. With the present pressure of business there would have been no chance of getting a separate day for this, and it would have been a waste of Parliamentary time not to have utilised the Friday which Mr Goulding had secured. You do me an injustice if you attribute to me any desire to show hostility to foreigners. My views are, indeed, entirely contrary, but I think that further measures are needed to deal with alien crime, and there are some aspects of the purely artificial and commercial form of alien immigration which undoubtedly need to be corrected. The Grand Committee will have every opportunity of discussing the whole question, and the House need not make up its mind upon it until the Report Stage is reached.

Yours very truly
WINSTON S. CHURCHILL

David L. Alexander[1] to WSC
(*Home Office Papers*)

15 May 1911   London Committee of Deputies of
                                    the British Jews
                                    19 Finsbury Circus

Dear Sir,

This Board has had under its consideration the two Alien Bills now before Parliament and I am asked to place before you the Board's views with regard to each of them. For the sake of convenience I enclose a copy of each Bill in which you will find set opposite to each section my Board's views on the same. You will see that my Board approves the whole of the Government Bill with the exception of Section 2, and that no objection will be raised even to that Section provided a proper right of appeal be given.

Yours faithfully
DAVID ALEXANDER
President

Memorandum by John Pedder
(*Home Office Papers*)

16 May 1911   Home Office

This[2] is important. The Jews officially approve the Govt Bill subject to one point on Clause 2 – as to obligation to give sureties. They want an appeal from the Summary Court Order: and they suggest the Court of Criminal Appeal or the K.B.D. That would be wrong: and their statement as to an existing right of appeal from an Expulsion Order is also wrong.

If any stress is laid on the point in Parliament, it might be possible to give an appeal to Quarter Sessions: but the alien should not be left free in the meantime, or he would simply disappear and defeat the whole clause.

Their views on Mr Goulding's Bill are also important and speaking generally helpful.

J.P.

---

[1] David Lindo Alexander (1842–1922), called to Bar 1866; President Jewish Board of Deputies.
[2] Referring to the views of the London Committee of Deputies of British Jews on the Aliens (Prevention of Crime) Bill; see above.

Memorandum by Sir Evelyn Ruggles-Brise
(*Home Office Papers*)

17 May 1911 Home Office

It would be absurd I think to give an Alien who fails to comply with an Order to find sureties a right to appeal against the Order. He would have to find sureties for the costs of the Appeal! If he or his friends are in a position to fight the matter why should they not comply with the order & be done with it. A recommendation is not equivalent to an Expn Order & a case of bona fide hardship can always be represented to S of S.

ERB

WSC note:
Keep them friendly. Put off till Cte.

WSC

* * *

Sir Arthur Bigge to WSC
(*Home Office Papers*)

30 April 1911 Buckingham Palace

My dear Churchill,
Enclosed is the text of the Address to be presented & read to the King on the 16th inst. His Majesty will be much obliged to you if you will draft a reply & he wishes me to mention to you some points to be brought out in it –
Please let it be short.
As an introduction HM wd like to say something to the effect that 'We are met together to celebrate the completion of the great work to stand for ever as a memorial to Queen Victoria & say all you can in her praise & honour as Queen & woman – If you can do it here, congratulate the sculptor Mr Brock[1] & the Architect Sir Aston Webb.[2]

---

[1] Thomas Brock (1847–1922), designer and sculptor of the Victoria Memorial. George V knighted him after the unveiling on 16 May 1911.
[2] Aston Webb (1849–1930), designed the architectural surroundings for the Victoria Memorial; architect of Admiralty Arch, the Royal College of Science and Technology, the completion of the Victoria and Albert Museum; knighted 1904.

Nearly ten years have passed before the work has been completed – In that period 'my beloved father' was not spared to see the consummation of the work in the initiation of which he was so personally interested – & make appreciative allusions to King Edward. Express great satisfaction 'to me & my family that my dear Cousin the German Emperor, accompanied by the Empress should be present'. Refer to the fact that he is the eldest Grandson of Queen V. for whom he always evinced love & veneration.

The Memorial is a testimony from the Motherland & the Oversea Dominions & Colonies to the Queen etc.

Personally the address seems rather a panegyric to King Edward!

HM would like an effective peroration: but I am afraid there is not much more to say!

I know you will forgive me for giving you these hints – & that if HM wishes to make alterations you will understand.

Yours very truly
ARTHUR BIGGE

I shall not expect anything from you until after the 7th May

AB

Draft Reply by WSC
(Home Office Papers)

[? May 1911]   Home Office

We are met together to celebrate the completion of the noble monument raised to Queen Victoria by Her people all over the world.

Ten years have passed since those who were chosen for this trust by my beloved father from the foremost men of both great parties in the State began their labours. Within that space of time we have had to mourn another loss. King Edward was not spared to guide the Committee to the end of their work. He had watched & aided its progress with tender interest & close attention. He did not live to see its consummation.

The Committee have deserved the public's approbation for the care and judgement which they have bestowed upon the honourable duty confided to them. The Memorial itself alike in beauty & situation does justice to the art of the sculptor & the skill of the architect. It now stands complete before our eyes to revive for us and to convey to our descendants the calm lustre and benignant fame which shine upon that happy age of British history, when a woman's hand held for a period which almost equalled the allotted space of human life the sceptre of the Empire, and when the simple virtues of a Queen comforted the hearts of nations.

The Dominions & Colonies beyond the seas which grew greatly in prosperity & strength during Her reign & whose loyalty centred even more directly upon Her August Person have from every part and quarter of the globe united to enshrine her memory: and this Monument represents the tributes & the blessings of races & regions more various in character & circumstance than have been combined before upon a common purpose.

It is a source of deep satisfaction to me & to my family that my dear cousin the German Emperor, accompanied by the Empress, is present at this historic ceremony. His Imperial Majesty is the eldest grandson of Queen Victoria whom he always loved and venerated with natural & cherished affection. Strong and living ties of kinship & friendship unite our Thrones and Persons. My people rejoice with me that he is here today to share in the unveiling of this Memorial.

I pray that this Monument may stand forever in London to proclaim the glories of the Reign of Queen Victoria, and to prove to future generations the sentiments of affection & reverence which Her people felt for Her & for Her memory. As time passes and the years unfold, events are revealed in their true character & proportion. We are sure that the tributes we pay today will not be disputed by posterity. No sovereign in history reigned so long over so many millions of mankind: no ruler saw so many wonderful changes come to pass or witnessed such a vast expansion in the scale & power of human arrangements: no reign in this Kingdom ever gathered up more carefully the treasure of the past, or prepared more hopefully the path of the future. No woman was ever held in higher honour. No Queen was ever loved so well.

Sir Arthur Bigge to WSC
(*Home Office Papers*)

12 May 1911   Buckingham Palace

Dear Churchill,

The King quite approves of your additions to the reply, and you will see that we have restored the fourth paragraph to its original state.

I also return you your draft.

You will, I suppose, now have the reply prepared ready for the King's use on the 16th, and that you will hand it to His Majesty.

Yours vy truly
ARTHUR BIGGE

*   *   *   *   *

Thomas Wiles[1] *to WSC*

17 May 1911   House of Commons

Dear Churchill,

At a meeting of London Liberal Members held today, I was desired to convey to you the following resolution which was carried unanimously 'that it is expedient that clause 4 dealing with Sunday closing be omitted from the Shops' Bill.' I may say that the feeling among our constituents is very strong against the special facilities which are being proposed for Jewish traders.

Yours very truly
THOMAS WILES

Stuart Samuel[2] *to WSC*

26 June 1911   Chelwood Vetchery
                                         Sussex

Dear Mr Churchill,

I consider it my duty as a supporter of the Government to draw your attention to the fact that the Jews are quite out of hand over Clause IV of the Shops Bill. The enclosed is but one evidence of it. I have written to say that at last Tuesday's meeting of the Committee you stated that the

---

[1] Thomas Wiles (1861–1951), Liberal MP South Islington 1906–18; PC 1916; Chairman of Port of London Authority; Chairman of Corn Exchange; Chairman of Anglo-Portuguese Colonial and Overseas Bank.

[2] Stuart Montague Samuel (1856–1926), a banker with Stuart Montagu & Co; Liberal MP for Whitechapel 1900–16; created baronet 1912.

Clause is not to be regarded as final & that you are prepared to consider suggestions for its amendment. I am bound to say that you have been misled by the Jewish Board of Deputies which is quite out of touch with Jewish sentiment in this matter. I have not been able to support their policy & that is why Mr Lionel de Rothschild[1] has represented their views on the Shops Bill. They have called a meeting for Thursday which I hope to attend and trust that an agreement may be arrived at. My own view is that the Clause as it appeared in the Shops (No 2) Bill is the least open to objection. In any case the Government would be free from obloquy & would not be open to the present well-founded charge of imposing the religious disability of an obligatory two days rest in seven. To my mind the objection of herding the Jews together has not much cogency for they already have a tendency to do so – without any very evil results.

Of course there is the expedient of allowing existing things to continue, whilst prohibiting an extension, but that will not remove the religious disability.

Forgive me addressing you at length, but the Jews are hard hit both by the Shops Bill & the National Insurance Bill, & are also apprehensive of the Aliens Bill. It would be undesirable to alienate their vote the large majority of which is cast on the Liberal side & I am anxious to avoid such a contingency if possible.

Yours very sincerely
STUART M. SAMUEL

The Archbishop of Canterbury to WSC

31 July 1911   Lambeth Palace

Private

Dear Mr Churchill,

I am receiving many communications on the subject of the Sunday Clauses in the Shops Bill. It is clear that there is a very widespread feeling that it will be really a retrograde step if it be enacted that in these particular cases the norm shall be that the shop is open and that the onus of getting a local order passed will rest on those who desire the shop to be closed. When the matter comes before the House of Lords this point will certainly have to

---

[1] Lionel Walter de Rothschild (1868–1937), eldest son of 1st Baron Rothschild; Liberal Unionist MP, Aylesbury 1899–1910; Trustee of British Museum from 1899; an author of zoological treatises.

be well thrashed out, and as a warm supporter of the Bill I cannot help hoping that you may find it possible before the Bill leaves the Commons to turn the process round so as to throw the onus of action upon those who desire to bring about the opening instead of upon those who desire to secure the restful day for the workers affected. I think it better to tell you this now than to let it all be postponed until the House of Lords discussions. I do not profess to have mastered technically all the intricacies of the Bill (I shall hope to do so in good time), but the matter I have referred to seems to me to be an outstanding principle of policy and fairness.

I am, Yours very truly
RANDALL CANTUAR

WSC to the Archbishop of Canterbury

1 August 1911   Home Office

Private

Dear Archbishop of Canterbury,

I thank you for your letter.

The Bill as it stands is an enormous advance upon anything hitherto attempted against Sunday trading. Except in a few specified areas and a very few trades it will be effectually prohibited all over the United Kingdom. Where the severe penalties and procedure of the new Bill do not apply, the Act of Charles II will continue in force. The opponents of Sunday trading are gaining enormously. They have never recognised in the smallest degree the advantages they secure. They have dwelt morosely on the one or two points where they have not got all they wish.

I have promised to consider before report whether a part at least of Part II of the 2nd Schedule can be inverted in the way you suggest; and of course it will be my desire to meet your wishes. But the opposition to this change may make it impossible. If, however, you are dissatisfied with the Sunday clauses as they eventually leave the House of Commons, and if they are further altered by the House of Lords – only one course will be open to me, and that one which has been strongly pressed upon me from many quarters. I shall drop the Sunday clauses wholly out of the Bill. I am indeed quite willing to do this now if I am assured that this is the wish of those who are opposed to Sunday trading.

If they prefer the present state of things – with the certain and continued growth of Sunday trading, and the growth consequently of the difficulties in the way of any future restrictions – gravely though I think them mistaken, I shall not press my view beyond a point where the main interests of the Bill are endangered.

Believe me, Yours vy truly
WINSTON S. CHURCHILL

*   *   *   *   *

G. R. Askwith to WSC

23 July 1911   Board of Trade

Dear Home Secretary,

I have written a brief memo on the initial stage,[1] which I think is what you wished: and I will send over addresses of the employers tomorrow. If you would wish me at this stage to develop further what I would do with the conciliation dept of the B of T I will do so, but it may be best to feel the way first. I have put on paper B. some broad points which you can keep to yourself or use at this stage as you think fit.

Yours
G. R. ASKWITH

Memorandum by WSC

[?] Late July 1911

There is grave unrest in the country. Port after port is called out. The police and the military are asked for at place after place. Fresh outbreaks continuously occur and will go on. The railways are not sound. Transport workers everywhere are getting to know their strength, while the 'hooligan'

---

[1] The initial stage of establishing new machinery for industrial conciliation.

element are causing riots: and those conversant of labour matters *in practice* anticipate grave upheaval. Serious crises have been in recent years, and very often lately, surmounted only by a narrow margin of safety and now specially a new force has arisen in trades unionism, whereby the power of the old leaders has proved quite ineffective, and the sympathetic strike on a wide scale is prominent. Shipping, coal, railways, dockers etc etc are all uniting and breaking out at once. The 'general strike' policy is a factor which must be dealt with.

While control can probably be maintained, even in a dozen or more simultaneous Tonypandys or Manchesters, control would be more difficult if the railways went, and adequate control must mean great uncertainty, destruction of property, and probably loss of life. Such protection or repression must be coupled with civil action for the lines of prevention and peace.

In *addition* to and not superseding all means at present available to the Board of Trade there should be either (a) a private meeting by the Prime Minister with the biggest employ*ers* of industry to ask their advice, not pseudo-commercial men, but the heads of great organizations in view of the interdependence of the great industries or (b) as the matter is urgent, an immediate appointment of a Committee under a chairman known to be impartial, non-political and conversant practically with labour questions consisting of (say) representatives of the Shipping Employers, the Shipbuilding Employers, the Railways, the Master Cotton Spinners, the Engineering Employers, the Iron and Steel Trades, the Coal Owners, the Master Builders, and Master Printers with Selected Members of the Parliamentary Committee of Trades Unions and (possibly) certain Labour Members of the House of Commons and others, with power to call witnesses, and to enquire into the present causes of unrest and existing disturbances with special reference to the Shipping and Coal Industries, and to report thereon: and make recommendations upon the subject (names to be published later but announcement to be made *at once* and (query) an appeal for peace pending the report).

Memorandum by G. R. Askwith

23 July 1911

The Board of Trade memorandum having been considered and the necessity of action being assumed it is desirable to consider the next steps, which would probably be meant to deal with (a) present crisis (b) the future. The future is the more important.

I think selected important employers should first be met: subsequently, but not yet, labour men. They should be asked to meet the Prime Minister as individuals, not as representatives. They will speak more frankly if there are few. It is easy to add desirable men and difficult to shed undesirables, so begin with the few. The Prime Minister could ask them at once privately and desire to see them on urgent public affairs. They will deem it an honour and due to their country and come at any cost. He need only fix time and place.

In addition to any points in the B of T memorandum he can briefly say that 1911 is not 1871 and the position evidently needs review – there has been strenuous effort by labour – young men are better educated and demand a better life – labour is realizing the idea of the sympathetic strike and its power, leading up to the general strike – the movement is becoming more national than formerly, hence the Head of the Government must take hold of the subject and enlist the cooperation of the biggest industries and the best men, both on the side of capital and labour.

It will be well to produce no cut and dried scheme but to lead them on, and make them see it is their problem, and that the solution must have the cordial support of labour too.

In the first instance there will be no cohesion among them, they may not even know each other; after a long talk it may be well to adjourn till the next day and ask them to meet together and consider things. It might be mentioned that Sir C. Macara's scheme had received support and they might consider it.

(NB They should be made to realize the gravity of the situation and if practicable tipped away from suggesting any course such as preventing of picketing or repression of organisation. It would be futile for them to agree on lines which labour would refuse to consider.)

The names I suggest in the *first* instance are:[1]

Mr F. L. Davis – Chairman, S. Wales Coal Conciliation Board.

Mr M. Cosh – Chairman, Scottish Coal Conciliation Board also a director North British Ry.

Mr Devitt[2] – Chairman, Shipping Employers.

Mr Booth[3] – Head of the great Liverpool Lines.

---

[1] The actual composition of the Industrial Council is printed in Lord Askwith's *Industrial Problems and Disputes*, pages 185–6.

[2] Thomas Lane Devitt (1839–1923), senior partner in the firm of Devitt and Moore; President of the UK Chamber of Shipping 1890; Chairman of the General Shipowners Society 1893; created Baronet 1916.

[3] Alfred Allen Booth (1872–1948), Director of Alfred Booth & Co; member of the Royal Commission on the Civil Service 1911–14; created Baronet 1916.

Sir Andrew Noble[1] – Engineering Employers
Sir Charles Macara – Cotton
Mr Henderson – Chairman Shipbuilders (Glasgow)
Mr Ree[2] – General Manager L & NWR
Mr A. Kaye Butterworth – General Manager NER

Later on for Labour I would suggest only:

Mr Henderson[3]
Mr Barnes
Mr Clynes
Mr Wilkie
Mr Smillie[4] (Scottish Coal)
Mr T. Richards[5] (Welsh Coal)
Mr Tom Ashton (Gen Miners Federation)
Mr Mullin[6] (Cotton)

The Conciliation dept must be

(a) non-political – There will be universal support of this.
(b) All its existing machinery should be retained, but there should be added assistants and an advisory semi-judicial board of reference, as per Macara's scheme, the chairman having status, etc.
(c) Statistics, Labour Exchanges, Trade Boards can remain in the Board of Trade, and the man looking after them be an Asst Secy there, but one man cannot be head of these and go about the country and be industrial Commissioner in addition to the routine of these divisions.
(d) Compulsion is out of the question at present. Conciliation must get public opinion behind it and be created or rather extended. The employers consulted should advise as to powers, if further are desired.

[1] Andrew Noble (1831–1915), in 1860 joined the firm of Sir W. G. Armstrong and Co, and was Chairman at the time of his death; knighted 1893; created Baronet 1902.

[2] Frank Ree (d. 1914), from 1909 he was General Manager of the LNWR and received a knighthood in 1913.

[3] Arthur Henderson (1863–1935) Labour MP Barnard Castle 1903–18; Widnes 1919–22; Newcastle 1923; Burnley 1924–31; Home Secretary 1924, in the first Labour Government; Secretary of State for Foreign Affairs 1929–31; President of the Disarmament Conference 1932–3; PC 1915.

[4] Robert Smillie (1857–1940), working-class leader; chiefly responsible for organizing the miners in Britain; President Scottish Miners' Federation 1894–1918; President Miners' Federation of Great Britain 1912–21; Labour MP Morpeth 1923–9. In 1917 Lloyd George offered him the controllership of food: he refused.

[5] Thomas Richards (1859–1931). A coal-miner from the age of twelve, he became Secretary of the South Wales Miners' Federation in 1898; Labour MP West Monmouthshire and Ebbw Vale 1904–20; PC 1918.

[6] W. Mullin, President of the United Textile Factory Workers' Association and General Secretary of the Amalgamated Association of Card and Blowing Room operatives.

(e) I think the whole could be done by administrative action – an Act of Parlt could follow if necessary – the cost would be small, not that of a half day's big strike – suddenness of action would restore confidence – details and objections I am prepared to deal with.

Objections that have been raised as yet.

(1) The Commissioner, if arbitrator, would become unpopular.

Answer: Why, more than existing arbitrators? He should arbitrate on wages as little as possible, and generally with assessors, but as a rule on small questions, as now, arbitration on wages would be referred to arbitrators ad hoc.

(2) Judicial forms and precedents would arise.

Answer: no more than now; why should a Commissioner suddenly develop 'red tape'?

(3) The Commissioner must be irremovable and might prove unsatisfactory or stay too long, till he was 80.

Answer: Nothing venture, nothing have; he could retire at 60 or 65, as a Civil Servant does.

(4) His salary being voted by Parliament, he must answer through a Parl^y chief.

Answer: Why so any more than the L.C.J., a Lord of Appeal, the Public Trustee, the Director of Public Prosecutions etc. The President of the Board of Trade could send him Party questions to supply answers and his vote be on the Treasury or the B of T like many others, and/or make him a cross-bench peer. An expert might be useful there.

(5) Who is to be Deputy Judge?

Answer: A Labour man; it will be a high post open to a first class labour man, who should have £2,000 or £2,500 a year at least in my opinion.

(6) The Board of Trade is doing very well.

Answer: The existing machinery can be used, taken out of the B of T, and it could then do much more. It can go back if the experiment fails, but the experiment is worth trying and is expected. The Board of Trade won't like it because the dept advertises them. I do not believe in such reflected credit.

(7) That Sir Charles Macara in his scheme is advertising himself.

Answer: This is the usual 'kind friend' criticism and is absolutely exaggerated. Sir Charles is very satisfied with his recent recognition, but for long he has found his work too heavy and sees no successor, particularly on the Cotton Conciliation Board. He has, I believe, hopes that the Commissioner might follow him in that important post as an outside and impartial chairman, and that he might also act on some of the

Coal Conciliation Boards as final referee: but this would be a matter of time and growing confidence in the man.

*   *   *   *   *

Home Office to Head Constable, Liverpool

TELEGRAM

9 August [1911]
3.45 pm

Your letter regarding strike. War Office are sending a battalion of troops tonight to Seaforth Barracks mentioned in your letter. In event of their being required they will have to be requisitioned by Magistrates in the usual way. You should see the Officer in Command as soon as possible. Another battalion has been ordered to stand by at Rhayader.

UNDER SECRETARY

Home Office to Head Constable, Liverpool

TELEGRAM

10 August [1911]
4.45 pm

Regiment of Scots Greys are being held in readiness at York. If they are actually required send requisition to General Officer Commanding, Western Command, Chester; at the same time inform General Officer Commanding, Northern Command, York.

UNDER SECRETARY

WSC to the King

TELEGRAM

[14 August 1911]   [Home Office]

Mr Secretary Churchill with great respect. He has received the following report from Head Constable, Liverpool. The situation is no better, rather worse. The dockers have not gone back to work and the shipowners have declared a general lockout from this afternoon to apply to all dock workers. There is a good deal of riotous disturbance particularly in the Irish quarter and a squadron of the Scots Greys is proceeding there – a body of Warwickshires will follow. The riot last night started with the hooligans not strikers but was quickly taken up by the latter. In view of this report two additional battalions of infantry, another regiment of Cavalry and the remaining squadron of Scots Greys have been ordered to proceed to Liverpool at once. Two more battalions will be moved to Lichfield to be available for Manchester if necessary and a third cavalry regiment will be held in readiness on the railway line at Tidworth. Aldershot has been told to have ten thousand men ready to move at short notice into London. Your Majesty's congratulations to the police force have been withheld pending a more complete cessation of the trouble.

WINSTON CHURCHILL

EXTRACT

'*The Employment of Military in the Rail Strike.*' *House of Commons Paper No 323 (1911)*

'On Friday August 11 the Lord Mayor requisitioned (from Officer Commanding at Seaforth Barracks) the aid of troops already there, and also requisitioned (from General Officer Commanding, Western Command) the second battalion held in readiness at Rhayader, and two squadrons of Scots Greys.

On Sunday 13 August a serious riot on St George's Hall Platform occurred, and on Monday 14 August a lockout was declared at the Docks. On the latter date the strength of the troops at Liverpool was made up to a full brigade of infantry and two regiments of cavalry, and Lieut-General Sir W. H. MacKinnon[1] proceeded to Liverpool and took command of the troops in Liverpool area.'

Lord Mayor of Liverpool and Mayor of Birkenhead to WSC
(*Home Office Papers*)

TELEGRAM

15 August 1911   The Town Hall
Liverpool

Copy

Strike so serious that ferry traffic may be suspended at any moment.

We think that you should consider desirability of sending a War Ship to Mersey with instructions that if need be Blue Jackets should work ferries.

LORD MAYOR LIVERPOOL AND MAYOR OF BIRKENHEAD

[1] William Henry MacKinnon (1852–1929), C-in-C Western Command 1910–15; entered army 1870; Colonel 1889; Director of Auxiliary Forces 1905–8; Director-General of the Territorial Forces 1908–10; Director of Recruiting War Office 1916; KCVO, KCB 1908; GCB 1916.

Captain Waring: I wish to ask the Home Secretary a question of which I have given him private notice, namely, whether it is a fact, as reported, that the troops fired on the crowd at Liverpool early this morning?

WSC: I am able to inform the House that the information I have received this morning shows the situation in London has improved. At the docks, I am informed, all sections of the men are returning to work, though not in full numbers. Men are also working at the wharves; and the employees of the Great Western Railway have come back. There are thus grounds for believing that all classes of transport workers are now beginning to realise the advantages which they have secured by the recent settlement and the folly of jeopardising them by any ill-considered action. If no untoward event should occur the Commissioner of Police hopes to continue to maintain order without the necessity of calling in military aid.

In Liverpool the situation yesterday was unsatisfactory. There was rioting in certain districts. The troops had to be called out, and the Riot Act was read. The statement that volleys were fired, to which currency has been given in the Press, is incorrect, but some individual shots were fired at the windows or roofs of houses from which missiles were being thrown at the troops. This morning the docks are closed and great numbers of men are out of work. The last reports I have received are favourable as regards the maintenance of order and the distribution of necessary food.

The House might like me to read a copy of a telegram received from the Head Constable, Liverpool, despatched at 11.33 today: –

'The Under-Secretary of State
  Home Office, London.
  'You need not attach any very great importance to the rioting of last night. It took place in an area where disorder is a chronic feature, ready to break out when any abnormal excitement is in force. The object of the riot was purely and simply attack on the police, whom they tempted into side streets where barricades of sanitary dustbins and wire entanglements were placed. The riot began about eight, and the troops were called out with natural reluctance on the part of the police officer in charge at 11.40. The mob pursued the same tactics, stoned troops and police from the windows and house tops, but troops and police worked admirably together, and reduced the neighbourhood to peace about 2.30 and the former returned to quarters. Twenty prisoners were taken from the streets and houses. The troops fired a few shots (officers' revolver shots I think) at the house tops, whence the stones came. Six privates of the

Yorkshire regiment and two constables received minor injuries. Both military and police behaved admirably, and the experience of working with the former has been valuable to the officers of the police, who will call the latter out more readily in future. A great deal of damage to houses and shops, especially public houses and provision shops, but food does not seem to have been the object, as the bread was thrown about the street. Troops engaged were Yorkshire regiment – 200 of all ranks.

HEAD CONSTABLE'

General MacKinnon telephoned at 12.30 p.m., after interviewing all his officers in command of sections, that last night serious rioting occurred in Homer Street, with which the police were unable to cope. As the police requisitioned, four companies of the Yorkshire regiment were sent to their assistance. The officer commanding showed very great forbearance, and, although called upon by the magistrate to take action, refrained from firing along the street on account of the women and children in the crowd. Bricks and other missiles were hurled from upper windows on the troops, and on further requisition of the magistrate to fire the officer commanding directed single shots to be fired at the most prominent individuals at the upper windows who were hurling missiles. The total number of shots fired were seven revolver shots by officers, five rifle shots. No casualties are reported to have resulted, and the disturbance was at once quieted down. The troops returned to barracks at 3 a.m. Three men were injured among the troops, but nothing serious. Bayonets were fixed, with their weapons at the 'charge', but no bayonet charge occurred, nor did they use their bayonets, as the crowd immediately dispersed down a side street. General MacKinnon reports that both officers and men showed the utmost forbearance, and were perfectly calm and collected.

In Manchester, at the request of the local authority, arrangements have been made for supplying troops if disturbances should develop, but up to now, I am glad to say, there has been no call for them.

W. Guy Granet[1] to WSC

15 August 1911
Secret

General Manager's Office
Midland Railway
Derby

Dear Mr Churchill,

I have some more definite information as to money coming from abroad, but I cannot pretend that it is ascertained to be accurate. I pass it on to you

[1] William Guy Granet (1867–1943), General Manager Midland Railways 1906–18; Director 1918; Chairman 1922; Chairman LMS 1924–7; knighted 1911; GBE 1923.

for what it is worth, confining myself to saying that I cannot help believing there is *some* truth in it.

The information is that the agent is a German named Bebel.

He was a waiter employed by the Glasgow & SWRwy in their *à la carte* Dept of the St Enoch Station Hotel.

He is now associated with Joe Larkin[1] a man who was prominent in the Belfast troubles 2 or 3 years ago. Bebel & Larkin were in Glasgow on the 9th & 10th inst:

The statement is made to me that the money Bebel has disbursed from the beginning of the strike at Liverpool up to the 10th inst has been as follows: –

J. H. Wilson[2] of the Sailors' & Firemen's Union	£1400
Tom Mann[3] (paid up to 8th inst)	800
J. A. French, Glasgow, of the Sailors & Firemen's Union	800
Gosling,[4] London	790
Davis, London. In connection with trams	600
Shinwell,[5] Glasgow – for propagation work in connection with the Goods Porters & Station Hands	300

I cannot help thinking that this statement is capable of verification by a first class detective, & that it is worth investigation.

Yrs sincerely

W. GUY GRANET

[1] James Larkin, who headed the Belfast dockers in the strike of 1907. With James Connolly he organized the Irish Transport Workers' Union.

[2] Joseph Havelock Wilson (1859–1929), a seaman; later President of the National Seamen's Union; Liberal MP Middlesbrough 1892–1900 and 1906–10, South Shields 1918–22; Wrote *My Stormy Voyage Through Life*.

[3] Thomas Mann (1856–1941), working-class leader. With Tillett, helped organize the London dock strike of 1891, and became the first president of the Docker's Union. In 1910–11 energetically advocated syndicalism and was one of the chief agitators in the 1911 strike movement. General Secretary Amalgamated Engineers 1918–21.

[4] Harry Gosling (1861–1930), apprenticed as a Thames waterman and lighterman; on the LCC 1898–1925; President TGWU; Labour MP Whitechapel 1923–30; Memoir: *Up and Down Stream*, 1927.

[5] Emanuel Shinwell (b. 1884). He was then, at the request of Havelock Wilson, organizing the Clydeside seamen in co-operation with agitators in all the ports. Shinwell was Labour MP Linlithgow 1922–4, 1928–31; Seaham 1935–50; Easington 1950 onwards; he was Minister of Fuel and Power 1945–47; Secretary for War 1947–50; Minister of Defence 1950–1.

Sir Edward Troup to Lord Mayor Liverpool
(*Home Office Papers*)

TELEGRAM

16 August 1911   Home Office

Copy

Your telephone message received 11.30 p.m. yesterday respecting ferry traffic. Arrangements have been made with Admiralty to send vessel for purposes of protection. With regard to your suggestion as to working of ferries, please furnish Secretary of State with a full report.

UNDER SECRETARY HOME OFFICE

WSC to Lord Mayor of Liverpool
(*Home Office Papers*)

TELEGRAM

11.40 am

16 August 1911   [Home Office]

Copy

You should not hesitate to apply to me for any further aid you may require in the difficulties with which you are coping. You will be promptly supported by the Government. I presume you will consider favourably the closing of public houses in all areas of disorder.[1]

WINSTON CHURCHILL

Lord Mayor of Liverpool to WSC
(*Home Office Papers*)

TELEGRAM

16 August 1911   [Liverpool]

Copy

We are much encouraged by your message. Will keep in communication with you as developments arise.

LORD MAYOR LIVERPOOL

[1] Home Office circular of 17 August 1911 asked authorities to bring to the attention of JPs the fact that they can close public houses if need be.

The King to WSC

16 August 1911

Accounts from Liverpool show that situation there more like Revolution than strike. Trust that the Government while inducing strike leaders and masters to come to terms will take proper steps to ensure protection of life and property.

Local feeling runs so high that you cannot expect reason to prevail yet, and a settlement must be forced on both parties. Could you not induce Labour leaders to assist or would they be afraid to be on the side of law and order.

Strongly deprecate the half hearted employment of troops. They should not be called upon except as a last resource but if called upon, they should be given a free hand and the mob should be made to fear them.

GEORGE R.I.

Lord Derby to WSC

15 August 1911   Grand Hotel
Confidential   Harrogate

Dear Churchill,

Nothing but urgent necessity would make me add to the many communications you have received with regard to the Liverpool riots – but an urgent telephone message from the Lord Mayor leaves me no alternative. I feel sure that he is wrong but the fact remains that he is of opinion that even now the serious position there is not realized, that it is no ordinary strike riot but that a revolution is in progress. He fears that tonight there may be no light in the town and that looting will be wholesale. I should hope the military forces will be sufficient to prevent this. But from what he tells me it is quite evident that both sides are determined to hold out – that feeling is very bitter – and that no settlement can be looked for locally. London is the very place where it can be arranged. I will speak frankly. From what he tells me the Board of Trade man who has been sent down is useless. He inspires no respect on either side and if something is not done, and done immediately, to secure the consideration of the position by some arbitrator of recognised position there can only be bloodshed and that on a large scale. The city is in a state of siege, the hospitals have but two days supply, and in 48 hours all the poor people will be face to face with starvation, and God alone knows what will happen when that moment arrives.

Please do not think that I am of opinion that you do not recognise the gravity of the position. I feel sure you do. I only repeat what I have been asked to tell you.

It is needless to say if I can be of any assistance, I am at your disposal. I am staying at Harrogate but a telegram giving any directions as to your wishes would be at once obliged & I could motor to Liverpool in 3 hours. Please treat this letter as strictly confidential as between you & me – especially about the B of T man.

Yours sincerely
DERBY

Hansard

16 August 1911   House of Commons

WSC: Although the situation in the London Docks shows no deterioration, a difficulty has arisen through a claim on the part of the men at the Albert Dock that they should be engaged outside the dock gates, in order that only union hands shall be taken on. This may be productive of trouble. At Liverpool, yesterday afternoon, an attack made by a violent mob on the prison vans had to be repelled by force, the troops were forced to fire; but after this event of which full reports have appeared in the Press, order was quickly restored and no further disturbance occurred during the evening or the night; and this morning when the last news was received all was still quiet. The convoys of food are being got out regularly. At Manchester business is practically at a standstill, but there has been no disturbance. Two battalions and a Cavalry regiment are held in readiness to proceed on the request of the local authorities. There was some disorder at Cardiff last night, but this morning all is reported quiet.

Mr Arthur Henderson: May I ask whether an order has been issued that in certain districts in Liverpool the people must be in their own homes by the hour of darkness, with all lights out, and on whose authority such an order has been issued?

WSC: I have no information upon that point at all, but I certainly think the local authorities should be supported in any precautionary steps they think necessary.

Sir C. Kinloch-Cooke[1]: Will the right hon Gentleman kindly inform the House how he comes to the conclusion that a distinction can be made between union and non-union men by being taken on at the dock gate?

---

[1] Clement Kinloch-Cooke (1854–1944). Unionist MP Devonport 1910–23; for Cardiff East 1924–9; Chairman Naval and Dockyard Committee 1910–24. Knighted 1905; created Baronet 1926. A man of wide literary attainments, he was editor at different times of the *Observer*, the *Pall Mall Gazette*, the *English Illustrated Magazine* and the *Empire Review*; a biographer of Queen Mary.

WSC: That is a technical matter. If the hon Gentleman fully understood the position at the London docks . . .

Sir C. Kinloch-Cooke: I do.

WSC: If the hon Gentleman does fully understand the position there is no need to answer the question.

Lord Mayor of Liverpool to Mayor of Birkenhead
(*Home Office Papers*)

TELEGRAM

17 August 1911   Liverpool

Copy

Received telegram from Home Secretary. You are authorised to apply for sailors from the *Antrim* either for the protection of docks or generally in aid of the civil power. Kindly communicate with me about united action.

LORD MAYOR LIVERPOOL

WSC to the King
(*Royal Archives*)

TELEGRAM

17 August 1911   Parliament Street

Sent in cypher

Mr Secretary Churchill with great respect there is a further improvement in the situation at the London Docks today.

Shipowners have been dissuaded from provocative action and men's leaders are urging the strikers who are still standing out to return and unload cargoes at once. It is possible that the Port of London will return to normal conditions shortly. Meanwhile the markets are well supplied and distribution is proceeding smoothly. The railway men's executives are conferring at the Board of Trade and the signal for a general strike on the railways has not yet been given. The measures taken to deal with that emergency are being concerted. Full protection will be given to all railway men willing to continue at work. And it is believed that the necessary services can in all circumstances be maintained. The following report has been received from Liverpool begins: 'The comparative quiet of yesterday continued through the night. The prison vans were taken by a different route yesterday on the suggestion of a Roman Catholic priest who said there would be trouble if the same route were followed. No particular trouble arose. Part of the tramway men came out yesterday. Attacks have been made on trams but nothing serious and the service is not very badly disorganised. The strike committee have called on the Electric Power Station men to come out at 2 p.m. today. The Chief Constable thinks it unlikely that they will comply.

If they do and the Power Station has to stop it will cut off power from Liverpool, Bootle and a large area around. One or two fires have broken out on vessels in the Docks apparently incendiarism but they were put out before great damage was done. The *Antrim* (First Class cruiser) has arrived in or off the Mersey. Disturbances of a serious character having broken out at Sheffield a battalion of the Gordon Highlanders was dispatched during the night and is now in the city.[1] The whole of the Guards brigade was brought to London last night and is now in Barracks. Although a spirit of unusual unrest and discontent is stirring the whole Labour world due mainly to the fact that wages have not in late years kept pace with the increased cost of living there is no ground for apprehension. The forces at the disposal of the Government are ample to secure the ascendancy of the Law. The difficulty is not to maintain order but to maintain order without loss of life. Preparations are also being made to swear in if necessary large bodies of Special Constables in London and the Provinces. Mr Churchill will report to Your Majesty later in the day.

W. Guy Granet to Edward Marsh

17 August 1911

General Manager's Office
Midland Railway
16 Great George Street

Dear Marsh,

I enclose a short report on the situation as it appears to me.

I would like Mr Churchill to know that I am most grieved & ashamed at an interview that is published with me in today's *Daily Mail*.

It contains just enough of truth to make it difficult for me to say it is a lie from beginning to end, but it perverts the whole tenor of my observations besides interpolating a great deal that I never said.

I intended merely to give them a few reassuring remarks so that the public should not think that the whole railway service would be at a standstill.

1. I never said that it would be a fight to a finish.

[1] The battalion was withdrawn on 23/4 August.

2. I never said that the Govt had offered us every available soldier.

3. I never said that the Govt was on our side except in this way. They were suggesting to me that they could make it hot for the Govt by saying that they were responsible for the whole situation. I said not at all, on the contrary the Govt have done all that could be done, and *so far as the principle of adhering to the conciliation scheme* they were necessarily on our side.

4. They left out the only thing to which I attached importance & which I thought might do good viz: that the Companies would be quite prepared to receive suggestions from the Board of Trade as to how the conciliation scheme could be improved.

5. As to the general communication to the press 'that the Rwy Coys having been assured that the Govt would provide adequate protection the Coys were prepared to carry on an effective tho' restricted service,' I am quite innocent, as we asked Mr Buxton's permission first, & he amended the wording of the communication.

But as to the interview I can only repeat my regret. Incidentally I may say that it made me say a lot of rubbish on internal matters which I never said & which is simply foolish. No more interviews for me.

Yrs sincerely
W GUY GRANET

Letter to Chief Constables
(*Home Office Papers*)

17 August 1911   Home Office

Draft

Sir,

I am directed by the Secretary of State to say that, in the event of a general railway strike or other serious emergency, it will be the duty of each Police Force to give effective protection to life and property and also to all railwaymen within their jurisdiction who wish to work. If the force at your command is not adequate for this purpose, it will be necessary to for you to have special constables sworn in, and the Home Secretary strongly recommends that you should take immediate steps to have suitable men ready to be sworn as special constables if necessity should arise. Men of trustworthy character and good physique should be chosen, and in the first instance you should if possible obtain the services of public spirited citizens whose position enables them to serve without pay. You should consider whether you can employ them most advantageously to take the place of constables withdrawn for special duty or to strengthen the police guards at railway stations and other points where disturbance may arise.

Where necessary the Government will contribute one-half of the pay of a certain number of paid special constables up to a maximum pay of 5/- or, if necessary, 6/- for each day of actual duty, provided that the constables be men of good character and thoroughly suited for the work (e.g. police pensioners, ex-soldiers, and others accustomed to discipline) and that the number for whom the Government will contribute will not exceed fifty per cent of the authorized strength of the Force except with the special sanction of the Home Secretary.

I am, Sir, Your obedient Servant
EDWARD TROUP

Dudley Ward[1] to the King
(*Royal Archives*)

17 August 1911   Post Office Telegraphs
                                                                House of Commons

TELEGRAM

Mr Dudley Ward's humble duty acting under authority which the Prime Minister gave Chief Whip this morning that in case of his absence Murray should arrange that Lloyd George assume complete control. The Chancellor and Ramsay Macdonald were brought together and the latter undertook to do his best to reopen negotiations with the men's executive union representative of all the railways who visited the Board of Trade this morning. Lloyd George made a tactful, diplomatic and hopeful speech this evening which was backed up by Ramsay Macdonald and Sir William Anson for opposition. Government have undertaken to appoint a commission of 3 consisting of a Capitalist, a representative of Labour and a chairman of distinction and impartiality who will at once sit and make a prompt report of their investigations. It is hoped that a further meeting will take place either tonight or tomorrow morning between the Executive union on the one hand and the Chancellor and President of Board of Trade on other.

[1] Dudley Ward (1885–1957); assistant Editor of *The Economist* 1910–12; Treasury 1914–19; Representative of Treasury at Peace Conference, 1919; CBE 1922.

Mayor of Birkenhead to WSC
(*Home Office Papers*)

TELEGRAM

17 August 1911   [Birkenhead]

Copy

Swearing in of Special Constables already proceeded with. Will not hesitate to take every step for safety of life and property. Will not hesitate to apply for more military aid if I think it needful. I appreciate very highly the support the Government offers me.

WILLMER MAYOR BIRKENHEAD

WSC to the King
(*Royal Archives*)

18 August [1911]   Parliament Street

TELEGRAM

With great respect. There seems little doubt that the Railway Strike will now be fought out. It is too soon at present to estimate what the extent of the disturbance to traffic will be. It is certain that while there is difficulty at all points a considerable service is still being maintained on all lines. Parliament has been adjourned until next Tuesday. The Home Secretary made the following Statement of general policy in explanation of the measures which the Government are adopting and will adopt. Begins: The Government are taking and will take all necessary steps make sure that supplies of food fuel and other essentials shall not be interrupted on the railways or at the ports and that all services which are vital to the life of the Community are maintained. They will do this not because they are on the side of the employers or of the workmen but because they are bound at all costs to protect the public from the dangers and miseries which famine and a general arrest of industry would entail. The means by which the millions of people in this island get their daily livelihood are highly artificial and any serious breakdown no matter from what cause would lead to the starvation of great numbers of the poorer people. It is not the well-to-do who would suffer either from dear food or a stoppage of railways and trams or from a failure of light, water or electric power. It is the working classes particularly in the great cities and those dependent upon them who would certainly be the victims and who would be quite helpless if the machinery by which they are fed and obtain wages were thrown seriously out of gear. Mr Churchill will receive later from the General Managers Committee a full report of the position on the Railways which he will forward to Your Majesty.[1]

WSC to the King
(*Royal Archives*)

TELEGRAM

18 August 1911   Parliament Street

Sent in cypher

With great respect the General Managers of all the Principal Railways have reported to the Home Secretary this evening that in spite of widespread secessions all the necessary services have been maintained over the whole system. Number of railwaymen of all grades on strike at present does not in their opinion exceed fifty thousand; by far the greater part of their staff are remaining at their posts. The managers have received many offers of service but have refrained for the present from availing themselves of these in order not to complicate the general situation and make peace more difficult. It has not yet been found necessary to divide the traffic assigning different areas to each railway and thus avoiding all duplication. There is a considerable reserve power in this available for a further strain. The movements of troops to the different threatened points continues and the enrolment of Special Constables proceeds at the various centres where disturbances have occurred. The Home Secretary has asked the War Office to furnish Your Majesty with a complete statement of the military movements.

He has been himself engaged all day among other things in endeavouring to settle the dispute at the London Docks and it is very near a settlement now. All the information which reaches him from many quarters shows that the situation is well in hand. No efforts will be spared to promote a peaceful settlement on honourable terms for the men at the earliest possible moment. Later. A complete settlement has been reached in regard to the Port of London difficulty and a very good spirit prevails between masters and men. The vessels will begin unloading meat for the London market which has been for some time sorely needed early tomorrow morning.

HOME SECRETARY

[1] The substance of this telegram was incorporated by WSC in his Memorandum of the same date (see pp. 1282-3).

Sir Frederick Ponsonby to WSC

18 August 1911   Bolton Abbey
                                                         Skipton

Dear Mr Churchill,

The King desires me to thank you for the many telegrams you have sent and to tell you how much His Majesty has appreciated the manner in which you have kept him informed of the different phases of the strike.

It is naturally a matter which interests the King very much and here where the newspapers do not arrive till the afternoon it has been a great advantage to receive telegrams, giving authentic details of the strike.

Yours very truly
F. E. G. PONSONBY

Memorandum by WSC

[18 August 1911]   [Home Office]

Copy

The Government are taking and will take all necessary steps to make sure that supplies of food, fuel and other essentials shall not be interrupted on the railways or at the Ports, and that all services which are vital to the life of the community are maintained. They will do this not because they are on the side of the employers, or of the workmen, but because they are bound at all costs to protect the public from the dangers and miseries which famine and a general arrest of industry would entail. The means by which the millions of people in this island get their daily livelihood are highly artificial and any serious breakdown, no matter from what cause, would lead to the starvation of great numbers of the poorer people. It is not the well-to-do who would suffer either from dear food or a stoppage of railways and trams, or from a failure of light, water or electric power. It is the working classes particularly in the great cities and those dependent upon them who would certainly be the victims, and who would be quite helpless if the machinery by which they are fed and obtain wages were thrown seriously out of gear. Workmen engaged in the Transport service cannot therefore in practice carry through strikes without interference in the same way as those employed in other kinds of work, and this, no doubt, imposes upon the Government and the public generally a special obligation to look after the wages & conditions of their labour. This duty will not be forgotten; but meanwhile the service of the nation must go forward. The law has already declared that it is a criminal offence to break a contract of employment where the effect will be to endanger life or to cause serious bodily injury. The Government believe that the arrangements which have been made to safeguard the working of the railways and to maintain order will prove effective. If not, other measures of an even larger scope will have to be taken promptly so that the transport of everything that is really necessary shall be assured. It must be clearly understood that there is no escape from these facts and that as they affect the food of the people and the safety of the country they are far more important than anything else.

WSC to Sir Edward Henry
(*Home Office Papers*)

19 August 1911

Copy

You must be prepared to release a large portion of the troops in London at short notice during next week for duty if required in other parts of the country. In these circumstances the recruitment of Special Constables must be pressed forward. Three classes will probably be necessary: (1) Those who volunteer to take regular spells of duty without pay; (2) Those who volunteer to remain at call for service in emergency and to do occasional spells of duty; and (3) Paid Constables. You should proceed at once and engage up to 3,000 trustworthy men, including Police Pensioners and persons having disciplined training, and these should do regular duty with your Force. All the extra men, so far as practicable, who were engaged for the Coronation, should be given preference and invited to rejoin during the present period. If you require additional clerical staff, you are to engage it without further reference to me. You are authorized to apply to the War Office for the services of 25 Staff College Officers to organise the Special Constables in London, and generally to assist in the administration of the Police Force. Pray let this proceed at once and report to me.

WSC

WSC to Chief Constable, Birkenhead
(*Home Office Papers*)

TELEGRAM

2.0 a.m. West Strand
[Saturday] 19 August 1911

Please report at earliest possible tomorrow (Saturday) by telegraph what proportion of Railway men and if possible how many have struck and how many remain at work at each Railway centre in your Police District and to what extent the goods trains and passenger trains respectively are running from the stations. Your telegram should reach the Home Office by 11 o'clock in the morning.

HOME SECRETARY

WSC to Mayor of Birkenhead[1]
(*Home Office Papers*)

TELEGRAM

6.20 a.m.   West Strand
19 August 1911

Secret

Government attach great importance at this junction to the enrolment of special constables, preferably unpaid, but if necessary you are authorized to enrol special constables on the terms of the Home Office letter dated the 17th instant. Please proceed actively with this, if you have any reason to apprehend trouble in your district report as soon as possible what steps you are taking and what numbers are registered. Applications for troops should not be made unless your resources in police and special constables are exhausted.

HOME SECRETARY

Chief Constable, Birkenhead, to WSC
(*Home Office Papers*)

TELEGRAM

19 August 1911   [Birkenhead]

Of 1031 railway men employed in this town 674 have struck. At the London and North Western Railway 230 men remain at work and 200 are on strike. At the Great Western Railway 52 men remain at work and 198 are on strike. Of the London and North Western and Great Western Joint Railways 38 men remain at work 92 are on strike. The Mersey Railway none working 400 suspended 100 on strike. This line is closed owing to inability to get coal to provide electric current. Cheshire lines 27 men working 84 men on strike; Midland 8 men working one on strike; Great Central

---

[1] This telegram was sent to all Chief Constables and Mayors in the disturbed areas, on a signal given at 4.30 p.m.

2 men working none on strike. The goods yard of the Great Central Railway is situated in the County Police District and therefore I can give no particulars. No goods trains are running on any line and no passenger trains except occasional ones on the London and North Western Joint Railways. Yesterday trains left on that line about 2 per hour but today so far only one train has been able to leave.

WSC to Mayor of Birkenhead
(*Home Office Papers*)

TELEGRAM

5.34 p.m. [Home Office]
19 August 1911

The military authorities have been charged with the duty of protecting the railroads and all railwaymen who continue at work and the general officers commanding the various military areas are instructed to use their own discretion as to whether troops are or are not to be sent to any particular point. The Army Regulation which requires a requisition for troops from a civil authority is suspended. The police and magistrates should co-operate in every possible way with the military, and it is essential that the police should give assistance in guarding the railways and should supply effective protection to railwaymen outside the railway premises.

HOME SECRETARY

Mayor of Birkenhead to WSC
(*Home Office Papers*)

TELEGRAM

6.0 pm [Birkenhead]
19 August 1911

Replying to your telegram of today I have to report that the number of special constables enrolled is 374, and that I am using every effort to obtain more. 50 Infantry have been withdrawn from the town. There have been several collisions between strikers and police. I do not consider that I have sufficient force at my disposal. If you cannot send me more military or naval support I cannot answer for the safety of life and property. I cannot maintain the various services of the Town as per my telegram of last evening.

Mayor of Birkenhead to Sir Edward Troup
(*Home Office Papers*)

TELEGRAM

11.30 pm   [Birkenhead]
19 August 1911

I have no reply to my telegram of this afternoon. Please send more troops at once. It is urgent. I cannot see my way to preserve life and property unless I get more assistance. Food supply running short.

WILLMER MAYOR BIRKENHEAD

WSC to the King
(*Royal Archives*)

TELEGRAM

19 August 1911   Parliament Street

With great respect Metropolitan Police reports show that perfect tranquillity and order prevail throughout the London District. Reduced but effective services of trains are working from all stations and ample supplies of provisions are coming in. The Port of London is working at its full activity. Great quantities of food particularly meat are being discharged. The Local Government Board report that no difficulty is experienced in feeding the 110,000 in their institutions throughout the metropolis and no complaint as to dearth of supplies have been received. Railway managers will give the Home Secretary a full report by this afternoon as to the general position on the railways and there is no doubt that in spite of a great deal of delay and inconvenience the whole railway system is working.

It is probable that a brigade from London will be sent into the Midlands during the course of the day. It will be replaced in London by another brigade drawn from the South Coast and Channel Islands. The enrolment of Special Constables is proceeding briskly at all centres where disturbances occurred. Detailed reports are now coming in from the Head Constables in all parts of the country as to the number of men who actually struck and the number of those working and these will be epitomised shortly. The Lord Mayor of Liverpool reports that he is being loyally supported by the magistrates, officials and large numbers of citizens. 3000 special constables have been sworn in and effective efforts are being made to deal with the critical situation which prevails in that city. He welcomes the appointment of the

Commission consisting of Mr T. P. O'Connor, Colonel Kyffin-Taylor[1] and Mr Shackleton and will give it every assistance. It is not certain how far the full pressure of the strike has made itself felt but all preparations are being made to cope with any further developments. The Chancellor of the Exchequer continues his efforts and exertion to procure a peaceful settlement and negotiations are still proceeding.

HOME SECRETARY

WSC to the King
(*Royal Archives*)

TELEGRAM

19 August 1911

Sent in cipher

With humble duty. Although it is true, taking the country as a whole, two thirds of the railway men are remaining out, the main features of the strike, as now disclosed, show that in important areas a very different proportion prevails.

Returns received from Chief Constables throughout the country show that in South Wales area practically seventy five per cent of the men are out. The triangle Bristol Gloucester Reading seems about half and half.

The great manufacturing provinces over the following area Carlisle Newcastle Grimsby Leicester Coventry Wolverhampton Crewe Chester Liverpool Bradford show at least sixty and probably seventy per cent of strikers. Over large parts of these areas 90 per cent of the drivers have come out.

Over the rest of England, there is inconvenience and dislocation but no serious stoppage except in cases of through trains cancelled through strike areas. London is quiet. Stoppage of goods trains in main strike areas perfectly complete. In some cases food and perishables are got through paralysed areas including population something like twenty millions comprising almost all the principal manufactures and they are dependant on Railways for food and raw materials.

Any prolonged interruption of traffic in these areas must involve comparative arrest of industry of all kinds coupled with severest famine.

[1] Gerald Kyffin-Taylor (1863–1949), Unionist MP for Kirkdale division of Liverpool 1910–15; Brigadier-General Royal Artillery 1917.

Figures of above are averages but in many important centres according to our returns all or almost all the men have left.

Negotiations which the Chancellor of the Exchequer is conducting are in a slightly more favourable position. Two Brigades have been sent to the Midlands and the North.

Newspapers report fatal riot at Llannelly. In view of situation the Prime Minister comes to London from York for a Cabinet Committee.

WSC to the King
(*Royal Archives*)

TELEGRAM

19 August 1911   West Strand

With great respect. A complete agreement between the employees and the companies having been reached by unanimous agreement the Railway Strike has been declared at an end. All railway men are returning to work.

The Secretary of State for War has ordered all troops to be sent back as soon as convenient to their districts and the Home Office has suspended the enrolment of special constables. The news today from every quarter showed that order was well maintained and even in districts where feeling ran high the railway men on strike took no part in any disturbance that occurred. The Chancellor of the Exchequer is principally responsible for the happy result.

WINSTON CHURCHILL

WSC to Mayor of Birkenhead
(*Home Office Papers*)

I a.m.   TELEGRAM

20 August   West Strand

Confidential

Copy

Railway Strike settled by unanimous agreement. Publish the fact that peace is made and be specially careful to avoid collisions with those who do not know this yet.

HOME SECRETARY

WSC to the King
(*Royal Archives*)

TELEGRAM

1 a.m.

20 August 1911   West Strand

Sent in cipher

Mr Secretary Churchill with great respect has to inform Your Majesty that reports from South Wales this morning show that everything is perfectly quiet. Order has been restored at Llanelly and the railwaymen are returning to work. The military officers report that the railwaymen were not themselves responsible for the rioting at Llanelly. The Commissioner of Police reports that everything is peaceful and quiet in London and that all arrangements are being made to facilitate the meeting of railway men in Hyde Park this afternoon. The troops are being withdrawn from the railway stations and other points and are being concentrated preparatory to returning home. The news from Liverpool and Birkenhead is that everything is quiet and orderly. It is expected that the settlement of the railway strike will promote a solution of the special difficulties which exist in those two places. Reports have been called for from all parts of the provinces. The dispute between the master lightermen and their employers was settled yesterday by conferences at the Home Office.

28234 89963 29823 90221 70212 35587 93446 28045
70624 55725 78236 03262 05299 46282 06838 48344[1]

WSC to the King
(*Royal Archives*)

20 August 1911

We shall know tonight whether the strike is really settled. Meanwhile no military movements will be made. If favourable news is received, as may be expected, and when it is quite clear that trouble is over, the Home Secretary would suggest a message expressing Your Majesty's satisfaction should be made public.

If agreeable to Your Majesty, he will prepare a short draft. He would also like to be authorized to convey a message of Your Majesty's appreciation to the Commissioner of the Metropolitan Police.

[1] Translation of this cipher not found in Chartwell Papers.

The King to WSC

TELEGRAM

20 August 1911   Bolton Abbey

Your telegram informing me that the Railway Strike has been declared at an end has given me the greatest satisfaction. I take this opportunity of thanking you for the very full accounts you have given me during this anxious time. Glad the troops are to be sent back to their Districts at once. This will reassure the public. Much regret unfortunate incident at Llanelly. Feel convinced that prompt measures taken by you prevented loss of life in different parts of the country. Trust in very short time normal state of affairs will be resumed.

GEORGE R.I.

WSC to Mayor of Birkenhead
(*Home Office Papers*)

TELEGRAM

12.20 pm   Home Office
20 August 1911

Copy

Please report to Home Office by 8 pm tonight whether order maintained and when men returning to work.

HOME SECRETARY

Mayor of Birkenhead to WSC
(*Home Office Papers*)

TELEGRAM

8.0 pm   . [Birkenhead]
20 August 1911

Copy

Today being Sunday it is difficult to judge exact position, but town is assuming normal condition. Wirral and Mersey Tunnel Railway service resumed, think other railways will resume tomorrow. Other labour may be Tuesday or Wednesday. Feeling entirely changed for the better. Special Constables who now number 444 have been withdrawn in order to avoid friction. Military pickets remain.

WILLMER MAYOR OF BIRKENHEAD

Chief Constable, Carmarthenshire to Home Office
(*Home Office Papers*)

TELEGRAM

9.50 p.m.
21 August 1911

Supplementary to Saturday's report by wire: attack made in afternoon on train which had passed through Llanelly station, under military protection, at railway cutting, sloping on either side to considerable height, near station. Train held up; engine driver roughly handled. Troops under Major Stuart quickly on scene, followed by 3 magistrates. Troops attacked on both sides by crowd on embankments hurling stones and other missiles. One soldier carried away wounded in head and others struck. Riot Act read. Major Stuart mounted embankment and endeavoured to pacify crowd. Stone throwing continued, crowd yelling at troops. Shots fired as warning,[1] no effect, attitude of crowd threatening and determined. Other shots fired, two men killed, one wounded, crowd fled. In evening, message received at railway station that house and business premises of Mr Thomas Jones, magistrate, attacked. Proceeded with all available police and about 100 troops requisitioned by magistrate, having only 40 constables, and dealt with riotous crowds in the town. Troops took no active part beyond accompanying police in case they might be overpowered. Several truncheon charges made until about 2 am. Business premises of Mr Jones gutted and much damage done. Meanwhile on line above railway station trucks looted and set on fire. Very considerable loss in property and damage. Trucks containing two cylinders of detonators caused violent explosion resulting in death of four people and injury to many. Later more troops arrived under Colonel Montressor, who cleared railway lines and sent troops to deal with attack on Docks Police Station. Order restored about 2 am Sunday. No further trouble since announcement of settlement.

[CHIEF CONSTABLE]

---

[1] Footnote in text: This is a mistake. No warning shots were fired, but as was proved at the inquest, a rifle was discharged accidentally before the order to fire was given.

Sir Edward Henry to Sir Edward Troup
(*Home Office Papers*)

21 August 1911   New Scotland Yard

Dear Troup,

The Special Constables who volunteered for Service have now been disbanded. They fall into three groups: –

1. Those who were attested.

2. Those who registered their names, but who not having been attested received no equipment.

3. Those who were attested as paid Constables.

I propose with the consent of the Secretary of State to call in the equipment issued, which consisted of truncheon, armlet and warrant card, except in the case of the honorary Special Constables in the first group, who would be permitted to retain the truncheon as a souvenir.

The total number of volunteers for duty was 8949. Of these 2158 honorary Constables and 351 paid Constables were attested.

Yours sincerely
E R HENRY

Note by Sir Edward Troup:
? Approve. ET 22/8/11
Initialled:
WSC 23/8

The King to WSC

TELEGRAM

22 August 1911   Studley Royal
                                                    Ripon

Very glad to hear last batch of strikers have come in and that strike is at an end. The police deserve the greatest credit for the admirable way in which they have dealt with situation created by strike during last few days.

GEORGE R.I.

WSC to the King
(*Royal Archives*)

23 October 1911   Home Office

Sir,

The very gracious words which your Majesty used to me yesterday will ever be remembered in my heart with a deep sense of pleasure & gratitude.

It has been a high honour to me to have stood so near to your Majesty during the moving and memorable events of the first year of a happily & brilliantly inaugurated reign. I have greatly valued the opportunities that have fallen to my lot of advising your Majesty upon the many important utterances to the public which have been necessary. I am profoundly sensible of the extreme personal kindness with which your Majesty has always treated me, and it is an immense encouragement to me to feel that as time has passed your Majesty has not been inclined in any way to withdraw the confidence which was so generously extended at the moment of your Majesty's accession.

In delivering my seals to your Majesty this morning I should be sensible of many regrets at ceasing to be your Majesty's principal Secretary of State, were it not for the fact that the great service of the sea upon which the life & honour of the realm depends is one with which your Majesty is so intimately associated by a life time of practical experience, & that I know I may recur to your Majesty for aid & support in the duties entrusted to me by your Majesty's gracious favour.

I am Sir, Your Majesty's faithful & devoted servant & subject

WINSTON S. CHURCHILL

*　*　*　*　*

Charles Bulbeck to WSC

[Undated]

Dear Mr Winston Churchill,

I want to thank you for sending me back home to my Mother and Father and I will always be a good boy and never take any coal or anything else again.

I remain, Yours respectfully

CHARLES BULBECK

17

Admiralty 1911

(See Main Volume II pp. 537–53)

———

WHEN Parliament reassembled on 24 October 1911, several changes were announced in the Cabinet:

	Previous	*October 1911*
Admiralty	McKenna	WSC
Home Office	WSC	McKenna
Privy Seal	Ripon	Carrington
Agriculture	Carrington	Runciman
Education	Runciman	Pease
Duchy of Lancaster	Pease	Hobhouse

Lady Randolph to WSC

1 October 1911   Glenmuick House

Dearest Winston,

You thrill me with curiosity. Is it a change of office? – I hope a good one. I shall look forward to seeing you in London the end of the week. My Connaught dinner is progressing – I so wish you and Clemmie were coming – but you are '*trop dans les grandeurs*' already!

It is icy here. Such a cold house and snow on the hills – I leave tomorrow and go to Newmarket next week. I wonder what you think of Italy and Turkey. I think the latter will give in; they are in a hopeless position, no navy; and how can they get their troops to Tripoli? Would they be allowed to go through Egypt? Well *au revoir* I am longing to see something of you and hear all your news – Sly Puss! at Balmoral they thought you were leaving early in order to visit your 'Mommer'! – How is the new car?

Love to Clemmie –

Oh! I played golf so well at Aboyne –

H. H. Asquith to Lord Crewe
(*Asquith Papers*)

EXTRACT

7 October 1911

. . . The First Lord ought to be in the H of Commons, and the Navy would not take kindly in the first instance to new organisation imported direct from the War Office.[1] On the whole, I am satisfied that Churchill is the right man, and he would like to go. . . .

WSC to the Master of Elibank

TELEGRAM

14 October 1911   33 Eccleston Square

Please tell PM of our conversation. I cannot feel that delay would be advantageous from public point of view. The Estimates should be brought before Cabinet in November and the Minister who is to be responsible for defending them must have some hand in shaping them to be master of the subject. There is no time to be lost. Naval estimates particularly govern both finance and policy not only one but two or three years ahead There is no time to be lost if this duty is to be effectively discharged this year. Chancellor of Exchequer authorises me to say that he feels this very strongly. Much inconvenience will result further from keeping two departments hanging in the wind and I should have thought the delay would be equally unpleasant and unsatisfactory for both ministers. I have been holding up appointments and decisions which ought fairly to be left to my successor and I should deprecate seriously new appointments at the Admiralty which might encumber the future and add to the difficulties of creating a war staff. If there is a long delay something is sure to leak out and this would be a real cause of mortification and be detrimental from every point of view. Such a change especially in times like these cannot be made too promptly once it is resolved on and the parties affected know. I hope the Prime Minister will consider these facts.

There is no difficulty about Home Office Bills. I am quite willing to conduct Shops Bill to its end, there are only three Parliamentary days of it left and the task is practically completed.

I have managed this Bill personally all through and it would not be right

[1] R. B. Haldane, who had recently been created Viscount Haldane of Cloan, was still Secretary of State for War. Lord Crewe was one of a number of Liberals who advocated his transfer to the Admiralty, in view of his success at the War Office.

for me to withdraw from it. McKenna is himself engaged this autumn with Insurance Bill and nothing wd be more natural than for me to finish Shops. The Mines Bill has always been in Masterman's charge who knows it thoroughly. There is nothing else this year worth speaking of. On the other hand surely the Minister who is to take charge of the Welsh Bill ought now to be preparing that and other Home Office legislation for next year.

I feel deeply for the Prime Minister in his difficulty and it is painful for me to have to press these points but I am sure that it is not only in the public interest but in McKenna's personal interest that changes should take place before Parliament meets.

Let me add that it would suit me not to move into Admiralty House till after Christmas as there are numerous small matters to be settled here and anyhow McKenna's convenience on such a point would be decisive for me but I daren't even put this house into the hands of agents for fear of starting rumours which would open a flood of spiteful gossip and canvassing deeply injurious and odious to all concerned.

CHURCHILL

Lord Knollys to Vaughan Nash
(*Asquith Papers*)

18 October 1911   Buckingham Palace

My dear Nash,

I am much obliged to you for your letter of today.

I *know* that the King will not allow anybody but himself to give the 'Seals' to W. Churchill's successor. In fact I don't see how anyone but the King could give them.

I hope therefore McKenna's resistance will be overcome, as if he does not agree to the transfer before 11th Nov, it cannot take place until the beginning of February, and this delay would certainly be unfair to Churchill.

Yrs sincerely
KNOLLYS

WSC to H. H. Asquith

23 October 1911

Copy

During the last few months circumstances, with which you are well acquainted, have forced me to consider the question of the country's food supply in the event of a general strike or of war. In either event the Home Secretary would be responsible for the maintenance of order throughout the country; in the event of war he might have to maintain order without the military assistance which is available in ordinary circumstances; and nothing would more inevitably lead to riots and disturbances than a shortage of the food supplies, or even a considerable rise in the price of necessaries due to mere panic. It is impossible, however great our naval superiority may be over an enemy, to say that that enemy would never gain a small local advantage or could by no possibility capture a few food ships: and if either of these events occurred in any part of the North Sea, it would cause alarm among shippers out of all proportion to the real danger, and insurance against war risks would be raised to a figure which would prevent food cargoes from being sent to London or our Eastern ports.

In view of this danger, it seemed to me necessary to consider how far the restriction of the importation of food by sea which would be caused by the fear of capture, even if the actual risk of capture were very small, could be prevented by providing a National Guarantee against the loss of ships bringing cargoes of food.

I found on inquiry that this matter had already (in 1908) been before a Departmental Committee of which Mr Austen Chamberlain was Chairman, and that the Committee reported generally against a National Guarantee for war risks; but on reading its report it appears that the Committee had not before it any well-considered scheme restricted in its scope to food and other necessaries; that its conclusions were reached with much hesitation; and that it negatives rather a previous general undertaking by the Government to indemnify against all war risks, than a special and restricted indemnity for food and raw material to be offered only when the emergency has actually arisen.

On the other hand, the Sub-Committee of the Committee of Imperial Defence on the Local Transportation and Distribution of Supplies in time of War, of which Colonel Seely is Chairman, expresses in its report the opinion that, if the facts now known had been in the possession of the Departmental Committee of 1908, 'their recommendations might have been other than they were,' and suggests that the question should not be regarded as closed.

I have consulted Mr McKenna on the subject – sending him a scheme of insurance which has been prepared by Sir F. Bolton and which at my request he showed me – and he writes: 'I have formed no bigoted opinion, but I am still not satisfied that Bolton's scheme would avoid the difficulties which are very fully stated in the Committee's report. (Sir F. Bolton's Scheme has been modified to meet these difficulties.) I suggest that you ask to have the matter reconsidered in the Committee of Imperial Defence.

The Department directly concerned is of course the Treasury, and I assume that George would agree to the question being re-opened.'

I confess that it seems to me that the matter should be further considered, but from a different point of view to that taken at the last inquiry. It should not be a question of a public guarantee to be announced before-hand, which is certainly open to grave objection. it is not even necessary to decide that in any circumstances a guarantee would be given. What seems to me essential is to be prepared for a situation in which, to save the country from high prices and consequent risk of civil disaster, the Government might be forced to give a guarantee. If that situation should arise, and no scheme is ready, some hasty and ill-considered scheme might have to be adopted which would be much less effective and involve much greater waste than if a good scheme of restricted operation had been carefully worked out before-hand. I suggest for your consideration that a Sub-Committee of the Committee on Imperial Defence should be appointed to examine the subject with a view to settling a scheme which should be kept secret and should be ready for adoption only if the actual circumstances of a future war rendered this necessary.

WSC to Lord Fisher

25 October 1911   Home Office

My dear Lord Fisher,
    I want to see you vy much. When am I to have that pleasure? You have but to indicate your convenience & I will await you at the Admiralty.

Yours vy sincerely
WINSTON S. CHURCHILL

Lord Fisher to WSC

26 October 1911   Grand Hotel National
                                                           Lucerne

Dear Winston,
    You have 'the desire of your heart' I think getting to the Admiralty and I now feel free to be with you again which of course is a pleasure as I dont forget past days which proved we had views in common and mutual regard!

You were very good to me! and I used so to enjoy my many lunches and dinners with you in Bolton Street! Well! dear old Cassel sent me a note that you had been enquiring about me so I sent him a telegram to say I would meet you in Paris any day you liked at the Hotel Meurice as I don't want to come to England – they would know then I was seeing you & I think perhaps best for you that this should not be the case! Only I am bound to tell you that only 5 minutes ago I got a letter from one of the most influential journalists in London that *'it is a well known fact that I have a great admiration for you and that of course you and I will be in close touch'*. So this rather shakes my idea of secrecy & I am quite ready to come to London to give you all the help in my power if you will send me a telegram to this Hotel. (Hotel National – Lucerne) and I shall go to the Curzon Hotel, Curzon Street Mayfair – where you can send me a note to await arrival to say *where* & *when* you would like to see me – perhaps you will prefer to come there. Also I had an immense letter from Spender before the news of your going to the Admiralty was announced & he being a safe & sure friend I wrote him a letter in reply suggesting for your consideration those who I *know* & can *guarantee* to serve you well.

If you take the advice there given I can ensure absolute and brilliant success in your administration – but they all inter-weave with each other so it's a case of *all or none!* A. K. Wilson is magnificent at sea but he has wrecked McKenna ashore – (of course I am writing to you the secrets of my heart now – I have not said this to a soul nor shall I!) – and he would just as certainly win a great Battle at sea as ever Nelson was certain! *That's a fact* until Sir John Jellicoe[1] commands the Home Fleet Wilson is our Admiralissimo! Jellicoe is as great as Nelson but he is not senior enough yet. You will see his name very prominent in the list I gave to Spender. Battenberg[2] is *ideal* for First Sea Lord – he has to perfection the German faculty of organising a great Naval Staff and in debates at the Committee of Imperial Defence you will find him incomparable but again this is dependent on your having Captain Mark Kerr[3] as your private Secretary – (he is now at the Admiralty

---

[1] John Rushworth Jellicoe (1859–1935), a Lord Commissioner of the Admiralty and Controller of the Navy 1908–10; commanded Atlantic Fleet 1910–11; commanded Second Division Home Fleet 1911–12; Second Sea Lord 1912–14; Commander of the Grand Fleet 1914–16 (at battle of Jutland); First Sea Lord 1916; Chief of Naval Staff 1917; Governor-General of New Zealand 1920–4; retired 1924; KCVO 1907; OM 1916; Viscount 1918; Earl 1925.

[2] Louis Alexander Battenberg (1854–1921), eldest son of Prince Alexander of Hesse; naturalized as Prince Louis of Battenberg in 1868; C-in-C Atlantic Fleet 1908–10; commanding Third and Fourth Divisions Home Fleet 1911; Second Sea Lord 1911–12; First Sea Lord 1912–14 when he resigned; in 1917 assumed the name Mountbatten; Earl of Medina 1917.

[3] Mark Edward Frederic Kerr (1864–1944), C-in-C Greek Navy 1913–15; of Adriatic Squadron 1916–17; Deputy-Chief Air Staff and Major-General RAF; retired from RN and RAF 1918; pioneer aviator who attempted to fly Atlantic 1919.

or rather Victoria Street) and on your having Captain Ballard[1] now commanding the Battleship *Britannia* in the Home Fleet as Director of Naval Intelligence – finding some place for Admiral Bethell[2] the present man – (that is to say when Sir A. Wilson leaves) –

However I wont repeat all I have said to Spender which I asked him to convey to you.

My love to your dear wife. If I come to London to see you I hope I shall meet her.

As for myself I am very happy.

'The World forgetting'

'Nor the World forgot'

I would offer to be your '*Chief of the Navy General Staff* – there is room for an immense 'coup' there but I don't want to embarrass' you.

Yours ever

FISHER

Lord Fisher to WSC

28, 29, 30 October [1911]   Reigate Priory
Surrey

Keep private till *the* day on which old Board leaves and New Board are in.
Y and E
NB The reduction must be sufficient to make the cost *well below* what engineer students formerly paid at Keyham College. This cuts the ground from under the feet of Barnes MP & Co.

———

Say – when 'making' the announcement that it is a prelude to entire abolition if this intermediate step is found to be successful.

———

Note here – the wisdom of carrying out these two manoeuvres off your own bat in the interregnum of Boards.

———

Don't make the offer yourself to Ottley.[3] He will refuse – allow me to speak to

———

[1] George Alexander Ballard (1862–1948), Director of Operations Division Admiralty War Staff. Admiral 1924.

[2] Alexander Edward Bethell (1855–1932), director of Naval Intelligence 1909–12; C-in-C East Indies 1912; Admiral commanding Coast Guard and Reserves 1918; second son of 2nd Baron Westbury, knighted 1912.

[3] Charles Langdale Ottley (1858–1932), Naval Attaché to the Maritime Courts 1899–1904, serving in the US, Japan, Italy, Russia and France; Director of Naval Intelligence 1905–7; Secretary of CID 1907–11; Rear-Admiral; knighted 1907.

him first & please guarantee Hankey[1] to succeed him – You can get the PM to promise this as he told Esher the other day he had the highest opinion of Hankey & meant to do something for him or words to that effect.

Don't commit yourself to *M* or *B*. – *till the very last hour* – one never knows what may turn up!

Don't move Bethell till *all* the moves are made. Make one big announcement of *all* the changes – as then you get rid of a mass of criticisms as it is seen how all the arrangements dove-tail with each other.

Get the 'House of Lords' fixed before the King leaves England

---

The *sooner* fixed with A.K.W. the *better* (but say to *him* – the 1st of Jany) as then no sudden action on his part would matter – the reason you give to him *& the one reason* – is the Estimates! & the very regretful necessity of his having to go on March 2 for age.

Let Ottley choose the two Deputies & his professional Secretary – Ottley being on the Retired List doesn't signify

---

Change *all* on the Board
Quite easy & very eligible candidates for No 3 & No 4 – Nos 1 & 2 you have arranged splendidly – as on reflection I am sure No 2 will run No 1!

I shld suggest *Peirse*[2] and *Kerr*

If you want to throw a sop to the Beresford party – give Custance the command in chief at Devonport but he will be mischievous – however it won't much signify.

---

[1] Maurice P. A. Hankey (1877–1963), denizen of the Cabinet offices; served in Naval Intelligence; Assistant Secretary Committee of Imperial defence 1908, Secretary 1912–38; Secretary War Cabinet 1916–18; held office in Chamberlain and Churchill Governments 1939–42; created Baron 1939.

[2] Richard H. Peirse (1860–1940), commanded First Battle Squadron Home Fleet 1911–12; C-in-C East Indies Station 1913–16; commanded Allied Naval Forces on Suez Canal 1914–16; knighted 1914. His son Richard was one of WSC's flying instructors in 1913.

Note to publish when you make the change known to *the new* Board (as a *fait accompli!*) that you are reverting to the ancient custom in taking up Quarters at an Hotel and this allows reversion to two other old institutions of value.

I. A Levée that always was held by the First Lord alone to see Officers at the Port or in the neighbourhood.

II. An evening reception to the Sisters & the Cousins & the Aunts!
NB A small dance acceptable if you invite me!
Take the *same* opportunity of the interregnum to make a speech somewhere that

I. You are giving your close personal attention to the question of opening up Commissioned Rank (Promotion to Lieutenants from Warrant Officers that is) of the *Blue Jackets & Marines*

II. and also to the various small items which though not constituting in themselves separately any great cause of complaint by the Lower Deck yet in the aggregate of these 'pin-pricks' cause a regrettable feeling of injustice & indifference to the far higher status of the men of the Lower Deck than 20 or 30 years ago when the various arrangements in question were no doubt necessary.
Fight *like hell* against increasing entry of cadets
The remedy is promote more Bluejackets & Marines from Warrant Officers.
NB You will have fearful opposition but you will have a Mutiny at the Nore if you dont handle the Lower Deck grievances & the grievances of the 39/40ths of the population whose sons cannot enter as Naval Officers because of the expense.
'The secret of successful administration is the intelligent anticipation of agitation'!

Submarines to be increased with an Admiral as a separate Service with the Destroyers under him also – but the days of the Destroyer are numbered

---

You can rely on Major General Nicholls, RMA[1] – now D.A.G. of Marines at the Admiralty as thoroughly loyal. *Private*

[1] William Charles Nicholls (1854–1935), Adjutant-General Royal Marines 1911–16; General 1914; knighted 1912.

Very few of the Marine Officers are!

Fighting Policy should be formed on *Navy* and not on *Army* views. 100,000 soldiers embarked in Transports – & kept *'en l'air'* – demobilize one million German soldiers – from the Vosges Frontier.
This is a fact given me by Moltke's[1] successor at the Hague Conference of 1899 – he was thinking then of the French landing an expeditionary force on a spot 90 miles from Berlin! At the time he told me this there never was any idea of the German Invasion of England.

Remark on Italian Invasion of Italy

Any plan shewn. . . .

Spectator
28 October 1911

We are afraid of Mr Churchill because he is weak and rhetorical. . . . his moods are not to be depended upon. We cannot detect in his career any principles or even any consistent outlook upon public affairs. His ear is always to the ground; he is the true demagogue, sworn to give the people what they want, or rather, and that is infinitely worse, what he fancies they want. No doubt he will give the people an adequate Navy if they insist upon it. We wish we could think that the Navy would be adequate, whether they insisted or not.

Memorandum by WSC

28 October 1911   Admiralty

Confidential

Adequate preparation for war is the only guarantee for the preservation of the wealth, natural resources, and territory of a State, and it can only be

---

[1] Helmuth Carl Bernhard von Moltke (1800–91), Chief of Prussian general staff from 1849; architect of German strategy in the Franco-German war of 1871.

based upon an understanding, firstly, of the probable dangers that may arise; secondly, of the best general method of meeting them as taught by the principles to be deduced from the events of history; and, thirdly, of the most efficient application of the war material of the era.

When war has actually broken out, the dangers to be faced have openly disclosed themselves, while the best general methods of meeting them and of applying the weapons available usually become obvious from the progress of hostilities, although too late as a rule to be of service to the losing side if not appreciated beforehand. The period of preparation is past.

In time of peace, however, preparation provides the only field wherein immediate and sustained action of a useful nature is possible, and the precision of modern appliances is such that a degree of scientific preparation may be reached which makes preparation in itself at once the most effective and cheapest form of defence. This standard of security is only really attainable, however, by an accurate estimate of the factors enumerated above, and except by chance, an accurate estimate can only be furnished by specially trained men. This is recognised in the organisation of all the more important combatant services in the world except the British Navy, in each of which a specially trained body or staff is established upon whose calculations and plans all expenditure is ultimately based, whether applied to administration, training, or supply. Unless the money required to give effect to these plans is forthcoming, no State can be regarded as having provided itself with the degree of preparation which is the surest and most truly economical form of defence, and, on the other hand, money spent for defensive purposes not in accordance with these plans is money wasted. But expenditure following the lines which they suggest may reasonably be considered as obtaining maximum value for the outlay because based upon the advice of experts.

In the past history of this country the Navy has carried out many maritime campaigns without the help of such a body of trained experts. But this is no proof either that such a body is not required under modern conditions, or that satisfactory results would not have often been obtained with less loss of life and waste of time if it had previously existed. In the periods of our greatest wars the operation and effect of war was very slow, and much less depended upon initial success than does now. Serious blunders were sometimes made, but there was time to rectify them, or the situation was saved at great cost of life by the superior seamanship and valour of our Fleets. Moreover, progress in naval architecture was so gradual that the science of naval strategy, as based upon the capabilities of ships and the science of administrative preparation as regards foreseeing their wants, were simple and unchanging. Throughout the three centuries which comprise the most active period of British naval warfare, the movements of the Fleets were entirely controlled by the wind, and the stores they required to fight and keep the sea were of practically the same nature. Even the armaments varied very slightly, the 18-, 24-, and 32-pr cast-iron smooth-bore guns remaining the standard line-of-battle weapons from first to last. No complications in the way of new weapons or appliances were introduced except in very minor details, and no new considerations or possibilities arose to modify or revolutionise war in consequence.

Finally, during long eras war was rather the rule than the exception, and the peace intervals which are the true periods of preparation were few and short.

In our own time all this is entirely changed. The scientific improvement of war material is so continuous that new conditions arise from year to year requiring consideration in any endeavours to realise our strategic position. Important fresh factors such as the submarine and aeroplane have appeared in the short interval of only five years which separates us from the most modern naval war and its lessons. Initial success has become of enormous importance and opportunities are not likely to occur for remedying initial blunders. And peace – the proper period of preparation for war – is the rule instead of the exception.

Nevertheless, the general principles remain unchanged and what is required is an understanding as to how they apply to modern conditions and developments. As already noted, all foreign States of importance act upon this and endeavour to base the work of preparation upon plans drawn up by expert staffs specially trained in this understanding. The organisation of our Navy is at present the only notable exception to the rule. The small number of officers employed upon the preparation of war plans at the British Admiralty have received no systematic training whatever in the broad strategic principles which all historians agree in emphasising as permanent in their application, or in the general tendency of the foreign politics of the day, or in the substance of the various treaties and agreements with other Powers which affect or limit our freedom of action as a belligerent, or our rights as a neutral. Service in the Fleet affords no more instruction on these important questions than service in a city office, and no other form of instruction is afforded. Only war itself, or the historical study of war can teach what results or effects may be expected from any particular variety of war policy such as blockade, attacks upon commerce, interruptions of lines of communication, or descents upon territory, and neither of these methods of instruction is open to our naval officers at the present day unless by private and unencouraged effort. In spite of this, an officer may find himself appointed to a position on the War Council in which his opinion in these matters may be required at any time, and may influence important decisions. Under the existing system, the majority of officers who reach the command of a battle-ship and are potential First Sea Lords have never read through the Declaration of Paris or studied the history of the blockade of Brest.

As a result of this condition of affairs there were no recognised plans for war at all at the Admiralty up till 1906, except a somewhat indefinite appropriation of mobilised cruisers as reinforcements for foreign stations, based upon the anticipated requirements of war with the Dual Alliance, but supposed to be applicable to emergencies in general. In 1906 a series of outline plans for war with Germany were drawn up by a very small committee of officers chiefly serving outside the Admiralty altogether, none of whom had received anything approaching to a sufficient training in the subject, except in so far as it might be imbibed from previous experience in the details of routine work in the existing Intelligence Department. These plans when issued for adoption were freely criticised by some of the officers whose duty it would have been to carry them out in war, but whose alternative suggestions were based upon no better opportunities for studying the subject and lacked any appearance of a better understanding of the situation. The result was a conflict of opinions leading to indecision and chaos that would have been disastrous in war. This state of affairs was exposed by the investigation of the Cabinet Committee, which enquired into the allegations advanced by Lord Charles Beresford on giving up his command, and formed the subject of comment in their finding. But no serious steps have ever been taken to remedy the primary and only vital defect in the system which produced such results, viz., an entire lack of training of the officers who are called upon to do the work. This extends to all ranks.

The contents of the Admiralty Record Office show how the views of one First Sea Lord may be utterly at variance with those of another. Each naturally recommends what he thinks best, but it is evident from a perusal of their minutes and their actions that many reached office without any previous study of the history of war. The result has often been an entire absence of continuity in Admiralty policy, with consequent financial waste. A certain First Sea Lord must have been responsible for the concurrence of the Admiralty in the futile strategic theories which prompted the building of the Palmerston forts with money that should have gone to the Navy. Another was responsible for the introduction of coast defence ships into a service whose whole policy during three centuries of successful war was to assume the offensive and fight out of sight of our coast altogether. And at least one of his successors must have agreed with this idea of abandoning the high seas to an enemy, for the considerable expenditure which was incurred on this type of ship was spread over a fairly extended period. Another, at a grave political crisis with France, recommended that our then powerful

Mediterranean Fleet should concentrate at Malta on the defensive in the event of hostilities breaking out. It would have been quite impossible for an officer of ordinary ability with a proper historical training to have committed any of these blunders, and there is no reason to suppose that ability was lacking. It is true, of course, that such cases may be the exception. The Navy has been fortunate in having many very capable men in the position of First Sea Lord who were fully equal to their responsibilities at all times. But there is no guarantee that such will be the case. At the best of times the field of selection for an officer to fill this post is very small, and it is not every man who is gifted with the strategical insight of a St Vincent[1] or a Barham.[2] But all might have their fitness for the position improved by training at an earlier period of their career, and the least capable would not be likely to go far wrong on important points if he had the advantage of a thoroughly competent staff. Under the existing system there is no guarantee against a repetition of such serious strategic blunders as were made during the Dutch wars, and only retrieved at great cost by the exceptional bravery of the officers and men in the Fleet. The situation is much the same. The technical training for war in the sea-going fleet of to-day is extremely good. But it would only be by chance that it was used to the fullest advantage upon a sound prearranged strategic plan. A competent strategist *might* occupy the position of First Sea Lord in the event of war no doubt, but not at all necessarily.

If an efficient and reliable War Staff is ever to be established at the Admiralty, whose work will be founded upon a sound knowledge of essential principles, and accepted by the Government as representing our defensive policy, the first requirement therefore will be to provide some system of proper training for the officers who are appointed to constitute it. From the technical point of view the training at sea is already excellent, and could be maintained at the same high standard if they spent a couple of months at sea in each year while serving on the staff. The rapidity of modern naval developments is such that some arrangement in this last respect has become absolutely necessary.

But, as already emphasized, no training on the historical or modern political side of the question exists at all. To these may be added the commercial side also. All this would require to be organized.

As regards education in the naval principles of strategy, which all historians agree to be permanent in their general application, it may perhaps be roughly estimated that a year's special course of study at the War College

---

[1] John Jervis (1735–1823), Naval commander; defeated Spanish fleet off Cape St Vincent 14 February 1797; created Earl of St Vincent 1797; First Lord of the Admiralty 1801–4.
[2] Charles Middleton, 1st Baron Barham (1726–1813), First Lord of the Admiralty 1805; Admiral 1795; created Baron 1805.

would answer the purpose. There is no text-book at present which could be taken as the standard for such a course, but the subject is fully treated by Mahan,[1] Colomb,[2] Corbett,[3] and others in a manner which would suffice, if properly handled, until an authorized text-book had been compiled from the material which may be extracted from their works. This course would have to include instruction also in the substance, scope, and general effect of all the most important Treaties and Agreements to which we are a party, such as the Declaration of Paris, &c. Taken as a whole, it would be the principal part of the War Staff training. The actual details of the course could be settled by the head of the War College in conjunction with the Directors of Naval Education, assisted, perhaps, by the advice of one of the University Professors of History.

A fair degree of instruction in the general political tendencies of important foreign Powers would be another essential requirement. Possibly this could best be provided by a two or three months attendance at the Foreign Office, under facilities for acquiring a sufficient grasp of foreign politics to give an understanding of current events and their possible effect on our interests. This ought not to present any real difficulties. In most other countries, the connection between the Ministry of Foreign Affairs and the War Staff of the Army and Navy is very close, which suggests itself as a proper state of affairs. It is true that the Admiralty has already one source of information on foreign affairs in the shape of the Naval Intelligence Department. But although the work done in that Department is very important, it is chiefly and rightly concerned with questions of a technical nature rather than with general policy.

A certain degree of acquaintance with the main features of the commercial and shipping interests upon which our national welfare so much depends – and about which the naval officers of the present day are with very few exceptions profoundly ignorant – would be a third necessary qualification, and could probably best be acquired by a short course in the Shipping Department of the Board of Trade, or attendance at Lloyd's.

With the technical knowledge acquired during sea service as a foundation, an officer who had thus added thereto a comprehensive understanding of the strategic principles of maritime war, of the general tendency of foreign

[1] Alfred Thayer Mahan (1840–1914), Admiral United States Navy; famous Naval historian and theoretician whose books on sea-power, particularly *The Influence of Sea-Power upon History*, published in 1890, and *Naval Strategy*, published in 1911, greatly influenced future generations of naval tacticians and leaders.

[2] Philip Howard Colomb (1831–99), writer on naval problems; devised night system known then as 'Colomb's flashing signals' and now as the 'Morse Code'; Rear-Admiral 1887; Vice-Admiral 1892.

[3] Julian Stafford Corbett (1854–1922), Naval historian whose work included *Drake and the Tudor Navy* (1898); History lecturer, Royal Naval War College, Greenwich 1902; knighted 1917.

politics, and of the commercial interests of the Empire would be well equipped for service on a War Staff. There would be nothing in such a course of training that would be beyond the capacity of any officer of ordinary intelligence.

But once in such a position he would have to be recognised and treated as a specialist if officers of good abilities were to be attracted to the work. To put him in a position of inferiority to those who receive special advantages for having qualified as specialists in other branches – chiefly through a natural gift for the theories of mathematics – would be fatal to the establishment of an efficient staff, and do more harm than good to the general interests of the Service. The work of a staff would never receive the confidence of officers afloat unless it was evident that the Admiralty regarded it as important by giving its members equivalent treatment to that accorded to other specialists. One of the reasons for the existing indifference of the junior ranks of the Navy to appointments at the Admiralty is a conviction that service at Whitehall is regarded by the Board as the performance of duties of an inferior description, because, in the matter of all advantages, it compares unfavourably with service at sea while imposing harder work. That this belief is deeply rooted is soon patent to anyone serving in the sea-going fleet who comes in touch with its inner sentiments. Great difficulty has often been experienced in finding an officer who would accept even the position of an Assistant Director of Naval Intelligence.

And not only the position of the individual, but the status of the Department would require to be established on a basis commensurate with the importance of its work. Having the responsibility of preparing the plans for war, it should be recognised as the Department which, under the First Sea Lord, was charged with the control of all general dispositions and movements of the Fleet, whether in war or peace. Preliminary distribution in time of peace is one important branch of preparation for war, and this fact is recognised in most foreign countries where the peace as well as the war movements of troops and ships are in the hands of the War Staffs. Moreover, the administrative practice and experience gained during peace in the details of transmitting orders and recording movements would be invaluable training for the prompt and efficient discharge of such duties in war. For it must be admitted that in war, the War Staff – of course under the First Sea Lord – should carry out this most important duty itself, without the intermediary of a civil clerical department. In time of peace, the present system, whereby the orders for the distribution of the Fleet with the movements consequent thereon are submitted by one Department, and, after having passed through a routine circuit, are carried out by another, is merely cumbersome. In time of war, the delay and possible confusion would be fraught with danger.

The relations between the War Staff and the mobilising and intelligence branches should be close, but it is doubtful whether any two of these should be combined in one Department. The responsibility of keeping war plans corrected up to date and attending to the movements of the Fleet would provide in itself enough work for efficient supervision by one head if fully and properly conducted.

The actual composition of the Staff as regards numbers could only in the end be determined by experience in connection with the amount of work to be done, but the nature of work would necessarily be such as to cause considerable fluctuations in the volume requiring immediate attention. For example, the Staff should draw up all the plans for manœuvres on a large scale. This would inevitably mean extra work at certain periods of the year. And in addition to this, it should be charged with the duty of making a careful study of all reports of manœuvres and exercises for the sake of noting such practical experience applicable to plans for war as they might embody. This would also call for extra work at certain periods. In former times, frequent reports of minor manœuvres planned and carried out in sea-going fleets were merely initialled in the NID, and passed on without comment, because the pressure of other work gave no time for a careful perusal. To provide for periods of special pressure in these or other matters, the organisation would have to allow for expansion when necessary. If fixed at a rigid limit as to numbers, the limit should be such that work at ordinary periods could be carried out by a 'nucleus crew,' or something approaching to it.

Moreover, an ideal Staff would be so constituted in relation to its work that time could be found for occasional practice exercises for the members on general plans set by the First Sea Lord. This custom prevails in nearly all military War Staffs including our own.

To get the best results, the gradation of a Staff should not be governed solely by naval rank, provided always that no officer was put in a position of subordination to a junior. Within certain limits, the best officers should be selected to fill positions to which they were suited irrespective of naval rank. This principle is also recognised not only in the appointment to the Board of Admiralty itself, but also in the positions of DNI or DNM, who are sometimes flag officers and sometimes Senior Captains. Instead of a Department constituted to consist of a Director, a certain number of Captains, and a certain number of Commanders or Marine Officers, the specification of a Staff therefore should be that of a Director, two or more Assistant Directors, and a certain number of Staff Officers, each of which position, with the duties and salaries attaching thereto, should be open to two naval ranks. For example, it might sometimes happen that a certain Commander was better qualified to fill a vacancy as an Assistant Director than any

Captain available at the time, or that a certain lieutenant was known to have special aptitude as a successor to a Commander leaving one of the subordinate appointments. In each case the appointment of the more junior rank should be permissible under regulations without a reduction in the salary appertaining to it. This would ensure the selection of the best available officers without adding to the cost of the Department, and at the same time provide an appreciable stimulus to ambition for service therein.

It it was decided to establish a War Staff somewhat on these lines, the question of the selection of the officers to be trained would first have to be solved. It might be found practicable to work it somewhat on the following general idea, modified afterwards as experience suggested: –

Firstly, an examination open to all lieutenants of over six years' seniority whether already specialists in other branches or not, and Captains of Marines of equivalent seniority. The object of this examination, which they would carry out on board their own ship under no supervision, would be to ascertain, firstly, their powers of drawing the right conclusions as to the probable results or effects of certain given situations or conditions of affairs during a maritime war, or before or after war. Secondly, their ability to express their views in writing clearly; and thirdly, their ability to draft an accurate report on some given subject as briefly as possible without omitting any essential point. It would not be so much the memory as *the power to reason upon facts the memory presented* that would be upon trial, and a mere knowledge of historical events would not be so important at this stage as a grasp of their consequences. No restrictions as to access to books of reference would therefore be imposed. This method of testing the reasoning faculty is recognised in the Military Staff examination of the German and British armies, in which candidates are usually asked to write an 'appreciation' of the situation on the eve of some particular campaign, or of the consequences to which some specified battle may have given rise. This is obviously a test of the reasoning powers rather than the memory, though the memory may play a part also.

A selection of the best papers sent in would then be made either by the Director of the Staff, or the Head of the War College, preferably the latter. The officers thus selected would be appointed to join the next annual Staff course at the College. The numbers annually admitted might for the first three or four years amount to six or eight, but at a later period half that would probably suffice to meet the yearly requirements. At the conclusion of the course at the College they would be noted as available for Staff appointments subject to a satisfactory report from the Head of the College. They would then return to sea till required. Vacancies on the Staff would be anticipated by the appointment of one of these officers six months in advance for a probationary period, including the attendance at the Foreign Office and Board of Trade suggested above, and a month or two at the Admiralty to learn the system and routine of work. At the end of this, his training as a fully qualified Staff Officer would be complete.

Appointments – except when temporary for special work – should always be for three years. For two months in each year each officer should serve at sea as a supernumerary in order to keep in touch with technical progress in the Fleet. This would be very essential to their real efficiency. During this period of absence from the Admiralty their Staff duties should be carried on for practice by their colleagues or subordinates, unless there was special reasons for a particular subject to remain in the hands of one officer, in which case he should take the necessary papers to sea with him, or they would be sent as occasion offered. At the end of a three years' Staff appointment an officer would always return to sea work for at least another three before again being available for service at the Admiralty.

The establishment of a War Staff somewhat on the above lines would be well received in the Navy as filling a want, and its work would be regarded with confidence. If press comments are any guide, it would receive approval outside the Service also, in quarters where naval subjects are studied and appreciated. Abroad it would be noted with attention, and tend to enhance the respect in which our Sea Service is held.

The creation of a War Staff would, in fact, mark one of the most notable advances in the Peace history of our Navy, and rank high with the many great reforms which have been introduced into its organisation during the early years of the twentieth century.

[WSC]

Memorandum by Sir Arthur Wilson

30 October 1911

The agitation for a Naval War Staff is an attempt to adapt to the Navy a system which was primarily designed for an army. There is a very general conception that because a great General Staff has been found a most successful instrument for the preparation of an army for war, especially in the case of the great General Staff presided over by Count von Moltke, which gave such extraordinary success to the Prussian armies in their Austrian and French wars, that therefore a Staff on similar lines must be a necessity for the Navy, but the conditions and the problems to be solved are so entirely different that no analogy can be drawn between them.

The conduct of wars on land depends mainly on the means of transport, and the supply of food and ammunition to the Army. Before a General can work out a plan of campaign or select the best line of operations, the Staff must make a most careful study of the topographical features of the country, the adaptation of the available means of transport, whether by railways or by motor-cars or other wheeled vehicles on ordinary roads, or pack animals across country. They must study bridging streams, the assistance or opposition they may expect from the inhabitants, and a multitude of other details which vary with every campaign, and must give the most careful consideration to the enemy's powers of attacking any part of the Army in superior force at any stage of the proceedings, and especially it must consider the means of defending its lines of communications, without which the Army cannot exist.

To determine all these matters, even for one campaign, requires a very large staff of highly trained officers, and it must be all worked out on paper from information obtained from a multitude of different sources, as no practical trial can be made of the proposed arrangements in peace time, except to a very limited extent.

Ships, on the other hand, contain in themselves all that they require for war, including accurate charts of every sea in which they are required to operate, so that they are ready to move anywhere at the speed ordered as soon as they can get steam ready, and up to the limit of their coal capacity they have no line of communications to defend.

To realise the difference in this part of the staff work in the two Services, imagine an order to be given simultaneously at this moment for a division of the Home Fleet to proceed to the North Sea and a Division from Aldershot to proceed to the coast of Norfolk, both prepared for instant battle. The first could be carried out within the limits of a single short telegram and without any preliminary plans. The second would require the consideration of many more details than anyone not conversant with the difficulties of moving large bodies of troops can think of. The provision and transport of tents, baggage, ammunition, food, horses, guns, the selection of camping ground, the timing and capacity of the trains, facilities for entraining and detraining men, loading and unloading stores, transport by road in various ways, and a hundred other matters must all be settled by the Staff beforehand or there would be hopeless confusion and great loss of time, and this even in time of peace in our own country. In war in an enemy's country the complications are of course infinitely greater.

In the movements of fleets there is nothing in the least analogous to all this, either in peace or war.

The requirements of the Navy are quite different. In the aggregate probably more thinking has to be done to produce an efficient Navy than an efficient Army, but it is on entirely different lines. The thinking in the Navy is mainly occupied with producing the most perfect ships, guns, and machinery, with crews trained and organised to make the most perfect use of them, and constantly practised under conditions approaching as nearly as possible to those of war.

All this requires an enormous thinking department, but the Staff that does this thinking is not called by that name. It is comprised of the principal members of every department of the Admiralty, supplemented by the Admirals, Captains, Executive Officers, and heads of the different departments in every ship afloat, all organised for one end.

The Navy has learned, by long experience, thoroughly to distrust all paper schemes and theories that have not been submitted to the supreme test of trial under practical conditions by the Fleet at sea, and the whole Admiralty has been gradually developed to make the most of the experience so gained.

The organisation of this huge staff to give every part of it the greatest freedom to think out its own work and at the same time to bring all departments into co-operation is necessarily a task of great difficulty, and one that requires constant adjustment to meet the changing conditions.

The process of thinking out a naval policy may be said to commence with the Intelligence Department, whose business it is to ascertain the strength of any possible enemy in ships, guns, men, training, &c, and the conditions under which they can be used to do us injury.

These are the data on which our whole policy must be framed. The Navy must be constructed and organised definitely with a view to meeting the actual forces of any combination of nations that is at all probable, as they are known to exist now, or as far as they can be foreseen for the future.

The working out of this problem is spread over every branch of the Admiralty, each of which deals with a part, as well as over the various schools for specialists and various squadrons and flotillas at sea.

The results are then brought to a focus, through the heads of the various departments of the Admiralty, to the members of the Board concerned, and in all matters relating to strategy and tactics and the actual use to be made of the Fleet in war they are still further focussed in the First Sea Lord as the principal adviser in these matters, who has a Naval Assistant, always one of the ablest Captains in the Navy, to assist him.

The preparation of war plans is a matter that must be dealt with by the First Sea Lord himself, but he has to assist him, besides his Naval Assistant, the Director of Naval Intelligence and the Director of Naval Mobilisation, and in the latter's department there is a war division consisting of a Captain and a Commander specially allocated to this work. The DNI and DNM, with the Assistant Secretary, form the War Council from whom the First Sea Lord obtains advice either by minutes on the papers or by verbal discussion as the occasion requires.

Another reason why a War Staff which is a necessary feature in Army organisation is unsuitable to the Navy is that, as it is impossible to produce conditions really resembling war in peace manœuvres on shore, Army policy must be framed principally from the records of past wars and the opinions of officers who have taken part in them, while Naval policy is based almost entirely on experiment and the results of actual practice at sea.

The Fleets, Cruiser Squadrons, Destroyer Flotillas, Submarines, Mine-layers, Mine-sweepers, &c, are continually carrying out experiments in tactics, gunnery, torpedo attacks, and all other operations of war under conditions far more closely resembling actual war than is at all possible with Army manœuvres. The difference between the two Services in this respect is enormous.

When a problem arises in the Army the only method in the majority of cases is to submit it for the opinion of the Staff because actual experiment is impossible, while in the Navy most problems are solved by actual trial by officers afloat.

Of course thinking, and often thinking of a very high order, is required to devise schemes for these experimental investigations and exercises, and for carrying them out, but the thinking is by no means confined to the Admiralty; probably the greater part is done by officers of all ranks serving at sea.

It is often suggested by advocates of a War Staff that special officers should be selected and trained for duty on the Staffs of the Admiralty and Admirals at sea.

Now a Staff in the naval sense is required by an Admiral to help him to do work that he has not time to do himself, and supply him with expert advice on technical subjects.

Thus he has in a large Fleet his Chief of the Staff or Captain of the Fleet to arrange the organisation, coaling, provisioning, and general duties of the Fleet: a Commander for Gunnery duties, a Flag Lieutenant for Signals, a Lieutenant for Wireless, an Engineer Captain, and sometimes one or two others. These are all available for any General Service duties that may be required in addition to their specialities, but no special Staff course could be made to suit them all.

The present system by which officers serve for two years in the different departments of the Admiralty and then go to sea circulates an immense amount of varied knowledge throughout the Fleet, and brings fresh sea-going experience to the Admiralty far better than any system of selecting special officers for Staff duties could.

The Service would have the most supreme contempt for any body of officers who professed to be specially trained to think. There is no Service where there is more thinking done, but officers are judged by what they can do when afloat.

The whole spirit and training of the Navy is to make officers, whatever their position, do their thinking for themselves, and to keep themselves ready to act instantly in all emergencies, and it is necessary that it should be so because the loss of five minutes in naval warfare would be generally of more importance than an hour in land warfare.

A.K.W.

WSC to J. A. Spender

[undated]   Admiralty

Copy

My dear Spender,

I have been so busy burrowing about in an apparently illimitable rabbit warren that I have not had a moment to thank you for sending me Fisher's most interesting letter, or to thank you for the kindly references to myself, which evidently called it forth. I have made a private note of its recommendations, and I now return it to you. As soon as I was appointed I wrote both to Fisher and Beresford, asking them to come and see me. I have had useful conversations with both, and I spent a very pleasant Sunday in Fisher's company. I am confident that I can look to him for any aid I may require.

Note by WSC

[November 1911]   Admiralty

Ld Fisher's proposals in letter to J. A. Spender of October 25 1911 written at Lucerne.

1st Sea Lord	Prince Louis.
2nd	Sir G. Callaghan.[1]
	(now 2nd in command Home Fleet.)
3rd	Briggs.[2]

[1] George Astley Callaghan (1852–1920), commanded 2nd Division Home Fleet 1910–11; C-in-C Home Fleet 1911–14; the Nore 1915–18; Admiral of the Fleet 1917; knighted 1909.
[2] Charles John Briggs (1858–1951), Third Sea Lord and Controller of Navy 1910–12; commanded 4th Squadron Home Fleet 1912–14; Admiral 1916; knighted 1913.

4th   Jerram.[1]
               (now 2nd in command Mediterranean.)
Wilson a Peer.
Egerton[2] to succeed P. Louis, Home Fleet.
Madden[3] „   „   Jerram.
Private Secretary. Capt Mark Kerr.
Troubridge[4] to succeed Slade[5] (E. Indies).
Jellicoe to be moved from Atlantic to 2nd in command Home Fleet.
Admiral Burney[6] as temporary Vice Admiral to succeed Jellicoe.
Ballard to be DNC – Bethell the first vacant job.

Sir Charles Ottley to WSC

1 November 1911   Committee of Imperial Defence

Private

Dear Mr Churchill,
    I saw the Prime Minister yesterday. He said that as soon as you were ready to deal with the matter a Sub-Committee of the CID was to be formed to investigate the question of forming a Naval War Staff. Mr Asquith added that he hoped you would yourself take the Chair, and he was inclined to think that Sir Arthur Wilson and Prince Louis of Battenburg should be members of the Sub-Committee. Lord Haldane and Sir William Nicholson[7] should, he added, be on the Sub Committee also, as well as Lord Esher. Captain Ballard should be called with other experts as witnesses.

[1] Thomas Henry Martyn Jerram (1858–1933), Second in Command Mediterranean Fleet 1910–12; Commander-in-Chief China Station 1913–15; commanded 2nd Battle Squadron 1915–16; at Jutland 1916; Admiral 1917; knighted 1914.
[2] George le Clerc Egerton (1852–1940); Second Sea Lord 1911–12; C-in-C Cape of Good Hope 1908–10; of Plymouth 1913–16; Admiral; knighted 1910.
[3] Charles Edward Madden (1862–1935), Fourth Sea Lord 1910–11; commanded 2nd and 3rd Cruiser Squadrons Home Fleet 1912–14; C-in-C Atlantic Fleet 1919–22; First Sea Lord and Chief of Naval Staff 1927–30; Admiral of the Fleet 1924; knighted 1916; created Baronet 1919; OM 1931.
[4] Ernest Charles Thomas Troubridge (1862–1926), Chief of the War Staff, Admiralty, 1911–12; Commanding Mediterranean Cruiser Squadron 1912–14; was court-martialed in September 1914 for apparently disobeying orders by breaking off pursuit of *Goeben* and *Breslau*. He was acquitted of all blame; Admiral 1919; knighted 1919.
[5] Edmond John Warre Slade (1859–1928), C-in-C East Indies 1909–12, sometime Vice-Chairman Anglo-Persian Oil Company; Admiral 1917; knighted 1911.
[6] Cecil Burney (1858–1929), commanded 5th Cruiser Squadron and Atlantic Fleet 1911; 3rd Squadron 1912–13; Second Sea Lord 1916–17; Admiral of the Fleet 1920; knighted 1913; created Baronet 1921.
[7] William Coldingham Masters Nicholson (1863–1932), Third Sea Lord 1919–20; Admiral 1925; knighted 1919.

Subject to the Prime Minister's approval it is also for consideration whether one or two other Cabinet Ministers might not also be on the Sub Committee, in order to ensure that any measures recommended would be certain of endorsement by the Government as a whole, and to give to the Sub Committee's conclusions all possible weight.

Will you please let me know as soon as you are ready to convene this Sub-Committee, and what your wishes are with regard to its reference & Constitution.

Yours very sincerely
C. L. OTTLEY

WSC to Lord Fisher
(Lennoxlove Papers)

2 November 1911   Plymouth

My dear Fisher,

I have settled nothing finally yet; but shall do so shortly. The new design is being worked out by Watts.[1] He liked the idea vy much. I gather that the 6″ secondary armament & its protection are defended on grounds of (a) the longer range of the new torpedoes & (b) the danger of the guns being injured in the general battle.

They appear to fit in vy conveniently with the superstructure. I will give the matter close attention.

I must tell you how much I valued the proof you gave me of your kindness in coming over so promptly to see me. I shall most sedulously endeavour to carry you with me in my administration of the Admiralty; & I have good hopes that I shall succeed, & that you will feel free to be a constant & ready counsellor.

I am vy much taken with the Mediterranean plan. There ought to be a Cte of the CID upon it.

Yours vy sincerely
WINSTON S. CHURCHILL

Lord Fisher to WSC

2 November 1911   Lucerne

My dear Winston,

I've just heard from Nicholson that I barely escaped in time – as when he got back to Admiralty after seeing me off – there was a telegram from Sandringham asking where I was! and so also it was opportune your putting

---

[1] Philip Watts (1846–1926), Director of Naval Construction, Admiralty 1901–12. Naval architect. Knighted 1905.

that paragraph in *The Times*. – As I didn't want any of the Royal pimps such as Sir George Armstrong[1] & co to give a malign colour to my sudden visit to England I wrote a curt letter to the King that you had expressed a wish to see me and both from private friendship as well as the public good I had broken my vow of absence in complying with your wish in the sure confidence I had in you that the Navy would be well served by you. To that short note of mine he has just sent me an immediate reply quite cordial and quite friendly. *I only tell you this that you may know all!* I am overwhelmed with letters from my very good and influential friends who direct public opinion but I have answered them not a word! Of course they one & all say you are coquetting with Beresford & co – so you have gained your object in the wording of *The Times* paragraph! I send this to Nicholson's private address 4 Paper Buildings – Temple E.C. but I don't here tell you the results of my own further calculations about 'parity of armament' and the *Non-Pareil* type of Dreadnought. I shall await the special messenger that Nicholson indicates as arriving Nov 23.

All I have to say in anticipation is that your views of cost and power are more than justified & I don't care a d——n what Watts says – anymore than I cared when the Dreadnought was conceived. (*NB* Send for the Blue book on the 'Dreadnought' design – if you can't get it by fair means – send for J. F. Phillips[2] – Sub-Librarian & he will give it you. *You ought to read it*) – '*Armour is vision*' dont ever forget those immortal 3 words! and *remember* only 2 types to concentrate on! The smallest Big-Ship and the Biggest Small-Ship(s)! but I expand this when your messenger comes.

You will win or lose according to your Board! Make no mistake about that!! ('united, determined, progressive') I give you credit for your flash of genius in thinking of Battenberg as Controller – He must be *compelled* and *can be* and I would not fail to have *Jerram* & *Mark Kerr* as 2nd & 4th Sea Lords. I have discovered an ingenious alternative to May[3] but I withhold it till I have thought a little more over it.

Anyhow I suppose you wont let a living soul know till the last moment.

There's a draft circular secreted somewhere that I wrote about the development of the present Naval War Council into a Naval War Staff – .

Further reflection only convinces me you have struck oil in selecting Ottley – but dont fail me, my dear Winston in having Hankey put in his place – *he is Napoleonic.*

[1] George Elliot Armstrong (1866–1940), journalist; sometime editor of *Globe;* ex-naval officer; succeeded father as 2nd Baronet 1907.
[2] James Falkner Phillips (–1933), Civil Servant; served in various posts Admiralty, Board of Invention & Research, Committee of Imperial Defence 1892–1932.
[3] William Henry May (1849–1930), C-in-C Plymouth 1911–13, Home Fleet 1909–11; Admiral of the Fleet 1913; knighted 1904.

I have carefully examined all my letters coming here. I don't think they have ever been tampered with. I hope you won't ever think I am ramming my advice down your throat! I have no axe to grind – I never want to set foot in England again! I am sick of all the d——d fools I've had to do with! and the d——d liars who have maligned me!

Yours always
F

I am probably going to America next August.

Give this pin to your new wife as a *gage d'amour!*

Postscript

When your Messenger comes here on Nov 23 I send you back by him a recapitulation of the *8 Big Things!*

I think you realized the wisdom of arranging your policy as a '*fait accompli*' in the interregnum of being off with the old love and before you are on with the new!

I hope you will tell them at the Mansion House on Nov 9 *to sleep quiet in their beds!*

Lord Fisher to WSC

4 November 1911　　　　　　　　　　　　　　　　　　　　Lucerne

Dear Winston,

I hope I am not bombarding you with too much advice. You need not take it – but I don't think I sufficiently emphasized in my letter this morning the advantage to you personally of having Battenberg as the predominating influence amongst the Sea Lords – with Poe[1] as First Sea Lord this would be the case but not with May who I think would resent his interference. However all depends on what you thought of Battenberg and if you decided on him.

Jellicoe won't at all like leaving the Atlantic Fleet but it is very desirable to get him as second to Bridgeman.[2]

If Callaghan succeeded Poe in the Mediterranean this would enable Jellicoe to be shifted – and Sir Henry Jackson could take Jellicoe's place in the Atlantic Fleet.

This gives you a free hand in the organisation of the Navy War Staff as the President of the War College (which Jackson now is) must be selected to fit in with Ottley and his coadjutors. You are not bound to find places for ex-Sea Lords any more than for ex-Cabinet Ministers so Egerton, Briggs &

---

[1] Edmund Poe (1849–1921), C-in-C, Mediterranean Station 1910–12; served in Navy for 52 years; Admiral; knighted 1906.

[2] Francis Charles Bridgeman-Bridgeman (1848–1929), C-in-C Home Fleet 1911; First Sea Lord 1911–12. Admiral; knighted 1908.

Madden can wait vacancies, but you *do* want to get Ballard in Bethell's place & so you can move Bethell into Battenberg's place – and if you take Jerram as Second Sea Lord you could put Briggs in his place.

I think it's sound to move Malta to Alexandria – I would not put A. K. Wilson on that Committee! Isn't it a big question of policy for the Cabinet and not for the Defence Committee – however you know best.

Of course in writing all the above I don't know what opinion you have formed of Battenberg. To my mind he is the ablest Admiral we have except Jellicoe and I repeat it was a flash of genius on your part to think of him for your most critical post – the man for the Ship-building Policy! *That's your knotty point!* The new War Staff will settle up all the rest and in Ottley you have a real 'Peach'! but let him choose his coadjutors & the new President of the War College –

Secrecy in all this is very important – and *do it altogether!* It makes it so much easier.

Yours
F

Dont trouble to answer this

I would have Mark Kerr in Madden's place not only because he is AI, but he fits in with Battenberg – and Phillpots[1] as *DNO* because he also would have to work with Battenberg & he was Battenberg's Chief of the Staff lately – and is AI, *and very much better than Leveson.*[2]

WSC to H. H. Asquith
(Asquith Papers)

5 November 1911 HMS *Enchantress*
Portsmouth

My dear Prime Minister,

The enclosed memo from Sir Arthur Wilson is decisive in its opposition not only to any particular scheme, but against the whole principle of a War Staff for the Navy. Ottley's rejoinder, wh I also send you, shows that it wd not be difficult to continue the argument. But I feel that this might easily degenerate into personal controversy, & wd in any case be quite unavailing. I like Sir Arthur Wilson personally & shd be vy sorry to run the risk of embittering relations wh are now pleasant. I therefore propose to take no public action during his tenure.

[1] Edward Montgomery Phillpots (1871–1952), Superintendent Signal Schools 1911; Naval Assistant to Second Sea Lord 1912, to First Sea Lord 1916; Admiral 1923.

[2] Arthur Cavanagh Leveson (1868–1929), Captain 1903; Rear-Admiral 1913; Vice-Admiral 1919; C-in-C China Station 1922–4; retired 1928.

If Wilson retires in the ordinary course in March, I shall be left without a First Sea Lord in the middle of the passage of the Estimates, & his successor will not be able to take any real responsibility for them. It is necessary therefore that the change shd be made in January at the latest, & that the King shd know this, & shd assent to a peerage being conferred, before he leaves for India.

I could, if it were imperative, propose to you a new Board for submission to the King at once. The field of selection for the first place is narrow; & since I have with a good deal of reluctance abandoned the idea of bringing Fisher back, no striking appointment is possible. I may however just as well enjoy the advantage of reserving a final choice for another month. At present therefore I will only say that Prince Louis is certainly the best man to be Second Sea Lord, that I find myself in cordial agreement with him on nearly every important question of naval policy, & that he will accept the appointment gladly.

I am preparing a letter to the King on the lines of what I have written above; & if you agree I will send it to him after we have had a talk on Tuesday. I wish also to propose to HM that as soon as the new Board of Admiralty has been reconstituted Beresford should be promoted to Admiral of the Fleet on the retired list, & that contingently upon this a baton of Admiral of the Fleet shd as a special distinction be conferred upon Fisher. I shd thus hope to start in the New Year with a united & progressive Board, & with the good will of both the factions whose animosities have done so much harm.

Meanwhile I am elaborating the scheme of a War Staff. It will probably comprise four distinct branches, all of which exist in imperfect combination at present: –

1) War Education, under the President of the War College;
2) War Information, under the Director of Naval Intelligence;
3) War Plans, under the Director of the War Division; and
4) War organization, under the Director of Naval Mobilisation: the whole associated in a 'War Staff Circle' (or Committee) under the Chief of the War Staff, who will be the servant of the Board of Admiralty as a whole, tho' brought in special contact with the First Sea Lord.

Ottley is preeminently fitted for the position of Chief of the War Staff; and if Hankey took his place on the CID neither you nor the Navy wd I believe suffer from the transfer. I wish to be authorized by you to approach Ottley on the subject this week.

I have come across one disconcerting fact: there is a shortage of 120 21″ torpedoes, meaning that 30 of our best destroyers wd have to go to sea without reserves of any kind other than the two they carry. This deficiency cannot be wholly repaired till April or May at the earliest.

I think you & Grey will have to make the Cabinet face the realities next Wednesday.

Yours vy sincerely
WINSTON S. CHURCHILL

WSC to Sir Charles Ottley

5 November 1911   Admiralty

[Copy]

Secret

My dear Ottley,

This is only a line to let you know that I am working steadily away at our ideas, and am turning now in my mind the questions of methods and men upon which they touch. You must not suppose that any delay will occur once I have made up my mind as to the precise action to be taken. There is no use, however, in making disturbances by halves, and it is with that in mind that I have refrained from pressing for the immediate appointment of the Committee or from sending for Captain Ballard. Everything that I have learned here makes me feel that the difficulties are not at all beyond my powers to remove. Once the plan is ready, individuals will not be allowed to stand in its way.

I sent your paper to the Prime Minister.

Yours vy sincerely
[WINSTON S. CHURCHILL]

Lord Fisher to WSC

6 November 1911   Lucerne

Dear Winston,

I've just been contemplating some of Repington's[1] ideas of Naval Strategy! Really these soliders are such d——d fools when they wade out to sea! They so soon get out of their depth & flounder about! Sea strategy is so simple that it completely deceives these great brains that have wet towels round their heads to make them think!

If you hold the Straits of Dover & Scapa Flow with an abundance of Submarines & Destroyers such as we possess and have a good Admiral in

[1] Charles A'Court-Repington (1858–1925). Military Correspondent for *The Times* 1905–18; Lieutenant-Colonel; served in Burma, Afghanistan, Sudan, South Africa; Military Attaché Brussels and The Hague 1899–1902.

perpetual charge of the East Coast with his own ear-marked flotillas of Submarines and Destroyers and attendant Cruisers then you can sleep quiet in your bed as regards any raid of the German Fleet – any bolt out of the blue I mean! And our Battle Squadrons never ought to be within Destroyer range of the German Coast. What is Destroyer range? (The German submarines can be ignored, those they have are only Coastal Vessels) Well! a German destroyer can only be mischievous at such a distance as enables her to get back to her Port before daylight for the English *Swifts* (we want more of that type) waiting off the rabbit holes at daylight would gobble them up on their return.

On the wide Ocean one *Indomitable* owing to her immense superiority of speed in a sea-way – (waves that are mountains to destroyers are nothing to her!) would overtake and lick up one after another any number of destroyers! As I said to you at Reigate she would be the Armadillo that put out her tongue & licked up the ants and the bigger the ant the more placid the digestive smile!

Of course the advantage of a Naval War Staff is that the Country aint ruined if you have a d——d fool as First Sea Lord. If you have a Barham as First Sea Lord he will dominate the War Staff. It never signifies anywhere whether you have a Board or a Committee – the ablest man runs the show! – A. K. Wilson had not been given 'the Prince' as you gave me! He would have given the Defence Committee a lovely plan – profoundly detailed and a wealth of clap-trap – but you dont think he would have been wise do you? to let out the real plan to 15 people & Repington with access to every secret drawer in the War Office & getting £500 a year from Government to assist him in being Military Correspondent of *The Times* & writing exasperating articles about the rottenness of the German Army!

As Admiral Mahan well wrote & Hanotaux[1] formerly French Minister of Foreign Affairs supported, England without any Foreign Office in the world suspecting what was going on or our own Foreign Office ever dreaming what was being effected brought 88 per cent of her sea power to bear upon Germany! How was it done? Not a d——d thing was ever put on paper and only *one* person engineered it! Of course you'll say that's damnable! Where was the Cabinet? The Cabinet don't understand sea fighting – of course they can manage a Boer War!

If you want Ottley mind you make him a KCB! he deserves it for his great services on the CID.

Yours always
F.

[1] Albert Auguste Gabriel Hanotaux (1853–1944), French Minister of Foreign Affairs 1894–5 and 1896–8; wrote in fifteen volumes *Histoire de la Nation Française*.

Duke of Connaught to Princess Louise
(*Royal Archives*)

8 November 1911

Government House
Ottawa

EXTRACT

... Personally I think Winston Churchill will do just as well at the Admiralty as McKenna & I don't think you will find him agree to a dangerous reduction of the Navy. I know him well & have done so for more than 17 yrs. I *loathe* his speeches, but he is young & impulsive still & 'all found' he is not a bad fellow & I know he is favourably much devoted to Georgy. ...

Lord Fisher to WSC

9 November 1911

Lucerne

Dear Winston,

Your kind letter from Devonport just come – I honestly think I can be a big help to you! I don't claim to be a genius but I know a d——d fool when I see him.

There are some '*vitals*' that I would die for!

I   '*Engineering*' the basis of the Naval Officer's education as now arranged.

II The just grievances to be dealt with in a liberal spirit of the blue-jackets and marines and especially the withholding from them of commissioned rank as at present. There are now a few niggardly hole & corner promotions and the recipients put away in useless places.

III The opening of the Navy to all by State paid education – with your splendid *Coup* as a prelude & *you to say so* – dont let it be forced on you! *Get the credit my dear Winston!*

The secret of successful administration is the intelligent anticipation of agitation!

I am quite confident that the '*Non-Pareil*' will work out half a million sterling *cheaper* and *50* per cent more powerful than the d——d hybrid you mentioned to me. Remember! *Never rely on an expert!* Old Watts will put in a whole lot of things that can certainly be rubbed out – *Common Sense* is all that is wanted. I've been doing a few more calculations & I *know* I'm right!

For God's sake dont have either armour or the 6 inch gun for the Anti-Torpedo armament. *It's silly utter rot!* Speed – *Big Gun* and *Cheapness* those are the 3 Fundamentals – & you can have them.

The *fulcrum* of your Admiralty lever is to have Battenberg as Controller. It was a pure flash of genius on your part to think of him in that capacity. Dont go back on that. I *insist on* it.

I also consider *Jerram & Mark Kerr* will be towers of strength. I've just had a wonderful letter about Jerram! besides my personal knowledge. *It's a great point with the public* to have all your Board *fresh from the Sea!* and Jerram & Kerr have nothing else but continuous sea service.

Now I'm prepared after careful thought to give you my Machiavellian idea as to First Sea Lord. Have Poe now Commder-in-Chief in Mediterranean! he has nearly 3 years to run before he retires – he is pliable and plastic and Battenberg your ablest brain would dominate the Sea Lords and play your game. Battenberg will be faithful because he has no friends at all – probably only you & me & Mark Kerr!

May will 'sell' you sooner or later – besides you can't get rid of him as he doesn't retire for about 10 years or more. I've thought this carefully out. Personally I should prefer May but *for you* I say Poe . . . May will be jealous of Battenberg – Poe won't.

Poe is A. K. Wilson's dear friend so you conciliate Wilson & Wilson is a power for 5 years at least – *a very great power if there is war!* Poe can do what he will with Wilson!

I am working up my notes for you for Nov 23 – I am sending this by a very safe & reliable route. Not this time by Nicholson –

Yours till charcoal sprouts!

FISHER

WSC to Prince Louis of Battenberg

10 November 1911

Copy   Admiralty

Secret

My dear Prince Louis,

I have had most satisfactory conversations with the King & the Prime Minister, & I see no reason at present for doubting that the arrangement which you regarded as agreeable to yourself will be carried into effect at the beginning of the New Year. It is however extremely important that no whisper should reach my present Board before the time for a regular communication arrives. Even such personal matters as the choice of a residence must remain in suspense!

I enclose you some plans I have had worked out secretly here for a new type of cruiser. A2 is the design approved by the Board for the contract to be put out in February. The advance on the *Queen Mary* consists roughly speaking in 1200 tons displacement put into wider armour and 6 in instead of 4 in anti-torpedo armament, together with 7000 added horsepower. My intention is that against this shd be considered A3 or A4.

A5 the original idea, wh I put before the Chief Constructor for a 30 knot 8.15 inch gunned vessel, is much too costly, but A4 seems to have enormous advantages over A2, & costs practically the same. Broadly speaking, the money & the weight are taken from the armour and put into the guns. The increase in muzzle energy is of course prodigious, & the governing principle, that yr own fire is the best protection against the enemy's, appears orthodox & sound. The armour, tho' less than the *Q Mary*, is (I think, – but am en-quiring) fully up to the existing Indomitables. If the type proves satisfactory, I contemplate building 4. Will you let me have yr views as soon as possible, & return me my enclosure, wh is a vy dangerous document.

Yours sincerely
[WSC]

Lord Fisher to WSC

10 November 1911 Lucerne

Dear Winston,

Your letter of Nov 8 just come is *very reassuring* because you tell me that you and Bg [Battenberg] absolutely agreed.

That makes me quite happy. I confess I think it *would* be a good thing if I had a further talk with you and of course I should love the *Enchantress* (*but not at sea!!!*) She's damnable at sea!

Dont you fail me my dear Winston at getting Hankey put in Ottley's place. *It's vital* to have him there both for your *personal* as well as the *public* welfare! and as he is a staunch admirer of yours it's so much the better. I know the Prime Minister values him prhps more than Ottley! So there *ought* to be no difficulty. Now I answer your questions:—

I.   I earnestly advise you to stick to your original impulse which was sent you from heaven & make Bg Controller instead of Briggs. You will find *for certain* that your *chief* worry will be the shipbuilding programme & the *estimates*, the *Controller is the controlling agent!* So for goodness sake as my earnest prayer, have Bg as Controller.

II. I *love Bridgeman!* he is what you say – a splendid sailor and a gentleman – but he has no genius whatever for administration. *However he would command immense confidence* so it would pay you to have him as First Sea Lord.

I again repeat to you – *May would sell you!* besides he and Bg could be at daggers drawn. *What you want really is for Bg's influence to pervade the Board!* Bg will stick to you – he has no friends at all but you & me – *remember that!* It's a d——d shame – but *it's true!*

Milne[1] is a *sneak* of the *dirtiest* kind! so pray have nothing to do with him and he is distrusted by everyone – he would be a great weakness to you just as much as Bridgeman would cast a 'halo' of integrity and firmness round the Board of Admiralty.

III. If you take Bridgeman as First Sea Lord then you must put *Sir George Neville*[2] in command of the Home Fleet – He is the only *fit* man *until Jellicoe gets senior enough.*

You may possibly think of Custance, but believe me he is quite unfit for so great a place & *Neville is A.I. Move May to Portsmouth* when Moore[3] leaves in the summer and give Custance Devonport. That will be a compliment to May and a d——d good thing for Custance.

IV. Pakenham[4] will be excellent as 4th Sea Lord – Warrender[5] is a bit off his head but this is *very private!* his brother died that way & he has a sister locked up! You must not breathe a word of this.

V. If you won't have Jerram as being too junior then *Sir Henry Jackson* would be a perfect *Second Sea Lord.* Have him!

VI. When dear old Watts sends you his answer you must trample on him and tell him to take out things as necessary so as to comply with your three elemental and vital conditions:—

---

[1] Archibald Berkeley Milne (1855–1938), C-in-C Mediterranean 1912–14; through confusion of orders allowed *Goeben* and *Breslau* to escape to Dardanelles at outbreak of war; equerry to George V 1910, to Edward VIII 1936, to George VI 1937; succeeded father as 2nd Baronet 1896; Admiral 1914; knighted 1904.

[2] George Neville (1850–1923), commanded 3rd and 4th Divisions Home Fleet 1909–11; Admiral 1913; knighted 1909.

[3] Arthur William Moore (1847–1934), representative of Britain at Anti-Slavery Congress in Brussels 1889; Member of Australia Defence Committee 1898–1901; C-in-C Cape of Good Hope 1901–4; C-in-C China Station 1906–8; C-in-C Portsmouth 1911–12; retired 1912; knighted 1902.

[4] William Christopher Pakenham (1861–1933), 4th Sea Lord 1911–13; commanded 3rd Cruiser Squadron 1913–17, Battle Cruiser Fleet 1917–19, North American and West Indies Station 1920–2; Admiral 1922; knighted 1916.

[5] George John Scott Warrender (1860–1917), commanded 2nd Cruiser Squadron 1910–12; 2nd Battle Squadron 1912–16; C-in-C Plymouth 1916–17. Married Maud Ashley, youngest daughter of 8th Earl of Shaftesbury 1894; succeeded father as 7th Baronet 1901; Vice-Admiral; knighted 1911.

    I. Cost. £1,995,000
    II. Speed. 30 knots
    III. Eight 15 inch guns.

N.B. I've been looking up what the 15 inch gun will do! It will 'stagger humanity'! Just glorious!

If you let these silly idiots frighten you into the 6 inch gun then I shall be bitterly disappointed – the argument don't hold water for having them. *Utterly silly.*

The 15 inch gun with big case shot will sweep everything into perdition up to the horizon! Believe me – it's all d——d rot about the 6 inch gun. Also if you put in everything that everyone wants for every sort of supposed battle then you'll have a ship costing about 5 millions sterling! You *must* have *cheapness* & the *big* gun & *speed!* let the rest alone – put in what 4 inch guns old Watts likes to fill up with but no more – and *reduce armour* and *increase* subdivision.

I have of course hours of talk that I think would be useful to you. Your first requisite is your Board. *You must* change them all. You must have each of them as your *man! There's* a devil a lot in that!

Yours always
FISHER

Beresford is a fool and you know how to 'fool' him! As I told you I will see you through anything.

I don't want to bore you with advice.

Lord Fisher to WSC

EXTRACT

10 November 1911   Lucerne

Dear Winston,

    You encourage me to write to you. You say you will weigh every word. Well! there are two pressing questions you ought to master at once, and especially before I see you. No use my ramming a lot of stuff down your throat when we meet unless you have verified my references.

    I. The Mobilization of the Fleet

    II. The protection of Commerce & Food Supply.

Your Estimates much affected by your right understanding of these two questions. So of early importance – Send for Captain Haworth-Booth RN.[1]

I don't quite know where he is – somewhere near London – *Have him at your*

---

[1] Francis Fitzgerald Haworth-Booth (1864–1935), Naval Representative for Commonwealth of Australia in England 1911–20. Rear-Admiral; knighted 1919.

private house like Bg because you must not be interrupted in the hour's lecture he gives you – it will spoil it. At the Admiralty always some one coming into the room – besides he won't feel his freedom there. Tell him to give you the same lecture he gave to the Prime Minister & the Committee of Defence on the Mobilization of the Fleet. He was the man who engineered it. He did all the spade work. Crewe said to me 'Have you many men like that in the Navy?' When he had finished! I said 'hundreds'! – *so there are!* Only it wants 'Favouritism' to develop them. I picked this man out right down at the bottom! he has had half his stomach cut out but his brain is like a hive of bees! –

Listen to him with admiration as he recounts how every officer & man has got his ticket for mobilizing. Devolution *in excelsis* – no rotten concentration at the Admiralty – Each Port Admiral has got the rope round his neck. *There's somebody to be hung for every little thing that may go wrong.*

Result: 375 vessels at 4 hours notice at sea and employed in manoeuvres lasting many weeks at the time of the Equinoctial gales. Not *one* lame duck. Not one mishap. Shoals & fogs & navigating without lights off the damnable West Coast of Scotland and Ireland.

II. Protection of Commerce & Food Supply.

Similarly send for Hankey – the incomparable Hankey – ask him to give you the 'Bovril' of Commerce Protection. I think they have A. K. Wilson's Memorandum & his Evidence before the Royal Commission on Food Supply which was splendid. There's an old woman called Sir Cyprian Bridge.[1] *The Times* gives him big print when he writes a letter. If his plan were followed – the Navy Estimates would be a hundred Millions! But you are going to be attacked on this & by friends – by clever ones like Alan Burgoyne[2] who knows more than all the House of Commons put together – so you want to digest the question. Simple un-utterable folly to build vessels costing £80 a ton – if you can hire vessels only costing £20 a ton or less! for the Commerce protection needed. . . .

Lord Fisher to WSC

11 November 1911   Lucerne

Dear Winston,

If you really wish to see me before we go to Naples which I think may be about Dec 22 from here, then I make the following suggestion for your

---

[1] Cyprian Arthur George Bridge (1839–1924), DNI 1889–94; C-in-C Australian Station 1895–8, of China Station 1901–4; retired 1904; Admiral 1903; knighted 1899.

[2] Alan Hughes Burgoyne (1880–1929), Conservative MP for Kensington North 1910–22, for Aylesbury 1924–9; Director of numerous companies and author of several books on naval subjects; knighted 1922; Honorary Treasurer of the Navy League 1909–13.

consideration, to have the *Enchantress* at Dartmouth on Friday Dec 15 & we could go down there by train (Mrs Winston also & say Lloyd George!) any time on Friday. I would come over on Wednesday & stay at the Curzon Hotel or else with Cassel. I very much want to see the College at Dartmouth for my own satisfaction about one or two points in the Engineering Instructions there. We could spend Saturday there & go on to Plymouth in the night and go up the Tamar River on Sunday and on Monday see the Mechanicians & Boy Artificers – two great innovations very near my heart – and I think it would interest you also – anyhow it would be extremely useful to you in fighting George Barnes MP for I turned the flank of the Trades Unions by those two simple reforms and at the same time did justice to some 30,000 stokers who were debarred from ever rising beyond the status of a blue-jacket & opened up Warrant Rank to them and the Boy-Artificers were suckled on Marine Engines instead of being brought in as Trades Union men brought up on bicycles and sewing machines! (However all this is a digression!) – I write now to see if you think the plan is feasible for Friday Dec 15 & I could arrange my movements accordingly. I think you will enjoy Dartmouth.

Yours always

FISHER

I compliment you on your Guildhall speech – it was first class! – What ever you do – get rid of Briggs as Controller. *He is a servile copyist!* He is one of those who adds on half an inch to the last design & he is timid! – *No originality – No push* – It is simply a scandal that the British Admiralty is now behind the whole world in Internal Combustion Propulsion – *Simply Scandalous!* It's the first time in Sea History that the British Navy has not led the way!

We were the first with the Water tube boiler – First with the Turbine – first with oil alone instead of coal – and if I had only remained one year longer at the Admiralty your 'Nonpareil' now being designed by Watts would have been driven like a Motor Car by the Captain on deck and only half a dozen d——d chauffeurs down below instead of 400 stokers and Engineers and it is all that d——d stupid timid Briggs! *You must always push the Experts over the precipice!* They are always straining at the gnat of *perfection* and swallow the camel of *un-readiness!* Half a loaf is better than no bread.

Germany is designing a Motor Cruiser that will go round the world without requiring to replenish fuel! Atlantic liners are now being constructed in profusion in Germany with internal combustion engines.

I persuaded a Millionaire friend of mine to scrap his whole fleet and substitute Motor-tramps! he is doing so. You save 78 per cent in fuel and gain 25 per cent in cargo space. No funnels – clear decks – No smoke to indicate you to the enemy when still below the horizon.

D——n Briggs!!!

PS *I open this letter again to thank you for your kind words at the Guildhall!*

Lord Fisher to WSC

13 November 1911   Lucerne

Dear Winston,

I feel just now like the Elephant's trunk which one moment picks up a pin and the next roots up an oak tree! I've just been revising a Sunday School Story for Sir N. Barnaby KCB.[1] (We are organizing 16 Millions of Sunday School pupils in England and the United States to sing hymns and say prayers & take home leaflets to their Mothers for an English speaking Federation!) '*The hand that rocks the cradle is the hand that . . . &c.*' And now a telegram from you for me to be at Plymouth where I suppose we shall discuss Millions of foot-tons at 6 miles range (the horizon is 7 miles!) Making German Dreadnoughts into tooth powder! when they can't reach the *Non-Pareil!* and the 3 *h*'s and the 3 *l*'s win the day!

For superiority of speed – preponderance of gun calibre and – and unity of armament (which means Fire Control *in excelsis*) enables you to

I Hit *First*	I *When* you *Like*
II Hit *Hard* and to fight	II *How* you *Like*
III Keep on Hitting	III *Where* you *Like*

You tell me Watts hasn't yet given you the design. What makes him so long I wonder. I hope he isn't messing about armour. Armour wants reducing. We are getting like the Knights of old!

You only want enough thickness of armour to make the shell burst outside, and in most places where armour is put you dont want it at all. And as for the Torpedo Bogey '*Size & Subdivision*' is the War Cry!

The First Class Cruiser *Hawke* rams the *Olympic* of 45,000 tons and makes a hole that a coach and horses can drive through but the *Olympic* takes no notice! – don't even heel one degree! and steams comfortably back to Southampton drawing about an inch more water! Watts & Co hate subdivision and so do the Officers and Crews! it's so d——d inconvenient! Nothing but pokey little spaces everywhere! '*It's not magnificent but it's War!*'

Not knowing where you might be I sent a private telegram in reply to

[1] Nathaniel Barnaby (1829–1915), naval architect; designed and built many warships; designed many offices in Whitehall; knighted 1885.

yours to the Resident Clerk (who I know can be trusted!) to inform you I will arrive at Charing Cross on Friday next at 3.28 pm and come to Plymouth to join you next morning by *10* am Express from Paddington unless I hear from you to the contrary at the Curzon Hotel, Curzon Street, Mayfair where I shall hide myself as I want to avoid seeing anyone at all, and get back straight here the moment I leave you at Plymouth.

Yours always
FISHER

WSC to Rear-Admiral Charles Madden

15 November 1911   Admiralty
                                                        (In the train)

Copy

Fourth Sea Lord:

The full explanation wh has reached me of the steps by wh the deficiency in 21″ torpedoes has been reached does not in any way alter the extremely unsatisfactory situation. It is essential that by the time all vessels are completed for service their full reserves of ammunition and torpedoes shd be simultaneously at hand. Any failure in this would be justly regarded as inexcusable by Parliament. It wd be pointed out that ships cost much more and take much longer to construct than torpedoes and that they are useless until these accessories are provided. If the facts were known nothing cd save the Admiralty from a charge of want of foresight, all the more serious when the immense liberality of recent Naval Estimates is considered. So far as the past is concerned the incident is closed by this minute.

To remedy the deficiency:—1) If the supply of 18″ torpedoes is complete, except as may be required for casual replacements (on which please report to me) I approve the stopping work on 18″ pro tem: and concentrating on the Mark I. 21″. 2) Overtime shd be worked continuously and fully on 21″ both in the new and old factories. 3) The proposal to spend £1500 on extra lathes is to be examined in detail by the Financial Secretary, who shd be asked to report whether the acceleration resulting will be worth the money. He shd also report in a similar sense upon the proposed overtime at Portsmouth and Portland.

Ammunition.

Report please on the time and expense required to complete the full reserves of ammunition for guns of all calibres.

Guns.

The deficiencies do not appear considerable, but I cannot judge till I know the scale of the reserves of each class. Please supply.

Mines.

This appears all right.

Small arms ammunition.

Do.

Automatic pistols.

Please report when decision as to pattern may be expected, what numbers will be required, what the cost will be, and when the complete issue cd be effected.

Rear-Admiral Charles Madden to WSC

15 November 1911   Admiralty

First Lord:

I attach a statement in reply to your questions on the shortage of Torpedoes and ammunition.

In your minute you refer to the want of foresight of the Admiralty which has led to the shortage. I trust you do not attribute any want of energy or foresight to the Heads of Departments who are responsible to me for supply i.e. the Director of Naval Ordnance, Superintendent of Ordnance Stores and the Director of the Torpedo Factory: they have I think shewn both energy and foresight in dealing with a difficult situation.

For the 3 years 1907, 1908 and 1909 – 364 eighteen inch Torpedoes were required for new ships and destroyers, in the following year 1910 the requirements jumped to 304 all to be of the new 21 inch type fitted with heaters, which introduced great additional complications in manufacture.

Until the Government's building policy was known in 1909 there was no reason to suppose that the Greenock Factory then building would be unable to meet requirements; as soon as the increased programme was known, the DNO [Director of Naval Ordnance] put forward proposals for increasing the Greenock Factory and hastening the work on the Loch Long Torpedo Range and when the works proposed in 1909 are completed, their capacity (assisted by the Weymouth works) will be about 700 Torpedoes of 21 inch Heater pattern per year. The existing shortage would have been avoided if these extensions had been proposed in 1908, but this was a year of great economy and a minimum building programme and it is most unlikely that such a scheme would have been approved if suggested.

Further, if the DNO's proposals of 1909 had been realised and the contractors for the Greenock extensions and Loch Long Range had kept to their dates I think the shortage would have been overtaken by the end of this financial year: and I consider the unsatisfactory position is due partly to their delay but mainly to

1. The 3 years heavy building programmes.

2. The adoption of the 21 inch heater Torpedo at a time of greatly increased requirements and while the Torpedo Factory was being removed from Woolwich to Greenock.

3. The policy of restricting overtime, when it offered the only means of overtaking the arrears.

C.M.

WSC to H. H. Asquith

16 November 1911   Admiralty

Copy

Prime Minister,

I have now to put before you my proposals for a new Board of Admiralty, & the changes consequent thereupon. Having now seen all the principal officers who might be considered candidates for such a post, I pronounce decidedly in favour of Sir Francis Bridgeman as First Sea Lord. He is a fine sailor, with the full confidence of the service afloat, and with the aptitude for working with and through a staff well developed. If, as would no doubt be the case, he should bring Capt de Bartolomé[1] as his Naval Assistant, I am satisfied that the work of this office wd proceed smoothly and with despatch. I have discussed the principal questions of strategy, administration & finance with him, and believe that we are in general agreement on fundamental principles. If you approve, I will write to Sir Francis & enter more fully into these matters in connection with an assumption by him of these new duties.

This appointment harmonizes, personally and administratively, with that of the new Second Sea Lord, Prince Louis of Battenberg, of whom I have already written to you, & of whose assistance I have the highest expectations. Rear-Admiral Briggs, the Controller & Third Sea Lord, has after a year just begun to acquire a complete knowledge of his vy extensive department, & I do not think it necessary to transfer him at the present time. He will be the only naval member of the old Board to remain. Rear-Admiral Madden is in any case leaving on the 5th of January, & I am advised from all quarters,

[1] Charles Martin de Bartolomé (1871–1941), 3rd Sea Lord and Controller of Navy 1918–19; Admiral 1929; knighted 1919.

including both the proposed First & Second Sea Lords, that the best man to fill his place is Capt Pakenham. This officer, who is vy highly thought of for his intellectual attainments, has also the rare distinction of having served throughout the Russian Japanese War, including the battle of the Tsushima.

The Home Fleet, wh becomes vacant, has not, unhappily, any candidate of clear & pre-eminent qualifications. Admiral Jellicoe is not yet sufficiently practised in the handling of fleets or sufficiently in command of the confidence of the Sea Service, to justify what wd seemingly be a vy startling promotion. I shall however be taking the perfectly straightforward & unexceptionable course in placing Vice-Admiral Sir George Callaghan, the present 2nd in command, who has been in almost daily control of the largest manoeuvres in the Home Fleet, and who has previously been second in command in the Mediterranean, in the place of Sir F. Bridgeman. Admiral Sir John Jellicoe will be his 2nd in command, & we shall thus be able to see what fitness he will develop for the succession.

It appears to me not merely important but necessary that these changes shd operate without delay. The draft Estimates have all arrived for discussion & a month of the most severe work governing the whole future policy of the next 2 years, awaits the Bd of Admiralty. This task can only be satisfactorily discharged if it is undertaken by men who come together with consenting minds, & who will find themselves responsible to the Cabinet & to Parlt for the immediate consequences of their decisions.

I wd therefore ask you to authorize me to approach all parties concerned without delay – unless some unexpected hitch occurs; I shall hope to submit the list to the King by telegraph not later than Wed next. The new Bd wd thus be fully constituted before the end of the present month.

Lord Northcliffe to WSC

16 November 1911   *The Times*

Very Private

My dear Churchill,

Read the following. I do not say where it comes from; but it comes from a very able writer.

'The French Ambassador[1] here has been repeating for the last three months, – *Nous allons vers la guerre!* I should be surprised if war were to come within the next six months, but I should not care to predict the maintenance of peace for much more than a year. The precarious position

[1] Pierre-Paul Cambon.

of German industry and the determination of the Prussian Junker class to force on, if possible, some foreign complication in order to prevent the destruction of Junker privileges by internal reform are, to my mind, the main elements in the situation. In different ways both of them make for war. Our interest is to see that we are not enticed into offending France by concluding a dupe's bargain with Germany and that we do not, by a show of ill-will towards Italy, consolidate the rickety Triple Alliance. Above all we must get our army into order and see that our reserves of weapons and ammunition are sufficient for all possible emergencies.'

Yours very sincerely
NORTHCLIFFE

WSC to Andrew Bonar Law
(Bonar Law Papers)

17 November 1911   Admiralty
My dear Bonar Law,

This is the first chance I have had to tell you how glad I was on personal grounds that you were chosen.[1] From your party's point of view a wise choice. From our standpoint a choice which makes me sure that if ever a national emergency makes party interests fade we shall find in the Leader of the Opposition one who in no fictitious sense places the country and the Empire first.

I hope the club may continue. Great tact will be necessary in the fixing of our meetings, and in the avoidance of bad moments. But no one can say that fortune has not, so far as public things are concerned, followed the footsteps of many of its members: or that the chance of including in its list a Prime Minister has become less good since our beginnings.

All good wishes to you from

Yours very sincerely
WSC

Andrew Bonar Law to WSC

18 November 1911   Pembroke Lodge
Private   Kensington
My dear Churchill,

I thank you very much for your kind letter & I am glad to think (as I have always thought) that though we are separated by party differences there is personal good-will between us.

I hope to see you at the Other Club on Thursday.

Yours sincerely
A. BONAR LAW

[1] Andrew Bonar Law was elected Conservative leader on November 13 in succession to A. J. Balfour. Austen Chamberlain and Walter Long had agreed together to stand aside.

Lord Fisher to WSC

1 *p.m.*   Lucerne
20 November 1911   In the train
Dear Winston,

In case *by any chance* Briggs does not remain then Waymouth[1] Captain of the *Triumph* who will shortly be an Admiral would make an excellent Controller. Make Watts give you a *cheaper* ship and I think in view of the immense *increase* of *gun power* in your new ships that you might only have 3 & take the money of the 4th for submarines *chiefly* & a few more destroyers.

I hope you wont be in any hurry for your new private Secretary as your present one can go on for a long time.

It will make all the difference in your life to have one who suits you *personally*.

Yours
FISHER

WSC to the King
(*Royal Archives*)

21 November 1911   [Admiralty]
Sent in Cypher

Mr Churchill with his humble duty to your Majesty. He had to apprize your Majesty a fortnight ago of the changes which it would be necessary to make in the Board of Admiralty in the New Year.

He now feels it will not be possible to delay them so long.

The interests of the State and of the service ask whether a new Board at the Admiralty should be appointed forthwith and that important questions of policy, which have to be dealt with at this season of the year, should be decided by those who will be effectively responsible both to your Majesty and to Parliament for the consequences of their decisions and not by a moribund Board. Although therefore no differences of any kind have yet been disclosed within the present board he humbly submits with the concurrence of the Prime Minister and the [blank space] for the gracious favour which your Majesty has always shown him the following proposals for the creation of a new Board and other changes consequent therein.

The whole of these changes should take effect immediately your Majesty's pleasure has been signified.

Admiral Sir Francis Bridgeman to be 1st Sea Lord.

Vice-Admiral HRH Prince Louis of Battenberg to be 2nd Sea Lord.

Rear-Admiral Briggs to continue as Controller.

[1] Arthur William Waymouth (1863–1936), inventor of the Waymouth-Cooke range finder; Captain 1902; Director of Naval Equipment 1912–14; commanded 7th Cruiser Squadron 1915; Admiral Superintendent Portsmouth Dockyard 1915–17; CB 1920.

Captain Pakenham to succeed Admiral Madden as 4th Sea Lord.

Sir George Callaghan to command the Home Fleet.

Sir John Jellicoe to command the 2nd Division.

Rear-Admiral Frederick Hamilton[1] to the 3rd Division.

Admiral Frederick Sturdee[2] to the Atlantic Fleet.

Rear-Admiral A. E. Bethell to the East Indies on being succeeded by Captain Ballard in the Intelligence Department.

It is proposed to announce at the same time that Vice-Admiral Sir George Egerton will be appointed to the first vacant command at a Home Port.

It is not without the gravest consideration that Mr Churchill submits to your Majesty these recommendations which he is confident are the best that can be made in the public interest.

He earnestly asks if your Majesty's assent may be made known by telegraph.

On your Majesty's assent being signified to these changes the Prime Minister will advise that a peerage be conferred upon Sir Arthur Wilson for his long and memorable services and that this should be announced at the same time as the appointments.

[WINSTON S. CHURCHILL]

WSC to Lord Stamfordham
(*Royal Archives*)

Tuesday   [Admiralty]
21 November 1911

Sent in cipher

My telegram last night. It should have been made clear that it is proposed that Burney should become Commander-in-Chief Atlantic Fleet with acting rank Vice-Admiral and that Sturdee should succeed him in Fifth Cruiser Squadron.

Lord Stamfordham to WSC
(*Royal Archives*)
TELEGRAM

21 November 1911   HMS *Medina*

The King approves of all your proposals for new Board of Admiralty and appointments which can be effected immediately and presumes peerage will be offered to Sir A. Wilson at once.

[1] Frederick Tower Hamilton (1856–1917), Rear-Admiral 1907; Inspector of Target Practice 1907–9; Commander of 5th Cruiser Squadron Atlantic Fleet 1909–11, Second and Third Fleets 1911–13; 2nd Sea Lord 1914–16; C-in-C Rosyth 1916–17; knighted 1911.

[2] Frederick Charles Doveton Sturdee (1859–1925), Rear-Admiral 1908; Rear-Admiral 1st Battle Squadron 1910; Commander of Second Cruiser Squadron 1912–13; Chief of War Staff 1914–15; C-in-C in action off Falkland Islands 1914; C-in-C the Nore 1918–21; knighted 1913; created Baron Sturdee of the Falkland Isles 1916.

WSC to the King
(*Royal Archives*)

23 November 1911   Admiralty

Sent in cypher

Mr Winston Churchill with his humble duty to Your Majesty expresses his deep sense of the unvarying kindness and support which Your Majesty accords to ministers engaged in the service of the Crown.

It is probable that the announcements will be made on Wednesday next.

Your Majesty has correctly divined the reason for the promotion of Burney to the Atlantic Fleet.

This appointment will be only till he is promoted Vice-Admiral, when Sturdee, whom Your Majesty will remember as Beresford's Chief of the Staff, will have his chance.

WSC to Sir Gerard Noel[1]

22 November 1911   Admiralty

[Copy]

Dear Sir Gerard Noel,

I was as unwitting as yourself when we met at dinner of the changes that impended, and I need not say that I am deeply conscious of the immense national importance of my new duties. Your congratulations are very welcome. Pray accept my thanks for your kindness.

I have read your letter of the 12th February, 1909, with great interest. Of course I am so new to the problems of the Admiralty that I do not feel entitled at the present time to express an opinion upon matters of such grave complexity. The new scheme of entry, to which you particularly allude, will in the near future reach a critical stage. I hope your fears may prove unfounded, but I will most carefully watch its progress and give your opinions full consideration. With what you say as to the fighting value of the ships known as pre-Dreadnoughts, I am in complete accord, and have expressed myself publicly in that sense in the last few years. I believe with you that many of them will prove to be of the greatest use in time of war, and it is far from my intention to allow the obsolescent ships to be reduced to such a

[1] Gerard Henry Uctred Noel (1845–1918), Commander of Home Fleet and Admiral-Superintendent Naval Reserves 1900–3; C-in-C China Station 1904–6, Nore 1907–8; Admiral of the Fleet 1908 until he retired 1915; KCMG 1898; KCB 1902; GCB 1913.

situation as would render them unfit to be brought forward in time of emergency to fill the gaps made in the early stages of a war. I will look most carefully into the question to which you allude as to the disarming of the East
Coast. As regards the administration, it is my intention to keep the closest
touch with all my colleagues on the Board, and to avail myself of their individual and collective advice. I am glad to have had the opportunity of
learning the views of an Officer of your long service and distinguished
abilities, and if you care to add anything, which the unceasing progress of
naval science may have rendered necessary, to the views expressed in your
previous letter, I shall study it most carefully.

[WSC]

Lord Fisher to WSC

22 November 1911   Lucerne

My beloved Winston,

You have said yourself War is our pre-occupation. So long as Callaghan
commands Home Fleet there would be no friction in appointing Bg from
Admiralty as Admiralissimo – When Callaghan's two years are up I presume
you will put Jellicoe in his place and then no need of an Admiralissimo – for
he is Head & Shoulders even above Bg! Bridgeman will confirm this – As
Bridgeman goes about that time you can make Bg his successor so that
smoothes over his not going as Callaghan's successor! *but the object of my letter
is that from this time forth you must make no appointment afloat for anyone senior to
Jellicoe* otherwise you will be in a fix in two years time when you wish him
to be Admiralissimo!

Isn't it all providential? In two years time is Armageddon! The Kiel Canal
finished. The German Navy at its best. The Austrian Dreadnoughts complete and France unready with her new ships, but we shall have our Jellicoe,
and our new batch of Winston's Submarines and Destroyers ready.

You won't forget them. *No sea going appointments senior to Jellicoe!* – And as
you withdraw Battleships from Mediterranean and Poe's time there expires
on April 30, 1913, you would replace him by a junior officer and do away
with the expense of Admiralty House at Malta.

I had a delightful letter from Bridgeman and he wrote so charmingly
about you that I have no fears as to your interview with him on Monday.

I hope you won't give me away to old Watts! He had a good object lesson
in the design he gave you because a few red ink corrections in the previous
design would have enabled tenders to be invited at once.

To deliberately invite tenders for a design you know to be faulty and damnably expensive is absolutely indefensible when a few months delay will give you the right ship. So I hope you will insist on a £1,995,000 ship, with 8—15 inch guns and 30 knots speed and d——n all the rest. Watts can make the rest of the details suit with this *all important* and *vital* condition that *armour* is to be replaced by *subdivision* 'in excelsis'! I wrote you a few hasty lines on telegraph forms at Boulogne I hope you got them.

Ask Troubridge about Waymouth's abilities for Controller – he knows him well.

There's a most delightful fellow & thorough gentleman called Sheppard,[1] Captain of the Battleship *Queen* in the Atlantic Fleet but he hasn't brains enough for you as your Private Secretary – and Heathcoat Grant[2] & George Cuthbert Cayley[3] and Allan Everett[4] – but you have heaps of time to choose and it *must* be a personal choice!

I hope you wont leave a single prospective appointment unannounced. You quite see the advantages I know.

Yours always
FISHER

WSC to Sir Edward Grey

22 November [1911]   Admiralty

[Copy]

Sir Edward Grey,

Capt Kell of the War Office secret service has given me the enclosed bundle of reports, which resulted from the action taken by him in conjunction with the Chief Constable during my tenure of the Home Office. Although there is a lot of 'stuff' mixed up with them, they are well worth looking through because they show that we are the subject of a minute and scientific study by the German military and naval authorities, and that no other nation in the world pays us such attention.

---

[1] Thomas Dawson Lees Sheppard (1866–1953), commanded 9th Cruiser Squadron December 1916 – January 1919; Rear-Admiral 1916; Admiral 1922; knighted 1922.

[2] Heathcoat Salusbury Grant (1864–1938), commanded *Diana, Kent, Black Prince,* and *Canopus*; Naval Attaché USA 1912–14; Fought at Coronel and Gallipoli; Vice-Admiral 1920; knighted 1919.

[3] George Cuthbert Cayley (1866–1944), Flag Captain, China Station 1910–13; Commodore, then Rear-Admiral in charge of Harwich 1914, 1917. Admiral 1926.

[4] Allan Frederic Everett (1868–1938). Captain of Fleet, Commodore on Staff of C-in-C Home Fleets and Grand Fleets 1913–15; Naval Secretary to First Lord of Admiralty 1916–18; Commanded 4th Light Cruiser Squadron 1918–19; 8th Light Cruiser Squadron 1919–21; C-in-C China Station 1924–5; Admiral 1926; knighted 1919.

Will you show them to Lloyd George when he dines with you tomorrow night?

I should add that Kell is thoroughly trustworthy and competent, & that of course the names and addresses of almost all the persons referred to are known.

The information is of course secret. A good deal more is accumulating through the warrant that I issued as Home Secretary for the inspection of correspondence. Please return.

WSC

Note by Sir Edward Grey

I hadn't time to look at this till today & Ll G has gone to Bath so I send it back to you.

EG

Engineer-Commander Taylor[1] to Lord Fisher

23 November 1911   HMS *Superb*
                                                Home Fleet

Dear Lord Fisher,

I have had a yarn with several Sub-lieuts (New Scheme) recently, and I gather from what they say that although they appear to have no dislike or objection to Engineering, *per se*, – not many of them will volunteer for E duties – they admit the work is interesting and well paid – but to use their own expression, '*they have been choked off*'.

None of them have done any Engineering since they became Sub-lieuts, and undoubtedly the impression they have got, and this appears to be a general feeling, is, that the Admiralty are not in earnest in regard to the Engineering part of the scheme.

I have gone over the recent Circular letter with them and pointed out that the Admiralty intentions are quite plain and that the Lieut E can rise to command like the other Specialist officers – But they are only half convinced. The fact is that there is still much prejudice against the Scheme, especially in my own branch – revived by the fact that the Sub-lieutenant is taken away from deck duties occasionally to do E duties, thus throwing more watch keeping on the other Lieuts – and that in the Engine room you now have two different kinds of commissioned officer doing the same duty – and the existing Engineer Officer does not like it. There is no doubt, despite all

---

[1] Charles Gerald Taylor (1864–1915), of whom Lord Fisher wrote in a letter to David Beatty in 1915: 'I feel the death of Engineer-Captain C. G. Taylor most acutely. You don't know what a faithful and loyal friend he was to me!' (Arthur J. Marder: *Fear God and Dread Nought*, Vol III, p. 146).

the regulations which have been issued, very little interest is taken in the Engineering training in the majority of ships.

At the same time I do not think there will be any shortage of Lieuts E. they may prefer the G T or N [Gunnery, Torpedo or Navigation] branches, but when these are full, they will rather specialise in E than not specialise at all: and in every term there are a certain number of enthusiasts who have made up their minds already to be Engineers.

I have no doubts about their capability and knowledge, we have all the material to make good Engineer Officers – if the training is properly carried out. I have one of these Sub lieuts now doing duty in the engine room of this ship – he is really excellent. *What I think is now required is that the Admiralty should show their determination in some way to have their orders and intentions carried out* – and they should round off some of the corners in the sea training. *There is only opposition because they think the Admiralty are weakening on the Scheme, and the recent alteration in the Marine portion has given this a fillip.*

I have seen Sir Francis Bridgeman lately and put some suggestions before him, which he approves of, and I think and trust will have carried out. He told me that he had strongly recommended my promotion at the end of the year – but I am a long way down the list and feel sure it will mean a big effort to get it. Do you think it is any use advocating that the existing Engineer Officers be fused with the 'Executive' line as far as is practicable – and that the pay and promotion question be investigated. I know this is a thorny question and you must be sick and tired of it – but I really think it is worth tackling.

You told me in one of your letters that you had once nominated Captain Napier[1] as the 1st Lord's private secretary – but for some reason it fell through. Could it not be resuscitated – we should have a real friend and upholder of the New Scheme at the Admiralty then.

Apologising for such a long letter, Believe me, Yours sincerely

C. G. TAYLOR

Lord Fisher to WSC

27 November 1911 Lucerne

Dear Winston,

I enclose you two first class letters just come – one from Sir Marcus Samuel[2] who explains to you what d——d fools you have got as Controller

[1] Charles Lionel Napier (1861–1934), commanded *Inflexible* 1909–11; *Monarch* 1912; Admiral 1922.

[2] Marcus Samuel (1853–1927), businessman, financier and founder of Shell Oil Company which later merged with The Royal Dutch Company. Lord Mayor of London 1902–3; knighted 1898; created Baronet 1903; Baron Bearsted 1921; Viscount Bearsted of Maidstone 1925.

and Engineer in Chief – timid as rabbits and silly as ostriches – and the other letter is from Engineer Commander Taylor of the *Superb* who you promised me you would see, promote, and make Head of the Engineering College at Keyham at Devonport. He is vital for it.

That ass Egerton has done irreparable mischief as Second Sea Lord. I hope he'll have appendicitis.

Yours always
FISHER

I hope all is prospering with your plans! I've not whispered a word to a soul about anything & not answered shoals of letters – not one –

WSC to the King
(*Royal Archives*)

TELEGRAM

27 November 1911 HMS *Medina*

Sent in Cipher

Mr Churchill with his humble duty submits the following names for new ships of this year's programme. Four battleships *Africa, Liberty, Assiduous, Oliver Cromwell.* Three second class cruisers *Birmingham, Lowestoft, Nottingham.* The name *Assiduous* was chosen before Mr Churchill assumed office.

The King to WSC
(*Royal Archives*)

TELEGRAM

27 November 1911

Sent by Cipher

The First Lord, Admiralty, London.

I approve of *Africa* for Battleship, also 3 submitted names of second class cruisers, but I cannot agree to *Liberty, Assiduous,* and *Oliver Cromwell.* I will send you 3 others.

GEORGE R.I.

I hope you will agree to the following names for the 3 remaining battleships, *Delhi, Wellington, Marlborough.*

GEORGE R.I.

Sir Charles Ottley to WSC

29 November 1911   Committee of Imperial Defence

Dear Mr Churchill,

I enclose a draft for the terms of reference of a sub-Ctee on national guarantee of war-risks of shipping bringing food to the United Kingdom. Will you please glance through it and see if it is what you wish.

As you doubtless recollect, the whole subject of national guarantee of war-risks of shipping was referred to a Committee (of wh Mr Austen Chamberlain was chairman) – 3 or 4 years ago. I was a member of that committee, as was also Sir G. Clarke.[1] The Committee as a whole reported adversely to any project for a national guarantee, George Clarke & I being the only dissentients.

I came to the conclusion at that date, that public opinion was not yet ready for any such measure. Ship-owners & under-writers who came before the Committee to give evidence, evinced a total lack of comprehension of the subject, and often crabbed the idea without knowing what its purport was!

But – in as much as the subject has so recently been dealt with, I think it might be well if you would speak to the Prime Minister, before I send him the Reference for approval; (if indeed you have not already done so).

Yours very sincerely

C. L. OTTLEY

Lord Selborne to WSC

29 November 1911   Brooks's
                                                    St James Street

Private

My dear Churchill,

Accept my very sincere congratulations on your appointment of Prince Louis.

He is the ablest officer the Navy possesses and, if his name had been Smith, he would ere now have filled various high offices to the great advantage of the country, from which he has been excluded owing to what I must characterise as a stupid timidity.

---

[1] George Sydenham Clarke (1848–1933), Secretary to Committee of Defence 1904–7; Governor of Bombay 1907–13, of Victoria 1901–4; Member of Air Board 1916–17; knighted 1893; created Baron Sydenham of Combe 1913.

He has in fact nearly had his naval career maimed because he is a Prince & because of his foreign relationships. I have stated what I think of his ability – I can only add that a better Englishman does not exist or one whom I would more freely trust in any post in any emergency. I think I know one of the special tasks you have in hand. I bequeathed that task as an urgent legacy to Fisher nearly seven years ago and gave him all the material for its fulfilment. To my surprise & disgust on my return from South Africa I found he had done nothing; I say 'surprise' because I thought it would have been a job after his own heart, but obviously I was wrong.

Prince Louis is just the man to help you.

Yrs sincerely
SELBORNE

Lord Fisher to WSC

29 November 1911   Lucerne

Dear Winston,

So glad to hear from you this morning that your '*Coup d'Etat*' arrives today! I now feel happy and content and relapse with relief into obscurity! – One thing I hope you wont forget as I think it so all important – To have No 2 associated with No 1 in CID Meetings in view of No 1 being possibly away and also because of the preponderance of Generals there. No less than 5! Both 1 and 2 always to attend – you can easily fix this with the PM.[1]

It's no use my harping on the new design of the *Non-Pareil!* You are bound to be guided by your experts – I *consider them d——d fools* – we should not have had the *Lion* if we had pursued the same course as they now recommend to you. Nor the Dreadnought. Nor Turbines before any Navy dared to think of them. Nor the Water-tube boiler when Sir W. Allan MP[2] said I was boiling the Stokers alive &c! – but I dont blame you. I am much concerned you should have a good Private Secretary but I've no doubt amongst them all they will find one you will like. My one great joy of all is that Jellicoe is safely in the right place. *You can sleep quiet in your bed!*

Of course I shall love to see you again as you dont mind how much I let fly! but you had better not ask me I think if it is at all likely to disturb susceptibilities amongst your new colleagues.

Of course they are all dear friends of mine but that is all the more reason to be careful.

[1] See below, *Sir Charles Ottley to WSC*, 12 December 1911, on p. 1356.
[2] William Allan (1837–1903), Liberal MP for Gateshead 1893–1903; was captured and imprisoned while running guns to blockaded Confederacy during American Civil War; knighted 1902.

Yes! as you say Beresford's speech as mischievous as it well could be and as you may suppose it's quoted in extenso in all the French & German newspapers!

Dont you bother to write again, though your letters are absolutely safe I think as they come direct in a sealed bag here via Laon & Basle I believe – & not through Paris – and mine to you I know go safely.

Yours always

F

Sir Charles Ottley to WSC

1 December 1911   Committee of Imperial Defence

Dear Mr Churchill,

I am issuing the Terms of Reference as approved and amended by you yesterday.

Inglefield[1] will be very useful as a witness, he has a real knowledge of the subject, and his later experience as secretary of Lloyds will give additional weight to his views. I agree however that it is undesirable to bring in any outside functionary as a member of the Committee, unless you are going to include several.

Yours very sincerely

C. L. OTTLEY

Lord Northcliffe to WSC

1 December 1911   *The Times*

Private

My dear Churchill,

The question of the suppression of news of naval movements in the newspapers, even at times like these, is I consider very important. In my judgment, it should be enforced tactfully but drastically. There are many reasons why it should be generally maintained at all times, not the least being the fact that if you suddenly impose censorship at times of extreme international complication it might be construed into a declaration of war. I am all for most drastic censorship before and during war, having due regard for the cables of the commercial classes.

---

[1] Edward Fitzmaurice Inglefield (1861–1945), Secretary of Lloyds 1906–21 succeeding Sir Henry Hozier, WSC's father-in-law; formerly served in Royal Navy; Rear-Admiral; knighted 1919.

I write this because Reginald Nicholson[1] of *The Times* told me yesterday that he was seeing the War Office people on the subject. It is essential that in this matter there should be co-ordination.

Yours very sincerely

NORTHCLIFFE

Lord Fisher to WSC

EXTRACT

3 December 1911   Lucerne

Dear Winston,

I trespass again on your patience for a few minutes before your New Board is constituted so that I may be free of any charge of endeavouring to influence you behind the backs of your new colleagues – my friends.

First of all I've heard from two Fleets of heartfelt joy *universal* at Bridgeman, Battenberg, Pakenham & *Jellicoe, but especially the last named! So that's all right.*

Now for 3 facts for those two Slugs you have now got as Controller and Director of Naval Ordnance who want you to perpetuate Battleships of the *Tortoise* type all armour and no speed and inadequate armament and d——d costly as compared with a *far cheaper, far faster* and *63 per cent more powerful ship!!*

How you can conscientiously permit contracts to be invited or orders given for a type of Battleship which you know that your own brilliant common sense instantly condemned on that Sunday night at Reigate I cant comprehend! Any delay is preferable to laying down obsolete and costly types! *But there need not be delay that will signify. We are two keels to one.* Now! You have a 37 per cent margin of delay

I. Send privately for Saxton Noble[2] London representative of the Elswick Firm, 8 Great George St, Westminster and ask him if his Firm entertains any idea of risk in manufacturing the new gun right off without trial. . . .

II. Mr Meyer[3] Secretary of the U.S. Navy has just announced that the new American Battleships to be laid down will have *oil fuel only* with a saving

---

[1] Reginald Nicholson (1859–1945), Manager of *The Times* 1911–15; Coalition Liberal MP for Doncaster 1918–22.

[2] Saxton William Armstrong Noble (1863–1942), Director of Sir W. G. Armstrong, Whitworth & Co, Mond Nickel Co, Whitehead Torpedo Companies; succeeded brother as 3rd Baronet 1937.

[3] George von Lengerke Meyer (1858–1918), United States Secretary of the Navy 1909–13; Postmaster-General 1907–9.

of *50* per cent (so he states) in the large Stoker personnel – *what a vista of economy! and of keeping the Sea! No going into harbour to coal!* Your ships will all tremble at giving up coal though every ocean swarms now with British Oil feeders – (one of them rammed the ship I went to America in last year at right angles). Please interview Sir Marcus Samuel.

III. Are you really going to build ships with fewer submerged Torpedo Tubes than the German new Battleships?

I say nothing of the increased personnel involved in the introduction of the 6 inch gun.

If you say what you want – you'll get it!

Cost £1,995,000 8 new-type guns – *only oil,* 30 knots speed. If they say they can't do it, go to another shop! Send for Professor Biles[1]! or tell Mr Gracie[2] of the Fairfield Works, he'll give it you! You have got to push these experts over the precipice. Dont trouble to answer.

Yours always
FISHER

WSC to Lord Fisher
(*Lennoxlove Papers*)

3 December 1911   Admiralty

My dear Fisher,

The *coup* was entirely successful, & is retrospectively a vy big event. I shall be with my new Board all this week. We have agreed on the main points. If the Germans increase that will be vy plain sailing for me, & it looks as if they wd. I am now working at 'concentration on the perfect types & in the decisive theatre', & I see daily the outlines of a really fine policy emerging. We must cut off an obsolete & obsolescent tail ('In peace a charge in war a weak defence') in order to develop teeth & claws of terrible strength.

The main obstacle to the 'improved 13.5' is that the present one is so awfully good. They are all in love with it & with an increased shell there is really nothing can stand against it yet. It is also bad to show your hand with only 1 card. Better wait a bit & have a squadron. Still matter is not settled yet.

Swifts are coming to the fore. B & B both like them. I have told Watts

---

[1] John Harvard Biles (1854–1933), Professor of Naval Architecture, Glasgow University 1891–1921; Assessor on Titanic Enquiry 1912; naval architect and manager of Clydebank Shipyard 1881–90.

[2] Alexander Gracie (1860–1930), Director Cammell Laird & Company, English Electric Company, Leeds Forge Company; knighted 1918.

they are to have *double* the oil of the old one. I wish you cd have seen the model of the new ships for this year. It conforms to almost every requisite wh we discussed together. I was extremely pleased with it: & am sure you wd like it vy much.

Did you say that you wd be at Lucerne till 20 *Jan?* If so I will fix up another *Enchantress* weekend about the middle of Jan! Let me know your intentions.

Troubridge is first favourite for Ch of Ws. Continue to write about things, I study all you say.

Always yours most sincerely
WINSTON S. CHURCHILL

Lord Fisher to WSC

6 December 1911   Lucerne

Dear Winston,

'*In peace a charge – in war a weak defence*'*!* is perfect! the worst of it is you wont remember these phrases! Think of those golden words in Keyham Dockyard that Sunday night returning from the *Monarch! Where are they now?* Yes! *ruthless elimination* and *effective concentration.!* Those are watch words of *Economy* and *Efficiency!*

I absolutely disagree with your two effete experts. They woke me at 4 am with a start! A nightmare! The British Fleet were Spithead Forts, splendid armour but they couldn't move! The first desideratum of all is *Speed!* Your fools dont see it – They are always running about to see where they can put on a little more armour! to make it safer! *You dont go into Battle to be safe!* No, you go into Battle *to hit the other fellow in the eye first* so that he cant see you! Yes! you hit him first, you hit him hard and you keep on hitting. *That's your safety!* You dont get hit back! Well! that's the improved 13½ inch gun! but disassociated from *dominating speed,* that gun is futile. Why? Because you want to fight *when* you like, *where* you like and *how* you like! and that only comes from *speed* – Big Speed – 30 knots – you dont care a d——n then whether your bottoms dirty or a compartment bashed in with a torpedo making you draw a foot more water because you have a big margin of speed over your Noah's Ark Dreadnoughts of 21 knots!

But the biggest stupidity of all in your two expert ostriches who are advising you is to talk of the inadvisability of showing your hand with only one card and better to have a squadron!! You must excuse me but really they *are* d——d fools! Why was the Dreadnought Policy a success? We pushed one specimen to completion with the utmost speed and *in a year and a day* from laying her first keel plate she was firing her guns! *Ready to fight!* The Germans paralysed for a year did what your fools recommend and started on four – a quartette.

We had our mistakes in one only and corrected them in those following. The Germans drew 2 feet too much water in *four* and tried to sell them to the Turks! Ask Burgoyne MP he'll tell you the inner history from his splendid spy in Germany. The one thing to do is to order Watts to produce a 30 knot ship with eight improved guns for £1,995,000 and if he cant do it (*of course he can!*) then order it from Gracie of the Fairfield Works (like you'd order a pound of sugar!) to be delivered in 2 years ready for fighting and you will get in Bacon then to make the guns. (he's going to knock out Vickers & Elswick! *Very secret* they are trying to buy him!).

Of course the Non-Pareil must be *oil only!* That's a *sine qua non* – I *do* hope you will see Sir Marcus Samuel at once – (telegraph The Mote, Maidstone, Kent) about his huge fleet of peripatetic oiling stations! It just makes me mad the way we are hanging back – *but you cant help it*. You must of course be governed by the advice of your experts.

Yes I *did* say to you I was going to Naples on Jan 20th and I have fixed up my plans definitely, but dont you bother about asking me to *Enchantress* – I think you have seen quite enough of me. *An Enthusiast is always a d——d bore!*

Remember '*Size and Subdivision*' is what you have got to ram down old Watts' throat, as opposed to armour. The new White Star Atlantic Liner is 1,000 feet long! *Hurrah!!* The poor fools are always thinking of making the ships fit the docks – *they are not thinking of winning the Battle!* The bigger the ship the cheaper – and of course the faster – The fighting and propelling portion costs £80 a ton – you shove on all the rest at £8 a ton! – *Shove it on!*

Yours always

FISHER

W. T. *Stead to WSC*

7 December 1911

The Review of Reviews
Kingsway

Private

Dear Mr Winston Churchill,

As you have been good enough to tolerate me writing once or twice when messages have come to me from the other side, I feel it is my duty to inform you that last night at the sitting of Julia's Circle, without any warning or expectation on our part, a message came purporting to come from your father, who professed himself to be very anxious about your need for sleep. He wanted you to be informed that he was very well pleased with the line you were taking, but he was very anxious as to the strain to which you were subjecting your nervous system. He implored us to beg you in his name to take more rest, to sleep, and not to rely upon any sedatives. With rest you would be all right. He was so urgent and so evidently anxious. I warned him that you might resent my intrusion if I sent you a message, he said he did not mind that so long as you got it.

So pray pardon me. I do not expect any acknowledgment of this letter. I have discharged my duty in sending it to you.

I am, Yours sincerely
WILLIAM T. STEAD

Lord Fisher to WSC

8 December 1911   Lucerne

Dear Winston,
It has got beastly cold here suddenly and it is 70° in the shade at Naples so we are off to the Excelsior Hotel at Naples on Dec 21st and I write to tell you as you had the kind intention of perhaps asking me on board *Enchantress* middle of January – so that is a pleasure to be foregone!

Dont trouble to answer.

I wish you all good luck. I have had most affectionate letters from your new Sea Lords and they are very appreciative of you! *so all promises well!*

Yours always
FISHER
PS I hope you will cultivate Alan Burgoyne and Edward Goulding MP. They are great friends of mine & *both A1.*

Sir Francis Hopwood to WSC

9 December 1911   13 Hornton Street

Very Confidential

My dear Churchill,
I think you would be well advised to base your negotiation for a new kind of Civil Lord – that is a man of affairs – on the precedent of the similar

appointees on the Council of the Secretary of State for India. Get a good business man, pay him & reward him well, no pension, & five years appointment. That would find you the Felix Schuster[1] or the late Sir James Mackay[2]! The Secretary to the Admiralty ought to be reformed into being the chef de Cabinet for all purposes but those of a high order of business and financial policy suitable for consideration by you and your new Civil Lord & through you & him by the Board of Admiralty. In this you will find a scheme useful to you & of value to the public service.

You kindly suggested that I should come to you in the new capacity. I replied that I should dearly like to work again with you & watch the development of your policy & enterprise in this new sphere. But I could not say more. I have been very much knocked about in the sea of official work & domestic trouble & I feel disposed to sit on the shelf allotted to me. Eighteen months ago, under severe pressure from the Ch of E & after receiving a letter from the Prime Minister (which George Murray advised gave me no alternative) I left the Civil Service proper & became a well paid member of a Royal Commission. I was put out of conceit of the move by the late & present King, by practically every other colleague of yours in the Cabinet & by the opposition leaders – A. Bonar Law for instance felt that I had sold myself for a little money! Then I was packed off to S. Africa under wretched circumstances to do the Duke of Connaught's tour & the business for him attending the inauguration of the Union. On my return the Treasury was to become vacant & George Murray strongly urged me to be a candidate. I did not apply for the post but it would be affectation to pretend that I did not know I was pressed in some quarters for the Secretaryship. If I was to be called upon to return from outside to the active ranks of the Civil Service then was the time & that was the post worthy of consideration. But the King wrote to me that he was informed that I was 'irreplaceable at the Development Commission' & to his disappointment could not be appointed to the Treasury. That form of refusal would in earlier days have raised the blush of modesty to my cheek! I have learned to appreciate it as merely a kindly form of negation of one's personal interest & advancement. A similar intimation under similar circumstances was given more than once at the Board of Trade, first in the case of a Railway Chairmanship & then twice on successive

[1] Felix Otto Schuster (1854–1936), German-born merchant banker; member of Council of India 1906–16; carried out a number of large and successful bank mergers to form National Provincial Bank 1919; Baronet 1906.

[2] James Lyle Mackay (1852–1932), Merchant; at the time in India to settle disputes between the railway companies and Railway Board. Partner in Mackinnon Mackenzie and Company; Vice-President Suez Canal Company; sat on many Government Committees; Knighted 1894; Created Baron Inchcape six months before this letter was written; Viscount Inchcape 1924; Viscount Glenapp of Strathnaver 1929; Earl of Inchcape 1929.

vacancies in the Railways Commission Court; the same thing happened at the Colonial Office when Botha & his friends asked that I should go to S. Africa as Governor-General; the same reply when it was a question of moving me from the Development Commission to the Treasury. (I must say that I never seriously supposed that Botha's proposal would be considered but he & his Cabinet did & when I was out last year they amused themselves at my expense by wondering why I was no longer wanted at the CO!)

You will appreciate the position. As I fully accept the compliment paid me as regards the Development Commission why should I leave it with its comparative ease & ten years appointment & go back into the rough & tumble of Departmental Government? As HMG said they wanted me at the Commission I have stuck to it loyally, worked at it, & its general administration is carefully laid out. Since I have been there I have refused, as you know, a good offer from Armstrong Whitworth & Co & a tremendous one, financially, of a partnership with Edgar Speyer. I declined both on the ground that HMG were good enough to attach importance to my remaining at my post. You will agree that I have performed my part & I need say no more.

All this is not written in any spirit of complaint, it is merely a brutal statement of a case made to drive it home to you that I am not unreasonable in wincing at your friendly suggestion. On public grounds you should look for a different class of man & on private grounds you should not hold me ungracious for not responding to your proposal.

The Government has been good enough from time to time to entrust me with a lot of odd & end work, Commission, Committee & otherwise & I shall be glad to do more. If I can be of any help to you in this way please think of me.

Ever yours sincerely
FRANCIS J. S. HOPWOOD

Sir Francis Hopwood to WSC

13 December 1911   13 Hornton Street

Confidential

My dear Churchill,

Many thanks for your letter couched in such friendly terms – almost thou persuadest me to be an Admiral! But this purely on personal grounds & not because I am convinced that you are right in pressing my nomination or that there is any public duty on my part to move again from the position to which I have been so recently assigned. Anyhow I am wrestling with the proposal as best I may & you shall have a definite reply without much delay. What does our friend the Ch of Ex say to it? You know how insistent he was that I should do the Development Commission & nothing else. Has he had enough of me? The recent intimation to HM referred to in my previous letter makes me doubt. If I am to embark on an entirely new line of life would the Prime Minister be benevolent & recommend me for some personal advancement? I recognise that had I remained Secretary to one of the Departments of State it would have been difficult for him to do so. I should have been one of a class & the members of the class must be dealt with on somewhat equal terms or claims & jealousies will arise. But I retired from the Civil Service, & I am nothing now but a Royal Commissioner appointed by Royal Warrant. My position is exceptional & isolated & no comparisons can be made. I had ten years service as a Permanent Under Secretary – a time fully equal to that for which such places are usually held prior to retirement. During those ten years, as you know, there was no lack of important movement either at the Board of Trade or Colonial Office. Within that period I had four or five Royal Commissions as well as two missions to Canada & two to South Africa. You might be good enough to consider this.

Then, as to the period of appointment: I should not mind giving up my present ten year appointment for one of five years if that was thought desirable. In my opinion it is very desirable that the man who is to hold the place you propose to create should not be 'permanent'. He should be 'Civil Lord' not 'Permanent Civil Lord'. Fresh blood may be required. That is one reason why I urge the analogy of the Indian Council.

If you relax your strong feeling in favour of the nomination of this particular individual I will suggest a name or two to you.

Ever yours sincerely

FRANCIS J. S. HOPWOOD

Sir Charles Ottley to WSC

12 December 1911   Committee of Imperial Defence

Dear Mr Churchill,

The Prime Minister desires me to say he approves your suggestion that the Second Sea Lord should attend the meetings of the Defence Committee; – in addition to the First Sea Lord and the DNI [Director of Naval Intelligence].

I have informed Prince Louis, and have sent him a file of the papers to be discussed on Thursday.

Yours vy sincerely

C. L. OTTLEY

J. S. Sandars to A. J. Balfour
(*Balfour Papers*)

EXTRACT

14 December 1911   4 Carlton Gardens

Confidential

My dear Chief,

I think you were interested in the appointment of a new Board of Admiralty which Winston brought into existence immediately on taking office. Various reasons were assigned for this unexpected action. And, if you will recollect, some of us thought that the most plausible reason was that the Government desired to have the services of McKenna at the Home Office, where Winston had been an undoubted failure, for the purpose of the forthcoming Welsh Disestablishment Bill. I understand the real reason was quite different.

Bridgeman, the new First Sea Lord came to see me on Sunday afternoon, and we had a very long talk. He told me that the Government has been profoundly dissatisfied with McKenna's want of information concerning the capacity of the Navy to undertake the tasks suggested for it at recent meetings of the Defence Committee. I pressed Bridgeman for a little more detail. I found out that he was darkly referring to the enquiry which the Defence Committee had made as to the protection which the Navy could afford to the passage of troops across the Channel. I rather expected that this was what he had meant. He told me that the Defence Committee had discovered that McKenna had neither informed himself of the subject independently, nor had he taken the trouble to collect the opinions of his Board, and that he was not himself able to throw any light upon the most pertinent enquiries, which, as you know, were necessary in view of the difficult situation in which the Government found themselves in September. Bridgeman told me that when he learnt this he was not in the least surprised. McKenna had always taken things very easily at the Board of Admiralty and had shown a growing indisposition to go into details concerning the manning of the Fleet and questions relating thereto. Of this he (Bridgeman) had particular knowledge, because as Second Sea Lord the manning of the Navy was in his particular department.

Bridgeman related to me that McKenna was highly indignant at his removal from the Admiralty, and that he had gone into the Home Office in the most irritated condition of mind, and full of resentment against the man who had taken his place. So much for that. I asked Bridgeman how he came to leave command of the Home Fleet. He said that Winston had sent for him, never mentioning what he wanted him for, and to his great surprise he was pressed to accept the post of First Sea Lord, although he had been Commander-in-Chief of the Home Fleet less than a year. He did his best to decline, but Winston was insistent. Winston told him that he was satisfied he should never be able to work with Wilson, and that he had satisfied himself that he could work with him (Bridgeman). In the result much against the grain Bridgeman had to consent. Winston apparently, in getting rid of McKenna's Board, displayed but little consideration. Wilson is very sore; and reserved man though he is, let Bridgeman know that he thought he had been very badly treated. Winston's first official act was to put into Bridgeman's hand the letter which he, Winston, had addressed to Wilson requesting him to relinquish his post, for Winston had declined to see Wilson. Bridgeman told me that the letter was a fine example of what a letter ought not to be under such circumstances, especially having regard to the high standing and conspicuous services of the outgoing First Sea Lord. He told me that it was a plain notice to quit, coupled with a solatium that he might have a peerage if he liked. The letter was sent, and of course under these circumstances, Wilson, without any grace whatever, promptly declined the honour. . . .

One word more about the Navy. I understand from Bridgeman that Winston in order to smooth his new official path, is anxious to make Charlie Beresford an Admiral of the Fleet. When this proposal was formerly mooted, McKenna consulted the Board and Bridgeman had advised against the appointment. I now told Bridgeman that if he thought Winston really meant to confer this honour upon Charlie, that he (Bridgeman) had better stand on one side, and that he should inform the First Lord that he had much better assume personal responsibility without reference to the opinions of his colleagues. But we both agreed that if Winston does make Charlie an Admiral of the Fleet, it will prejudice him much in the eyes of Fisher. . . .

A. J. Balfour to WSC

16 December 1911   Whittingehame
Private

My dear Winston Churchill,

Forgive my not having answered your most kind letter earlier. I am, by original sin, a reluctant and unpunctual correspondent; and my recent wanderings – the first fruits of liberty – have not improved my habits. I feel very remorseful.

I can most truly assure you that never – not even during the hottest moment of political controversy – [have I] been the least tempted to allow public differences to destroy private friendships. On that score you need have no feeling of regret for any episode in the past: nor do I think that you have the smallest reason to reproach yourself with anything in the nature of the 'faults of [?]' of which you speak. I at least recall no case in which I had reason to feel aggrieved. Even had such existed, your letter would have made enough – more than enough – amends! –

I am glad you have gone to the Admiralty. A fresh eye at this moment is all important. To say nothing of organisation, mere mechanical invention is modifying tactics, and (I suspect) even strategy, with bewildering rapidity. Do we (*eg*) grasp in all extents, the effect which submarines, owned by the weaker navy, may have in restricting the power over lines of communication which 'command of the sea' is supposed to confer on the stronger navy?

They may not greatly hinder commerce – but how about large military expeditions over sea? But this is an unpardonable digression in a letter which was intended only to convey my sincere thanks for what you have written.

Yrs sin

A. JAMES BALFOUR

William Royle to WSC

18 December 1911   Elmwood
Rusholme

Private & Confidential

Dear Mr Churchill,

I am sorry you could not join us at lunch tomorrow as it would have been a real pleasure for your friends to have met you once more.

As a working politician I want to have a word with you on the foreign policy of the Government & its effect on our party. In the ranks of the Liberal party there is without the shadow of a doubt widespread dissatisfaction & the cause ought if possible to be removed without delay.

I have no hesitation in saying that nine out of ten Liberals would say if questioned 1) that we take up a hostile attitude as regards Germany, that the Lloyd George speech in July was unwarranted & that Sir Edward Grey's speech was unsympathetic in his references to Germany 2) That in respect of the treaty of 1907 we occupy a subservient position in Persian matters, leaving the initiative to Russia & England humbly acquiescing & playing a very poor 'second fiddle'.

Of course Lancashire has an enormous trade with Persia & this has come to a complete standstill. I enclose two letters from today's *Guardian* which speak for themselves & represent Liberal opinion here.

In confidence I may say we expect an election in 'North West' Manchester early in the new Year & in the present feeling we shall suffer severely.

May I be allowed to say that your voice which has been silent for months is very much missed in these anxious days when foreign affairs occupy so much of public attention?

I wondered whether you had a message which would allay anxiety in these matters I have mentioned & which you would allow to be published & if you could add the hope that in the near future years there might be a reduction in the cost of armaments it would be a welcome message for this Christmas time.

With kindest regards, Sincerely yours
WM ROYLE

WSC to William Royle

20 December 1911　　　　　　　　　　　　　　　　　Admiralty

[Copy]

Private & Confidential

My dear Mr Royle,

I was very sorry I could not come over to see you when I was so near Manchester; I should greatly have welcomed the opportunity of a talk with you. I am not surprised that our foreign policy causes disappointment to some of our friends. The explanation of it, however, is very simple. It is dictated by one conception, namely, national safety. The very rapid growth of the German Navy, stimulated year after year by successive expansions of their Fleet Law, constitutes the main preoccupation in the minds of those responsible for the security of the country. The union of a Navy of such great power with the largest Army in Europe will be a most sinister and disquieting fact, especially when we consider that these gigantic engines of destruction will not be wielded by a Government in Germany which can be said to be in any real sense a democratic Government, with Ministers responsible to Parliament, but by a military and bureaucratic oligarchy supported by a powerful Junker landlord class. In these circumstances we have to be very careful not to open up new lines of divergence with other great Powers, and it is in this light, and with due consideration for these circumstances, that you must study our policy in the Mediterranean and in Persia. I am very sorry for the Persians, but for six years they have been indulging in the delights of anarchy, and, after all, Russian influence has for many years been the established predominating influence in the northern province, which, I may remind you, includes the capital. Before the Anglo-Rumanian agreement was made, not even the most Jingo politician wd have dreamt of our questioning her position in this respect. I earnestly hope that with the new year better relations between England and Germany may begin; but I am not sanguine. If Germany were to slacken her preparations for Naval War by any substantial or definite step there would be an immediate *détente* in Europe, and the revulsion of feeling in England would be extraordinary. She has it in her own hands, without endangering her own security or liberty at all, to terminate at once the distressing tension which now exists. Any step that she may take in that direction we will instantly respond to, not only by words and sentiments, but by action. Even if she adhere to her present Fleet Law with the gigantic Navy which it gives her, I should hope that some slight diminution of our Naval Estimates will be possible within the next two years, and certainly there would be a feeling of comparative relief. The indications however seem to point to another large addition being made to her naval forces with special reference to ourselves, and in these circumstances we shall of course have to face the real facts and take precautions accordingly. My voice is silent on these subjects because the open discussion of them can only rarely be beneficial. There is no use making soft and honeyed speeches which have no relation to real fact. They do no good, and events move on unaffected by them.

I am sure that if the Chancellor of the Exchequer had not made the speech he did Germany would have got France in a corner by herself and forced her to choose between a great humiliation and war. There is, I think, no reason to doubt that beyond a certain point the French, deeply apprehensive as they are of German strength, would have found it incompatible with national honour to yield. Of course you may say that if these facts be true the evil day is only postponed. Well, that at any rate is a great deal. I do not believe in the theory of inevitable wars. All the world is changing at once, and it may be that in a few years time that the democratic forces in Germany will again have greater control of their own Government, and that the landlord ascendancy which now exists will be replaced by more pacific and less formidable elements. Then, too, Russia is recovering from her disasters in Manchuria, and that also is a great corrective to aggressive action on the part of Germany.

You have a right from your position in our party organization in Manchester to receive a full expression of views from me on these subjects. I know I can count upon you to use my letter only with complete discretion.

Yours vy sincerely
WINSTON S. CHURCHILL

WSC to the Master of Elibank
(Elibank Papers)

20 December 1911   Admiralty
Secret

My dear Alick,

Sir Max Aitken is desirous of being appointed one of the British Commissioners on the Imperial Commission to investigate the trade resources of
the Empire. He has asked Locker-Lampson[1] to put this before me, and I
have received the enclosed letter from the latter. If Aitken were appointed
he would vacate his seat at Ashton-under-Lyne and retire for the time being
from politics altogether. He is really a very advanced Liberal and it is only
an accident that sent him into politics on the Tory side. An election at Ashton-
under-Lyne might be extremely convenient to you especially if it were
brought off at an appropriate moment. As I hear with great misgivings that
North West Manchester will be vacant in January, I feel it very necessary
that you should have something up your sleeve to repair any loss we might
suffer in that quarter. I have talked it over with the Chancellor of the
Exchequer and he thinks very highly of the project. I like Aitken myself
personally, and he is certainly a man of very high commercial ability as well
as being thoroughly patriotic and public spirited. The matter seems to me
to be pressing as otherwise the Commissioners may be all appointed, and the
opportunity may have passed.

I am writing to you also by this mail on another subject which is causing
me great and increasing anxiety. Many thanks for sending me the cuttings
from your press bureau, it is certainly an excellent institution, and I will not
fail to take the fullest advantage of it.

Yours vy sincerely
WINSTON S. CHURCHILL

Charles A'Court-Repington to WSC

25 December 1911   Maryon Hall
                                                              Hampstead
My dear Churchill,

Many thanks for your nice letter. We have done a couple of campaigns
together and I am glad to think that you accept me as an ally for a third. I
count on you to let me know when I can bear a hand.

Yes, war is all one, and its principles are eternal. I can realise some of

[1] Oliver Stillingfleet Locker-Lampson (1880–1954), conducted *Empire Review*; Lieut-
Commander in RNAS 1914; Commander 1915; served with armoured cars on many fronts
1914–18; Russian representative to the Ministry of Information 1918; Conservative MP,
North Huntingdonshire 1910–22, Handsworth 1922–45.

your difficulties with the sailors and the need for going slow at first, but I have a confident hope that the best men will rally to you and that the head of the Navy will be as serviceable, when your work is done, as the arm is today. I do not know any more urgent or more fruitful work that any British statesman could undertake.

Wishing you a fair wind and all good luck for the coming year.

I am, Yours very sincerely

C. A'C. REPINGTON

Sir Francis Hopwood to WSC

25 December 1911   13 Hornton Street

My dear Churchill,

I saw Chalmers[1] today about some Development business and he incidentally gave me a considerable shock by telling me that I should forfeit my pension rights if I took a five year appointment at the Admiralty. He says they can neither allow the five years to count for pension or give me any pension at the end of it. This will never do. My pension rights are now worth an annuity of £700 a year and about £2500 cash. . . . It would be dreadfully improvident to let this drop. . . . I don't think it could be justified.

Please don't have me gazetted until we find a way round this difficulty, – to get in the *Gazette* would be most awkward.

It seems that I should have also lost my pension had I gone to Bengal. That is because I should have been paid out of Indian funds.

The trouble here is that any appointment short of one that will take me to 60 (9 years) is 'temporary' service and so non-pensionable.

Sorry to worry you with letters.

Ever yours sincerely

FRANCIS T. S. HOPWOOD

H. H. Asquith to WSC

26 December 1911   Archerfield House
Dirleton

Private

My dear Winston,

Aitken is quite impossible. I take it that his Canadian record is of the shadiest, and when (at the instance of the Tories) he was made a Coronation

---

[1] Robert Chalmers (1858–1938). Permanent Secretary of Treasury and Auditor of the Civil List 1911–18; Governor of Ceylon 1913–16. Knighted 1908; PC (Ireland) 1916; created Baron Chalmers of Northiam 1919.

knight, Albert Grey[1] wrote to us that throughout the Dominion there was a howl of indignation and disgust.

This, I need not say, is for your own consumption only.

Yours ever
HHA

PS As there is no present prospect of other provision being made for Lambert,[2] your new man will have to be an *additional* Civil Lord. I do not know whether this necessitates an Order in Council, but it would be well to obtain the King's consent. Hopwood, of course, is the best man for the job, but you should be careful in advance to get Ll George's concurrence (as he is sensitive about the Development Commn) and to arrange with the Treasury as to fixing the rate of H's salary, which I assume will be personal to himself.

Lord Fisher to WSC

30 December 1911   Lucerne

My beloved Winston,

Your letter came a few minutes ago and has departed this life in accordance with your wishes.

I cannot congratulate enough over Hopwood! Nor will *he* ever regret it, for the possibilities of his new office are *immense!* (Remember I found 10,000 cane bottom chairs in store when a post card to Maple's would have got a million if necessary by the next train. These chairs represented a storehouse, storehouse men – a foreman – a clerk at the Admiralty – and additional Clerk in the Auditor Gerent's department & so on & so on! Blankets rotted never used, tumblers, water closets &c. . . . but alas! *No oil!*. . . . *What won't Hopwood do?* So you see how glad I am you have cut Briggs in two – (I wish you'd cut him altogether – however I comfort myself with the thought that after all you yourself will do the 'plunging' as you have so nobly done in regard to the *Super-Swifts!* and thank God! you've knocked off 2 Dartmouths you ought to have knocked 4! *Totus Porcus!!* but still I admit you must play up to your 'seals'!

I deeply regret your halting steps about the Submarines. It is time we have an enormous lead! Forgive me for being egotistical but every d——d soul was dead against them – all my colleagues and all the Navy – and

---

[1] Albert Henry George Grey (1851–1917), 4th Earl Grey; Administrator of Rhodesia 1894–7; Director of Chartered Company 1898–1904; Governor-General and C-in-C of the Dominion of Canada 1904–11.

[2] George Lambert (1866–1958), Liberal MP for South Molton 1891–1924, 1929–31; Liberal National 1931–45; Civil Lord of the Admiralty 1905–15; PC 1912; created Viscount Lambert of South Molton 1945.

Beresford calling them 'playthings' in official letters and the Submarine Officers & men being disparaged and ridiculed.

You say 'But I got no encouragement to spend the additional £400,000' – still less was there in those past years to spend a million! but do please believe me that they are *the the one strategical* and *tactical requirement* both in a War with Germany and to attract the United States to us! When you get 1200 ton submarines with a radius of 5,000 miles and a gun armament and self sustained for 2 months then America knows that with England as an Ally no German *coup-de-main* on Brazil is feasible and our help as regards any future American Japanese complications would be decisive. The ordinary Naval Officer aint brought up to generalize – you must get home Captain S. S. Hall[1] of the *Diana* as soon as you can! Dear old A. K. Wilson got rid of him as he was a d——d sight too pertinacious! Put those 4 Submarines in with only a 'token' sum in the Estimates and then you can pay for them out of the invariable half a million sterling that is returned by the Admiralty to pay off the National Debt.

Tell Hopwood every Head of a Department jams on a big sum to make himself safe, as there is always a hell of a row if he under-estimates. Whereas he ought to be praised. '*From a little – take a little*' is a lovely proverb! Economy is the secret of efficiency as every ounce is made use of and the parasites die for want of sustenance! Put in those 4 submarines with a token sum so *as to get authority for ordering them.*

30 Knots for the February Cruiser *is lovely* – I could kiss you!!! but you are pusillanimous for not plunging with the 'improved' gun! and for allowing the '*Armour Fetish*' to dominate you.

    I. Cost. £1,995,000

    II. Speed. 30 Knots

    III. 10" *'improved'* guns and 10 Submerged Torpedo Tubes.

and *sacrifice armour* and have *Size & Subdivision! That's all pure common sense!* Modern Strategy & Modern Tactics *demand* the above type! *Oil only! – I only pray you wont be fore-stalled by the Germans!*.

From the time I knew you well & had those *tête à tête* lunches in Bolton Street I have consistently maintained that you were 'ideal' for the Admiralty, *because you are a brave man!* The whole secret of Admiralty success is 'plunging' – it stupefies foreign Admiralties. You get a great lead, and a stern chase to pick up *is Hell!*

Not to spend one penny on Argonauts, Canopi and Majestics is splendid of you! and your project for putting the 4th Division in full commission without a proclamation is equally excellent. *N.B.* Mind you 'run' Alan Burgoyne MP, he

---

[1] Sydney Stewart Hall (1872–1955), commanded *Diana* 1910–12, *Roxburgh* 1914; Submarine Service 1906–10, 1915–18; Admiral 1929.

is of inestimable value to you in controlling public opinion, and they have a new man called Hannon[1] as Secretary of the Navy League who is just doing wonders in extending the ramifications of their journalism, and also they possess a first class spy at Berlin whose name you can get if you want it. That 150,000 a year you propose to spend on '*the pick of the Fleet Reserve*' will probably bring you more credit than all else you do.! – I fully share your opinion of Duff[2]–and I am delighted you have *pleased yourself* as to Beatty[3]....
I *so* hope you will be able to keep all your secrets! See how brilliantly effective was the 'coup' abt your New Board of Admiralty! It dumb founded and dazed and was swallowed like an oyster – as delicious!

You ask me as to '*Winston the Silent*' about Beresford? *Of course you are right* – He is getting low down when collaborating with Bottomley, MP.! Isn't it odd that in reading your letter just come I can see Beresford through a telescope in the *Osborn* in this harbour from my balcony in the Hotel! he is en route to Egypt I believe for some complaint he has of which I forget the name – but women often have it after a baby! No, my dear Winston you are right – *ignore him!*

It delights me more than I can say that you are pleased with your 'seals' and that they work well with you. '*United – determined – progressive*'*!* But your Controller & Director of Artillery are old women! However *you'*ll do their work! and I *just simply* '*revel*' in the thoughts of Hopwood! *You are splendid!* my *dear Winston!*

I hope you have seen Jellicoe. Quite likely you will be disappointed. He is so quiet – *but he has all the Nelsonic attributes* I. *Self-reliance* II. Fearlessness of Responsibility III. Fertility of Resource IV. Power of Initiative! He ordered the *Lion* when everyone shivered! He will win the Battle of Armageddon on Oct 21 1914. (*Make a note of that date!*) as he will automatically succeed Callaghan as Commander in Chief of the Home Fleet in 2 years time, at Nelson's age at the Battle of Trafalgar! It wont be a victory dear Winston that Jellicoe will accomplish! it will be 'annihilation'! but there must be an additional half a million sterling per annum for Submarines and be sure to

---

[1] Patrick Joseph Henry Hannon (1874–1964), General Secretary of the Navy League and editor *The Navy* 1911–18; Conservative MP Moseley 1921–50; President, National Association of British Manufacturers 1935–53; sometime Director of Daimler Co; James Booth & Co; BSA; President of Aston Villa Football Club; knighted 1936.

[2] Alexander Ludovic Duff (1862–1933), Director of the Mobilization Division of Admiralty War Staff 1911–14; Rear-Admiral, 4th Battle Squadron 1914–17; Director of Anti-Submarine Division 1917; Assistant Chief of Naval Staff 1918–19; Admiral 1921; C-in-C China Station 1919–22. Retired 1925; knighted 1918.

[3] David Beatty (1871–1936), Rear-Admiral 1910; Naval Secretary to First Lord 1912; Commander, 1st Battle Squadron 1912–16; Vice-Admiral 1915; Commander, Grand Fleet, 1916–19; First Lord 1919–27; Admiral of the Fleet 1919; knighted 1914; created Earl Beatty, Viscount Borodale and Baron Beatty of the North Sea 1919; PC 1927.

talk to *S. S. Hall* of the *Diana* when you come to the Mediterranean at Whitsuntide! –

I hope you will shift Malta to Alexandria. It will be an immense 'coup'! *It is common sense.* What a history has Alexandria! The key of the Mahommedan World. *It locks up the East!* When I was First Sea Lord, a second class cruiser grounded in the act of entering on a stormy day. I wrote a private note to Cromer and asked him to dig a Dreadnought Channel – he *did* – it cost an un-mentionable sum. Not a newspaper ever had a word of it. *Send for the Chart & see the old passage & the new!* It's an eye opener. I told Cromer *he was a man!* as the great Napoleon said

     '*Les hommes sont rares!*'

Do come to Naples and do go to Alexandria at Whitsuntide! –

I have a great personal friend in a *very high* position at Berlin – an American – but I have *such absolute and complete confidence in Grey* that I sleep quite quiet in my bed as to German intentions in regard to Portuguese *East Africa,* and I think it wiser for *my friend's sake* to say nothing either to you or to Grey.

I send this letter by a route far safer than the Embassy at Rome. Dont forget to lower the cost of cadets *below* what was formerly paid by Engineer Students at *Keyham College.*

Yours till charcoal sprouts!

F.

WSC to the King
(*Royal Archives*)

TELEGRAM

31 December 1911

First Lord submits that it is not intended that Chief of the Staff should compete in rank or authority with the First Sea Lord whose principal assistant he will be.

An officer of middle rank was therefore indicated. Admiral Troubridge was specially desired by the First Sea Lord and the Second Sea Lord entirely approved. Admiral Beatty will succeed him as Private Secretary. Hopwood gives up his present appointment and is transferred to Admiralty at same salary and pension rights. He is excluded from Parliament and is entirely non-political in character.

Precedent 1882 was when Lord Northbrook appointed present Lord Rendel[1] as additional Civil Lord though for somewhat different duties to those now contemplated. All above changes are urgently required.

[1] George Wightwick Rendel (–1902), Managing partner of the Elswick Ordnance Works 1858; Professional Civil Lord 1882-5. WSC appears to have confused him with the first Baron Rendel (1834-1913).

The King to WSC
(*Royal Archives*)

TELEGRAM

31 December 1911

I approve proposed constitution of War Staff and of Hopwood's appointment to the new post which has been created.

G.R.I.

*   *   *   *   *

On 29 September 1911 Italy declared war on Turkey and invaded Tripolitania and Cyrenaica. The two provinces were successfully occupied and formally annexed to Italy on November 5.

Djavid Bey[1] to WSC

28 October 1911   Constantinople

Dear Mr Churchill,

My belief in your sincere friendship for Turkey and the Young Turks leads me to speak of a very important matter today.

After the Constitution in Turkey those that believed in the beginning of a close friendship between England and Turkey saw with regret the misunderstanding that prevented it. I need not speak of its different causes here. Only the true friends of England in Turkey never ceased from trying to remove it. The actual circumstances appear to be a good occasion for success. The attack of one of the triple alliance powers on our territory has turned the public opinion greatly against the triplice. The pro-English statesmen in Turkey and pro-Turkish statesmen in England could profit of this occasion.

Knowing and believing you occupy an important and influential position among our friends in England I will beg you to join our effort using your influence in bringing out this friendship. Has the time arrived for a permanent alliance between the two countries? On what basis could it be attempted? Will you please write me your personal views on the matter? They will

[1] Djavid Bey (–1926), Turkish financier; resigned in May 1911 as Minister of Finance; sometime Minister of Finance under Enver Pasha. Was hanged by Kemal Ataturk in 1926.

be considered entirely personal and unofficial. But I will consider myself happy if we can prepare a possible ground for official purposes.

Believe me Sir to be, Yours truly

DJAVID

WSC to Sir Edward Grey

4 November 1911   HMS *Enchantress*

Secret

Copy

My dear Grey,

I have thought a good deal since the Cabinet abt an arrangement with Turkey. I cd not help feeling that our colleagues were rather inclined to treat a little too lightly the crude overture wh the T Govt have made. You have of course been looking at the present situation entirely from an Armageddon point of view, and I frankly confess that in spite of many misgivings and much repugnance that aspect has held sway in my mind. But the course of events has strongly altered and is perhaps to alter more strongly still the European situation. The Morocco dispute is settled. Germany has recoiled. It may well be several years before the gt antagonism recurs. Italy has behaved atrociously; and I cannot myself measure what the feelings of our countrymen will be as the news of those abominable massacres, resulting as they do from an act of wanton and cynical aggression, is amplified and confirmed. I am sure, judging by what I hear from every quarter, that all the strongest elements in Liberal opinion must be stirred against the Italians. On the other hand there is, as you know so well, a strong historical pro-Turkish party among Conservatives throughout the country. The combination of these two forces, normally in equipoise, wd afford a basis for political action of a vy decided character. Turkey has much to offer us.

In fixing our eyes upon the Belgian frontier and the North Sea we must not forget that we are the greatest Mahometan power in the world. We are the only power who can really help her and guide her. And if she wants to turn to England and Russia, and if R herself is anxious for an assocn wh shd carry T in some sort of way into the system of the Triple Entente, the proposition ought not to be lightly pushed aside. We may ask ourselves whether we have not more to gain from Turkish friendship than from Italian policy; and still more whether we have not more to apprehend from the consequence of throwing T than of throwing Italy into the arms of Germany.

T is the greatest land weapon wh the Germans cd use agst *us*. Italy is not likely to be worth much for or agst anyone for some time to come. There is also this extremely practical fact – never was a great power more utterly at our mercy than is Italy today, or than she will be during the continuance of this Tripolitan war. You therefore occupy the rare and remarkable position, both in the H of C and in the Mediterranean, of being able to issue commands wh will not be disregarded.

All this is not intended to advocate a T alliance at the present time, but to emphasise the importance of two steps – first a sympathetic and respectful consn of the T appeal, and 2ndly a clear protest against the vile massacres of women and little children wh have dishonoured the Italian arms. Whatever happens you cannot win the gratitude of Italy. Br public opinion is too plainly apparent for that. But a turn, or even a gesture, might produce a lasting impression on the Mahometan world. There can be no doubt which way we shd have leaned but for our position agst Germany. And what I am wondering now is whether we are not at the present time strong enough to confront G and at the same time develop a purely Br policy in the Orient. I wish you had a good man at Constantinople.

At the next Cabinet you shd I think take up a vy strong position abt military consultations with the French. There cd have been no war unless the Germans had violated the neutrality of Belgium and invaded France in undisguised aggression. In such circs the Cabinet have an absolute right to have a free choice between peace and war; and they cd not have had that choice, nor can they retain it, without constant and detailed communications between the Br and Fr military authorities.

I had been meaning to write to you abt Turkey for 2 or 3 days, and I now send you a letter from Djavid wh has just reached me.

Yrs vy sincerely
WSC

Sir Edward Grey to WSC

9 November 1911   3 Queen Anne's Gate

Private

Dear Churchill,

I quite agree about the reply to Turkey. Of course I didn't mean it to be brusque like my thumb nail sketch of it to the Cabinet.

A reply made of 'Sugar and spice and all that's nice' has now been drafted: you shall see it [in] time and you will I am sure never have read anything more mellifluous.

Yours sincerely

E. Grey

WSC to Djavid Bey

19 November 1911   Admiralty

Copy

My dear Djavid Bey,

It is a great pleasure to me to receive your letter, the importance of which I fully recognise. So far as the present lamentable struggle is concerned, we have definitely declared our neutrality, and it is not to be expected that we shall alter a policy so gravely decided. My answer therefore to your question must be that at the present time we cannot enter upon new political relations. In the future the enormous interests which unite the two great Mussulman Powers, should keep us in touch. That is our wish; the feeling of British public opinion, as you will have seen from recent manifestations of it, opposes no barrier to that wish, if only the Turkish Government will not alienate it by reverting to the oppressive methods of the old regime or seeking to disturb the British status quo as it now exists and you and your friends, whom I remember to have met with so much pleasure, should bear in mind that England, almost alone among European states, seeks no territorial expansion, and that alone among them she retains the supremacy of the sea. We earnestly desire to revive and maintain our old friendship with Turkey, wh while we retain the supremacy of the sea shd be a friendship of value.

I must apologise for the delay in answering yr letter, wh was due to the importance of its nature.

Yours very sincerely

[Winston S. Churchill]

*   *   *   *   *

While he was First Lord, WSC used the Admiralty yacht, HMS *Enchantress*, as a mobile office to inspect the fleet and naval installations along the coast.

The ship had a complement of 196 officers and ratings. When WSC first came on board in November 1911 she was commanded by Captain W. G. E.

Ruck Keene,[1] MVO, RN. She was commanded by Captain H. Lynes,[2] RN from 1912–13.

The *Enchantress* was laid up during World War I but was recommissioned in January 1919 at Portsmouth. Her crew was paid off in December 1934 and six months later she was sold to Dover Industries Limited, Dover.

HMS Enchantress *Log Book*
(*Admiralty Archives*)

EXTRACT

1st Visit

5 November 1911	10.30 *am*	WSC inspected ship and ship's company at Cowes.
6 November 1911		Cowes to Portsmouth.
	9.15 *am*	WSC left ship to go to Submarine Depot.
	11.30 *am*	WSC returned on board.
	1.25 *pm*	WSC left ship to inspect Portsmouth Dockyard.
7 November 1911	8 *am*	WSC left ship. Portsmouth.

2nd Visit

10 November 1911		WSC and party came on board Portsmouth *pm*.
11 November 1911		*Enchantress* escorted King and Queen, in HMS *Medina*, out of Portsmouth harbour, on their way to Delhi Durbar.
12 November 1911		WSC on board, steamed from Portsmouth to Portland.
13 November 1911	8.35 *am*	WSC left ship for HMS *Neptune*, on return to Portsmouth from Portland.

[1] William George Elmhirst Ruck Keene (1867–1935), Commander 1901; Captain 1906; Rear-Admiral 1918; retired 1927.

[2] Hubert Lynes (1874–1942), served in the Naval Ordnance Department 1903–5; at Whale Island for experimental work 1908–10; commanded Admiralty Yacht 1912–13, H.M.S. *Penelope* 1914–17; commanded Ostend forces at Zeebrugge April 1918; retired 1919; Rear-Admiral, retired, 1922.

3rd Visit

17 November 1911	afternoon	Devonport. WSC and party arrived.
18 November 1911	3.5 *pm*	WSC launched HMS *Centurion*. Devonport.
19 November 1911	late *pm*	WSC and party left ship, Devonport.

4th Visit

25 November 1911	7.15 *pm*	Portsmouth. WSC and party arrived.
26 November 1911		WSC on board. Portsmouth, left at 8 *am* for Cowes. WSC landed at Cowes at 10.45 *am*. Ten past noon WSC returned on Board. *Enchantress* returned to Portsmouth.
27 November 1911	8 *am*	WSC inspected *Falcon* TBD [Torpedoboat destroyer] and left *Enchantress* finally before noon.

5th Visit

9 December 1911	4 *pm*	Portsmouth. WSC and party arrived.
10 December 1911		WSC on board. Portsmouth.
11 December 1911	9.15 *am*	Board of Admiralty inspecting Royal Naval Barracks, Portsmouth. *Excellent* and *Vernon* in morning, RMLI and Naval Hospital in afternoon.
	4.30 *pm*	WSC left ship.